Calling All Cooks

**Telephone Pioneers of America
Alabama Chapter No. 34**

AT&T Pioneers, Alabama Chapter 34
3196 Hwy 280 E., Room 316S–Desk 639
Birmingham, Alabama 35243

Regular Edition
ISBN 10: 0-9787283-0-0
ISBN 13: 978-0-9787283-0-4

Special Hard Cover Edition
ISBN 10: 0-9787283-6-X
ISBN 13: 978-0-9787283-6-6

Calling All Cooks is published by
Favorite Recipes Press in collaboration
with AT&T Pioneers, Alabama Chapter
34. Favorite Recipes Press works
with top chefs, food and appliance
manufacturers, restaurants and resorts,
health organizations, Junior Leagues,
and nonprofit organizations to create
award-winning cookbooks and other
food-related products. Favorite Recipes
Press is an imprint of Southwestern
Publishing House, 2451 Atrium Way,
Nashville, Tennessee 37214.
Southwestern Publishing House
is a wholly owned subsidiary of
Southwestern/Great American Inc.,
Nashville, Tennessee.

Christopher G. Capen, President,
    Southwestern Publishing House
Sheila Thomas, Publisher,
    Favorite Recipes Press
Kristin Connelly, Managing Editor
frpbooks.com | 800-358-0560

1st printing	Nov. 1982	44,000 copies	14th printing	Feb. 1993	25,000 copies
2nd printing	Feb. 1983	33,000 copies	15th printing	Oct. 1994	25,000 copies
3rd printing	Apr. 1983	40,300 copies	16th printing	Nov. 1995	20,000 copies
4th printing	Nov. 1983	25,000 copies	17th printing	Feb. 1998	20,000 copies
5th printing	Aug. 1984	35,000 copies	18th printing	Aug. 2001	25,000 copies
6th printing	Apr. 1985	27,000 copies	19th printing	Feb. 2005	25,000 copies
7th printing	Oct. 1985	28,000 copies	20th printing	Mar. 2010	5,000 copies
8th printing	Sept. 1986	52,500 copies	21st printing	Jun. 2011	3,000 copies
9th printing	Oct. 1987	21,500 copies	22nd printing	Mar. 2012	5,000 copies
10th printing	May 1988	20,500 copies	23rd printing	Nov. 2014	5,000 copies
11th printing	Nov. 1988	25,000 copies	24th printing	Nov. 2017	5,000 copies
12th printing	Oct. 1989	25,000 copies	25th printing	Nov. 2020	5,000 copies
13th printing	May 1991	25,000 copies			

Special Hard Cover Edition   Mar. 2010   3,000 copies

AT&T Pioneers
Alabama Chapter No. 34

2020 EXECUTIVE COMMITTEE MEMBERS

Bell Rogers—President
Felicia Carter Johnson—Vice President
Mary B. Williams—Immediate Past President
Terri Keeton—Secretary
Karen Howze-Samuels—Treasurer
Ricky Rivers—Member-at-Large
Rosemary Parker—Member-at-Large
Tara Carnahan—Member-at-Large
Adrienne Gray—Member-at-Large
Mabel Smartt—Member-at-Large-Decatur
Mona Burdick—Member-at-Large-Montgomery
Todd Freshwater—Member-at-Large-Anniston
Shelia Goodwin—Member-at-Large-Birmingham South Cahaba
Anthony Sarradet—President, Mobile Council
Cora Underwood—President, Birmingham Life Member Club

2020 COMMITTEE CHAIRMEN

Sara Cooley—Cookbooks
Waylon Pickens—Chaplain
Naomi Watkins—Fundraising
Ricky Rivers—Environmental
Cynthia Portis—Education/Awards
Felicia Carter Johnson/Rosemary Parker—Membership
Susan Conway/Virginia Mayo—Military/Veterans
Dottie Steelreath/Tara Carnahan—Newsletter
Adrienne Gray—Policies, Procedures, Bylaws
Cheryl Pritchett—Communications Director
Mary Williams/Janie Davis—Pals/Volunteer Now
Cathy Kelley/Jamelle Prewitt—Special Projects
Rickey Morgan—Website
Betty Willingham—Advisor

TELEPHONE PIONEERS OF AMERICA
1982-1983

ALABAMA CHAPTER NO. 34

President ....John I. Wood, Jr.

Vice-President... Cliff Cagle

Pioneer Administrator.. Evelyn Kilgo

COUNCILS PARTICIPATING

Anniston Council
Birmingham Central Council
Birmingham Life Member Club
Birmingham East Council
Birmingham South Council
Riverchase Council
Birmingham West Council
Decatur Council
Jasper Club
Huntsville Council
Mobile Council

Mobile Life Member
Bon Secour Life Member Club
Montgomery Council
Montgomery Life Member Club
Opelika Club
Phenix City Club
Tri-Cities Council
Tuscaloosa Council
Tuscaloosa Life Member Club
Selma Club
Selma Life Member Club

ACKNOWLEDGMENT

My thanks to everyone who contributed recipes, some of which have been handed down from generation to generation.

A very special thank you to those of you who devoted endless hours to assemble our treasures.

Thank you to all of the Council Presidents and their cookbook committees who worked so diligently to collect these recipes.

To all of you . . . . . thank you again.

Peggy Autry

Pioneers' Legacy

The Pioneers' legacy is long and inspiring. It all began in 1911 with just 734 members (including Alexander Graham Bell). In the beginning, friendship and fellowship were what it was all about, according to industry people recalling the facts, traditions, and memories of the early history of the telephone. But those who wrote the original Pioneers' purpose were forward-thinking in adding that it would also encourage "such other meritorious objects consistent with the foregoing as may be desirable." That became what would make the Pioneers different from other industry groups.

One of those "meritorious objects" translated into community service. Chapters, councils, and clubs began their own initiatives, mostly working with children's groups. By 1958, community service was established as the Pioneers' "New Tradition."

Today, the organization is the world's largest group of industry-specific employees and retirees dedicated to community service. Pioneers volunteer more than 15 million hours annually, responding to the individual needs of their communities.

Alabama Pioneers published the first *Calling All Cooks* (known as the yellow cookbook) in 1982. This well-known and loved Alabama cookbook has sold over 580,000 copies. Profits from its sale, as well as the sales of later *Calling All Cooks* cookbooks, continue to fund community-service initiatives across the state of Alabama.

TELEPHONE PIONEERS OF AMERICA
1982-1983
ALABAMA CHAPTER NO. 34

President . . . . John I. Wood, Jr.*
Vice-President. Cliff Cagle*
Pioneer Administrator . . . . Evelyn Kilgo*

COUNCILS PARTICIPATING

Anniston Council	Mobile Life Member Club
Birmingham Central Council	Bon Secour Life Member Club
Birmingham Life Member Club	Montgomery Council
Birmingham East Council	Montgomery Life Member Club
Birmingham South Council	Opelika Club
Riverchase Council	Phenix City Club
Birmingham West Council	Tri-Cities Council
Decatur Council	Tuscaloosa Council
Jasper Club	Tuscaloosa Life Member Club
Huntsville Council	Selma Club
Mobile Council	Selma Life Member Club

*Deceased

TABLE OF CONTENTS

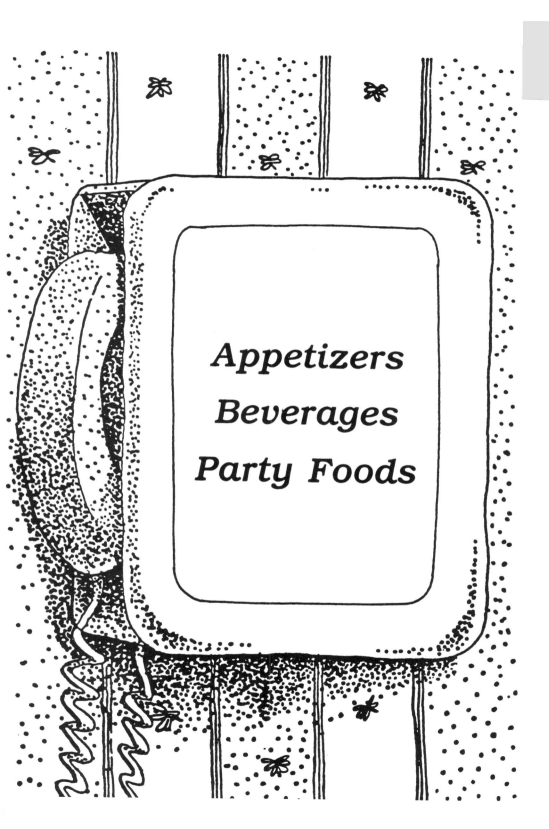

Appetizers
Beverages
Party Foods

SPICE CHART

Spices should be stored in airtight containers away from the heat of the stove or in the refrigerator. Add ground spices toward the end of the cooking time to retain maximum flavor. Whole spices may be added at the beginning but should have a small amount of additional spices added near the end of cooking time also.

Allspice	Pungent aromatic spice, whole or in powdered form. It is excellent in marinades, particularly in game marinade, or in curries.
Caraway seed	Use the whole seeds in breads, especially rye, and with cheese, sauerkraut and cabbage dishes.
Celery seed	Use whole or ground in salad dressings, sauces, pickles or meat, cheese, egg and fish dishes.
Chili powder	Made from dried red chili peppers, this spice ranges from mild to fiery depending on the type of chili pepper used. Used especially in Mexican cooking, it is a delicious addition to eggs, dips and sauces.
Cinnamon	Ground from the bark of the cinnamon tree, it is delicious in desserts as well as savory dishes.
Coriander	Seed used whole or ground, this slightly lemony spice adds an unusual flavor to soups, stews, chili dishes, curries and desserts.
Curry powder	A blend of several spices, this gives Indian cooking its characteristic flavor.
Cumin	A staple spice in Mexican cooking. Use it in meat, rice, cheese, egg and fish dishes.
Ginger	The whole root used fresh, dried or ground is a sweet, pungent addition to desserts or oriental-style dishes.
Mustard (dry)	Ground mustard seed brings a sharp bite to sauces or may be sprinkled sparingly over poultry or other foods.
Nutmeg	Use the whole spice or a bit of freshly ground for flavor in beverages, breads and desserts. A sprinkle on top is both a flavor enhancer and an attractive garnish.
Pepper	Black and white pepper from the pepperberry or peppercorn, whether whole, ground or cracked, is the most commonly used spice in or on any food.
Poppy seed	Use these tiny, nutty-flavored seeds in salad dressings, breads, cakes or as a flavorful garnish for cheese, rolls or noodle dishes.
Turmeric	Ground from a root related to ginger, this is an essential in curry powder. Also used in pickles, relishes, cheese and egg dishes.

A HAPPY HOME RECIPE

4 c. love	5 Tbsp. hope
2 c. loyalty	2 Tbsp. tenderness
3 c. forgiveness	4 qt. faith
1 c. friendship	1 barrel laughter

Take love and loyalty; mix it thoroughly with faith. Blend it with tenderness, kindness and understanding. Add friendship and hope; sprinkle abundantly with laughter. Bake it with sunshine. Serve daily with generous helpings.

ARTICHOKE FRITTATA

2 Tbsp. olive oil	1/4 lb. shredded Cheddar
1/2 c. chopped onion	cheese
1 clove mashed garlic	2 Tbsp. minced parsley
1 (14 oz.) can artichoke	1/2 tsp. salt
hearts	1/8 tsp. pepper
1/4 c. bread crumbs	1/4 tsp. oregano
1/4 lb. shredded Swiss	1/8 tsp. Tabasco sauce
cheese	4 eggs

1. Saute onion and garlic in oil, till limp. Remove from heat. 2. Drain and chop artichoke hearts; add to onion and garlic. 3. Beat eggs; add to mixture. 4. Add remaining ingredients and mix well. 5. Pour in greased 7x11 inch pan; bake at 350° for 1/2 hour. Let cool first, then cut in squares. Good for parties or holidays as appetizers.
Joan Beiers, Huntsville Council

STUFFED BACON ROLLS

1 tsp. minced onion	1 egg, well beaten, plus
1 stick butter	enough milk to measure 1 c.
1 pkg. stuffing mix	Bacon

Saute onion in butter; stir in stuffing mix. Remove from heat; add liquid and mix thoroughly. Wrap 1 full teaspoon in 1/2 strip bacon. Place on ungreased baking sheet; bake at 450° until bacon cooks.
Fran Rhodis, Montgomery Council

BEEF AND BACON DELIGHTS

2 lb. beef franks
1 lb. bacon, sliced

1 (1 lb.) box light brown sugar
Toothpicks

Cut franks in halves. Wrap a slice of bacon around each frank half. Secure with toothpick. In crock-pot place a layer of wrapped franks and a layer of brown sugar. Cover and cook slowly for 2-3 hours, stirring occasionally.

Dot Beadlescomb, Birmingham Central Council

CREAMY STUFFED CELERY

3 stalks celery
1 (3 oz.) pkg. cream
  cheese, softened
1 Tbsp. finely chopped
  pimiento-stuffed olives

1 Tbsp. finely chopped onion
1 Tbsp. finely chopped
  sweet pickle
1 Tbsp. finely chopped pecans
1 1/2 tsp. mayonnaise

Wash celery, and cut into 3 inch pieces. Combine remaining ingredients, mixing well. Stuff the celery pieces with cream cheese mixture. Yield: 9 celery pieces.

Regina Cash, Anniston Council

CHEESE BALL

2 (8 oz.) pkg. cream
  cheese

2 pkg. pressed ham or beef
4 green onions
Chopped nuts (optional)

Chop onions and meat; mix into cream cheese and roll into ball. Optional: Roll in chopped nuts.

Charlotte East, Mobile Council

CHEESE BALL

1 lb. Velveeta cheese
1 (8 oz.) pkg. cream cheese
1 small jar olives

1 bunch green onions
1 small jar Armour dried beef

Mix 1 pound Velveeta cheese, cream cheese, olives (chopped) and green onions (chopped); roll into ball. Chop up dried beef (blender does perfectly) and roll cheese in the dried beef. Chill in refrigerator 1 hour before serving. Serve with crackers (Sociables, Town House or your favorite). Optional ingredients: Pecans, chives or pimento.

Linda Mizell, Tuscaloosa Council

4

CHEESE BALL

2 (8 oz.) pkg. cream cheese
1/4 or 5 oz. can crushed pineapple, drained
1/4 c. each finely chopped bell pepper and onion
2 c. pecans, chopped
1 Tbsp. seasoned salt (use a little more)

Whip up cream cheese with fork until creamy. Put in all ingredients except 1 cup pecans; mix and form in ball and roll in remaining pecans. Wrap in aluminum foil and let it set overnight. (This is very important, so onion and bell pepper taste will not be so strong.)

Carol D. Adams, Mobile Council

CHEESE BALL

1 (8 oz.) pkg. cream cheese, softened
1/4 c. mayonnaise
2 (4 oz.) cans deviled ham
2 Tbsp. chopped parsley
1 tsp. minced onion
1/4 tsp. dry mustard
1/4 tsp. Tabasco sauce
1/2 c. chopped nuts

Beat cheese and mayonnaise until smooth; stir in next 5 ingredients. Cover; chill several hours. Form into ball; roll in nuts to coat.

Margaret W. Keith, Huntsville Council

BLUE CHEESE BALL

8 oz. cream cheese
2 oz. Blue cheese
3 Tbsp. chopped celery
1/4 c. chopped onion
2 Tbsp. dried parsley
2 Tbsp. dried chives (optional)

Mix all ingredients; form in ball. Roll in chopped pecans or walnuts; chill.

Mary Norris, Mary Louise Sharp,
Birmingham Central Council

CHEESE BALLS

1 stick oleo
3 c. plain flour
Dash of salt
1 (8 oz.) pkg. dates
8 oz. Cheddar cheese
Pecan halves

Grate cheese. Melt butter; mix cheese and butter. Add flour and salt; mix well. Pinch off little bit of dough. Put half dates and half of pecans and wrap around with dough. Bake at 375° for 15 to 20 minutes.

1567-82   Mae Kennedy, Montgomery Council   5

CHEESE CRISPS

2 c. grated sharp cheese
2 or 3 drops of Tabasco
  sauce
2 c. plain flour

2 c. chopped pecans or
  2 c. Rice Krispies (I
  prefer Rice Krispies)
1 (8 oz.) stick margarine

Cream margarine; add grated cheese. Add flour, Tabasco and Rice Krispies. Roll in small balls the size of a quarter. Flatten with fork. Sprinkle with paprika; bake 10-12 minutes in 350° oven (until light brown). Bake on ungreased pan.

Della Pearl Dukes, Retired,
Bon Secour Life Chapter

CHEESE HOOIES

1 stick oleo
1/4 lb. strong American
  cheese

1 c. plain flour
1 tsp. salt
Good dash of red pepper

Grate cheese into butter; cream well together. Add salt and red pepper, then work in flour until thoroughly blended. Knead on a board until smooth; roll into long thin rolls (about size of quarter) and refrigerate until chilled. When chilled, slice thin and bake on a cookie sheet in 350° oven until hooies are beginning to turn brown (8-10 minutes). These can be frozen and you do not even have to let them thaw out.

Mrs. Guy Pippin, Anniston Council

CHEESE PUFF

1 (8 oz.) pkg.
  refrigerator biscuits

1/4 lb. cubed sharp
  Cheddar cheese
Oil for deep frying

Separate biscuits; cut each into thirds. Wrap dough around cheese cubes; seal well. Fry in hot fat 2 or 3 minutes until brown. Yield: 30 appetizers.

Mrs. Jeri Nuss, Decatur Council

KATHY'S CHEESE SNACKS

13 oz. Cracker Barrel
  cheese
1 can green chiles
  (unpeeled, roasted)
1/2 tsp. prepared mustard

1/2 tsp. Worcestershire
  sauce
3 eggs
Salt and pepper to taste
Little bit of garlic powder

Put chiles in 13x9 inch pan; cover with grated cheese. Mix the other ingredients and spread on top of cheese and chiles. Sprinkle with paprika; cook for 30 to 40 minutes at 350°.

Joan Sims, Birmingham South Council

CHEESE STICKS (MICROWAVE STYLE)

6 Tbsp. butter/margarine
3/4 c. Cheddar cheese,
  grated
3/4 c. flour
1/4 tsp. salt
2-3 drops hot Tabasco sauce

Cream butter/margarine and Cheddar cheese together; mix in other ingredients. Pour onto well floured surface and roll out to about 1/8 inch thick. Cut out thin strips and lay on wax paper or paper towels or cookie sheet. Microwave on high for 3-5 minutes.

Dina Johnson, Birmingham South Council

ROY AND EDNA ADAMS' CHEESE STRAWS

1 stick melted oleo
1 lb. grated New York
  sharp Cheddar cheese
2 c. plain flour
1/2 tsp. salt
1/2 tsp. red or cayenne
  pepper (more if you want
  cheese straws hot)

Mix well. Put into cookie press, using the star attachment. Bake at 400° for 10 minutes or until crisp. Store in tins. Will keep for several months.

Jane Killian, Birmingham South Council

JALAPENO CHEESE SQUARES

4 c. grated Cheddar
  cheese
4 eggs, beaten
1 tsp. minced onion
4 jalapeno peppers,
  seeded and chopped

Combine all ingredients; mix well. Spread in an ungreased 8 inch square pan. Bake at 350° for 30 minutes. Cut into 1 inch squares. Yield: 64 squares.

Gloria H. Ramage, Birmingham South Council

CHICKEN FINGERS

Chicken breast
Buttermilk
Egg

Flour
Salt
Pepper

Wash chicken breast; debone and cut into 1 to 2 inch strips, following the grain while cutting the meat. Marinate in buttermilk overnight or a few hours. Beat egg until fluffy (can add a few drops of water). Dip each strip of meat in egg mixture, then shake each one in a small paper bag containing the flour, salt and pepper. Deep fat fry at 250° to 300° until golden brown, or skillet with oil. Drain on paper towel.

Bonnie Mayfield, Anniston Council

BAKED CHICKEN LIVER AND BACON

1 lb. chicken livers
3 Tbsp. Dijon mustard

10 to 12 slices bacon, cut
  in halves
1/2 c. cracker crumbs

Dip chicken livers lightly in mustard. Wrap a half slice of bacon around each, and secure with a wooden pick. Coat livers with crumbs. Place in an 8 inch square baking dish; bake at 425° for 25 minutes. Yield: 6 to 8 appetizer servings.

Linda Mitchell, Decatur Council

SAUCY CHICKEN LIVERS

1 lb. chicken livers
Salt
Pepper

1/4 c. melted butter
  or margarine
1 c. dry bread crumbs
Lemon Curry Dip

Lemon Curry Dip:

1 c. chicken broth or
  bouillon
1/3 c. freshly squeezed
  orange juice
1 Tbsp. cornstarch
3 Tbsp. brown sugar

1 Tbsp. butter or margarine
1/2 tsp. curry powder
2 tsp. freshly grated lemon peel
3 Tbsp. freshly squeezed
  lemon juice

Rinse livers in cold water and dry on paper towel. Cut into bite size pieces. Sprinkle livers with salt and pepper; dip in melted butter and coat with bread crumbs. Place on cold broiler pan 3 to 5 inches from source of heat in cold broiler. Broil 5 to 6 minutes on each side until crisp. Serve hot with Lemon Curry Dip. Appetizers for 8 or may be

8

served as a light supper.

Lemon Curry Dip: Thoroughly combine broth, orange juice and cornstarch. Add brown sugar, butter and curry; bring to boil over medium heat, stirring constantly. Boil 2 to 3 minutes. Add lemon peel and juice; set aside and keep warm. I put the Lemon Curry Dip in fondue to keep warm. Dip in the livers and you may enjoy dipping crusty French bread in dip. Delicious.

Bonnie Summers, Huntsville Council

CHINESE CHICKEN WINGS

50 wings (cut off tips)	1/2 c. soy sauce
1 tsp. dry mustard	1/3 c. salad oil
1 tsp. Accent	1/8 tsp. garlic powder
1 Tbsp. molasses (overflowing)	1 chopped medium onion

Mix all ingredients together and cover in refrigerator 7 to 8 hours to marinate. Turn over once or twice. Place on cookie sheet and bake 1 hour at 350° in shallow pan. (Try 40 minutes.)

Bonnie Summers, Huntsville Council

DIP FOR CHIPS

1 c. sour cream	2 dill pickles, finely chopped
2 (3 oz.) pkg. cream cheese	1 tsp. Worcestershire sauce
1/4 lb. chipped beef, finely chopped	2 tsp. prepared horseradish
	Dash of lemon juice
	Dash of pepper

Blend all ingredients. May add little milk for desired consistency.

A. M. Robertson, Huntsville Council

ARTICHOKE DIP

1 can artichoke hearts, drained and chopped	1 c. grated Parmesan cheese
1 c. Hellmann's mayonnaise	Melba rounds or other snack crackers

Mix artichoke hearts, mayonnaise and cheese. Place in small glass serving dish. Bake at 300° for 30 minutes. Serve with crackers.

Lisa Reinhard, Birmingham Central Council, Louise Trotman, Life Member, Birmingham Central Council

AVOCADO DIP

3 large ripe avocados,
    peeled and mashed
1 Tbsp. chili powder
1 tsp. taco sauce

3 Tbsp. lemon juice
2 Tbsp. mayonnaise
1/2 tsp. salt
2 Tbsp. finely chopped onion

Combine all ingredients, mixing well. Serve with taco chips. Makes 2 cups.

B. Hall, Huntsville Council

MEXICAN AVOCADO DIP

1 can refried beans with
    peppers or bean dip
2 Tbsp. lemon juice
2 or 3 ripe avocados
1/2 tsp. salt
1/4 tsp. pepper
8 oz. c. sour cream
1/2 c. mayonnaise

3/4 pkg. taco seasoning mix
1 large bunch new chopped
    onion (green and all)
3 firm red tomatoes, cubed
1 can chopped black olives
8 oz. Cheddar cheese,
    grated
Tortilla chips

Blend avocados, lemon juice, salt and pepper together until all lumps are removed. Mix sour cream, mayonnaise and seasoning mix together. Heat refried beans and layer in bottom of glass baking dish. Put a layer of avocado mix on top, then a layer of sour cream mix. Then layer onion, tomatoes, black olives and cheese in same fashion. Melt cheese in 325° oven until desired consistency is obtained.

Diane Lassiter, Huntsville Council

BAKED BEEF DIP

1 c. chopped pecans
2-4 tsp. melted butter
2 (8 oz.) pkg. cream
    cheese, softened
1/4 c. milk

2 (2 1/2 oz.) jars
    dried beef, minced
1/2 tsp. garlic salt
1 (8 oz.) carton sour cream
4 tsp. finely minced onion

Saute pecans in butter until lightly browned. Drain on paper towels. Set aside. Combine remaining ingredients; mix well. Spoon into greased 1 1/2 quart baking dish. Top with pecans; bake at 350° for 20 minutes or until bubbly. Serve hot with assorted crackers or Bugles. Works best when kept warm in chafing dish.

Mary Jo Murphy, Riverchase Council

BEAU MONDE DIP

1/2 c. sour cream
1/2 c. mayonnaise

Spices: Beau Monde, onion
salt, garlic salt, dill weed

This dip is made strictly by taste. Start with the above ingredients; add dashes of each spice, then put in refrigerator for about 30 minutes and then taste again. The taste changes as the spices mingle. It's best when made 24 hours in advance. Excellent as a vegetable dip or served with potato chips.

Sheilah Miller, Birmingham East Council

BROCCOLI DIP

2 pkg. chopped broccoli
1 small onion, chopped
1 can cream of mushroom
  soup

1 small can mushroom pieces
1 stick butter or margarine
2 rolls of Kraft garlic cheese
2 ribs celery, chopped

Saute onions, celery and mushrooms in butter; add cheese and soup. Separate, cook and drain broccoli and add to mixture. Service with crackers or potato chips.

Rita Finley, Huntsville Council

CAULIFLOWER DIP

1 c. mayonnaise
6 oz. Blue cheese

1 clove garlic
1 tsp. Worcestershire sauce

Mix together and refrigerate overnight. Serve with raw cauliflower or other vegetables.

Susan Ruskin, Montgomery Council

CHEESE DIP

1 (8 oz.) pkg. Velveeta
  cheese
1 chopped jalapeno pepper
  (optional)

1 (10 oz.) can Ro-Tel with
  tomatoes and green
  chilies

Pour can of Ro-Tel into small saucepan; add cheese and pepper, if desired. Cook over low heat until cheese is melted. Serve with Tostitos and Doritos.

Brenda McKinney Reeves,
Birmingham South Council

HOT CHEESE DIP

1/2 stick margarine
4 Tbsp. flour
2 Tbsp. chili powder
1 tsp. paprika
1 tsp. cumin

1/4 tsp. garlic powder
1/4 tsp. dry mustard
2 c. milk
8 oz. Velveeta or American
   cheese
1 Tbsp. catsup

Melt margarine; add dry ingredients and stir in the milk and continue stirring until thick. Add cheese and catsup; stir until cheese melts. Serve warm with chips, etc.

Juanita Davis, Birmingham Central Council

CON QUESO DIP

1 lb. Velveeta cheese,
   cubed
1 (16 oz.) can tomatoes,
   drained and chopped

1/4 c. chopped onion
1 tsp. chili powder
1 (4 oz.) can whole green
   chilies, drained and chopped

Combine all ingredients; cook over low heat until cheese melts. Serve hot with green pepper strips, carrot and celery sticks, French bread cubes or tortilla chips.

Anna Lee Hickman, Tri-Cities Council

CHILI CHEESE FONDUE

1 lb. hamburger (grease
   drained after frying)
1 lb. cheese (American),
   cut in small pieces

1 can green peppers, cut up
1 can tomatoes and jalapeno
   peppers
1 tsp. Worcestershire sauce
1/2 tsp. chili powder

Stir constantly until cheese melts in slow cooker. Cook on high for 1 hour. Serve with tortilla chips.

Jane Patterson, Riverchase Council

CLAM DIP

3 (3 oz.) pkg. cream
   cheese
1 (8 oz.) can minced
   clams, drained

1 tsp. dry mustard, or
   more to taste
Red pepper, salt, onion
   juice, Tabasco to taste

Heat all ingredients in double boiler until well mixed. Serve in chafing dish with chips or crackers.

Dede McNeal, Huntsville Council

HOT CLAM DIP

3 Tbsp. butter
1 small onion, chopped

1/2 bell pepper, chopped
1 pimento, chopped

Cook the preceding ingredients for 3 minutes and add:

1 (8 oz.) can minced
  clams, drained
1/2 lb. Velveeta cheese,
  cubed

4 Tbsp. catsup
1 Tbsp. Worcestershire
1 Tbsp. milk
1/4 tsp. cayenne pepper

When cheese melts; stir until smooth.
Jo Tidwell, Huntsville Council

DEBBIE'S HOT CRAB DIP

3 Tbsp. butter
1 medium onion, finely
  chopped
1/2 green pepper,
  finely chopped
1 (6 oz.) can crabmeat

1/4 lb. Old English
  cheese, cubed
4 Tbsp. catsup
1 Tbsp. Worcestershire sauce
1 Tbsp. milk
Dash of salt, pepper and
  garlic salt

Melt butter and add onion and green pepper. Saute for 3 minutes. Add crab, cheese, catsup, Worcestershire and milk. Cook until cheese is melted. Season with salt, pepper and garlic salt to taste. If preferred, dip can be seasoned with Tabasco for hotter taste. If cooking for more than 4-6, recipe should be doubled.
Dianne Bledsoe, Birmingham Central Council

CRABMEAT MORNAY

1 stick butter
4 or 5 green onions,
  chopped
1/2 c. finely chopped
  parsley (fresh)
2 Tbsp. flour
1 pt. half & half

1/2 lb. Swiss cheese, grated
1 Tbsp. sherry
Red pepper to taste
Salt to taste
1 lb. lump crabmeat
  (fresh, not canned)

Melt butter in heavy pot; saute onions and parsley. Blend in flour, half & half and cheese, stirring until cheese is melted. Add other ingredients and gently fold in crabmeat. Can be served in a chafing dish with Melba toast rounds or in party shells.
Anne Spragins, Birmingham East Council

CURRY DIP FOR VEGETABLES

1 c. mayonnaise	1 tsp. garlic salt
1 tsp. curry powder	1 tsp. prepared horseradish
1 tsp. tarragon vinegar	

Combine all ingredients; mix well and chill. This is pretty served in a small hollowed out purple cabbage and surrounded with fresh vegetables such as broccoli, cauliflower, carrots, zucchini, celery, cucumber, bell pepper, radishes, etc.

Linda Jones, Riverchase Council

DILL AND SOUR CREAM DIP

1 c. sour cream	1 tsp. flaked onion
1 c. mayonnaise	3 tsp. or more parsley,
1 1/4 tsp. crushed dill weed	dried or fresh

Mix all ingredients and let stand at least 1 hour. Serve as a dip with potato chips. Some add chopped cucumber and/or shrimp to this tasty and economical dip.

Selina Dyess, Huntsville Council

FANTASTIC DIP

1/4 tsp. red pepper	2 boxes chopped broccoli
2 Kraft garlic cheese rolls	1 medium onion, chopped
1 can mushroom soup	1 can sliced mushrooms
	2 tsp. butter

Saute onions and mushrooms in butter. Melt cheese in mushroom soup. Cook broccoli by directions. Combine all in chafing dish. Serve hot with chips or crackers.

Selene Patterson, Birmingham South Council

FRESH FRUIT DIP

1/2 c. sugar	Grated rind and juice
1/4 c. cornstarch	of 1 orange
1/2 tsp. salt	Grated rind and juice
2 eggs, beaten	of 1 lemon
1 c. pineapple juice	6 oz. softened cream cheese

Combine everything but cheese in the top of a double boiler; cook over medium heat, stirring constantly until smooth and thickened. Remove from heat; cool. Beat cream cheese until fluffy; add cooked mixture, beating until well blended. Chill. Serve with wedges of fresh fruit.

Debbie Tucker, Birmingham East Council

GUACAMOLE DIP OR SALAD

2 large avocados
1/2 c. chopped onion
3 seeded chopped
  jalapeno peppers

1 large chopped, peeled tomato
Salt to taste
Lettuce
Tortilla chips

Mix first 5 ingredients and mash well. Serve on lettuce with tortilla chips.

Edwina Hicks (Mrs. Jimmy),
Montgomery Council

HORSERADISH DIP

1 c. California Dip:
  1 env. onion soup mix
  and 1 pt. sour cream

Pinch of snipped parsley
1 Tbsp. horseradish
2 Tbsp. milk

Combine 1 cup California Dip with 1 tablespoon horseradish and 2 tablespoons milk. Sprinkle top with snipped parsley. Makes 1 cup.

Becky Cook, Huntsville Council

PARMESAN PARTY DIP

2 c. dairy sour cream
1 c. shredded sharp
  natural Cheddar
  cheese

1/2 c. grated Parmesan cheese
4 crispy cooked bacon
  slices, crumbled
1/4 c. green onion slices

Combine sour cream and cheese; mix well. Stir in bacon and onion; chill. Garnish with additional green onion, if desired. Serve with vegetable dippers or chips.

Frances Crenshaw, Birmingham East Council

PARTY DIP

1 (3 oz.) pkg. soft
  cream cheese
1 Tbsp. light cream
  (half & half)
1 Tbsp. chili sauce

2 tsp. grated onion
1/4 tsp. salt
1/8 tsp. dry mustard
Few drops of Worcestershire
  sauce
Dash of pepper

Early in day blend cream cheese, light cream, chili sauce, onion, salt, mustard, Worcestershire sauce, pepper until smooth and creamy. Refrigerate until ready to serve. Makes 1/2 cup.

1567-82
    Aileen Hardin, Riverchase Council

PECAN DIP OR SPREAD

1 c. chopped pecans
1 jar dried beef,
  chopped fine
2 tsp. onion flakes
1/2 tsp. salt to taste
  (optional)

1 (8 oz.) pkg. cream cheese
1/2 c. sour cream
1/2 c. chopped green pepper
Pepper to taste
1 tsp. butter

Saute pecans in butter. Mix well with remaining ingredients. Bake in small casserole dish or pan for 20 minutes at 350°. Serve on party rye or various crackers.

Joy Brewer, Riverchase Council

SHRIMP DIP

1 (8 oz.) pkg. cream
  cheese
1/3 c. mayonnaise
2 Tbsp. chili sauce
2 Tbsp. grated onion

2 Tbsp. lemon juice
1 tsp. Worcestershire
  sauce
1/2 lb. cooked shrimp
Pinch of salt

Soften cream cheese. Chop shrimp. Mix all ingredients. Serve with crackers or chips.

Ms. Bill Wheeler, Birmingham South Council

SPINACH DIP

1 (10 oz.) pkg. frozen
  chopped spinach
1 pkg. Knorr vegetable
  soup mix

1 (8 oz.) carton sour cream
1 c. mayonnaise
1 medium onion, chopped
1 can water chestnuts, chopped

Thaw spinach and drain thoroughly. Squeeze all water out of spinach. Mix all ingredients and refrigerate. Keeps well for several days.

Jane Knox, Montgomery Council

DIP FOR RAW VEGETABLES

8 oz. cream cheese
1/3 c. French or Thousand
  Island dressing

2 Tbsp. catsup
2 tsp. finely chopped onion

Mix together and serve chilled as a dip for peppers, carrots, celery, radishes, sliced cucumber or squash, mushrooms, etc.

Barbara Munson, Birmingham South Council

WATER CHESTNUT DIP

1 (8 oz.) carton sour cream
1 c. mayonnaise
2 (8 oz.) cans water
   chestnuts, drained and
   finely chopped

1/4 c. chopped onion
1/4 c. chopped parsley (fresh)
3/4 tsp. soy sauce
1/2 tsp. salt

Combine all ingredients in a medium bowl; stir well. Chill. Serve dip with potato chips or crackers.

Vinnie Mae Lyon, Birmingham Central Council

DEVILED EGGS

4 hard cooked eggs
2 tsp. mayonnaise or
   salad dressing
1 tsp. lemon juice
1/4 tsp. grated onion

1/2 tsp. dry mustard
1/2 tsp. Worcestershire sauce
1/2 tsp. pepper
1/2 tsp. salt
Paprika

Halve eggs lengthwise. Remove yolks; mash. Add mayonnaise, lemon juice, onion, mustard, Worcestershire sauce, salt and pepper; beat until fluffy. Refill egg whites. Garnish with parsley or paprika. Serves 4.

Frances Harris, Birmingham South Council

CHINESE EGG ROLLS

1 1/2 c. finely chopped
   raw shrimp
1 c. finely chopped celery
1 (8 1/2 oz.) can water
   chestnuts, finely chopped
1/2 c. finely chopped
   green onions
1 clove garlic

2 Tbsp. soy sauce
2 Tbsp. cornstarch
1/4 tsp. ginger
6 Tbsp. oil
Egg Roll Skins: 1 c. unsifted
   flour, 1 c. water, 2 eggs,
   1 Tbsp. corn oil

Prepare egg roll skins; set aside. In large skillet heat 3 tablespoons corn oil over medium heat; add shrimp, celery, water chestnuts, green onion and garlic. Cook 1 to 2 minutes or until shrimp turn pink. Stir in soy sauce, cornstarch and ginger. Spread 2 tablespoons filling down center of each skin. Tuck sides over filling and roll up, securing with wooden pick if necessary. In skillet heat remaining 3 tablespoons corn oil; add egg rolls, a few at a time, and brown on all sides.

Brenda Etheredge, Mobile Council

ZIPPY FRANKS

1 lb. frankfurters
1 (10 oz.) jar currant jelly
1/2 c. mustard
1 Tbsp. horseradish

Melt a 10 ounce jar of currant jelly with 1/2 cup mustard, 1 tablesoon of horseradish. Add 1 pound frankfurters, cut into 1 inch pieces. Heat and serve.
Mendolyn Dean, Montgomery Council

GAZPACHO

4 large ripe tomatoes, peeled and chopped
1/2 cucumber, chopped
1/4 c. green peppers, chopped
4 Tbsp. salad oil
1 c. tomato juice
1/2 tsp. salt
1/2 tsp. grated onion
1/2 tsp. fresh lemon juice
Fresh ground pepper
Dash of Tabasco sauce

Blend all ingredients in blender; blend well and cool. Serve ice cold.
Thelma Nelson, Birmingham East Council

APPETIZER HAM BALL

2 (4 1/2 oz.) cans deviled ham
3 Tbsp. chopped stuffed green olives
1 Tbsp. prepared mustard
Tabasco to taste
1 (3 oz.) pkg. cream cheese
2 tsp. milk

Combine first 4 ingredients; form into a ball on serving dish. Chill. Blend cream cheese and milk; frost ball with mixture. Keep chilled. Serve with assorted crackers.
Sammie Jackson, Huntsville Council

HAM AND CHEESE ROLL UPS

Ham slices
Cream cheese, softened

Spread cream cheese on ham slices. Roll ham up; cut diagonally into 1 1/2 inch sections. Secure with toothpicks.
Juelene Humphrey, Huntsville Council

HAM AND CHEESE PUFFS

Ham Mixture:

1 c. canned deviled ham
2 tsp. prepared mustard
1/2 tsp. Worcestershire
 sauce

1/4 c. mayonnaise
1 tsp. onion, finely grated
1 tsp. baking powder

Cheese Mixture:

3/4 c. Cheddar cheese,
 grated
1 beaten egg

1 tsp. onion, grated
1 tsp. baking powder

Trim crust from thin sliced white bread; cut each slice into 4 squares. Toast squares on one side. Turn over and spread thin layer of butter on each square before applying mixtures. Apply ham mixture first; spread to edge of squares. Top with cheese mixture. At this point, canapes may be frozen. When ready to serve, remove from freezer and place under broiler until topping puffs and is brown. Serve at once. Canapes should not be removed from freezer until ready to serve. Do not allow them to thaw.

Elsie Hard, Riverchase Council

HAM ROUND

1 c. baked ham, ground
1/2 c. chopped hazelnuts
1/2 c. chopped olives

Mayonnaise
Rye rounds
A few capers

Mix ham, nuts and olives with mayonnaise. Pile on rye rounds. Sprinkle with capers.

Susan Ruskin, Montgomery Council

HANKY PANKIES

1 lb. sausage
1 lb. ground beef
1 lb. Velveeta cheese

1 tsp. oregano
1 loaf pantry rye bread

In skillet brown sausage, ground beef and oregano. Drain well. Add cheese. Melt with beef and sausage. Spoon out on rye bread. Place on cookie sheet to freeze. When ready to serve, place in 350° oven until mixture is warm or cheese mixture has melted.

Louise Sexton, Montgomery Council
Dianne Dean, Montgomery Council

LOBSTER ROUNDS

2 c. lobster	Salt
1 hard boiled egg, chopped	Pepper
	Mayonnaise
1 tomato, peeled, drained and chopped	Wheat rounds
	Cucumber slices

Mix lobster, egg, tomato, salt, pepper and mayonnaise. Pile on wheat rounds. Garnish center with cucumber slices.

Susan Ruskin, Montgomery Council

MEAT BALLS
(For Hors D'Oeuvres)

2 lb. hamburger meat	2/3 c. brown sugar
1 c. chopped onions	3 Tbsp. butter
1 c. chopped bell peppers	1/2 c. bread crumbs
1 can tomato soup	1/2 c. Parmesan cheese, grated

Saute 1/2 cup onions and 1/2 cup bell peppers in butter; add tomato soup and brown sugar. Let simmer. This sauce turns reddish-brown. Take hamburger meat, 1/2 cup onion, 1/2 cup bell pepper, bread crumbs and cheese; mix together. Knead several times. Roll into small bite size meat balls. Broil; drain off grease. Put meat balls in sauce. Let simmer all day. These can be frozen. Just take out of freezer and put in refrigerator to thaw the day before you wish to serve. Serve in fondue pot.

Sheilah Miller, Birmingham East Council

SWEET AND SOUR MEAT BALLS

Meat Balls:

1 env. onion soup	1/2 c. dry oats or 2 slices bread, crumbled
2 lb. ground meat	

Mix the above and make into small meat balls. Place on cookie sheet and brown in 400° oven for about 20 minutes. Drain.

Sauce:

1 or 1 1/2 c. apricot nectar	2 Tbsp. mustard
1 c. catsup	3/4 c. brown sugar
2 Tbsp. horseradish	1/2 c. vinegar

Blend all and cook slowly for about 10 minutes before adding meat balls. Simmer for 10-15 minutes.

Sherry Lonnergan, Anniston Council

GREAT NACHOS

1 pkg. Doritos
1 can chili with beans

1 can chili without beans
2 c. shredded cheese

Layer Doritos, chili and cheese on large plate. Microwave 7 minutes on high or bake in 350° oven 30-40 minutes.
Pati Cheney, Birmingham East Council

OLIVE CHEESE APPETIZERS

3 c. grated Cheddar cheese
2 (4 1/2 oz.) cans black
olives, chopped
1 c. mayonnaise

1/2 c. chopped onion
1/4 tsp. curry powder
2 loaves Pepperidge Farm
rye bread

Mix first 5 ingredients together. Toast one side of bread. Spread mixture on other side of toast. Heat under broiler. Serve hot.
Louie Spear, Montgomery Council

OLIVE CHEESE PUFFS

6 oz. Monterey Jack cheese,
grated (about 1 1/2 c.)
3/4 c. flour
1/4 c. butter or margarine,
softened

2/3 c. small stuffed
green olives
2 Tbsp. fine dry bread
crumbs
Paprika

Mix together cheese, flour and butter until crumbly. Shape small amount of dough around each olive. Roll balls into bread crumbs; sprinkle with paprika. Refrigerate 1 hour. Place on ungreased baking sheet. Bake in 350° oven 20 to 25 minutes. Serve warm. Makes about 3 dozen.
Aileen Hardin, Riverchase Council

OYSTERS WILLIAMS' STYLE

2 pt. oysters and liquid
1 env. Good Seasons
salad dressing
1 oz. white wine

2 oz. soy sauce
1/4 c. oil
1/4 c. red cider vinegar

Mix all ingredients together. Place oysters in baking sheet and pour mixture over them. Broil for 15 minutes. Serve with your favorite cracker.
Mary Lynn Williams, Mobile Council

PARMESAN SESAME STICKS

12 slices of bread,
  crusts removed
1/4 c. butter, melted

1/4 c. Kraft Parmesan
  cheese
2 Tbsp. sesame seeds

Cut each slice of bread into 4 sticks and place on ungreased cookie sheets; brush with butter, then sprinkle with cheese and sesame seeds. Bake at 350° for 10-15 minutes until golden brown. Yield: 4 dozen.

Becky Woo, Birmingham South Council

SPICED PINEAPPLE PICKUPS

1 (20 oz.) can pineapple
  chunks
3/4 c. vinegar
1 1/4 c. sugar

Dash of salt
6 to 8 whole cloves
1 (4 inch) piece stick
  cinnamon

A day or so ahead: Drain syrup from pineapple chunks. To 3/4 cup syrup add vinegar, sugar, salt, cloves, cinnamon. Heat 10 minutes. Add pineapple chunks. Bring to a boil. Refrigerate until time to serve. To serve, drain pineapple chunks. Serve them ice cold with picks.

Donna Bertoldi, Huntsville Council

NEW POTATO HORS D'OEUVRES

2 dozen new potatoes
  (tiniest size)
1/2 c. sour cream

Chopped green onion,
  bacon bits or caviar

Cook potatoes with their skins on in boiling, salted water until done. When cool enough to handle, cut the potatoes in halves and scoop out a small cavity with a spoon or melon baller. Fill the cavity with sour cream and top with chopped onion, bacon bits or caviar. Serves 8 to 10 people.

Flo Thompson, Montgomery Council

POTPOURRI PILE

1 can ripe pitted black
  olives, chopped
1 can green chilies,
  chopped
2 ripe tomatoes, chopped

1/2 tsp. wine vinegar
Dash of Tabasco
1 Tbsp. olive oil
2 to 3 chopped green onions
Dash of garlic

Mix and chill. Serve with large Fritos.

Dianne Dean, Montgomery Council

SAUSAGE BALLS

3 c. Bisquick
2 c. grated cheese

1 lb. sausage (room
  temperature)

Mix ingredients together and form into balls. Bake in 400° oven about 15 to 20 minutes. I use mild sausage and mild cheese. (You can use hot sausage and sharp cheese.)

Shirley Hunter, Tuscaloosa Council

SAUSAGE BALLS IN CHUTNEY SOUR CREAM SAUCE

1 lb. mild bulk sausage
1 c. sour cream

1/4 c. sherry
1/2 c. chutney, chopped fine

Roll sausage into balls and cook in heavy skillet until well browned and done. Remove sausage and drain grease. Put sour cream, chopped chutney and sherry into skillet. Cook gently for few minutes; do not boil. Put sausage into chafing dish and pour sauce over. Serve with toothpicks.

Fran Rhodis, Montgomery Council

"SHRIMP ARNAUD"

2 lb. cooked shrimp
1/4 c. minced celery
1/4 c. green onions, minced
1/2 c. prepared Creole
  mustard

1/2 c. vinegar
1/4 c. olive oil
Crushed red pepper, to taste
1 Tbsp. salt

Combine all ingredients except shrimp and mix thoroughly. Pour over shrimp. Marinate at least an hour. Serves 6.

Mrs. Thelma M. Nelson, Birmingham Council

SHRIMP COCKTAIL

1/2 c. catsup
1/2 c. chili sauce
1/2 tsp. horseradish

3-4 drops of Tabasco sauce
1/2 lb. shrimp, cooked
  and cleaned

Mix catsup, chili sauce, horseradish and Tabasco sauce; shake well. Arrange shrimp on lettuce. Cover with sauce. Yield: 4 servings.

Flo Thompson, Montgomery Council

SHRIMP DELIGHT

1 lb. fresh boiled shrimp
1 (8 oz.) pkg. cream
  cheese
1 Tbsp. mayonnaise
1/4 - 1/2 tsp. garlic powder

1 Tbsp. catsup
1 1/2 tsp. Worcestershire sauce
1 Tbsp. lemon juice
2 Tbsp. grated onion
1 Tbsp. dill seed

Chop shrimp, reserving some whole ones for garnish. Combine all other ingredients except dill seed and blend well. Add chopped shrimp. Shape as desired and chill several hours. Garnish with whole shrimp and dill seed.

Alexine S. Becker, Montgomery Council

NIPPY SHRIMP

1 c. cleaned, cooked
  shrimp
1/2 clove garlic, crushed

1/2 c. chili sauce
8-10 slices bacon

Combine shrimp and garlic; pour chili sauce over. Cover; refrigerate several hours. Cut bacon slices in halves and fry until partially cooked. Drain. Wrap each shrimp in bacon piece. Secure with toothpick. Set oven at broil; broil 2-3 inches from heat until bacon is crisp. Makes 16-20 appetizers.

Jeannie Riddles, Riverchase Council

PICKLED (SNACK STYLE) SHRIMP

2 1/2 lb. shrimp
1/2 c. celery tops
3 1/2 tsp. salt
1/4 c. mixed pickling
  spices
1 pt. sliced onions

7 or 8 bay leaves
1 1/4 c. salad oil
3/4 c. white vinegar
2 1/2 Tbsp. capers and juice
2 1/2 tsp. celery seed and
  a dash of hot sauce

1. To 2 1/2 pounds shrimp add boiling water to cover. Add 1/2 cup celery tops, 3 1/2 teaspoons salt and 1/4 cup mixed pickling spices. Cook shrimp 10 to 12 minutes. 2. Drain shrimp; cool with cold water. Peel and remove black line; rinse. 3. Alternate cleaned shrimp and sliced onions (you'll need about 1 pint sliced onions). Add 7 or 8 bay leaves; you are now ready for the sauce. 4. Combine 1 1/4 cups salad oil, 3/4 cup of white vinegar, 1 1/2 teaspoons salt, 2 1/2 tablespoons capers and juice, 2 1/2 teaspoons celery seed and a dash of hot sauce (Tabasco). Mix well and then pour over shrimp and onions. 5. Cover dish and store

in refrigerator at least 24 hours. Pickled shrimp will keep well for at least 2 weeks in refrigerator (but they won't last long once you taste them).

Mary Fairchild, Mobile Council

SALMON ROLL

1 (1 lb.) can salmon (2 c.)
1 (8 oz.) pkg. cream
  cheese, softened
1 Tbsp. lemon juice
2 tsp. grated onion
1 tsp. prepared horseradish
1/4 tsp. liquid smoke
1/2 c. chopped pecans
1/4 tsp. salt
3 Tbsp. snipped fresh
  parsley

Drain and flake salmon, removing skin and bones. Combine salmon, cream cheese, lemon juice, onion, horseradish, salt and liquid smoke. Mix thoroughly; chill several hours. Combine pecans and parsley. Shape salmon mixture into 1 large mound or 2 small rolls. Roll in nut mixture. Chill; serve with crackers.

Billie Bays, Decatur Council

SPINACH BALLS

2 boxes frozen spinach,
  cooked and drained
  very dry
1 small bag Pepperidge
  Farm herb stuffing
2 large onions, chopped fine
6 eggs, beaten
1/2 c. Parmesan cheese,
  grated
1/2 tsp. black pepper
1 Tbsp. Accent
1 Tbsp. garlic salt
1/2 tsp. thyme
3/4 c. butter, melted

Mix together; shape into small balls. Place on cookie sheet. Freeze until solid. Put in bags in freezer. Defrost before serving; bake at 350° for 20 minutes. Makes 100 small balls. These are colorful and add to the spirit of Christmas or Saint Patrick's Day. Even spinach-haters love these, too.

Lisa Reinhard, Birmingham Central Council

SWEET - SOUR COCKTAIL BITES

1 c. packed brown sugar
3 Tbsp. all-purpose flour
2 tsp. dry mustard
1 c. unsweetened
  pineapple juice
2 tsp. soy sauce
2 Tbsp. pure vegetable oil
2 large green peppers, cut in
  1 inch square pieces
1/2 c. vinegar

1567-82

Smoked sausage links,
cocktail franks or
sliced frankfurters

2 (15 1/2 oz.) cans pineapple
chunks in unsweetened juice
(drain and reserve 1 c.
juice for sauce)

Drain pineapple; reserve 1 cup juice for sauce. In saucepan blend sugar, flour and mustard. Stir in pineapple juice, vinegar and soy. Cook and stir until thick and bubbly. Heat oil in large skillet over medium heat; add green peppers. Saute 2 minutes, stirring occasionally. Remove. Reserve. Add sausage or franks to skillet. Cook until lightly browned. Pour sauce in skillet with sausage and bring to a boil. Add pineapple and green peppers. Heat through. Serve in chafing dish with wooden picks. Serves 12.

Berniece Peterson, Birmingham South Council

STUFFED CHERRY TOMATOES

1 (8 oz.) pkg. cream
cheese
2 medium cucumbers
1/8 tsp. cayenne pepper

1/4 tsp. salt
1/8 tsp. white pepper
2 dozen cherry tomatoes
Capers

Peel and seed the cucumbers. Chop finely and cover with salted ice water for 10 minutes. Drain well. Mix with cream cheese (at room temperature). Add seasonings. Seed and drain the tomatoes; do not peel. Take a thin slice from the bottom so tomatoes will stand upright. Stuff with mixture. Top with a caper.

Donna Bertoldi, Huntsville Council

BENEDICTINE SANDWICH SPREAD

1 medium onion, peeled
and cut into chunks
1 cucumber, peeled and
cut into chunks

2 (8 oz.) pkg. cream
cheese, softened
1/4 tsp. salt
3 drops green food coloring

Position knife blade in processor bowl; add onion and cucumber. Process 3 to 5 seconds. Stop processor, and scrape sides with a rubber spatula. Process 3 to 5 additional seconds or until vegetables are finely chopped. Remove vegetables and drain well. Position plastic blade in bowl. Cut cream cheese into about 1 inch pieces; place in processor bowl. Process 8 to 10 seconds or until smooth. With processor running, add vegetables and salt through food chute; process 20 to 25 seconds or until well combined. Add food coloring; process about 5 seconds. Scrape sides; process 5

26

seconds or until well combined. Spoon mixture into a covered container, and chill thoroughly. Spread on pumpernickel bread and top with lettuce leaves, if desired. Yield: About 2 1/2 cups.

Faith Kirby, Anniston Council

SANDWICH SPREAD

1/2 lb. Velveeta cheese	Dash of salt
Mayonnaise	Minced onion to taste
1 pimento, chopped	3 hard cooked eggs, chopped

Blend cheese with enough mayonnaise to make a soft spreading consistency. Add remaining ingredients. Spread on whole wheat bread.

Flo Thompson, Montgomery Council

CORNED BEEF SPREAD

1 can corned beef	1 pkg. Lipton onion soup
1 small carton sour cream	2 Tbsp. mayonnaise

Mix all of the above ingredients together in a large mixing bowl. Put in refrigerator until cool. Makes delicious spread for sandwiches on rye bread. Serve with pickled onions or sweet pickles.

Wanda Lynch, Montgomery Council

JALAPENO CHEESE SPREAD

1 (8 oz.) pkg. cream cheese, softened	1 c. grated Cheddar cheese
1 (8 oz.) carton sour cream	3 to 4 jalapeno peppers, chopped finely

Mix well. Serve with crackers.

Pauline Woodham, Mobile Council

PARTY CHEESE SPREAD

10 oz. sharp "cold pack" cheese	2 Tbsp. chopped onion
8 oz. cream cheese	2 Tbsp. chopped bell pepper
2 Tbsp. butter	1 Tbsp. Worcestershire sauce
2 Tbsp. chopped pimento	1 tsp. lemon juice

Cream cheeses and butter together till well blended; add other ingredients and mix well. Serve with assorted crackers.

Nancy Morgan, Decatur Council

PIMIENTO CHEESE SPREAD

4 c. (1 lb.) shredded
  extra-sharp Cheddar
  cheese
1 (4 oz.) jar pimiento,
  drained
3/4 c. chopped pecans
1/2 c. mayonnaise

12 pimiento-stuffed
  olives, diced
2 Tbsp. dry sherry
1 Tbsp. olive juice
1 tsp. sugar
1/2 tsp. pepper
1/2 tsp. hot sauce

Combine all ingredients and stir well. Chill. Yield: About 4 cups.

R. Cash, Anniston Council

GAIL'S COOKED PIMENTO CHEESE

1: Bring to boil -

1 Tbsp. margarine
1/4 c. vinegar

3/4 c. water

2: Add (while still boiling), mixed:

3 Tbsp. sugar

1 Tbsp. flour

3 Add 2 eggs, beaten, while still boiling. Pour over:

1 box grated cheese
  (about 1 lb.)

1 small pimento

Cook over low heat. Pour sugar and flour mixture in slowly. Mash pimento before adding to cheese.

Anne Spragins, Birmingham East Council

HAM, PINEAPPLE, CREAM CHEESE FILLING

1 can chunky ham
1 small can crushed
  pineapple, well drained

Mayonnaise to moisten
1 pkg. cream cheese
Few chopped pecans

Good for sandwiches for coffees or lunch.

Suzanne Beaty, Riverchase Council

DEVILED HAM SNACK

1 large can deviled ham
1 large pkg. cream cheese

About 12-15 olives, chopped

Allow cream cheese to soften. Mix all ingredients. Good on rye bread or as a dip with Club crackers.

Judy Bejarano, Birmingham West Council

28

TUNA PATE

Blend together:

1 (8 oz.) pkg. softened cream cheese
2 Tbsp. chili sauce
2 Tbsp. parsley
1/2 tsp. Tabasco sauce
2 (6 1/2 oz.) cans tuna, drained
1 tsp. minced onion

Pack into a 4 cup mold and chill at least 3 hours. Unmold. Serve with crackers.

Debbie Tucker, Birmingham East Council

TUNA WALNUT SPREAD

1 (6 oz.) can tuna
1 (3 oz.) pkg. cream cheese
1/2 onion
Pickle relish (to taste)
Chopped walnuts
Lemon juice

Combine tuna, well drained, cheese, a little lemon juice, chopped onion, chopped walnuts and pickle relish. Serve with crisp crackers.

Mendolyn Dean, Montgomery Council

ASPARAGUS PINWHEELS

Use 1 can of green asparagus spears, drained on paper towels. Mix well one 8 ounce package of regular cream cheese (not whipped - needs to be at room temperature to mix), about 3 small green onions (use part of the blade), chopped fine (use more or less to taste), about 1/4 teaspoon dill weed (you don't want to overpower, as the dill weed flavor absorbs after mixture sets), about 1 tablespoon mayonnaise (more or less), to make mixture more spreadable. Use Nature's Own honey and wheat or Millbrook honey crushed wheat bread - I find this is tastier than white bread and the fresher the bread, the easier to work with.

Trim crusts from bread (this will probably be enough spread for about 12 slices). Roll bread fairly thin with glass or rolling pin. Spread about 1 tablespoon of cream cheese mixture on the bread (more or less of mixture as you see how much you need). Place asparagus spear on bread and roll, sealing end of bread with cheese mixture, then remove excess and spread with finger. To hold shape, roll in waxed paper as you finish each roll, then wrap in foil and cool in refrigerator overnight. Each roll can be cut into 5 pieces to make a nice bite size pinwheel.

I find the cream cheese mixture is better if you mix it the night before you spread it on the bread. The cream

1567-82

cheese seems to have more time to absorb the onion and dill flavors. Remove from refrigerator in plenty of time to get to room temperature before spreading.

Barbara Hill, Birmingham Central Council

ASPARAGUS ROLL UPS

Cream together:

8 oz. cream cheese
4 oz. Blue cheese
1 egg

1 can asparagus spears, drained

Cut crust from large loaf of white or whole wheat bread. Roll each slice of bread thin with rolling pin; spread with cheese mixture. Add asparagus spear and roll up. Partially freeze for easier slicing. Cut each piece in fourths and secure with toothpick. Dip in melted oleo. Freeze at this point if desired. Bake frozen for 15 minutes in 400° oven.

Guy Pippin, Anniston Council

CARROT SANDWICHES

2 (8 oz.) pkg. cream
  cheese
4 small carrots
1/2 c. chopped pecans

1 Tbsp. onion juice
Salt
Pepper
Mayonnaise
Brown bread

In mixer cream the cheese and add grated carrots, onion juice, salt, pepper and enough mayonnaise to moisten. Add pecans. Trim bread. Spread filling and roll like jelly roll. Chill or freeze before slicing. Freezes well.

Beverly Hearn, Riverchase Council

CHEESE SANDWICH

2 (8 oz.) pkg. cream
  cheese
2 green onions (tops
  and all), chopped

6 Tbsp. mayonnaise
6 strips bacon, cooked crisp
1 c. Parmesan cheese, grated
Few drops of Tabasco
20 slices bread

Let cheese come to room temperature. Fry bacon crisp; crumble. Chop onions; add rest of ingredients; mix well. Cut 20 slices of bread in triangles; toast on one side. Put filling on other side. May be put in freezer and kept until needed. Few minutes before serving, run in oven and broil a few minutes until bubbly. Makes 80 triangles.

30   Jane Knox, Montgomery Council

HAM AND CHEESE SANDWICHES

1 (1/2 lb.) pkg. ham   1 pkg. Swiss cheese
  (4 long slices)   (4 long slices)

Cut ham and cheese in small pieces about the size of roll. Use about 3 packages of ready to serve rolls of 24 to a package.

Sauce:

1 stick oleo   2 Tbsp. poppy seed
2 Tbsp. sugar   2 Tbsp. salad mustard
1 Tbsp. grated onion   Salt/pepper to taste

Melt oleo and add ingredients in order. Break pan of ready to serve rolls in 3 rows. Slice each row open; lay aside. Spread sauce on both sides; add a small slice of cheese and ham. Fold rolls back together and place back in pan until ready to serve. Bake if fresh rolls at 250° for 20 minutes, or if frozen at 250° for 30 minutes. Can be made ahead of time and frozen.

Marcella James, Tri-Cities Council

HOT HOAGIE SANDWICH

1 can Tender Chunk ham,   1/4 tsp. garlic salt
  turkey or chicken   3 Tbsp. butter
1/4 c. mayonnaise   1/2 long loaf French bread
1/4 c. sour cream   6 oz. grated Cheddar
2 Tbsp. chopped onion   cheese
2 Tbsp. chopped parsley   1/4 c. ripe olives (optional)
                                Bell pepper

Combine first 6 ingredients. Slice bread lengthwise. Butter bread and spread with meat mixture. Cover with cheese and garnish with bell pepper and ripe olives. Broil until cheese melts.

Diane N. Jones, Birmingham East Council

PINK PARTY PINWHEELS

1 small can crushed   1 small jar strawberry
  pineapple   preserves
1 (8 oz.) pkg. cream   2 loaves of unsliced bread
  cheese   Few drops of red food coloring

Place pineapple in colander; press out all juice with a fork. Combine pineapple, softened cream cheese and preserves in a bowl. Slice bread in thin layers lengthwise. Roll out with rolling pin on a damp cloth. Trim crust from edges. Spread each slice with a thin coat of butter, then add a thin layer of cream cheese mixture. Roll up; wrap in foil and freeze. Before serving, slice thinly. Will thaw in about 15 minutes.

Linda Prince, Huntsville Council

TUNA PUFF SANDWICHES

1 (7 oz.) can tuna, drained and flaked
1 1/2 tsp. prepared mustard
1/4 tsp. Worcestershire sauce
1/4 c. mayonnaise

1 1/2 tsp. grated onion
2 Tbsp. chopped green pepper (optional)
3 hamburger buns (split) or English muffins
Tomato slices

Topping:

1/2 c. mayonnaise

1/4 c. shredded cheese

Blend first 6 ingredients. Pile onto bun halves. Add tomato slice and top with cheese mixture. Broil 4 inches from heat until topping puffs and browns. Makes 4-6.

Becky Woo, Birmingham South Council

VEGETABLE SANDWICH

3 tomatoes
1 cucumber
1 green pepper
1 carrot
1 small onion
1 tsp. Worcestershire sauce

1 tsp. paprika
1/2 tsp. mustard
1 tsp. salt
1 c. mayonnaise
3 tsp. gelatin
1/4 c. cold water

Grind all vegetables in chopper; drain. Add seasonings. Dissolve gelatin in water in top of double boiler and heat. Add to vegetables and mix. Chill for several hours or overnight before making sandwiches.

Sharon Crabtree, Tuscaloosa Council

KOLIVA

1 c. cracked wheat
1 c. water
1/2 c. almonds

1/2 c. raisins
1 Tbsp. cinnamon
3 Tbsp. apple juice

Pour 1 cup boiling water over 1 cup cracked wheat;

cover and let stand 20 minutes. Add raisins, nuts, cinnamon and apple juice. Serve as cereal for breakfast. Serve as dessert or snack.

Jean Weaver, Mobile Council

PARTY CRUNCH MIX

1/2 c. margarine, melted
2 qt. popped corn
2 c. small pretzels
2 c. bite-sized crispy
   corn squares

1 (3 oz.) can chow mein
   noodles
1/2 c. grated Parmesan
   cheese

Pour margarine over combined remaining ingredients; mix lightly. Spread on ungreased 15 1/2 x 10 1/2 inch jelly roll pan. Bake at 250° for 1 hour, stirring occasionally. Makes 11 cups.

Frances Crenshaw, Birmingham East Council

SUGAR AND SPICED NUTS

2 c. pecan halves
1 egg white
1/4 c. sugar

1 tsp. cinnamon
Dash of salt

Put pecans in large bowl. Put in unbeaten egg white. Mix well with spoon until all halves are coated with egg white. Mix sugar and cinnamon and salt, then sprinkle over above mixture. Mix well again. Pour on ungreased cookie sheet; bake in preheated 300° oven for 30 minutes.

Peggy Hunter, Anniston Council

NORWEGIAN SUGARED NUTS

1 lb. shelled mixed nuts
   (or 4 c. pecans)
2 tsp. butter
1/4 c. butter

2 egg whites
1 c. sugar
1/4 tsp. salt
1/4 tsp. cinnamon (or to taste)

Arrange nuts in a shallow pan; add the 2 teaspoons butter. Cook until brown in 325° F. oven (similar to roasting pecans). Remove from pan; cool. Melt the 1/4 cup butter in the pan. Beat the egg whites until moist peaks form. Combine sugar, salt, cinnamon; fold into egg whites. Stir nuts into mixture. Spread them out over the melted butter, forming 1 layer. Bake 40 minutes at about 350°.

Annie Belle Whitlock, Montgomery Council

GLAZED PEANUTS

1 c. sugar
1/2 c. water

2 c. raw nuts

Place all ingredients in saucepan; cook over low heat until thick syrup. Spread on cookie sheet; roast at 250° for 15 or 20 minutes, or until peanuts are roasted as you like them. Separate the peanuts if they stick together.

Donna B. Byron, Montgomery Council

CANDIED PECANS

1 c. sugar
1/2 c. cold water
3/4 tsp. salt

1 tsp. vanilla
1 tsp. cinnamon
1 lb. shelled pecans

Combine all ingredients in a skillet except pecans; simmer for 4 minutes or until mixture spins a small thread from spoon. Remove from heat; stir in pecans. Continue stirring until syrup forms a sugar coating over pecans. Gently separate nuts on wax paper while cooling. Yield: 1 pound.

Eugenia Metzger, Tri-Cities Council

FRIED PECANS

4 c. pecan halves
1 1/2 qt. water

1/2 c. sugar
1/4 c. Wesson oil

Bring water to boil in large saucepan; add pecans and cook 1 minute. Empty pecans in colander and run hot water over them. Stir pecans in the sugar until sugar dissolves. Heat Wesson oil until hot; add pecans. Fry until brown, stirring continuously. Spoon pecans to paper towels; sprinkle with salt. Allow to completely cool before placing in a container.

Virginia H. Greene,
Birmingham Central Council

PARTY PECANS

8 c. pecans
1 stick margarine

4 tsp. Worcestershire sauce
1/2 tsp. garlic salt

Melt margarine; add Worcestershire sauce and garlic salt. Heat pecans in 250° oven in a shallow pan; pour heated pecans into a large bowl. Drizzle mixture over nuts; stir well. Return to oven; toast 1 hour at 250°. Rice and Corn Chex may be substituted for some of the nuts.

34   Charlene Brown, Montgomery Council

SPICED PECAN HALVES

1 c. sugar
1/2 tsp. cinnamon
1/3 c. evaporated milk

2 c. pecan halves
1 tsp. vanilla

Boil sugar, cinnamon and evaporated milk to soft ball stage; add pecan halves and vanilla. Put onto wax paper and let dry.

Edna Johnson, Birmingham South Council

BAKED CARAMEL CORN

1 stick margarine
1 c. brown sugar

1/2 tsp. salt
1/4 c. light Karo syrup

Bring above to boil and boil for 5 minutes. Then add:

1/2 tsp. vanilla

1/4 tsp. soda

Stir well. Pour over 3-4 quarts popped popcorn; mix well. Peanuts or pecans are optional. Use large oven pan and grease with butter. Pour popcorn mix in pan; bake at 275° for 20 to 30 minutes.

Beverly Durham, Mobile Council

CAROL'S POPCORN BALLS

1/3 c. light molasses
3/4 c. sugar
1/4 c. water
1/4 tsp. vinegar

1/4 tsp. salt
1 1/2 Tbsp. margarine
6 c. popped corn

Cook ingredients except margarine until it registers 270° F. on candy thermometer. Remove from heat; add margarine. Pour over popcorn. Shape into balls.

Dave Stewart, Mobile Council

GARLIC BUTTERED POPCORN

3 c. freshly popped corn
1/4 c. butter

1 clove garlic, split
1 Tbsp. chopped parsley

Place butter and garlic in small saucepan; heat until butter is melted. Remove garlic and stir in parsley. Pour butter mixture over popcorn and toss lightly. Very good with cocktails.

Fran Rhodis, Montgomery Council

1567-82

CHRISTMAS POPCORN BALLS

8 c. popped popcorn
1 c. natural cereal
1/2 c. pancake syrup

1/2 c. firmly packed brown
  sugar
1/2 tsp. salt
1/4 c. butter or margarine

Lightly grease a large bowl; add the popcorn and cereal. Mix well. In a heavy medium saucepan combine syrup, sugar and salt. Cook, stirring occasionally, over medium-high heat until mixture comes to a boil. Cook, stirring frequently, to hard ball stage (260°) or until small amount of mixture dropped into very cold water forms a hard ball which holds its shape, but is pliable. Remove from heat; add butter, stirring until melted. Pour over the popcorn mixture, mixing well. Cool slightly; shape to form balls, each about 3 inches in diameter. Place on wax paper. Cool thoroughly. Wrap securely in plastic wrap. Makes 6 to 8 popcorn balls.

Flo Thompson, Montgomery Council

PEANUT BUTTER POPCORN

6 qt. popped corn
1 c. sugar
1/2 c. honey

1/2 c. white corn syrup
1 c. peanut butter
1 tsp. vanilla

Place popped corn in large pan. Place in warm oven (225°). In a saucepan combine sugar, honey and corn syrup. Bring to a boil, stirring constantly; boil for 2 minutes. Remove from heat; stir in peanut butter and vanilla. Mix well. Pour over warm popped corn and mix well.

W. A. Davis, Riverchase Council

BANANA CRUSH

4 c. sugar
6 c. water
Juice of 5 oranges
Juice of 2 lemons

1 (46 oz.) can unsweetened
  pineapple juice
5 bananas, crushed
Soda or 7-Up

Boil sugar and water for 3 minutes. Mix orange juice, lemon juice, pineapple juice and bananas until smooth; stir in syrup. Freeze. Fill serving glasses half full with frozen mixture, beating with spoon. Fill glasses with soda, stirring to mix. Yield: 30 servings.

Elouise Buzzard, Mobile Council

VERY BLOODY MARY

1 (No. 5) can tomato juice	2 1/2 tsp. Worcestershire sauce
3/4 c. beef consomme	1 tsp. celery salt
1/2 tsp. Tabasco	1 tsp. salt
1/2 tsp. lemon juice	1/2 tsp. pepper

Combine all ingredients; mix well. Makes 1 1/2 quarts. To mix drinks, fill glass with ice and pour in 1 or more ounces of vodka. Add mix and stir slightly. Garnish with a wedge of lime and/or celery stick.

Larry York, Montgomery Council

BEWITCHING BREW

1 c. powdered milk	3 c. water
Dash of salt	3 Tbsp. sugar
3 Tbsp. cocoa	1/4 tsp. cinnamon

Combine solid ingredients; add water and mix well. Heat thoroughly.

Bea Windham, Montgomery Council

CAFE DIABLO

3 c. strong hot coffee	8 whole cloves
1/4 c. plus 2 Tbsp. brandy	4 orange twists
	4 lemon twists
1/4 c. Triple Sec	4 (2 inch) cinnamon sticks

Fill 4 mugs with 3/4 cup hot coffee each. Combine next 3 ingredients in a medium saucepan. Heat mixture until hot, not boiling. Ignite and pour 3 1/2 tablespoons into each mug. Place 1 orange twist and 1 lemon twist in each mug. Garnish each serving with a cinnamon stick.

Debbie Tucker, Birmingham East Council

EGGNOG
(40 cups)

1 dozen eggs, beaten separately	1 pt. liquor
	1 qt. whipping cream
1 c. sugar	Grated nutmeg

Beat the egg yolks and 1/2 cup sugar until thick and lemony; add liquor very slowly, beating constantly. Beat egg whites until foamy; add remaining sugar and beat until stiff, but not too dry. Fold into the yolk mixture. Fold in

1567-82

stiffly whipped cream. Refrigerate 1 hour before serving. Pour into punch bowl and sprinkle with nutmeg.

Betty Parker, Montgomery Council

ELDERFLOWER "CHAMPAGNE"

4 large heads elderflowers
1 1/2 lb. sugar (3 1/2 c.)

2 Tbsp. vinegar
1 gal. water
2 lemons

Put the flowers, sugar, vinegar and water into a large bowl. Squeeze the juice from the lemons and cut the shells into quarters. Add lemon juice and segments; cover and let stand for 24 hours, stirring or shaking occasionally with a wooden spoon. Strain into screw-topped bottles. Chill before serving. It's the softest, subtlest drink ever. May be served with a dash of vodka or white rum.

Thena B. Jenkins, Decatur Council

MOCK PINK CHAMPAGNE

1/2 c. sugar
1 c. water
1 c. grapefruit juice
1/2 c. orange juice
1/4 c. grenadine syrup

1 (28 oz.) bottle ginger ale, chilled
Twists of lemon peel
Stems on maraschino cherries

Combine sugar and water in saucepan; simmer uncovered, stirring constantly, until sugar is dissolved, about 3 minutes. Cool. Mix with juices and grenadine in punch bowl. Chill. Just before serving, add ginger ale, pouring slowly down side of bowl. Serve over ice in sherbet glasses. Trim with peel and cherry. Great for ladies' lunch or brunch.

Sandi Watts, Birmingham East Council

CHRISTMAS CORDIAL

1 qt. grape or cranberry
  juice
1 qt. water
1 c. white sugar
1/2 tsp. nutmeg

1/2 tsp. cinnamon or
  1 stick cinnamon
1 tsp. whole cloves
Juice of 1 lemon

Combine all ingredients. Simmer for 10 minutes. Remove cinnamon stick. Bottle. Add an ice cube to each glass when served. Yield: 2 quarts.

Flo Thompson, Montgomery Council

HOT CHOCOLATE MIX

1 (8 qt.) box Carnation
   instant milk
1 (6 oz.) jar Coffee-mate

1 (2 lb.) box Quik
1 box confectioners sugar
   (sifted)

Mix all ingredients thoroughly. Fill mug or cup 1/3 full with mix. Pour boiling water over mix and stir.

Kitty Logan, Anniston Council

MULLED CIDER

3 qt. apple cider
1 c. sugar
1 c. brown sugar

1 tsp. allspice
1/2 tsp. cloves
2 Tbsp. butter

Boil all ingredients together for about 5 minutes. Add 4 quarts orange juice and butter. Add stick of cinnamon when served, if desired.

Margaret W. Keith, Huntsville Council

STRAWBERRY DAIQUIRI

1 (8 oz.) carton frozen
   strawberries

1 (6 oz.) can frozen limeade
Light Bacardi rum

Place strawberries and limeade in blender. Fill blender with crushed ice. Pour rum (measured in limeade can) over ice. Blend to desired consistency. For a special dash, add pieces of soft peppermint to mixture before blending ingredients. Or add 2 tablespoons of creme of coconut for a tropical taste.

Celeste B. Mathews,
Birmingham South Council

WATERMELON DAIQUIRIS

Pulp from 2 1/2 lb.
   watermelon, seeded,
   cut into pieces and
   chilled
1 c. plus 2 Tbsp. dark rum

1/2 to 2/3 c. fresh lime
   juice, or to taste
3 Tbsp. superfine granulated
   sugar
3 tsp. orange-flavored liqueur

In a blender or food processor fitted with the steel blade, puree the watermelon, the lime juice, the sugar, the orange-flavored liqueur and the rum until the mixture is smooth and divide the mixture among chilled stemmed glasses. Makes 6 drinks.

Katherine Creamer, Mobile Council

LEMONADE COOLER

2 env. lemon-lime
   flavored drink powder
1 1/3 c. sugar

2 qt. water
3 (6 oz.) cans frozen
   lemonade concentrate
2 oranges or limes, sliced

Combine drink powder, sugar and water; stir until sugar is dissolved. Pour into ice cube trays and freeze. Add water to lemonade concentrate, according to directions on can. Place 2 or 3 frozen green cubes in tall glasses or jumbo paper cups; fill with lemonade. Garnish with a slice of orange or lime slice. Makes 3 quarts lemonade.

Wanda Ange, Birmingham East Council

KAHLUA
(Coffee Liqueur)

4 c. water
4 c. sugar
2 oz. instant coffee

1 qt. vodka (100 proof)
1 vanilla bean

Add water and sugar; boil for 5 minutes. Add 2 ounces instant coffee; boil for 5 minutes. Remove from heat; add 1 vanilla bean. Allow to cool. Add 1 quart vodka (100 proof). Let set 2-3 weeks. This makes 1/2 gallon.

Sheilah Miller, Birmingham East Council

PUNCH

2 lb. sugar
1 medium bottle lemon juice

1 qt. grape juice
2 (qt. size) bottles Canada Dry

Put sugar in saucepan; add 2 cups of water. Let it get just warm enough to melt sugar. Cool. Add lemon juice and grape juice. Do not add ginger ale until ready to serve. Use either ice cubes or ice mold.

Mary C. Martin, Birmingham East Council

PUNCH

1 fifth vodka
1 fifth white Yago

2 (48 oz.) cans pineapple juice
2-4 bottles ginger ale

Mix all ingredients. Can be served with ice ring in punch bowl.

Belinda J. White, Riverchase Council

40

PUNCH

2 large cans unsweetened
  pineapple juice
2 large cans "hot" water
2 qt. ginger ale

6 pkg. lemon-lime Kool-Aid,
  unsweetened (or flavor
  to give desired color)
6 c. sugar

Mix Kool-Aid and sugar in hot water until completely diluted. Add pineapple juice and freeze in large container. At serving time, remove from freezer and place in punch bowl. Pour ginger ale over frozen mixture and mix. Recipe may be halved. Serves 50.

Mary Ann Davis, Anniston Council

EASY PUNCH

3 pkg. (any flavor)
  Kool-Aid
3 c. sugar

1 large can pineapple juice
2 cans water (more if needed)
3 bottles 7-Up

Combine all ingredients except the 7-Up. Just before serving, add 7-Up. Makes about 40 cups. Pour over crushed ice. Use different flavor of Kool-Aid for occasions.

Willadean Cooley, Tuscaloosa Council

CIDER MILL PUNCH

1/2 gal. apple cider
2 c. orange juice
1 c. lemon juice
1/4 c. honey

2 1/2 inch cinnamon stick
5 whole cloves
1/4 tsp. allspice
1 1/2 tsp. butter

Bring to a boil; cover and simmer 1 hour. Makes about 3 quarts.

Faith Kirby, Anniston Council

HOT APPLE CIDER PUNCH

4 c. apple cider
2 c. cranberry juice
1 c. orange juice

1 (12 oz.) can apricot
  nectar
1 c. sugar

Heat all ingredients in a saucepan and simmer 20 minutes. Serves 20 to 25.

Linda L. Unger, Riverchase Council

CHAMPAGNE PUNCH

1 c. sugar   1 c. water

    Boil for 3 minutes and cool. Add:

1 c. lemon juice   1 bottle sparkling water
1 bottle sauterne   2 oranges, sliced
1 bottle pink champagne

        Elsie Hard, Riverchase Council

CHRISTMAS PUNCH

3 pkg. Kool-Aid (cherry,   2 large (10 oz.) bottles 7-Up
   strawberry, lemon)   4 c. sugar
1 large can pineapple juice   5 qt. water

       Lindie Rice, Tuscaloosa Council

CRANBERRY JUICE PUNCH

1 (3 oz.) pkg. cherry jello   1 (6 oz.) can frozen lemonade
1 c. boiling water   or pineapple-orange juice
1 (1 qt.) can cranberry   (condensed)
   cocktail juice, chilled   3 c. cold water

    Pour over ice. Add one 1 pint 12 ounce bottle of ginger ale and fruit-flavor sherbet, if desired.
       Bertha Capps, Birmingham East Council

CHRISTMAS PUNCH

1 regular size box   1 qt. pineapple juice
   cherry jello   1/4 pt. ReaLemon juice
2 c. boiling water   1 orange
2 c. sugar

    Dissolve jello in boiling water; add sugar and juices. Add enough water to make a gallon. Slice an orange into thin pieces. Peel off the rind and drop the fruit into the punch bowl. Refrigerate until ready to use.
       Sammie M. Jackson, Huntsville Council

HOT CRANBERRY PUNCH

2 1/2 c. cranberry juice
2 c. pineapple juice
2 c. water
1/2 c. brown sugar

1 Tbsp. whole cloves
1/2 Tbsp. allspice
1 Tbsp. cinnamon

Dissolve brown sugar in cranberry juice, pineapple juice and water. Pour into a coffee pot (8 cup coffee pot). Put cloves, allspice and cinnamon in the basket of coffee pot. Perk till good and hot. Makes 8 cups.

Brenda McGee, Birmingham South Council

FROZEN PUNCH

1 (48 oz.) can grape drink
1 (48 oz.) can pineapple-
  grapefruit drink
1 (12 oz.) bottle 7-Up

1 (6 oz.) can frozen
  lemonade concentrate
3 (6 oz.) cans water
1/2 c. (about) sugar

Mix all ingredients together; place in large aluminum pan. Place pan in freezer; stir every hour until completely frozen and resembles crushed ice. Will keep for weeks. Yield: 18 servings.

Virginia Mayo, Mobile Council

FRUIT PUNCH (YELLOW)

1 large can pineapple juice
3 small cans frozen orange
  juice (add water as
  directed on can)
2 qt. water

1/2 c. frozen lemon juice or
  1/2 dozen lemons, juiced
1 (6 oz.) pkg. lemonade
  mix (dry)
2 1/2 c. sugar

Mix well and freeze. Makes 1 1/2 gallons. Serves 50 people. Remove from freezer; let thaw at least 3 hours. Before serving, add 1 quart ginger ale.

Hazel Campbell, Birmingham South Council

LEMON-LIME PINEAPPLE PUNCH

2 pkg. lemon-lime Kool-Aid
2 c. sugar
2 qt. water

1 (36 oz.) can pineapple juice
  (if unsweetened, use 1 more
  c. sugar)
1 (32 oz.) bottle ginger ale

Mix ingredients. Yield is little over a gallon. Freeze punch in ice trays for ice.

Margie Judge, Mobile Council

1567-82

OPEN HOUSE PUNCH

2 c. sugar
2 c. water
1 (46 oz.) can apricot
nectar
1 (46 oz.) can unsweetened
pineapple juice
1 1/2 c. lemon juice
1 small can frozen orange
juice, mixed according
to directions on can
2 qt. ginger ale

Combine sugar and water; heat until dissolved. Cool and chill. Add other juices. Chill until ready to serve. Gently combine with cold ginger ale in punch bowl. Garnish (is very pretty with frozen ring). Serves 50.
Betty Gray, Montgomery Council

PARTY PUNCH

2 pkg. cherry Kool-Aid
1 (16 oz.) can frozen
orange juice
1 large can pineapple juice
2 c. sugar
1 gal. water
1 (16 oz.) can frozen lemonade

Mix all ingredients well. Can be served over ice or may be frozen to a slush consistency. To freeze, put in plastic milk jugs and store in freezer. Shake occasionally until punch is a slush. Shake jugs well and pour in punch bowl to serve. Different flavors of Kool-Aid can be used to change flavor.
Ann Ackerman, Birmingham South Council

PINEAPPLE-RASPBERRY CREAM PUNCH

2 qt. pineapple juice
4 (28 oz.) bottles
ginger ale
2 qt. vanilla ice cream
2 qt. raspberry sherbet

Pour pineapple juice and ginger ale over ice cream and sherbet and stir until melted and blended. Makes 2 dozen 4 ounce servings. Double all ingredients to serve 50.
Sandra Tutt, Montgomery Council

HOT SPICED PERCOLATOR PUNCH

10 cups:

3 c. pineapple juice
3 c. cranberry juice
1 1/2 c. water
1/3 c. brown sugar
1 1/2 tsp. whole cloves
1 stick cinnamon
1/8 tsp. salt

30 cups:

9 c. pineapple juice
9 c. cranberry juice
4 1/4 c. water

1 c. brown sugar
4 1/2 tsp. whole cloves
4 sticks cinnamon
1/4 tsp. salt

Combine juice, water, sugar and salt in coffee pot. Place spices in coffee pot basket; perk and serve hot.
Dot Beadlescomb,
Birmingham Central Council

SLUSH PUNCH

1 pkg. strawberry jello
1 pkg. cherry jello
1 1/2 c. sugar

1 large can pineapple juice
1 can frozen limeade
1 can frozen lemonade
1 qt. ginger ale

Dissolve gelatin as directed on package; add the frozen limeade diluted to make 1 quart, also lemonade. Put in freezer and freeze, stirring all along. Just before serving, add ginger ale and ice cubes if needed. Serves about 50.
Nancy Murray, Birmingham South Council

SLUSH

7 c. warm water
1 (3 oz.) pkg. strawberry
   jello
2 c. strong tea

1 large can frozen lemonade
1 large can orange juice
1 c. sugar
1 pt. vodka

Mix all together and put into covered container and freeze. Use a blender and mix with 7-Up until it is slushy. Serve.
Barbara Seegmiller, Decatur Council

STRAWBERRY PUNCH

1 large can pineapple juice
2 pkg. strawberry Kool-Aid
1 gal. water

1 small can frozen lemonade
   (undiluted)
1 pt. frozen strawberries
3 to 4 c. white sugar

Mix Kool-Aid and water; add remaining ingredients and mix well. Freeze overnight. Remove from freezer several hours before serving. Serve slushy. Serves 40-50.
Louise Couch, Birmingham South Council

1567-82

TROPICAL FRUIT PUNCH

2 pkg. cherry or
  strawberry jello
8 c. boiling water
1 c. sugar
1 1/2 c. lime or lemon juice

2 c. or 1 (No. 3) can
  pineapple juice
5 c. orange juice (fresh
  or frozen)
1 1/2 qt. Sprite or 7-Up

Stir jello in 2 cups boiling water until dissolved; add sugar, 6 cups cold water, lime juice, pineapple juice, orange juice. Chill. Add Sprite or 7-Up when ready to serve. Serves about 20.

Dora Murray, Mobile Council

ALMOND TEA

3 c. water
2 c. sugar
Juice of 3 lemons

1 tsp. vanilla
1 tsp. almond
2 c. strong tea

Boil sugar and water together and add rest of ingredients. Serve hot. Serves 12 cups.

Mrs. Vonda Cook, Riverchase Council

FRUITED TEA

4 tea bags or 3 Tbsp.
  loose tea
2 qt. plus 2 c. water
1 1/2 c. sugar

Juice of 3 lemons, strained
1 tsp. vanilla extract
1 tsp. almond extract

Make tea, using 2 cups water. Remove bags or leaves. Add sugar, lemon juice and extracts. Add remaining water when ready to serve. Heat and serve. Yield: 20 servings.

Flo Thompson, Montgomery Council

INSTANT SPICED TEA

1/2 c. instant lemon
  flavored tea
1 to 1 1/2 c. sugar
2 c. Tang

2 tsp. ground cinnamon
1 tsp. ground cloves
1 small pkg. sweetened
  lemonade mix

Mix all of the above together. Use 2 teaspoons of tea mixture to 1 cup hot water.

Nancy Williams, Anniston Council

RUSSIAN TEA

1 gal. water
2 sticks cinnamon
3 whole cloves
2 c. sugar

5 tsp. tea or 3 small tea bags
1 (16 oz.) can frozen orange
   juice
1 (16 oz.) can frozen lemonade

Boil tea, cinnamon and cloves in water for 2 minutes. Remove tea bags, cinnamon and cloves; add sugar and juices, mix and serve hot. Makes 1 gallon.

Sammie M. Jackson, Huntsville Council

RUSSIAN TEA

2 c. sugar
1 c. Tang
1/2 c. instant tea
2 tsp. ground cinnamon

1 small pkg. lemonade mix
   (about 1/2 c.)
1 tsp. ground cloves
1 tsp. whole cloves

Use heaping tablespoonful in cup of boiling water.

Lindie Rice, Tuscaloosa Council

WASSAIL

2 qt. apple juice or cider
1 pt. cranberry juice
3/4 c. sugar
1 tsp. aromatic bitters

2 sticks cinnamon
1 tsp. whole allspice
1 small orange, studded
   with whole cloves
1 c. rum (optional)

Put all ingredients in crock pot; cover and cook on high for 1 hour, then on low for 4 to 8 hours. Serve warm from crock pot. Makes good holiday drink. Makes about 12 cups.

Betty Chilton, Birmingham East Council

WASSAIL PUNCH

1/2 gal. natural apple juice
   (this juice will be cloudy)
1 can frozen apple juice
   concentrate
1 qt. Wagner's orange
   breakfast drink

5 sticks cinnamon bark
12 whole cloves (or
   ground to taste)
2 sliced oranges
Sugar to suit your taste

Mix juices, spices and concentrate together and heat in large pan. When the mixture begins to steam, add sugar, 1/2 cup at a time, until it is sweet enough for your taste. Slice orange over the top of the punch and simmer for at least an

1567-82

hour. Serve. If a punch bowl is used, heat the bowl with very hot water before adding punch. You may use spiced apple slices to decorate punch before serving.

Bertha Capps, Birmingham East Council

WEDDING PUNCH

4 c. Simple Syrup
8 c. pineapple juice
A sprig of mint

1 c. strained lemon juice
2 qt. Canada Dry ginger ale
Ice

All juice may be prepared and mixed early, but ginger ale is best added at the time of serving. This recipe makes 5 quarts of punch, 50 servings.

Simple Syrup: Cook sugar and water in equal proportions. For above recipe cook 4 cups sugar and 4 cups water to a thin syrup. Cool and store in refrigerator for use when needed.

Faith Kirby, Anniston Council

VODKA SLUSH

1 (6 oz.) can frozen orange juice concentrate, thawed and undiluted
2 (6 oz.) cans frozen lemonade concentrate, thawed and undiluted

2 (6 oz.) cans frozen limeade concentrate, thawed and undiluted
1 c. sugar
3 1/2 c. water
2 c. vodka
2 (28 oz.) bottles lemon-lime carbonated beverage, chilled

Combine first 6 ingredients, mixing well. Freeze 48 hours, stirring occasionally. For each serving, spoon 3/4 cup frozen mixture into a tall glass; fill with carbonated beverage. Serve at once. Yield: About 16 (8 ounce) servings.

Linda Austin, Tuscaloosa Council

WINE

Use equal part water and berries or fruit. Cut or mash fruit; boil water and pour over it. Let stand 4 days and strain. Sweeten to taste. Let stand 4 or 5 more days; strain again. If not sweet enough, add more sugar. Let stand 6 weeks before bottling. Be sure it is through working. If you make it in cool weather, let stand another week before straining.

48   Mary Edna Fife, Montgomery Council

GRAPE WINE

3 large cans frozen
  Welch's grape juice

3 c. sugar
1 pkg. yeast

Dissolve yeast in warm water; add to juice and sugar. Add water to make 1 gallon. Work 6 days, then strain several times. Bottle. Six days is maximum.

        Helen Gorff, Birmingham West Council

CULLMAN STRAWBERRY WINE

3 1/2 lb. fresh strawberries
1/8 lb. chopped white raisins
4 1/2 lb. invert sugar
1 campden tablet

1 gal. water
1/4 pkg. all-purpose
  wine yeast
3 Tbsp. sodium metabisulphite

Take fresh strawberries (if slightly overripe, the better), stem and mash in non-metallic container. Boil water and stir in sugar. While water is cooling, mix sodium metabisulphite with cool water and rinse fermentation container. Pour rinse down drain. Next, break up campden tablet; mix with sugar and water, and add mashed strawberries (pulp and all juice) with chopped raisins. Let set covered overnight. (If you have hydrometer, adjust water and sugar for a 24° on brix scale.) At room temperature (70° F. to 78° F.), add yeast and let aerobic fermentation begin for 2 days. Transfer to non-metallic cask; fit with air lock and let work for 6 months in dark cool area. Check air lock periodically for bubbling. Transfer with siphon (except last inch of liquid which contains settlings) to sterile containers and store in cool area. Serve chilled and once chilled, keep chilled until used up. Do not use in metallic implements or container after fermentation begins. For drier wine, cut sugar to 3 1/2 pounds per gallon.

        George Ponder, Decatur Council

** NOTES **

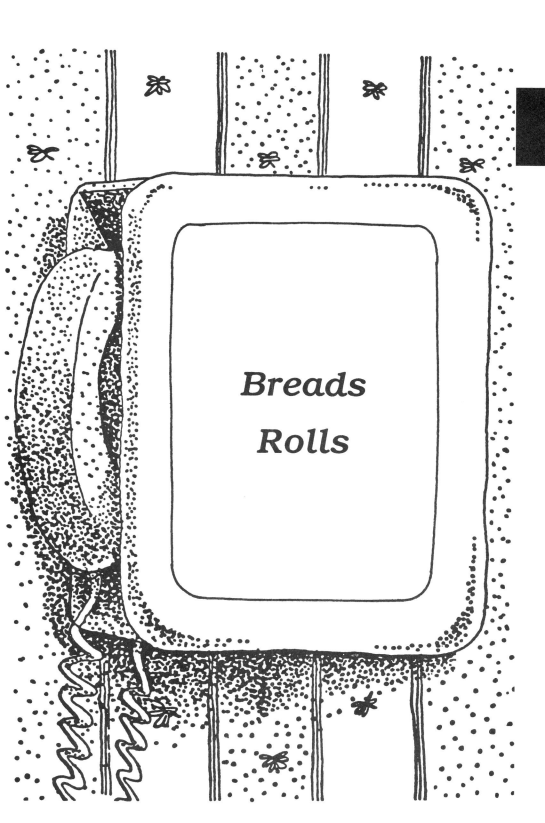

Breads

Rolls

BREAD BAKING GUIDE

The pleasure of baking homemade bread is matched only by eating it, except when something goes wrong. Most problems can be determined and easily avoided the next time.

Problem...	Cause...
Bread or biscuits are dry	Too much flour; too slow baking; over-handling
Bread has too open texture or uneven texture	Too much liquid; over-handling in kneading
Strong yeast smell from baked bread	Too much yeast; over-rising
Tiny white spots on crust	Too rapid rising; dough not covered properly while rising
Crust has bad color	Too much flour used in shaping
Small flat loaves	Old yeast; not enough rising or rising much too long; oven temperature too hot
Heavy compact texture	Too much flour worked into bread when kneading; insufficient rising time; oven temperature too hot
Coarse texture	Too little kneading
Crumbly texture	Too much flour; undermixing; oven temperature too cool
Yeasty sour flavor	Too little yeast; rising time too long
Fallen center	Rising time too long
Irregular shape	Poor technique in shaping
Surface browns too quickly	Oven temperature too hot
Bread rises too long during baking and is porous in center and upper portion of loaf	Oven temperature too cool

BREADS, ROLLS

ANGEL BISCUITS

5 c. flour, sifted
1 tsp. soda
3 tsp. baking powder
1/4 c. warm water
1 c. shortening

1/3 c. sugar
2 tsp. salt
1 pkg. dry yeast
1 1/2 c. buttermilk

Sift dry ingredients together; cut in shortening. Dissolve yeast in warm water and combine with buttermilk and then add this to dry ingredients. Stir well and then knead. Add more flour if necessary. Roll out on floured board about 1/2 inch thick; cut with biscuit cutter. Brush tops with melted butter. Bake at 450° until a golden brown. Cut out biscuits may be frozen on cookie sheets until hard and then placed in plastic bags and kept in freezer until needed.

Mrs. P. A. Garrett, Huntsville Council

ANGEL BISCUITS

1 pkg. dry yeast
1/4 c. warm water
2 1/2 c. plain flour
1/2 tsp. baking soda
1 tsp. baking powder

1 tsp. salt
2 Tbsp. sugar
1/2 c. shortening
1 c. buttermilk

Dissolve the yeast in warm water. Mix the dry ingredients. Cut in shortening as for biscuit dough. Add buttermilk and yeast mixture; blend thoroughly. Turn the dough out onto a floured cloth and knead as for regular biscuits. Roll out and cut biscuits. Place biscuits in a greased pan. Let dough rise for a few minutes before baking for 12-15 minutes at 400°.

Virginia H. Greene,
Birmingham Central Council

BISCUITS

4 c. self-rising Red Band
   flour
12 heaping Tbsp. lard

1 1/3 c. buttermilk (maybe
   a little more)
1 Tbsp. baking powder

Mix all ingredients; drop by spoon onto ungreased baking sheet. Do not use Crisco; use lard in the box. Bake at 400°.
1567-82   Jo Ardis, Anniston Council   51

BEER BISCUITS

4 c. Bisquick   1 (12 oz.) can beer
3 Tbsp. sugar

Stir all ingredients together; drop into hot muffin pan (greased). Cook 20 minutes at 375°. Makes 16 biscuits. Serve with roast, ham.

Eleanor Herring, Anniston Council

BUTTER-ME-NOT BISCUITS

2 c. Bisquick   8 oz. sour cream
1 stick butter or margarine   Water

Preheat oven to 425°. Mix first 3 ingredients; add just enough water to moisten. Form into a ball on a floured cloth and knead 10 times; pinch off enough dough for the size biscuit you want and roll in your hand. Place on ungreased baking sheet; bake 10 minutes. Makes 8 to 12 biscuits.

Martha Gordy, Riverchase Council

BUTTERCUP BISCUITS

2 sticks butter   2 c. presifted self-rising flour
                                8 oz. sour cream

Blend butter and sour cream until creamy; add flour. Place by teaspoon into buttercup-sized biscuit pans. Makes about 4 dozen. Bake at 350° for 30-35 minutes or until golden brown.

Kathy Geiger Jones, Tri-Cities Council

BUTTERMILK BISCUITS

2 c. self-rising flour   1/4 c. oil
3/4 c. buttermilk

Preheat oven to 400° F. Mix above ingredients with tablespoon. Coat hands with flour and spoon dough into your hand and roll biscuits in palms. Place on greased pan and cook about 8-10 minutes or until golden brown. Yield: Approximately 10-12 biscuits. Delicious.

LaVaughn Jarvis, Birmingham South Council

CHEESE BISCUITS

1 c. sharp Cheddar cheese	1 c. flour
1 stick butter	1 c. Rice Krispies

Mix all together; roll into small ball and put on cookie sheet. Bake at 375° for 15 or 20 minutes.

Mae Kennedy, Montgomery Council

CINNAMON BISCUITS

2 c. biscuit mix	2 tsp. cinnamon
1/2 c. brown sugar	2/3 c. milk

Topping:

3/4 c. powdered sugar	3 tsp. milk
1 tsp. vanilla	

Mix biscuit mix, brown sugar and cinnamon in mixing bowl: add milk. Drop by tablespoon onto greased pan; bake at 400° for 10 to 15 minutes.

Topping: Mix ingredients together; spread on top of biscuits while hot. Nuts and raisins may be added to biscuits, if desired.

Mrs. Jack E. Gentte, Sr.,
Montgomery Council

DROP BISCUITS

1 1/2 c. Martha White self-rising flour	1/2 c. Crisco oil Approx. 1/2 c. dairy fresh buttermilk

To flour add Crisco oil; stir, then add enough buttermilk to mix. Dough should be soft enough to drop easily. Drop by tablespoons onto a pan greased with bacon drippings and spoon just a dot or two of bacon grease on top of each. Bake in hot oven (450°) till brown. (Grated cheese added is a treat.)

Emma Husley, Mobile Council

FROZEN BISCUITS

5 c. flour	1 c. shortening
1/2 c. sugar	2 pkg. yeast
1 tsp. salt	1/2 c. warm water
1 tsp. soda	2 c. buttermilk
3 tsp. baking powder	

1567-82

Sift dry ingredients together; cut in shortening. Dissolve yeast in warm water; add to milk. Add milk to dry mixture; mix well. Turn onto floured surface; fold over (working in small amount of flour) several times. Pat or roll out to desired thickness; cut and place on greased cookie sheet and freeze. As soon as biscuits are frozen, if desired, roll each in melted (room temperature) butter; put them in freezer bags or freezer containers. Defrost 30 minutes before baking; bake at 400° until brown. Yield: 60 to 80 small biscuits, or you may wish to cut them larger. The size cutter (glass) I used produced a nice medium size biscuit and the yield was 35.

Tommie H. Smith, Montgomery Council

MAYONNAISE BISCUITS

1 c. self-rising flour   3 heaping Tbsp. mayonnaise
1/2 c. milk

Mix all ingredients well; drop by spoonfuls into muffin tin. Bake 15 minutes in 400° oven. Makes 6.
Note: If desired, biscuits may be rolled and cut; just decrease milk.

Jean Chandler, Mobile Council

OLD FASHIONED HOMEMADE BISCUITS

2 c. self-rising flour   1/4 tsp. soda
1 c. buttermilk   1 tsp. sugar
1/2 Tbsp. baking powder   8 Tbsp. pure lard

Mix dry ingredients together; add pure lard and buttermilk and knead for several minutes, until dough is smooth and pliable. Roll out biscuits with hands (put flour over hands before each biscuit is rolled). Or roll dough out on floured board or cloth and cut biscuits to desired size. Serve piping hot with butter, jam or cheese. Makes a convenient snack for children.

Eleanor Gearhart, Montgomery Council

SARRAH'S FOOD PROCESSOR BUTTERMILK BISCUITS

2 1/2 c. flour   1/2 tsp. soda
3 tsp. baking powder   1/3 c. shortening
1 tsp. salt   1 c. buttermilk

Combine dry ingredients; add shortening and blend. Add milk and blend. Knead on floured board and cut. Bake at 425° until brown.

Anne Spragins, Birmingham East Council

TANGY CHEDDAR BISCUITS

Dough:

2 c. sifted white flour
1/2 c. vegetable shortening
1/2 c. milk
1 Tbsp. baking powder
1 tsp. salt

6 oz. finely grated Cheddar
  seasoned with garlic
  powder
1/4 c. milk, warmed
1/4 c. melted butter

Begin by sifting together the flour, baking powder and salt. Work with a pastry knife until coarse. Add the shortening and work again. Form a well and add the 1/2 cup milk all at once. Work until stirrable with a fork. Roll the dough out to a 1/4 inch thickness and about an inch apart on a greased cookie sheet. Place grated Cheddar cheese on half the circles, and cover with the remaining circle of dough. Brush with melted butter and milk; bake at 450° for 12 minutes. Makes 14 biscuits.

Alma Pitt, Decatur Council

SOUR CREAM BISCUITS FOR TWO

1/2 c. sour cream
1/2 stick butter

1 c. Bisquick

Melt butter. Mix all ingredients; spoon into 9 inch pie pan and bake.

Edna P. Traylor, Life Member, Mobile Council

YEAST BISCUITS

1 pkg. yeast
2 Tbsp. warm water
4 Tbsp. sugar
3 tsp. baking powder
1 1/2 tsp. salt

1 tsp. soda
1 c. shortening
5 c. flour
2 c. buttermilk

Dissolve yeast in water; cut shortening in flour. Add buttermilk and yeast; knead and put in a covered bowl in refrigerator. When chilled, roll out and cut. Bake at 400° for 10 minutes. Dough may be refrigerated for several days.

Sharon Crabtree, Tuscaloosa Council

APRICOT WALNUT BREAD

1 c. dried apricots
1 1/2 c. boiling water
2 1/2 c. flour
3 tsp. baking powder
1/2 tsp. salt

1 egg
1 tsp. vanilla
1/2 c. oil
1 c. sugar
3/4 c. walnuts

Cut apricots with scissors into small pieces. Pour boiling water on and let set until slightly cool. Add remaining ingredients and stir only until moistened. The batter should be lumpy. Spoon into greased pans. Makes 3 small or 1 large loaf. Bake small loaves 35-40 minutes at 325°. Bake large loaf 45-50 minutes at 350°. After baking, cool 10 minutes, then turn out. Let cool completely, then wrap in Saran Wrap and store at least 12 hours before slicing. This bread falls apart after freezing, but it stays moist for a long time.

Betty Chilton, Birmingham East Council

BANANA BREAD

2 c. sugar
3/4 c. oleo
2 eggs
3 c. sifted all-purpose
   flour
1 1/2 tsp. baking powder

1/2 tsp. salt
1 1/2 tsp. soda
1 1/8 c. buttermilk
1/2 tsp. vanilla flavoring
1 1/2 c. mashed bananas
1 c. chopped pecans

Cream oleo; add sugar. Beat in eggs, one at a time. Sift dry ingredients together; add alternately with buttermilk. Add vanilla and bananas and nuts. Bake in loaf pans (2 big pans or 4 small loaf pans). Bake at 350°. When cake is done, cake will turn loose from side of pans.

Ann Sellers, Tuscaloosa Council

BISHOP BREAD

3 eggs
1 c. sugar
1 c. plain flour
1 tsp. baking powder
1/4 tsp. salt

1 c. chopped dates
1 c. chopped nuts
1 tsp. vanilla
2 Tbsp. peach brandy
(optional)

Mix 1/4 cup flour with dates and nuts. Mix all together and bake in loaf pan at 325° for 1 hour. This is good sliced with cream cheese between slices. Cut into finger slices.

Mickey Wash, Tri-Cities Council

BREAD - DINNER ROLLS OR LOAF BREAD

1 c. milk, scalded
1/4 c. sugar
1/4 c. oil
1 tsp. salt
1/4 c. lukewarm water

2 pkg. yeast
1 egg, beaten
4 c. plain flour (use
  more if needed to
  make dough stiff)

Dissolve yeast in lukewarm water. Mix sugar, oil, salt and milk in large mixing bowl; cool to lukewarm. Add egg and yeast. Mix well; add 3 cups flour and beat vigorously. Add remaining cup of flour. Cover with foil or Saran Wrap and let rise in a warm place. Should rise to top of bowl. Turn out on heavily floured board and knead until dough is smooth and easy to handle. Make into 2 loaves or 2 dozen rolls. Bake at 450° until golden brown.

M. C. Arndt, Birmingham South Council

BREAD STICKS

1 stick oleo
1/4 tsp. garlic salt
1 Tbsp. sesame seed

1 Tbsp. poppy seed
1 pkg. of 8 hot dog buns

Cut buns into 6 strips. Melt oleo, adding garlic salt. Brush all sides of bread with this and sprinkle sesame and poppy seed over bread sticks. Bake in 250° oven for 2 1/2 hours. These can be frozen and you do not have to let them thaw.

Mrs. Guy Pippin, Anniston Council

BREAD STICKS

1 large loaf sandwich
  white bread
2 1/2 sticks oleo
1 tsp. curry powder
2 garlic buds

Dash of garlic salt
Durkee's seasoned salt
Dash of Tabasco
1 or 3 drops of
  Worcestershire sauce

Melt oleo. Crush garlic buds and mix all ingredients except bread. Butter bread on both sides with mixture; slice into strips. Bake at 275° for 1 hour until bread sticks are free from moisture.

Jane Knox, Montgomery Council

BROCCOLI BREAD

1 loaf frozen bread dough
1/2 lb. Provolone cheese
1/2 lb. sliced pepperoni
   (or salami)
1/2 lb. shredded
   Mozzarella cheese

1 box chopped broccoli
1 clove garlic
1 Tbsp. olive oil
Sauteed onions and
   mushrooms (optional)

Cook broccoli in garlic clove and olive oil; set aside. Let the frozen bread dough rise, then roll out to size of cookie sheet. Place a layer of Provolone cheese, then pepperoni, then broccoli. Top with Mozzarella cheese. Roll up in a jelly roll fashion and place on oiled cookie sheet; slash top and bake at 350° for 1/2 hour or until golden brown. Serves 4-5 people.

Kim Kizziah, Birmingham Central Council

BUTTER BRAID BREAD

1 c. milk
1/2 c. butter
1/3 c. sugar
2 tsp. salt
6-7 c. all-purpose flour

2 pkg. active dry yeast or
   2 cakes compressed yeast
1/4 c. warm water
3 eggs, beaten
Poppy seeds or sesame seeds

Heat milk and pour over butter, sugar and salt. Sprinkle or crumble yeast into water; let stand a few minutes and stir to dissolve, then stir into milk mixture. Add beaten eggs and 3 cups flour; beat until smooth, then stir in enough flour to make a stiff dough. Turn into lightly floured board and knead well. Put into greased bowl; cover and let rise until double in bulk. Punch down and turn out on board. Divide dough in half; cut each half into 3 equal pieces; roll in rolls about 18 inches long and braid. Brush with melted butter and sprinkle with seeds. Let rise until double and brush with egg white and water. Bake in preheated 375° oven for 30-35 minutes. Makes 2 loaves.

Bobbie Robertson

BUTTERMILK BREAD

6 c. unsifted plain
   flour (about)
3 Tbsp. sugar
2 1/2 tsp. salt
1/4 tsp. baking soda

1 pkg. yeast
1 c. buttermilk
1 c. water
1/3 c. margarine

Combine 2 cups flour, sugar, salt, baking soda and undissolved yeast. Heat buttermilk, water and margarine over low heat until liquids are warm. (Mixture will appear curdled.) Add dry ingredients; beat for 2 minutes at medium speed, scraping bowl occasionally. Add 1 cup flour; beat at high speed for 2 minutes. Stir in enough flour to make a soft dough. Turn onto floured board; knead about 8 to 10 minutes. Place in greased bowl; grease top. Cover; let rise until doubled in size (about 1 hour). Punch down; turn onto floured board. Divide dough into half; shape into loaves. Place each in a greased 8 1/2 x 4 1/2 x 2 1/2 inch loaf pan; cover and let rise until doubled, about 1 hour. Bake at 375° about 35 minutes or until brown. Remove from pans and cool on wire racks.

Betty Pinson, Decatur Council

CORN LIGHT BREAD

1 egg	1 1/2 c. sour buttermilk
2 c. corn meal	1/2 tsp. soda
1/2 c. flour	1/8 tsp. salt
1/2 c. sugar	

Beat egg; add sugar and milk. Sift flour, salt, soda and corn meal into mixture. Pour into an iron skillet; bake in a slow oven.

Mattie Singleton, Retired,
Birmingham Central Council

BEEF SAUSAGE CORN BREAD

1/2 lb. beef sausage	1 egg
2 c. self-rising white corn meal mix	1 1/2 c. milk
	2 Tbsp. beef sausage drippings

Heat oven to 375°. Place sausage in large skillet and fry until browned on all sides. Remove sausage from skillet and cut each in quarters. Place corn meal mix in large mixing bowl, stirring with wooden spoon. Add egg, milk and beef drippings from skillet. Stir in sliced sausage. Grease a 9 inch round baking pan (with shortening) and pour in batter. Bake 30 to 40 minutes or until golden brown. Serves 8.

Muriel P. Hayes, Montgomery Council

CORN BREAD FOR TWO

1 c. Martha White corn
    meal (self-rising)
3/4 c. buttermilk

1 Tbsp. sugar
4 Tbsp. bacon drippings
1 egg

Mix corn meal, buttermilk, sugar and egg. Melt bacon drippings in small skillet in 500° oven. Pour drippings in batter and stir thoroughly. Pour batter into hot skillet; bake at 500° for 10 to 15 minutes.

Diane M. Cook, Montgomery Council

INCREDIBLE CORN BREAD

2 c. chopped onion
1 c. melted butter
1 (8 oz.) carton sour cream
1 c. shredded Cheddar
    cheese
1 1/2 c. self-rising
    corn meal

2 Tbsp. sugar
1/4 tsp. dill weed
2 eggs
1 (8 1/2 oz.) can creamed corn
1/4 c. milk
1/4 c. oil
Dash of hot sauce

Saute onions in butter; add in cheese and sour cream. Melt cheese and remove from heat; set aside. Combine all other ingredients until moistened; pour in lightly greased 9 inch square pan. Spread sour cream mixture over batter; bake at 375° for 30 minutes.

Deborah D. Sellers, Birmingham South Council

JALAPENA CORN BREAD

1 1/2 c. corn meal
1 heaping Tbsp. flour
3 tsp. salt
1/2 tsp. soda
1 c. buttermilk
2/3 c. salad oil

2 eggs, beaten
1 small can cream style corn
    (optional)
3 to 6 jalapenos, chopped
1/2 green pepper, chopped
4 to 5 green onions, chopped
1 1/2 c. grated Cheddar cheese

Mix corn meal, flour, salt and soda; add buttermilk, oil, eggs and corn. Beat and mix well. Stir in jalapenos, green pepper and onions. Grease 9x14 inch baking dish with butter; heat well. Pour in half of batter; sprinkle with half of cheese and repeat. Bake at 375° for 35 minutes or until done. Yield: 8 servings.

Barbara Griffin, Birmingham West Council

MEXICAN CORN BREAD

1 c. sweet milk
1 c. corn meal
2 eggs, well beaten
1 large can cream style corn

1/2 lb. hamburger meat
1 large onion, chopped
1/2 lb. grated cheese (8 oz.)
4 hot peppers

Grease skillet and preheat. Brown hamburger and drain. Mix corn meal, eggs, milk and corn. Sprinkle corn meal on hot skillet. Pour 1/2 of batter in skillet; add onions, cheese, meat and pepper. Pour remainder on top; bake at 350° for 45-50 minutes. Bread will turn loose from skillet better if allowed to cool first. Good!!!

W. D. Cameron, Tuscaloosa Council

NON-GREASY CRACKLIN CORN BREAD

Combine:
2 c. self-rising corn meal
1/2 c. flour
1 egg
4 Tbsp. corn oil

1 (2 oz.) bag Golden Flake
or similar pork skins
(crush skins in hands or
any way you desire)

Add buttermilk to make thin batter. Pour into 9 inch greased iron skillet; bake at 450° until brown on top.

Dennis Lackey, Anniston Council

SOUTHERN CORN BREAD

2 c. sifted corn meal
1 tsp. baking powder
1 tsp. salt
1 c. buttermilk

1 small egg
1 2 c. water
1 Tbsp. fat
1/2 tsp. soda

Sift corn meal, baking powder and salt together in mixing bowl. Mix soda with buttermilk and add to dry ingredients. Add egg and beat well. Add water to make a medium-thick batter. Grease skillet with fat and pour batter in and bake at 450° for 25 minutes.

Willadean Cooley, Tuscaloosa Council

SOUR CREAM CORN BREAD

1 c. self-rising corn meal
1 stick margarine (1/2 c.)
1 c. sour cream

1 c. cream corn
2 eggs, well beaten
1/4 medium grated onion

Melt margarine in iron skillet; coat pan sides with

margarine. Mix other ingredients till blended. Add remaining margarine into batter and mix well. Pour into hot skillet; bake in 350° to 400° oven for 35 to 40 minutes.

Freida Elkourie, Birmingham South Council

SOUR CREAM CORN BREAD

1 c. self-rising corn bread
1/2 c. salad oil
2 eggs
1 small can cream style corn
1 small carton sour cream

Mix meal, oil, eggs and corn thoroughly; fold in sour cream. Pour into greased pan and bake at 450° F. about 20 minutes. Test in the middle of bread with toothpick to be sure it is done.

Shirley Wood, Birmingham South Council

SWEET POTATO CORN BREAD

2 c. self-rising corn meal
1/4 tsp. salt
1 Tbsp. self-rising
  flour
1 egg
1 c. sweet or buttermilk
2 medium sweet potatoes
1 1/2 Tbsp. oil

Mix first 5 ingredients together with a fork until blended. Peel and cut sweet potatoes into cubes. Boil until tender. Stir with a fork. When tender, add to corn bread mix; stir and put in small skillet and bake at 350° for approximately 20 minutes or until brown on top. Grease skillet before adding mix.

Jake Armstrong, Birmingham East Council

APPLESAUCE - RAISIN BREAD

1 c. applesauce
1/2 c. oil
1 c. sugar
1 3/4 c. flour, sifted
1 tsp. baking soda
1/2 tsp. salt
1 tsp. cinnamon
1/2 tsp. cloves
1/2 tsp. nutmeg
1 egg, slightly beaten
1 c. raisins

Preheat oven to 325° F. Mix the applesauce, oil and sugar. Sift in the flour, baking soda, salt, cinnamon, cloves and nutmeg. Mix well after each addition; add the slightly beaten egg and the raisins. Mix, then pour into a greased and floured 8x4 inch loaf pan. Bake 1 hour and 20 minutes, or until done.

Ellen S. McDowell, Riverchase Council

62

CAROL'S OATMEAL DILL BREAD

2 Tbsp. instant
  minced onion
1/2 c. water
2 c. large curd creamed
  cottage cheese
3 Tbsp. butter or
  margarine
1/4 c. sugar

2 tsp. salt
3 1/2 c. sifted all-purpose
  flour
2 eggs
2 pkg. dry yeast
1 c. quick or old fashioned
  oats, uncooked
2 Tbsp. dill seed
1/2 tsp. soda

Combine onion and water in a large bowl. Combine cottage cheese, butter, salt, sugar, soda and onion water. Add 2 cups flour, eggs and yeast; beat 2 minutes. Stir in oats, dill seed and remaining flour. Cover and let rise in a warm place until double in size (about 1 hour). Stir batter down. Place in 2 greased deep 1 1/2 quart casseroles or souffle dishes. Brush tops with melted butter; let rise uncovered in warm place until double in size. Bake in preheated 350° oven about 35 minutes; remove from casseroles. Brush tops with melted butter and sprinkle with salt.

Dave Stewart, Mobile Council

CHEESE/DATE BREAD

1 c. grated mild
  Cheddar cheese
1 beaten egg
1 1/2 c. pitted chopped
  dates
1/2 c. milk
1 tsp. vanilla extract

3 c. flour, sifted
1/2 c. sugar
3/4 c. hot water
3/4 tsp. salt
4 tsp. baking powder
1/4 c. vegetable shortening
3/4 c. chopped pecans

Soak the dates in very hot water; allow it to cool. Drain and set aside. Melt the shortening and set it aside to cool. Sift the flour, sugar, salt and baking powder into a bowl; blend well. Blend the cheese and pecans thoroughly. To the date-water mixture add the shortening, vanilla, egg and milk; mix well. Slowly, by forming a well in the dry ingredients, add the date mixture. Mix thoroughly and turn it into a greased loaf pan; bake at 350° for 60-70 minutes.

Alma Pitt, Decatur Council

CINNAMON BREAD

2 pkg. yeast
1/4 c. warm water
1 c. milk
1/4 c. shortening
1/2 c. sugar
1 tsp. salt

5-6 c. plain flour
2 eggs
2 tsp. melted butter
1 Tbsp. cinnamon
1/3 c. sugar

Soften yeast in water. Scald milk and add shortening, 1/2 cup sugar and salt; stir in 2 cups flour and beat until smooth. Add yeast and eggs; beat, and then add enough flour to make a soft dough. Put on floured board and knead until satiny. Place in a greased bowl; brush top with melted fat and cover and let rise in warm place until doubled in bulk, about 2 hours. Divide dough in half; knead and set aside for 5 minutes. Roll into a rectangle about 1/4 inch thick, 6 inches wide and 16x18 inches long. Spread with butter; sprinkle the cinnamon and 1/3 cup sugar on; roll up lengthwise, like jelly roll. Place in 2 greased loaf pans, smooth side up. Let rise until tripled in bulk, about 1 1/2 hours. Bake at 350° for 15 minutes and then 325° for 35 minutes.

Ann Curry, Tuscaloosa Council

COLBY BREAD

2 1/2 c. shredded Colby
  cheese
2 1/4 c. whole milk, scalded
1 pkg. active yeast
2 tsp. salt

1 Tbsp. vegetable shortening
5 1/2 c. white flour
1/8 c. melted butter
1/4 c. very hot water
2 Tbsp. sugar

Soften the yeast in the hot water. Mix the sugar, salt and shortening together. Add scalded milk and beat until smooth. Mix in the yeast; slowly add the remaining flour, stirring constantly until smooth. Mix in the cheese to form a dough and roll briskly on a flour dusted surface; set aside for 12 minutes. Roll the dough into a ball and then roll in a greased bowl. Cover and let rise for 45 minutes. Roll the dough on a floured surface and shape into loaves. Place in greased loaf pans and let rise until doubled in bulk. Bake 40-45 minutes at 350°.

Alma Pitt, Decatur Council

CREAM CHEESE BREAD

Bread:

1 c. sour cream	2 pkg. dry yeast
1/2 c. melted butter	4 c. all-purpose flour
2 eggs, beaten	1 tsp. salt
1/2 c. sugar	1/2 c. warm water

Filling:

2 (8 oz.) pkg. cream cheese (room temperature soft)	1/8 tsp. salt
	3/4 c. sugar
1 egg, beaten	2 tsp. vanilla

Combine cream cheese and sugar, then add rest of ingredients. Note: Filling is easier to handle when mixed night before and refrigerated until morning.

Bread I: Day before baking: 1. Heat sour cream over low heat; stir in sugar, salt and butter. Cool to luke-warm. 2. Sprinkle yeast over warm water in large mixing bowl, and stir until dissolved. 3. Add sour cream mixture, eggs, flour and mix well. 4. Cover tightly and refrigerate overnight. Make sure bowl size allows for rising.

Bread II: Next day: 1. Divide dough into 4 equal parts; roll each part on a well floured board into 12x8 inch rectangle. 2. Spread 1/4 cream cheese filling on each rectangle, almost to edge. 3. Roll jelly roll fashion. Pinch ends together and fold under. 4. Place on greased baking sheet with seam side down; cover and let rise (about 1 hour). 5. Bake at 375° for 12 to 15 minutes, or until light brown.

Glaze (optional):

2 c. powdered sugar	2 tsp. vanilla
4 tsp. milk	

Garnish with pecans, if desired. Great warm or cold.
Portia Finch, Birmingham Central Council

DILLY CASSEROLE BREAD

1 pkg. dry yeast	2 1/4 to 2 1/2 c. sifted flour
1 c. creamed cottage cheese	1/4 c. warm water
	2 Tbsp. sugar
1 Tbsp. butter	1 Tbsp. minced onion
2 tsp. dill seed	1 tsp. salt
1/2 tsp. baking soda	1 egg

Dissolve yeast in water. Heat cottage cheese to

lukewarm. Combine. Add other ingredients and 1 cup flour. Stir or beat until well blended; add enough flour to make stiff dough. Cover; let rise in warm place until doubled (50 to 60 minutes). Stir down dough. Turn into well greased 1 1/2 quart casserole; let rise until light (30 minutes). Bake in 350° oven about 50 minutes. Brush with butter; sprinkle with salt.

Peggy Blevins, Anniston Council

GREEK EASTER BREAD

3 pkg. powdered yeast
1/2 c. water
8 c. sifted flour
1 c. sugar
1 c. Crisco
6 eggs

1 tsp. cinnamon
1 tsp. mastiha
1 tsp. powdered mahleb
1 1/2 c. milk
2 Tbsp. vegetable oil

Dissolve yeast in 1/2 cup warm water; set aside. Place flour, sugar and Crisco in large bowl; blend, rolling by hand, to feel like corn bread. Add 5 beaten eggs and remaining ingredients; knead well. Place in pan and cover. Let stand in warm place until double in size. Knead very lightly again and let rise. Divide into 3 loaves and place each loaf in pan. Brush with beaten egg and sprinkle with sesame seed; bake 30 minutes at 350°.

Mary C. Martin, Birmingham East Council

MAPLE GINGERBREAD

1 c. maple syrup
3 Tbsp. shortening
1 tsp. ginger

1 tsp. soda
2 c. flour (or till stiff)
1 c. boiling water

Mix syrup, shortening, ginger and soda with flour, then beat well by adding boiling water. Bake quickly in oven. Molasses may be used.

Hison A. Harris, Riverchase Council

"JEW BREAD"

1 lb. light brown sugar
4 eggs
2 c. sifted self-rising flour

2 c. chopped pecans
2 tsp. vanilla flavoring

Beat the 4 eggs into brown sugar; steam over double boiler until sugar is melted, about 10 minutes. Remove from
66

heat and add flour, nuts and vanilla. Mix well. Preheat oven to 350°. Pour mixture into long 9x12 inch or 10x14 inch pan; bake until brown, about 25 minutes. Cut into 1 or 2 inch squares when cool.

Margaret L. Gibson, Mobile Council

MONKEY BREAD

4 cans (10) biscuits
1 1/2 c. brown sugar
1 Tbsp. cinnamon
1 1/2 sticks butter

Cut biscuits into fourths and coat with sugar and cinnamon mixture. In saucepan melt 1 1/2 sticks butter, 1 1/2 cups brown sugar and 1 tablespoon cinnamon. Place 1/2 biscuits in greased Bundt pan; add 1/2 cup chopped pecans or 1/2 cup raisins. Pour half of liquid over this. Repeat with remaining ingredients; bake 35-40 minutes at 350°.

Cynthia Lee, Tuscaloosa Council

MONKEY BREAD (PLUCKIN' BREAD)

2 pkg. dry yeast
1 c. lukewarm water
1 egg
4 Tbsp. sugar
1/2 tsp. salt
3 1/2 c. flour
1 stick oleo

Dissolve yeast in lukewarm water; add egg, sugar, salt and flour. Let rise to double (approximately 45 minutes). Punch down; roll out to 1/4 inch and cut in strips. Melt oleo and dip strips. Place in any form into tube pan; let rise for 20 minutes. Bake for 30 minutes at 325°.

(For a special touch, after dipping strips in oleo, roll in cinnamon-sugar mixture.)

Frances Coleman, Huntsville Council

NUT BREAD

1 1/2 c. sour cream (1 pt.)
2 c. white sugar
2 eggs
1 tsp. baking soda
1 tsp. soda
1 tsp. vanilla
3 c. sifted flour
1 c. nutmeats (English walnuts or pecans)

Grease and flour loaf pans. Make 2 loaves. Bake at 350° for 50 to 60 minutes.

Linda Matthews, Tuscaloosa Council

COUNTRY ONION BREAD

2 c. self-rising meal
1/2 c. self-rising flour
1 tsp. salt
1 egg

1 1/2 c. milk
3 Tbsp. bacon drippings
2 c. onion, coarsely chopped

Add milk and egg to corn meal mix; stir until well blended. Add onions and melted bacon drippings. Pour into well greased iron skillet. Bake in preheated 425° oven 20 to 25 minutes.

Billy Dees, Montgomery Council

ONION CHEESE BREAD

6 c. bread flour
2 pkg. active dry yeast
2 c. milk
6 oz. process Swiss
   cheese, grated

1/2 c. sugar
1 small onion, grated fine
1/2 stick margarine
1 Tbsp. salt
1 egg

In saucepan heat milk, cheese, sugar, margarine and salt till cheese melts (cool to 115° to 120°). In large bowl combine 2 cups flour and yeast; add cheese and milk mixture to flour. Add onion and egg; beat 3 minutes at high speed. By hand stir in enough flour to make a soft dough. Turn out on lightly floured surface; knead till smooth and elastic. Cover and let rise in large bowl in a warm place until double in size. Punch down dough; turn out on lightly floured surface. Divide and form into loaves. Makes 3-4 small or 2 large loaves. Cover and let rise until double in size; bake 10 minutes at 400°; reduce oven to 350° and bake 20-25 minutes more. Brush tops with margarine.

Dot Beadlescomb, Birmingham Central Council

ORANGE CRANBERRY BREAD

2 c. flour
1/2 tsp. salt
1/2 tsp. soda
1 1/2 tsp. baking powder
1 c. sugar

2 Tbsp. butter
Orange juice
1 egg
1 c. nuts
1 c. raw cranberries

Place 2 tablespoons butter in cup. Add boiling water to butter to equal 1/4 cup; add fresh orange juice to make 3/4 cup. Add 1 egg to dry ingredients, then add liquid and mix to blend. Add 1 cup nuts and 1 cup raw cranberries, cut in halves. Mix; pour in bread pan. Bake 1 hour at 325°.

Bonnie Summers, Huntsville Council

ORANGE-NUT BREAD

2 1/4 c. sifted enriched
    flour
2 1/4 tsp. baking powder
1/4 tsp. soda
3/4 tsp. salt
3/4 c. sugar

3/4 c. chopped California
    walnuts
2 Tbsp. melted shortening
    or salad oil
1 beaten egg
3/4 c. orange juice
1 Tbsp. grated orange peel

Use 350° oven. Sift dry ingredients into a large mixing bowl; add nuts, melted shortening, egg, orange juice and grated peel. Stir till mixture is dampened, but not smooth. (Have shortening at room temperature so it won't separate from other ingredients.) Pour into 8 1/2 x 4 1/2 x 2 1/2 inch loaf pan; bake in moderate oven (350°) for 55 minutes.

Jean Whitworth, Huntsville Council

PEPPER-CHEESE BREAD

1 pkg. yeast
1/4 c. hot water
2 1/2 c. plain flour
1 tsp. salt
1/4 tsp. soda

1 c. sour cream
1 egg
1 c. shredded cheese
1/2 tsp. pepper
2 Tbsp. sugar

In large mixing bowl dissolve yeast in hot water; add half the flour, then egg, sugar, salt, soda and sour cream. Blend for 1/2 minute with mixer on low speed, then blend for 2 minutes on high speed. Stir in rest of flour, cheese and pepper. Divide dough evenly in two 1 pound coffee cans (well greased). Let rise in a warm place for 1 hour and 45 minutes. Bake at 350° for 40 minutes.

Debbie Tucker, Birmingham East Council

POPPY SEED BREAD

3 c. plain flour
2 1/3 c. sugar
1 1/2 tsp. salt
1 1/2 Tbsp. baking powder
3 eggs

1 1/2 c. milk
1 1/2 c. cooking oil
1 1/2 Tbsp. poppy seed
1 1/2 tsp. each vanilla,
    almond, butter flavoring

Glaze: Heat until sugar dissolves and pour over bread -

1/2 tsp. each vanilla,
    almond and butter
    flavoring

1/4 c. orange juice
3/4 c. sugar

Grease 2 loaf pans; bake at 325°. Mix all ingredients with mixer. Bake 1 hour or until brown; let cool 10 minutes. Pour glaze over bread while still in pan. Leave in pans about 1 hour.

Kay Ard, Birmingham Central Council

POTATO RUSKS

1 c. Irish potatoes, creamed	1 c. shortening
1 c. sugar	4 eggs, beaten
1 yeast cake	1 tsp. salt
1/2 c. tepid water	4-5 c. flour
	Confectioners sugar

At night cream potatoes, and while hot, add 1 cup sugar. Dissolve 1 yeast cake in tepid water. When both have cooled, mix well and cover with cloth until morning. For 1:00 luncheon, make up dough at 7:00 A.M. as follows: To shortening add eggs, salt and yeast; add flour to make like tea cake dough and set aside to rise. Three hours before serving, make into rolls. Bake in 350° oven for about 20 minutes or until golden brown. When ready to serve, brush with butter and sprinkle with confectioners sugar. Yield: About 3 dozen rolls.

Note: Handle rolls gently; do not use any more flour or handle any more (when rolling out to cut) than absolutely necessary. In warm weather, 2 to 2 1/2 hours are required for rising before baking.

Ann Ervin, Montgomery Council

MOIST PUMPKIN BREAD

2/3 c. shortening	2 tsp. soda
2 2/3 c. sugar	1 1/2 tsp. salt
4 eggs	1 tsp. ground cinnamon
1 (16 oz.) can pumpkin	1 tsp. ground cloves
2/3 c. water	2/3 c. chopped pecans
3 1/3 c. all-purpose flour	2/3 c. chopped dates
1/2 tsp. baking powder	

Cream shortening; gradually add sugar, beating well. Add eggs; mix well. Stir in pumpkin and water. Combine flour, baking powder, soda, salt, cinnamon and cloves; add to creamed mixture, mixing well. Fold in pecans and dates. Spoon into 2 well greased and floured 9x5x3 inch loaf pans; bake at 350° for 1 hour and 10 minutes or until bread tests done. Yield: 2 loaves.

Elaine Rindt, Riverchase Council,
Margie Lavender, Riverchase Council

RYE BREAD

1 c. milk
2 Tbsp. honey
1 Tbsp. sugar
1 Tbsp. salt
1 Tbsp. margarine
3/4 c. warm water
  (105° to 115° F.)
1 pkg. or cake yeast

1 Tbsp. caraway seeds
  (optional)
2 1/2 c. unsifted rye flour
2 1/2 c. unsifted white
  flour (approx.)
1/4 c. corn meal
1 egg white
2 Tbsp water

Scald milk; add honey, sugar, salt and margarine. Cool to lukewarm. Measure warm water into large bowl. Sprinkle yeast in; stir in till yeast has dissolved. Add lukewarm milk mixture. Add caraway seeds and rye flour. Beat well; add enough white flour to make a soft dough. Turn dough out onto lightly floured board; knead until smooth and elastic, about 7 minutes. Place in greased bowl, turning to grease top. Cover; let rise in warm place, free from draft, until doubled in bulk, about 1 1/2 hours. Punch down and turn out onto lightly floured board. Divide dough in half; form each piece into a smooth ball. Cover; let rest 10 minutes. Flatten each piece slightly. Roll lightly on board to form tapered ends. Sprinkle 2 greased baking sheets with corn meal. Place breads on baking sheets. Combine egg white and water; brush breads. Let rise, uncovered, in warm place, free from draft, for 35 minutes. Bake in hot oven (400° F.) for 25 minutes. Cool on wire racks.

Cora Nelson, Decatur Council

SPOON BREAD

1 1/2 c. finely grated
  Cheddar cheese
4 egg whites
4 egg yolks
2 c. scalded milk

1 c. yellow corn meal
1/4 c. butter
1/2 tsp. salt
1 tsp. sugar

Stirring constantly, slowly mix the scalded milk and corn meal. Stir until thick and smooth. Beat the egg yolks and remove corn meal from the heat. Mix the egg yolks and corn meal mixture. Slowly, blend in the cheese, salt, sugar and butter and beat until smooth. Beat the egg whites till they peak, and fold into the mixture. Turn into a buttered casserole dish and bake for 35-40 minutes in a 375° oven.

Alma Pitt, Decatur Council

STEAMED BROWN BREAD

1 c. corn meal
1 c. stirred graham
  or whole wheat flour
1 c. sifted enriched
  white flour
1 tsp. salt
1 tsp. baking powder

1 tsp. soda
3/4 c. dark molasses or
  6 Tbsp. light molasses
  and 6 Tbsp. brown sugar
2 c. buttermilk or sour milk
1 c. seeded raisins

Use 450° oven. Add corn meal and graham flour to white flour sifted with salt, baking powder and soda; add molasses, buttermilk and raisins; beat thoroughly. Half-fill 3 greased 1 pound coffee cans or five 1 pound baking powder cans; cover tightly. Steam 3 hours on rack in covered pan, using small amount of boiling water. Remove cover; place in very hot oven (450°) for 5 minutes before removing from can.

Christine Turner, Huntsville Council

STRAWBERRY BREAD

3 c. plain flour
1 tsp. salt
2 c. sugar
1 tsp. soda
3 tsp. cinnamon

1 1/4 c. chopped pecans
2 (10 oz.) pkg. frozen
  strawberries, thawed
1 1/4 c. cooking oil
3 eggs, beaten

Sift dry ingredients together in large mixing bowl; add pecans and mix. Make a well in the center. Mix the remaining ingredients; pour into well. Stir enough to dampen all ingredients and then pour into 2 greased loaf pans. Bake in 350° oven for 1 hour.

Edith Fields, Mobile Council

WHOLE WHEAT BREAD

2 1/2 c. warm water
2 Tbsp. dry yeast
3 Tbsp. unrefined corn
  germ oil

4 Tbsp. unsulphured molasses
5 to 5 1/2 c. whole wheat flour
1 1/2 tsp. sea salt
1 c. bran flakes

Dissolve the yeast in warm water. Add the oil and molasses. Mix the flour and salt; add the liquids. Mix well with hands, adding a little more flour if needed. Cover and let rise until double (about 1 1/2 hours). Knead down; shape into 2 loaves. Place in oiled loaf pans; allow to rise again until nearly doubled. Bake 10 minutes at 400°; reduce the heat to 350° and bake 20 minutes more. Cool on rack. This is a simple delicious bread. It works well for beginners or old hands.

Rita Finley, Huntsville Council

SPICED ZUCCHINI BREAD

3 c. all-purpose flour
2 tsp. soda
1 tsp. salt
1/2 tsp. baking powder
1 1/2 tsp. ground cinnamon
3/4 c. finely chopped
   walnuts

3 eggs
2 c. sugar
1 c. vegetable oil
2 tsp. vanilla extract
2 c. coarsely shredded
   zucchini
1 (8 oz.) can crushed
   pineapple, well drained

Combine flour, soda, salt, baking powder, cinnamon and nuts; set aside. Beat eggs lightly in a large mixing bowl; add sugar, oil and vanilla; beat until creamy. Stir in zucchini and pineapple. Add dry ingredients, stirring only until dry ingredients are moistened. Spoon batter into 2 well greased and floured 9x5x3 inch loaf pans. Bake at 350° for 1 hour or until done. Cool 10 minutes in pan before removing; turn out on rack and cool completely. Yield: 2 loaves.

Mrs. Libby Pilling, Decatur Council

BUBBLE BUNS

1/2 c. finely chopped
   walnuts
1/3 c. sugar

1/3 c. mayonnaise
1 pkg. (10) refrigerated
   biscuits
1/2 tsp. cinnamon

Grease ten 2 1/2 inch muffin pan cups. In small bowl combine nuts, sugar and cinnamon. Separate biscuits. Cut into quarters; shape into balls. Coat each with mayonnaise, then roll in walnut mixture. Place 4 in each muffin pan cup. Bake in 400° oven 15 to 17 minutes or until browned. Serve warm. Makes 10.

June Crowe, Anniston Council

CROUTONS

Use 4 slices each of:

White bread   Jewish dill bread
Whole wheat bread   Jewish rye bread

Dice bread. Sprinkle to taste with any/all of the
following seasonings:

Italian seasoning   Celery salt
Garlic salt   Butter-flavored salt seasoning
Parsley flakes   Parmesan cheese

While tossing bread cubes lightly, pour 1 cup melted
butter (or oleo) over them. Place in large baking pan and
bake in slow oven for approximately 45 minutes or until
bread is light brown and crispy. Toss occasionally while
baking to ensure that croutons are browning evenly.
Ruby Pruett, Riverchase Council

HUSH PUPPIES

2 c. self-rising meal   1 tsp. baking powder
1 c. self-rising flour   1/2 can beer
2 c. chopped onions   1 c. buttermilk
4 Tbsp. Crisco   1 egg

Mix meal, flour and baking powder; add Crisco, onions,
egg and beer. Then stir in buttermilk gradually until you
can dip out in small balls. (If needed, add small amount of
buttermilk.) Fry in deep fat until golden brown.
Dot Curry, Tuscaloosa Council

SQUASH PUPPIES

2 c. meal (yellow)   2 eggs
1 c. flour   Buttermilk
1 c. squash   1/2 tsp. salt
1 large onion   1/4 tsp. black pepper

Boil squash until tender. Put squash, onion and eggs
in blender (liquefy). Mix dry ingredients; add liquid from
blender mix; add buttermilk (beer optional) until loose
consistency. (If consistency is firm, puppies will be rough
instead of smooth.) Use self-rising meal and flour. Let set
1 hour before cooking. Cook in deep fat cooker (Fry
Daddy) until brown, approximately 2 to 3 minutes.
E. E. Hodges, Huntsville Council

BACON MUFFINS

2 c. flour
6 slices bacon
2 Tbsp. bacon fat

1 Tbsp. sugar
1 c. milk
1 egg, well beaten

Sift dry ingredients together. Chop bacon in small pieces. Blend thoroughly into flour mixture. Make a deep well in center. Combine remaining ingredients; blend thoroughly. Pour, all at once, into center of well. Mix just until ingredients are moistened; spoon into muffin tins. Bake at 400° for 12-15 minutes. Makes 12 muffins.

Dorothy Hayes, Birmingham Central Council

BRAN MUFFINS

1 (15 oz.) box Raisin Bran
3 c. sugar
5 c. plain flour
5 tsp. soda

2 tsp. salt
1 c. melted margarine
  (2 sticks)
4 eggs, beaten
1 qt. buttermilk

Mix all dry ingredients in a very large bowl; add margarine, eggs and buttermilk and mix well. Bake in greased muffin pan at 400° for 15-20 minutes (center of muffin should rise when done). The mix can be kept in tight container in refrigerator for up to 6 weeks.

Joanne Whitten, Birmingham South Council

BLUEBERRY MUFFINS

2/3 c. shortening
1 c. sugar
3 eggs
3 c. all-purpose flour

2 1/2 tsp. baking powder
1 tsp. salt
1 c. milk
1 c. fresh blueberries

Cream shortening; gradually add sugar, beating until light and fluffy. Add eggs, one at a time, beating well after each addition. Combine flour, baking powder and salt; add to creamed mixture alternately with milk, beginning and ending with flour mixture. Stir in blueberries. Spoon batter into greased muffin pans, filling 2/3 full. Bake at 375° for 20 to 25 minutes. Yield: About 2 dozen.

Note: Batter may be stored in refrigerator 2 weeks before baking.

Faith Kirby, Anniston Council

CHEESE MUFFINS

1 c. grated American cheese
1 egg
2 c. sifted white flour
3 Tbsp. melted, cooled shortening
3 tsp. baking powder
1 c. milk
1 tsp. salt

Sift the flour with the baking powder and salt and then mix with 3/4 cup of the cheese. Mix the egg, shortening and milk together, and then stir into the cheese mixture with a fork. Spoon about 2/3 full into greased muffin pans and sprinkle the remaining cheese on. Bake in 425° oven for 25 minutes until brown.

Brenda Stewart, Decatur Council

CINNAMON BRAN MUFFINS

3 c. bran cereal (raisin or whole bran)
1 c. boiling water
2 1/2 c. flour
3/4 c. sugar
2 1/2 tsp. baking soda
1 1/2 tsp. cinnamon
1/2 tsp. salt
2 eggs
2 c. buttermilk
1/2 c. oil
1/2 c. currants or raisins

In large bowl stir cereal with water; moisten evenly. Set aside to cool. Stir together flour, sugar, cinnamon, baking soda and salt; set aside. Stir eggs, buttermilk, oil and currants into cereal mixture until well blended; stir in flour mixture until well blended. Bake or store for future. Before using, stir to distribute currants. Fill muffin cups 2/3 to 3/4 full. Bake in preheated 425° oven 20 minutes or until tops spring back. Makes 24 to 30. Batter will keep in airtight container (in refrigerator) approximately 4 weeks.

Shirley Du Pont, Birmingham South Council

EASY YEAST MUFFINS

1 pkg. dry yeast, dissolved in 2 c. warm to hot water
1/2 c. sugar
3/4 c. Crisco shortening
1 egg, beaten
4 c. self-rising flour

Beat eggs; mix in sugar and Crisco. Add flour. Stir yeast and water; pour into other ingredients and mix with a spoon. Butter muffin pan with quite a bit of butter and fill 3/4 full with dough. Bake in a 400° oven for 15 minutes or as brown as you like. Store remaining dough in covered bowl in refrigerator. It will stay good for about a week.

Sandy Horn, Riverchase Council

MUFFIN MIX

2 c. All-Bran cereal
2 c. Shredded Wheat
  (3 biscuits)
1 c. shortening
3 c. sugar
4 eggs, beaten slightly

5 c. sifted flour
2 tsp. salt
4 1/2 tsp. soda
1/2 tsp. baking powder
1 qt. buttermilk

Add 1/2 cup boiling water to Shredded Wheat and All-Bran. Cream shortening and sugar; add eggs and cereal. Sift dry ingredients and add flour alternately with buttermilk. Dates, raisins, apples, etc., chopped, may be added at baking time. Bake at 400° for 20 minutes. Mix keeps in refrigerator up to 6 weeks. Bake as needed.

Vinnie Mae Lyon, Birmingham Central Council

ORANGE JUICY MUFFINS WITH HONEY SPREAD

2 c. Bisquick baking mix
2 Tbsp. sugar
1 egg
1 tsp. grated orange peel
2/3 c. orange juice

2 Tbsp. sugar
1/4 tsp. ground cinnamon
1/8 tsp. ground nutmeg
Honey Spread*

Heat oven to 400°. Grease bottoms only of 12 medium muffin cups. Mix baking mix, 2 tablespoons sugar, the egg, orange peel and orange juice; beat vigorously 30 seconds. Fill muffin cups about 2/3 full. Mix 2 tablespoons sugar, the cinnamon and nutmeg. Sprinkle each muffin with about 1/2 teaspoon sugar mixture; bake 15 minutes. Serve with Honey Spread. Makes 12 muffins.

*Honey Spread: Beat 1/2 cup margarine or butter, softened, and 1/2 cup honey until fluffy.

Pat Canter, Birmingham Central Council

PINEAPPLE MUFFINS

1 (8 oz.) can crushed pineapple
1/2 c. all-purpose flour
1/3 c. firmly packed
  brown sugar
1/4 tsp. ground cinnamon
1/2 c. butter or margarine,
  melted and divided

2 c. all-purpose flour
1/2 c. sugar
1 Tbsp. baking powder
1/2 tsp. salt
1 egg, beaten
3/4 c. milk

Drain pineapple, reserving 1 4 cup juice. Combine 1/2 cup flour, brown sugar, cinnamon and 1/4 cup butter; stir well. Combine next 4 ingredients. Combine egg, milk, remaining 1/4 cup butter and reserved pineapple juice; stir well. Make a well in center of dry ingredients; add liquid ingredients, stirring just until moistened. Spoon batter into greased and floured muffin pans, filling half full. Spoon pineapple over batter and sprinkle with cinnamon mixture. Bake at 375° for 30 minutes. Yield: 16 muffins.

Tip: If you grease more muffin cups than you need, fill the empty cups with water to keep grease from baking on.

Donna M. Walker, Birmingham Central Council

RAISIN-BRAN MUFFINS

1 (15 oz.) box Raisin
    Bran (or closest size)
3 c. self-rising flour
3 c. sugar

4 eggs, well beaten
1 c. oil
1 qt. buttermilk
1 c. raisins (optional)

In a very large bowl combine Raisin Bran, sugar and flour; add buttermilk, oil, eggs and raisins. Stir well. Pour into greased muffin tins and bake at 375° for 15-20 minutes. This mixture will keep refrigerated for 5-6 weeks and can be baked as needed.

Lashawn Hopson, Birmingham East Council

REFRIGERATOR BRAN MUFFINS

2 c. buttermilk
1/2 c. oil
2 eggs
3 c. bran flake cereal
    with or without raisins

2 1/2 c. Pillsbury's Best all-
    purpose or unbleached flour
1 1/2 c. sugar
1 1/2 tsp. soda
1 tsp. salt
1/2 c. chopped nuts

Heat oven to 400° F. Line muffin cups with paper liners. In large bowl combine butter, milk, oil and eggs; beat well and add remaining ingredients, stirring just until moistened. Fill prepared muffin cups half full; bake at 400° F. for 20 to 25 minutes until golden brown. Yield: 36 muffins. Mixture will keep for approximately 2 weeks in refrigerator.

Mary McCulley, Birmingham East Council

*   *   *   *   *

People who want by the yard but try by the inch should be kicked by the foot.

WHOLE WHEAT MUFFINS

1 c. sifted all-purpose flour
1 c. sifted whole wheat
 flour
1/2 tsp. salt
1 Tbsp. plus 1 tsp.
 baking powder

1/2 c. brown sugar, packed
1 c. milk
2 eggs, slightly beaten
1/3 c. oil
1/2 c. nuts, coarsely
 chopped

Grease 12 large muffin cups. In large mixing bowl combine flours, salt, baking powder and brown sugar. Combine milk and eggs; add to dry mixture. Stir in oil and nuts; stir just until dry ingredients are moistened. Spoon batter into pans, 3/4 full. Bake at 425° for 15 minutes. Makes 12 large muffins. Freeze leftovers.

Rubie Nelson, Montgomery Council

PANCAKES

1 c. all-purpose flour
2 tsp. baking powder
1 Tbsp. sugar
1/2 tsp. salt

3/4 c. milk
2 Tbsp. melted butter
 or margarine
2 eggs, beaten

Mix flour, baking powder, sugar and salt; add melted butter and milk to beaten eggs. Add dry ingredients. Stir just enough to dampen flour. Do not beat too much! Adjust amount of milk to make batter thin enough to pour. Cook on hot griddle. An electric skillet which produces a constant heat gives best results. Set at 380°.

Jack Pickell, Birmingham Central Council

PANCAKES

1 1/2 c. self-rising flour
1/4 to 1/2 tsp. baking
 powder

1 egg
4 Tbsp. cooking oil
1 1/4 to 1 1/2 c. milk

Maple Syrup:

2 c. water
4 c. sugar
1/2 c. brown sugar

1 tsp. vanilla flavoring
1 tsp. maple flavoring

Bring water and sugar to a boil; boil about 1 minute. Remove from heat and add flavorings.

Bonnie Mayfield, Anniston Council

POTATO PANCAKES

2 potatoes, peeled
1 small onion, chopped fine
1 egg

1/4 c. all-purpose flour
1 tsp. chopped parsley
Salt and pepper to taste

Grate potatoes fine. Combine all ingredients and mix well. Drain excess liquid. Spoon into frypan containing hot oil. Flatten into pancake shape. Brown slightly on one side then flip and brown other side. Drain on paper towel. Serves 2.

Raymond Unger, Riverchase Council

PERFECT PASTRY

Into mixing bowl sift together:

3 c. sifted all-purpose
  Gold Medal flour
1 Tbsp. sugar

3/4 tsp. salt
1/2 tsp. baking powder

Cut in 1 1/4 cups shortening till mixture resembles small peas. Combine 1 beaten egg, 5 tablespoons water and 1 tablespoon vinegar. Sprinkle 4 tablespoons of mixture over flour mixture and mix lightly with fork. Add 4 more table-spoons egg mixture; continue mixing till pastry just holds to-gether. Gather dough together with hands and press into ball. Wrap in clear plastic. Wrap; chill 15 minutes. Divide dough into 4 parts. Roll out between clear plastic wrap. Makes 4 crusts. Freezes well.

Margean H. Uptain, Birmingham South Council

DINNER ROLLS

2 c. self-rising flour (sift)
1/2 tsp. sugar

1 c. sweet milk
1/4 c. mayonnaise

Mix above ingredients together; drop in greased muffin tins and cook 12 minutes at 450°.

Becky Cook, Huntsville Council

DORIS' COAST GUARD ROLLS

2 pkg. dry yeast
1 1/2 c. warm water
1/2 c. shortening
3/4 c. sugar
2 tsp. salt

1 c. boiling water
1 c. cold water
4 eggs, beaten
7 1/2 c. flour (bread
  flour is best)

Dissolve yeast in warm water. Cream together in large bowl shortening, sugar and salt. Add boiling water and mix. Add yeast and water mixture and mix. Add cold water and mix. Add eggs and mix. Add flour and mix thoroughly. (May have to add additional flour if mixture is too wet.) Cover and refrigerate 3 hours before making out. Roll on floured board and cut with biscuit cutter. Spread melted butter or margarine on each side and fold to 1/2 circle. Cover and place in greased pan in warm place for 2 1/2 hours (more if needed to rise). Bake at 400° for 15 minutes. Half of recipe makes quite a lot of rolls. Dough may be kept in refrigerator before making out for as long as 7 days. The older the dough, the longer it will take to rise before baking.
Anne Spragins, Birmingham East Council

EASY   REFRIGERATOR   ROLLS

2 c. warm water
2 pkg. active dry yeast
1/2 c. sugar
1/4 c. soft shortening

2 tsp. salt
1 egg
6 1/2 to 7 c. sifted flour

Dissolve yeast in warm water; stir in sugar, salt, shortening and egg. Mix flour in until dough is easy to handle. No kneading necessary. Grease top of dough and put in refrigerator before using. Shape about 2 hours before serving. Bake at 400° for 12 to 15 minutes. Makes 4 to 5 dozen medium rolls. This mixture can also be used for basis of cinnamon or pecan rolls.
Carolyn G. Blackburn,
Birmingham Central Council

EASY   DOUBLE   RISE   ROLLS

2 c. warm water
2 pkg. yeast
2 sticks melted oleo
1 tsp. salt
2/3 c. sugar

6 eggs
6 c. plain flour, unsifted
   (one 2 lb. bag flour
   equals 6 c.)

In large bowl dissolve yeast in warm water; add salt, sugar, oleo and eggs. Mix well, then add all flour. Stir till mixed well (dough will be sticky). Cover; let rise till double. Punch down. Pour onto floured board and knead just till not sticky anymore. Shape into ping-pong size balls for cloverleaf rolls or roll out to 1/2 inch thick and cut with biscuit cutter. Let rise till double again. Bake at 350° for 15 minutes. Makes about 6-8 dozen rolls. Recipe can be halved easily. Dough can be stored in refrigerator up to 2 weeks.

Joan M. Johnson, Birmingham Central Council

EVELYN HUNTERS' ICEBOX ROLLS

3/4 c. milk
1/4 c. Crisco
1/4 c. sugar
1 tsp. salt
1/4 tsp. soda

1 (1/4 oz.) pkg. dry yeast
1/4 c. lukewarm water
1 egg
Plain flour (see instructions)

Melt Crisco; add milk, sugar and salt. (Do not get real hot.) Mix 1 package yeast and 1/4 cup lukewarm water; add to above mixed ingredients. Add enough flour to make a thin batter. Put in warm place; let rise. Add egg, soda, baking powder and enough flour to make dough. Keep in refrigerator 2 or 3 days. Do not use too much flour, just enough to handle. Put dough on flour and knead. Roll out; let rise about 2 hours. Makes about 1 1/2 dozen medium size rolls.

Maxine Lawley, Birmingham South Council

HERB ROLLS

3/4 c. butter
1 tsp. sweet basil
1 tsp. tarragon

1/2 tsp. chopped parsley
12 brown and serve rolls

Soften butter; season with basil, tarragon and parsley. Mix and mix and mix more. Slice rolls in quarters, but only halfway through, separating slices a little and spread on both sides with herb mixture. Heat until rolls are lightly browned.

Ann Ervin, Montgomery Council

ICEBOX ROLLS

1 pkg. yeast
1/4 c. warm water
1 tsp. sugar
4 1/2 c. all-purpose
    flour

1/3 c. sugar
1 tsp. salt
1/2 c. shortening
2 eggs
1 c. sweet milk

Put yeast in lukewarm water and add 1 teaspoon sugar; set aside. Sift flour twice. Put shortening, sugar, salt and milk in saucepan. Heat until shortening melts; cool to luke-warm. In mixing bowl add eggs and yeast. Add flour and mix well with cool milk. Cover; put in refrigerator over-night. Use as needed. When used, knead dough; roll out and cut with small cutter. In a small pan melt some shorten-ing; dip rolls in melted shortening and place on cookie sheet. Let rise 1 hour before cooking. Cook in preheated 325° to 350° oven until brown, approximately 20-25 minutes.

Maggie McCullough, Birmingham Council

24 INDIANA CHEESE ROLLS

1 c. grated mild Cheddar cheese	1 Tbsp. fresh lemon juice
1 egg white	1 whole egg
1/4 c. very hot water	3 c. white flour
1 pkg. active yeast	1/4 c. warm water
1/4 c. vegetable shortening (or more)	1/2 c. sugar
	1/8 c. melted butter
	1/2 tsp. salt

Soften the yeast in hot water and set aside. Into a large bowl pour warm water and mix in 3/4 cup of flour. Mix the softened yeast and mix it with the flour until smooth. Cover and let stand in a warmed corner for an hour. Mix to-gether the grated cheese, lemon juice and shortening until smooth. Add the salt and sugar and cream until fluffy. Beat the egg yolks and slowly add to the mixture. Divide the re-maining flour in thirds and mix until smooth and blended into the mixture. Turn the dough onto a flour dusted sheet of waxed paper and allow to rest for 7 minutes approximately. Knead the dough thoroughly and roll into a ball. Roll the ball into a greased bowl and cover. Allow to stand for 45 minutes until the dough rises and doubles. Punch. Knead quickly and allow to rest 7 minutes. Roll out the dough to a 1/4 inch thickness and cut into approximately 3 to 4 inch squares. Fold to form triangles and place on greased cookie sheets. Brush with butter and bake for 40-50 minutes at 350°.

Jan Brady, Decatur Council

INSTANT ROLLS

1 env. dry yeast, dissolved in 1/4 c. warm water	1/4 c. sugar
1 egg, beaten	1 c. warm water
	4 c. sifted self-rising flour
	3/4 c. oil

Mix all ingredients together; cover in Tupperware bowl;

place in refrigerator and use as needed. Fill greased muffin tins 3/4 full and bake at 450° until brown.

Note: I usually mix and bake immediately.

Charlotte Johnson, Huntsville Council

JIM'S ROLLS

1 pkg. yeast	1/4 c. oil
1 Tbsp. sugar	1/2 c. warm water
1 Tbsp. water	2 1/2 c. plain flour
1/4 c. sugar	

Dissolve yeast, sugar and 1 tablespoon water. Beat sugar, oil and 1/2 cup warm water. Dissolve the ingredients together and stir in flour. Let rise 1 hour. Punch down then roll out and cut into squares. Pat center with butter or oil, then fold over and let rise again. Bake at 300° for 20 minutes.

Jim Loggins, Decatur Council

PLAIN ROLL DOUGH

1 pkg. active dry yeast or 1 cake compressed yeast	1/4 c. shortening
	1 tsp. salt
	3 1/2 c. sifted all-purpose
1/4 c. water	flour
1 c. milk, scalded	1 egg
1/4 c. sugar	

Soften active dry yeast in warm water (110°), compressed yeast in lukewarm water (85°). Combine milk, sugar, shortening and salt; cool to lukewarm. Add 1 cup of the flour; beat well. Beat in softened yeast and egg. Gradually add remaining flour to form soft dough, beating well. Cover and let rise in warm place (82°) till double (1 1/2 to 2 hours). Turn out on lightly floured surface and shape as desired.

Emma Arnold, Decatur Council

POTATO ROLLS

Mix together:

1/2 c. sugar	1 Tbsp. salt
2 pkg. dry yeast	1 1/2 c. warm water (not real hot)

Mix yeast with sugar and salt; add water and mix. I set this in a pan of warm water to keep ingredients from

84

cooling off too quickly. Let this stand till it starts to get bubbly. Then mix these ingredients together:

1/2 c. oleo or butter (soft)	1/2 c. cooked and mashed
2 eggs	unseasoned potatoes (cool)

(I beat eggs separately for a minute.) Mix all together then add to above ingredients (yeasts and etc.). Using large bowl of mixer, start adding flour, 6 1/2 cups unsifted flour. You will be able to mix all but about 1 cup with mixer. Finish with your hands till dough turns loose from bowl. Dump dough in larger bowl that has been lightly greased. Flatten dough on top. Grease with oleo. Cover well (I place foil over bowl, then lay towel on top), set in warm place to rise. After dough is double in bulk (about 2 1/2 hours), punch down. You can pinch off part of dough and make out in rolls (as you do biscuits). Let rise for about 1 1/2 to 2 hours. Place rest of dough in refrigerator. Will keep 2 or 3 days, but punch dough down each day.

Marcia Freeman, Birmingham East Council

REFRIGERATOR ROLLS

2 c. lukewarm water	1 egg (room temperature)
1/2 c. sugar	1/4 c. shortening
1 1/2 tsp. salt	6 1/2 to 7 c. plain flour
2 pkg. dry yeast	

Mix water, sugar and salt together; add yeast and stir until dissolved. Add beaten egg and shortening. Add flour (2-3 cups at a time) and stir until well blended, but do not knead. Shape dough into desired rolls. Cover with cloth; let rise 1 1/2 to 2 hours. Bake at 400° for 12-15 minutes. Dough can be kept in refrigerator for 2-3 days.

Glenn C. Gibson, Decatur Council

ROLLS

2 medium size potatoes	1 c. sugar
1 pkg. yeast	1 tsp. salt
3/4 c. warm water	1 1/2 c. milk
1 c. lard	7 c. plain flour

Boil potatoes; mash to make 1 cup. Add package yeast to 3/4 cup warm water; stir and leave standing. Using large bowl add:

1 c. lard	1 c. sugar
1 c. hot mashed potatoes	1 tsp. salt

Add alternately 7 cups plain flour and 1 1/2 cups milk. Mix well. Refrigerate about 3 hours before using. Roll out and cut into circle about 1/2 inch thick. Spread with melted butter; bake at 350° for 15 or 20 minutes.

Mary McCulley, Birmingham East Council

ROLLS

1 c. hot tap water	3 c. self-rising flour
1/4 c. Wesson oil	1 pkg. dry yeast
1/4 c. sugar	1 egg

Mix together 1 cup hot tap water, 1/4 cup Wesson oil, 1/4 cup sugar. Sift together 1 cup self-rising flour and 1 package dry yeast and mix with above ingredients. Beat 1 egg slightly and add to above mixture. Add 2 more cups self-rising flour. Put in greased Tupperware bowl and cover. Refrigerate for 2 hours or more; knead dough down, then pinch off for rolls or roll out on floured cloth. Put in greased pan. Will take 2 hours to rise, less time in hot weather. Bake at 450° till brown. Dough will keep at least 4 days in refrigerator.

Margie Lavender, Riverchase Council

SPOON ROLLS

2 c. warm water	3/4 c. melted margarine
1 pkg. dry yeast	1 egg, beaten
1/4 c. sugar	4 c. self-rising flour

Dissolve yeast in warm water (using a spoon). Add remaining as listed. Grease muffin pan (I use margarine); fill about 1/2 full. Bake at 425° about 20 minutes. Mixture will be soupy and will not need to rise. It may be kept in refrigerator for several days.

Opal Kemp, Mobile Council

TOMATO-CHEESE ROLLS

1 yeast cake	1 tsp. onion juice
1 Tbsp. sugar	Melted butter
3/4 c. tomato juice	2 1/4 c. sifted flour
1 tsp. salt	3/4 c. grated cheese

Crumble yeast into bowl; add sugar. Heat tomato juice until lukewarm; stir into yeast mixture. Let stand for 5 minutes; add salt, onion juice and 3 tablespoons butter. Add half the flour; beat until smooth. Add remaining flour; beat until smooth. Brush top with butter; cover closely with damp cloth. Let stand in warm place until doubled in bulk. Turn onto floured cloth; roll into circle 1/4 inch thick. Brush with butter; sprinkle with grated cheese. Cut into 16 pie-shaped pieces. Roll each from wide edge toward point. Brush with butter; let rise for 30 to 50 minutes. Bake at 400° until brown. Yield: 16 servings.

Virginia Mayo, Mobile Council

TWO DOZEN NO-WORK ROLLS

1 c. grated Cheshire cheese	1 Tbsp. milk
2 1/2 c. flour	1/2 c. water
3 Tbsp. sweet butter	3 Tbsp. sugar
1 pkg. active yeast	1 tsp. salt
1 egg yolk	1/4 c. butter, melted
3/4 c. milk	

Place the salt, yeast, sugar and about 1 1/2 cups of the flour in a large mixing bowl and blend thoroughly. In a pan, heat 3/4 cup of milk, the water and 3 tablespoons of butter. Slowly add the milk mixture to the flour mixture and beat with an electric mixer for 2 to 3 minutes at medium speed. Slowly blend in another cup of flour and beat at high speed for 1 to 2 minutes. Stop beating when sticky dough is formed. Note: It is acceptable to add more flour if needed. The dough should be placed in a greased bowl and covered. Allow to rise for an hour.

Punch the dough. Roll onto a flour dusted surface and divide evenly in two. Take half the dough and roll out into a medium sized rectangle. Brush with melted butter and top with half the cheese; cut into at least 8 sections through the width and cut those sections into thirds and twist. Repeat for the other half of the dough. Place on greased cookie sheets and brush with remaining butter, egg yolk and milk mixture. Let stand for 20-30 minutes and bake for 5-10 minutes at 425°.

Alma Pitt, Decatur Council

VERY EASY ROLLS

6 c. flour
2 pkg. dry yeast
1 c. shortening
1/2 c. sugar

1 c. lukewarm water
1 c. boiling water
2 eggs
3 tsp. salt

Cream sugar, salt and Crisco; add boiling water. Dissolve yeast in lukewarm water; add eggs and stir. Add yeast to mixture. With spoon, blend in flour. Refrigerate for 6 to 8 hours. Roll, shape and let rise in a warm place about an hour. Bake at 450° for 10 to 15 minutes. Use only what you need. Dough will keep for weeks in the refrigerator. Just like Mammy's Angel Biscuits, only easy!

Debbie Tucker, Birmingham East Council

** NOTES **

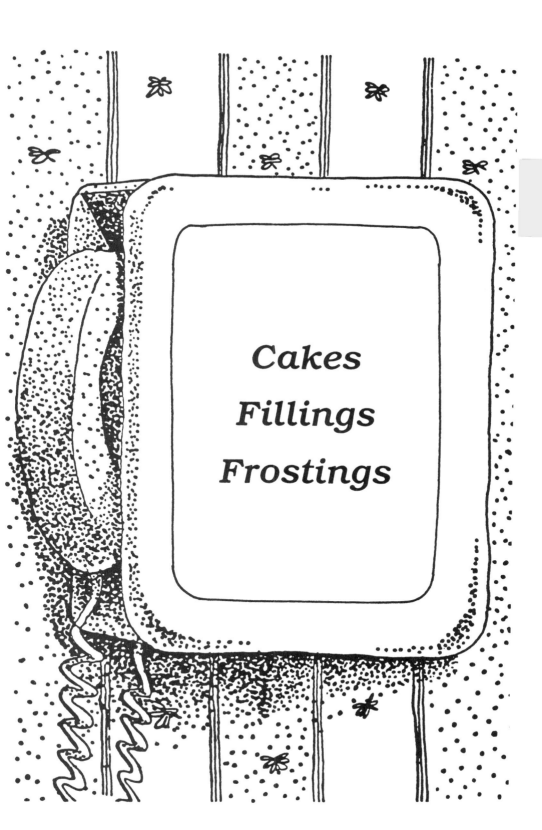

Cakes

Fillings

Frostings

CAKE BAKING GUIDE

Problem...	Cause...	
	Butter-Type Cakes	**Sponge-Type Cakes**
Cake falls	Too much sugar, liquid, leavening or shortening; too little flour; temperature too low; insufficient baking	Too much sugar; over-beaten egg whites; egg yolks underbeaten; use of greased pans; insufficient baking
Cake cracks or humps	Too much flour or too little liquid; overmixing; batter not spread evenly in pan; temperature of oven too high	Too much flour or sugar; temperature too high
Cake has one side higher	Batter spread unevenly; uneven pan; pan too close to side of oven; oven rack or range not even; uneven oven heat	Uneven pan; oven rack or range not level
Cake has hard top crust	Temperature too high; overbaking	Temperature too high; overbaking
Cake has sticky top crust	Too much sugar or shortening; insufficient baking	Too much sugar; insufficient baking
Cake has soggy layer at bottom	Too much liquid; eggs underbeaten; undermixing; insufficient baking	Too many eggs or egg yolks; underbeaten egg yolks; undermixing
Cake crumbles or falls apart	Too much sugar, leavening or shortening; batter undermixed; improper pan treatment; improper cooling	
Cake has heavy, compact quality	Too much liquid or shortening; too many eggs; too little leavening or flour; overmixing; oven temperature too high	Overbeaten egg whites; underbeaten egg yolks; overmixing
Cake falls out of pan before completely cooled		Too much sugar; use of greased pans; insufficient baking

CAKES, FILLINGS, FROSTINGS

<u>Do not</u> grease the sides of cake pans!!!
How would you like to climb a greased pole?

AMBROSIA CAKE

1 box Duncan Hines
  lemon supreme cake mix
1 small size box instant
  pineapple pudding mix

4 whole eggs
3/4 c. Crisco oil
1 (10 oz.) bottle 7-Up

Filling:

1 (6 oz.) pkg. frozen
  coconut
1 large can crushed
  pineapple
Juice of 1 medium lemon
1/2 c. orange juice

5 Tbsp. flour
2 c. sugar
1/2 c. chopped pecans
10 chopped maraschino
  cherries

Mix box of cake mix, pudding mix, oil and eggs; beat well. Add 7-Up last. Do not beat too hard or long after adding 7-Up, as the batter will be very light. Divide into 3 layers and bake at 350° until done. Cool layers, then put layers together with filling.

Filling: Mix flour, lemon juice and orange juice; add sugar and pineapple. Cook until slightly thick. Remove; add coconut. Cook a few minutes more. Remove from stove and add pecans and cherries; cool slightly and spread on layers of cake.

Mary Jo Waters, Birmingham Central Council

AMBROSIA SHORTCAKE

1 pkg. instant lemon
  pudding
1 can mandarin orange
  slices (save juice)
1 banana, thinly sliced

1/2 c. sweetened coconut
1/2 pt. whipping cream
1 medium sponge or angel
  food cake

Mix lemon pudding as directed on package; add whipped cream, oranges, bananas and coconut. Cover bottom of flat baking dish with slices of cake. Sprinkle some of orange juice on cake; add half pudding mixture and repeat with slices of cake, juice and remainder of pudding. Chill several hours before serving.

1567-82   Mrs. O. O. Prickett, Selma Pioneer Unit

ANALGAMATO CAKE

1 box yellow cake mix
Yolks of 8 eggs
2 c. sugar
1 c. butter

1/2 lb. seeded raisins
2 c. chopped pecans
1 c. grated coconut

Bake cake according to directions on box; stir together and cook 8 eggs, 2 cups sugar and 1 cup butter. Cool and add 1/2 pound seeded raisins, 2 cups chopped pecans and 1 cup grated coconut. Frost cake.

Elizabeth Maddox, Mobile Council

ANGEL FOOD CAKE

1 c. cake flour
1 1/2 c. sugar
1 1/2 c. egg whites

1/2 tsp. salt
2 1/2 Tbsp. cold water
1 1/2 tsp. cream of tartar
1 tsp. vanilla

Sift flour and 1/2 cup sugar together. Place egg whites in large bowl; add salt and water. Whip till frothy. Add cream of tartar; whip until mixture stands in peaks. Whip in remaining sugar. Fold in a portion of the flour mixture; add vanilla. Add remaining flour mixture. Pour batter into an ungreased angel food cake pan; bake 40 to 50 minutes at 350°. Invert cake pan until cake is cool.

Joyce Reavis, Decatur Council

APPLESAUCE-NUT CAKE WITH CARAMEL FROSTING

3/4 c. butter
1 c. granulated sugar
1 c. brown sugar
3 large eggs
3 c. applesauce
3 1/2 c. sifted flour
2 tsp. baking powder

1 tsp. salt
3/4 tsp. ground cloves
1 tsp. ground nutmeg
3 tsp. ground cinnamon
1 lb. seedless raisins
1 1/2 c. chopped pecans

Cream butter and sugar; add eggs and applesauce and beat well. Combine dry ingredients and stir in. Add raisins and pecans and mix well. Spoon batter into 10 inch greased and floured tube pan; bake at 325° for 2 hours or until cake tests done.

Caramel Frosting:

3 c. sugar

1 level Tbsp. all-purpose flour
1 c. sweet milk

In an iron skillet brown 1/2 cup sugar. Let first

90

mixture of remaining sugar, flour and milk come to a good boil and mix in browned sugar; stir real well. Cook to soft ball stage and stir in 1 1/2 sticks of margarine and heat until creamy and frost cake. This is a favorite cake with all. Moist; keeps well.

Emma Gray, Decatur Council

APPLE DAPPLE CAKE

3 c. flour
1 tsp. salt
1 tsp. soda
1 1/2 c. pecans,
    chopped fine

1 c. Wesson oil
2 c. sugar
3 eggs
2 tsp. vanilla
3 c. raw apples, chopped fine

Mix oil, sugar, eggs and vanilla. Sift together flour, salt, soda and add to first mixture. Fold in pecans and apples. Bake in tube pan at 350° for 1 hour.

Sauce:

1 c. brown sugar
1/4 c. milk

3/4 c. oleo

Mix and cook 3 minutes; pour over cake while cake is hot. Let cake cool before removing.

Helen Mitchell

APPLE NUT CAKE

3 c. diced apples
1 c. chopped pecans
2 c. sugar
3 c. self-rising flour

1 c. Crisco oil
3 eggs
1 tsp. vanilla

Mix all ingredients together with hands; bake at 350° for 1 hour or until done in Bundt pan. This is very good made 2 or 3 days ahead.

Glaze:

1/2 c. sugar
1/4 c. water

1/2 tsp. vanilla

Bring to boil and brush on warm cake.

Brenda Etheredge, Mobile Council

1567-82

DRIED APPLE CAKE

1 c. butter or oleo
2 c. sugar
4 egg yolks, unbeaten
1 tsp. vanilla
1 c. buttermilk

2 1/2 c. sifted all-purpose
flour
1/2 tsp. salt
1 tsp. baking soda
4 egg whites, stiffly beaten

Frosting:

1 1/2 c. sugar
1 small can Pet milk

1 stick oleo

Boil 5 minutes, then add:

1 c. stewed dried apples
1 c. coconut

1 c. chopped pecans
1 tsp. vanilla

Mix well. Frost cool layers.

Cake: Cream butter and sugar until fluffy; add egg yolks, one at a time, and beat well after each. Add vanilla and mix well. Sift together flour, salt and soda. Add alternately with buttermilk to butter mixture, beating after addition until smooth. Fold in beaten egg whites. Pour into three 8 or 9 inch layer pans that have been greased and floured. Bake at 350° for 30 to 40 minutes; cool before frosting.

Note: The secret to the flavor of this cake is to use home-dried apples. Twenty-four hours in a tightly covered cake cover before cutting enhances flavor. Freezes very well.

Sue Loyd, Anniston Council

EASY APPLE CAKE WITH CREAM TOPPING

1 (20 oz.) can apple
fruit filling
2 c. all-purpose flour
1 c. sugar
1 1/2 tsp. baking soda

1 tsp. salt
2 eggs, beaten
1 tsp. vanilla
2/3 c. cooking oil
3/4 c. chopped walnuts

Spread apple fruit filling over bottom of 9x13 inch pan. Combine flour, sugar, soda and salt; sprinkle over fruit filling. Blend beaten eggs, vanilla, oil and 1/2 cup of the walnuts and pour over ingredients in the pan. Stir with fork only until blended. Smooth batter evenly in the pan. Bake at 350° F. for 40-50 minutes, or until cake springs back when lightly touched. Pour hot Cream Topping over warm cake; sprinkle with remaining walnuts. Serve warm or cold. (Topping follows on next page.)

Cream Topping:

1 c. sugar
1/2 tsp. baking soda

1/2 c. commercial
   sour cream

Combine sugar, sour cream and baking soda in saucepan; cook over medium heat, stirring constantly until mixture comes to a boil. Remove from heat and pour over warm cake.

Diane Lassiter, Huntsville Council

FRESH APPLE CAKE

1 1/4 c. corn oil
2 c. sugar
3 eggs, well beaten
3 c. plain or cake flour
1 tsp. salt

1 tsp. soda
2 tsp. vanilla flavor
1 c. chopped pecans
3 or 4 medium red
   Delicious apples

Icing:

1/2 c. oleo
1 c. light brown sugar

1/4 c. evaporated milk
1 tsp. vanilla flavor

This cake needs to be prepared at least 3 days in advance of serving. Combine first 3 ingredients in order given above. Next peel, core and chop enough fresh apples to make 3 cups (3 or 4 medium apples) and add to mixture; also add chopped pecans. In separate bowl sift 3 or 4 times 3 cups flour, salt and soda. Add to apple mixture; stir well and add vanilla flavor. Grease 11x14 inch pan; cover bottom with wax paper. Pour cake onto the wax paper and put in cold oven and then set oven at 325° for 45 minutes.

Icing: Heat oleo and brown sugar over low heat, then add evaporated milk; let come to full boil. Remove from heat and cool, then add 1 teaspoon vanilla flavor; pour over cake.

Elaine Hunt, Birmingham Central Council

APRICOT BRANDY CAKE

3 c. white sugar
1/2 lb. oleo
6 eggs
3 c. flour
1/4 tsp. soda
1/2 tsp. salt
1 c. sour cream

1/2 tsp. rum flavoring
1 tsp. orange flavoring
1/4 tsp. almond flavoring
1/2 tsp. lemon flavoring
1 tsp. vanilla flavoring
1/2 c. apricot brandy

Cream butter, sugar and eggs, one at a time. Sift dry ingredients together - flour, salt and soda. Alternate eggs, flour and sour cream; add flavoring and brandy. Bake in tube pan, well greased and floured, at 325° for 1 1/2 hours.

Sarah Louise Gray, Life Member,
Tri-Cities Council

BANANA NUT CAKE

2 1/2 c. sifted cake flour
1 2/3 c. sugar
1 1/4 tsp. baking powder
1 1/4 tsp. soda
1 tsp. salt

2/3 c. Crisco
1/3 c. buttermilk
1 1/4 c. mashed bananas
1/3 c. buttermilk
2 large unbeaten eggs
2/3 c. chopped nuts

Frosting:

1 box plus 2 c. sifted
  confectioners sugar
3/4 c. Crisco

Scant 1/2 c. evaporated milk
Dash of salt
1 tsp. maple flavoring

Sift together first 5 ingredients; add next 3 ingredients and beat vigorously for 2 minutes. Add next 2 ingredients and repeat beating for 2 minutes. Fold in chopped nuts and bake in greased and floured pans for 30-35 minutes at 350°. Makes three 8 inch layers or two 9 inch layers.

Frosting: Mix all ingredients and beat vigorously for 20 minutes; spread over cooled layers. The maple flavored frosting compliments the banana cake beautifully.

Carolyn Arnold, Huntsville Council

BANANA PINEAPPLE CAKE

3 c. plain flour
2 c. sugar
1 tsp. soda
1 tsp. salt
1 1/2 c. diced bananas

1 (8 oz.) can crushed
  pineapple with juice
1 1/2 c. salad oil
3 eggs
1 1/2 tsp. vanilla

Mix all ingredients together (do not use mixer). Put in greased and floured tube pan; bake at least 1 hour and 20 minutes at 350°. Cool completely before removing from pan.

Mildred Parker, Huntsville Council

BANANA SPLIT CAKE

1 stick melted butter
2 c. graham cracker
  crumbs
2 c. confectioners
  sugar
2 eggs

2 sticks butter
5 or 6 bananas
1 large can crushed
  pineapple, drained
1 large container Cool Whip
Chopped nuts and cherries

Mix the first 2 ingredients in bottom of dish like crust. Beat confectioners sugar, eggs and 2 sticks of butter in electric mixer for 5 or 6 minutes or until fluffy. Pour this mixture over the crust. Slice bananas and cover the mixture; add pineapple (drained) over bananas; cover mixture with Cool Whip. Spread chopped nuts and cherries over top. Refrigerate.

Kathryn Robertson, Tuscaloosa Council

BETTER THAN SEX

1 box Duncan Hines butter
  cake mix (yellow)
1 (8 oz.) pkg. chocolate
  chips (sweet)
1 (8 oz.) pkg. pecans,
  chopped
1 box instant French
  vanilla pudding

1/2 box German's chocolate
  (unsweetened), grated
1 (8 oz.) carton sour cream
1/2 c. Wesson oil
1/2 c. milk (sweet)
4 eggs
1 stick butter or margarine

Icing:

1 (8 oz.) pkg. cream
  cheese (room temperature)
1 box confectioners sugar

1 tsp. vanilla
Nuts and coconut (optional)

Mix all ingredients in cake mix and mix. Pour in greased and floured tube or Bundt pan; bake 1 hour at 350° or until done.

Icing: Cream cheese and sugar until smooth; add vanilla, nuts and coconut.

Mary C. Martin, Birmingham East Council

BLACKBERRY CAKE

2 c. white sugar
1 c. butter
2 tsp. cinnamon
2 tsp. allspice
3 c. flour

2 tsp. nutmeg
2 c. blackberries
5 eggs
2 tsp. soda in 6 Tbsp.
  sour milk

1567-82

Put blackberries in blender and blend; set aside. Mix sugar and butter. Add eggs and spices. Add alternately the blackberries and flour. Lastly, add soda and milk; bake at 375° for 40 minutes.

Olive Crow, Mobile Council

BLUEBERRY BUCKLE

1/2 c. shortening	1/2 c. milk
1/2 c. sugar	2 c. fresh blueberries
1 well beaten egg	1/2 c. sugar
2 c. sifted enriched flour	1/2 c. sifted enriched flour
2 1/2 tsp. baking powder	1/2 tsp. cinnamon
1/4 tsp. salt	1/4 c. butter or margarine

Use 350° oven. Thoroughly cream shortening and 1/2 cup sugar; add egg and mix well. Sift 2 cups flour, baking powder and salt; add to creamed mixture alternately with milk. Pour into well greased 11 1/2 x 7 1/2 x 1 1/2 inch pan. Sprinkle blueberries over batter.

Combine 1/2 cup sugar, 1/2 cup flour, cinnamon and butter till crumbly; sprinkle over blueberries. Bake in moderate oven (350°) for 45 to 50 minutes. Cut in squares. Serve warm. Makes 8 to 10 servings.

George Burns, Huntsville Council

BLUEBERRY CAKE AND CREAM CHEESE FROSTING

1 box cake mix	1 can blueberry pie filling

Frosting:

1 (8 oz.) pkg. cream cheese	1/2 c. powdered sugar
1 large Cool Whip	1/2 c. sugar

Bake 2 layer regular cake; split layers. Use blueberry pie filling to stack.

Frosting: Combine all ingredients. Put some blueberry pie filling in middle of cake. Keep in refrigerator.

Cathy Porter, Tuscaloosa Council

BROWN RAISIN CAKE

1 1/2 c. brown sugar	1 tsp. cinnamon
1 1/2 c. water	1 tsp. cloves
1 c. raisins	3 Tbsp. shortening
1/2 tsp. nutmeg	1 tsp. salt

| 3 c. flour | 3/4 tsp. baking powder |
| 1 1/2 tsp. soda | Nutmeats and citrus fruits |

Boil together for 3 minutes the brown sugar, water, spices and shortening for 3 minutes; cool. Sift together flour, soda, baking powder and salt; mix with cooled liquid mixture. One teaspoon vanilla may be added, also nuts and citrus fruits (candied). Bake in a 350° oven in a tube pan for about 40 minutes, or test for doneness. When cake is cooled, drizzle with powdered sugar icing.

Mrs. John D. Hall, Birmingham Central Council

BUTTERMILK CAKE

1 c. shortening (Crisco)	4 eggs
2 c. sugar	2 1/4 c. flour
1/2 tsp. soda	1 c. buttermilk
1/4 tsp. salt	1/2 tsp. baking powder
1/2 tsp. vanilla	

Cream sugar and shortening; add eggs, one at a time. Mix soda in buttermilk and add to batter. Add vanilla and all flour and baking powder and remaining ingredients. Mix well; pour in large tube cake pan, well greased and floured. Bake 1 hour and 10 minutes at 350°. This will also make 3 layers for a stack cake. If tube pan is small, make 1 dozen cupcakes.

Irene Whiddon, Birmingham West Council

MRS. EDGAR'S BUTTERMILK CAKE

4 1/3 c. all-purpose flour	1/4 tsp. baking soda
1 3/4 c. butter (3 1/4 sticks)	1 Tbsp. vanilla or 1 tsp.
3 1/3 c. sugar	vanilla and 1 tsp. almond
8 eggs	flavor*
	1/2 c. buttermilk

Note: Recipe may be cut down to smaller proportions.
*Note: Lemon may be used in place of almond with the vanilla.

Have all ingredients at room temperature. One needs a strong arm or electric beater when making this cake. Start oven 10 minutes before baking; set to moderate slow (325° F.). Butter well a tube pan; dust with flour. Sift flour, then measure. Measure butter and soda into a 4 quart mixing bowl and cream until smooth and soft. Add flavorings, then sugar gradually, creaming thoroughly. Cream with rotary beater if you do not use an electric beater. Add

1567-82

eggs, one at a time, beating well after each. Now clean off
beater; remove and use wooden spoon. Then add flour and
milk alternately in 2 or 3 portions, beginning and ending
with flour and beating until thoroughly blended after each
portion. Bake an hour and 15 to 30 minutes, or till cake
tests done with toothpick.

Annette Turner

BUTTERNUT CAKE

2 c. self-rising flour
1 c. oil
4 eggs

2 c. sugar
1 c. milk
1 tsp. vanilla butternut
   flavoring

Icing:

1 box confectioners sugar
1 stick oleo
8 oz. cream cheese

1 tsp. vanilla butternut
   flavoring
1 c. nuts

Beat eggs and oil, then add all other ingredients.
Cook 20-25 minutes at 350° in two 9 inch pans or three 8
inch pans. Ice when cooled.

LaDon S. Young, Birmingham Central Council

BUTTER PECAN CAKE

3 Tbsp. butter
1 1/3 c. chopped pecans
2/3 c. butter, softened
1 1/3 c. sugar
2 eggs

2 c. all-purpose flour
1 1/2 tsp. baking powder
1/4 tsp. salt
2/3 c. milk
1 1/2 tsp. vanilla extract

Butter Pecan Frosting:

3 Tbsp. butter, softened
3 c. powdered sugar
3 Tbsp. plus 1 tsp. milk

3/4 tsp. vanilla
Reserved toasted pecans

Melt 3 tablespoons butter in 13x9x2 inch pan; stir in
pecans and bake at 350° for 10 minutes. Cool. Cream
softened butter in large mixing bowl; gradually add sugar,
beating until light and fluffy and sugar is dissolved. Add
eggs, one at a time, beating well after each addition. Combine flour, baking powder, salt; add to creamed mixture alternately with milk, beginning and ending with flour mixture. Stir in vanilla and 1 cup pecans; reserve remaining
pecans for frosting. Pour into 2 greased and floured 9 inch

cake pans. Bake at 350° for 30 minutes. Cool cake 10 minutes in pans. Remove and cool completely. Frost with icing.

Frosting: Cream butter; add sugar, milk and vanilla, beating until light and fluffy. Stir in pecans.

Jeannie Riddles, Riverchase Council

CARROT CAKE

2 c. plain or cake flour	1/2 c. chopped nuts
2 tsp. cinnamon	3 c. carrots, grated
2 tsp. soda	1 c. Wesson oil
2 c. sugar	3 eggs

Frosting:

1 box confectioners sugar	1 (8 oz.) pkg. cream cheese, softened
1 stick soft margarine	2 tsp. vanilla
	1/2 c. chopped nuts

Sift flour, cinnamon, soda and sugar together 3 times. Put Wesson oil and eggs in mixer; beat until fluffy. Add grated carrots, then blend in dry ingredients; add nuts. Pour batter into three 9 inch pans; bake at 350° for 35 minutes.

Frosting: Combine sugar, cream cheese and margarine. Add vanilla and nuts. Frost each layer completely.

Virginia H. Greene, Birmingham Central Council

CARROT PINEAPPLE CAKE

1 1/2 c. all-purpose flour	2/3 c. oil
1 c. sugar	2 eggs
1 tsp. baking powder	1 c. finely shredded raw carrot
1 tsp. soda	1/2 c. crushed pineapple with syrup
1 tsp. cinnamon	1 tsp. vanilla
1/2 tsp. salt	

In large mixer bowl stir together dry ingredients; add oil, eggs, carrot, pineapple and vanilla. Mix till all ingredients are moistened. Beat with electric mixer 2 minutes at medium speed. Pour batter into greased and lightly floured 9x9x2 inch pan. Bake in 350° oven about 35 minutes; cool. Frost with Cream Cheese Frosting.

Cream Cheese Frosting:

1 (3 oz.) pkg. cream cheese	4 Tbsp. butter or oleo
	1 tsp. vanilla

1567-82

A dash of salt
1/2 c. chopped pecans

2 1/2 c. sifted powdered
sugar

Cream together cream cheese, softened, and softened butter or oleo. Beat in vanilla and salt. Gradually add powdered sugar; blend in well. Stir in pecans.

Eunice Eatman, Tuscaloosa Pioneer Unit

CARROT PUDDING CAKE

1 pkg. (2 layer size)
 yellow cake mix
1 pkg. (4 serving size)
 vanilla flavor instant
 pudding and pie filling
4 eggs
1/3 c. water

1/4 c. oil
3 c. grated carrots
1/2 c. raisins, finely chopped
1/2 c. chopped walnuts
1/2 tsp. salt
2 tsp. ground cinnamon

Blend all ingredients in large mixing bowl; beat 4 minutes at medium speed of electric mixer. Pour into 2 greased and floured 8x4 inch loaf pans. Bake at 350° for 45 to 50 minutes, until cakes spring back when lightly pressed and begin to pull away from sides of pans. Do not underbake. Cool in pans 15 minutes; remove and cool on racks. Frost with Orange Cream Cheese Frosting.

Orange Cream Cheese Frosting: Blend 1 tablespoon butter or margarine with one 3 ounce package cream cheese and 1 teaspoon grated orange rind until smooth. Alternately add 2 1/2 cups sifted confectioners sugar and 1 tablespoon orange juice, beating after each addition until smooth.

Faye King, Huntsville Council

CHEESECAKE SUPREME

1 1/4 c. graham cracker
 crumbs
1/4 c. sugar
1/4 c. melted butter or
 margarine
5 (8 oz.) pkg. cream
 cheese, at room
 temperature

1 3/4 c. sugar
3 Tbsp. flour
2 tsp. grated lemon peel
1 Tbsp. grated orange peel
5 whole eggs
2 egg yolks
1/4 c. heavy cream

Pineapple Glaze:

1 Tbsp. cornstarch
2 Tbsp. sugar

1 (8 1/2 oz.) can
 crushed pineapple

Heat oven to 500° F. Work graham cracker crumbs,

sugar and butter together until well blended. Butter a 9 inch spring form pan and press crumb mixture over the bottom and about 2 1/4 inches up the sides of the pan. In the large bowl of an electric mixer combine cheese, sugar, lemon peel, flour and orange peel on low speed. Add whole eggs and egg yolks, one at a time, beating well after each addition. Add cream and beat at medium speed just until mixture is smooth. Pour cheese mixture into prepared pan; bake for 10 minutes. Reduce oven temperature to 200°F. and continue baking for 1 hour. Remove from oven and cool on wire rack away from drafts. Refrigerate until cold. When cold, remove rim of pan and place cake on a serving plate. Top with Pineapple Glaze. Serves 12 to 14.

Pineapple Glaze: Combine cornstarch and sugar in a small saucepan; gradually stir in undrained pineapple. Cook on moderately low heat, stirring constantly, until thickened. Add a few drops of yellow food coloring, if desired. Remove from heat; stir occasionally. Cool before using.

Ada Mae Tant, Birmingham South Council

CHERRY TOPPED CHEESECAKE

1 pkg. Duncan Hines yellow cake mix	4 eggs
	1 1/2 c. milk
2 Tbsp. oil	3 Tbsp. lemon juice
2 (8 oz.) pkg. cream cheese, softened	3 tsp. vanilla
	1 (1 lb. 5 oz.) can cherry
1/2 c. sugar	pie filling

Preheat oven to 300°. Reserve 1 cup of dry cake mix. In large mixing bowl combine remaining cake mix, 1 egg and oil (mixture will be crumbly). Press crust mixture evenly into bottom and 3/4 way up the sides of a greased 13x9x2 inch* pan. In same bowl blend cream cheese and sugar. Add 3 eggs and reserved cake mix; beat 1 minute at medium speed. At low speed slowly add milk and flavorings; mix until smooth. Pour into crust; bake at 300° for 45-55 minutes until center is firm. When cool, top with pie filling; chill before serving. Store in refrigerator; freeze covered with foil. Makes a 13x9 inch* cheesecake.

*Cheesecake can also bake in two 9 inch pans for 40-50 minutes.

Teresa Petty, Huntsville Council

CHOCOLATE CHEESECAKE

1/4 c. chocolate wafer or graham cracker crumbs (18 wafers or 16 squares)
2 Tbsp. sugar
3 Tbsp. butter, melted

2 (8 oz.) pkg. and 1 (3 oz.) pkg. cream cheese, softened
1 c. sugar
1/4 c. cocoa
2 tsp. vanilla
3 eggs
Coconut Pecan Topping

Heat oven to 350°. Stir together crumbs and 2 tablespoons sugar; mix in butter. Press mixture evenly in bottom of ungreased 9 inch spring form pan. Bake 10 minutes and cool. Reduce oven to 300°. Beat cream cheese in large mixer bowl; gradually add 1 cup of sugar and the cocoa, beating until fluffy. Add vanilla and beat in eggs, 1 at a time. Pour over crumb mixture; bake until center is firm, about 1 hour. Cool to room temperature. Spread topping and refrigerate 3 hours. Loosen edge from pan and remove.
(Note: For best results, use food processor.)

Coconut Pecan Topping:

2 Tbsp. butter
1/3 c. light cream, or evaporated milk
2 Tbsp. brown sugar

2 egg yolks or 1 egg
1/2 tsp. vanilla
1/2 c. chopped pecans
1/2 c. flaked coconut

Cook butter, cream, sugar and egg yolks in small saucepan over low heat; stir in vanilla, pecans and coconut; cool.

Yvonne Stokes, Birmingham West Council

EASY CHEESECAKE

1 box yellow cake mix (any brand)

1 stick butter or margarine
2 eggs

Topping:

1 (8 oz.) pkg. cream cheese
2 eggs

1 box confectioners sugar
1 tsp. vanilla

Preheat oven to 350°. Mix cake mix, butter and eggs until smooth; spread in bottom of 9x14 inch pan. Mix topping ingredients and pour on top of cake mix mixture; bake about 40 to 45 minutes or until firm. Cool and serve.
Note: Cake will fall in center while cooling.

Sharon Harris, Birmingham Central Council

MINI CHEESECAKES

3 (8 oz.) pkg. cream
  cheese, softened
1 c. sugar

5 whole eggs
1 tsp. vanilla

Topping:

1 c. sour cream
1/4 c. sugar

1/2 tsp. vanilla
Smucker's strawberry
  or cherry preserves

Mix together all the ingredients except for the topping. Pour the ingredients into miniature cupcake or candy paper cups until the cup is approximately 3/4 full. Bake in 300° F. oven for 30 to 40 minutes. Do not brown; cool.

Topping: Mix together all the ingredients for the topping except for the preserves. Spread a small amount on top of each cup. Add a drop of preserves in the middle of each cup and put back into the oven for 5 minutes. Freezes well.

Beverly McCoy, Montgomery Council

OLD FASHIONED CHEESE CAKE DELUXE

Crust:

1 1/2 pkg. graham crackers
2 Tbsp. sugar

4 Tbsp. butter

Filling:

1 1/2 lb. cream cheese
1 1/2 c. sugar
16 oz. sour cream
2 tsp. vanilla

1 can Eagle Brand sweetened
  condensed milk
8 eggs
2 Tbsp. lemon juice

Crush graham crackers and add sugar; mix in 10 inch spring form pan with melted butter. Pat down and form crust on bottom and partly up sides of pan. Beat softened cream cheese until smooth; add sugar, sour cream, milk, lemon juice and vanilla; add eggs, one at a time, until thoroughly mixed. Bake at 325° for 1 hour and 10 minutes. Shut oven off and leave in oven for 1 hour; remove and cool to room temperature, then refrigerate. When cake is cooled, top with pineapple, cherry or strawberry prepared pie filling. (This cake freezes very well.)

D. J. Del Guercio, Riverchase Council

STRAWBERRY CHEESE CAKE

First Layer:

1 1/4 c. graham cracker   1 stick melted butter
  crumbs

Second Layer:

1 (8 oz.) pkg. softened   1 c. powdered sugar
  cream cheese   2 to 3 Tbsp. milk

Third Layer: Use 1 cup chopped pecans.

Fourth Layer: Use 1 package Dream Whip. (Chill and serve with Fifth Layer.)

Fifth Layer: Drop spoonfuls of sweetened strawberries on top.

Mary Ann Davis, Anniston Council

CHERRY SUPREME CAKE

1 box cherry cake mix   3/4 c. oil
1 (3 oz.) pkg. cherry   3/4 c. water
  jello   4 eggs

Icing:

1/2 c. hot water   2 Tbsp. butter
1/2 pkg. (3 oz.)   2 c. confectioners sugar
  cherry jello

Mix cake mix, jello, oil, water and eggs. Bake 1 hour like pound cake at 350°.

To make icing, the hot water should dissolve the jello, butter and sugar; if not, place over low heat to dissolve. Poke holes in cake and pour icing over it. The longer it sets, the better it gets.

Lavelle D. Willingham, Riverchase Council

CHESS CAKE

1 box yellow cake mix   1 egg, beaten
1 stick melted margarine

Mix and press in 9x13 inch loaf pan.

8 oz. cream cheese   1 box confectioners sugar
3 eggs

Mix well and pour over batter; bake at 375° for 10 minutes; turn down to 325° for 30 minutes.

104   Mrs. John Pilling, Decatur Council

BLACK FOREST CAKE

Combine one package (2 layer size) chocolate cake mix, one 21 ounce can cherry pie filling, 1/4 cup oil and 3 eggs. Beat well until batter is smooth. Pour into a greased, floured 12 cup Bundt pan and bake in preheated 350° oven 45 minutes or until cake is done. Cool in pan 25 minutes, then invert onto rack to finish cooling. Decorate and serve with 1 can cherry pie filling and whipped cream.

Debbie Tucker, Birmingham East Council

CHESS CAKE (OOEY-GOEY BARS)

1 chocolate cake mix   1 egg
1 stick margarine

Frosting:

1 (8 oz.) pkg. cream   2 eggs, slightly beaten
   cheese (room temperature)   1 1/2 tsp. vanilla
1 box powdered sugar   1/2 c. chopped pecans

Melt margarine in 9x13 inch pan. Beat egg into margarine, then sprinkle in cake mix. Mix well with fork and press down until evenly spread. Beat the frosting ingredients well and pour onto cake mixture. Bake at 350° for 40-45 minutes.

Lashawn Hopson, Birmingham West Council

CHOCOLATE CAKE

1 c. water   1/4 tsp. cinnamon
1/2 c. shortening   2 eggs, beaten
1 stick margarine   1 c. buttermilk
2 Tbsp. cocoa   1/2 tsp. soda
2 c. plain flour   1 tsp. vanilla
2 c. sugar   1/4 tsp. salt

Bring first 4 ingredients to a boil; pour over the remaining 8 ingredients. Mix well; bake in a 9x12 inch greased and floured pan at 350° for about 30 minutes. Frost while still warm.

Frosting:

1 stick margarine   6 Tbsp. sweet milk
3 Tbsp. cocoa

Bring to a boil; pour over 1 box confectioners sugar, 1

teaspoon vanilla and 1 cup chopped pecans. Spread on warm cake. (This cake freezes very well.)
Mrs. Bobby H. Henson,
Birmingham Central Council

CHOCOLATE CHIP CAKE

3/4 c. oil
1 small box instant vanilla
   pudding mix
4 eggs
1 Tbsp. vanilla
5 oz. chocolate syrup

1 pkg. butter flavored
   cake mix
1 (8 oz.) carton sour cream
   (1 c.)
1 (6 oz.) pkg. chocolate chips
1/2 c. melted butter

Mix oil, pudding, eggs, vanilla, sour cream, butter and cake mix. Divide cake mixture equally into 2 bowls. Add chocolate chips to one mixture and chocolate syrup to the other. Swirl ingredients in individual bowls. Pour into greased Bundt pan; bake at 325° for about 1 hour. No icing needed.
Carolyn Arnold, Huntsville Council

CHOCOLATE DUMP CAKE

1 stick butter
4 eggs
1 c. self-rising flour

1 c. sugar
1 large can chocolate syrup

Icing:

1 c. sugar
1/2 stick butter

1/4 c. milk
2 Tbsp. cocoa

Combine all ingredients in an ungreased 9x13 inch pan; bake at 350° for 30 minutes. Frost while cake is still warm.
Icing: Combine all ingredients in a heavy saucepan; boil for 1 minute and then beat until creamy. Pour over hot cake.
Susan Pruitt, Birmingham East Council

CHOCOLATE FUDGE CAKE

1/2 c. butter, softened
1 (16 oz.) pkg. brown
   sugar
3 eggs
3 (1 oz.) squares unsweetened chocolate, melted

2 1/4 c. sifted cake flour
2 tsp. soda
1/2 tsp. salt
1 c. commercial sour cream
1 c. hot water
1 1/2 tsp. vanilla extract
Frosting (recipe follows)

Cream butter; gradually add sugar, beating well. Add eggs, one at a time, beating well after each addition. Add chocolate, mixing well. Combine flour, soda and salt; gradually add to chocolate mixture alternately with sour cream, beating well after each addition. Add water, mixing well; stir in vanilla extract. (Batter will be thin.) Pour batter evenly into 2 greased and floured 9 inch cake pans. Bake at 350° for 45 minutes or until cake tests done. Let cool in pans 10 minutes; remove layers from pans, and place on wire racks to complete cooling. Spread frosting between layers and on top and sides of cake. Yield: One 9 inch layer cake.

Frosting:

4 (1 oz.) squares
  unsweetened chocolate
1/2 c. butter

1 (16 oz.) pkg. powdered
  sugar, sifted
1/2 c. milk
2 tsp. vanilla extract

Combine chocolate and butter; place over low heat until melted, stirring constantly. Combine sugar, milk and vanilla in a medium mixing bowl; mix well. Set bowl in a large pan of ice water, and stir in chocolate mixture, then beat at high speed of portable mixer until spreading consistency. Yield: Frosting for one 9 inch layer cake.

Faith Kirby, Anniston Council

CHOCOLATE MOUNDS CAKE

2 c. flour
2 c. sugar
1 c. water
1 tsp. salt
1 tsp. baking powder
2 eggs

3/4 c. sour cream
1/4 c. shortening
1 1/4 tsp. baking soda
1 tsp. vanilla
4 oz. melted chocolate

Preheat oven to 350°. Lightly grease two 8 inch round cake pans. In a large bowl combine all the dry ingredients, mixing well. Add chocolate, water, beaten eggs, shortening and vanilla. Beat for 2 minutes at high speed, stirring well. Pour into cake pans and bake for 40-45 minutes. Cool cake completely and slice layers in halves with a string.

Filling:

1 (12 oz.) pkg. frozen
  coconut (not fresh or dry)

1 3/4 c. granulated sugar
4 oz. sour cream

Mix thoroughly and spread between each layer.

Frosting:

2 c. sugar
1/4 c. Crisco
Pinch of salt

2/3 c. milk
2 squares Baker's chocolate
    or 3 Tbsp. cocoa
1 tsp. vanilla

Put all the ingredients in a heavy saucepan and bring to bubbling boil. Set aside to cool. When cooled, beat with mixer until glossy and of spreading consistency. Frost the sides and top of cake generously.

Mrs. Hazel Driggers, Retired, Life Member,
Anniston Council

CHOCOLATE PUDDING CAKE

1 stick oleo or margarine
1 c. pecans
1 c. plain flour
1 (8 oz.) pkg. cream cheese
1 c. Cool Whip
1 c. powdered sugar

1 (3 3/4 oz.) pkg. instant
    vanilla pudding mix
1 (3 3/4 oz.) pkg. instant
    chocolate pudding mix
2 1/2 c. milk
1 Hershey's bar

1. Melt 1 stick oleo and mix in 1 cup chopped pecans and 1 cup plain flour. Press down in 12 x 7 1/2 inch Pyrex baking dish and bake for 20 minutes at 350°. 2. Mix one 8 ounce package cream cheese, 1 cup Cool Whip and 1 cup powdered sugar; spread on cooled crust. 3. Mix one (3 3/4 ounce) package instant vanilla pudding, 1 package instant chocolate pudding mix and 2 1/2 cups cold milk; spread on layer 2. 4. Spread on remaining Cool Whip and grate 1 Hershey's bar on top. Refrigerate. Delicious.

P.S. This appears to be a complicated recipe, but is simple and fun to make.

Louise (Teske) Colvin, Jasper Club

CHOCOLATE SHASTA CAKE

Sift together in large bowl 2 cups sugar and 2 cups flour. Put in saucepan:

1 stick oleo
4 Tbsp. cocoa

1/2 c. Crisco
1 c. water

Melt and bring to rapid boil; stir into sugar mixture. Mix together:

1/2 c. buttermilk
1 tsp. soda

1 tsp. vanilla
2 eggs, slightly beaten

Mix into other ingredients; pour into greased 11x16

inch pan; bake 15-18 minutes at 400°.

Icing: Start making icing 5 minutes before cake is done. Melt together -

1 stick oleo   6 Tbsp. Pet milk
4 Tbsp. cocoa

Bring to boil and remove from heat; add:·

1 box confectioners sugar   1 c. pecans
1 tsp. vanilla

Beat well and spread over cake while still hot. Leave in pan to ice.

Doris A. Boyd, Anniston Council

CHOCOLATE SHEATH CAKE

2 c. sugar   1 c. water
2 c. flour   1/2 c. buttermilk
1/4 tsp. salt   2 eggs, beaten slightly
1 stick butter or   1 tsp. soda
   margarine   1 tsp. powdered cinnamon
1/2 c. shortening   1 tsp. vanilla extract
4 Tbsp. cocoa

Icing:

1 stick margarine   1 box confectioners sugar
   or butter   1 tsp. vanilla
4 Tbsp. cocoa   1 c. chopped nuts
6 Tbsp. milk

Sift together in large bowl the sugar, flour and salt. In saucepan place margarine, shortening, cocoa and water. Bring to a rapid boil and pour over flour mixture; stir well. Add, mixing by hand, the remaining ingredients. Batter will be quite thin. Pour in greased 16x11 inch pan, or 2 smaller pans and bake at 350° for 20 minutes.

Icing: Combine margarine, cocoa and milk. Bring to a rapid boil; remove from heat and add to confectioners sugar, vanilla and nuts. Beat well. Spread icing over cake in pan while hot. Cool thoroughly before cutting. Makes 32 two-inch squares.

Carole Foshee, Riverchase Council

CHOCOLATE SWIRL CAKE

1 box Duncan Hines
  yellow cake mix
1 (4 oz.) pkg. vanilla
  instant pudding mix

2/3 c. Mazola oil
4 eggs
3/4 c. water
1 c. Hershey's syrup

Mix first 2 ingredients. Make well in center and add oil, eggs, water; beat 2 minutes by hand (do not use mixer). Take 1/2 of mixture and add chocolate syrup; set aside. Pour half of batter in greased and floured tube pan. Add chocolate mixture; top with remaining mixture. Take knife and swirl. Bake at 350° for 45-50 minutes. Let cool 20 minutes before removing from pan.

            Grace M. Laney, Decatur Council

COFFEE CHOCOLATE CAKE

1 c. butter
2 c. sugar
3 egg yolks, separated
3 squares unsweetened
  chocolate

2 c. sifted flour
1/2 tsp. salt
2 tsp. baking powder
1 c. double strength coffee
1 tsp. flavoring

Cream sugar and butter; cream well and add beaten egg yolks. Add chocolate that has been softened over hot water. Sift all dry ingredients together alternating with coffee; add flavoring. Add nuts and fold in beaten egg whites. Bake in 3 greased and floured pans at 350°.

    Icing:

2 squares unsweetened
  chocolate, melted
  over hot water

1 1/2 (3 oz.) pkg. cream cheese
2/3 Tbsp. milk
2 1/4 c. powdered sugar
1/8 tsp. salt

Cream together cream cheese, milk, sugar and salt; add melted chocolate and cream together. Let cake cool before icing cake.

        Lola E. Johnson, Birmingham Central Council

DEVILS FOOD CAKE

1 1/2 c. flour
1 1/4 c. sugar
1/2 c. cocoa
1 1/4 tsp. soda
1/4 tsp. cream of tartar

1 tsp. salt
2/3 c. shortening
1 c. milk
1 tsp. vanilla
2 eggs

Mix together dry ingredients in mixing bowl; add shortening and 3/4 cup milk. Beat on medium speed for about 2 minutes. Add 1/4 cup milk, vanilla and eggs. Beat 2 more minutes. Pour in two prepared cake pans to make 2 layers. Bake at 350° for about 25 minutes. Frost with white frosting, chocolate, caramel or may be put together with whipped cream or Cool Whip and refrigerate.

Blanche Hooper, Anniston Council

GERMAN CHOCOLATE'S COUSIN CAKE

1 box yellow cake mix
1 pkg. vanilla instant
  pudding
1 (8 oz.) carton sour cream
4 eggs
1/2 c. oil

1/2 c. water
6 oz. semi-sweet
  chocolate chips
1 bar German's chocolate,
  grated
1 c. pecans

Mix cake mix, pudding, sour cream, 4 eggs, 1/2 cup oil, 1/2 cup water together. Add chocolate chips, chocolate bar (grated) and 1 cup pecans. Bake at 350° for 1 hour in tube or Bundt pan.

Valencia Lanier, Riverchase Council

HERSHEY BAR CAKE

1 large (8 oz.) plain milk
  chocolate Hershey's bar
2 sticks butter
2 c. sugar
4 eggs

2 1/2 c. flour, sifted
1/4 tsp. salt
1/4 tsp. soda
1 c. buttermilk
2 tsp. vanilla
2 c. chopped nuts

Preheat oven to 325°. Line tube pan with wax paper. Soften Hershey's bar until limp, not runny, and soften butter at room temperature. Cream butter and chocolate; add eggs and vanilla. Mix sugar and then dry ingredients alternately with buttermilk, beginning and ending with flour. Save some flour to mix with nuts so they won't sink when added to batter; bake in tube pan for 70 minutes.

Evelyn Howard, Decatur Council

HERSHEY'S DISAPPEARING CAKE

1/4 c. butter
1/4 c. shortening
2 c. sugar
1 tsp. vanilla
2 eggs
3/4 c. Hershey's cocoa

1 3/4 c. unsifted all-purpose flour
3/4 tsp. baking powder
3/4 tsp. baking soda
1/8 tsp. salt
1 3/4 c. milk

Generously grease and flour two 9 inch round cake pans. Cream butter, shortening, sugar and vanilla until fluffy; blend in eggs. Combine cocoa, flour, baking powder, baking soda and salt in bowl; add alternately with milk to batter; blend well. Pour into pans; bake at 350° for 30 to 35 minutes or until cake tester inserted in center comes out clean. Cool 10 minutes; remove from pans. Use cocoa in your favorite frosting recipe, too!

Frosting:

2 c. sugar
3 Tbsp. cocoa

1 stick oleo
1 Tbsp. white corn syrup

Cook on moderate heat, stirring until it comes to a boil. Boil 2 minutes. Beat in blender until consistency to spread over cake.

Lera Lee, Tuscaloosa Pioneer Unit

HOT FUDGE CAKE

3/4 c. sugar
1 c. flour
2 Tbsp. cocoa

1 1/2 c. milk
3 Tbsp. melted butter
1 tsp. vanilla

Topping:

1/2 c. sugar
1/2 c. brown sugar

1/4 c. cocoa

Mix cake ingredients in bowl or casserole dish (must be deep). Mix topping and sprinkle onto cake mix. Pour 1 1/2 cups water over both. Do not stir. Bake 45 minutes at 350°. Serve while hot.

Rosa M. Thornton, Huntsville Council

HOT FUDGE SUNDAE CAKE

1 c. plain flour
3/4 c. granulated sugar
2 Tbsp. cocoa
2 tsp. baking powder
1/4 tsp. salt
1/2 c. milk

2 Tbsp. salad oil
1 tsp. vanilla
1 c. chopped nuts
1 c. brown sugar, packed
1/4 c. cocoa
1 3/4 c. hot tap water
Vanilla ice cream

Heat oven to 350°. In ungreased square 9x9x2 inch pan stir together flour, granulated sugar, 2 tablespoons cocoa, baking powder and salt. Mix in milk, oil and vanilla with fork till smooth; stir in nuts. Spread evenly in pan. Sprinkle with brown sugar and 1/4 cup cocoa. Pour hot water over batter; bake 40 minutes. Let stand 15 minutes. Spoon into dessert dishes or cut into squares. Invert squares on plate. Top with ice cream and spoon sauce over each serving.
Carol Blackwood, Birmingham Central Council

MARBLE CAKE

1 c. Snowdrift shortening
3 c. sugar
6 eggs
3 c. sifted cake flour

1/4 tsp. soda
1 c. buttermilk
1 tsp. vanilla extract
1/2 tsp. salt
1 (5.5 oz.) can chocolate syrup

Cream together shortening and sugar; add 1 egg at a time, beating well after each addition. Sift together flour, salt and soda; add to creamed mixture alternately with buttermilk, beginning and ending with buttermilk. Add vanilla extract and blend well. Pour half the batter mixture into well greased and floured 10 inch tube pan; add chocolate syrup to remaining batter. Pour chocolate mixture over top of other batter and fold in gently with spatula for marble effect. Bake at 350° for 1 hour and 10 minutes. Cool on wire cake rack. Frost as desired. Makes one 10 inch cake.
Donna M. Walker, Birmingham Central Council

MARBLE CHIFFON CAKE

Preheat oven to 325°. Sift ample amount of Softasilk cake flour on square of paper. Stir these until smooth. Cool:

1/4 c. cocoa
1/4 c. sugar

1/4 c. boiling water
1/4 tsp. red food coloring,
    if desired

Step 1: Measure (level measurements throughout) and sift together in mixing bowl:

2 1/4 c. sifted Softasilk
  cake flour (spoon lightly
  into cup, don't pack)

1 1/2 c. sugar
3 tsp. baking powder
1 tsp. salt

Make a well and add in order:

1/2 c. Wesson oil
5 unbeaten egg yolks
  (medium size)

3/4 c. cold water
2 tsp. vanilla

Beat until smooth with spoon, or beat with electric mixer on medium speed for 1 minute. Step 2: Measure into large mixing bowl 1 cup egg whites (7 or 8) and 1/2 teaspoon cream of tartar. Beat until whites form very stiff peaks by hand, or with electric mixer on high speed for 3 to 5 minutes. Do not underbeat. Egg whites are stiff enough when a rubber scraper drawn through leaves a clean path. Step 3: Pour egg yolk mixture gradually over beaten egg whites, gently folding with rubber scraper just until blended. Do not stir.
Place 1/2 the batter in another bowl; pour cocoa mixture gradually over it, gently folding until blended. Immediately pour alternate layers of light and dark batters into ungreased tube pan (10x4 inches). Bake 55 minutes in slow moderate oven (325°) then increase to 350° for 10 to 15 minutes, or until top springs back when lightly touched. Immediately turn pan upside down, placing tube over neck of funnel or bottle. Let hang, free of table, until cold. Loosen from sides and tube with spatula. Turn pan over. Hit edge lightly on table to loosen. Makes 16 to 20 servings.
Ernestine Gudgen (Mrs. R. E.),
Birmingham South Council

MARBLE MILK CHOCOLATE CAKE

1 pkg. yellow cake mix
1/4 tsp. soda
1 c. dairy sour cream
1 (8 oz.) pkg. cream
  cheese
3 eggs

1 pkg. milk chocolate or
  fudge frosting mix
1/3 c. lukewarm water
1 to 2 Tbsp. cream or milk
Nut halves if desired

Preheat oven to 350°. Using solid shortening or margarine, generously grease and flour a 12 cup fluted pan. In large bowl blend first 5 ingredients; beat 2 minutes at highest speed. In small bowl blend frosting mix and water 1 minute at lowest speed. Beat 2 minutes at high speed; remove

1 cup frosting and drop over batter in 5 or 6 places. Cover remaining frosting; set aside. With mixer at low speed, swirl frosting into batter, turning bowl 3 times. Pour into prepared pan. Bake 55 to 60 minutes. Cool upright in pan 45 minutes. Turn onto serving plate; cool completely. Stir cream into remaining frosting until spreading consistency. Spoon over top of cake. Garnish with nuts.

Linda Crear, Riverchase Council

THE PERFECT CHOCOLATE CAKE

Cake:

1 c. unsifted unsweetened
  cocoa
2 c. boiling water
2 3/4 c. sifted all-purpose
  flour
2 tsp. baking soda
1/2 tsp. salt

1/2 tsp. baking powder
1 c. butter or regular
  margarine, softened
2 1/2 c. granulated sugar
4 eggs
1 1/2 tsp. vanilla extract

In medium bowl combine cocoa with boiling water, mixing with wire whisk until smooth. Cool completely. Sift flour with soda, salt and baking powder. Preheat oven to 350° F. Grease well and lightly flour three 9 x 1 1/2 inch layer cake pans. In large bowl of electric mixer, at high speed, beat butter, sugar, eggs and vanilla, scraping bowl occasionally, until light, about 5 minutes. At low speed, beat in flour mixture (in fourths), alternately with cocoa mixture (in thirds), beginning and ending with flour mixture. Do not overbeat. Divide evenly into pans and smooth top. Bake 25 to 30 minutes, or until surface springs back when gently pressed with fingertip. Cool in pans 10 minutes. Carefully loosen sides with spatula; remove from pans; cool on racks.

Filling:

1 c. heavy cream, chilled
1 tsp. vanilla extract

1/4 c. unsifted
  confectioners sugar

Whip cream with sugar and vanilla; refrigerate. To assemble cake: On plate, place a layer, top side down; spread with half of cream. Place second layer, top side down; spread with rest of cream. Place third layer, top side up to frost.

Frosting:

1 (6 oz.) pkg. semi-sweet
  chocolate pieces
1/2 c. light cream
1567-82

1 c. butter or regular margarine
2 1/2 c. unsifted confectioners
  sugar

In medium saucepan combine chocolate pieces, cream and butter; stir over medium heat until smooth. Remove from heat. With whisk, blend in 2 1/2 cups confectioners sugar. In bowl set over ice, beat until it holds shape. With spatula, frost sides first, covering whipped cream; use rest of frosting on top, swirling decoratively. Refrigerate at least 1 hour before serving. To cut, use a thin-edged sharp knife; slice with a sawing motion. Serves 10 to 12.

Betty Willingham, Birmingham South Council

PETER PAUL MOUND CAKE

Cake:

1 box devils food cake mix (make 3 layers and slice horizontally when cool)

1 c. sugar
1 c. milk
24 large marshmallows
1 (14 oz.) pkg. cocoanut

Icing:

1 stick margarine
2 c. sugar
1/2 c. milk

3 Tbsp. cocoa
1 tsp. vanilla

For cake: Melt at medium heat; put this mixture between layers of cake. For icing: Bring to boil for 1 minute, spread on top and sides of cake. Icing recipe may also be used as fudge.

Delores Champion Dugger, Decatur Council

STAR MARBLE CAKE

3/4 c. shortening
1 tsp. vanilla
3 tsp. baking powder
1 c. milk
3 squares chocolate
1/4 c. boiling water

2 c. sugar
3 c. flour
1/2 tsp. salt
6 egg whites, beaten
4 Tbsp. sugar
1/4 tsp. baking soda

Cream shortening, 1 1/2 cups sugar and 2 tablespoons milk. Sift flour, salt and baking powder; add to creamed mixture alternately with remaining milk. Beat egg whites stiff, with remaining 1/2 cup sugar. Fold into batter. To melted chocolate add 4 tablespoons sugar, boiling water and soda. Divide cake batter in half. To one half add chocolate mixture, place by alternate spoonfuls in pans and bake at 350° for 30 minutes.

Sandra Crenshaw, Mobile Council

SWEET CHOCOLATE TEA CAKE

1 (4 oz.) pkg. Baker's
  German's sweet chocolate
2 3/4 c. sifted cake flour
1 3/4 c. sugar
1 tsp. salt
3 eggs plus 1 egg yolk

3/4 tsp. cream of tartar
1/2 tsp. soda
1/4 tsp. cinnamon
1 c. soft butter or margarine
3/4 c. milk
1 tsp. vanilla

*Sweet Chocolate Glaze (if desired):

1 (4 oz.) pkg. Baker's
  chocolate
1 Tbsp. butter or margarine
3 Tbsp. water

1/2 tsp. vanilla
1 c. sifted confectioners
  sugar
Dash of salt

Heat chocolate over hot water until partially melted. Remove from heat and stir rapidly until melted; cool. Sift flour with sugar, salt, cream of tartar, soda and cinnamon. Sift shortening; add flour mixture, milk and vanilla. Mix until all flour is dampened. Beat 2 minutes at medium speed of electric mixer or 300 vigorous strokes by hand. Add eggs, yolk and chocolate. Beat 1 minute longer or 150 strokes by hand. Pour into a 9 or 10 inch tube pan that has been greased and floured on sides and tube and lined on bottom with wax paper. Bake in moderate oven (350° F.) about 1 hour and 5 to 10 minutes or until cake tester inserted in center comes out clean and cake is free from sides of pan. Cool in pan 15 minutes; loosen from tube and sides, and remove from pan. Glaze while warm, if desired.

*Melt chocolate and butter in water over low heat. Combine sugar and salt. Add chocolate mixture gradually, blending well. Add vanilla. Makes 1 cup glaze, or enough to cover top of a 9 inch layer, a 9 or 10 inch tube cake, a cake roll or a loaf cake.

Sherry A. Liles, Future Pioneer
Tri-Cities Council

TUNNEL OF FUDGE CAKE

2 sticks butter
1/2 c. Crisco
6 eggs
1 1/2 c. sugar

2 c. chopped nuts
2 c. flour
1 (12 1/2 oz.) pkg. double
  Dutch frosting

Cream butter and Crisco at high speed; add eggs, one at a time, beating well. Gradually add sugar; continue creaming at high speed until fluffy. Add flour, frosting and nuts; mix by hand until well blended. Pour mixture into well greased and floured Bundt pan; bake at 350° for 60-65 minutes. Cool for 2 hours before removing from pan.

Dorothy Hayes, Birmingham Central Council

TURTLE CAKE

1 box German's chocolate
  cake mix
1 (14 oz.) bag caramels
3/4 c. butter

1/2 c. evaporated milk
1 c. chopped pecans
1 c. chocolate chips
Chocolate frosting (optional)

In saucepan, over low heat, melt caramels with butter and milk. Mix cake according to directions. Pour half of batter into a greased and floured 13x9 inch pan; bake at 350° for 15 minutes. Remove from oven; top with chocolate chips and pecans. Pour second half of cake batter over top. Bake 20 minutes at 350°. May frost if desired. May be prepared a couple of days in advance.

Margaret Morrow, Birmingham Central Council

WHITE CHOCOLATE CAKE

4 oz. white chocolate
1/2 c. boiling water
1 c. butter or
  margarine
2 c. sugar
4 egg yolks, unbeaten

1 tsp. vanilla
2 1/2 c. sifted Swans Down
  cake flour
1/2 tsp. salt
1 tsp. baking soda
1 c. buttermilk
4 egg whites, stiffly beaten

Melt chocolate in boiling water; cool. Cream butter and sugar until fluffy. Add egg yolks, one at a time, and beat well after each. Add melted chocolate and vanilla; mix well. Sift together flour, salt and soda; add alternately with buttermilk to chocolate mixture; beat well. Beat until smooth. Fold in whites. Pour in 3 deep 8 or 9 inch layer pans, lined on bottoms with paper. Bake in moderate oven (350° F.) for 30 to 40 minutes; cool. Frost top and sides.

Rich White Chocolate Frosting (double frosting):

4 oz. white chocolate
Dash of salt
2 Tbsp. butter

3/4 c. confectioners sugar
2 Tbsp. hot water
1 egg yolk
1/2 tsp. vanilla

Melt chocolate; blend in sugar, salt and hot water. Add yolk; beat well. Add butter, 1 tablespoon at a time, beating thoroughly after each. Stir in vanilla.

Rosemary Parker, Birmingham Central Council

COCA-COLA CAKE

1 c. margarine, softened
2 c. all-purpose flour
1 3/4 c. sugar
3 Tbsp. cocoa
1 tsp. soda

1 tsp. vanilla
2 eggs
1/2 c. buttermilk
1 c. Coca-Cola
1 1/2 c. miniature
  marshmallows

Combine all ingredients except marshmallows in large mixing bowl; blend at low speed in mixer. Blend well, then add marshmallows by hand. Pour batter into greased 13x9 inch pan; bake at 350° for 35 minutes or until toothpick comes out clean; cool 15 minutes and then spread icing.

Coca-Cola Icing: Combine 1/2 cup margarine, 3 tablespoons cocoa, 1/3 cup Coca-Cola and 1 box confectioners sugar; beat until smooth, then stir in 1 cup chopped pecans and spread on cake.

Becky Cook, Huntsville Council

COCONUT CAKE

Every Southern woman prides herself on her cake-making skill. This elegant coconut cake might well grace a very special dinner table or a church supper.

2 3/4 c. sifted cake flour
4 tsp. baking powder
3/4 tsp. salt
3/4 c. butter or shortening
1 1/2 c. sugar

4 egg whites (at room
  temperature)
1 tsp. vanilla
1 tsp. almond extract
1 c. milk or coconut milk

Measure flour, baking powder and salt; sift together 3 times. Cream butter; add 1 cup sugar, blending well. Beat egg whites until fluffy; add remaining sugar gradually, beating until stiff peaks form. Add flavorings to milk; add milk mixture alternately with flour mixture to creamed mixture. Beat well; fold egg white mixture into batter. Pour batter into 3 greased round 8 inch cake pans; bake in 350° oven for 25 to 30 minutes. Cool on cake racks.

White Frosting:

2 c. sugar
1/8 tsp. salt
1 tsp. white vinegar

3 egg whites
1/2 tsp. vanilla
1/2 lb. fresh or frozen coconut

Combine sugar, 1 cup water, salt and vinegar in heavy saucepan; cook over medium heat, stirring constantly, until clear. Cook, without stirring, to 242° on candy thermometer or until mixture forms thin thread when dropped from

1567-82

spoon. Beat egg whites until stiff; add hot syrup, beating constantly. Continue beating until frosting holds shape; add vanilla. Spread frosting between cake layers, topping with coconut. Cover top and side of cake with frosting; sprinkle with remaining coconut. Yield: 8-10 servings.

Joyce Reavis, Decatur Council

COCONUT CAKE

2 c. sifted cake flour
1 1/2 c. sugar
1/2 c. shortening
1 tsp. salt
2/3 c. milk

3 tsp. baking powder
2 eggs, unbeaten
1/2 c. milk
1 tsp. vanilla

Cream by hand or with mixer 2 minutes, sugar, shortening, salt, flour and 2/3 cup milk, then stir in baking powder. Add eggs, 1/2 cup milk and flavoring, then beat at medium speed for 2 minutes. Pour in two 9 inch cake pans; bake in 375° oven for 25 minutes.

Fluffy Coconut Frosting: Combine in top of double boiler -

3/4 c. sugar
1/4 c. light corn syrup
2 egg whites

2 Tbsp. water
1/4 tsp. cream of tartar
1/4 tsp. salt

Cook over boiling water, beating constantly until mixture stands in peaks. Remove from heat. Add 1 teaspoon vanilla; beat until of spreading consistency. Sprinkle coconut on frosted cake.

Peggy Blevins, Anniston Council

COCONUT CREAM CAKE

1 box Duncan Hines
   yellow cake mix
1 c. sour cream

1/4 c. oil
3 eggs
1 (8 1/2 oz.) can
   cream of coconut

Mix well; bake at 350° for about 25 minutes. Makes 3 layers. Mix:

1 (6 oz.) can frozen
   cream of coconut

1 can water (using cream
   of coconut can)
1 Tbsp. sugar

Heat to near boil. Drizzle over each layer before icing. (Icing on next page.)

120

Icing for Coconut Cream Cake:

1 (8 oz.) pkg. cream
  cheese
2 Tbsp. milk

1 (6 oz.) can frozen
  cream of coconut
1 Tbsp. vanilla
2 boxes powdered sugar

Mix and spread evenly.
Mrs. Libby Pilling, Decatur Council

HOLIDAY COCONUT CAKE

1/3 c. shortening
1/3 c. butter, softened
1 3/4 c. sugar
3 c. cake flour
3 1/2 tsp. baking powder
3/4 tsp. salt

1 1/3 c. milk
2 tsp. vanilla extract
4 egg whites
Lemon Filling (recipe follows)
Fluffy Frosting
Freshly grated coconut

Cream shortening, butter and sugar until light and fluffy. Sift together flour, baking powder and salt; add to creamed mixture alternately with milk, beating well after each addition. Stir in vanilla. Beat egg whites until stiff and fold into batter. Pour batter into 3 greased and floured 8 inch cake pans; bake at 350° for 30 minutes. Cool completely. Spread Lemon Filling between layers. Frost top and sides of cake with Fluffy Frosting and sprinkle with coconut. Yield: One 8 inch layer cake.

Lemon Filling:

1 c. plus 2 Tbsp. sugar
1/4 c. cornstarch
1 c. plus 2 Tbsp. water

2 egg yolks, slightly beaten
2 Tbsp. butter
3 Tbsp. lemon juice
1 Tbsp. grated lemon rind

Combine sugar and cornstarch; gradually stir in water. Cook over medium heat, stirring constantly, until mixture thickens and boils; boil 1 minute. Slowly stir a small amount of the hot mixture into egg yolks; add to hot mixture in saucepan. Boil 1 minute longer, stirring constantly. Remove from heat and continue stirring until smooth; stir in butter, lemon juice and rind. Cool. Yield: About 2 cups.

Fluffy Frosting:

1 c. sugar
1/3 c. water
1/4 tsp. cream of tartar

2 egg whites
1/2 tsp. vanilla extract
1/2 tsp. almond extract

Combine sugar, water and cream of tartar in a heavy saucepan; cook over low heat without stirring until syrup

1567-82
121

spins a 6 to 8 inch thread. Beat egg whites until soft peaks form. Continue to beat egg whites, and slowly pour in syrup mixture. Add flavorings; beat well. Yield: Enough for one 8 inch cake.

Faith Kirby, Anniston Council

RAVE REVIEWS COCONUT CAKE

1 pkg. (2 layer size) yellow cake mix
1 pkg. (4 serving size) Jell-O brand vanilla flavor instant pudding and pie filling
1 1/3 c. water
4 eggs
1/4 c. oil
2 c. Baker's Angel Flake coconut
1 c. chopped walnuts or pecans

Blend cake mix, pudding mix, water, eggs and oil in large mixer bowl*. Beat at medium speed of electric mixer 4 minutes; stir in coconut and walnuts. Pour into 3 greased and floured 9 inch layer pans; bake at 350° for 35 minutes. Cool in pans 15 minutes; remove and cool on rack. Fill and frost with Coconut-Cream Cheese Frosting.

Coconut-Cream Cheese Frosting:

4 Tbsp. butter or margarine
2 c. Baker's Angel Flake coconut
1 (8 oz.) pkg. cream cheese
2 tsp. milk
3 1/2 c. sifted confectioners sugar
1/2 tsp. vanilla

Melt 2 tablespoons butter in skillet; add coconut. Stir constantly over low heat until golden brown. Spread coconut on absorbent paper to cool. Cream 2 tablespoons butter with cream cheese; add milk and sugar alternately, beating well. Add vanilla; stir in 1 3/4 cups of the coconut. Spread on tops and sides of cake layers; sprinkle with remaining coconut.

*High altitude areas, increase water to 1 3/4 cups and add 1/4 cup flour.

Imogene Davis, Birmingham Central Council

BISCUIT COFFEE CAKE

4 (10 count) cans biscuits
3/4 c. sugar
1 tsp. cinnamon
1/4 c. chopped nuts

Cut biscuits in 1/4 size pieces. Mix all above together in large mixing bowl and pour in greased Bundt pan. In double boiler mix 3/4 cup butter and 1 cup sugar; bring to boil. Pour over cake; bake at 350° for 40 to 45 minutes;

wait approximately 10 minutes before removing. Served while still warm is better to me.

Note: I use Hungry Jack biscuits.

Edith Dixon, Birmingham South Council

COWBOY COFFEE CAKE

2 1/2 c. sifted enriched
   flour
1/2 tsp. salt
2 c. brown sugar
2/3 c. shortening

2 tsp. baking powder
1/2 tsp. soda
1/2 tsp. cinnamon
1/2 tsp. nutmeg
1 c. sour milk
2 well beaten eggs

Use 375° oven. Combine flour, salt, sugar and shortening; mix till crumbly. Reserve 1/2 cup mixture. To remaining crumbs, add baking powder, soda and spices; mix thoroughly. Add milk and eggs; mix well. Pour into 2 waxed paper lined 8x8x2 inch baking pans; sprinkle with reserved crumbs. Chopped nuts and cinnamon may be sprinkled over crumbs. Bake in moderate oven (375°) for 25 to 30 minutes.

Jerry Gambel, Huntsville Council

HUNGARIAN COFFEE CAKE (ARANYGALUSKA)

1 c. sour cream
1/2 c. sugar
1 tsp. salt
2 cakes yeast
3 eggs
1/2 c. soft butter

4 1/2 c. flour
1/2 c. melted butter
1 c. chopped walnuts
3/4 tsp. cinnamon
1 c. sugar

Mix sour cream, sugar, salt and yeast; stir until yeast dissolves. Add eggs, softened butter and half flour. Mix well and add rest of flour. Turn dough out on floured board and knead until smooth for about 10 to 15 minutes. Place in greased bowl; cover and let rise in warm place until double in bulk for about 1 1/2 to 2 hours. Punch down. Turn over and let rise again for about 45 minutes. After second rising, form into walnut sized balls. Dip in melted butter and roll in sugar and walnuts-cinnamon mixture. Place in layers in 10 inch greased tube pan; let rise 45 minutes. Bake 40 to 50 minutes at 375°.

Catherine F. Pittman, Mobile Council

QUICK CINNAMON NUT COFFEE CAKE

1 pkg. canned biscuits
1/2 c. sugar
6 Tbsp. margarine

1 Tbsp. cinnamon
1/2 c. chopped nuts

Melt margarine in small pan over low heat; measure and mix sugar and cinnamon in small bowl. Remove margarine from heat; dip biscuits, one at a time, in margarine, then roll in cinnamon and sugar mixture. Place in tube pan overlapping biscuits in a circle. Sprinkle with nuts and remaining sugar and cinnamon; bake at 450° for 10-12 minutes.

Donna Cox, Birmingham East Council

SOUR CREAM COFFEE CAKE

1 stick oleo or butter
1 c. sugar
2 eggs
2 c. flour

3/4 tsp. soda
1 1/2 tsp. baking powder
1 c. sour cream
1 tsp. vanilla

Topping:

1/2 c. brown sugar
1 tsp. cinnamon

1/2 c. chopped nuts

Cream butter and sugar; add eggs. Add to creamed mixture sifted dry ingredients; mix well. Add alternately with sour cream and vanilla. Pour half of batter in greased and floured square pan. Sprinkle brown sugar mixture over batter. Pour remaining batter into pan; bake at 350° for 40 minutes. Allow cake to cool in pan 20 minutes before turning out.

Louanna C. Killian, Birmingham Life Members

DATE-NUT CAKE

1 c. sugar
1/2 c. shortening
2 eggs
2 c. flour
1 pkg. pitted dates,
   chopped

1 c. pecans, chopped
3/4 c. buttermilk
1 tsp. soda
1 tsp. vanilla
1 orange (grated rind only)

Cream sugar and shortening; add eggs, one at a time, beating well. Add soda to buttermilk. Mix alternately with flour to above mixture. Add vanilla, orange rind, nuts and dates which have been sprinkled with a little flour. Pour into heavy skillet and bake 1 hour at 300° or until done. (Topping follows on next page.)

124

Topping: Combine 1 cup sugar with juice of 2 oranges and let sugar dissolve thoroughly. Do not cook. While cake is warm, pour carefully over the top so it will soak into cake gradually.

Annette Turner

DUMP CAKE

1 (20 oz.) can crushed pineapple
1 (20 oz.) can cherry pie filling

1 yellow cake mix
3/4 c. melted butter
1/2 c. cocoanut
1 c. pecans, chopped

Dump pineapple and pie filling in bottom of oblong pan. Smooth out. Sprinkle cake mix evenly over this. Pour melted butter, then sprinkle cocoanut and pecans on top. Bake at 350° for 1 hour. Serve in pan.

Martha Cantrell, Birmingham East Council

FAVORITE CAKE

3 c. sifted cake flour
4 tsp. baking powder
1/4 tsp. salt
1 c. butter

2 c. sugar
1 tsp. vanilla
4 eggs
1 c. milk

Have all ingredients at room temperature. Sift flour 3 times with baking powder and salt. Cream butter thoroughly, using medium speed of mixer; add sugar gradually. Cream well; add vanilla. Add eggs, one at a time, beating well after each. Using low speed of mixer; add dry ingredients, alternating with milk. Pour into 2 greased and floured 9 inch pans. Bake in a 375° oven 25 minutes. Frost with Fluffy Custard Frosting. Serves 12.

Ruby Tolbert, Montgomery Council

FIG CAKE

1 c. buttermilk
1 c. cooking oil
3 eggs
1 1/2 c. sugar
2 c. cake flour
1 tsp. soda

1 tsp. salt
1 tsp. vanilla
1 tsp. cinnamon
1 tsp. allspice
1 c. chopped pecans
1 c. fig preserves, drained and chopped

Sauce:

1/2 c. buttermilk	1 c. sugar
1/2 tsp. soda	3/4 stick margarine

Combine liquids; sift dry ingredients together and add to liquids. Mix well. Add nuts and figs. Pour into floured stem cake pan and bake at 300° for 1 hour; turn top side up after removing from pan.

Sauce: Cook mixture to soft ball stage; beat until slightly cooled. Pour over cake.

Mrs. Arthur Lane, Birmingham South Council

FRIENDSHIP CAKE

1 c. juice (from a friend)	1 c. chopped pecans (no juice)
	1 c. sugar

Place the above ingredients in a 1/2 gallon glass jar. Stir with a wooden spoon. Leave at room temperature and stir every 3-4 days. Two weeks later, add 1 cup crushed pineapple (no juice) and 1 cup sugar. Stir every 3-4 days. Two weeks later add 1 cup maraschino cherries and 1 cup sugar. Leave at room temperature. Stir every 3-4 days. Two weeks later (6 weeks from beginning), drain juice from fruit; use 1 cup to start cake. (Give 1 cup to a friend.)

1 1/2 c. Crisco oil	3 1/2 c. self-rising flour
3 c. sugar	1 can coconut
3 eggs	3 c. well drained fruit
1 tsp. soda	2 c. chopped nuts (floured)
2 tsp. vanilla	

Use canned fruit. Combine oil, sugar and eggs; add dry ingredients, vanilla, fruit, nuts and coconut. Bake in large tube pan or loaf pan; bake at 350° for 1 hour and 15 minutes.

Louise Sisco

CHRISTMAS FRUIT CAKE

1 c. sugar	Pecans, walnuts, almonds
2 sticks margarine	2 tsp. allspice
4 c. flour	2 Tbsp. cinnamon
8 eggs	2 Tbsp. nutmeg
1 glass grape jelly	1 lb. crystallized cherries
1 c. grape juice	1 lb. crystallized pineapple
	1 lb. mixed fruits

Cream sugar and margarine well; add yolks of eggs,

one at a time; add spices, add jelly and add juice. Add flour plus fruits. Fold in whites of eggs. Will bake in 3 pans 2 hours at 270°. Can decorate with nuts and fruits.

Lola E. Johnson, Life Member,
Birmingham Central Council

CITRUS CAKE

3 c. sifted cake flour
2 c. sugar
1 c. milk
4 eggs
3 tsp. baking powder
1/2 tsp. salt

1 c. butter or margarine
1 tsp. vanilla extract
1/2 tsp. almond extract
1 small can concentrated
  orange juice
Confectioners sugar

Cream butter, adding sugar gradually in small bowl. In large bowl sift flour, baking powder and salt. Add 1 egg at a time to creamed mixture, blending well after each addition. Mix creamed mixture with milk and flavorings alternately to flour mixture. Blend well after each addition. Bake in preheated 350° oven from 45 to 55 minutes.

Glaze: Melt 1/2 can of concentrated orange juice with confectioners sugar to taste over low heat until sugar has dissolved. Place glace over warm glaze over cake after cake has cooled 15 minutes.

Jevenari Marshall, Riverchase Council

DIABETIC FRUIT CAKE

1/2 c. raisins
5 dates or prunes,
  finely chopped
5 figs, chopped
16 dried apricot halves,
  finely chopped
1 orange rind, grated
1/2 c. oleo

2 eggs
1 1/4 c. plain flour
1/2 tsp. soda
1 tsp. baking powder
1/4 tsp. cinnamon
1/4 tsp. nutmeg
1/8 tsp. cloves
1 tsp. vanilla

Combine raisins, dates or prunes, figs, apricots and orange rind in small bowl. Set aside. Cream oleo until light and fluffy. Add eggs and vanilla; stir in flour, soda, baking powder and spices. Pour in fruit mixture and beat until blended. Bake at 325° for 45-55 minutes. Cool and store in airtight container for 3 days. Freezes well.

Mickey Wash, Tri-Cities Council

FRUIT CAKE RECIPE

1 lb. walnuts	2 lb. candied cherries
1 lb. pecans	1 tsp. nutmeg
1 lb. raisins	1 tsp. cloves
1 lb. candied pineapple	1 tsp. mace
1/2 lb. citron	2 tsp. cinnamon
1/4 lb. lemon peel	2 tsp. soda
1/4 lb. orange peel	1 lb. butter
1 lb. dates	1 lb. sugar
1 lb. flour	10 eggs, separated
1 c. white Karo	1/2 c. grape juice

Break up nutmeats and cut fruit in small pieces, except cherries, which are left whole. Mix 1/2 flour with fruit and nuts. Sift other 1/2 with spices and soda several times. Cream sugar and butter; add egg yolks, syrup and grape juice. Fold in beaten egg whites, then floured fruits; add rest of flour. Pour into pans that have been lined with brown paper. Bake at 275° until done, about 2 hours and 20 minutes. Leave in pans to cool before turning out.

Faith Kirby, Anniston Council

FRUIT COCKTAIL CAKE

1/2 c. sugar	1 (17 oz.) can fruit cocktail
2 c. flour	2 eggs
	1 tsp. vanilla

Mix sugar and eggs; add flour and juice from fruit. Mix well; add fruit and vanilla. Pour into pans; bake at 350° or 375° until golden brown.

Icing:

1 stick butter	1 small can Pet milk
1 c. sugar	

Boil these 3 ingredients about 10 minutes. Add:

1 c. coconut	1 c. nuts

Mix well, then top cake.

Peggy Hunter, Anniston Council

JAPANESE FRUIT CAKE

2 c. sugar
1 c. butter
4 eggs, well beaten
3 c. flour
1 c. milk (butter)

1 c. nuts (pecans)
1 c. raisins
1 tsp. baking powder
1 tsp. cinnamon
1 tsp. cloves

Add butter and sugar, then eggs. Sift flour, baking powder and cloves. Add together with coconut milk or water, then raisins and nuts. Bake in 3 layers at 350° until done.

Topping:

1 coconut
1 lemon
1 orange

2 c. sugar
1 c. coconut milk or 1 c.
    boiling water

Add lemon, orange and sugar, 1 cup of coconut milk or 1 cup of boiling water; add coconut. Put on cake when removed from oven while hot.

Edgar McFarlen, Huntsville Council

PORK FRUIT CAKE

1 1/4 lb. fresh ground pork
2 boxes raisins
4 c. nuts
1 Tbsp. allspice
1 Tbsp. cloves
1 Tbsp. cinnamon

2 lb. sugar
6 eggs
5 c. flour (use 1/2 c. over
    nuts and raisins)
2 tsp. soda
1 pt. wine

Mix flour, soda and spices. Cream pork and sugar; add eggs, one at a time. Add wine, flour alternately. Add floured nuts and raisins; mix well. Line bottom of pan with greased brown paper. Bake at 250° for 1 1/2 hours or until done. Remove paper when done.

Mrs. Ed. H. Lindley, Birmingham South Council

UNBAKED FRUIT CAKE

1 lb. vanilla wafers
1 lb. shelled pecans
1 lb. raisins
1 lb. candied cherries
1 lb. English walnuts

1 can condensed milk
1 lb. dates
1 lb. coconut
1 lb. candied pineapple
1 lb. small marshmallows

Grind in crust vanilla wafers. Cut candied fruits into small pieces. Mix all ingredients except milk and

1567-82

marshmallows. Melt marshmallows in milk and mix with other ingredients. When well mixed, pack in buttered angel food cake pan or in small loaf pan. When cool, remove from pan. (Can freeze.)

Peggy Sweetman, Life Member,
Huntsville Council

GEORGIA SPECIAL CAKE

1 box Duncan Hines
  butter cake mix
4 whole eggs
1 (11 oz.) can mandarin
  oranges with juice
1/2 c. Wesson oil

1 large can crushed
  pineapple with juice
1 small pkg. instant vanilla
  pudding
1 large Cool Whip
3/4 c. chopped pecans
1 small can coconut (optional)

Mix cake mix, oranges with juice and oil; add eggs, one at a time, in electric mixer. Cook in 3 cake pans, greased and floured, 20 to 25 minutes at 325°.

Frosting: Mix pudding and pineapple together; fold in 1 large Cool Whip; add 3/4 cup pecans and 1 small can coconut (optional). Mix in electric mixer until smooth. Frost tops and sides.

Mrs. Carl E. Cutchin (Ernestine), Phenix City

GOOEY BUTTER CAKE

1 stick oleo
2 eggs

1 yellow Deluxe II cake mix

Frosting:

2 eggs
1 box confectioners sugar

1 (8 oz.) pkg. cream
  cheese

Melt in 9x13 inch pan 1 stick oleo. Mix 2 eggs and yellow Deluxe II cake mix; spread over oleo. Mix 2 eggs and box of confectioners sugar and 8 ounces cream cheese and spread over layer of cake mix. Bake at 350° or until brown.

Margaret Medders, Tuscaloosa Pioneer Unit

130

GRAPE JUICE LAYER CAKE

1 (18 1/2 oz.) pkg.
  white cake mix
1/2 tsp. almond flavoring
1 tsp. grated lemon peel
1/2 c. Concord grape juice
1/2 c. water

3 Tbsp. cornstarch
1/4 tsp. salt
1/2 c. sugar
4 Tbsp. lemon juice
1 Tbsp. butter or margarine

Frosting:

1 egg white
3/4 c. sugar

3 Tbsp. Concord grape juice
1/2 tsp. light corn syrup

Prepare cake mix according to package directions, adding almond flavoring and lemon peel. Bake in 2 greased and floured 8 inch round cake pans; cool. In the top of a double boiler, combine 1/2 cup Concord grape juice, water, cornstarch, salt and 1/2 cup sugar. Cook over direct heat until thickened, stirring constantly. Place over boiling water; cook 15 minutes, stirring occasionally. Add lemon juice and butter; blend. Cool. Spread between layers of cake. Combine egg white, 3/4 cup sugar, 3 tablespoons Concord grape juice and corn syrup in top of double boiler. Beat at high speed 1 minute with electric mixer. Place over boiling water; be certain that water does not touch bottom of pan. Beat at high speed for 7 minutes until frosting holds stiff peaks. Pour into large bowl; beat 1 minute longer. Use to frost cake.

Anna Lee Hickman, Tri-Cities Council

HARVEY WALLBANGER CAKE

Cake:

1 pkg. orange cake mix
1 (3 3/4 oz.) pkg. instant
  vanilla pudding mix
4 eggs

1/2 c. cooking oil
1/2 c. orange juice
1/2 c. liquor Galliano
2 Tbsp. vodka

Glaze:

1 c. powdered sugar (sifted)
1 Tbsp. orange juice

1 Tbsp. Galliano
1 tsp. vodka

Cake: In large bowl combine cake mix and pudding mix. Add eggs, oil, orange juice, Galliano and vodka. Beat with electric mixer 1 2 minute on low speed, then beat on medium speed for 5 minutes, scraping bowl frequently. Pour into greased and floured 10 inch tube pan; bake in 350° oven for 45 minutes. Cool in pan 10 minutes; remove to rack. Pour on glaze while cake is still warm.

Glaze: Combine powdered sugar, orange juice, Galliano and vodka.

Sue Fehrenbach, Birmingham Central Council

"HEAVENLY HASH" CAKE

2 sticks margarine	4 eggs
1 c. chopped pecans	1 1/2 c. flour
2 c. sugar	3 Tbsp. cocoa
Vanilla to taste	1 c. miniature marshmallows
(approx. 1 tsp.)	

Place margarine, sugar, eggs, cocoa, flour, vanilla and nuts together and mix well. Put in a 9x12 inch baking dish and bake it for 50-60 minutes at 300° to 350°. While cake is still hot, put marshmallows on top.

Heavenly Hash Icing:

3 Tbsp. cocoa	6 Tbsp. evaporated milk
1 stick margarine	Vanilla to taste
1 box confectioners sugar	

Melt margarine and cocoa in a boiler; add milk, sugar and vanilla. Mix well and pour over cake before it cools. Put back in oven for just a minute or so.

Shirley Wood, Birmingham South Council

HONEY CAKE

3 eggs, beaten	3 c. flour
1 c. sugar	1 tsp. baking soda
1/2 c. oil	1 tsp. baking powder
1 c. Tom's honey	1/2 tsp. cinnamon
1 c. strong coffee	1/4 tsp. ginger
1 peeled, grated apple	1/2 tsp. salt
1 c. nuts, chopped	1 c. raisins

Beat eggs, sugar and oil. Mix coffee into honey. Mix dry ingredients and add to egg-oil mixture. Alternating with coffee and honey mix. Add nuts and raisins and grated apple. Bake 1 hour at 350° in a well greased tube pan. If you can't get Tom Underwood honey, another works well.

Mrs. Hal Wiley, Tri-Cities Council

HUMMINGBIRD CAKE

3 c. all-purpose flour
   (plain)
2 c. sugar
1 tsp. salt
1 tsp. soda
1 tsp. cinnamon
3 eggs, beaten

1 1/2 c. salad oil
1 1/2 tsp. vanilla
1 (8 oz.) can crushed
   pineapple, drained
1 c. chopped nuts
2 c. chopped bananas

Mix by hand. Combine dry ingredients; add eggs and salad oil; stir until well mixed. Add vanilla, pineapple, bananas and nuts. Spoon batter into large greased and floured sheet pan. Bake at 350° for 40 to 45 minutes.

Icing: Combine -

1 box confectioners sugar
1/2 c. margarine

8 oz. cream cheese
1 tsp. vanilla

Sprinkle 1 cup chopped nuts on top of icing.
Freida Elkourie, Birmingham South Council

ICE CREAM CAKE

1 2/3 c. evaporated milk
2 egg yolks
2 c. sugar
Juice of 2 lemons

2 Tbsp. flour
4 egg whites, stiffly beaten
1 small box graham
   crackers, crushed

Chill milk until icy; whip with chilled beater in chilled bowl. Cook and stir yolks, sugar, lemon juice and flour until mixture thickens. Set aside to cool. Fold egg whites into whipped milk; fold into cooled custard. Sprinkle cracker crumbs in bottom of 8 or 10 inch cake pan; cover with custard. Freeze until ready to serve. Yield: 10 servings.
Flo Thompson, Montgomery Council

ICE CREAM CAKE

1 box angel food cake mix
1/2 gal. vanilla ice cream
1 tall can crushed
   pineapple

1 pt. frozen strawberries,
   thawed
1 c. chopped pecans
2 env. Dream Whip (optional)
Red food coloring (optional)

Make cake according to box directions. Crumble cake up with hands; mash cake up into softened ice cream. Stir in pineapple, strawberries and nuts. Pour into tube pan;

freeze. Remove from pan. Frosting optional. Frost with Dream Whip tinted with few drops of red food coloring.

Doris W. Petty, Birmingham South Council

ITALIAN CREAM CAKE

1 stick oleo (soft)	1 tsp. soda
1/2 c. shortening	1 c. buttermilk
2 c. flour (Gold Medal all-purpose)	1 Tbsp. vanilla
	1 small pkg. coconut
2 c. sugar	1 c. chopped pecans
5 eggs	

Cream oleo and shortening; add sugar and beat well. Add eggs, one at a time. Add flour, soda and buttermilk alternately with sugar and shortening mixture. Add vanilla, coconut and bake in three 9 inch pans for 40 minutes at 350°.

Cream Cheese Frosting: Soften one 8 ounce package cream cheese at room temperature. Beat until smooth with 1/2 stick oleo. Add 1 box confectioners sugar and 1 tablespoon vanilla. Beat until smooth; add nuts and beat 1 minute. Spread on each layer on the tops and sides.

Harold Busby, Mobile Council

BLACKBERRY JAM CAKE

1 tsp. baking soda	3 c. unsifted all-purpose flour
1 c. buttermilk	
1 c. butter or margarine, softened	1/2 tsp. cinnamon
	1/4 tsp. cloves
1 c. sugar	1/4 tsp. nutmeg
1 c. firmly packed brown sugar	1 c. blackberry jam (without seeds - use good quality jam)
4 eggs	

Stir baking soda into buttermilk; set aside. In large mixer bowl cream butter or margarine and sugars until light and fluffy (medium speed). Add eggs, one at a time; beat well. In medium bowl combine flour, cinnamon, cloves and nutmeg; add alternately with buttermilk to egg mixture, beginning and ending with flour. Stir in jam. Bake at 350° till done.

P.S. Ice with Butter Cream Frosting.

Marcia Freeman, Birmingham East Council

JAM CAKE

1 c. raisins, chopped	3 c. flour
1 c. pecans, chopped	1 tsp. soda
1 c. coconut	4 tsp. spices (cloves
1 c. blackberry jam	and cinnamon)
1 c. buttermilk	1 1/2 c. butter or oleo
2 c. sugar	6 eggs

Cream butter and sugar; add well beaten eggs. Add milk and dry ingredients and alternately add remaining ingredients and mix thoroughly. Bake in very thin layers (3 or 4) at 300° F.

Filling:

3 c. sugar	1/2 c. raisins
1 tsp. soda	1/2 c. blackberry jam
1 c. buttermilk	1/2 c. coconut
1 c. butter	2 tsp. vanilla
1 c. chopped pecans	

Mix all ingredients and cook until thick. Stir to keep from burning.

Bertha Ross, Decatur Council

JAM CAKE

1/2 c. butter	1 1/4 tsp. soda
2 c. sugar	1 tsp. vanilla
1 c. buttermilk	1/2 tsp. nutmeg
3 c. flour	1/2 tsp. salt
3 eggs	2 c. jam

Cream butter, sugar and salt. Sift and add flour, soda and nutmeg. Beat in eggs. While beating, gradually add buttermilk and vanilla, then the jam. Pour in well greased tube pan; bake at 300° for 45 to 50 minutes. (If cake is baked longer than 45-50 minutes, it usually falls in the middle.) While cake is still hot, pour half of the following over it:

1/4 lb. butter	1 c. sugar
1/3 c. milk	1/4 tsp. salt
1 tsp. nutmeg	

Bring these ingredients to a hard boil and then pour half of it over the cake as mentioned above. Cool the remainder until soft ball appears when dropped in water and then glaze.

Mr. Dave McConnell,
Birmingham Central Council

KENTUCKY WONDER CAKE

2 1/2 c. self-rising flour
2 c. sugar
1 1/2 c. oil
4 eggs, separated

1 small can crushed
  pineapple, undrained
2 1/2 tsp. cinnamon
1 1/2 tsp. nutmeg
1 c. chopped pecans

Combine all ingredients except egg whites and pecans. Beat well and add pecans. Fold in stiffly beaten egg whites. Pour in greased tube pan and bake at 350° for 1 hour or until done. This cake is great to use for a brunch or coffee, and travels well for picnics and family gatherings.

Gloria H. Ramage, Birmingham South Council

LANE CAKE

1 1/2 c. butter or
  margarine
4 c. sugar
3 1/2 c. sifted flour
3 tsp. baking powder
1 c. milk

2 tsp. vanilla
8 eggs, separated
1 c. chopped raisins
1 c. chopped nuts
1 c. coconut
1 c. wine or bourbon

Cream 1 cup butter and 2 cups sugar together until fluffy and light. Sift flour with baking powder. Add flour mixture to creamed mixture alternately with milk; add 1 teaspoon vanilla. Fold in stiffly beaten egg whites. Spoon batter into three 9 inch greased and floured layer cake pans; bake at 350° for 20 to 30 minutes or until cakes test done. Beat egg yolks slightly. Add remaining sugar and butter; cook in double boiler until thick, stirring constantly. Add raisins, nuts and coconut. Stir in remaining vanilla and wine. Spread filling thickly between layers of cake and on top and sides.

Joyce Reavis, Decatur Council

HONEY LEMON LAYER CAKE

1/2 c. shortening
1 c. honey
2 eggs
2 c. sifted cake flour

3/4 tsp. salt
1/4 c. milk
2 Tbsp. lemon juice

Cream shortening and honey; add eggs, one at a time, and beat well after each addition. Sift together flour and salt. Add lemon to milk to make sour. Add the sifted dry ingredients alternately with sour milk; add egg mixture. Pour into 2 greased 8 inch layer cake pans; bake at 350°

136

for 25 to 30 minutes or until cake tests done. Glaze with Honey-Cream Cheese Frosting.

Bobby Blair, Birmingham East Council

LEMON APRICOT NECTAR CAKE

1 box lemon supreme	3/4 c. corn oil
cake mix	1/2 c. sugar
4 eggs	1 c. apricot nectar

Preheat oven to 325°. Grease and flour round tube pan. Mix ingredients together in order given; bake for 1 hour. As soon as cake is removed from oven, pour on glaze (below) while cake is still very hot.

Glaze: Use 1 cup powdered sugar and the juice of 1 lemon.

Redonna G. Leckie, Birmingham West Council

LEMON CHRISTMAS CAKE

1 lb. butter or oleo	1 1/2 oz. lemon extract
2 c. sugar	1/2 lb. candied cherries,
6 eggs	chopped
4 c. all-purpose flour	1/2 lb. candied pineapple,
1 qt. pecans, chopped	chopped

Cream butter and sugar; add eggs, one at a time, beating well after each addition. Save 1 cup of flour to dredge fruit and nuts. Gradually add 3 cups flour to mixture. Add flavoring; add fruit and nuts. Put into 1 large or 2 small tube pans. To bake, start baking in a cold oven, at 325° for 15 minutes. Reduce heat to 300° for 1 hour; reduce to 275° for 10 minutes.

Marilyn Dees

LEMON CREAM CAKE

1 (8 oz.) pkg. cream cheese	2 1/4 c. unsifted flour
1/2 c. shortening	3 tsp. baking powder
1 1/4 c. sugar	1 tsp. salt
3 eggs	1 c. milk
2 Tbsp. grated lemon peel	1/4 c. lemon juice
	1/3 c. sugar

Preheat oven to 350°. Blend cream cheese and shortening until fluffy. Beat in 1 1/4 cups sugar; add eggs, one at a time, beating well after each. Add lemon peel, flour, baking powder, salt and milk. Blend at low speed just until

1567-82

blended, scraping bowl. Pour batter into greased 10 inch tube pan; bake 45-50 minutes. Combine lemon juice and sugar. Pour over hot cake, allowing to run down edges between cake and pan. Cool 30 minutes; remove from pan; cool. Sprinkle with powdered sugar.

Jeannie Riddles, Riverchase Council

LEMON FILLING CAKE

Cake:

3 c. sifted flour	2 c. sugar
3 tsp. baking powder	1 tsp. vanilla
1/4 tsp. salt	4 eggs, separated
1 c. shortening	1 c. milk

Lemon Filling:

3/4 c. sugar	1/3 c. lemon juice
2 Tbsp. cornstarch	1/2 c. water
1/8 tsp. salt	1 egg, beaten
1 Tbsp. grated lemon rind	1 Tbsp. butter

Frosting:

1/2 c. butter	1/2 tsp. grated lemon rind
3 c. powdered sugar	2 1/2 Tbsp. lemon juice
	2 Tbsp. cream

Cake: Stir flour, baking powder and salt together. Cream shortening, sugar and vanilla until fluffy; add beaten egg yolks and beat thoroughly. Add dry ingredients and milk alternately in small amounts, beating well after each addition. Beat egg whites until stiff and fold into batter. Pour into three 9 inch pans and bake at 375° about 30 minutes.

Filling: Thoroughly mix sugar, cornstarch and salt; add remaining ingredients and blend. Cook over boiling water; stir constantly until thickened. Cool; spread between cooled layers.

Frosting: Cream butter; add remaining ingredients and blend until fluffy. Spread on top and sides of cake.

Mrs. G. W. Bates, Birmingham South Council

MALCAMATION CAKE

2 c. sugar
2 c. butter
9 egg whites
1 c. milk

3 1/2 c. plain flour
3 tsp. baking powder
1 tsp. vanilla

Filling:

3 c. sugar
1 lb. butter
4 c. nuts

9 egg yolks
1 c. coconut water
2 c. grated coconut

Cream butter and sugar until light and fluffy; add vanilla. Sift flour and baking powder; add to butter mixture with milk. Beat egg whites until stiff; fold in batter. Pour into greased and floured pans; bake at 350° for 35 minutes.

Filling: Boil sugar, butter, egg yolks, coconut water until thick enough to spread. Remove from heat; stir in pecans and coconut. Spread between layers.

Hattie Pinson, Birmingham West Council

MAYONNAISE CAKE

3 c. unsifted flour
1 1/2 c. sugar
1/3 c. cocoa
2 1/4 tsp. baking soda

1 1/2 c. mayonnaise
1 1/2 c. water
1 1/2 tsp. vanilla

Sift together dry ingredients. Stir in mayonnaise. Gradually stir in water and vanilla until smooth and well blended. Pour into prepared pans (two 9 inch layers or one 9x13 inch pan). Bake at 350° about 30 minutes or until cake springs back when touched. Frost with chocolate icing or with cream cheese icing.

Nancy Morgan, Decatur Council

MARDI GRAS PARTY CAKE

2/3 c. Nestle's butterscotch
   morsels
1/4 c. water
2 1/4 c. sifted Pillsbury's
   Best all-purpose flour
1 tsp. salt
1 tsp. soda

1/2 tsp. double acting
   baking powder
1 1/4 c. sugar
1/2 c. shortening (part
   butter may be used)
3 unbeaten eggs
1 c. buttermilk or sour milk

Melt butterscotch morsels in water in saucepan; cool. Sift flour with salt, soda and baking powder; set aside. Add

1567-82

sugar gradually to shortening, creaming well. Blend in eggs; beat well after each. Add melted butterscotch; mix well. Add dry ingredients alternately with buttermilk, beginning and ending with dry ingredients. Blend well after each addition. (With mixer, use a low speed.) Turn into two 9 inch or two 8 inch (at least 1 1/2 inches deep) round layer pans, well greased and lightly floured on bottoms. Bake at 375° for 25-30 minutes; cool. Spread filling between layers and on top to within 1/2 inch of edge. Frost sides and top edge with Seafoam Frosting or whipped cream. Makes two 9 inch layers.

Butterscotch Filling: Combine 1/2 cup sugar and 1 tablespoon cornstarch in 2 quart saucepan; stir in 1/2 cup evaporated milk, 1/3 cup water, 1/3 cup Nestle's butterscotch morsels and 1 beaten egg yolk. Cook over medium heat, stirring constantly, until thick. Remove from heat; add 2 tablespoons butter, 1 cup coconut, chopped, and 1 cup pecans or walnuts, chopped; cool.

Seafoam Frosting: Combine in saucepan 1/3 cup sugar, 1/3 cup firmly packed brown sugar, 1/3 cup water and 1 tablespoon corn syrup. Cook until a little syrup dropped in cold water forms a soft ball (236° F.). Meanwhile, beat 1 egg white with 1/4 teaspoon French's cream of tartar until stiff peaks form. Add syrup to egg white in slow steady stream, beating constantly until thick enough to spread.

Pam Moman, Birmingham South Council

MILKY WAY CAKE

8 (1 11/16 oz.) chocolate
   covered malt-caramel
   candy bars
1/2 c. melted butter or
   margarine
1 1/2 c. sugar
1/2 c. butter or
   margarine, softened

4 eggs, separated
1 tsp. vanilla extract
1 1/4 c. buttermilk
1/2 tsp. soda
3 c. all-purpose flour
1 c. chopped pecans
Milk Chocolate Frosting

Combine candy bars and 1/2 cup melted butter in saucepan; place over low heat until candy bars are melted, stirring constantly. Cool. Cream sugar and 1/2 cup softened butter until light and fluffy; add egg yolks, one at a time, beating well after each addition; stir in vanilla. Combine buttermilk and soda; add to creamed mixture alternately with flour, beating well after each addition. Stir in candy bar mixture and pecans. Fold in stiffly beaten egg whites. Pour batter into a greased and floured 10 inch tube pan; bake at 325° or 1 hour and 35 minutes or until well done. Let cool in pan 1 hour; remove from pan, and complete cooling on wire rack. Frost with milk chocolate frosting. Yield: One 10 inch cake.

Opal Moffitt, Tuscaloosa Pioneer Unit

MISSISSIPPI MUD CAKE

2 sticks butter, melted	1 1/2 c. plain flour
1/2 c. cocoa	1 1/2 c. pecans, chopped
4 eggs, slightly beaten	1 tsp. vanilla
2 c. sugar	1/2 tsp. salt

Topping:

Miniature marshmallows	1/2 c. milk
1 box powdered sugar (sifted)	1/3 c. cocoa
	1 stick butter, melted

Mix together butter and cocoa; add eggs and sugar to butter and cocoa mixture. Blend flour, pecans, vanilla and salt into the above; bake 35 minutes at 350° in a greased 9x13 inch oblong pan. Cover with miniature marshmallows and place in oven to melt marshmallows. Combine powdered sugar, 1/2 cup milk, 1/3 cup cocoa and 1 stick butter and mix until smooth, then spread on cake.

Nanette Stinson, Montgomery Pioneer Unit

MORAVIAN SUGAR CAKE

1/2 c. warm water (110°)	1/2 tsp. salt
1/2 tsp. sugar	1/2 c. melted, cooled butter
2 pkg. active dry yeast	2 eggs
3/4 c. warm water (110°)	3 c. flour
1/2 c. sugar	1 c. brown sugar
2 Tbsp. dry milk	1 tsp. cinnamon
1/4 c. instant mashed potatoes (dry)	1/2 c. melted, cooled butter

Add yeast to warm water and sugar; set aside until yeast bubbles. Add next 7 ingredients plus 1 cup of the flour. Beat 2 minutes on medium speed. With wooden spoon, add 2 remaining cups flour. Place in a greased bowl; turn once to grease top of dough. Cover and let rise until double, about 1 hour. Punch dough down and put in greased shallow pan(about 17x12x1 inches). Let rise 30 minutes. Spread evenly in pan; sprinkle evenly with brown sugar and cinnamon. Make shallow indentations with fingers and dribble with last 1/2 cup melted and cooled butter. Let rise 30 minutes and bake until golden brown, about 12 to 15 minutes at 375°.

Mrs. William M. (Carolyn) Johnson,
Birmingham Central Council

MYSTERY HOT PUDDING CAKE

1 c. sifted all-purpose
   flour
2 tsp. baking powder
1/4 tsp. salt
3/4 c. sugar
2 Tbsp. cocoa
1/2 c. milk

2 Tbsp. shortening, melted
1 c. chopped nuts
1 c. brown sugar, packed
1/3 c. cocoa
1 3/4 c. hot water
1 tsp. vanilla

A rich tasting fudge dessert. Easy to make and very inexpensive. The sauce forms a pudding over the cake while baking. Sift together into bowl flour, baking powder, salt and cocoa; stir in milk and shortening, melted. Blend in chopped nuts. Spread in 9 inch square pan. Sprinkle with mixture of brown sugar and cocoa. Pour over entire batter 1 3/4 cups hot water. Add vanilla to hot water before pouring over batter. Bake at 350° (moderate oven) for about 45 minutes. Makes about 9 servings.

During baking, cake mixture rises to top and chocolate sauce settles to bottom. Invert squares of pudding on dessert plates. Dip sauce from pan over each serving, or the entire pudding can be inverted in a deep serving platter. Serve warm, with or without whipping cream on top.

Carl Caffin, Tuscaloosa Pioneer Unit

OATMEAL CAKE

1 c. oats
1 stick oleo

1 1/4 c. boiling water

Pour boiling water over oats and oleo; let stand 20 minutes. Add:

1 c. white sugar
1 c. brown sugar
2 eggs

1 1/2 c. flour, sifted
1 tsp. soda
1/2 tsp. cinnamon

Mix well and bake in greased and floured sheet pan for about 35 minutes at 350°.

Topping:

1/2 c. white sugar

1 stick oleo

1 small can Angel
  Flake coconut

1/4 c. Pet milk
1 c. nuts, chopped

Melt oleo; add other ingredients and mix well. Spread over baked cake and broil until light brown.

Edith Fields, Mobile Council

OLD FASHIONED SHORT CAKE

5 egg whites
5 egg yolks
1 c. plain flour
1/4 tsp. salt

1/2 c. sugar
1/3 c. sugar
1/2 tsp. baking powder
1 tsp. vanilla

Beat egg whites until stiff; add 1/2 cup sugar and then beat a little longer. Add 1/3 cup sugar to egg yolks and beat until thick. Fold in the egg white mixture; add flour, salt and baking powder. Mix well, then add vanilla. Pour mixture into two 9 inch ungreased pans and bake at 350° for 25 to 30 minutes. Cool; remove from pans by running a case knife around edges of pan and with egg turner loosen cake from bottom of pan. Stack cake with strawberries and whipped cream.

Louise Eley, Decatur Council

1-2-3-4 CAKE

1 c. shortening
1 c. milk
2 c. sugar
3 c. flour

3 tsp. baking powder
4 eggs
1 tsp. vanilla

Cream shortening and sugar. Separate eggs; add beaten yolks to mixture and beat well. Add flour and baking powder alternately with milk. Add vanilla; fold in stiffly beaten egg whites. Bake in tube pan at 325° for approximately 1 hour 10 minutes, or may be baked in two 9 inch layer pans.

Mary Norris, Birmingham Central Council

1-2-3-4

1 c. flour
1 stick oleo (soft)
1/2 c. nuts, chopped
1 (8 oz.) pkg. cream
  cheese

1 c. powdered sugar
1 large carton Cool Whip
2 pkg. instant pudding
  (1 lemon, 1 vanilla)
3 c. cold milk

1567-82

143

Layer I: Mix flour, oleo and nuts; pat in bottom of 13x9 inch pan. Bake 15 minutes at 350°, then cool in refrigerator. Layer II: Beat cream cheese till soft; add 1 cup powdered sugar and add 3/4 large carton Cool Whip. Whip until well blended. Add to Layer I. Layer III: Mix 2 packages instant pudding with 3 cups of milk. Put on Layer II. Layer IV: Use rest of Cool Whip and top off with chopped nuts.

Note: Chocolate pudding is also good.

Karen Crowe, Riverchase Council

100 HOLE CAKE (ORANGE)

1 yellow cake mix
1 pkg. lemon instant
  pudding

4 eggs
3/4 c. Crisco oil
3/4 c. orange juice

Mix all ingredients together; bake at 325° in oblong pan 45 minutes. Leave in pan. Punch 100 holes in cake. Pour icing over cake while warm.

Icing:

2 c. 10X sugar
2 Tbsp. butter

1/3 c. + 2 Tbsp.
  orange juice

Cook over low heat until melted.

Martha Cantrell, Birmingham East Council

CANDY ORANGE SLICE CAKE

Cream 1 cup oleo or butter and 2 cups sugar. Add 4 eggs, 1 at a time, beating each one. Combine in bowl:

1/2 c. buttermilk and
  1 tsp. soda

3 1/2 c. flour

Add:

1 lb. dates, chopped
2 c. chopped nuts

1 lb. candy orange slices,
  chopped

Add to creamed mixture 1 1/3 cups or 1 can Angel Flake cocoanut. Makes stiff dough. Bake at 350° for 2 1/2 or 3 hours. Pour 2 cups powdered sugar and 1 cup orange juice over while hot.

Bertha Capps, Birmingham East Council

144

GRECIAN ORANGE CAKE

Cake:

1 box yellow cake mix
1 pkg. instant lemon
   pudding

4 eggs
3/4 c. corn oil (scant)
3/4 c. water

Icing:

2 c. confectioners sugar
2 Tbsp. melted butter

1/3 c. + 2 Tbsp. frozen
   concentrated orange juice

Cake: Place all ingredients in mixer. Turn mixer on low; beat for 2 minutes, scraping sides of bowl constantly. Pour into greased and floured tube and bake at 325° for 45 minutes.

Icing: Combine 2 cups confectioners sugar, 1/3 cup plus 2 tablespoons frozen concentrate of orange juice, 2 tablespoons melted butter. When hot cake is taken from oven, punch about 100 holes in cake with ice pick, punching through to bottom of pan, and pour icing mixture over hot cake and let stand in tube pan until cold.

Betty Havard, Mobile Council

MANDARIN ORANGE CAKE

1 Duncan Hines butter
   recipe cake mix
4 eggs

1 (6 oz.) can undrained
   mandarin oranges
1/2 c. oil

Icing:

1 large box instant
   vanilla pudding

1 large can crushed pineapple
1 (9 oz.) Cool Whip

Mix cake ingredients together approximately 2 minutes. Bake at 350° about 30 minutes in a greased and floured 11x13 inch pan or in 2 round cake pans.

While cake is baking, prepare icing by mixing instant pudding and pineapple and then refrigerating. When cake is cool, add Cool Whip to pudding and pineapple mixture. Frost cake and refrigerate.

Holly Woodard, Riverchase Council

ORANGE DATE NUT CAKE AND GLAZE

Cake:

1 c. butter or Crisco
   shortening
2 c. sugar

4 eggs
4 c. plain flour
1 1/2 c. buttermilk

1567-82

145

2 c. chopped pecans
1 box chopped dates

1 tsp. soda
2 Tbsp. grated orange rind

Glaze:

1 c. orange juice
2 c. white sugar

2 Tbsp. orange rind

Cake: Cream butter and sugar; add eggs, one at a time. Dissolve soda in buttermilk; add flour and milk alternately. Lightly flour dates and nuts, then add to mixture with orange rind. Bake in a greased, floured tube pan at 1 1/2 hours at 325°.

Glaze: Mix orange juice and sugar and orange rind. Do not heat, but let stand at room temperature until sugar is dissolved. Pour over hot cake while it is still in the tube pan. Let stand for several hours before removing from pan while warm.

Mrs. John R. Criswell (Evelyn), Mobile Council

ORANGE DELIGHT CAKE

Cake:

1 box yellow cake mix
1 box lemon instant
   pudding mix

3/4 c. Wesson oil
3/4 c. water
4 eggs

Icing:

2 c. confectioners sugar
2 Tbsp. melted butter

1/3 c. plus 2 Tbsp. frozen
   orange juice

Cake: Mix well. Bake in angel food cake pan which has been greased and floured. Bake 45 minutes at 325°.

Icing: Mix and pour over cake while cake is warm.

Delores Champion Dugger, Decatur Council

NUTTY ORANGE CAKE

1 large orange, pulp and
   rind (reserve juice
   for topping)
1 c. raisins
1/2 c. finely chopped
   salted peanuts
1/4 c. milk

2 c. flour
1 tsp. soda
1 tsp. salt
1 c. sugar
1/2 c. shortening
3/4 c. milk
2 eggs

Grind together first 3 ingredients; set aside. Add shortening and 3/4 cup milk to sifted dry ingredients; beat 2 minutes. Add 2 eggs and 1/4 cup milk; beat 2 minutes more.

146

Fold in ground fruit and nuts. Pour into greased 13x9x2 inch greased pan; bake at 350° for 40-50 minutes.

Topping: Drizzle 1/3 cup orange juice over warm cake. Combine 1/3 cup sugar, 1 teaspoon cinnamon and 1/4 cup ground salted peanuts and sprinkle over cake.

Jane Day, Birmingham Central Council

NELL'S PARADISE CAKE

1/2 c. butter or margarine	1 tsp. vanilla
1 c. sugar	1 small can crushed pineapple
2 c. plain flour	1 c. chopped nuts
1 tsp. soda	1 c. chopped dates with sugar
2 tsp. baking powder	2 eggs

Add nuts and dates last. Makes 2 layers.

Icing:

2 c. sugar	1 c. coconut
1 c. sweet milk	1/2 c. butter
1 c. dates	1 tsp. vanilla

Cook just long enough to melt butter.

Ann Smith, Tuscaloosa Pioneer Unit

PEA PICKING CAKE

1 box Duncan Hines yellow cake mix	1 small box vanilla instant pudding

Mix these 2 ingredients together; add:

4 eggs	1 can mandarin oranges with juice
1 (12 oz.) bottle Crisco oil	

Mix well; cook in layer or tube pan at about 325° for 40 minutes.

Icing for above:

3 small pkg. vanilla instant pudding mix	1 (13 oz.) Cool Whip 1 large can crushed pineapple

Drain pineapple; add all ingredients together and mix. Spread on cool cake.

Mrs. Libby Pilling, Decatur Council

PECAN PIE CAKE

1 yellow cake mix   1/2 c. melted butter
1 egg

Mix above ingredients real well. Reserve 2/3 cup of batter. Pour the rest of the batter into a 9x13 inch pan and bake for 15 minutes or until brown at 325°. Then mix:

1 1/2 c. white Karo syrup   1/2 c. dark brown sugar,
2/3 c. batter   packed
3 eggs   1 tsp. vanilla flavoring
                                      1 to 2 c. chopped pecans

Pour filling on top of crust and cook about 1 hour at 325°.

Rosemary Parker, Birmingham Central Council

PEANUT BUTTER CAKE

1/2 c. margarine   2 tsp. baking powder
1 1/3 c. sugar   1 tsp. salt
1/4 c. peanut butter   1 c. milk
1 tsp. vanilla   1 (10 oz.) jar strawberry
2 eggs   preserves
2 c. flour

Heat oven to 350°. Cream margarine and sugar until light and fluffy; add peanut butter, vanilla and eggs. Beat well. Combine flour, baking powder and salt; add alternately with milk to creamed mixture, mixing well after each addition. Pour into 2 greased and floured 8 or 9 inch layer pans and bake at 350° for 35 to 40 minutes; cool 10 minutes. Remove from pan. Spread 2/3 cup preserves between layers. Frost with Peanut Butter Frosting.

Peanut Butter Frosting:

1/4 c. margarine   1/2 tsp. salt
1/4 c. peanut butter   2 1/2 c. sifted confectioners
1 tsp. vanilla   sugar
                                      3 Tbsp. milk

Cream margarine; blend in peanut butter, vanilla and salt. Add sugar alternately with milk, beating until light and fluffy.

Peggy Blevins, Anniston Council

PINA COLADA CAKE

1 pkg. yellow cake mix
1 (3 3/4 oz.) pkg. instant
  vanilla pudding mix
4 eggs

1/2 c. non-alcoholic pina
  colada bottled drink mix
1/2 c. light rum
1/3 c. cooking oil
1/2 c. flaked coconut

Topping:

1 qt. pineapple sherbet
1/2 c. light rum

1 (8 1/4 oz.) can crushed
  pineapple, drained

In large bowl mix cake mix, pudding mix, pina colada mix, 1/2 cup rum, oil and eggs; blend well. Beat 2 minutes. Fold in coconut. Pour into well greased and floured 10 inch fluted tube pan; bake at 350° for 50-55 minutes. Cool 15 minutes in pan. Invert onto rack; cool. Soften sherbet; blend in 1/2 cup rum. Fold in pineapple; freeze. Serve atop cake slices.

Anna Lee Hickman, Tri-Cities Council

PINA COLADA CAKE

1 box yellow cake mix
1 can Eagle Brand milk
Cool Whip

1 creme of coconut
  pina colada mix
1 pkg. frozen coconut

Cook yellow cake mix in sheet pan; leave in pan. Cool. Punch holes with fork. Mix milk, creme of coconut pina colada and pour over cake. Mix frozen coconut and Cool Whip and top cake. Chill.

Frank Jones, Tuscaloosa Pioneer Unit

PINEAPPLE CHOCOLATE PUDDING-CAKE

1 (1 lb. 4 oz.) can
  crushed pineapple
2 c. sifted flour
1 c. sugar
1 1/2 tsp. baking soda
1/2 tsp. salt
1/4 tsp. cinnamon

1/4 tsp. nutmeg
1 (4 oz.) pkg. sweet cooking
  chocolate, chopped
1 c. chopped nuts
1/2 c. chopped raisins
2 eggs, slightly beaten
1/3 c. butter or margarine,
  melted

Grease a 9 inch tube pan; line the bottom with brown paper. Drain pineapple thoroughly; there will be a generous cupful. Reserve 3/4 cup of the pineapple syrup. Sift together the flour, sugar, baking soda, salt, cinnamon and nutmeg into a mixing bowl; stir in the chocolate, pecans and

1567-82

raisins. Add the slightly beaten eggs, drained pineapple, reserved 3/4 cup pineapple syrup and the melted butter. Stir enough to moisten all the flour; turn into the prepared tube pan. Bake in a moderate 350° oven 1 hour and 10 minutes. Place cake in pan on wire rack to cool for 15 minutes. Loosen edges and center with spatula or small knife. Turn out; remove paper. Turn right side up. Allow to stand on rack until cold. Cover tightly and store 12 hours before serving.

Nell Chaffin, Tuscaloosa Pioneer Unit

PINEAPPLE-DELIGHT CAKE

1 box yellow cake mix
1 stick margarine, melted
1 egg
1 small can crushed
    pineapple
2 Tbsp. cornstarch
1 (8 oz.) pkg. cream
    cheese, softened
2 eggs
1 box confectioners sugar

Mix first 3 ingredients in large mixing bowl; pat in bottom of 13x9 inch greased pan. Slowly cook pineapple and cornstarch until clear; pour over cake. Beat cream cheese, eggs and sugar. Pour over pineapple; bake at 350° until golden brown, approximately 45 minutes.

Sara Staggs, Birmingham West Council

PINEAPPLE-NUT LOAF CAKE

3 sticks margarine
    (1 1/2 c.)
1 1/2 boxes powdered
    sugar
6 eggs
1 tsp. vanilla extract
1 tsp. lemon juice
4 c. all-purpose flour
1 (20 oz.) can crushed
    pineapple, drained
2 c. chopped pecans

Cream margarine; add sugar and beat well. Add eggs, 2 at a time, and beat well after each addition. Add vanilla and lemon juice. Stir in flour and mix well. Add pineapple (after juice has been drained). Add 1 1/2 cups pecans and mix well. Use 10 inch tube pan, greased and floured. Sprinkle remaining pecans in pan and spoon batter into pan. Bake for 1 1/2 hours at 350°. Yield: One 10 inch tube cake.

Pat Cochran, Birmingham South Council

PINEAPPLE NUT SPICE CAKE

2 1/2 c. sifted self-rising
  flour
2 c. sugar
1 1/2 c. Crisco oil
4 egg yolks
1 small (8 1/2 oz.) can
  crushed pineapple
  and juice

2 Tbsp. hot water
2 tsp. cinnamon
1 tsp. butter extract
1 tsp. coconut extract
1 tsp. vanilla extract
1 c. chopped nuts
4 egg whites, beaten
1 1/2 tsp. nutmeg

Combine all ingredients except nuts and egg whites. Beat well, and then add nuts. Fold in egg whites. Pour into greased and floured tube pan. Place in cold oven; set oven at 325° and bake 1 hour and 15 minutes. Let cool 15 minutes before removing from pan.

C. T. (Dub) Emerson, Huntsville Council

PINEAPPLE SUPREME CAKE

3 c. cake flour
1/2 c. butter or margarine
2 1/4 c. sugar
1/2 c. Crisco oil
3 tsp. baking powder
1/2 tsp. salt

4 eggs
1 c. milk
1 Tbsp. vanilla extract
1 Tbsp. lemon flavor
1 (3 1/8 oz.) box vanilla
  Jell-O pudding mix

Frosting:

1 (8 oz.) box Philadelphia
  cream cheese
1 (16 oz.) box
  confectioners sugar

1 Tbsp. vanilla extract
1 (15 oz.) can crushed
  pineapple, drained

Cream butter and sugar until fluffy; add eggs, one at a time, to mixture. Add flour, salt and baking powder alternately with milk, flavoring and oil, beating until smooth. Add Jell-O pudding mix and beat until smooth. (For best results, use electric mixer; beat 10 minutes.) Pour batter into 3 greased and floured 9 inch layer pans; bake at 350° for 30 minutes. (Cool layers before frosting.)

Frosting: Mix cream cheese, confectioners sugar and flavor until smooth. After icing each layer, sprinkle drained pineapple over layers.

Elizabeth H. Allen, Birmingham South Council

SWEDISH PINEAPPLE CAKE

2 c. white sugar
2 c. plain flour
2 eggs
1 tsp. vanilla
1 1/2 tsp. soda

1/2 tsp. salt
2/3 c. chopped nuts
1 (20 oz.) can crushed
   pineapple and juice

Mix all together by hand. Pour into a 13x9 inch ungreased pan; bake at 350° for 35 minutes. Do not overcook. (I use self-rising flour.)

Frosting:

1 (8 oz.) pkg. cream
  cheese
1/2 c. oleo

1 box confectioners sugar
Chopped nuts

Mix all above ingredients with mixer. Spread while still warm. Sprinkle with nuts.

Eileen Bevis, Tri-Cities Council

PINEAPPLE UPSIDE-DOWN CAKE

5 Tbsp. butter
1 c. brown sugar,
  firmly packed
1 (No. 2) can (2 1/2 c.)
  pineapple slices or
  peach halves, drained

Pecan halves
Maraschino cherries
1 (1 lb. 2 oz.) pkg.
  yellow cake mix

For electric frypan. Preheat frypan to 225° F. Melt butter. Add brown sugar and mix well. Spread evenly over bottom of frypan. Arrange fruit and nuts over sugar mixture. Prepare cake mix according to directions; spread evenly on top of fruit. Cover frypan, with vent open. Bake for 30 minutes or until cake is dry on top. While cake is still hot, loosen around edges with a spatula. Place plate or tray over frypan and invert to remove cake. Lift off frypan. Serve warm or cold with whipped cream.

Jamima Edney, Birmingham South Council

PISTACHIO CAKE

Preheat oven to 350°. Grease and flour pan. Mix 1/2 cup nuts and 1/2 cup chocolate chips. Sprinkle in bottom of pan (Bundt pan). Mix together:

1 pkg. instant pistachio
  pudding

1 pkg. yellow cake mix
1/2 c. sugar

1/2 c. oil   4 eggs
1 c. water

Mix 2 minutes or more. Take out 1 cup of batter and mix in 5 ounce can of chocolate syrup. Pour batter in pan. Then pour chocolate batter around top. Run knife through batter; bake 1 hour. Let it set in pan 10 minutes before taking out.

Rosemary Parker, Birmingham Central Council

PLUM CAKE

2 c. self-rising flour
2 c. sugar
2 jars strained plum
  baby food
3 eggs

1 tsp. ground cloves
1 tsp. cinnamon
1 c. oil
Pecans

Mix all ingredients together with a spoon (do not use mixer). Bake in greased and floured Bundt pan 50 minutes at 350°.

Bonnie Hall, Mobile Council

POPCORN CAKE

1 c. granulated sugar
1/2 c. heavy cream
1/3 c. white corn syrup
1 tsp. vanilla extract

1/3 tsp. soda
12 c. popped corn
1 Tbsp. butter

Combine granulated sugar, cream, white corn syrup, butter; cook until it will spin a thread or 234° F. Remove from heat; stir in 1 teaspoon vanilla, 1/3 teaspoon soda. Pour over 12 cups popcorn at once. Pack in an ungreased tube pan. After this sets, turn out and decorate as desired with candy corn, nutmeats, gumdrops or other candy. Slice cake to serve.

Mona Maze (Mrs. David C.),
Birmingham South Council

POPPY SEED CAKE

1 pkg. Duncan Hines
  yellow cake mix
1 pkg. banana cream or
  coconut cream instant
  pudding

4 large eggs
1/2 c. Wesson oil
1 c. hot water
1/4 c. poppy seeds

1567-82

Mix all together and beat for 4 minutes with electric mixer. Turn into greased and floured tube pan; bake 50 minutes in preheated 350° oven. Turn out and eat warm or cool. It's great.

Joan Waters, Huntsville Council

BUTTERSCOTCH POUND CAKE

8 oz. cream cheese
2 1/4 c. sugar
6 eggs
1/2 tsp. salt
1 c. chopped pecans

1 c. butter
2 1/2 c. all-purpose flour
1 Tbsp. vanilla
1 (6 oz.) pkg. butterscotch
  bits

Cream the sugar, butter and softened cream cheese; add eggs, one at a time, beating well after each addition. Add flour gradually, continuing to beat well. Add vanilla. Fold in chopped pecans and butterscotch bits; bake at 325° for 20 minutes in a well greased Bundt or tube pan. Lower oven to 300° and cook for 1 1/2 hours.

June Crowe, Anniston Council

CHERRY NUT POUND CAKE

1 1/2 c. shortening
3 c. sugar
6 eggs
1/2 tsp. almond
  flavoring

1/2 tsp. vanilla flavoring
3 3/4 c. plain flour
3/4 c. milk
5 oz. maraschino cherries,
  well drained and chopped

Cream together shortening and sugar until very creamy and beat 10-15 minutes. Add eggs, one at a time, beating well after each addition. Add 1/2 teaspoon vanilla and 1/2 teaspoon almond flavoring and blend well. Alternate flour with milk, mixing well after each addition. Fold in cherries. Pour into large greased tube pan. Place in cold oven; set oven at 275° and bake for 2 hours and 10 minutes. Cool thoroughly and frost.

Frosting:

8 oz. cream cheese
1 lb. confectioners sugar
1 tsp. almond flavoring
1 tsp. vanilla flavoring

1/2 stick margarine
1 c. coconut
1 c. chopped walnuts
5 oz. maraschino cherries,
  drained and chopped

Frosting: Blend margarine and cream cheese until smooth (allow them to reach room temperature for easy blending). Gradually add confectioners sugar and beat until smooth. Add 1 teaspoon each of vanilla and almond flavoring and mix well. Fold in nuts, cherries and coconut; spread over cake. Reserve several whole cherries and little coconut to decorate the frosted cake, if desired.

Fay Clark, Decatur Council

CHOCOLATE CHIP POUND CAKE

1 box Duncan Hines
  yellow cake mix
1 small box instant
  vanilla pudding

4 eggs
1/2 c. oil
1/2 pt. sour cream

Mix above ingredients together for 7 minutes. Combine 1/2 cup chocolate chips, 1/2 cup light brown sugar and 1 1/2 cups chopped pecans. Pour half mixture of cake into greased Bundt or tube pan. Sprinkle half the nut mixture over dough. Add balance of cake mixture and the rest of nut mixture. Bake at 350° for 50 minutes.

P.S. It is often surprising to find what heights can be attained merely by remaining on the level.

Barbara Spivey, Mobile Council

CHOCOLATE POUND CAKE

2 sticks margarine
1/2 c. Crisco
3 c. sugar
5 whole eggs
1/4 tsp. salt

1 tsp. baking powder
1/2 c. cocoa
1 tsp. vanilla
1 1/4 c. sweet milk
3 c. cake flour

Mix dry ingredients. Cream butter, sugar and Crisco; add eggs, one at a time, beating after each. Add milk and dry ingredients and flavoring. Cook at 300° for 1 1/2 or 2 hours. Do not open oven door until 1 1/2 hours is up.

Chocolate Icing (if desired):

2/3 c. Pet milk
2 c. sugar

1/4 c. cocoa
1/4 tsp. salt

Mix and boil fast for 2 minutes. Take off; add vanilla and butter. Beat with mixer until creamy.

2/3 c. margarine
  (1 stick)

1 tsp. vanilla

Dilla Samuel, Anniston Council

COCONUT POUND CAKE

3 c. sugar
2 sticks oleo
1/2 c. Crisco
6 eggs
3 c. flour

1 c. milk
1/2 tsp. vanilla
1/2 tsp. almond or
   coconut flavoring
1 (3 1/2 oz.) can Angel
   Flake coconut

Cream oleo and Crisco; add sugar gradually. Add eggs, 1 at a time, beating 2 minutes after each. Add flour alternately with milk; blend in flavoring and coconut until well mixed. Pour in tube pan; bake at 350° F. for 1 1/4 hours (or until done). Do not preheat oven.

Mattie Singleton, Birmingham Central Council

CREAM CHEESE POUND CAKE

1 (8 oz.) pkg. cream
   cheese
6 medium eggs
3 c. granulated sugar

3 sticks margarine
1 tsp. vanilla flavoring
3 c. cake flour (box kind)

(May add chopped nuts.) Soften and mix cream cheese and margarine; stir in sugar. Add eggs and vanilla flavoring; blend until smooth. Stir in cake flour. Blend mixture until doughy texture. Pour in Bundt pan and bake for 1 1/2 hours at 300°.

Glaze (if desired):

1/2 box confectioners
   sugar
1/2 stick butter

1 (3 oz.) pkg. cream cheese
1 tsp. vanilla
1 Tbsp. milk (until consistent)

Cream and blend together until fluffy.

J. S. Cole, Birmingham Central Council

CRUSTY POUND CAKE

1 1/2 c. butter, softened
3 c. sugar
6 eggs
1 Tbsp. vanilla extract

1 tsp. almond extract
3 c. all-purpose flour
1/2 tsp. salt

Cream butter well in a large mixing bowl; add sugar gradually, mixing until texture is fine and mealy. Add eggs, one at a time, beating after each addition. Add flavorings. Combine flour and salt; stir flour mixture into batter, beating until flour is moistened. Do not overbeat. Pour into a

156

greased and floured 10 inch tube. Bake at 325° for 1 hour and 25 minutes, or until a toothpick inserted comes out clean and cake shrinks slightly from sides of pan. Cool in pan 15 minutes. Turn out onto a wire rack; turn right side up and complete cooling. Yield: One 10 inch cake.

Willie Mae Crews, Birmingham East Council

DOWN HOME POUND CAKE

1 lb. butter
2 2/3 c. sugar
3 1/2 c. sifted all-
  purpose flour

8 eggs
8 Tbsp. coffee cream
  (canned milk will do)
1 tsp. vanilla

Separate eggs. Whip whites; add 6 level tablespoons sugar and refrigerate until rest of cake is mixed. Cream butter and remaining sugar, beating until very light (this is important). Add egg yolks, 2 at a time, beating well after each addition. Add flour and cream alternately, beating until mixture is light. Add vanilla. Fold in egg whites. Bake in greased and floured tube pan at 300° about 1 hour 25 minutes or until done. For a smaller recipe, halve the recipe and bake 1 hour in loaf pan.

Emma Arnold, Decatur Council

LEMON APRICOT POUND CAKE

Cake:

1 pkg. lemon cake mix
4 eggs

1/2 c. sugar
1/2 c. Wesson oil
1 c. apricot nectar

Glaze:

1 c. sifted confectioners
  sugar

5 Tbsp. lemon juice

Cake: Mix and beat 2 minutes. Bake in Bundt pan in 350° oven for 1 hour.
Glaze: Mix glaze and pour over warm cake.

Billie Harrison, Decatur Council

LEMON BUTTERMILK POUND CAKE

3 sticks oleo or butter
2 1/2 c. sugar
4 eggs

3 1/2 c. flour
1/2 tsp. salt
1 c. buttermilk

1567-82

1 Tbsp. lemon extract   1/2 tsp. baking soda, dissolved
                                      in 1 Tbsp. hot water

Generously grease tube pan. Preheat oven to 325° F. Cream butter until light and fluffy. Gradually add sugar and cream well until smooth. Add eggs, one at a time, beating well after each addition. Sift flour and salt together. Dissolve soda in hot water and add to buttermilk. Alternately add flour and milk to butter mixture; blend well. Add lemon extract and blend. Pour mixture evenly into tube pan. Shake pan to even it further. Place in preheated oven and bake undisturbed for 1 hour. Cool in pan or remove as soon as possible and pour a glaze of lemon juice and confectioners sugar over cake while still warm.

Debra T. Bean, Riverchase Council

MAPLE PECAN POUND CAKE

3 c. plain flour (plus 1/2   1 c. butter
  tsp. soda and dash of   3 Tbsp. maple flavoring
  salt)   1 c. chopped pecans
6 egg yolks   6 beaten egg whites
3 c. sugar   1 c. sour cream

Cream well butter and sugar; add egg yolks, 1 at a time, and beat well after each one. Add flour alternately with sour cream; add flavoring and nuts. Fold in egg whites. Bake in greased and floured tube pan 1 1/2 hours at 300°; cool well in pan.

Rachel Carroll, Decatur Council

ORANGE JUICE POUND CAKE

2 sticks butter*   1 tsp. vanilla flavor
1/2 c. Crisco   1 tsp. almond flour
2 c. sugar   6 Tbsp. orange juice
6 eggs   (better if fresh squeezed)
3 c. flour (plain)   1/2 tsp. salt

*May use margarine. Cream butter and Crisco; add sugar and beat till creamy. Sift flour and salt together; add flour to butter, sugar and Crisco. Batter will be thick. Add orange juice; add eggs, one at a time, beating after each. Add flavor; bake at 300° about 1 1/2 hours.

Bobbye Jones, Montgomery Council

PINEAPPLE POUND CAKE

1/2 c. shortening
1/2 lb. butter or oleo
2 3/4 c. sugar
6 large eggs
3 c. sifted flour

1 tsp. baking powder
1/4 c. milk
1 tsp. vanilla
3/4 c. undrained crushed
   pineapple

Glaze:

1/4 c. butter or oleo
1 1/2 c. powdered sugar

1 c. crushed pineapple,
   drained

Cream butter, shortening and sugar; add eggs, one at a time, beating thoroughly after each addition. Add flour sifted with baking powder, large spoonful at a time, alternately with milk. Add vanilla. Stir in crushed pineapple and juice; blend well. Pour in greased and floured tube pan. Place in cold oven; turn oven to 325° and bake for 1 1/2 hours until top springs back when touched lightly. Run knife around edge and remove carefully from pan; cool 10 minutes.

Glaze: Combine butter, powdered sugar and drained pineapple and pour over cake.

Edith Fields, Mobile Council

PSYCHEDELIC POUND CAKE

1/2 c. Crisco
1 stick margarine
3 c. sugar
3 c. flour
1/2 tsp. baking powder
1 c. milk
5 eggs

1 tsp. lemon extract
1 tsp. vanilla
Food coloring: Yellow,
   green, red (use as much
   as desired to make shades
   you desire - start with
   1 drop)

Cream shortening and butter together; add sugar, then eggs. Sift flour and baking powder together and add to batter alternately with milk. Add flavoring. Mix batter well. Separate batter in 3 bowls. Color each bowl desired colors. Grease and flour large tube pan. Pour colored batter alternately into pan; set in cold oven and set at 375° for 10 minutes, then reduce heat to 350° and cook for 1 hour 10 minutes.

Marian Turnipseed, Birmingham West Council

SEVEN-UP POUND CAKE

1 1/2 c. butter
5 eggs
3 c. sugar

3 c. sifted plain flour
2 Tbsp. lemon extract
3/4 c. 7-Up

Cream butter and sugar until fluffy; add eggs, one at a time. Combine well. Add flour. Beat in lemon extract and 7-Up. Pour mixture into well greased Bundt or tube pan; bake 1 to 1 1/4 hours at 325°.

Peggy Hawkins

SOUR CREAM POUND CAKE

1/4 c. water
1/4 c. sugar
4 eggs
1/2 c. Crisco oil

1/2 pt. sour cream
1 all butter Duncan Hines
  yellow cake mix

Mix eggs and cake mix; add sugar, oil, water and beat until smooth. Fold in sour cream. Preheat oven to 375° and cook for 45 minutes.

Sharon Simpson, Decatur Council

SWEET CREAM POUND CAKE

1/2 lb. butter (2 sticks
  real butter)
3 c. sugar, divided
6 eggs, separated

1 tsp. vanilla
1 c. whipping cream
  (don't whip it)
3 c. cake flour

Have all ingredients at room temperature. Grease and flour a deep 10 inch tube pan. Cream butter well; add 2 cups sugar and cream until light and fluffy. Add beaten egg yolks and mix well. Sift cake flour 3 times and then measure. Alternate, adding cake flour and whipping cream, starting and ending with flour. Beat well after each addition. Add vanilla and mix well. Beat egg whites with rotary beater until soft peaks form. Gradually add remaining 1 cup sugar to egg whites to make a stiff meringue. Fold egg whites mixture into batter. Pour batter into greased and floured tube pan. Put pan in a cold oven and set temperature at 325°. Bake 1 1/2 hours or until cake is golden brown and tests done. Let cake stand in pan for 15 minutes. Loosen sides with a knife and invert pan over cake rack Allow to cool thoroughly before slicing. Ummm - Good!

Jane Spear, Riverchase Council

160

PUMPKIN SPICE CAKE

4 eggs
2 c. sugar
1 c. oil
2 c. plain flour
2 tsp. soda

2 tsp. cinnamon
1/2 tsp. salt
2 c. pumpkin or 1 can
Nuts (optional)

Mix eggs, sugar and oil; beat and add remaining ingredients. Grease and flour long pan; bake at 350° for 40 minutes. Round Bundt pan requires 60 minutes. Serve with Hot Caramel Sauce:

1 stick oleo
1/2 c. white sugar

1/2 c. brown sugar
1/2 c. cream

Mix together. Bring to a boil; continue stirring and boil for 5 minutes. Pour over Pumpkin Spice Cake when serving.

Linda Barnette, Birmingham South Council

PRISM CAKE

1 pkg. orange jello
1 pkg. cherry jello
1 pkg. lime jello
3 c. boiling water
1 1/2 c. cold water
1 c. pineapple juice

1/4 c. sugar
1 pkg. lemon jello
1/2 c. cold water
1 c. graham cracker crumbs
1/4 c. butter, melted
2 1/2 pt. carton whipped cream

Prepare the first 3 packages of jello separately, using 1 cup hot water and 1/2 cup cold water for each. Pour into 8x8x2 inch pans and chill until firm. Combine pineapple juice and sugar and heat until sugar is dissolved. Remove from heat and dissolve lemon jello in hot liquid. Add remaining 1/2 cup cold water. Chill until just syrupy. *Mix crumbs with melted butter; press crumb mixture smoothly over bottom of pan or glass dish. Whip the 2 1/2 pints cream and pour into the syrupy lemon gelatin. Cut the firm orange, cherry and lime jello into 1/2 inch squares. Lift jello out of pans with wide spatula, dipped in hot water. Fold into whipped cream mixture, then pour into container. Chill at least 8 hours. If desired, this may be covered with 1/2 cup cream whipped and sweetened.

(*Optional.)

Nana Clark, Anniston Council

PRUNE CAKE

3 eggs
1 1/2 c. sugar
1 c. Wesson oil
2 c. plain flour
1 c. buttermilk
1 c. cooked prunes,
   chopped

1/2 c. nuts, chopped
1 tsp. soda
1 tsp. salt
1 tsp. cinnamon
1 tsp. nutmeg
1 tsp. allspice
1 tsp. vanilla

Sift flour and spices. Mix first 3 ingredients in mixing bowl with mixer. Add flour alternately with milk. Fold in prunes and nuts. Grease and flour 9x13 inch pan; bake 1 hour at 300°.

Buttermilk Icing:

1 c. sugar
1/2 c. buttermilk
1/2 tsp. soda

2 tsp. syrup (white Karo)
1/4 lb. oleo
1/2 tsp. vanilla

Boil until soft ball forms and pour over hot cake.
Faith Kirby, Anniston Council

PRUNE CAKE

4 1/2 c. flour
2 1/4 c. sugar
2 1/4 tsp. soda
1/2 tsp. salt

2 tsp. each cinnamon,
   allspice, nutmeg, cloves
2 c. Wesson oil
2 c. buttermilk
1 c. prunes, cooked, mashed

Put all dry ingredients in mixing bowl, then add liquid and prunes. Bake at 350° for 25 minutes. Makes 3 layers.

Filling and Icing:

1 1/2 c. sugar
1/2 lb. butter

7 egg yolks
6 Tbsp. cornstarch

Cook in double boiler until thick, then add:

1 c. chopped nuts, toasted
1 c. chopped raisins

1 c. fresh grated cocoanut
1 Tbsp. vanilla

Mrs. Rosemary Parker,
Birmingham Central Council

PUMPKIN CAKE ROLL

3 eggs
1 c. granulated sugar
2/3 c. pumpkin
1 tsp. lemon juice
3/4 c. flour
1 tsp. baking powder

2 tsp. cinnamon
1 tsp. ginger
1/2 tsp. nutmeg
1/2 tsp. salt
1 c. finely chopped pecans

Filling:

1 c. powdered sugar
2 (3 oz.) pkg. cream cheese

4 Tbsp. butter or oleo
1/2 tsp. vanilla

Beat eggs on high speed of mixer for 5 minutes; gradually beat in granulated sugar. Stir in pumpkin and lemon juice. Stir together flour, baking powder, cinnamon, ginger, nutmeg and salt. Fold into pumpkin mixture; spread in greased and floured 15x10x1 inch pan. Top with 1 cup finely chopped pecans. Bake at 375° for 15 minutes; turn out on towel sprinkled with powdered sugar. Starting at narrow end, roll towel and cake together; cool. Unroll. Mix filling ingredients and spread over cake. Roll and chill. Makes about 8 servings.

Note: Cake should be refrigerated and improves after day or more.

Ruth Apperson, Decatur Council

RAINBOW CAKE

1 pkg. orange jello
1 pkg. cherry jello
1 pkg. lime jello
3 c. hot water
1 1/2 c. cold water
1 c. pineapple juice
1/4 c. sugar
1 pkg. lemon jello

1/2 c. cold water
1 c. graham crackers
    (2 c. graham crackers)
1/4 c. melted butter
    (1/2 c. melted butter)
2 c. heavy cream
1/2 c. heavy cream
    (optional) for icing

Prepare the lime, orange and cherry jello in separate 8x8 inch pans, using 1 cup boiling water and 1/2 cup cold water each. Combine pineapple juice and sugar; heat until sugar is dissolved. Remove from heat and dissolve lemon jello in hot liquid; add 1/2 cup cold water. Chill until just syrupy (do not let it get beyond the syrupy stage). Mix crumbs with melted butter. Press crumb mixture smoothly over bottom of a 9 inch spring form pan. Whip 2 cups cream and pour lemon jello into whipped cream. Cut the firm orange, cherry and lime jello into cubes, about 1/4 inch square. (Dip sharp knife into hot water after each cut.)

1567-82

Run hot knife around edge of tray. Lift out jello with wide spatula (hot water dipped). Fold into whipped cream mixture, then pour into spring form pan. Chill 8 hours in refrigerator. Remove sides of pan before serving. If desired, frost with 1/2 cup of whipped cream.

Anne Spragins, Birmingham East Council

RED VELVET CAKE

1 box white cake mix	3 Tbsp. cocoa
1 env. Dream Whip	2 large bottles red food color
3 eggs	1 1/3 c. liquid

In large mixing bowl mix dry ingredients, cake mix, cocoa and Dream Whip. In 2 cup measuring cup add food color; add enough milk to make 1 1/3 cups liquid. Add to dry mixture. Add eggs and beat 4 minutes with hand mixer. Bake at 350° in 4 layers, 20 minutes. Remove from pans and let cool.

Frosting:

3 c. sweet milk	4 Tbsp. cornstarch

Cook in double boiler till thick to pudding consistency. Set in refrigerator to cool. In large bowl beat:

1 c. shortening (I use Crisco)	1 c. margarine
	2 c. XXX sugar

Gradually add sugar. Cream shortening and margarine; beat until it looks like whipped cream. Then add cool milk mixture and beat well. This cake needs to be kept cool. Serves 12.

Marie P. Williams, Mobile Council

RED VELVET CAKE

2 1/2 c. sifted cake flour	1 1/2 c. sugar
1/2 tsp. salt	2 (1 oz.) bottles red food
3 Tbsp. instant chocolate	coloring
mix	1 tsp. vanilla
1/2 c. butter	1 c. buttermilk
2 eggs	1 Tbsp. white vinegar
	1 tsp. soda

Sift together flour, salt and instant chocolate mix. Cream butter and sugar. When well creamed, beat in whole eggs, one at a time. Blend well and add food coloring and vanilla. Mix buttermilk, vinegar and soda; add alternately

164

with dry ingredients to the creamed mixture. Blend at low speed on electric mixer between each addition. Grease and line two 9 inch cake pans. They must be 1 1/2 inches deep as cake rises high. Pour in batter and bake in preheated 350° oven about 30 minutes or until done; don't overbake. Remove from oven and cool on racks 15 minutes. Remove from pans and continue cooling on racks before frosting. Frost with Mystery Icing.

Mystery Icing:

4 Tbsp. flour
1 c. sweet milk
1 c. granulated sugar
1 stick margarine

1/2 c. other non-liquid
  shortening
3 tsp. vanilla
1/4 tsp. salt

Blend flour and milk. Cook until mixture thickens to consistency of cream; cool, but don't chill. Cream sugar, margarine and other shortening, adding salt and vanilla. Add the slightly cooked flour mixture and continue beating until fluffy. Spread generously between layers and over all the cake. This makes a large gorgeous red cake with icing that never hardens. Sure to be a conversation piece.
Jewel Edney, Riverchase Council

REUNION CAKE-PIE

1 c. dark corn syrup
1 c. chopped pecans
3 eggs, beaten
1 tsp. vanilla extract
2/3 c. sugar or packed
  light brown sugar
Dash of salt
2 Tbsp. butter or
  margarine, melted
1/4 c. shortening

1/2 c. sugar
1 egg, beaten
2 tsp. vanilla extract
1 c. sifted cake flour or
  1 c. sifted all-purpose
  flour minus 1 Tbsp.
1/4 tsp. salt
3/4 tsp. baking powder
1/4 c. milk

1. Make pie layer: Into medium bowl combine corn syrup, pecans, eggs, vanilla, sugar, dash of salt and 2 tablespoons melted butter. Mix well. 2. Pour pecan mixture into a lightly greased 9 inch pie pan. Bake in preheated 400° F. oven for 15 minutes. 3. Prepare cake layer: In a large bowl, cream 1/4 cup shortening with 1/2 cup sugar, beating until light and fluffy. Beat in egg and vanilla. 4. Add flour mixed with salt and baking powder alternately with milk, beginning and ending with flour. Beat just until all is combined. 5. Pour cake batter over baked pecan layer. Return to oven; lower heat to 375° F. and bake about 30

minutes or until cake springs back when lightly touched with finger. Cool on rack. 6. When cake-pie is cool, decorate surface with confectioners sugar lightly sifted through a lace paper doily. Cut into wedges to serve. A spoonful of whipped cream on top of each serving is a generous touch. Makes 6 to 8 servings.

Eileen Bevis, Tri-Cities Council

RUM CAKE

1 (18 1/2 oz.) pkg. yellow cake mix
1 (3 3/4 oz.) pkg. Jell-O instant vanilla pudding mix
4 eggs

1/2 c. cold water
1/2 c. Wesson oil
1 c. chopped pecans or walnuts
1/2 c. Bacardi dark rum (80 proof)

Glaze:

1/4 lb. butter
1/4 c. water

1 c. granulated sugar
1/2 c. Bacardi dark rum (80 proof)

Preheat oven to 325° F. Grease and flour 10 inch tube or 12 cup Bundt pan. Sprinkle nuts over bottom of pan. Mix all cake ingredients together. Pour batter over nuts; bake 1 hour. Cool. Invert on serving plate. Prick top. Drizzle and smooth glaze evenly over top and sides. Allow cake to absorb glaze. Repeat till glaze is used up.

For glaze, melt butter in saucepan; stir in water and sugar. Boil 5 minutes, stirring constantly. Remove from heat; stir in rum.

Optional: Decorate with whole maraschino cherries and border of sugar frosting or whipped cream. Serve with seedless green grapes dusted with powdered sugar.

Charlie Mills, Decatur Council

SCOTTISH SHORTBREAD

1 lb. unsalted butter
1 c. sugar

3 c. Wondra cake flour
1 c. plain flour

Cream butter; gradually add sugar and beat for 10 minutes on high speed of mixer. Gradually add flour. Press into ungreased 11x18 inch pan; bake at 350° for 20 minutes, then bake at 325° for 40 minutes. Cut into squares while hot.

Mary Ann Aycock, Riverchase Council

7-UP CAKE

1 box yellow cake mix
4 eggs
3/4 c. salad oil

1 box vanilla or pineapple
    instant pudding
1 (10 oz.) bottle 7-Up

Topping:

2 eggs, beaten
1 1/2 c. sugar
1 Tbsp. flour

1 stick butter
1 (No. 2 or 13 1/4 oz.)
    can crushed pineapple,
    undrained

Combine and beat well:
1 box yellow cake mix
4 eggs

3/4 c. salad oil
1 box vanilla or pineapple
    instant pudding

Add, beating well, one 10 ounce bottle 7-Up. Pour into well greased and floured 9x13x2 inch pan.

Topping: To beaten 2 eggs, add -

1 Tbsp. flour
1 stick butter

1 can pineapple
1 1/2 c. sugar

Cook until thick, stirring constantly. Take from fire and stir in 1 can coconut. Pour while warm over warm cake.
Lee Johnson, Huntsville Council

SKILLET CAKE

1/2 c. shortening
1 c. sugar
3 eggs
3/4 c. milk

2 c. flour
1 Tbsp. vanilla
1/2 tsp. salt

Topping:

1 c. brown sugar
1 Tbsp. cinnamon

2 Tbsp. butter
2 Tbsp. flour

Icing:

1 c. confectioners sugar

2 Tbsp. milk

Cream shortening and sugar until light and fluffy; add eggs, one at a time. Add flour, salt, vanilla, milk and nuts. Pour in pan and put topping on. Mix topping with pastry blender or fork. After placing topping on cake mix (10 inch skillet), take spoon and push to bottom of pan so topping will bake into the cake. Bake 45 minutes at 350°. Mix confectioners sugar and milk and place on top of cake after it is cooled.
1567-82   Harold Busby, Mobile Council

SNOWBALL CAKE

2 env. Knox unflavored
  gelatine
1 c. crushed pineapple
1 c. pineapple juice
1 c. sugar

1 large angel food cake
3 small pkg. whipped topping
Juice of 1 lemon
1 can coconut
1/2 tsp. salt

Dissolve gelatine in 4 tablespoons of cold water; add 1 cup boiling water. Let partially cool. Combine pineapple juice, pineapple, sugar, salt and lemon juice. Add to gelatine mixture. Let partially congeal in refrigerator. Prepare whipped topping and fold in congealed mixture. Save part of topping to ice cake with coconut mixed with it.
      Helen Dickmann, Decatur Council

SORRY CAKE

2 c. Bisquick
4 eggs, slightly beaten
1 box light brown sugar

1 tsp. vanilla
2 c. chopped nuts

Combine ingredients and bake 35 minutes at 350°. Use 9x12 inch greased and floured pan. Sprinkle with powdered sugar while warm. Cool in pan; cut in squares. We love it for breakfast, but it's good as a quick dessert.
      Debbie Wootan

SOUR CREAM BANANA PECAN CAKE

Cake:

1/2 stick oleo
1 1/3 c. sugar
2 eggs
1 tsp. vanilla
2 c. sifted flour
  (plain)

1 tsp. baking powder
1 tsp. soda
3/4 tsp. salt
1 c. sour cream
1 c. ripe bananas, mashed
1/2 c. pecans, chopped

Cream butter and sugar; add eggs, one at a time. Add vanilla. Sift dry ingredients together and add to creamed mixture alternately with sour cream. Add bananas and pecans and mix well. Pour into greased and floured 13x9 inch pan; bake at 350° for 40 minutes.

Frosting:

1 1/2 sticks oleo
3/4 c. brown sugar, packed

6 Tbsp. evaporated milk
3 1/2 c. confectioners sugar
1 1/2 tsp. vanilla

Heat butter and brown sugar over low heat, stirring constantly until sugar melts; blend in milk. Cool. Gradually beat in confectioners sugar until spreading consistency. Add vanilla.

Eloise Bennett, Decatur Council

SPUD CAKE

2 c. sugar
1 c. butter
4 eggs
1 c. mashed potatoes
1 tsp. cinnamon
1 tsp. nutmeg
1 tsp. vanilla
1 tsp. lemon juice

1/2 c. chocolate (Hershey's cocoa)
2 c. all-purpose flour
2 tsp. baking powder
1 c. pecans, chopped
1 (16 oz.) jar cherries, halved
1/2 c. cherry juice
1 c. raisins, soaked in hot water or warm Bacardi rum

Separate eggs. Mix egg yolks and butter; add mashed potatoes. Sift sugar, cinnamon, nutmeg and add. Add and mix well vanilla and lemon juice. Sift chocolate, all-purpose flour, baking powder and mix well to previously mixed ingredients. Add pecans, cherries, cherry juice and raisins. Lastly, add stiffly beaten egg whites. Pour into well greased and floured Bundt pan; bake 45 minutes at 375°.

Z. T. Daniels, Birmingham Central Council

EASY STRAWBERRY CAKE

1 large box strawberry jello
1 large pkg. frozen strawberries, sliced

1 medium size Cool Whip
1 large angel food cake

Use pound cake pan. Tear 1/2 angel food cake into pieces. Put in cake pan. Mix jello with 2 cups hot water. Mix thawed strawberries with jello mixture. Pour 1/2 mixture over cake. Spread 1/2 Cool Whip on cake. Tear other 1/2 of cake into pieces. Pour remainder of jello mixture over cake. Refrigerate overnight. When ready to use, put cake pan into hot water a few seconds. This will loosen cake. Turn out on plate; top with remainder of Cool Whip.

Nila Swann, Birmingham Central Council

STRAWBERRY PECAN CAKE

1 box Duncan Hines
  white cake mix
1 small box strawberry jello
1 c. Wesson oil
1/2 c. milk

4 eggs
1 c. frozen strawberries
1 c. coconut (optional)
1 c. pecans

Icing:

1 stick margarine
1 box confectioners
  sugar

1/2 c. drained strawberries
1/2 c. pecans
1/2 c. coconut (optional)

Mix cake mix and jello together dry. Add oil, milk and eggs, one at a time. Use mixing instructions on back of cake mix box. Add remaining ingredients; bake in 3 layers at 350° for approximately 25-30 minutes or one 9x13 inch pan. Cool thoroughly before frosting. Cream sugar and butter and add other ingredients and spread on cake.

Ladon S. Young, Birmingham Central Council

SUGARPLUM LOAF

1 3/4 c. sugar
3/4 c. shortening
4 eggs
3/4 c. buttermilk
1 tsp. orange extract
1 Tbsp. lemon juice
1 (3 1/2 oz.) can
  flaked coconut

1 (8 oz.) pkg. chopped dates
1 c. chopped orange slice
  candy
1 1/2 c. chopped pecans
4 c. all-purpose flour
1 tsp. soda
Dash of salt
Glaze (recipe below)

Cream sugar, shortening and eggs until light and fluffy and stir in buttermilk, orange extract and lemon juice. Set aside. Combine coconut, dates, orange slice candy and pecans; set aside. Combine flour, soda and salt; sprinkle over fruit mixture, mixing well. Stir into creamed mixture. Line bottom of two 9x5x3 inch loaf pans with waxed paper; grease waxed paper and sides of pans. Spoon batter into pans; bake at 300° for 1·hour and 50 minutes or until done. Cool in pans 5 minutes. Punch holes in top of loaves with a toothpick. Remove from pans; drizzle glaze over top of loaves. Wrap tightly in foil to store. Yield: 2 loaves.

Glaze: Combine 1 cup powdered sugar, 2 to 3 tablespoons orange juice and 1/2 teaspoon orange extract, blending until smooth. Yield: About 1/2 cup.

Vinnie Mae Lyon, Birmingham Central Council

SWEET POTATO LOAF CAKE

1 1/2 c. sugar
1/2 c. vegetable oil
2 eggs
1/3 c. water
1 3/4 c. all-purpose flour
1 1/2 tsp. ground cinnamon
1 tsp. ground nutmeg
1 tsp. soda
1/2 tsp. salt
1 c. cooked, mashed
   sweet potatoes
1/2 c. chopped pecans
1/2 c. raisins

Combine sugar, oil, eggs and water; beat at medium speed of electric mixer just until combined. Combine next 5 ingredients; add to egg mixture, mixing just until moistened. Stir in sweet potatoes, pecans and raisins. Spoon batter into 2 greased and floured 1 pound coffee cans or loaf pans; bake at 350° for 1 hour or until a wooden pick inserted in center comes out clean. Let cool in cans 10 minutes; remove from cans to complete cooling. Yield: 2 loaves.

Mary M. Howell, Anniston Council

TOMATO SOUP CAKE

3/4 c. shortening
1 1/2 c. sugar
1 c. tomato soup
3/4 c. water
1 tsp. soda
3 c. flour
3/4 tsp. salt
3 tsp. baking powder
1 1/2 tsp. cinnamon
1 tsp. cloves
1 1/2 tsp. nutmeg
1 1/2 c. raisins
1 1/2 c. chopped nuts

Blend shortening and sugar. Combine tomato soup, water and soda. Add to first mixture the dry ingredients. Stir in raisins and nuts. Place in greased pan at 350° for 45 minutes.

Bonnie Summers, Huntsville Council

UGLY DUCKLING PUDDING CAKE

Cake:

1 pkg. (2 layer size)
   yellow cake mix
1 pkg. (4 oz. serving size)
   Jell-O lemon flavor instant
   pudding and pie filling
1 (16 oz.) can fruit
   cocktail, including syrup
1 c. Baker's Angel
   Flake coconut
4 eggs
1/4 c. oil
1/2 c. firmly packed
   brown sugar
1/2 c. chopped nuts (optional)

Blend all ingredients except brown sugar and nuts in

1567-82

large mixer bowl. Beat 4 minutes at medium speed of electric mixer. Pour into greased and floured 13x9 inch pan. Sprinkle with brown sugar and nuts; bake at 325° for 4 minutes or until cake pulls away from sides of pan. Do not underbake. Cool in pan 15 minutes. Spoon hot Butter Glaze over warm cake. Serve warm or cool with prepared Dream Whip whipped topping, if desired.

Butter Glaze: Combine 1/2 cup each butter or margarine, granulated sugar and evaporated milk in saucepan; boil 2 minutes. Stir in 1 1/3 cups Baker's Angel Flake coconut.

Daisy M. Singleton, Jasper Club

UNCOMMONLY GOOD CAKE

In large mixing bowl, mix:

1 pkg. yellow cake mix   1/2 c. melted butter
   (not pudding)   2 eggs
1 c. peanut butter

Stir until dough holds together; press in bottom of ungreased 9x13 inch pan, reserving 1/3 of dough. In heavy saucepan combine:

1 (12 oz.) pkg. semi-sweet   1 (15 oz.) can condensed milk
   chocolate chips   2 Tbsp. butter
                      1/2 tsp. salt

Melt over low heat, stirring constantly. Remove from heat and add:

1 c. flaked coconut   2 tsp. vanilla
1 c. chopped pecans

Spread over dough. Crumble remaining 1/3 dough on top; press lightly. Bake at 325° for 20-25 minutes until brown.

Mrs. Buddy Gulledge, Anniston Council

UPSIDE DOWN PEAR CAKE

1 (1 lb.) can pear halves   1 tsp. nutmeg
1/4 c. melted butter   4 eggs
1/4 c. sugar   1 pkg. white cake mix
12 pecan halves   1 (3 oz.) pkg. lemon or
10 cherry halves   lime flavored gelatin
3/4 c. vegetable oil   1 tsp. lemon extract

Heat oven to 350° F. Drain pears and reserve 3/4 cup of the pear syrup. Pour melted butter in bottom of

3/4 x 9 x 2 inch cake pan. Combine sugar, nutmeg and sprinkle over butter. Arrange pecans and cherries over bottom of pan. Combine cake mix, gelatin, oil, the 3/4 cup pear syrup, eggs and lemon extract in a large bowl. Beat 4 minutes at medium speed. Pour batter carefully over pears in pan; bake 55 minutes or until cake pulls away from edge of pan. Let cool about 5 minutes and turn out onto a serving tray.

Maggie Sivley, Decatur Council

VANILLA WAFER CAKE

2 sticks margarine
2 c. sugar
1 (12 oz.) box vanilla
  wafers, crushed
6 eggs
1/2 c. milk
1 Tbsp. vanilla
2 pkg. frozen coconut
2 c. pecans, chopped

Cream margarine and sugar; add 1 egg at a time. Add crushed vanilla wafers, alternating with milk. Add pecans and coconut. Bake in tube pan 1 1/2 hours at 325°.

P.S. Always do what is right. This will gratify some people and astonish the rest.

Barbara Spivey, Mobile Council

WATERGATE CAKE

1 pkg. white cake mix
1 pkg. instant pistachio
  pudding
1 c. Crisco oil
1 c. club soda
3 eggs
1/2 c. nuts, added after
  first 5 ingredients

Mix well at medium speed. Pour into greased, floured 9 inch pans (two). Bake 40-50 minutes at 325°.

Frosting:

1 (9 oz.) container
  Cool Whip
1 pkg. instant pistachio
  pudding
1 medium can crushed
  pineapple and juice
1 c. miniature marshmallows
1/2 c. nuts

Mix. Frost cake. Refrigerate.

Bertha Capps, Birmingham East Council

WINE CAKE

1 box Duncan Hines
  yellow cake mix
1 box instant vanilla
  pudding mix

3/4 c. Wesson oil
1 tsp. nutmeg
4 eggs (room temperature)
3/4 c. blackberry wine

Preheat oven to 375°. Grease a Bundt or 10 inch tube pan. In large mixing bowl put all ingredients and beat on medium speed for 4 minutes; bake for 45 minutes. Glaze cake while still warm.

Glaze:

1/4 tsp. nutmeg
1 c. confectioners sugar

1 Tbsp. butter
Few Tbsp. wine

Drizzle glaze over cake while still warm.
Margie Lavender, Riverchase Council

YELLOW LOAF CAKE

2 c. sugar
1 c. shortening
6 eggs
1/2 tsp. salt

2 c. flour
1/4 tsp. nutmeg
1 tsp. lemon extract

Mix sugar, shortening, 4 eggs and salt; beat with mixer for approximately 2 or 3 minutes. Add flour and 2 eggs. Beat additional 2 minutes; add nutmeg and extract. Pour in tube pan that has been greased and floured. The batter will be thick. Cook in 325° oven for 1 hour and 10 minutes or until cake tester comes out clean. Cake will have a good crust. Cool 10 or 15 minutes before removing from pan.

Maggie McCullough

ZUCCHINI CAKE

3 eggs
2 c. sugar
1 c. oil
2 c. coarsely grated
  zucchini
2 c. flour
1 tsp. baking powder

1 tsp. baking soda
1 tsp. salt
3 tsp. vanilla
1 tsp. cinnamon
1 c. nuts
1 c. raisins

Beat eggs; add sugar, oil and vanilla and salt. Sift dry ingredients together; add zucchini, nuts and raisins. Bake at 350° about 1 hour.
Bonnie Summers, Huntsville Council

174

CAKE FROSTING

3 boxes powdered sugar
  (add 1 box at a time)
1 1/2 c. Crisco shortening
3/4 c. cold water

1 tsp. clear vanilla
  (Liberty and Food World -
  imitation vanilla)
1 dash of salt

(Add 1 teaspoon white vinegar or 1 teaspoon lemon juice if too sweet.) Mix in mixer 3-4 minutes. May need to add teaspoon of water. (Will keep on shelf 3-4 weeks.)

Mary C. Martin, Birmingham East Council

CARAMEL ICING

2 c. sugar
1/2 c. sugar
1 Tbsp. flour

1 stick margarine
1 small can evaporated milk

Brown 1/2 cup sugar in iron skillet. While this is browning, add all other ingredients in a thick cooker and bring to boil. Mix browned sugar and let it all cook together 2 minutes. Remove from heat and beat till ready to put on cake. (Good on yellow or spice cake.) Try it. Very easy and good.

Doris Holder, Decatur Council

CHOCOLATE CAKE ICING

1 stick butter or margarine
4 Tbsp. cocoa
6 Tbsp. buttermilk

1 box powdered sugar
1 tsp. vanilla
1 c. chopped pecans

1. Melt butter. 2. Stir in 4 tablespoons cocoa and add all the buttermilk. 3. Bring to a rapid boil. 4. Add 1 box powdered sugar. 5. Add teaspoon of vanilla. 6. Add chopped pecans. 7. Stir thoroughly and spread over cake while icing is still hot.

Barbara S. Mason

CHOCOLATE ICING

2 c. sugar
3 Tbsp. cocoa
1 stick butter

1 small can Carnation milk
1 tsp. vanilla

Mix all ingredients except vanilla. Cook 3 minutes; remove from heat and add vanilla. Cool. For fudge candy, cook 5 minutes.

Earline Thornton, Tuscaloosa Pioneer Unit

1567-82

CHOCOLATE ICING

1 c. sugar
1 heaping Tbsp. cocoa
Dash of salt
1/2 c. milk

1/2 tsp. vanilla
1/2 stick margarine
Confectioners sugar

In saucepan mix first 3 ingredients together; add margarine and milk. Boil briskly for 3 minutes. Add vanilla. Let cool, then add enough confectioners sugar to spread.

Janice Bass, Riverchase Council

COCONUT FROSTING

1 (8 oz.) carton sour cream
1 1/2 or 2 c. sugar

12 oz. coconut (2 packs frozen coconut)

Margie Judge, Mobile Council

CREAM CHEESE CAKE FROSTING

1 pkg. cream cheese
1 box powdered sugar

1 stick butter
1 1/2 c. pecans

Mix cream cheese, powdered sugar and butter, then add pecans.

Margie Judge, Mobile Council

FLUFFY CUSTARD FROSTING
(Frosting for Favorite Cake)

2 Tbsp. flour
3/4 c. milk
3/4 c. butter

3/4 c. sugar
1/8 tsp. salt
1 tsp. vanilla

In a saucepan add a small amount of milk to flour. Stir, making a smooth paste. Add remaining milk; cook over medium heat, stirring constantly, until mixture boils and thickens. Cool. Cream butter, using medium speed of mixer. Gradually add sugar and salt; beat well. Add cooled milk mixture. Whip until light and fluffy. Add vanilla.

Ruby Tolbert, Montgomery Council

FUDGE FROSTING

1/2 c. shortening
2 c. sugar
3 oz. unsweetened chocolate

2/3 c. sweet milk
1/2 tsp. salt
2 tsp. vanilla

Mix all ingredients except vanilla in boiler; heat to rolling boil. Stir occasionally. Boil 1 minute without stirring. Place pan of frosting in bowl of ice water; beat until smooth and spreading consistency. Stir in vanilla.

Elizabeth Cornwell, Birmingham Central Council

1-2-3 FUDGE SAUCE

1 medium can Carnation
   milk
1 tsp. vanilla

2 c. sugar
6 Tbsp. cocoa

Mix and bring to a boil; boil for 5 minutes. Remove from heat. Serve over cake or ice cream.

Barbara Roper, Huntsville Council

HONEY-CREAM CHEESE FROSTING

1 (3 oz.) pkg. cream cheese
1 Tbsp. honey

2 1/2 c. sifted
   confectioners sugar

Blend cream cheese with honey; gradually add sugar and beat well until smooth. Frost when cake cools.

Bobby Blair, Birmingham East Council

HOT FUDGE CAKE SAUCE

12 oz. (2 c.) semi-sweet
   chocolate pieces
12 oz. evaporated milk

1 1/2 pt. marshmallow
   cream
2 Tbsp. cocoa

In double boiler combine chocolate pieces and milk, stirring to blend. Add cocoa; blend well. Beat in marshmallow cream until blended. Keep sauce hot in double boiler until ready to serve. To serve, take 1 piece of cake and place in serving bowl. Place a square of vanilla ice cream on top of cake. Place another piece of cake on top of ice cream. Spoon hot fudge sauce over top of cake; top with whipped cream and complete with a cherry.

Auretha Karrh, Decatur Council

LEMON CHEESE FILLING

4 layer cake:

6 egg yolks
1 1/2 c. sugar
4 Tbsp. flour
3/4 c. soft oleo
Juice of 2 lemons
1 large can crushed
    pineapple including juice

2 layer cake:

2 egg yolks and 1 whole egg
1 c. sugar
3 Tbsp. flour
1/2 c. (1 stick) oleo
Juice of 1 lemon
1 small can crushed
    pineapple including juice

Mix all ingredients in boiler and cook until thick (not very long). Spread between layers of cake. Can be used as icing, but does not get hard.

Mary Norris, Birmingham Central Council

LIGHT BUTTER CREAM FROSTING

1 1/2 c. margarine
1 3/4 c. shortening
    (Crisco)
4 lb. powdered sugar
3/4 tsp. salt
7 Tbsp. nonfat dry milk
3/4 c. water
2 Tbsp. vanilla

Cream margarine and shortening at medium speed until soft and creamy. Add powdered sugar, salt and nonfat dry milk to creamed mixture. Combine water and vanilla; add slowly to creamed mixture. While beating at slow speed; beat until moisture is absorbed. Scrape down bowl; beat at medium speed 3-5 minutes.

Mary C. Martin, Birmingham East Council

MILK CHOCOLATE FROSTING

1 1/2 c. sugar
1 c. evaporated milk,
    undiluted
1/2 c. melted butter
    or margarine
1 (6 oz.) pkg. semi-sweet
    chocolate pieces
1 c. marshmallow cream
2 Tbsp. milk

Combine sugar, evaporated milk and butter in a heavy saucepan; cook over medium heat until mixture reaches soft ball stage (237°). Remove from heat; add chocolate pieces and marshmallow cream, stirring until melted. Add milk and stir until smooth. Yield: Frosting for one 10 inch cake.

Opal Moffitt, Tuscaloosa Pioneer Unit

PARTY CAKE ICING

1/3 c. water
1 1/2 lb. powdered
  confectioners sugar

1 c. Crisco
1/4 tsp. vanilla extract

Beat ingredients until smooth; add desired food coloring to any amount of mixture for decorating. Double recipe if large cake.

Wanda Kanaday, Mobile Council

PEANUT BUTTER ICING

2 c. sugar
1/2 c. peanut butter
2/3 c. sweet milk

1/2 c. shortening
2 tsp. vanilla

Combine sugar and peanut butter; add melted shortening and milk. Boil 2 minutes, stirring constantly. Remove from heat; add vanilla and beat until creamy. If too thick, add a little milk.

Anniston's Sots, Anniston Council

QUICK CHOCOLATE ICING

1/4 c. milk
1/4 c. cocoa

1/4 stick oleo
1 c. sugar

Mix all above ingredients in a heavy saucepan; boil 1 minute. Remove from heat and beat to spreading consistency. Add 1 teaspoon vanilla while beating. Especially delicious on yellow sheet cake. This recipe does better if used on sheet cakes.

Jim Chaffin, Tuscaloosa Council

QUICK TRICK FUDGE SAUCE

1 c. Hershey's instant
  cocoa mix

1/3 c. boiling water
1 Tbsp. butter or margarine

Blend instant cocoa mix, water and butter. Serve over ice cream, puddings or cake-type desserts. Yield: 3/4 cup sauce.

Barbara Roper, Huntsville Council

7 MINUTE ICING (WHITE)

3/4 c. sugar
1/3 c. white Karo
1/4 tsp. cream of tartar
1/4 tsp. salt
2 Tbsp. water
2 egg whites

Mix all ingredients in top of double boiler. Beat with electric mixer for 7 minutes. Recipe may be doubled.
Louise Willoughby, Tuscaloosa Council

SEVEN MINUTE ICING

1 1/2 c. sugar
5 Tbsp. cold water
1 Tbsp. syrup
Dash of salt
2 egg whites
1 c. small marshmallows
1 tsp. vanilla

Mix all ingredients and cook in a double boiler, beating with electric mixer until it stands in peak. Add vanilla and spread on cake.
Lemmie Cochran, Montgomery Council

WHITE MIRACLE FILLING

1 c. milk
1/2 c. flour
Pinch of salt
1 c. sugar
1 c. shortening
1 Tbsp. vanilla

Cook flour, milk and salt until thick; cool. Beat sugar, shortening and vanilla until fluffy. Add cooled first mixture to sugar and shortening. Beat until very fluffy. Spread between layers of cake and use your favorite icing on top.
Mary Norris, Birmingham Central Council

WHITE CREAMY ICING

1 box + 2 c. powdered
   sugar
1 tsp. white vanilla
   flavoring
1/4 tsp. salt
1 c. shortening
1/3 c. hot (tap) water

Blend first 4 ingredients; add hot water slowly until desired consistency. Beat 5 to 10 minutes. Good to use when decorating a cake.
Mary Norris, Birmingham Central Council

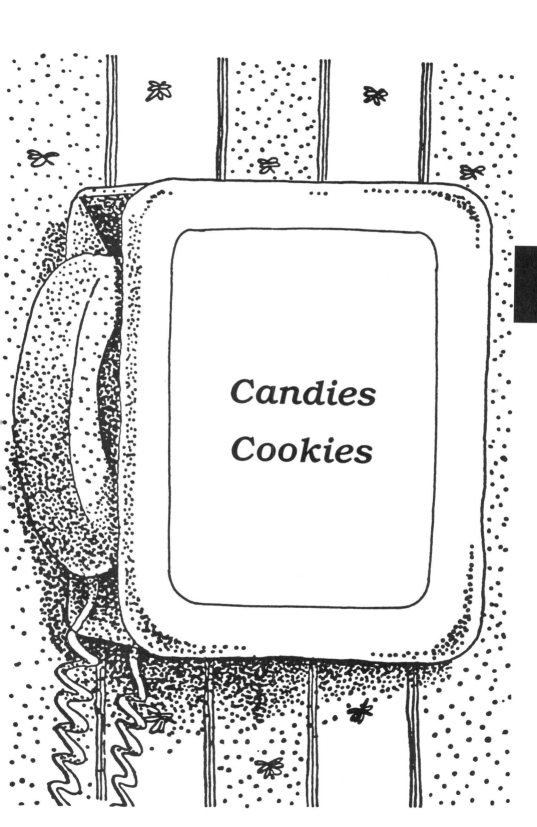

Candies

Cookies

CANDY CHART

PRODUCT	TEST IN COLD WATER*	DEGREES F. ON CANDY THERMOMETER			
		SEA LEVEL	2000 FEET	5000 FEET	7500 FEET
FUDGE PENUCHE AND FONDANT	SOFT BALL (can be picked up but flattens)	234° to 240°	230° to 236°	224° to 230°	219° to 225°
CARAMELS	HARD BALL (holds shape unless pressed)	232° to 248°	238° to 244°	232° to 238°	227° to 233°
DIVINITY, TAFFY AND CARAMEL CORN	HARD BALL (holds shape though pliable)	250° to 268°	246° to 264°	240° to 258°	235° to 253°
BUTTERSCOTCH AND ENGLISH TOFFEE	SOFT CRACK (separates into hard threads but not brittle)	270° to 290°	266° to 286°	260° to 280°	255° to 275°
BRITTLES	HARD CRACK (separates into hard and brittle threads)	300° to 310°	296° to 306°	290° to 300°	285° to 295°

* Drop about 1/2 teaspoon of boiling syrup into one cup water, and test firmness of mass with fingers.

CAN SIZE CHART

Can Size	Can Number	Cups
8 ounces		1
10 1/2 ounces		1 1/4
12 ounces		1 1/2
14 - 16 ounces	300	1 3/4
16 - 17	303	2
20 ounces	2	2 1/2
29 ounces	2 1/2	3 1/2
46 ounces		5 3/4
6 1/2 to 7 1/2 pounds	10	12 - 13

CANDIES, COOKIES

BUCKEYE BALLS

1 1/2 c. creamy peanut
  butter
1/2 c. lightly salted butter
  or margarine (at room
  temperature)
1 tsp. vanilla extract

1 (16 oz.) pkg. confectioners
  sugar
1 (6 oz.) pkg. semi-sweet
  chocolate pieces
1 Tbsp. solid vegetable
  shortening

Line baking sheet with wax paper. In a medium sized bowl mix peanut butter, vanilla, butter and sugar with hands to form a smooth dough. Mixture will be very stiff. Shape dough into balls using 2 teaspoons for each. Place on wax paper and put in refrigerator. In the top of a double boiler over simmering, not boiling, water, melt chocolate and shortening together. When smooth, pour into a small bowl or measuring cup. Remove peanut butter balls from refrigerator. Insert a wooden toothpick into ball and dip into melted chocolate so that 3/4 of ball is covered. Return to wax paper, chocolate side down, and remove pick. Repeat with all balls. Refrigerate on wax paper 30 minutes or longer, until chocolate is firm, not sticky. To store, remove balls from wax paper and place in plastic containers, with wax paper between layer. Makes about 5 dozen candies, 89 calories each.

Mary Ann Davis, Anniston Council

BUTTER CREAMS

1/2 c. butter, softened
1 (1 lb.) pkg. powdered
  sugar, sifted
2 Tbsp. milk

1 tsp. vanilla extract
1/4 tsp. salt
4 (1 oz.) squares
  unsweetened chocolate
1 Tbsp. melted paraffin

Cream butter; gradually add sugar, beating well. Stir in milk, vanilla and salt. Chill mixture overnight or until firm. Shape into 3/4 inch balls. Combine chocolate and paraffin in top of a double boiler. Place over hot water, stirring until chocolate is melted. Using 2 forks, quickly dip each ball of candy into chocolate mixture. Place on waxed paper and refrigerate until chocolate is firm. Yield: About 5 dozen.

Jean Cater, Birmingham South Council

BUTTERSCOTCH CANDY

3/4 c. chow mein noodles
3/4 c. chopped pecans, roasted

2 (6 oz.) pkg. butterscotch morsels

Melt butterscotch morsels over 2 cups water in double boiler. Do not boil water. After melted, add noodles and pecans.

Dian Cornelson, Mobile Council

BUTTERSCOTCH LOG

1 (6 oz.) pkg. Nestle's butterscotch flavored morsels

1/3 c. sweetened condensed milk
1/2 tsp. vanilla
1/3 c. chopped pecans

Melt over hot (not boiling) water one 6 ounce package (1 cup) Nestle's butterscotch flavored morsels. Remove from water; stir in 1/3 cup sweetened condensed milk, 1/2 teaspoon vanilla. Add 1/3 cup chopped pecans; chill till firm enough to handle. Form into 12 inch roll on waxed paper. Roll tightly in waxed paper to shape evenly. Unroll and mark surface lengthwise with tines of fork; brush with slightly beaten egg white. Press pecan halves into roll to completely cover surface. Wrap in waxed paper; chill. Cut in 1/2 inch slices with sharp knife. Makes about 2 dozen.

Lera Lee, Tuscaloosa Council

CARAMEL CANDY

3 c. sugar
1 c. sweet milk
Pinch of soda

1/2 stick oleo
1 c. nuts
1 tsp. vanilla

Caramelize 1 cup sugar in heavy iron skillet; bring to boil in another heavy saucepan sugar, milk and pinch of soda. Add slowly the caramelized sugar and bring to the soft boil stage. Remove from heat and beat to thick consistency. Add nuts and pour into buttered platter. Let cool and cut into squares.

Jim Chaffin, Tuscaloosa Council

CHOCOLATE COVERED CHERRIES

6 Tbsp. butter, softened
2 1/2 c. sifted powdered
   sugar
1 1/2 tsp. milk
1/4 tsp. vanilla extract

About 48 maraschino cherries
   with stems
1 (12 oz.) pkg. semi-sweet
   chocolate morsels
1 Tbsp. shortening

Cream butter; gradually add sugar, beating well. Blend in milk and vanilla. Chill mixture for 2 hours or until firm. Drain cherries; dry on absorbent paper towels. Place bowl of sugar mixture in a bowl of ice to keep mixture chilled. Shape a small amount of sugar mixture around each cherry. Place on waxed paper lined cookie sheet; chill about 2 hours or until firm. Melt chocolate and shortening in top of double boiler. Dip each cherry by the stem into chocolate. Place on a waxed paper lined cookie sheet; chill until firm. Store cherries in a cool place. Yield: About 4 dozen.

Betty Chilton, Birmingham East Council

CHOCOLATE CREAM STICKS

3 oz. unsweetened
   chocolate
3/4 c. butter
1 1/2 c. sugar

3 eggs
3/4 c. plain flour
3/4 c. pecans, chopped

Preheat oven to 350°. Melt chocolate and butter over low heat; add other ingredients, blending well. Spread evenly in a greased and floured 9x13 inch pan; bake 20 minutes. Cool completely.

6 Tbsp. butter, softened
3 c. confectioners sugar

3 Tbsp. milk
1/2 tsp. vanilla extract

Mix. Spread evenly and chill. Top with 4 ounces semi-sweet chocolate and 4 tablespoons butter. Melt together and spread on top. Refrigerate until firm. Cut into finger-like sticks. Keep refrigerated. Yield: Approximately 4 dozen.

Margie Lavender, Riverchase Council

CHOCOLATE COATED COCONUT BALLS

2 boxes confectioners sugar
1 large pkg. coconut
1 can Eagle Brand milk

1 stick oleo
1-4 c. chopped pecans

Coating:

1 pkg. chocolate chips
1567-82

1 stick paraffin

Oleo should be at room temperature. Add milk, coconut and nuts. Mix well with hands and roll in small balls. Put on cookie sheet and let set for few hours.

Coating: Put paraffin in double boiler. When melted, add chocolate chips. When all is melted, leave on fire on low heat in double boiler. Stick toothpicks in coconut balls and dip in chocolate. Put on wax paper. After setting a couple of hours, put in glass gallon jar and keep in cool place. Makes over a hundred balls.

Elsie Thrasher

CHOCOLATE PEANUT BUTTER BALLS

2 sticks butter
1 c. crunchy peanut butter
1 box confectioners sugar
2 c. graham cracker crumbs

1 c. coconut
1 c. chopped nuts
1 pkg. chocolate bits
1/4 stick paraffin (1 oz.)

Melt butter; add peanut butter and sugar. Blend well. Add remaining ingredients and mix. Roll in balls. Melt chocolate and paraffin; dip balls in this, then put on rack to cool.

Lera Lee, Tuscaloosa Council

CHOCOLATE COVERED PEANUTS

2 c. salted Spanish
  peanuts
1 (6 oz.) pkg.
  chocolate morsels

1 (6 oz.) pkg. butterscotch
  morsels
2 Tbsp. peanut butter

Melt peanut butter, chocolate and butterscotch in a large pan; add peanuts and stir well. Drop onto wax paper and refrigerate.

Kaye Campbell, Birmingham South Council

CHRISTMAS FRUIT FANCIES

3 c. granulated sugar
1 c. white corn syrup
1 1/2 c. coffee cream
1 tsp. vanilla
1 c. Brazil nuts

1 c. whole pecans
1 c. walnuts, broken
1 c. candied cherries,
  cut in halves
1 c. candied pineapple

Cook sugar, syrup and cream to soft ball stage; remove from range. Beat until thick (color will change slightly). Continue beating. Add 1 teaspoon vanilla. Slowly add nuts, cherries and pineapple. Mixture will be thick and sticky.

184

Pack into loaf pan and chill. After a few hours, the sticky syrup becomes firm and creamy. Store 24 hours. Slice 1/2 inch thick. Cut each slice in finger lengths. Will keep for months.

Marcella James, Tri-Cities Council

CRUNCHIES (MICROWAVE STYLE)

1 (6 oz.) pkg. butterscotch   1/4 c. peanut butter
  morsels   3 1/4 c. corn flakes

Melt butterscotch morsels on 70% power for 2-4 minutes. Mix ingredients together; spoon out on wax paper to cool and harden.

Dina Johnson, Birmingham South Council

CORN FLAKE KISSES

2 egg whites   1/2 c. peanuts or walnuts
1/4 tsp. salt   1 1/2 c. crisp corn flakes
2/3 c. sugar

Beat egg whites and salt until just stiff enough to hold moist peaks. Add sugar gradually at about 1 heaping tablespoon at a time. Continue to beat after each addition until whites are very stiff. Mix in peanuts using a fork, then fold in corn flakes. Drop by teaspoonfuls onto an ungreased unglazed brown paper on cookie sheet. Bake in slow oven (300°) for 30 minutes. Remove from paper to cake racks immediately. Makes about 3 dozen kisses.

Candy Harp

DATE BALLS

2 c. Rice Krispies   2 pkg. chopped dates
1 stick oleo   1 c. chopped pecans
2 c. confectioners sugar

Put the stick of oleo in a pan over medium heat and then add the dates and stir in and remove the pan from the stove; add pecans and Rice Krispies. Roll the dates into 1 inch balls, then roll it into a separate bowl with the confectioners sugar.

Deborah Hyatt, Riverchase Council, Hazel Campbell, Birmingham South Council, Joan Sims, Birmingham South Council

1567-82

DATE NUT CANDY

2 c. sugar
1 c. dates
2 Tbsp. butter

1 c. evaporated milk
1 c. nuts

Boil sugar and milk until forms soft ball in cold water. Add dates and nuts and butter. Boil until candy cooks away from sides of pan. Beat until stiff enough to roll. Put on a cold damp cloth; roll into roll and refrigerate.

Peggy Blevins, Anniston Council

DIVINITY CANDY

5 c. sugar
1 c. light corn syrup
1 c. water

2 tsp. vanilla
4 egg whites
3 c. chopped nuts

Combine light corn syrup, water and sugar. Boil to 265° (hard ball stage). Beat egg whites stiff and gradually beat in boiling syrup. Whip until it begins to stiffen. Add vanilla and nuts; drop on wax paper. Makes about 150 pieces.

P.S. A generation ago when a person finished a day's work he needed rest, now they need exercise.

Janet Everett, Mobile Council

DIVINITY FUDGE

2 c. sugar
1/2 c. corn syrup
1/2 c. water
3/4 c. candied cherries

2 egg whites
3/4 c. blanched almonds
1 Tbsp. almond or lemon
   extract

Put the sugar, water and corn syrup into a saucepan; stir the mixture over the heat and let boil without stirring to the light crack stage (265°). While it is cooking, beat the whites of eggs stiffly, and when the syrup is ready, pour it over them, beating constantly. Beat until creamy; add nuts, cherries and extract. Pour into buttered pans.

Bettye Ferguson, Huntsville Council

CHOCOLATE DIVINITY

5 c. granulated sugar
1 c. light corn syrup
1 c. water
1/2 tsp. salt
4 egg whites

2 tsp. vanilla
4 squares (4 oz.) unsweetened
  chocolate, melted
1/2 c. chopped nuts

In a 3 quart saucepan combine sugar, corn syrup, water and salt. Cook, stirring constantly, until sugar dissolves. Continue cooking over medium heat without stirring to hard ball stage (260°). Meanwhile, in large bowl, beat egg whites until stiff peaks form. Gradually pour syrup over egg whites, beating at high speed. Add vanilla and beat until candy begins to hold shape (5 to 6 minutes). Beat in chocolate; beat 2 to 3 minutes if necessary. (Note: Watch it carefully; it gets hard all of a sudden.) Pour into buttered 15 x 10 1/2 inch pan. Spread evenly and top with nuts. Cut in squares when firm. Yield: About 36 pieces.

Grace Davis, Mobile Council

FRUIT CHEWS

1 c. sugar
2 eggs
1/4 c. soft butter
1 c. Bisquick

1 c. chopped dates
1 c. chopped maraschino
  cherries
1 c. chopped nuts

Mix sugar, eggs and butter; add Bisquick. Fold in dates, cherries and nuts. Put into well greased pan; bake at 350° for 30 minutes. Cool for 10 minutes. Remove from pan easily as cookies are very tender. Sprinkle with powdered sugar.

Betty Lancaster, Birmingham South Council

FRUIT ROCKS

2 1/2 qt. pecans, chopped
1 1/2 lb. candied
  cherries (whole)
1 lb. candied pineapple,
  chopped
1/2 lb. butter
1 c. sugar

2 1/2 c. flour
5 eggs
1/2 tsp. each cloves,
  allspice, cinnamon, nutmeg
1/2 c. wine
1 Tbsp. syrup

Cream butter and sugar; add eggs and flour (to which spices have been added) alternately with wine and syrup. Add fruit and nuts which have been floured with additional flour (about 2 1/2 cups). Refrigerate overnight. Drop by teaspoon on greased baking sheet; bake at 350° until light brown. Mixture will keep in refrigerator several days before baking.

Jo Ann Williams, Birmingham West Council

2-MINUTE FUDGE

Power level: High. Microwave time: 2 minutes total.

1 box confectioners
  sugar
1/2 c. cocoa
1/4 tsp. salt

1/4 c. milk
1 Tbsp. vanilla extract
1/2 c. (1/4 lb.) butter
1 c. chopped nuts

In 1 1/2 quart casserole stir sugar, cocoa, salt, milk and vanilla together until partially blended (mixture is too stiff to thoroughly blend in all dry ingredients). Put butter over top in center of dish. Microwave at high 2 minutes, or until milk feels warm on bottom of dish. Stir vigorously until smooth. If all butter has not melted in cooking, it will as mixture is stirred. Blend in nuts; pour into wax paper lined 8x4x3 inch dish. Chill 1 hour in refrigerator or 20 to 30 minutes in freezer. Cut into squares. Makes about 36 squares.

Mary C. Martin, Birmingham Central Council

FUDGE NUGGETS

2 c. sugar
1 c. Pet milk
1/2 c. oleo
2 (6 oz.) pkg.
  chocolate chips

3/4 c. plain flour
1 c. graham cracker
  crumbs
1 tsp. vanilla
1 c. nuts

In saucepan add sugar, cream and oleo. Bring all three of these to a full rolling boil; boil for 10 minutes, stirring now and then. Remove from heat. Blend well the chocolate chips and flour and graham cracker crumbs and nuts, to the above cream, sugar and oleo mixture; add vanilla. Pour into buttered platter and let cool before cutting.

Jim Chaffin, Tuscaloosa Council

GRANDMA'S CHOCOLATE CANDY

3 c. sugar
4 Tbsp. cocoa
1 c. milk

1 Tbsp. butter or margarine
1 tsp. vanilla flavoring
1 1/2 c. crunchy peanut
   butter

(The more milk you put in, the longer it has to be boiled.)

(Option: Instead of peanut butter, you can use chopped pecans.)

Mix sugar, cocoa and milk together and bring to a boil. Mixture is done when it is dropped into water and it makes a ball. When mixture is done, take off heat and stir in vanilla and then the peanut butter. Stir until peanut butter is blended into mixture. Let cool about 8 to 10 minutes and then drop with tablespoon onto wax paper. Let it stand until completely cooled. Makes 24.

Brenda P. Bearden, Riverchase Council

RAYMOND'S CHRISTMAS FUDGE
(Brazil Nut Fudge)

4 1/2 c. sugar
1 large can evaporated milk
3 (5 oz.) plain chocolate
   bars
2 (6 oz.) pkg. semi-sweet
   chocolate bits

1 1/2 tsp. salt
1 (8 oz.) jar marshmallow whip
1 c. Brazil nut pieces
1 tsp. vanilla

Bring sugar and milk together to boiling point; cook over medium heat 4 1/2 minutes (clock), stirring occasionally. Break chocolate bars into pieces; mix with semi-sweet pieces, marshmallow whip and salt in large bowl. Pour hot sugar and milk mixture over, 1/2 at a time, mixing thoroughly after each addition. Let stand until cool; add nuts and vanilla and pour in large buttered pan (about 8x12 inches). Cool in refrigerator and cut into pieces. Makes lots and keeps beautifully.

Raymond Gudgen, Birmingham South Council

CHOCOLATE CANDY

5 c. sugar
1 large can Pet
   evaporated milk
2 sticks butter

1 large pkg. chocolate chips
1 tsp. vanilla flavoring
1 jar marshmallow cream
Nuts (optional)

1567-82

Combine sugar, evaporated milk and butter; bring to a boil over medium heat. Use a heavy metal pot if possible. Leave heat setting at medium and continue to cook for 10 minutes. Remove from heat and add chocolate chips, marshmallow cream and vanilla flavoring; stir until smooth and creamy. Pour into large buttered pan to cool. Nuts may be added or placed on top.

Betty W. Sanders, President,
Birmingham Central Council

BUTTERMILK FUDGE

2 c. buttermilk	2 tsp. baking soda
1 c. butter (do not	4 c. sugar
substitute margarine)	2 c. chopped pecans
4 Tbsp. light Karo syrup	2 Tbsp. vanilla

Put first 5 ingredients in large pot (4-6 quarts). Place on low heat, stirring until sugar is melted. Cook to 236° F. on candy thermometer, or until forms soft ball when dropped in cold water. Remove from heat and cool to lukewarm. Beat until mixture begins to thicken and loses its gloss. Quickly pour into buttered dish, approximately 12x14 inches. Cut into squares when firm, but still warm. Makes approximately 3 pounds.

Mamie E. Smith, Mobile Council

TWO FLAVOR FUDGE

2 c. light brown sugar	1 (16 oz.) pkg. Nestle's
1 c. sugar	butterscotch morsels
1 c. evaporated milk	1 (16 oz.) Nestle's semi-
1/2 c. butter or oleo	sweet chocolate morsels
1 jar marshmallow cream	1 c. chopped walnuts or pecans
	1 tsp. vanilla

Combine in saucepan brown sugar, evaporated milk and butter or oleo; bring to full boil over moderate heat, stirring occasionally. Boil for 10 minutes; remove from heat and add marshmallow cream, butterscotch morsels, semi-sweet chocolate morsels. Stir until smooth; blend in chopped walnuts or pecans and vanilla. Pour into 9 inch greased pan.

Lera Lee, Tuscaloosa Council

DOUBLE FUDGE FANCIFILLS

Filling:

1 (8 oz.) pkg. cream cheese, softened	1 Tbsp. cornstarch
	1 egg
2 Tbsp. margarine or butter	2 Tbsp. milk
1/4 c. sugar	1/2 tsp. vanilla

Base:

1 pkg. devils food cake mix (with pudding in mix)	3 eggs
	1/3 c. oil
	1 c. water

Heat oven to 350° F. Grease and flour 13x9 inch pan. In small bowl blend all filling ingredients; beat at highest speed until smooth and creamy. Set aside. In large bowl blend cake mix, eggs, oil and water until moistened. Beat 2 minutes at highest speed. Pour half of batter into pan. Pour cream cheese mixture over batter, spreading to cover. Pour remaining batter over cream cheese mixture; bake at 350° for 45 to 55 minutes. Cool completely. Frost with fudge frosting.

Donna Campbell, Anniston Council

MARY BALL FUDGE

1 large can Pet milk	1/2 lb. butter
5 c. sugar	2 c. nuts
3 pkg. chocolate bits	1 jar marshmallow cream
	Vanilla to taste

Mix sugar and milk together; bring to boil and boil exactly 9 minutes. Remove from heat; stir in chocolate bits, butter and marshmallow cream. Stir until melted and mix well. Add vanilla and nuts. Yield: About 5 pounds.

Helen Gorff, Birmingham West Council

PEANUT BUTTER FUDGE

2 c. sugar	3 Tbsp. white Karo
1/2 c. milk	1/2 c. peanut butter
1/4 stick margarine	1 tsp. vanilla

Cook sugar, milk, margarine and syrup until it forms a soft ball in cold water; remove from heat and add peanut butter and vanilla. Beat until creamy. Pour on buttered pan; let set until firm before cutting into squares.

Glenda Whitcomb, Birmingham East Council

PEANUT BUTTER FUDGE

1 stick margarine
2 (1 lb.) boxes
  confectioners sugar
1 (1 lb.) jar peanut butter

1 tsp. vanilla flavoring
1 jar marshmallow creme
1 large can Pet milk
Optional: 1 c. chopped pecans

Melt butter; add Pet milk and gradually stir in both boxes sugar. Cook until a small ball forms when dropped into a cup of cold water; remove from heat. Add remaining ingredients; stir until well mixed and pour into square dish. Cut into squares. Add nuts, if desired.

Sonja Martin, Anniston Council

HAYSTACKS
(Sometimes referred to as Grasshoppers)

1 bag butterscotch morsels   1 can chow mein noodles

Melt butterscotch morsels in top of double boiler. Mix in noodles to a good consistency. Drop by spoonfuls onto wax paper and cool.

Redonna G. Leckie, Birmingham West Council

HEAVENLY DELIGHT

1 c. white corn syrup
1 1/2 lb. candied pineapple
1/2 lb. chopped pecans
1/2 lb. chopped Brazil nuts

3 c. white sugar
1 1/2 c. cream or undiluted
  evaporated milk
1 1/2 lb. candied cherries
1/2 lb. chopped walnuts

Cook sugar, corn syrup and cream or milk to the firm ball stage; beat until almost ready to lose glossiness. Add chopped fruit and nuts. Mold into buttered or waxed paper lined pans. Garnish the top with pineapple or nuts, if desired. Let set in refrigerator until hard. Cut into slices after 24 hours. Store in refrigerator until ready to use. Yield: 5 1/2 pounds.

Mrs. P. A. Garrett

HONEY BALLS

1 c. honey
1 c. peanut butter

2 c. dry milk solid (dry
  powdered milk)
1 c. corn flakes, crushed

Cream honey and peanut butter; mix with milk solids. Shape in balls. Roll in crushed corn flakes.

192   Willadean Cooley, Tuscaloosa Council

IRISH POTATO CANDY

1 medium sized potato   1 small jar peanut butter
1 box powdered sugar

Boil potato until well done; take peeling off and mash well. Mix powdered sugar with potato until it is thick enough to roll out (takes about one 1 pound box). Sprinkle dough board with powdered sugar; roll out and spread with peanut butter. Roll up, wrap in wax paper and refrigerate until cool enough to slice.

Bobbie D. Thompson, Decatur Council

FAST 'N FANCY MACAROONS

5 1/3 c. (14 oz. bag)   1 (14 oz.) can Borden's Eagle
   Baker's Angel Flake   Brand sweetened
   coconut   condensed milk
                    2 tsp. vanilla

Combine all ingredients, mixing well. Drop from teaspoon 1 inch apart on well greased baking sheets; bake at 350° for 10 to 12 minutes or until lightly browned. Remove at once from baking sheets, using moistened spatula. Makes about 5 dozen.

Variations: Chocolate-A-Roons - Fold in 4 squares semi-sweet chocolate before baking. Nut-A-Roons: Add 1 cup chopped pecans before baking. Raisin-A-Roons: Add 1 cup raisins before baking. Chip-A-Roons: Add 1 cup Baker's chocolate flavor baking chips before baking.

Paulette Carroll

MARTHA WASHINGTON BALLS

2 boxes confectioners sugar   1 can Eagle Brand
2 sticks butter   condensed milk
2 c. pecans   1 (6 oz.) pkg. semi-sweet
1/4 block paraffin   morsels

Mix together sugar, melted butter, pecans and milk. Roll into balls. Melt paraffin and morsels in a double boiler. Use a toothpick to dip balls in chocolate.

Delesia Garner, Birmingham West Council

MILLIONAIRES

2 c. chopped pecans	1 (12 oz.) bar Baker's
2 Tbsp. milk	German's chocolate
1 (14 oz.) bag caramels	1/4 bar paraffin

Melt caramels over low heat with milk; stir in pecans. Drop by teaspoons onto buttered wax paper. Chill in refrigerator. Melt chocolate with paraffin in double boiler. Dip caramels in chocolate. Put on buttered wax paper and cool.

Ann Sellers, Tuscaloosa Council

CHOCOLATE OATMEAL CANDY

1/2 c. milk	4 Tbsp. cocoa
1 stick margarine	1 tsp. vanilla
2 c. sugar	

Mix all ingredients and boil for 1 1/2 minutes. Stir in 2 1/2 cups 1-minute oats. Drop by teaspoonfuls on buttered wax paper.

Bertha Capps, Birmingham East Council

OLD FASHIONED CANDY

Syrup:

6 c. Domino granulated sugar	3 c. water
	3/4 tsp. cream of tartar

Cook these ingredients quickly without stirring to 290° F.

Candied Apples or Pears: Add a few drops of red food coloring. Place pan in hot water to keep syrup from hardening. Begin dipping skewered apples or pears at once. Cool on greased surface. Makes enough to coat 9 medium apples or pears.

Brenda Stewart, Decatur Council

ORANGE BALLS

1 (6 oz.) can orange juice, undiluted	1 box powdered sugar
	1 can coconut
1 stick margarine (room temperature)	1 c. chopped nuts
	1 box vanilla wafers, crushed

Mix juice, margarine and sugar in mixer; refrigerate 1 hour. Add nuts and wafers; roll into balls the size of a small walnut and then roll in coconut. Makes 16 dozen.

194   Regenia Colburn, Tuscaloosa Council

PARTY MINTS

1 large egg white, unbeaten
1 ball of margarine (size of
  large egg)

1 (1 lb.) box confectioners
  powdered sugar
3-6 drops of oil of peppermint

Cream the above ingredients together; shape with pastry tube or with hands. Add extra sugar and knead to shape with hands. Add a little milk if mixture does not work well in a pastry tube or for extra decorations. Divide mixture and color as desired. Use a small paint brush to add leaves on hand shaped mints.

Faith Kirby, Anniston Council

10 MINUTE PEANUT BRITTLE (MICROWAVE)

1 c. sugar
1/2 c. light corn syrup
1/8 tsp. salt
1 tsp. soda

1 to 1 1/2 c. roasted salted
  peanuts
1 Tbsp. butter or oleo
1 tsp. vanilla

Combine sugar, syrup and salt in 2 quart casserole or mixing bowl; microwave at high 5 minutes. Stir in peanuts; microwave 2 to 5 minutes, stirring after 2 and 4 minutes until syrup and peanuts are lightly browned. Stir in butter, vanilla and soda until light and foamy. Spread to 1/4 inch thickness on large well buttered cookie sheet. Makes 1 pound.

Terry Dillard, Riverchase Council

PEANUT BRITTLE

1 c. sugar
1/2 c. light Karo syrup
1/2 c. water
2 c. peanuts

1 tsp. butter
1/2 tsp. vanilla flavoring
1 tsp. soda

In a large (#7) cast iron skillet on medium heat (#6 or #7), cook sugar, syrup and water until a small amount will form a soft ball when placed in cool water. Add peanuts, stirring constantly, until peanuts reach a hard crack stage. Remove from heat and quickly add butter, vanilla and soda. Soda will cause foam. Stir until it is well mixed. Pour on a buttered aluminum foil sheet. Thin to a single peanut thickness; cool. For more candy, repeat the process.

Jimmy Warren, Decatur Council

ORANGE PEANUT BRITTLE

1 c. sugar
1 c. raw peanuts
1 c. light corn syrup

2 Tbsp. coconut
1 Tbsp. orange rind
1 tsp. soda

Combine sugar, peanuts and corn syrup in a heavy Dutch oven; cook over medium heat, stirring constantly, to soft crack stage (about 290°). Remove from heat; stir in coconut and orange rind. Add soda and stir well. Spread mixture thinly on a warm buttered jelly roll pan (15x10x1 inch). (Work quickly.) Let cool and break into pieces. Yield: 1 pound.

Gloria H. Ramage, Birmingham South Council

PEANUT BUTTER - OATMEAL CANDY

2 c. sugar
1 stick margarine
3/4 c. evaporated milk
1 tsp. vanilla

1 c. peanut butter
3 c. oatmeal, uncooked
Optional: Coconut or nuts

Bring sugar, margarine and milk to a boil over medium heat. When it starts bubbling, cook about 4 more minutes, stirring constantly. Remove from heat and add remaining ingredients; drop by teaspoonfuls onto waxed paper.

Carol Britt, Anniston Council

PEANUT BUTTER KRISPIES

2 c. Cocoa Krispies
1/2 c. sugar

1/2 c. white Karo syrup
1 big jar crunchy peanut
    butter

Bring to boil sugar and Karo syrup. Mix peanut butter and Cocoa Krispies; pour hot syrup over. Drop by teaspoonfuls on cookie sheet. Do not cook.

Edna Watters, Montgomery Council

COATED PECANS

2 c. pecans
1 c. sugar
5 Tbsp. water

1/8 to 1/4 tsp. salt
1 1/2 tsp. vanilla
1 1/2 tsp. cinnamon

Roast pecans 10 to 12 minutes at 300°. In large saucepan combine remaining ingredients; cook on high approximately 2 minutes or until forms soft ball in water. Remove from heat; add pecans and stir by hand until sugared. Pour out on wax paper and separate.

Jeanne Anderson, Montgomery Council

CREAMY PECANS

1/2 c. brown sugar, packed	1/4 c. sour cream
	1/2 tsp. vanilla
1/4 c. white sugar	1 1/2 c. pecans

Cook sugars and sour cream over low heat, stirring constantly, until it forms soft ball in water. Remove from heat and add vanilla and pecans. Stir until coating forms on nuts and spoon onto wax paper.

Mary Ann Davis, Anniston Council

PECAN CLUSTERS

5 c. sugar	4 c. nuts
1 stick butter	1 1/2 lb. chocolate kisses*
1 large can Pet milk	1 (9 oz.) jar marshmallow
1/2 tsp. salt	cream

Combine sugar, milk, butter and salt; boil 7 minutes. Stir constantly; set off heat. Add nuts, chocolate kisses and marshmallow cream. Mix well. Drop on wax paper. Makes about 6 pounds.

*Peel kisses before starting candy.

Patti Smith, Anniston Council
Peggy Hunter, Anniston Council

PECAN LOG

1 box vanilla wafers	1 1/2 c. confectioners sugar
1 c. chopped pecans	
1 can condensed milk	1/2 c. cherries (optional)

Crumble vanilla wafers; add 3/4 cup confectioners sugar, pecans and milk. Mix together. Texture should be sticky. Add cherries, if desired. Roll into log and use remaining confectioners sugar to roll logs in. Wrap in wax paper and refrigerate.

Janet Humphries, Riverchase Council

BUTTERMILK PRALINES

2 c. sugar
1 c. buttermilk
2 Tbsp. light corn syrup
1 c. butter (not margarine)

1 tsp. soda
1 tsp. vanilla
1/8 tsp. salt
1 c. coarsely chopped pecans

Combine sugar, buttermilk, syrup, butter and soda in heavy buttered 4 quart saucepan; bring to boil over medium heat, stirring constantly, until sugar dissolves. Cook, without stirring, to 236° or until soft ball is formed when small amount is dropped in cold water. Remove from heat; add vanilla and salt; beat vigorously until candy thickens and begins to lose its gloss. Stir in pecans; drop by teaspoonfuls onto waxed paper. Place waxed paper on newspaper and pralines will come up easily.

Margaret Welch Keith, Huntsville Council

CREAM PRALINES

1 (1 lb.) box light
   brown sugar
1/3 tsp. salt
3/4 c. evaporated milk

1 Tbsp. butter (margarine)
1/2 lb. pecan halves (2 c.)
1/2 tsp. vanilla

In 2 quart saucepan combine sugar, salt, milk and butter; stir over low heat until sugar is dissolved. Add pecan halves. Increase heat to medium; continue cooking and stirring to soft ball stage (234°). Remove from heat; stir in vanilla and cool 5 minutes. (Meanwhile, place large sheet of foil on counter surface; crimp edges for dropping patties.) Stir rapidly until mixture begins to thicken and coats pecans lightly. Drop rapidly from spoon (1 tablespoon for large or 1 teaspoon for small patties). If mixture becomes too stiff, add few drops of water (hot). Let patties cool before removing from foil. Yield: 40 small or 20 large.

Marie P. Williams, Mobile Council

ROCKY ROAD CANDY

1 (6 oz.) pkg. semi-sweet
   chocolate pieces
1 (1 oz.) square
   unsweetened chocolate
1 Tbsp. butter
2 eggs

1 1/4 c. confectioners sugar
1/2 tsp. salt
1 tsp. vanilla
2 c. salted peanuts
2 c. miniature marshmallows

Melt chocolate pieces, chocolate and butter in large saucepan over low heat, stirring until smooth; remove from

heat. Beat eggs until foamy. Mix in sugar, salt and vanilla. Blend in chocolate mixture; stir in peanuts and
marshmallows; drop by teaspoonfuls onto waxed paper. Chill
2 hours or until firm. Store in refrigerator; remove just
before serving. Makes about 4 dozen candies.

Virginia L. Hutchens, Montgomery Council

SORGHUM SYRUP CANDY

1 c. pure sorghum syrup   1 tsp. vanilla
2 c. parched shelled   1/4 stick butter
  peanuts, crushed

Boil syrup until drops are firm when dropped in ice
water (2-4 minutes). Remove from heat; stir in butter and
vanilla flavoring. When butter is melted, stir in crushed
parched peanuts. Place in buttered container until cool.
Candy should be about 3/4 inch thick in container. When
cool, cut into small pieces.

Randy Ham, Birmingham South Council

SPONGE CANDY (MICROWAVE STYLE)

1 c. sugar   1 Tbsp. vinegar
1 c. dark corn syrup   1 Tbsp. baking soda

Mix sugar, syrup and vinegar. Microwave 3 minutes
on high; stir. Microwave for 4 1/2 minutes and test to see
when reaches 300°. Add baking soda when candy is done.
Stir well. (To test for doneness, drop some in cold water.
If brittle, it's ready.) Pour out onto buttered foil; let set
till firm.

Dina Johnson, Birmingham South Council

SUGARPLUMS

1/2 c. (1 stick) butter   5 c. confectioners sugar
  (not oleo)   1 tsp. vanilla
1/4 c. whipping cream

Cream butter thoroughly; add sugar slowly. Continue
beating until light and crumbly. Add cream and vanilla;
beat until completely blended. Shape into small balls and
press a pecan half or a maraschino cherry into each ball.
Pretty tinted pink or green. Keep in refrigerator. Yield:
1 1/2 pounds.

Joella Bradford, Huntsville Council

WHITE CANDY

2 1/4 lb. white chocolate
1 large jar dry
  roasted peanuts
2 c. Rice Krispies

2 c. Cap'n Crunch peanut
  butter cereal
2 c. miniature marshmallows
  (white or colored)

Heat chocolate in 200° oven until it is soft to touch. Mix dry ingredients in large bowl; add soft chocolate. Stir entire mixture until coated with chocolate. Spoon onto wax paper. Let dry. Store in an airtight container. Makes 85 to 100 pieces of candy.
          Mrs. JoAnn Thompson, Decatur Council

ALMOND COOKIES

6 c. plain flour
2 1/2 c. shortening*
2 1/2 c. sugar
1 Tbsp. baking powder

2 Tbsp. almond flavoring
1/2 tsp. salt
5 eggs
Whole almonds (untoasted)

Cream together eggs, sugar and shortening; add flavoring and set aside. Sift together flour, salt and baking powder; gradually add flour to sugar mixture, blending well after each addition. Roll teaspoonfuls into balls and place on ungreased cookie sheet. Press whole almond on top of each cookie and brush with egg white; bake at 350° for 10-12 minutes or until lightly browned.
    *Half butter may be used.
          Becky Woo, Birmingham South Council

APPLESAUCE COOKIES

1 pkg. (2 layer size)
  spice cake mix
1 c. raisins

1/2 c. cooking oil
1/2 c. applesauce
1 egg

In large bowl combine all ingredients; beat at medium speed of electric mixer for 1 minute. Drop from teaspoon onto ungreased cookie sheet; bake at 350° for 12-15 minutes. Yield: 6 dozen.
          Janice Bass, Riverchase Council

*   *   *   *   *

It is a funny thing about life. If you refuse to accept anything but the best you very often get it.

BANANA BARS

1 pkg. Pillsbury yellow
  cake mix
1 1/4 c. thinly sliced
  ripe bananas

1 c. buttermilk or sour milk
1/4 c. cold coffee
2 eggs

Frosting:

1 1/3 c. powdered sugar
1/4 tsp. salt

1 Tbsp. butter or margarine
2 to 3 Tbsp. cold coffee

Preheat oven to 350°. Grease 15x10 inch jelly roll pan or 13x9 inch pan. In large bowl blend first 5 ingredients; beat 2 minutes at highest speed. Pour into greased pan; bake 25 to 35 minutes or until bar springs back when touched lightly in the center; cool. Mix frosting ingredients until smooth; frost bars. Yield: About 3 dozen bars.

Fay King, Huntsville Council

VERY THIN BENNE COOKIES (SESAME)

1/4 lb. softened butter
3/4 c. plain flour
1 1/2 c. light brown sugar
1 tsp. vanilla

1 egg
1 c. toasted benne seeds
  (sesame)
1/4 tsp. baking powder
1/4 tsp. salt

Mix and drop on aluminum foil covered cookie sheet about size of nickel; let it run. Bake at 350° until brown. Let cool on foil.

Virginia Bowen, Birmingham South Council

BROWN SUGAR CHEWS

1 egg
1 c. light brown sugar
1 tsp. vanilla

1/2 c. sifted flour
1/4 tsp. salt
1/4 tsp. soda
1 c. nuts

Beat egg; add sugar and vanilla. Blend in dry ingredients. Add nuts; pour into well greased 8 inch square pan. Bake in 350° oven 18 to 20 minutes. Allow to cool. Should still be slightly soft when removed from oven. Makes 16 squares.

Linda Crocker, Mobile Council

BROWNIES WITH ICING

Brownies:

2 sticks margarine	2 c. plain flour
3 or 4 Tbsp. cocoa	2 eggs
1 c. water	1/2 c. buttermilk
2 c. white sugar	1 tsp. soda

Icing:

1 stick margarine	1 box powdered sugar
6 Tbsp. buttermilk	1 tsp. vanilla
3 or 4 Tbsp. cocoa	1 c. pecans, chopped

Brownies: Bring to boil margarine, cocoa and water; pour over 2 cups of sugar and 2 cups of flour. Add and mix eggs, buttermilk and soda; bake at 300° on a greased and floured pan for 45 minutes to 1 hour.

Icing: Bring to a boil margarine, buttermilk and cocoa; remove from fire and add powdered sugar, vanilla and cup of pecans (chopped). Pour over hot cake. Do not try to stack.

Mrs. John R. Criswell, Mobile Council

BLOND BROWNIES

2 2/3 c. flour	3 eggs
2 1/2 tsp. baking powder	1 (6 oz.) pkg. chocolate chips
1/2 tsp. salt	1 (6 oz.) pkg. butterscotch
2/3 c. butter	chips
1 (1 lb.) box light brown sugar	1 c. chopped pecans

Sift flour, baking powder and salt together and set aside. Melt butter and brown sugar in saucepan; cool. When cool, add eggs, one at a time. Add flour mixture; add chips and nuts last. Spread in a jelly roll pan; bake at 350° for 25 to 30 minutes. Do not overcook. Batter is very thick. Cut in squares when cool.

Margie Lavender, Riverchase Council

BOILED COOKIES

2 c. sugar	1/4 tsp. salt
1/2 c. cocoa	3 c. quick cooking oatmeal
1/2 c. milk	2 tsp. vanilla
1/2 c. butter	1 c. chopped pecans (optional)

Mix sugar, cocoa, salt, milk and butter in large sauce-pan; cook and stir over medium heat till mixture comes to full rolling boil. Boil 3 minutes. Remove from heat; add oatmeal and vanilla and nuts. Stir until cool or proper consistency to drop by teaspoonfuls on wax paper. Makes 3 dozen.

Beverly Bowles, Montgomery Council

BROWN SUGAR COOKIES

1 c. oleo
1 box sugar and 1/2 c.
  extra
4 eggs
8 Tbsp. sweet milk
1 tsp. baking powder

1 Tbsp. soda
1 tsp. salt
Vanilla or black walnut
  flavoring
Nuts

Beat all these together and then add 1 cup flour at a time till too thick to stir. Put on tables and keep kneading in flour. This altogether will take almost 7 cups flour. Put in 2 rolls and wrap in waxed paper and chill overnight. Bake on ungreased cookie sheet.

Barbara Davis, Decatur Council

BROWN SUGAR SQUARES

1 egg
1 c. brown sugar
1 tsp. vanilla
1/2 c. sifted flour

1/4 tsp. salt
1/4 tsp. soda
1 c. chopped nuts

Blend egg, brown sugar and vanilla; do not beat. Quickly stir in flour, soda and salt; add nuts and spread in buttered 8 inch square pan. Bake at 350° for 18 to 20 min-utes. Cool in pan. Cut in squares.

Mae B. Jordan, Retired,
Birmingham Central Council

BUTTER COOKIES

1 lb. butter
1 c. sugar
1 tsp. vanilla

4 c. flour
Pinch of salt
1 egg, well beaten

Butter should be at room temperature. Cream butter well and add sugar gradually, egg and flour gradually. Make into roll; wrap in wax paper and store in refrigerator overnight or until well chilled. Slice thin and bake on ungreased cookie sheet at 375° for 10-12 minutes.

Hints: Beat 1 egg white and after cookies are cooled, brush with egg whites and sprinkle chopped pecans or red and green decorator candy.

Judith C. Hussey, Birmingham South Council

BUTTER NUT BALLS

Cream:

1 c. butter
1 c. sugar
2 egg yolks

3 c. flour (sifted)
2 tsp. lemon extract
1/4 tsp. salt

Form into small balls; dip into slightly beaten egg whites, then into ground nuts. Place on greased cookie tin and press candied cherry on top. Bake 10 minutes at 400° F.

Louise Mooney, Mobile Council

CHERRY-PECAN COOKIES

1 c. oleo
1 c. powdered sugar (sifted)
1 egg
2 1/2 c. all-purpose flour

1/4 tsp. cream of tartar
1 c. candied cherries,
    halved or chopped
1/2 c. chopped pecans

Cream oleo, sugar and egg; add flour and cream of tartar. Add cherries and pecans. Drop by teaspoonfuls or roll and place on lightly greased cookie sheet. Bake at 350° for 10 to 12 minutes or until lightly browned.

Ann Sellers, Tuscaloosa Council

CHOCOLATE CHIP COOKIES

1/3 to 1/2 c. shortening
1/2 c. granulated sugar
1/4 c. brown sugar,
    firmly packed
1 egg, well beaten
1 c. sifted flour

1/2 tsp. salt
1/2 tsp. soda
1 (6 oz.) pkg. chocolate
    chips
1/2 c. nuts, chopped (optional)
1 tsp. vanilla

Cream shortening; add sugars and cream together until light and fluffy. Add egg and mix thoroughly. Sift flour with salt and soda; add and mix well. Add chocolate chips (nuts) and vanilla; mix thoroughly. Drop from teaspoon onto ungreased baking sheet about 2 inches apart. Bake at 375° for approximately 10 minutes (until tops start getting brown). Remove from oven; cool and enjoy! Yield: About 1 1/2 dozen.

Carol Higdon, Riverchase Council

CHOCOLATE GLORIFIED COOKIES

1/2 c. Crisco	1 c. sugar
3 Tbsp. cocoa	1 c. plain flour
2 eggs	1 c. chopped nuts
1 tsp. vanilla	

Icing:

4 Tbsp. butter (at room temperature)	1 tsp. vanilla
	3 Tbsp. cocoa
3 c. powdered sugar	4 Tbsp. hot milk

Cream Crisco and sugar; add eggs, one at a time, mixing well. Add cocoa, flour and nuts; mix well. Bake at 350° for 25 minutes in 8 1/2 x 11 inch rectangular pan. Remove from oven and place large marshmallows 1 inch apart on top of cake and place back into oven to soften (about 5 minutes). When soft, press down with spoon. Cool and top with icing.

Bonnie Golden, Anniston Council

CHOCOLATE CHIP OATMEAL COOKIES

1/2 c. butter	3/4 c. sifted flour
6 Tbsp. firmly packed brown sugar	1/2 tsp. soda
	1/2 tsp. salt
6 Tbsp. granulated sugar	1 c. oats
3/4 tsp. vanilla	1 (6 oz.) pkg. (1 c.) semi-sweet chocolate chips
1 egg	

Beat butter, sugar and vanilla until creamy; beat in egg. Sift flour, soda and salt; add to mixture. Stir in oats and chocolate pieces. Drop onto lightly greased cookie sheet. Bake in preheated 375° oven 8-10 minutes. Makes 3 dozen.

Peggy Y. Hughes, Birmingham South Council

CHOCOLATE PEPPERMINT BARS

2 squares unsweetened chocolate	3 Tbsp. butter or oleo
	5 tsp. milk
1/2 c. butter or oleo	1 tsp. peppermint extract
2 eggs	1 1/2 oz. unsweetened chocolate
1 c. sugar	
1/2 c. sifted flour	1 1/2 Tbsp. butter or oleo
1/2 c. chopped almonds	1 Tbsp. peppermint candy, crushed
1 1/2 c. sifted confectioners sugar	

Combine 2 ounces chocolate and 1/2 cup oleo in saucepan; cook over low heat till melted. Remove from heat and cool. Beat eggs and 1 cup sugar in bowl till thick and lemon colored, using mixer at high speed. Blend in chocolate mixture and flour till smooth. Stir in almonds. Spread in greased 8 inch square pan; bake at 350° for 25 minutes; cool. Combine confectioners sugar, 3 tablespoons oleo, milk and extract; beat till smooth. Spread on brownies; cover and chill in refrigerator till firm. Melt 1 1/2 ounces chocolate with 1 1/2 tablespoons oleo over hot water; cool slightly and spread carefully over cream layer. Sprinkle with crushed peppermint candy; cut in 2x1 inch bars. Makes 32.

Ann Johnson, Montgomery Council

CHRISTMAS COOKIES

Light oven, get bowl, spoons and ingredients; grease pan, crack nuts, remove 10 blocks, seven toy autos and one wad of chewing gum from kitchen table. Measure 2 cups of flour; remove Johnny's hands from flour, wash flour off him, measure 1 more cup flour to replace flour on floor. Put flour, baking powder and salt in sifter. Answer doorbell. Return to kitchen. Remove Johnny's hands from bowl. Wash Johnny. Answer phone; return. Remove 1/4 inch salt from greased pans, grease more pans. Look for Johnny. Answer phone. Return to kitchen and find Johnny. Remove his hands from bowl. Wash shortening, etc. off him. Take up greased pan and find nut shells in it. Head for Johnny, who flees, knocking bowl off table. Wash kitchen floor. Wash table. Wash kitchen walls! Wash dishes. Wash Johnny. Call baker. Lie down! Happy Holidays.

A. M. Robertson, Huntsville Council

CHRISTMAS SNOWCAPS

3 egg whites	Dash of salt
1/8 tsp. cream of tartar	3/4 c. granulated sugar
1/2 tsp. peppermint extract	2/3 c. diced, candied cherries

Beat egg whites, to which cream of tartar has been added, until stiff but not dry; add sugar gradually and beat until well blended and smooth. Save some of the cherries for topping; add the rest to egg mixture. Cover cookie sheet with plain brown paper; drop mixture by teaspoonfuls onto paper. Bake at 325° about 20 minutes. Let stand a few minutes after removing from oven. Top cookies with remaining cherries. Yield: About 30 cookies.

Peggy Autry, Birmingham South Council

CINNAMON GRAHAM-CRACKER COOKIES

1 box cinnamon graham
  crackers
1 stick pure butter

1 stick margarine
1/2 c. sugar
Pecans (as many as desired)

Take a 13x9x2 inch pan and spread aluminum foil in the inside; place a single layer of crackers on the foil. In a pan melt your 2 sticks of butter; add sugar and bring to a boil. Boil 3 to 4 minutes. Pour over graham crackers. Sprinkle pecans on top; bake at 350° for 10 minutes. Remove from oven; let cool. Break into pieces and eat.

Melba McSwain, Decatur Council

COCOA KISS COOKIES

1 c. softened margarine
2/3 c. sugar
1 tsp. vanilla
1 2/3 c. all-purpose
  flour

1/4 c. cocoa
1 c. chopped pecans
1 (9 oz.) pkg. Hershey's
  silver wrapped kisses
Confectioners sugar

Cream margarine, sugar and vanilla. Mix flour and cocoa; blend into creamed mixture. Add pecans; beat on low speed until well blended. Chill dough in freezer 20 minutes; roll into ball and mash. Put kiss in middle and roll back into ball; bake on ungreased cookie sheet at 375° for 10-12 minutes. Cool and remove to wire rack. Cool completely and roll in confectioners sugar.

Charlotte Adair Smith, Birmingham East Council

CREAM CHEESE COOKIES

1 stick oleo
1 (3 oz.) pkg. cream
  cheese
1 c. sugar
1 egg yolk

1/2 tsp. vanilla or
  almond extract
2 1/2 c. sifted flour
Pecan halves

Cream shortening; add cream cheese and sugar. Add egg yolk, extract and flour, and mix well. Dip small amounts onto cookie sheet far enough apart to allow for spreading. Place pecan half in center of each cookie. Bake about 15 minutes at 350°.

Jane Knox, Montgomery Council

NUTTED DATE BARS

1 c. dates	1 Tbsp. melted shortening
1 c. nuts	1 Tbsp. lemon juice
2 eggs	4 Tbsp. flour
1 c. powdered sugar	1/2 tsp. salt

Chop dates and nuts fine. Beat eggs lightly and add powdered sugar, melted shortening, lemon juice, flour and salt. Combine 2 mixtures; spread onto greased baking pan 1/4 inch thick. Bake in moderate oven (325°) for 20 minutes and cut in strips while hot. Roll in powdered sugar.

Sandra Surrett, Anniston Council

EASY COOKIES

1/2 c. margarine	2 3/4 c. flour
1/2 c. Crisco	2 Tbsp. sugar
1 1/2 c. sugar	2 tsp. cinnamon
2 eggs	

Cream butter, shortening, sugar and eggs; after mixed well, add flour gradually. Roll into balls. Place on ungreased cookie sheet and bake at 400° until golden. Bake longer for crisp cookie.

Marcia Freeman, Birmingham East Council

15 MINUTE COOKIES

2 c. sugar	2 c. oats
1/4 c. margarine	1/2 c. peanut butter
1/2 c. milk	1 tsp. vanilla
4 Tbsp. cocoa	

Combine sugar, butter, cocoa and milk; boil 1 minute. Stir in oats, peanut butter and vanilla. Drop from spoon onto waxed paper. Yield: 20 servings.

Note: One cup nuts may be substituted for 1 cup oats.

Janice Bass, Riverchase Council

FORGET 'EMS

2 egg whites	1/2 tsp. vanilla
3/4 c. sugar	1 c. chopped nuts

Preheat oven to 400°. Beat egg whites. Add sugar, vanilla and nuts. Spoon on greased cookie sheet. Place in oven; turn oven off and forget 'em until oven cools completely.

208   Verlan Harden, Montgomery Council

"FORGOTTEN" COOKIES

2 egg whites, at room
  temperature
1/4 tsp. cream of tartar
1/8 tsp. salt
2/3 c. sugar

1 tsp. vanilla extract
1 (6 oz.) pkg. miniature
  chocolate chips (regular
  sized chips can be used)
1 c. broken pecans

Preheat oven to 350°. Beat egg whites and cream of tartar. Add sugar gradually and beat until sugar is dissolved. Add remaining ingredients. Drop by teaspoonfuls on cookie sheets. Place all cookies in the oven at one time. When you place the cookies in the preheated oven, turn off the oven immediately and leave overnight to dry out. (In other words, "forget" about them until morning.) Remove with spatula. These are beautiful cookies. Made very small, they are lovely for teas or receptions. Makes about 5 dozen.

Jann LeCroy, Birmingham Central Council

FORGOTTEN CRISPY COOKIES

2 1/2 c. powdered sugar
4 egg whites
1 tsp. cream of tartar

1 tsp. vanilla
1 c. chopped nuts

Beat everything but nuts 15 minutes; add nuts and drop by teaspoonfuls on cookie sheet. Cook at 225° for 1 hour; turn oven off; leave in oven till cool.

Edna Watters, Montgomery Council

AUNT BOBBIE'S FRUIT COOKIES

1 c. brown sugar
1/2 c. butter
4 eggs
1 glass brandy
3 tsp. soda, dissolved
  in 3 tsp. milk

1 lb. dates, candied cherries,
  candied pineapple
6 c. or 1 1/2 lb. pecans
1 1/2 lb. white raisins
1 tsp. cinnamon
1 tsp. nutmeg
3 c. sifted all-purpose flour

Add 1 cup flour to fruit and nuts. Cream sugar and butter; add brandy, then soda and milk and well beaten egg yolks. Add flour, nuts and spices. Beat egg whites and fold in batter. Drop in small cookies; bake 20 minutes at 300°. Makes 12 dozen.

Ann Smith, Tuscaloosa Council

1567-82

FRUIT COOKIES

1 c. brown sugar
1 stick oleo
2 eggs
1 1/2 tsp. soda, dissolved
  in 1 1/2 Tbsp. milk
1/3 c. whiskey or brandy
1 1/2 c. flour (sifted)

1/2 tsp. cinnamon
1/2 tsp. cloves
1/2 tsp. nutmeg
1/2 lb. candied cherries
1/2 lb. candied pineapple
3 c. pecans
1 box white raisins

Mix thoroughly; drop on cookie sheet and cook at 300° for 20 minutes. (If flour is mixed with candied fruits, it will keep them from sinking to bottom.)

Bonnie Summers, Huntsville Council

DROP FRUIT CAKE COOKIES

1 c. brown sugar
1/2 lb. oleo (2 sticks)

4 eggs, beaten

Cream sugar and oleo together, then add eggs.

3 tsp. soda, dissolved in
  3 Tbsp. sweet milk
1 lb. dates (chopped or cut)
1 lb. cherries (cut)
6 c. pecans (or less),
  chopped

1 lb. white raisins (or less)
1 lb. candied pineapple (cut)
2 tsp. cinnamon
3 c. flour
1 Tbsp. vanilla
1/2 tsp. salt

Add 1/2 of extra flour to fruit (plus 1 cup) or little more than 1/2 cup of flour. Mix well and drop with teaspoon on cookie sheet; bake 20 minutes at 300°. (Grease cookie sheet lightly.)

Patti Smith, Anniston Council

SARRAH'S FUDGE SQUARES

1 c. Crisco
2 c. sugar
4 eggs
2 c. flour

3 Tbsp. cocoa
1 tsp. vanilla
Nuts

Cream sugar and Crisco; add eggs, one at a time. Mix flour and cocoa together. Add to first mixture. Add vanilla and nuts; bake at 350° for about 30 minutes.

Anne Spragins, Birmingham East Council

FUDGE SQUARES

1 stick butter	1 1/4 c. sugar
2 oz. bitter chocolate	1/8 tsp. salt
(or 1/3 c. cocoa plus	3 eggs, beaten
1 Tbsp. butter)	1 tsp. vanilla
1/2 c. flour	3/4 c. chopped nuts
	(walnuts or pecans)

Melt butter and chocolate. Sift flour, sugar and salt; add to melted butter and chocolate. Stir into mixture eggs, vanilla and nuts. Bake in preheated 350° oven for 25 minutes. Serves 6.

Mary Ruth Wood, Life Member,
Birmingham South Council

GERMAN TOWN COOKIES

1 c. brown sugar	1 c. pecans
1 c. white sugar	1 tsp. baking soda
1 c. butter or margarine	1 tsp. baking powder
2 eggs	1/4 tsp. salt
1 c. oatmeal	2 1/2 c. flour
1 c. coconut	1 tsp. vanilla extract

Mix sugars, margarine and eggs. Sift dry ingredients together, then add to first mixture. Add oats, coconut and pecans last to the mixture. Roll into balls the size of a walnut and flatten. Bake at 350°. Makes about 80 cookies.

Mrs. John R. Criswell (Evelyn), Mobile Council

GINGERBREAD BOYS

1 c. shortening	5 c. flour
1 c. sugar	1 1/2 tsp. baking soda
1/2 tsp. salt	1 Tbsp. ground ginger
1 c. molasses	1 tsp. ground cinnamon
2 Tbsp. white vinegar	1 tsp. ground cloves
1 egg, beaten	

Cream shortening, sugar and salt; stir in molasses, vinegar and egg. Sift together and add remaining ingredients. Chill mixture overnight. Divide dough into fourths. Roll one part of dough at a time on a floured board to 1/8 inch thickness. (Refrigerate dough you are not using.) Cut out gingerbread boys with sharp cookie cutter. Place on greased cookie sheet and bake at 375° about 6 minutes. Cool slightly;

remove carefully. Decorate as desired. Cookies will keep several months in airtight container and indefinitely in freezer. Makes 55-65 small boys.

Henrietta Sanders

GINGERSNAPS

2 c. sifted enriched flour	3/4 c. shortening
1 Tbsp. ginger	1 c. sugar
2 tsp. baking soda	1 egg
1 tsp. cinnamon	1/4 c. molasses
1/2 tsp. salt	Granulated sugar (extra)

Set oven at 350°. Mix and sift first 5 ingredients. Sift again twice; return to sifter. Beat shortening until creamy. Add 1 cup sugar gradually, continuing to beat. Beat in egg and molasses. Sift about 1/4 of the flour mixture over the molasses mixture; stir to blend well. Repeat until all flour mixture is added. Form teaspoons of dough into small balls by rolling lightly between palms of hands. Roll balls in extra sugar. Place about 2 inches apart on ungreased baking sheets. Bake 12 minutes or until tops are slightly rounded and crackly. Cool on racks. Makes about 48.

Donna M. Walker, Birmingham Central Council

GRANDMA WYATT'S COOKIES

1 c. Crisco	1/4 tsp. cream of tartar
1 c. sugar	1/2 tsp. soda
1 egg	1 capful vanilla
1/4 tsp. salt	Icing: Powdered sugar
2 c. sifted flour	and milk

Beat together Crisco, sugar, egg and 1/4 teaspoon salt. Add 2 cups sifted flour, cream of tartar, soda and capful vanilla. Roll dough out on waxed paper and use favorite cookie cutters. (Tip: Dough will rise, so roll fairly thin.) Bake at 350° until golden brown.

Icing: After cookies cool, ice with powdered sugar, using 1 tablespoon milk until desired consistency is reached.

Nancy Wyatt, Tuscaloosa Council

HAPPY TUMMY COOKIES

1/2 c. shortening
1 c. firmly packed
  brown sugar
1 egg
3 Tbsp. milk
1 tsp. vanilla
1 1/4 c. sifted all-purpose
  flour

1/2 tsp. soda
1/4 tsp. salt
2 c. Quaker 100% natural
  cereal (with raisins
  and dates)
1 box chopped dates
1 c. English walnuts

Beat shortening, sugar, eggs, milk and vanilla together until creamy. Sift together flour, soda and salt; add to creamed mixture. Blend well; stir in the 100% natural cereal, the box of dates and the cup of nuts. Drop by teaspoonfuls onto greased cookie sheets; bake in preheated moderate oven (350°) for 10 to 12 minutes.

Faith Kirby, Anniston Council

ICEBOX COOKIES

1 1/2 c. Crisco
1 c. brown sugar
1 tsp. cinnamon
1 1/2 tsp. soda
1 c. broken pecans

1 c. white sugar
2 eggs
1/2 tsp. salt
4 1/2 c. plain flour

Cream the shortening and add sugar gradually. Add beaten eggs and mix well. Add all dry ingredients, which have been sifted together 3 times, and mix with nuts. Make into rolls and keep in refrigerator. When ready to bake, slice very thin and bake in moderate oven (350° or 375°).

Barbara Davis, Decatur Council

KOLACZKI (LITTLE CAKES) POLISH COOKIES

1 c. butter
6 oz. cream cheese
1/4 tsp. vanilla

2 1/2 c. flour
1/2 tsp. salt
Jam

Cream butter and cream cheese until fluffy; beat in vanilla. Combine flour and salt. Add to butter mixture, blending well. Chill dough until easy to handle. Roll dough to 1/4 inch thickness on floured surface; cut out 2 inch circles. Place on ungreased floured surface. Make a thumbprint about 1/6 inch deep in each cookie; fill with jam. Bake in 350° oven for 15 minutes or until lightly browned on edges.

Art Lipski, Birmingham Central Council

LEMON CHEESE BARS

1 Duncan Hines pudding
  recipe yellow cake mix
1 (8 oz.) pkg. cream
  cheese, softened

1/3 c. sugar
1 tsp. lemon juice
2 eggs
1/3 c. oil

Mix dry cake mix, 1 egg and 1/3 cup oil until crumbly; reserve 1 cup. Pat remaining mixture lightly in an ungreased 13x9x2 inch pan; bake 15 minutes at 350°. Beat cheese, sugar, lemon juice and 1 egg until light and smooth. Spread over baked layer; sprinkle with reserved crumb mixture; bake 15 minutes longer. Cool. Cut into bars.

Nancy S. Black, Decatur Council

MAGIC COOKIE BARS

1/2 c. butter or margarine
1 1/2 c. graham cracker
  crumbs
1 (14 oz.) can Eagle
  Brand milk

1 (6 oz.) pkg. semi-sweet
  chocolate morsels
1 (3 1/2 oz.) can flaked
  coconut
1 c. chopped nuts

Preheat oven to 350° (325° for glass dish). In 13x9 inch baking pan melt butter. Sprinkle crumbs over butter; pour Eagle Brand milk evenly over crumbs. Top evenly with remaining ingredients; press down gently. Bake 25 to 30 minutes or until lightly browned. Cool thoroughly before cutting. Store loosely covered at room temperature. Makes 24 bars.

Donna Campbell, Anniston Council

MERINGUE COOKIES

2 egg whites
2/3 c. sugar
1/2 c. coconut

1 c. chopped pecans
1 c. chocolate chips

Preheat oven to 350°. Get oven real hot. Beat egg whites stiff. Add remaining ingredients and fold until blended. Drop on foil-lined cookie sheets by teaspoonfuls. Place in oven and turn heat off; leave for at least 3 to 4 hours. These cookies should come out crispy. It is important that your oven is very hot and you leave these cookies in until your oven is cold. Otherwise, your cookies will come out moist and soft.

Lela Milam, Anniston Council

MY MAN COOKIES

4 sticks butter
2 c. white sugar
1 box brown sugar
4 eggs
2 Tbsp. vanilla
4 c. flour

2 Tbsp. soda
2 Tbsp. baking powder
2 tsp. salt
4 c. quick cook oatmeal
2 c. coconut
2 c. pecans, chopped

Cream butter, white sugar, brown sugar together, then add eggs and vanilla. Combine flour, soda, baking powder and salt; blend into sugar mixture. Add oatmeal and mix, then add coconut and pecans. Drop by teaspoon on greased cookie sheet. Bake at 350°; do not overbake.

M. C. Arndt, Birmingham South Council

M & M COOKIES

1/2 c. Crisco
1/2 c. brown sugar
1/4 c. sugar
1/2 tsp. vanilla
1/4 tsp. water
1 egg

1 c. + 2 Tbsp. sifted flour
1/2 tsp. soda
1/2 tsp. salt
3/4 c. M & M's plain chocolate
    candies or nuts or raisins

Blend in Crisco and sugar; beat in vanilla, water and eggs. Sift remaining dry ingredients together; add to sugar and egg mixture; mix well and stir in M & M's. Drop from teaspoon onto ungreased baking sheet; bake at 375° for 10 to 12 minutes. For additional color, press extra M & M's into cookies before baking. Some candies crack.

Edna Johnson, Birmingham South Council

MAPLE COOKIES

1 1/4 c. packed light
   brown sugar
1/2 c. butter or oleo
2 c. unsifted all-purpose
   flour
3/4 c. uncooked oats
   (quick or old fashioned)

1 egg, beaten
2 Tbsp. milk
1 tsp. maple flavoring
1 tsp. baking soda
1/2 tsp. salt
1/8 tsp. ground ginger

Beat butter and sugar until light and fluffy with mixer at medium speed. Reserve 1/3 cup flour. Add remaining flour to butter and sugar at slow speed. Add oats, egg, milk, maple flavoring, soda and salt; mix well. Form 1 inch balls. Combine reserved flour and ginger; roll balls in and place on ungreased cookie sheet. Bake in 375° oven 10 to 12 minutes. Cookie tops will be cracked.

Note: Cookies are best when not overcooked.

Ruth Apperson, Decatur Council

OATMEAL BROWNIES

2 c. sugar
4 Tbsp. cocoa
1/2 stick oleo
1 Tbsp. vanilla

1/2 c. milk
1/2 c. peanut butter
2 c. oats (I use 3-minute oats)

Mix first 5 items together and after mixture comes to boil on top of stove, cook for 2 minutes on medium heat. Remove from stove and add peanut butter and oats. Beat well when cools a little. While beating, drop from spoon on wax paper. Let cool about 5 minutes and eat all you can. (Very rich.)

Doris Holder, Decatur Council

OATMEAL COOKIES

1 c. shortening
1 c. brown sugar
1 c. white sugar
1 1/2 c. flour (plain)
3 c. oatmeal

1 c. nuts
2 eggs
1 tsp. salt
1 tsp. soda
1 tsp. vanilla

Cream shortening and sugar; add eggs. Sift flour, salt and soda together. Add oatmeal, nuts and vanilla; roll in wax paper. Chill in refrigerator overnight. Cut in 3/4 inch slices and bake for 15 minutes at 350°.

Lois Harris, Tuscaloosa Council

CHOCOLATE OATMEAL COOKIES

2 c. sugar
2 Tbsp. cocoa
1/2 c. milk
1/2 c. butter or margarine

1/2 c. peanut butter
2 c. uncooked rolled oats
1 tsp. vanilla

Put 2 cups of sugar in a boiler; add 2 tablespoons of cocoa. Stir. Add 1/2 cup of milk. Add 1/2 cup of butter or margarine. Stir. Put the boiler on the stove. Turn heat to low; cook until it starts to boil. Stir as it cooks. Boil about 2 minutes; remove from stove. Add 1/2 cup of peanut butter; add 2 cups of rolled oats. Stir until well mixed. Add 1 teaspoon of vanilla; let cool. Drop on plate by spoon and refrigerate. Makes 3 or 4 dozen cookies.

Dwayne Cook, Huntsville Council

LACE OATMEAL COOKIES

1/2 c. butter
1/2 c. sugar
2 Tbsp. cream

3/4 c. minute oatmeal
1/4 c. flour

Melt butter and remaining ingredients; drop by spoonfuls on a cookie sheet. Bake 10 minutes in 350° oven. They are very thin. Take out of oven and cool 1/2 minute, then roll around handle of wooden spoon. They will not roll if too hot or too cool. These are good flat also if you don't have the time or patience to roll.

Gloria H. Ramage, Birmingham South Council

OATMEAL MACAROONS COOKIES

1 c. shortening
1/2 tsp. salt
1 c. granulated sugar
1 c. light brown sugar
1 Tbsp. vanilla

2 eggs, unbeaten
1 2/3 c. flour
1 tsp. baking soda
3 c. quick oatmeal, uncooked
1 c. chopped pecans

Mix thoroughly the shortening, sugars, vanilla and eggs. Sift together the flour, soda and salt, then add to first mixture. Fold in oats and nuts. All oats and nuts should be thoroughly moistened. Mixture will be stiff. Form balls of mixture using a teaspoon on a greased cookie sheet. Bake 10 to 15 minutes at 350°. Makes about 4-5 dozen cookies.

Mrs. John R. Criswell (Evelyn B.),
Mobile Council

ORANGE BALLS

1 box vanilla wafers,
   chopped fine
1 stick margarine
1 small (6 oz.) can
   frozen orange juice

1 box confectioners
   sugar*
1 c. pecans
1 c. coconut

Cream butter, sugar, wafers, pecans and orange juice; form into balls. Roll into coconut. Roll in powdered sugar.

1567-82

May be refrigerated or frozen.

*Need to save a little sugar to roll the balls in, or buy another box.

Sheilah Miller, Birmingham East Council

COLONIAL PEANUT OATMEAL COOKIES

1 c. shortening
1 c. granulated sugar
1 c. light brown sugar
1 tsp. vanilla
2 eggs

1 1/2 c. sifted flour
1 tsp. soda
3 c. rolled oats
1/2 lb. salted Spanish peanuts

Cream shortening; add sugar gradually. Add vanilla and eggs and beat well. Sift flour and soda; add to mixture. Add rolled oats and peanuts; mix well. Shape dough into small balls. Bake on lightly greased cookie sheet for about 7 minutes at 425°.

Edith Fields, Mobile Council

PEANUT BUTTER COOKIES

1/2 c. shortening (half
   butter or margarine),
   softened
1 c. crunchy peanut butter
1/2 c. granulated sugar
1/2 c. brown sugar, packed

1 egg
1 1/4 c. all-purpose flour*
3/4 tsp. soda
1/2 tsp. baking powder
1/4 tsp. salt

Mix thoroughly shortening, peanut butter, granulated sugar, brown sugar and egg; blend in flour, soda, baking powder and salt. Cover and chill. Heat oven to 375°. Shape dough into 1 inch balls. Place on lightly greased baking sheet. With fork dipped in flour, flatten in crisscross pattern. Bake 10 to 12 minutes. This recipe can be doubled and 1/2 of dough frozen.

*If using self-rising flour, omit soda, baking powder and salt.

Carol Bradley, Riverchase Council

PECAN BALLS

1/2 c. butter
3 heaping Tbsp.
   confectioners sugar
1 c. + 2 Tbsp. flour

1 tsp. vanilla flavoring
1 c. floured pecans
1 Tbsp. water

Cream butter and sugar; blend well. Add flour and nuts. Add flavoring and water last; blend well. Roll into balls the size of walnut. Bake on greased cookie sheet approximately 15 minutes. Roll balls in powdered sugar.

Lola E. Johnson, Retired,
Birmingham Central Council

PECAN CHEWIES

·2 sticks oleo
1 c. granulated sugar
1 c. light brown sugar
2 eggs, well beaten

2 c. self-rising flour
1 c. pecans
2 tsp. vanilla flavoring

Preheat oven to 300°. Melt butter in large pan; add sugars and blend well. Add well beaten eggs. Stir well; add 2 cups flour and stir until there are no lumps. Add pecans and vanilla. This mixture is more like cake batter. Pour into long pan 1 1/2 to 2 inches deep that has been greased and dusted with flour; cook approximately 25-30 minutes. This recipe should be mixed by hand and not with mixer; cut into squares while hot and take up while hot.

Juanita Grimes, Birmingham West Council

SAND TARTS

1 c. butter
5 Tbsp. powdered sugar
2 c. flour

2 tsp. vanilla
1 1/2 c. chopped nuts

Cream butter and sugar. Work flour, vanilla and nuts into creamed mixture; form into balls. Bake in 350° oven for 30 minutes. Roll tarts in powdered sugar as soon as they are removed from oven.

Sharon Crabtree, Tuscaloosa Council

SESAME COOKIES

1 c. Parkay margarine
2 c. flour
1/2 tsp. salt
1 tsp. almond extract

Sesame seeds
Kraft strawberry preserves
1/4 c. sugar

Cream margarine, sugar, flour and salt; add almond extract. Take teaspoon size of mixture and roll into ball, then roll in sesame seeds. Make indent in middle of ball and fill with preserves. Bake in 400° oven approximately 10 minutes.

Jackie Tunink, Mobile Council

SKILLET COOKIES

2 Tbsp. butter
1 c. finely cut pitted dates
1 c. sugar
2 eggs

3 c. Kellogg's Rice Krispies
1/2 c. chopped nuts
Confectioners sugar

Melt butter in skillet; add dates, granulated sugar and eggs. Cook over low heat, stirring constantly until mixture forms a ball. Remove from heat; cool slightly. Stir in Rice Krispies and nutmeats, mixing well. Sprinkle a piece of waxed paper lightly.

Mary C. Martin, Birmingham Central Council

SPRITZ COOKIES

2 c. sifted cake flour
  or 1 7/8 c. all-purpose
  flour
3/4 c. butter or margarine

1/2 c. sugar
1 egg yolk
1/2 tsp. almond extract
1/4 tsp. salt

1. Sift flour; measure. Add salt and resift. 2. Cream butter until fluffy. 3. Add the sugar to the butter gradually and beat. Add the egg yolk and almond extract; blend well. 4. Combine the flour into the creamed mixture. Make into a smooth dough. Chill until firm. 5. Preheat oven to 375°. Lightly oil baking sheet. 6. Select cookie press; pack with dough. Shape cookies on sheet and press with fork. 7. Garnish with a cherry or nut, if desired. 8. Bake 8 to 10 minutes until very delicately browned. Yield: About 3 dozen.

Helen Smith, Birmingham Council

SUGAR COOKIES

1 c. Crisco
1 c. butter
1 c. sugar
1 c. confectioners sugar
4 c. plain flour

2 eggs
1 tsp. soda
1 tsp. salt
1 tsp. cream of tartar
2 tsp. vanilla

Cream butter and Crisco; add sugar and eggs. Mix dry ingredients. Mix well and roll in little ball. Coat with sugar; bake at 350° for 8-10 minutes.

Frances Elrod, Anniston Council

OLD FASHIONED TEA CAKES

2 c. sugar
2 eggs
1 c. shortening (half
   butter and half Crisco)
1/2 c. milk

Pinch of salt
Nutmeg to taste
3-5 c. flour
3 level tsp. baking powder

Cream sugar and shortening; add eggs and mix well. Add 3 cups of flour (mixed with baking powder, salt and nutmeg) alternately with milk. Add enough flour until stiff enough to roll dough. Roll on floured board; cut out and place on greased cookie sheet. Bake at 375° approximately 15 minutes or until brown.

Pat Ozenne, Retired,
Birmingham Central Council

DROP TEA CAKES

1 1/2 c. sugar
4 eggs
1 1/3 c. melted shortening
   (not oil)

2 tsp. vanilla
3 c. flour
3 tsp. baking powder
1 tsp. salt

Using wooden spoon (not mixer) mix eggs and sugar very well. Add melted shortening; mix well. Stir in vanilla. Sift dry ingredients together and add to batter; mix well. Drop by rounded tablespoon onto buttered cookie sheet; bake at 350° approximately 10 minutes. Remove when brown around edges.

(Note: Do not substitute oil for melted shortening as it will not work.)

Nancy Morgan, Decatur Council

** NOTES **

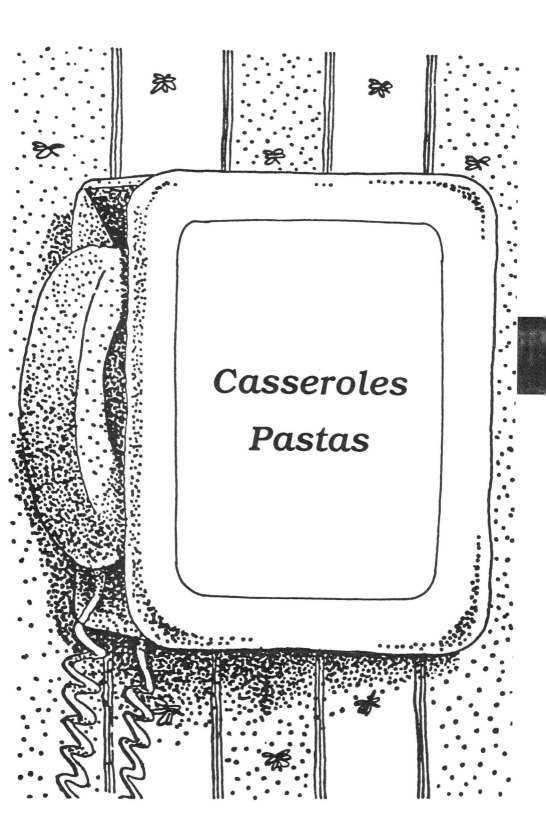

Casseroles

Pastas

HERB CHART

Use fresh whole herbs when possible. When fresh herbs are not available, use whole dried herbs that can be crushed just while adding. Store herbs in airtight containers away from the heat of the stove. Fresh herbs may be layered between paper towels and dried in the microwave on High for 2 minutes or until dry.

Basil	Can be chopped and added to cold poultry salads. If the recipe calls for tomatoes or tomato sauce, add a touch of basil to bring out a rich flavor.
Bay leaf	The basis of many French seasonings. It is added to soups, stews, marinades and stuffings.
Bouquet garni	A bundle of parsley, thyme and bay leaves tied together and added to stews, soups or sauces. Other herbs and spices may be added to the basic herbs.
Chervil	One of the traditional *fines herbes* used in French cooking. (The others are tarragon, parsley and chives.) It is good in omelets and soups.
Chives	Available fresh, dried or frozen, it can be substituted for raw onion or shallot in nearly any recipe.
Garlic	One of the oldest herbs in the world, it must be carefully handled. For best results, press or crush the garlic clove.
Marjoram	An aromatic herb of the mint family, it is good in soups, sauces, stuffings and stews.
Mint	Use fresh, dried or ground with vegetables, desserts, fruits, jelly, lamb or tea. Fresh sprigs of mint make attractive aromatic garnishes.
Oregano	A staple, savory herb in Italian, Spanish, Greek and Mexican cuisines. It is very good in dishes with a tomato foundation, especially in combination with basil.
Parsley	Use this mild herb as fresh sprigs or dried flakes to flavor or garnish almost any dish.
Rosemary	This pungent herb is especially good in poultry and fish dishes and in such accompaniments as stuffings.
Saffron	Use this deep orange herb, made from the dried stamens of a crocus, sparingly in poultry, seafood and rice dishes.
Sage	This herb is a perennial favorite with all kinds of poultry and stuffings.
Tarragon	One of the *fines herbes*. Goes well with all poultry dishes whether hot or cold.
Thyme	Usually used in combination with bay leaf in soups, stews and sauces.

ROCKY'S RECIPE (Or Bachelor's Old Fashioned Oatmeal)

3/4 c. cold water

1 pkg. old fashioned instant oatmeal

1. Remove pan from cabinet. 2. Fill 3/4 full with cold water. 3. Place on stove on high heat. 4. Bring water to vigorous boil. 5. Empty contents of 1 package Quaker's old fashioned instant oatmeal into salad bowl using care not to spill any on counter top. 6. Add boiling water to contents of bowl while stirring gently. 7. Let oatmeal savour water while cleaning up mess. 8. Enjoy with glass of cold milk. Energy and time saving variations of above recipe: Skip steps 1-4 - see step 5. Replace above step 6 with step 6A. Fill bowl with hot tap water from sink. See above for steps 7 and 8.

Rocky Sullivan, Decatur Council

ASPARAGUS CASSEROLE

2 cans asparagus
2 c. cheese, grated
4 eggs, boiled and chopped
1/4 c. flour
1/4 c. butter

2 c. milk
1 tsp. salt
1/8 tsp. black pepper
Mushrooms (optional)
 (1 small can)

In shallow baking dish alternate asparagus with 1 1/2 cups of cheese, eggs and mushrooms in 2 layers. Set aside. Melt butter in medium saucepan; blend in flour. Gradually stir in milk, salt and pepper and small amount of juice from asparagus. Bring to boil while stirring; boil 1 minute. Pour sauce over casserole and top with remaining cheese. Bake at 375° for 25 minutes or until cheese is brown.

Walter McLeod, Mobile Council

ASPARAGUS CASSEROLE

1 can asparagus spears
 (drain and reserve liquid)
1 can cream of mushroom
 soup

4 hard boiled eggs
3/4 lb. Cheddar cheese
12 saltine crackers
3/4 c. milk

Cut cheese in small cubes. Chop eggs. Crumble 4 crackers in bottom of buttered casserole dish; add layer of cheese, eggs, asparagus and soup. Alternate layers until all

1567-82

is used. Pour milk and 2 teaspoons asparagus juice over all.
Sprinkle with rest of crackers. Bake at 350° for 25 minutes.
Jaunita Grant, Montgomery Council

ASPARAGUS   CASSEROLE

1 large can asparagus	1 (10 1/2 oz.) can cream
2 boiled eggs	of mushroom soup,
1 c. grated cheese	undiluted
1 small can English peas	1/2 stick butter or margarine

In saucepan mix butter, cheese and soup; simmer till
melted. Layer mixture; bake at 375° for 30 minutes or till
done.
Patsy Mitchell, Birmingham East Council

CHEESE   AND   ASPARAGUS   CASSEROLE

2 (15 oz.) cans asparagus	6 Tbsp. flour
or 2 (10 oz.) pkg. boiled	3/4 tsp. salt
frozen asparagus (do not	1/8 tsp. white pepper
drain either one)	2 c. coarsely grated sharp
1 pt. light cream	Cheddar cheese
6 Tbsp. butter or margarine	1 c. poultry stuffing mix

Preheat oven to 400° F. Drain canned asparagus liquid
or asparagus cooking water into a quart measure and add
enough light cream to measure 3 cups. Melt 4 tablespoons
butter over moderate heat and blend in flour. Add the 3
cups liquid and heat, stirring constantly, until thickened.
Add salt, pepper and 1 cup cheese; cook and stir until
cheese is melted. Arrange asparagus in a buttered shallow 2
quart casserole and top with cheese sauce. Toss remaining
cheese with stuffing mix. Sprinkle over sauce and dot with
remaining butter. Bake, uncovered, 10-12 minutes, until
bubbly and touched with brown. Makes 4 servings.
Sandra Tutt, Montgomery Council

EGGS   SUNSHINE

6 eggs	White Cream Sauce
3 English muffins	

White Sauce:

3 Tbsp. butter	1/8 tsp. pepper
3 Tbsp. flour	1 c. milk
1/4 tsp. salt	

Boil eggs; separate yolks from whites. Chop whites finely and set aside. Chop yolks finely and set aside.

White Sauce: Melt butter over low heat; blend in flour and seasonings. Stir until smooth and bubbly; add milk and bring to a boil, stirring constantly. (If sauce is too thick, add milk.)

Just before serving, combine chopped egg whites and White Sauce. Serve sauce over toasted buttered English muffin halves and top each with about 2 tablespoons of chopped egg yolks.

William M. Johnson, Jr.
Birmingham Central Council

DEVILED EGG CASSEROLE

Use 8 hard boiled eggs, deviled with:

1/3 c. mayonnaise	1/4 tsp. curry powder
1/2 tsp. paprika	1/4 tsp. dry mustard

Sauce:

2 Tbsp. flour	1 can cream of shrimp soup
4 Tbsp. butter	1 can cream of mushroom soup
1 small jar dried beef	1 (8 or 9 oz.) can Pet milk

Cook sauce on low until thick; remove. Add 1/2 cup grated sharp cheese, one 4 ounce jar pimento. Stir. Line casserole dish with eggs. Pour sauce over. Top with buttered cracker crumbs; bake at 350° for 15-20 minutes.

Jane Chastain, Montgomery Council

FLUFFY OVEN EGGS AND BACON

1/2 lb. bacon (about 12 slices)	1/2 lb. chopped onion
	3 eggs
1/2 c. Bisquick baking mix	1/4 tsp. salt
1 1/4 c. milk	1/2 c. shredded Cheddar cheese
1/8 tsp. pepper	

Heat oven to 375°. Grease 1 1/2 quart round casserole. Cut bacon slices into thirds. Cook and stir bacon in 10 inch skillet over medium heat until almost crisp. Add onion. Cook, stirring frequently, until bacon is crisp; drain. Spread bacon and onion in bottom of casserole. Beat baking mix, eggs, milk, salt and pepper with hand beater until almost smooth. Slowly pour egg mixture over bacon; sprinkle with cheese. Bake uncovered until knife inserted in center comes out clean, about 35 minutes. Makes 4 to 6 servings.

June Crowe, Anniston Council

IMPOSSIBLE BACON PIE

12 strips bacon, fried
   and crumbled
1/3 c. chopped onions
1 c. grated Swiss cheese
4 eggs, slightly beaten

2 c. milk
1 c. Bisquick baking mix
1/8 tsp. pepper
1/3 tsp. salt
1/2 c. chopped bell pepper
   (optional)

Preheat oven to 400°. Lightly grease pie plate. Fry bacon until golden brown. Blot off excess grease with paper towel; crumble. Sprinkle bacon, onions, cheese and peppers on bottom of plate. Mix eggs, milk, Bisquick, pepper and salt together until smooth (blender - 15 seconds on highest speed, hand mixer - 1 minute on regular speed). Pour mixture into pie plate; bake 35-40 minutes or until knife inserted in center comes out clean. Great for breakfast! Yield: 6-8 servings.

Tammy Taylor, Birmingham South Council

BUTTER BEAN PIE

1 lb. dry butter beans,
   cooked (do not drain
   juice off)
2 lb. ground beef
1 large onion

1 bell pepper
1 can tomatoes
Salt and pepper to season
Pie crust

Brown ground beef, then drain. In large deep roasting pan spread layer of ground beef, then layer of butter beans, layer of thinly sliced onion and bell pepper. Repeat all 4 layers. Pour can of tomatoes on top of layers. Sprinkle with seasoning. Top with your favorite pie crust. Make pie crust a little thicker than usual. Bake in 375° oven for about 45 minutes to 1 hour, or until crust is brown.

Marian Turnipseed, Birmingham West Council

CALICO BEANS

1/2 lb. ground beef
1/2 lb. bacon, diced
1 large onion, chopped
1/2 c. catsup
2 tsp. salt
2 tsp. prepared mustard
4 tsp. cider or white
   vinegar

3/4 c. firmly packed light
   brown sugar
1 (30 oz.) can pork and beans
1 (15 oz.) can garbanzo
   beans, drained
1 (10 oz.) pkg. frozen lima
   beans, thawed
1 (15 oz.) can kidney beans,
   drained

Cook ground beef, bacon and onions in large skillet until onions are tender. Drain only if there is a large amount of fat. Stir in catsup, salt, mustard and vinegar. Combine remaining ingredients in a 3 quart casserole. Stir in meat mixture. Cover; bake at 350° for 40 minutes or until bubbly. Garnish with strips of crisp bacon if desired.

Mary Ann Davis, Anniston Council

GREEN BEAN CASSEROLE

2 cans cut green beans, drained
1 (5 oz.) can water chestnuts
1 small can mushrooms, thinly sliced

1 medium onion, chopped
1 can cream of mushroom soup
1 can cream of celery soup
Salt to taste
1 c. grated Cheddar cheese

Use 1 1/2 or 2 quart buttered casserole. Layer half the beans, chestnuts, mushrooms and onion. Cover with half the soups, salt and cheese. Repeat the layers, topping with cheese. Bake at 350° to 375° (depending on your oven) for 30 minutes. Makes 6-8 servings.

Allene Hartzog, Montgomery Council

GREEN BEAN CASSEROLE

2 cans beans* or 1 qt. fresh beans, cooked
2 Tbsp. bacon drippings

2 medium onions, chopped
1 clove garlic, chopped

Saute onions in bacon drippings; add beans and chopped garlic. Add 1 cup water and simmer for 1 hour. Pour in dish.

Topping:

1/2 stick butter
1/2 c. bread crumbs

1/2 c. broken pecans

Melt butter; add bread crumbs and pecans. Sprinkle salt and stir. Saturate bread and pecans well. Spread over bean mixture.

*If you buy beans, buy Blue Lake canned beans.

Mrs. Russell Lou Guthrie, Montgomery Council

FRANCES BROCCOLI CASSEROLE

2 pkg. frozen chopped
  broccoli
2 beaten eggs
1 c. mayonnaise
1 c. sharp Cheddar
  cheese, shredded
Salt and pepper to taste

1 can condensed mushroom
  with chicken or celery soup
1 tsp. Worcestershire sauce
1 tsp. minced onion
1 stack Ritz crackers,
  crumbled
Butter

    Cook broccoli; drain. Combine all ingredients except crackers and butter. Grease with butter all sides of baking dish to be used. Pour in mixture and top with Ritz crackers, crumbled, and pat with butter. Bake for 45 to 50 minutes at 350° or until brown. May be reheated and will remain soft.

    Adeline Rodgers, Montgomery Council

IMPOSSIBLE VEGETABLE PIE

1 pkg. frozen broccoli,
  thawed and drained
  (do not cook)
1/2 c. onion
1/2 c. green pepper

1 c. grated cheese
3/4 c. Bisquick
1 1/2 c. milk
3 eggs
1 tsp. salt and pepper

    Lightly grease a pie plate. Put broccoli, onion, green pepper and grated cheese into pie plate. Combine Bisquick, milk, eggs, salt and pepper; pour over vegetables. Cook at 400° for 40 minutes.

    Carole Smith, Tuscaloosa Council

ITALIAN BROCCOLI CASSEROLE

2 (10 oz.) pkg. frozen
  chopped broccoli
2 beaten eggs
1 can Cheddar cheese soup

1/2 tsp. crushed oregano
1 (8 oz.) can stewed tomatoes
3 Tbsp. grated Parmesan
  cheese

    Combine eggs, Cheddar cheese soup and oregano; stir in drained tomatoes and cooked broccoli. Pour into 10x6x2 inch baking dish; sprinkle with Parmesan cheese. Bake uncovered at 350° for 30 minutes.

    Ginger Seaman, Mobile Council

MARY'S BROCCOLI CASSEROLE

2 pkg. broccoli, cooked
  by pkg. directions
1 medium onion, chopped
1 can mushroom soup
1/2 c. milk

1/2 c. rice, cooked by
  pkg. directions
3/4 stick oleo
Salt and pepper to taste
Sharp cheese, grated

Mix soup and milk. Cook onion in oleo. In casserole dish, put broccoli, onion mixture, soup mixture, then rice and sprinkle grated cheese on top; cook for 30 minutes at 350°.

Emma Rousseau, Huntsville Council

BROCCOLI CASSEROLE

1/2 c. chopped celery
1 c. mushroom soup
1 c. cream of chicken soup
1 small jar Cheez Whiz

1/2 c. chopped onion
Salt and pepper to taste
1 pkg. frozen chopped
  broccoli
1 c. steamed rice

Cook celery and butter until clear; add soups, cheese, broccoli, onions, salt and pepper. Put rice in buttered casserole dish. Pour mixture over rice. Cook in 350° oven for 10 minutes.

Mrs. Libby Pilling, Decatur Council

BROCCOLI CASSEROLE

3 pkg. broccoli, drained
2 Tbsp. flour
2 Tbsp. sugar
2 Tbsp. butter

1 tsp. salt
4 oz. grated cheese
1 c. sour cream

Topping:

2 c. corn flakes

1/2 stick margarine

In double boiler mix flour, sugar, butter and cheese together; stir until melted. Add 1 cup sour cream and mix with broccoli.

To make topping, mix 2 cups corn flakes with 1/2 stick margarine; put on top. Bake for 30 minutes at 350°.

Debbie Hearn, Birmingham East Council

BROCCOLI CASSEROLE

2 boxes frozen broccoli, chopped
1/2 c. milk

1/2 lb. American cheese, grated (can use Velveeta)
1 can cream of chicken soup
1 c. bread crumbs

Place broccoli in a well buttered large casserole dish. Combine soup and milk; pour over broccoli. Sprinkle with bread crumbs and cheese. Bake at 350° for 40-45 minutes. or until done. Prick broccoli with fork to see if tender. Serves 8.

K. Leggett, Huntsville Council

BROCCOLI CASSEROLE

20 oz. chopped broccoli
1 can cream of mushroom soup
1 c. mayonnaise
2 beaten eggs

1/2 chopped onion
4 Tbsp. melted butter
Salt and pepper to taste
1/2 pkg. herb Pepperidge Farm stuffing mix

Cook and drain broccoli. Combine broccoli and all remaining ingredients. Pour in 9x13 inch pan and top with cheese; sprinkle more stuffing on top. Bake at 350° for 35 minutes.

Kitty Maxey, Montgomery Council

RUTH SPITZER'S BROCCOLI CASSEROLE

1 stick margarine
1 large onion
1 can mushroom soup

1 pkg. (roll) Kraft garlic cheese
2 boxes (pkg.) broccoli

Cook chopped onion in margarine until onion is glossy. Add mushroom soup and cheese; cook over low heat until cheese is melted. Pour over cooked broccoli in baking dish. Bake until cheese is bubbly.

Patsy S. Dean, Mobile Council

BROCCOLI CASSEROLE

2 (10 oz.) pkg. frozen chopped broccoli, cooked and drained
2 beaten eggs
1/2 c. milk
1 can cream of celery soup (undiluted)

2 c. shredded sharp Cheddar cheese
1 tsp. Worcestershire sauce
1 Tbsp. finely chopped onion
Salt and pepper to taste
Cracker crumbs
1 c. mayonnaise

Combine all ingredients except cracker crumbs in large bowl. Pour into a greased 13x9 inch pan. Cover with cracker crumbs; bake at 350° for about 45 minutes. Serves 8 to 10 people.

Wanda Ange, Birmingham East Council

BROCCOLI CASSEROLE

2 pkg. frozen broccoli,
   cooked and drained
3/4 c. celery
3/4 c. onion
1/2 c. bell pepper
2 cans mushroom soup
8 oz. Cheez Whiz
3 c. cooked rice

Saute celery, onion and bell pepper in 1 stick butter. Mix and bake at 350° for 30 minutes.

Shirley Adams, Birmingham East Council

BROCCOLI AND CHICKEN CASSEROLE

6 chicken breasts, cooked
   and boned
2 pkg. broccoli
2 cans cream of chicken
   soup, undiluted
1 c. mayonnaise
1 tsp. lemon juice
1 tsp. curry powder
Cheddar cheese, grated
Ritz crackers, grated or
   crushed

Cook broccoli for a few minutes and put on bottom of casserole dish. Top with bite size pieces of chicken. Mix all other ingredients together and pour sauce over chicken and broccoli. Sprinkle with cheese and top with Ritz crackers. Bake 30-40 minutes at 350° F.

Mabel Bene (Mrs. K. J. Bene),
Birmingham Central Council

BROCCOLI-PEAS CASSEROLE

2 (10 oz.) pkg. frozen
   chopped broccoli
2 (17 oz.) cans green peas
1 can cream of mushroom
   soup or cream of celery
   (prefer mushroom)
1 c. mayonnaise
1 tsp. salt
1/2 tsp. pepper
1 c. shredded sharp
   Cheddar cheese
1 medium onion, chopped
2 eggs, beaten
1/2 c. crushed round
   Ritz crackers

Cook broccoli according to package; drain. Arrange 1 package of cooked broccoli in a greased 2 quart casserole dish. Cover with peas. Mix soup, mayonnaise, salt, pepper,

1567-82

cheese, onion and eggs to make sauce. Pour half of sauce over broccoli and peas. Add rest of broccoli and top with remaining sauce. Sprinkle crushed crackers on top. Bake at 350° for 30 minutes. Makes 8 servings.

Libby McDowell, Montgomery Council

BROCCOLI AND RICE CASSEROLE

1 pkg. frozen broccoli
1 c. white rice
1/2 c. chopped bell
  pepper
1/2 c. chopped onion

1/2 c. chopped celery
1 stick margarine
1 can cream of mushroom soup
1 can Cheddar cheese soup

Cook broccoli as directed on package. You can cook rice ahead of time. Saute onions, celery and bell pepper in margarine. Mix all ingredients, including soups, and pour into casserole dish. Bake at 350° until bubbly.

Margie Judge, Mobile Council

BROCCOLI-RICE CASSEROLE

2 (10 oz.) pkg. frozen
  chopped broccoli
1 small onion, chopped
2 Tbsp. melted oleo
3 c. cooked rice

1 (10 oz.) can cream of
  chicken soup, undiluted
1/2 c. milk
1 (8 oz.) American cheese
  spread, cubed

Cook broccoli according to package directions; drain well and set aside. Saute onions in oleo until tender. Add soup, milk and cheese. Cook over medium heat, stirring constantly until cheese melts. Stir in rice and broccoli. Pour into a 2 quart greased casserole; bake at 350° for 30 minutes.

Lila Stovall, Decatur Council

BROCCOLI AND RICE (MICROWAVE)

1/2 c. chopped onion
1/2 c. chopped celery
1 (10 oz.) can cream of
  mushroom soup
1 (10 oz.) can cream of
  chicken soup
1 (8 oz.) jar Cheez Whiz

Salt and pepper
Paprika
2 (10 oz.) pkg. frozen
  chopped broccoli
1 c. uncooked rice
1 (4 oz.) can sliced
  mushrooms

1. Cook rice according to cookbook instructions (long rice). 2. Broccoli should be cooked in package for 6-8 minutes (punch holes in top of box). 3. Cook onion, celery

and 1 tablespoon butter in microwave oven for 3 minutes. The measuring cup can be used to cook this combination in. 4. Mix onion, celery, broccoli, rice, Cheez Whiz and soups together in the country cooker. Add mushrooms and sprinkle with paprika. 5. Heat the mixture 5 minutes on medium high (8) or until bubbly. Yield: 10 servings.

Bonnie Mayfield, Anniston Council

BAKED EGG CASSEROLE

4 slices white bread
1 c. Cheddar cheese
  (grated coarse)
2 Tbsp. oleo
3 eggs

1/2 tsp. salt
1/4 tsp. Worcestershire
  sauce
1 1/3 c. milk
Paprika

Trim crust and break in small pieces. Grease 1 1/2 quart casserole. Alternate layers of bread and cheese. Begin with bread (4 layers in all). Beat eggs; add salt and Worcestershire sauce, paprika and milk. Pour over bread and cheese; dot with butter and sprinkle with paprika. Cover and place in refrigerator 10 or more hours. Bake at 350° and cook 1 hour. Put in cold oven and turn on heat to keep from breaking dish. Cook until solid, not soupy. Serve hot! Very good!

Patti Smith, Anniston Council

BAKED MACARONI AND CHEESE SQUARES

1 pkg. or 2 c. elbow
  macaroni
8 oz. shredded sharp
  Cheddar cheese
1 3/4 c. milk

3 eggs
2 Tbsp. chopped pimiento
2 tsp. chicken flavor instant
  bouillon or 2 chicken
  flavor bouillon cubes

Preheat oven to 350°. In medium saucepan cook macaroni according to package directions; drain. In same saucepan add remaining ingredients except 1/2 cup cheese; mix well. Cook and stir over medium heat 3 to 5 minutes, until bouillon dissolves and cheese melts. Turn into a well greased 8 or 9 inch square baking dish. Top with remaining cheese; bake 20 to 25 minutes or until bubbly. Let stand 10 minutes before serving. Cut into squares. Makes about 9 servings. Refrigerate leftovers.

Betty Chilton, Birmingham East Council

BRITISH CASSEROLE - QUICK STYLE

1 box macaroni and
  cheese mix
1 small onion, chopped
1 small bell pepper, chopped
1 Tbsp. celery seeds
2 eggs

1/2 to 1 c. milk
Salt and pepper to taste
1 c. any kind of cheese
  you prefer
1 can of 5 biscuits

Boil macaroni until tender; drain. In a large bowl mix macaroni, onion, bell pepper, celery seeds, eggs, salt and pepper and gradually pour in milk to make mixture slightly soupy. Mix in cheese well. Pour into a casserole dish. Pull biscuits apart and lay flat on top of casserole. Bake at 350° until biscuits are golden brown. Serve hot!

Cheryl Glasco, Birmingham South Council

BRUNCH CASSEROLE

2 c. croutons
1 c. shredded cheese
  (natural or sharp)
4 eggs, slightly beaten
2 c. milk
1/2 tsp. salt

1/2 tsp. prepared mustard
1/2 tsp. onion powder
Dash of pepper
4 slices bacon, crisped,
  drained and crumbled

Preheat oven to 325°. In bottom of a greased 10x6 inch baking dish combine croutons and shredded cheese. Combine eggs, milk, salt, mustard, onion powder and pepper. Mix until blended. Pour over crouton mixture. Sprinkle bacon over top of casserole. Bake 55 minutes. Serves 4 to 6. Serve with fresh fruit, hot rolls and coffee.

Faith Kirby, Anniston Council

CHEESE CASSEROLE

6 oz. Velveeta cheese
2 oz. sharp cheese
3/4 stick oleo or butter

16 oz. large curd cottage cheese
2 heaping Tbsp. flour
4 eggs, beaten

Cut cheese and butter into small cubes. Combine with all other ingredients. Bake in a greased 2 quart baking dish at 350° for approximately 1 hour. Let set about 5 minutes and cut into squares. Can be cooked ahead of time for 40 minutes, then reheated for 20 minutes. Serves 8.

Sammie M. Jackson, Huntsville Council

234

CHEESE AND MACARONI CASSEROLE

1 box elbow macaroni
1 can mushroom soup
1 small can mushrooms
  (stems and pieces)
1 c. mayonnaise

1/4 c. chopped bell pepper
1/4 c. pimento
1/4 c. onions
1 lb. grated cheese

Cook macaroni and drain; add all ingredients together and mix with macaroni except with cheese on top. Bake at 350° for 30 minutes.

Debbie Hearn, Birmingham East Council

CHEESE PUDDING CASSEROLE

10 slices white bread
2 c. grated sharp cheese
3 eggs, well beaten
1 tsp. salt

1 tsp. dry mustard
2 c. milk
1 stick oleo

Trim crust from bread; cut each slice into 9 pieces. Melt oleo and dip each piece in oleo. Place layer of bread on bottom of baking dish; add a layer of cheese. Repeat until both are used. Mix remaining ingredients; beat well. Pour over bread-cheese layers. Refrigerate for 8 hours. Bake at 350° for 1 hour. Yield: 6-8 servings.

Virginia Mayo, Mobile Council

CHEESE STRATA

12 slices bread (crusts
  removed and buttered
  on both sides)
3/4 lb. Cheddar cheese,
  grated
6 eggs

4 c. milk
3/4 tsp. dry mustard
1 Tbsp. grated onion
3/4 tsp. salt
Dash of cayenne pepper

Butter 8x13 inch casserole. Place layer of buttered bread in bottom of casserole. Cover with all the grated cheese. Add another layer of bread (the remaining 6 slices). Beat eggs; add rest of ingredients. Mix and pour over bread; sprinkle with paprika and place in refrigerator at least 1 hour or overnight. Remove from refrigerator and let dish get room temperature. Bake at 350° for 1 hour. Serves 6. Best served as soon as removed from oven.

Izola Wood, Mobile Council

MACARONI CASSEROLE

1 (12 oz.) pkg. macaroni
1 small can pimento
2 cans cream of mushroom
  soup
1 c. mayonnaise
1 small chopped onion
1 stick margarine
1 lb. Cheddar cheese
Salt to taste

Cook macaroni according to directions on package until tender, but not soft. Chop pimento, onion and cheese. Combine all ingredients while macaroni is hot. Bake in 300° oven for 30 minutes. Delicious!

Note: This may be prepared a day or two in advance and refrigerated until ready to cook.

Evelyn Howard, Decatur Council

MACARONI AND CHEESE

2 1/2 c. water
1 tsp. salt
1 c. uncooked macaroni
1/4 lb. sharp cheese
1/4 lb. mild Cheddar cheese
4 Tbsp. melted butter
2 eggs, beaten
2 c. milk
1/2 tsp. salt

Bring water and 1 teaspoon salt to boil; add macaroni and cook until tender (8 minutes). Drain and let cool. Put a layer of macaroni in a baking dish and cover with layer of cheese. Repeat. Dip melted butter over the macaroni. Combine eggs, milk and 1/2 teaspoon salt. Pour over macaroni and bake at 350° for 30 minutes.

Brenda Etheredge, Mobile Council

MACARONI AND CHEESE

1 pkg. macaroni (cook
  about 5 minutes in
  salted water)
3/4 lb. Cheddar cheese,
  cut into 1 inch cubes
1 1/2 c. milk (or more
  if needed)
2 Tbsp. Mazola margarine
2 eggs, well beaten

Pour cooked macaroni into an oblong Pyrex dish; add margarine and let melt. Stir. Add milk, cubed cheese; distribute well through macaroni. Pour the 2 well beaten eggs on top, and stir just a little. Bake in 350° oven about 20-25 minutes, or until it bubbles up and is lightly browned on top. Do not overcook. This is my mother's recipe and it is really delicious. Use as a meat substitute and serve it with green beans, slaw and sliced tomatoes, or any other vegetable you like.

Dot Elder, Tuscaloosa Council

MACARONI AND CHEESE CASSEROLE

1 c. macaroni
1 can cream of chicken soup
1/2 c. mayonnaise
1 c. grated sharp cheese

1 small onion, finely chopped
2 Tbsp. finely chopped
  green pepper
2 Tbsp. chopped pimento

Cook macaroni until done. Mix other ingredients and macaroni. Pour into casserole; cook 35 to 40 minutes in 350° oven.

Grace Green, Anniston Council

MACARONI AND CHEESE DELUXE

1 (8 oz.) pkg. macaroni
2 c. cottage cheese
8 oz. sour cream
1 egg, beaten

3/4 tsp. salt
Dash of pepper
2 c. grated Cheddar
Paprika

Cook macaroni according to package directions. Drain; rinse and set aside. Combine next 6 ingredients. Add macaroni and stir well. Spoon into lightly greased 2 quart casserole. Sprinkle with paprika; bake at 350° for 45 minutes. Yield: 6 to 8 servings.

Gloria H. Ramage, Birmingham South Council

SMACK-ARONI AND CHEESE

1 (8 oz.) pkg. macaroni,
  cooked and drained
1 c. cubed Longhorn
  cheese, divided
1 c. cubed Swiss cheese,
  divided

3/4 c. grated Parmesan
  cheese, divided
Salt and pepper to taste
1 Tbsp. melted butter
1 Tbsp. all-purpose flour
1 c. milk

Place half of macaroni in a greased 2 quart casserole; top with half of Longhorn and Swiss cheese and 1/4 cup Parmesan cheese. Sprinkle with salt and pepper; repeat layers. Combine butter, flour and milk in a small saucepan; bring to a boil over low heat, stirring constantly. Remove from heat; pour sauce over casserole and top with remaining Parmesan cheese. Bake at 350° for 30 minutes. Yield: 8 to 10 servings.

Rachel Key, Montgomery Council

CHICKEN CASSEROLE

4 or 5 large chicken
  breasts
3 cans chicken soup
1 (8 oz.) carton sour
  cream

1/4 c. chicken broth
3 cylinders Ritz crackers
  (1/2 box if crackers are
  loose)
1 1/2 sticks margarine

Boil chicken; save broth. Remove bone from chicken. Cut into bite size pieces. Place pieces in bottom of large flat Pyrex dish. Mix soup, cream and chicken broth and heat until well blended; pour over chicken. Cover with crushed Ritz crackers, well coated in melted margarine. Bake at 350° for 30 to 35 minutes.

Earline Thornton, Tuscaloosa Council

CHICKEN CASSEROLE

3 chicken breasts, cooked
  and chopped
3 stalks chopped celery
1 chopped onion
1 c. Minute rice
1 can cream of chicken soup

1/2 c. water
1/2 tsp. salt
1/2 tsp. pepper
1/2 tsp. lemon juice
3/4 c. mayonnaise
1/2 c. potato chips

Mix ingredients together; top with potato chips. Bake at 350° for 40 minutes.

Dorothy Hayes, Birmingham Central Council

CHICKEN CASSEROLE WITH ALMONDS

3 or 4 lb. fryer
1 c. sour cream
1 can celery soup
1 can mushroom soup

1/2 c. almonds
1 tube crackers
1 Tbsp. poppy seed
1 stick oleo, melted

Boil chicken without salt; bone and skin. Cut in bite size. Mix soup, sour cream and almonds with chicken. Put in a buttered baking dish; cover with cracker crumbs. Pour melted oleo over cracker crumbs; add poppy seed and bake until it bubbles (350°). (Can be frozen until ready to serve. Then add the oleo, cracker crumbs and poppy seed.)

Marcella James, Tri-Cities Council

CRUNCHY CHICKEN CASSEROLE

3 c. chopped, cooked
   chicken
1/2 c. slivered almonds
1 (8 1/2 oz.) can water
   chestnuts, thinly sliced
1/4 c. chopped pimiento
1/4 tsp. celery salt
1/8 tsp. pepper

1/8 tsp. paprika
1 Tbsp. chopped parsley
1 (10 3/4 oz.) can cream.
   of mushroom soup, undiluted
1/2 c. French fried onion
   rings, crumbled
1/2 c. shredded sharp
   Cheddar cheese

Combine all ingredients except onion rings and cheese; pour into a greased 1 1/2 quart casserole. Sprinkle onion rings and cheese over top; bake at 350° for 30 minutes. Yield: 6 servings.

Faith Kirby, Anniston Council

CURRY CHICKEN BROCCOLI CASSEROLE

2 pkg. frozen broccoli
4 chicken breasts,
   cooked and boned
2 c. cream of chicken
   soup, undiluted

1 c. mayonnaise
1 tsp. lemon juice
3/4 tsp. curry powder
1/2 c. shredded sharp
   American cheese
1 Tbsp. toasted bread crumbs

Cook and drain broccoli; arrange in baking dish. Place chicken on top. Mix soup, mayonnaise, lemon juice and curry powder and pour over chicken. Sprinkle with cheese. Combine bread crumbs and melted butter and pour on top of cheese. Bake 30 minutes at 350°. May be made day before if needed and refrigerated.

Celeste Bouchillon, Anniston Council

CHICKEN CASSEROLE

4 chicken breasts, boiled
   with 1/4 stick butter
1 (8 oz.) pkg. Pepperidge
   Farm stuffing (herb
   seasoned)

1 can cream of celery soup
1 can cream of chicken soup
1 egg
1 stick margarine

Mix herb seasoned stuffing with 1 stick margarine (melted) and 1 egg. Mix 1 can cream of celery soup with 3/4 cup chicken broth. Mix 1 can cream of chicken soup with 3/4 cup chicken broth. Place in a casserole dish 1 layer of stuffing, 1 layer chicken, cream of celery soup, 1 layer of stuffing, 1 layer chicken, cream of chicken soup and the rest of the stuffing on top. Bake at 325° for 1 hour.

Sara Waldrop, Birmingham South Council

CHICKEN CASSEROLE

6 chicken breasts,
  halved and deboned
Bacon strips

Dried beef slices
1 can mushroom soup
1 (8 oz.) carton sour cream

Wrap chicken with strips of bacon. Use a 9x13 inch size pan. Cover bottom with dried beef slices. Place chicken on dried beef. Mix soup and sour cream and spoon over chicken; cover with foil. Refrigerate overnight; bake 3 hours at 275°.

Gladys Coker, Mobile Council

CHICKEN CASSEROLE

1/2 c. butter
6-8 chicken breasts
1/4 c. sherry
2 cans cream of chicken
  soup
1/2 c. mayonnaise

1 Tbsp. parsley flakes
6 c. cooked rice
  (yellow rice mix)
1 c. sour cream
1 tsp. paprika

Skin chicken before baking. Place butter in 9x13 inch baking dish at 350° and melt. Sprinkle chicken with salt and pepper and seasoned salt. Roll chicken in melted butter and pour sherry over chicken. Bake at 350° for 1 hour. Allow to cool, then bone chicken. Take leftover broth and place in mixing bowl; add soup, sour cream and remaining ingredients, except rice. Cook rice by package directions while boning chicken. Put rice in baking dish; pour 1/2 of sour cream mixture over rice. Place chicken on top, then pour remaining mixture over chicken. Place in oven and bake at 350° for 30-40 minutes. Can make through step 8 and freeze or refrigerate, then bake before serving.

Edwina Hicks (Mrs. Jimmy), Montgomery Council

CHICKEN CASSEROLE

2 Tbsp. olive oil
4 chicken breasts, skinned
2 Tbsp. flour
Salt and pepper (1/4 tsp.
  each)

1 c. dry vermouth
1/2 c. water
2 tomatoes, peeled and sliced
1 green pepper, sliced in rings
1 medium onion, thinly sliced

Use casserole dish large enough to lay the chicken in one layer. Lightly brown the chicken in a skillet, but not until done. Remove from the pan and set aside. Add the flour to the oil left in the pan and lightly brown it. Add the vermouth, water, salt and pepper and bring to a boil. Additional water may be needed to make a thin sauce. In the casserole dish, layer half the tomatoes, onions and peppers, in that order. Put the chicken on top and layer the remaining vegetables on top of the chicken. Pour the sauce over the ingredients in the dish and cover tightly with foil. Bake in a moderate oven (325°) for 40 to 45 minutes. With rice and a salad, you have a complete meal.

Diane M. Cook, Montgomery Council

CHICKEN CASSEROLE

2 to 3 c. cooked chicken, diced
4 hard boiled eggs, chopped
2 c. cooked rice
1 1/2 c. celery, chopped
1 small onion, chopped
1 c. mayonnaise
2 cans mushroom soup
1 (3 oz.) pkg. slivered almonds or 1 c. chopped pecans
1 tsp. salt
2 Tbsp. lemon juice
1 c. bread crumbs
2 Tbsp. margarine

Mix all ingredients except bread crumbs and margarine. Place mixture in buttered 9x12 inch pan or casserole. Brown bread crumbs lightly in margarine. Sprinkle over casserole. Refrigerate overnight; remove from refrigerator 1 hour before cooking. Bake 40-45 minutes at 350°. Serves 8.

Mattie Tynes, Montgomery Council

CHICKEN CASSEROLE

1 large baking hen (4 to 6 lb.)
1 (8 oz.) pkg. rice
1 large onion
3/4 stick butter
4 Tbsp. flour
2 cans cream of mushroom soup
1 c. milk
1 large can mushrooms, chopped
Salt and pepper to taste
1 lb. sharp cheese

Cook hen; cool and chop in bite size pieces. Blend flour and milk; add mushrooms, soup, salt and pepper to taste. Cook rice and layer sauce, rice, chicken and cheese. Two layers. End with cheese. Bake at 325° to 350° until bubbly. Serves 10-12.

Edna P. Killen, Tri-Cities Council

CHICKEN CASSEROLE

1/4 c. chopped bell pepper
2 small pkg. wide
  noodles, cooked
1 small onion, chopped
2 cans mushroom soup,
  undiluted
1 tsp. salt
1 c. crushed soda crackers

1 c. shredded sharp cheese
2 c. cooked chicken, chopped
4 hard boiled eggs, chopped
1 c. mayonnaise
1 (3 oz.) pkg. slivered almonds
1 Tbsp. lemon juice
1 1/2 c. chopped celery

Mix all ingredients except crackers and 1/2 to 1/4 cup shredded sharp cheese. Put into a large casserole dish. Refrigerate overnight. Remove from refrigerator 1 hour before baking. Sprinkle cracker crumbs, then cheese. Bake in 350° oven for about 35 to 45 minutes.

Kay Boyett, Montgomery Council

CHICKEN AND BROCCOLI CASSEROLE

2 whole breasts and 6
  thighs, cooked, diced
2 pkg. chopped broccoli,
  cooked
2 cans cream of chicken
  soup

1 c. mayonnaise
1 Tbsp. lemon juice
1 tsp. curry powder
1 stick melted butter or oleo
1 pkg. Pepperidge Farm
  herb dressing

Place diced chicken in 3 quart shallow casserole dish; top with broccoli. Mix soup, lemon juice, mayonnaise and curry powder. Pour over chicken and broccoli. Sprinkle herb dressing over top. Pour melted butter over all and cook at 350° for 30 minutes. Cover lightly with aluminum foil to keep topping from browning too rapidly. Serves 12.

Rochelle Yarbrough, Montgomery Council

CHICKEN-BROCCOLI CASSEROLE

1 cooked, boned chicken
2 c. chopped broccoli
1 can cream of chicken
  soup
1/4 pkg. Pepperidge Farm
  herb dressing

1/2 c. mayonnaise
1/2 stick butter
1 tsp. lemon juice
1/4 tsp. curry powder
1/4 c. chicken broth

Place chicken in long shallow pan. Sprinkle chopped broccoli, which has been cooked 5 minutes and drained. Mix soup, lemon juice, chicken broth, curry and mayonnaise well; pour over chicken and broccoli. Sprinkle dressing over top; spoon melted butter over all. Bake at 350° for 30 minutes.

Dana C. Lesher, Birmingham South Council

CHICKEN ORIENTAL CASSEROLE

2 c. cooked chicken
2 c. chopped celery
1 medium onion
1 can water chestnuts
2/3 c. mayonnaise

1 can cream of chicken soup
1/4 tsp. salt
1/4 tsp. pepper
2 c. crushed potato chips

Boil chicken and cut in pieces. Mix soup and mayonnaise with chicken. Add rest of the ingredients, but only half of the potato chips. Blend well. Pour into buttered casserole dish; sprinkle with remaining potato chips. Bake at 400° for 15 minutes. Good served with rice.

Kathy Ward, Montgomery Council

CHICKEN PIE

Cut up a large fryer. Cover with water. Add salt and a little red pepper. Cook until meat is ready to fall from the bones. Boil 3 eggs and slice. Make a thick white sauce with:

1 stick butter
2 c. milk
Salt and pepper

3/4 c. flour
1 c. chicken broth

Add sauce to chicken and eggs; pour into a pan lined with pie crust. Top with biscuits; dot with butter and bake at 425° until brown.

Debbie Tucker, Birmingham East Council

CHICKEN-RICE CASSEROLE

3 c. (or more) cooked,
  diced chicken
1 pkg. Uncle Ben's long
  grain and wild rice,
  cooked
1 can cream of celery
  soup, undiluted
1 jar chopped pimentos

1 medium onion, chopped
1 can French style green
  beans, drained
1 c. mayonnaise
1 can water chestnuts,
  sliced
Salt and pepper to taste

Mix all ingredients. Pour into 3 quart casserole; bake at 350° for 25-30 minutes.

Ann Johnson, Montgomery Council

CHICKEN AND RICE CASSEROLE

1/4 onion, minced
1 medium bell pepper,
  in strips
1 Tbsp. butter or
  margarine

1 can chicken broth
1 can boned chunk chicken
1/2 c. uncooked rice
1/2 c. shredded American
  cheese

In medium casserole dish melt butter; add onions and peppers and let simmer until tender, about 5 minutes. Add broth and the can of chicken, flaked. Add rice and cheese. Stir well. Bake in 350° oven, covered, for 1 hour.

Kathy Leake, Birmingham Central Council

CHICKEN SCALLOP

1 can chicken rice soup
1 can mushroom soup
1 (13 1/2 oz.) can
  evaporated milk

2 c. cut up cooked
  chicken
1 medium can chow mein
  noodles

Combine above ingredients and place in greased 1 1/2 quart casserole. Sprinkle crushed potato chips on top; bake at 350° for 1 hour.

Sammie M. Jackson, Huntsville Council

COMPANY CHICKEN CASSEROLE

1 1/2 c. uncooked
  Minute rice
1/4 c. margarine
1/2 c. celery, diced
1 (2 1/2 oz.) jar sliced
  mushrooms
4 to 6 chicken breasts
1 c. water

2 (10 3/4 oz.) cans soup
  (any combination of cream of
  mushroom, cream of celery
  or cream of chicken)
1 (6 oz.) can water chestnuts,
  sliced
1 (1.75 oz.) pkg. Lipton
  onion soup mix

Sprinkle dry rice into bottom of large well greased flat baking dish. Saute celery and mushrooms in margarine in small pan. In large bowl combine cans of soup, mushrooms, celery, margarine and water chestnuts. Shake the unopened envelope of onion soup mix to mix well. Add half of envelope to soup mixure in bowl. Stir well. Pour mixture over dry rice. Place chicken breasts, skin side up, over soup. Pour water over all this. Sprinkle other half of dry onion soup mix onto chicken. Cover; bake at 350° for 1 1/2 hours. Yield: 4 to 6 servings.

Linda (Hannah) Shattuck, Tuscaloosa Council

CORN BREAD CASSEROLE

4 to 6 chicken breasts
1 can cream of
  celery soup
1 can cream of
  chicken soup

1 c. chicken broth
2 boiled eggs
1 stick melted margarine
1 pan (8 or 9 inch) corn
  bread

Cook (boil) chicken breasts until done; save 1 cup broth. Pull chicken off bones; cut in bite size pieces. Set aside. After baking corn bread, let cool. Crumble up corn bread fine and pour melted margarine over corn bread. Mix well; set aside. To meat add 1 cup chicken broth, both cans soup. In bottom of baking dish put a little more than half corn bread, then spoon meat mixture on next mixture. Then sliced boiled eggs, and top with remaining corn bread. Bake at 325° till bubbly.

Agnes Trott, Montgomery Council

CREAMY CRUNCHY CHICKEN AND RICE BAKE

1 (8 oz.) jar Cheez Whiz
  pasteurized process
  cheese spread
1 1/2 c. hot cooked rice
2 c. chopped, cooked
  chicken

1 (10 oz.) pkg. frozen
  peas, cooked and drained
  (English peas)
1 (2.8 oz.) can Durkee's
  French fried onions

Combine process cheese spread and rice; mix well. Add chicken, peas and half of onions; mix lightly. Pour into 1 1/2 quart casserole. Bake at 350° for 15 minutes. Top with remaining onions; continue baking 5 minutes or until onions are lightly browned. Makes 4 to 6 servings.

Jane Courington, Montgomery Council

EASY CHICKEN AND RICE

2 whole chicken breasts,
  split and boned
  (about 1 1/2 lb.)
1 (4 oz.) can sliced
  mushrooms, drained
  (optional)

2 Tbsp. butter or margarine
1 can cream of chicken soup
1 1/2 c. water
1 1/2 c. quick cooking
  rice, uncooked

In skillet brown chicken and mushrooms in butter; stir in soup, water, 1/4 teaspoon salt, dash of pepper. Cover; simmer 20 minutes; stir in rice. Simmer 10 minutes more until liquid is absorbed. Stir often. Makes 4 servings.

1567-82   Louise Cox, Montgomery Council

SARRAH'S GREEN NOODLE CHICKEN CASSEROLE

5-6 lb. chicken, cooked,
  skinned, boned and diced
1 stick butter
1 c. chopped onion
1 c. celery
1/4 c. bell pepper

1 pkg. green noodles
1 can cream of mushroom soup
1 can cream of chicken soup
1 can sliced mushrooms
1/2 lb. Velveeta cheese
Parmesan cheese

Cook, skin, bone and dice chicken. Saute onion, celery and pepper in butter until tender. Cook noodles in chicken stock; drain, leaving about 1 cup stock in noodles. Mix the 2 cans of soup, sliced mushrooms and Velveeta cheese with the sauteed vegetables and chicken. Toss with the noodles (add more stock if needed). Sprinkle with Parmesan cheese and bake at 350° for about 1 hour.

Anne Spragins, Birmingham East Council

LAYERED CHICKEN CASSEROLE

1 1/2 lb. diced, cooked
  chicken
6 hard cooked eggs
2 cans condensed cream
  of mushroom soup
1/4 c. milk
1/2 c. chopped celery

1/4 c. finely chopped onions
1/4 tsp. salt
1/2 tsp. pepper
1/2 tsp. paprika
1 1/2 c. cracker crumbs
5 Tbsp. butter or
  margarine
1/2 c. chopped green peppers

In a medium bowl combine mushroom soup, milk, celery, green pepper, onion, salt, pepper and paprika. Mix well. Set aside. In a greased casserole cover bottom with 1/2 pound diced chicken. Slice hard cooked eggs; arrange slices over chicken. Spread 1/2 the soup mixture over eggs. Top with 1/2 cup cracker crumbs evenly. Repeat layers twice, using remaining chicken, eggs, soup mixture and cracker crumbs. Drizzle with butter or margarine. Bake at 375° for 1 hour. Serves 6.

Mrs. Jeri Nuss, Decatur Council

MACARONI AND CHICKEN CASSEROLE

1 c. uncooked elbow
  macaroni
1 c. diced, cooked chicken
1 (10 3/4 oz.) can cream
  of mushroom soup,
  undiluted

1 c. milk
1/2 (8 oz.) pkg. process
  cheese spread, diced
2 hard cooked eggs, chopped
2 Tbsp. chopped pimento

Combine all ingredients and spoon mixture into buttered 1 1/2 quart casserole. Cover dish and place in refrigerator overnight. Remove casserole from refrigerator and allow to set at room temperature 1 hour; cook at 350° with cover for 1 hour and 15 minutes.

Barbara Spivey, Mobile Council

MEXICAN CHICKEN CASSEROLE

6 chicken breasts, boiled
1 large taco Doritos
1 1/4 c. chicken broth
1 c. grated cheese
1/2 c. chopped green
  peppers
3/4 c. chopped onions
2 cans cream of chicken
  soup
1 can Ro-Tel tomatoes
1 tsp. garlic salt
1 Tbsp. chili powder

Remove skin from chicken and debone. Dice into fairly large pieces. Put aside in bowl. Put Doritos in bowl and pour chicken broth over them. Let them stand for 5 minutes stirring occasionally. Grease large casserole. Put in casserole by layers, 1/3 Doritos, 1/2 green peppers, 1/2 onions, 1/2 chicken and 1/3 cheese, ending up with Doritos on top. Mix together 2 cans cream of chicken soup, can tomatoes and peppers, garlic salt and chili powder; pour over top. Bake at 350° for 45 minutes. Sprinkle with remaining cheese after taking out of oven.

Denetiza Wilkes, Riverchase Council

PARTY CHICKEN CASSEROLE

4 1/2 whole cooked and
  deboned chicken breasts
1 small can sliced water
  chestnuts
2 cans cream of mushroom
  soup
1 c. mayonnaise
1 chopped pimiento
3/4 c. celery, finely chopped
3/4 c. onion, finely chopped
1/2 pkg. Pepperidge Farm
  stuffing mix
1/2 c. chicken broth
1/2 tsp. poultry seasoning
Salt and pepper to taste
Lemon pepper seasoning to
  taste

Mix all ingredients together and fill a 3 quart casserole and top with stuffing and moisten with broth. Can be fixed the day before the party. Bake at 350° uncovered for 40-50 minutes. Serves 8-10 people.

Joyce Hobbs, Huntsville Council

QUICK CHICKEN POT PIE

4 chicken breasts
1 can cream of
  chicken soup
1 small onion, chopped
1 small can English peas,
  drained (optional)

Salt and pepper to taste
1 or 2 cans buttermilk biscuits
4 to 6 Irish potatoes, peeled
  and sliced into 1/4 inch
  circles
1 or 2 Tbsp. cornstarch

Cover chicken with water in pot; add onions, salt and pepper and cook until chicken is tender. Remove chicken to cool. Pull into small pieces. Add soup and slices of potatoes and cook until potatoes are tender, but not falling apart. Mix cornstarch with 1/4 cup of cold water until smooth. Pour into hot mixture to thicken. Add chicken (without bones) and peas to the potatoes. Spray deep baking dish with Pam. Pour mixture into dish. Open cans of biscuits and place over top of hot chicken and potato mixture. Bake at 400° until biscuits are brown.

Mrs. John R. Criswell, Mobile Council

CORN CASSEROLE

2 cans Green Giant
  Mexicorn
1 pkg. Mahatma yellow rice
  in a box (use only 1 pkg.)

1 stick margarine
1 can cream of celery soup
1 c. sharp cheese

Prepare rice according to instructions on package. Add margarine; stir until melted. Add corn and soup. Grate 1 cup or more sharp cheese. Combine with mixture; bake 30 minutes at 350°. Remove from oven; sprinkle some cheese on top and sprinkle some paprika for color.

Jan Cook, Anniston Council

CORN CASSEROLE

1 medium size onion,
  chopped
1/2 bell pepper, chopped
1 c. instant rice
2 cans Mexican corn

2 cans cream of mushroom
  soup
1 c. butter or margarine
1 c. water
1 c. grated cheese

Saute onion and bell pepper in butter in large cooking dish. Add 1 cup water; bring to boil. Add 1 cup instant rice. Cover and let stand for 5 minutes. Add corn and cream of mushroom (golden cream of mushroom may be substituted for more spicy flavor). Sprinkle top with grated cheese. Bake in 350° oven 30 minutes. Salt and pepper to taste.

Gertrude Cheatwood,
Birmingham South Council

CORN CASSEROLE

2 (12 oz.) cans Niblets
  corn, drained
1 medium onion, chopped
1 green pepper, chopped
1 stick margarine

2 c. cooked rice
1 can mushroom soup
1 small jar pimento, chopped
2 Tbsp. Worcestershire sauce
1 c. grated cheese

Saute onion, pepper in margarine. Combine all ingredients in casserole dish (except cheese). Bake 30 minutes or until bubbly. When almost done, top with grated cheese.

Debbie Hearn, Birmingham East Council

CORN CASSEROLE

1 medium onion, chopped
1 green pepper
1 stick margarine
4 Tbsp. flour
2 c. cooked rice
2 c. whole kernel corn

2 c. canned tomatoes
2 hard cooked eggs, chopped
1 tsp. Worcestershire sauce
1/2 tsp. Tabasco sauce
1 1/2 tsp. salt and pepper

Brown onions and pepper in margarine; add all other ingredients and mix well. Pour in greased casserole dish and cover with grated cheese. Place in 375° oven until cheese melts.

Doris Beasley, Mobile Council

GOOD CORN

2 cans Green Giant
  Mexicorn, well drained
1 can sliced mushrooms,
  drained

2 cans cream of mushroom soup
4 oz. Cracker Barrel sharp
  cheese, grated
Plenty of black pepper

Slowly heat all ingredients until cheese melts and is hot.

Edwina Hicks (Mrs. Jimmy),
Montgomery Council

CORN CASSEROLE

2 eggs
1/4 c. milk
1/2 c. cracker crumbs
1 (17 oz.) can cream
  style corn
1/4 c. melted butter
  or margarine
1/4 c. grated carrot

1/4 c. chopped green pepper
1 Tbsp. chopped celery
1 Tbsp. chopped onion
1/8 tsp. hot sauce
1/2 tsp. sugar
1/2 tsp. salt
1/2 c. shredded Cheddar
  cheese

Combine eggs and milk; beat until well blended. Add cracker crumbs; set aside until all liquid is absorbed. Add remaining ingredients except cheese to cracker crumb mixture, stirring well. Spoon mixture into a greased 1 quart casserole. Bake at 350° for 45 minutes; sprinkle with cheese while hot. Yield: 4 to 5 servings.

Rita Finley, Huntsville Council

CORN CASSEROLE

1 can yellow cream corn
1/4 c. chopped onion
1 c. crushed crackers
3 Tbsp. chopped pimiento

1 egg
1 c. milk
1 Tbsp. butter
Salt and pepper to taste

Melt butter; add onions and saute. Add corn, milk, egg, pimiento and cracker crumbs. Bake in greased casserole 50 minutes at 350°. Top with buttered bread crumbs.

Lois Harris, Tuscaloosa Council

CORN CASSEROLE

2 cans white shoe peg
  corn, drained
1 stick butter

1 small carton whipping cream
2 Tbsp. flour
Salt and pepper

Melt butter in baking dish; add corn, whipping cream and salt and pepper. Blend in flour; bake at 350° for 45 minutes until light brown.

Linda Lindley, Birmingham Central Council

CORN AND TOMATO CASSEROLE

8 slices bacon, cut in halves
2 c. soft bread crumbs
2 c. peeled, chopped
  fresh tomatoes

1 medium size green pepper,
  chopped
3 c. fresh corn, cut from cob
1/4 tsp. salt

1/4 tsp. pepper
1/4 tsp. sugar

1/4 c. butter or margarine,
melted

Place half of bacon in a shallow 2 quart casserole, and top with 1 cup bread crumbs. Layer half of tomatoes, green pepper and corn over bread crumbs; sprinkle with half of salt, sugar and pepper. Repeat layers of the vegetables and the seasonings. Combine the melted butter and remaining 1 cup bread crumbs, stirring well. Spoon evenly over casserole. Top with remaining bacon; bake at 375° for 40 to 45 minutes or until bread crumbs are golden. Yield: 8 servings.

Margie Lavender, Riverchase Council

QUICK CORN CASSEROLE

1 large can cream
   style corn
1 large can whole style
   corn

1/2 c. chopped bell peppers
1 Tbsp. butter or
   margarine
Salt and pepper to taste

Preheat oven to 375°. Mix all of the above ingredients and place in a 1 1/2 quart casserole dish; bake until top is slightly brown.

Jean R. Jordan, Montgomery Council

RICE AND CORN CASSEROLE
(Microwave Cooking)

1 (5 oz.) pkg. yellow rice
1 can cream of celery soup
1 stick oleo

1 (12 oz.) can Green
   Giant Mexicorn
1 c. grated Cheddar cheese

In a 2 quart casserole cook rice and water according to directions on package on high setting on microwave for 5 minutes, covered. Reduce heat to 50% power; cook for 12 minutes, still covered. Add remaining ingredients except cheese. Mix well. Sprinkle cheese on top; heat 2 minutes or until cheese melts.

Jeanette Granthum, Montgomery Council

SWISS CORN BAKE

1 pt. canned whole
   kernel corn
1 (6 oz.) can evaporated
   milk (2/3 c.)
2 beaten eggs

2 Tbsp. finely chopped onions
Dash of pepper
1 c. shredded process Swiss
   cheese (4 oz.)
1 c. soft bread crumbs
2 Tbsp. melted butter

Boil corn, uncovered, 20 minutes before tasting or using. Drain well. Combine corn, evaporated milk, eggs, chopped onions, pepper and 3/4 cup of shredded cheese. Turn mixture into a 10 x 6 x 1 1/2 inch baking dish or a 1 quart casserole. Toss bread crumbs with melted butter and remaining 1/4 cup shredded Swiss cheese. Sprinkle over corn mixture; bake at 350° for 25 to 30 minutes. Garnish with green pepper rings, if desired. Makes 4 to 6 servings.

Myrtle Parks, Opelika Council

BOND CRABMEAT AND EGGPLANT

1 large-medium eggplant	1 stalk celery (adjust to taste)
Salt to taste	1 egg
About 3/4 stick oleo	About 2-3 c. cracker or
1 small onion (adjust	bread crumbs
to taste)	1 can lump or claw crabmeat

Cook eggplant in salted water until tender; drain and mash. Combine and saute celery and onion in butter until tender. Combine cracker crumbs, sauteed vegetables and eggplant. Add slightly beaten egg and crabmeat (using liquid in can). Dot with oleo. Bake at about 375° until top is slightly browned, about 30 minutes.

Betty Floyd Parker, Montgomery Council

EGGPLANT CASSEROLE

1 eggplant	1 minced garlic clove
2 c. celery, chopped	2 slices bread, finely
1 c. chopped onion	chopped
1 egg, well beaten	Salt to taste
1/2 stick melted butter	Dash of cayenne pepper

Boil eggplant in water until tender; allow to cool and then peel. Remove seed and chop. Saute onion and celery in the butter until tender. Combine eggplant, celery and onion in bowl and add well beaten egg and finely chopped bread and cheese. Season with salt and pepper; mix well. Place in buttered casserole and cover with cracker crumbs and dots of butter; bake at 350° about 25 minutes, until crumbs are browned. You might like to add 1/2 pound of cooked shrimp, or 1/2 pound of cooked (and crumbled) sausage to above. Add before baking. You may prefer cracker crumbs instead of the chopped bread.

Mary C. Martin, Birmingham East Council

252

EGGPLANT CASSEROLE

1 large eggplant, peeled and sliced

Spaghetti sauce (home cooked or Ragu brand)

Slice eggplant and sprinkle with salt and let stand for 10 minutes. Rinse and dry. Saute in oil until almost done. Layer in casserole and pour sauce over and top with cheese. Bake for 30 minutes at 350°.

Sara Lindsey, Riverchase Council

EGGPLANT CASSEROLE

1 eggplant
1 small onion, chopped
1 can condensed
  mushroom soup

1 can small shrimp
  (fresh are better)
1 1/2 c. grated Cheddar cheese
Salt and pepper to taste
1/2 c. cracker crumbs

Peel and cube eggplant; cook in very little water with salt and chopped onion. Cook until soft; drain and save liquid. Mash and add undiluted soup, shrimp, salt and pepper. Top with cracker crumbs and cheese. Use liquid only if dry while cooking - rarely needed. Cook about 1 1/2 hours in 350° oven. Serves 4-6.

Ruth Turner, Mobile Council

EGGPLANT CASSEROLE

1 eggplant
1 1/2 c. grated sharp cheese
1 1/2 c. cracker crumbs
1 1/2 c. milk

4 eggs
1 tsp. salt
1/2 tsp. pepper
1 stick oleo, melted

Cook eggplant until mushy; drain. Add all ingredients, reserving 1/2 cup cheese, 1/2 cup crumbs and small amount oleo. Mix well. Pour into baking dish; sprinkle with reserved cheese, crumbs and melted butter. Bake at 325° to 350° for 30 minutes.

Jane Paulk, Montgomery Council

EGGPLANT CASSEROLE

5 or 6 slices toasted
  bread, cut in small pieces
1 medium eggplant, cut in
  cubes and parboiled

1 lb. hot sausage, cooked
  and drained
1/2 c. diced celery
1/2 c. diced bell pepper

1 c. chopped green onions
1 can stewed tomatoes,
   drained

1 c. sharp cheese, cut in
   small pieces

Grease 2 quart baking dish; cover bottom with bread crumbs, then add eggplant, celery, bell pepper, onions, sausage and tomatoes. Cover and bake at 350° for 45 minutes. Add remaining bread crumbs and cheese. Return to oven for 3 or 4 minutes until the cheese melts. Serve hot.

Peggy Kersh, Birmingham South Council

MARY'S EGGPLANT CASSEROLE

1 large eggplant
1/4 stick margarine
1 small onion
1 stalk (or less) celery
1/4 c. water

1/4 bell pepper (or more)
1 c. toasted bread crumbs
1/4 c. grated cheese
2 medium tomatoes
Salt and pepper to taste

Split eggplant in half; remove inside (ice cream scoop okay). Place margarine in skillet; add onion (minced) and eggplant. Start cooking, then add water, celery (chopped), bell pepper (chopped); let cook until vegetables are tender, then add tomatoes and grated cheese. Then stir in toasted bread crumbs and place into empty eggplant shells. Add or garnish with chopped tomatoes and bake until tomatoes are done. (Browned ground beef may be added if meat casserole is desired.) These may be served at this time or frozen and reheated to be served later.

O. W. Scott, Gadsden Council

VENISON AND EGGPLANT CASSEROLE

1/2 lb. ground venison
   (steak or venison
   hamburger)
1 medium eggplant, diced
1 onion, chopped

3 Tbsp. chopped parsley
1 (8 oz.) can tomato sauce
1/2 tsp. paprika
1 tsp. salt
Corn flakes

Mix all ingredients (except corn flakes). Pour into 1 1/2 quart casserole; cover with corn flakes and bake at 350° for 1 hour.

Eleanor Gearhart, Montgomery Council

CHEESE GRITS

2 1/2 c. milk
3/4 c. regular grits
1/2 c. margarine

1/2 tsp. salt
1/3 c. Parmesan cheese
1 (5 oz.) jar sharp
 process cheese spread

Bring milk to a boil; add grits and cook until thickened (about 10 minutes), stirring often. Stir in margarine, salt and cheese; spoon into lightly greased 1 quart casserole dish and bake at 325° for 20 minutes. Serves 6 to 8 people.

Gloria H. Ramage, Birmingham South Council

CHEESE GRITS

1 c. grits
1/2 c. butter or margarine
3 eggs, beaten

2/3 c. sweet milk
1/2 lb. Cheddar cheese,
 grated
1 (6 oz.) roll bacon cheese

Cook grits according to package. Add butter and bacon cheese to hot grits; blend well. Cool. Combine eggs with milk and stir into grits. Pour into greased 2 quart casserole. Sprinkle with cheese; bake 30 or 40 minutes at 325°.

Mary Edna Fife, Montgomery Council

GARLIC GRITS CASSEROLE

1 c. grits
4 c. water
1 tsp. salt

1 stick margarine
1 stick Kraft's garlic cheese
2 eggs

1. Cook grits in water and salt. 2. Add chopped margarine and cheese; stir to dissolve. 3. Add small amount to eggs. 4. Return to grits; stir to mix. 5. Pour in buttered casserole dish. 6. Bake at 350° until brown, about 1 hour.

Bonnie Mayfield, Anniston Council

BACHELOR'S CASSEROLE

1 (1 lb.) can tomatoes
3 Tbsp. vegetable oil
2 large onions, chopped
1 green pepper, chopped
1 1/2 lb. ground beef
1/2 c. uncooked rice

2 tsp. salt
1/2 tsp. chili powder
1/4 tsp. sweet basil
1/4 tsp. marjoram
1/8 tsp. pepper

Saute onions and green pepper in vegetable oil until

tender; add ground beef and brown well. Drain off excess grease. Stir in remaining ingredients; pour into greased 2 quart casserole. Bake covered at 350° for 45 minutes. Uncover and bake 15 minutes more. Serves 6-8.

W. F. Ary, Huntsville Council

BARBEQUE BEAN CASSEROLE

1 lb. ground beef	1 Tbsp. Worcestershire sauce
1/2 c. chopped onion	2 Tbsp. vinegar
1/2 tsp. salt	1/4 tsp. Tabasco (optional)
1/4 tsp. black pepper	1 (1 lb. 12 oz.) can
1/2 c. catsup	pork and beans

Brown beef and onion; pour off fat. Add remaining ingredients. Pour into 1 1/2 quart casserole dish; bake at 350° for 30 minutes.

Nanette Stinson, Montgomery Council

BEEF 'N CORN CASSEROLE

1 lb. ground beef	1 (12 oz.) can whole kernel
1/2 c. chopped onion	corn, drained
1 (8 oz.) pkg. cream	1/4 c. chopped pimento
cheese, cubed	1/4 tsp. salt
1 can condensed cream	Dash of pepper
of mushroom soup	1 (7.5 oz.) can refrigerated
	buttermilk biscuits

Brown meat; drain. Add onion; cook until tender. Add cream cheese and soup, mixing well. Stir in corn, pimiento and seasonings; pour into 1 1/2 quart casserole. Separate dough into 10 biscuits; cut each in half, forming 20 half-circles. Place biscuits, cut side down, around edge of casserole. Bake at 375° for 20 to 25 minutes or until biscuits are browned. Makes 6 servings.

Debbie Hearn, Birmingham East Council

BEEF NOODLE CASSEROLE

1 Tbsp. butter	1 (6 to 8 oz.) pkg. noodles
1 1/4 lb. ground steak	1/2 pt. sour cream
1 clove garlic, minced	3 oz. cream cheese,
2 cans tomato sauce	softened
1 tsp. sugar	Chives
Salt and pepper to taste	Grated Cheddar cheese

Melt butter in large pan; brown meat and garlic. Add

tomato sauce, sugar, salt and pepper; cook about 20 minutes. Cook noodles by package directions. Combine sour cream, cream cheese and chives. In casserole alternate layers of meat, cheese and noodles until all are used. Top with cheese and bake at 350° until hot and bubbly. Can be made day before and heated thoroughly. Serves 6-8.

Miriam B. Vinson, Riverchase Council

BEEF AND WATER CHESTNUT CASSEROLE

3 lb. ground chuck
2 tsp. salt
1 tsp. black pepper
1 tsp. Italian seasoning
1 c. onion, chopped
2 (6 oz.) cans tomato paste
2 1/2 c. water
1 c. celery, chopped

1/4 c. bell pepper, chopped
2 (8 1/2 oz.) cans water
  chestnuts, sliced
2 c. cooked rice (cooked as
  directed on pkg.)
1 (4 oz.) can evaporated milk
3 Tbsp. melted margarine
  or butter
2 c. crushed soda crackers

Brown beef lightly, stirring all the time. Add next 6 ingredients and cook covered on low heat for 1 hour. Add celery, peppers and water chestnuts; cook 15 minutes, leaving vegetables a little crunchy. Remove from heat; add rice and evaporated milk. Place in long shallow casserole. Sprinkle with buttered cracker crumbs. Bake in preheated 350° oven for 25 to 35 minutes. This casserole may be divided into smaller portions and frozen for later use. Serves 10. Approximately 48¢ per serving. (First Place winning recipe.)

Faith Kirby, Anniston Council

CANNELLONI

1/2 lb. ground beef
1/4 c. chopped onion
3 eggs, beaten
1/4 c. parsley
8 manicotti shells,
  uncooked
1 (8 oz.) can tomato
  sauce

1 (4 oz.) pkg. Mozzarella
  cheese
1/4 lb. sausage
1/2 c. Parmesan cheese
1/4 tsp. oregano leaves
1/2 tsp. garlic salt
2 (16 oz.) cans tomatoes
1/4 c. water

Brown meat; drain. Add onion; cook until tender. Stir in 1/4 cup Parmesan cheese, eggs and seasonings. Fill manicotti shells; place in 10x6 inch baking dish. Pour in combined tomatoes and tomato sauce and water over manicotti;

sprinkle with remaining Parmesan cheese. Cover with aluminum foil; bake at 350° for 1 hour. Top with Mozzarella cheese. Continue baking until cheese is melted. Serves 4.

Becky Cook, Huntsville Council

CHEESE AND PASTA IN A POT

2 lb. lean beef (ground)	8 oz. shell macaroni
Vegetable oil	1 1/2 pt. dairy sour cream
2 medium onions, chopped	1 (1/2 lb.) pkg. sliced
1 garlic clove, crushed	Provolone cheese
1 (14 oz.) jar spaghetti	1 (1/2 lb.) pkg. Mozzarella
sauce	cheese, sliced thin
1 (1 lb.) can stewed	1 (3 oz.) can sliced broiled
tomatoes	mushrooms (optional)

Cook ground beef in a little vegetable oil in a large deep frying pan until brown, stirring often with a fork; drain off any excess fat. Add onions, garlic, spaghetti sauce, stewed tomatoes and undrained mushrooms; mix well. Simmer 20 minutes or until onions are soft. Meanwhile, cook macaroni shells according to package directions; drain and rinse with cold water. Pour half the shells into a deep casserole dish. Cover with half the tomato-meat sauce. Spread half the sour cream over sauce. Top with slices of Provolone cheese. Repeat, ending with slices of Mozzarella cheese. Cover casserole; bake at 350° for 35 to 40 minutes. Remove cover; continue baking until Mozzarella cheese melts and browns slightly. Serves 8.

Becky Cook, Huntsville Council

CHEESEBURGER CASSEROLE

2 lb. ground beef	1 can mushroom pieces
1 onion, diced	1 large can cut green beans
1 bell pepper	1 can crescent rolls
1 stalk celery, diced	1 egg
1 tsp. season salt	1 (12 oz.) pkg. sharp
1 tsp. garlic salt	Cheddar cheese
1 large can tomato sauce	Paprika

Brown ground beef and onion in a skillet; pour off all fat from the ground beef. Add to ground beef and onions the bell pepper, celery, season salt, garlic salt, tomato sauce and mushrooms. Let this simmer while you dice the cut green beans. Add the green beans and continue to simmer this mixture. Take the crescent rolls and form a crust in a deep casserole dish. You can use a rectangular baking pan

258

if you desire, but this may require 2 cans of crescent rolls.
A see-through Pyrex dish is best to use, so you can tell when
the crust is brown on the bottom. Remove mixture from heat.
Beat the egg and grate the cheese. Spread the beaten egg
over the crust and sprinkle a little cheese on the crust.
Pour the mixture into the crust. Put the remaining cheese
over the top; bake at 425° until cheese is melted and crust is
golden brown.

Eusebia C. Sanderson,
Birmingham Central Council

CHEESEBURGER PIE

1 c. Bisquick baking mix
1/4 c. cold water
1 lb. ground beef
1/2 c. chopped onion
1/2 tsp. salt
1/4 tsp. pepper
2 Tbsp. Bisquick
   baking mix
1 Tbsp. Worcestershire
   sauce
2 eggs
1 c. small curd creamed
   cottage cheese
2 medium tomatoes, sliced
1 c. shredded Cheddar
   cheese (about 4 oz.)

Heat oven to 375°. Mix 1 cup baking mix and the water
until soft dough forms; beat vigorously 20 strokes. Gently
smooth dough into ball on floured cloth-covered board.
Knead 5 times. Roll dough 2 inches larger than inverted pie
plate (9 x 1 1/4 inches). Ease into plate; flute edge, if
desired. Cook and stir ground beef and onion until beef is
brown; drain. Stir in salt, pepper, 2 tablespoons baking
mix and the Worcestershire sauce. Spoon into pie crust.
Mix eggs and cottage cheese; pour over beef mixture. Arrange tomato slices in circle on top; sprinkle with Cheddar
cheese. Bake until set, about 30 minutes. Makes 6 to 8
servings. High altitude directions (3,500 to 6,500 feet): Use
boiling water to make dough. Bake about 35 minutes.

Sherry A. Liles, Tri-Cities Council

CHINESE CHUCK CASSEROLE

1 lb. ground chuck
1 medium onion, diced
1 can cream of mushroom
   soup
1 can cream of chicken soup
1 can water
1/2 c. raw rice
1 can chow mein noodles

Brown ground chuck and onion; add soups, water and
rice. Bring to a boil; pour into a casserole dish and bake 25
minutes at 350° F. Add the chow mein noodles and bake 10
minutes longer. Yield: 6 servings.

1567-82   G. Roper, Birmingham East Council   259

CONEY ISLAND CASSEROLE

1 (8 oz.) pkg. macaroni	2 cans herb tomato sauce
1 pkg. wieners	Cheddar cheese
1 lb. ground meat	1 Tbsp. oil

Preheat oven to 350°. Cook macaroni according to package directions; drain. Slice wieners; brown in 1 table-spoon oil; drain. Brown hamburger meat in drippings; drain. Mix hamburger meat, wieners, tomato sauce, shredded cheese and macaroni. Place in baking dish. Garnish with shredded cheese. Bake 40 minutes.

Eulene Miller, Mobile Council

CORNED BEEF CASSEROLE

1 (12 oz.) can corned beef, crumbled	1 c. milk
1/4 lb. chopped American cheese	1/2 c. chopped onion
1 can cream of chicken soup	1 (8 oz.) pkg. noodles, cooked and drained
	3/4 c. buttered bread crumbs

Combine all ingredients except noodles and bread crumbs. Alternate layers of meat mixture with noodles in 2 quart casserole; top with bread crumbs and bake 30 minutes in 375° oven.

Jamima Edney, Birmingham South Council

CORN BREAD PIE

1 lb. ground beef	1 small onion, chopped
1 can tomato soup	1/2 tsp. salt
1 can Niblet corn, drained	1 tsp. pepper
1/2 medium bell pepper, chopped	1 Tbsp. chili powder
	Water

Corn Bread Topping: Mix together -

3/4 c. self-rising meal	1 egg, beaten
1/4 c. flour	2 Tbsp. bacon drippings
About 1/2 c. milk	

(Should be soupy.) Brown ground beef; drain off fat. Add onion, bell pepper, chili powder, salt and pepper. Add tomato soup and about 3/4 can of water. Stir together and simmer about 15 minutes. Slowly spoon Corn Bread Topping over beef mixture and bake till brown, about 20 minutes at 350° F.

Helen Glass, Birmingham West Council

COTTAGE PIE

1 large onion
3 carrots
1 1/2 lb. hamburger
2 Tbsp. flour
Salt, pepper

2 Tbsp. Worcestershire sauce
1 c. beef bouillon
1 lb. potatoes
3 Tbsp. butter
Milk or cream

Slice a large onion and fry in beef drippings or shortening until softened, but not browned. Add 3 thinly sliced carrots and 1 1/2 pounds crumbled hamburger. Stir until it starts to turn brown, then sprinkle with 2 tablespoons flour and season with salt, pepper and 2 tablespoons of Worcestershire sauce. Add about 1 cup bouillon; cover and simmer for about 30 minutes. Transfer to an ovenproof dish, and top with creamy mashed potatoes, obtained by boiling 1 pound peeled, quartered potatoes for about 20-25 minutes, then sieving and mixing with 3 tablespoons of butter and enough milk or cream to form a soft puree. Season with salt and pepper and, using a fork, smooth the top with lots of butter. Bake at 375° for 20 minutes; brown under a hot broiler if necessary; the top should be golden.

Ginger H. Bryars, Birmingham Central Council

COUNTY FAIR CASSEROLE (SOUTHERN LIVING)

1 (8 oz.) pkg. elbow
  macaroni
1 lb. ground beef
1 c. chopped onion
1 tsp. salt

1/4 tsp. pepper
1 can cream of celery soup
1 (8 oz.) carton sour cream
1 can English peas, drained

Cook macaroni according to directions; drain well. Combine ground beef, onion and seasonings in a skillet; saute until meat is lightly browned, stirring to crumble. Drain grease. Stir in cream of celery soup; cover and simmer 10 minutes. Stir in macaroni and remaining ingredients; bake in a lightly greased 2 1/2 quart casserole dish for 35 minutes at 350°. Serves 8 people.

Debbie Hearn, Birmingham East Council

CROWD PLEASER CASSEROLE

1 1/2 lb. ground beef
1 c. chopped onion
1 (16 oz.) can whole
  kernel corn, drained
1 c. cream of chicken soup

1/4 c. pimento
1/2 tsp. salt
1/2 tsp. pepper
1 c. sour cream
1 (10 oz.) pkg. noodles, cooked
1 c. buttered bread crumbs

Brown meat and onions; add all other ingredients and bake at 350° for 20 minutes. Then add bread crumbs and bake 10 minutes more.

P.S. "There is one nice thing about working for the Lord", says the minister, "The pay isn't much, but the retirement plan is fantastic!"

Barbara Spivey, Mobile Council

FIRECRACKER CASSEROLE

2 lb. ground beef
1 large onion, chopped
2 Tbsp. chili powder
2 tsp. ground cumin
1 tsp. salt

1 (15 oz.) can chili beans
6 frozen tortillas, thawed
1 1/2 c. shredded Monterey Jack
1 1/2 c. shredded Cheddar
1 (10 oz.) can Ro-Tel tomatoes

Cook ground beef and onion until done; drain drippings. Add chili powder, cumin and salt. Stir well. Cook over low heat 10 minutes. Spoon meat mixture into casserole dish (13x9x2 inches). Layer beans, tortillas and cheeses over meat mixture. Pour Ro-Tel tomatoes on top. Cover baking pan and refrigerate overnight; bake uncovered at 350° for 1 hour. Yield: 8 to 10 servings.

Gloria H. Ramage, Birmingham South Council

ETTA'S GOULASH

1 lb. ground beef
1 small onion
1 can corn
1 can tomatoes

1 can pinto beans
1 c. cooked macaroni
1 c. catsup
Salt and pepper to taste

Brown ground beef and onions; drain oil. Add all other ingredients. Cook on medium heat about 30 minutes.

Charles-Etta Smith, Huntsville Council

GROUND BEEF CASSEROLE

1 lb. ground beef
1 small onion, chopped
2 cans tomato soup
1 can tomatoes

2 c. uncooked macaroni
4 slices cheese
1 Tbsp. Worcestershire
Salt to taste

Brown ground beef and onion; drain. Combine tomato soup, tomatoes, cooked macaroni and Worcestershire; add to ground beef and onion. Put into greased 2 quart casserole dish; top with cheese; bake at 350° for 25-30 minutes.

262   Donna Campbell, Huntsville Council

GROUND BEEF-NOODLE CASSEROLE

1 1/2 lb. ground chuck
1 medium onion, finely
 chopped
1 (5 oz.) pkg. large noodles

2 small cans tomato sauce
Oregano
Celery salt
1 c. shredded Cheddar cheese

Brown ground chuck with onions; season to taste with salt, pepper, celery salt and stir well. Add tomato sauce and simmer while noodles cook in separate saucepan. When noodles are cooked, stir them in ground beef mixture and oregano. Pour in casserole dish; top with cheese and place in hot oven 5 to 7 minutes.

Donna Cox, Birmingham East Council

GROUND CHUCK OR ROUND CASSEROLE

1 1/2 lb. ground chuck
1 medium onion
1 can cream of celery soup

Tater tots
1 can cream of mushroom soup,
 diluted with 1/2 can water

Crumble meat over bottom of large flat casserole pan. Slice onions on top of meat; add the celery soup, undiluted, and spread over onions. Then put on a layer of tater tots. Then add the can of mushroom soup with 1/2 can water (diluted). Bake in 350° oven 1 hour 15 minutes.

Gladys Coker, Mobile Council

HAMBURGER BEAN CASSEROLE

1 lb. hamburger
1/4 lb. bacon
1/2 c. onion
1 can kidney beans
1 can green lima beans
1 can pork and beans

1/2 c. catsup
1 Tbsp. prepared mustard
2 Tbsp. vinegar
3/4 c. brown sugar
Salt and pepper to taste

Combine hamburger, bacon and onion and fry all together. Drain. Combine with bean mixture. Cook in crock pot on low for 4 to 5 hours, or bake in 350° oven for 1 to 1 1/2 hours. Great dish for church suppers, family reunions, backyard picnics, etc.

Kay Atkisson, Montgomery Council

HAMBURGER-CORN CASSEROLE

1 1/4 lb. hamburger	1 (6 oz.) pkg. noodles
3/4 c. onion	1 c. sour cream
1 large can whole kernel	1 small jar pimento
corn	1/4 tsp. salt
1 can cream of mushroom	1/4 tsp. pepper
soup	1/2 tsp. Accent
1 can cream of chicken soup	

Topping:

1 c. bread crumbs	1/4 c. butter

Brown meat and onions until tender; drain. Add corn and all other ingredients. Mix well, then add cooked noodles and put in casserole dish. Top with bread crumbs. Melt butter; pour over top. Sprinkle with paprika; bake at 350° for 45 minutes.

Charlene Brown, Montgomery Council

HAMBURGER STROGANOFF

2 lb. ground beef	1/2 tsp. pepper
1/2 c. butter	1 tsp. Worcestershire
1 (4 oz.) can sliced	sauce
mushrooms, drained	1/4 c. flour
1 c. chopped onion	1/3 c. chili sauce
1 clove garlic, minced	1 1/2 c. dairy sour cream
2 tsp. salt	

Brown ground beef in half of the butter; add remaining butter, mushrooms, onion, garlic, salt and pepper. Saute until onions are tender. Add Worcestershire sauce; stir in flour, then chili sauce. Just before serving, blend in sour cream. Serve hot over noodles or spaghetti. Serves 6 to 8.

Dianne Lassiter, Huntsville Council

HOMINY PIE

3/4 lb. ground beef	1 tsp. flour
1 (12 oz.) can tomatoes	1 (16 oz.) can hominy
1/2 tsp. chili powder	1 c. grated Cheddar
1 medium onion, chopped	cheese

Brown meat and add flour, tomatoes and seasoning. In separate pan brown onions and hominy with a little margarine or vegetable oil. Add meat mixture; place in greased casserole. Bake at 350° for 30 minutes. Sprinkle with cheese.

"Pot" Harris, Tuscaloosa Council

HUNGRY JACK-BEEF CASSEROLE

1 lb. ground beef
1 tsp. salt
1 (16 oz.) can pork
  and beans
3/4 c. Kraft barbecue sauce

2 Tbsp. brown sugar
1 Tbsp. instant minced onion
1 (9.5 oz.) can Hungry Jack
  biscuits
1 c. Cheddar cheese, shredded

Preheat oven to 375°. Brown beef and drain grease. Stir in next 5 ingredients; heat until bubbly. Pour into a 2 quart casserole dish. Cut biscuits in halves to form 20 half circles. Place cut side down around edge of casserole; sprinkle with cheese and bake 25-30 minutes. Serves 4-6.

Sammie M. Jackson, Huntsville Council

HUSBAND'S DELIGHT

1 lb. ground beef
1 garlic clove or salt
1 tsp. sugar
Pepper to taste
2 cans tomato sauce

5 scallions (spring onions)
1 (8 oz.) pkg. small noodles
1/2 c. grated Cheddar cheese
1 small pkg. cream cheese
1 carton plain yogurt

Brown beef and drain; add garlic, pepper, sugar and tomato sauce. Cover and simmer about 15 minutes. Cook noodles and drain. Finely chop tops and bottoms of scallions and mix with cream cheese and yogurt. Layer noodles, meat sauce, cream cheese mixture and grated cheese in 2 quart baking dish, ending with cheese on top. Bake about 20 minutes to heat thoroughly at 350°. Best mixed the day before. Serves 8 with seconds. Freezes well.

Janet Eversole, Birmingham South Council

ITALIAN CASSEROLE

1 lb. ground meat
2 Tbsp. bacon drippings
1 medium onion, chopped
2 garlic cloves, minced
1 c. tomato juice

1 c. chopped parsley
1 can whole kernel corn
1 Tbsp. olive oil
1 box noodles (3 scant c.),
  cooked
1/2 lb. sharp cheese, grated

Brown meat in bacon fat. Simmer tomato juice and parsley 5 minutes. Cook noodles; drain and measure. Mix all ingredients, folding in cheese and noodles last. Season to taste with salt. Put in 1 1/2 to 2 quart casserole; bake 1 1/2 hours at 325°. Serves 6.

Mrs. W. R. Chambless, Life Member,
Birmingham Council

JOHNNIE'S QUIK FIX

1/2 c. chopped onion
1/2 c. chopped green
  pepper
1/2 c. chopped celery
1 (7 1/4 oz.) box
  macaroni and cheese mix

1 (16 oz.) can whole
  kernel corn
1 (8 oz.) can tomato sauce
Lawry's seasoning salt
1 lb. ground beef

Fix macaroni and cheese mix according to package directions. Brown meat in skillet. Blend onions, pepper, celery and seasoning salt. Stir and taste for flavor. Season to personal taste. Heat oven to 350°. Mix meat and macaroni dinner in casserole dish. Add drained corn and tomato sauce. Stir thoroughly. Place in preheated oven for 15 minutes. Serve as main dish with tossed salad.

Jim South, Selma Council

MARZETTI

1 1/2 lb. ground beef
1 green bell pepper,
  chopped, or 1/2 pepper
1 large onion, chopped
2 stalks celery, chopped
1 can tomato soup
1 can mushroom soup
1 can water

2 Tbsp. bacon drippings
1 tsp. salt and pepper
1 Tbsp. sugar
1/4 tsp. chili powder
Dash of garlic
Grated cheese for top
1 (10 oz.) pkg. 1/4 inch
  noodles, cooked and drained

Use bacon drippings; cook onions, celery, bell pepper and meat in large skillet. Add soups and water and seasoning for about 15 minutes; cook and drain noodles and mix with meat mixture and put in large casserole that has been buttered. Put cheese on top of casserole and bake in 350° oven for 45 minutes covered; uncover and cook 15 minutes more. Serves about 10 people.

Ernestine Gudgen, Birmingham South Council

MEAT BALL CASSEROLE

1 1/2 lb. ground meat
3/4 c. rolled oats,
  uncooked
1 c. evaporated milk

1 Tbsp. instant onion flakes
1 tsp. salt
1/2 tsp. pepper

    Sauce:

1 c. catsup
2 Tbsp. vinegar

1/2 c. water
2 Tbsp. sugar

Combine meat, oats, milk, onion flakes, salt and pepper. Mix well; shape into 8 large meat balls. Place in 2 quart casserole. Combine catsup, vinegar, water, sugar and pour over top of meat balls; bake at 350° for 1 1/2 hours.

Curtis Whitman, Montgomery Council

MEXICAN CASSEROLE

2 lb. hamburger meat
1 medium onion
1 large or 2 medium
  cans enchilada sauce*
2 cans cream of mushroom
  soup
1 can water

2 small cans green chilies
  (if whole chilies used,
  chop them up)
3/4 lb. grated Longhorn
  cheese
1 dozen corn tortillas
  (not canned type)

Brown hamburger and onion and add enchilada sauce and simmer. In saucepan combine soup, water and green chilies; simmer until soup is smooth. Grease casserole dish; line with tortillas. Add a layer of meat mixture, soup mixture and cheese, another layer of tortillas, then meat mixture, soup mixture and cheese. Continue layering ingredients until all used, ending with cheese on top. Bake in 350° oven for 1 hour. Makes a great meal with just tossed salad and crackers.

Note: If "hot" enchilada sauce is used, the casserole will be very hot - I use "mild".

Peggy Sweetman, Huntsville Council

MEXICAN CASSEROLE

1 lb. ground hamburger
  meat
1 (15 oz.) can Ranch
  Style beans
1 (10 3/4 oz.) can cream
  of chicken soup
7 tortillas, broken in
  bite size

1 (10 3/4 oz.) can cream
  of mushroom soup
1 (10 oz.) can Ro-Tel tomatoes
  with green chilies
1 medium onion, chopped
About 1 1/2 c. grated
  cheese or less

Crumble meat in bottom of 9x13x2 inch Pyrex dish; add 1 can of soup. Add beans and chopped onion, 1/2 of tortillas, 1/2 of cheese, Ro-Tel tomatoes, other can of soup, rest of tortillas, rest of cheese. Bake at 350° for 1 hour.

Donna Griffin, Mobile Council

MIMIE'S GOULASH (WINTER STEW)

2 c. diced potatoes
1 can kidney beans
1 can stewed tomatoes
1 lb. ground beef

1/2 c. diced onion
2 c. water
1 tsp. chili powder

Brown ground beef and onion; drain well. In large boiler add all remaining ingredients and ground beef. Bring to boil; cover and simmer 30 minutes. Makes 6-8 servings of hearty "soup-stew". Great on cold winter nights.

Darion Browning, Birmingham South Council

MOUSSAKA (A GREEK DISH)

Meat Sauce:

2 Tbsp. butter or
  margarine
1 1/2 lb. ground
  chuck or lamb
1/2 tsp. dried oregano
  leaves
1/2 tsp. cinnamon

Dash of pepper
1 c. finely chopped onion
1 clove garlic, crushed
1 tsp. dried basil leaves
1 tsp. salt
2 (8 oz.) cans tomato sauce

Have ready:
2 eggplants (1 lb. 4 oz.),
  washed and dried

Salt
1/2 c. butter or margarine,
  melted

Meat Sauce: In hot butter in 3 1/2 quart Dutch oven, saute onion, chuck, garlic, stirring until brown, 10 minutes. Add herbs, spices, tomato sauce; bring to boiling, stirring. Reduce heat; simmer, uncovered, 1/2 hour.

Halve unpared eggplants lengthwise; slice crosswise, 1/2 inch thick. Place in bottom of broiler pan; sprinkle lightly with salt; brush lightly with melted butter. Broil 4 inches from heat, 4 minutes per side, or until golden.

Cream Sauce:

2 Tbsp. butter or
  margarine
1/2 tsp. salt
2 c. milk
2 Tbsp. flour

2 eggs
1/2 c. grated Parmesan cheese
1/2 c. grated Cheddar cheese
2 Tbsp. dry bread crumbs
Dash of pepper

Make Cream Sauce: In medium saucepan melt butter; remove from heat and stir in flour, salt and pepper. Add milk gradually. Bring to boil, stirring until mixture is thickened. Remove from heat. In small bowl, beat eggs with wire whisk. Beat in some hot cream-sauce mixture; return mixture to saucepan. Mix well; set aside. Preheat oven to 350°.

To assemble casserole: In bottom of a shallow 2 quart 12 x 7 1/2 x 2 inch baking dish, layer half of eggplant, overlapping slightly. Sprinkle with 2 tablespoons each grated Parmesan and Cheddar cheeses. Stir bread crumbs into meat sauce; spoon evenly over eggplant in casserole, then sprinkle with 2 tablespoons each Parmesan and Cheddar cheeses. Layer rest of eggplant slices, overlapping, as before. Pour cream sauce over all. Sprinkle top with remaining cheese. Bake 35 to 40 minutes or until golden brown and top is set. If desired, brown top a little more under broiler, 1 minute; cool slightly to serve. Cut in squares. Makes 12 servings.

Martha Hatcher, Montgomery Council

NOODLES ITALIAN STYLE

2 Tbsp. vegetable oil
1 small clove garlic,
  pressed (optional)
4 (8 oz.) cans tomato
  sauce with mushrooms
1/2 tsp. sugar
1/4 tsp. dried basil leaves
1 lb. medium egg noodles,
  cooked and drained
8 oz. Mozzarella cheese,
  sliced

1/4 c. coarsely chopped
  parsley
1 lb. Ricotta cheese
1/3 c. sliced onions
  (or chopped)
1 lb. ground round beef
1/4 tsp. salt
1/4 tsp. dried oregano leaves
2 Tbsp. grated Parmesan
  cheese

Heat oven to 375°. In a large saucepan over moderate high heat, heat oil and brown onion and garlic lightly. Add ground beef and cook, stirring frequently, until no longer pink. Reduce heat to moderate low and stir in tomato sauce, sugar, salt, basil and oregano. Simmer, uncovered, 15 minutes. In an ungreased shallow 3 quart rectangular baking dish spread half the cooked noodles and top with half the meat sauce mixture. Sprinkle with 1 tablespoon Parmesan cheese and 2 tablespoons of the chopped parsley. Dot with half the Ricotta. Repeat with remaining noodles, sauce, Parmesan cheese, Parsley and Ricotta. Arrange Mozzarella slices over top of casserole. Bake 15 to 20 minutes, or until Mozzarella is melted and lightly browned. Serves 8.

Martha Hatcher, Montgomery Council

"OLE" SKILLET SUPPER

1 Tbsp. cooking fat
1 lb. ground beef
2 c. cooked rice
1 (1 lb.) can tomatoes
  and juice
1 tsp. salt
1/8 tsp. black pepper
1/2 to 3/4 tsp. chili
  powder (to taste)
1 large onion, grated
1 c. corn bread mix
  (I use 1 1/2 c.)

1. Melt cooking fat in 9 inch skillet; add ground beef. Cook till browned. Add rice, tomatoes, salt, pepper, chili powder (double if you like it hot) and onion. Mix well, breaking tomatoes and meat in small pieces. 2. Cook until piping hot and liquid is absorbed. 3. Top with corn bread batter made from corn bread mix. 4. Bake at 425° F. about 25 minutes. Add a bit of water to meat mixture if baking time exceeds 30 minutes.

Theresa Elkourie, Birmingham East Council

PICADIA

1 to 1 1/2 lb. ground
  chuck
1 to 1 1/2 lb. sausage
1 onion
1 bell pepper
Garlic salt
1 can whole tomatoes
3 bay leaves
1 c. olives, chopped
  (with pimentos)
1 c. raisins
2 packs yellow rice
1 can English peas

Saute onion and bell pepper; add ground chuck and sausage and garlic salt. Cook until meat browns. Add tomatoes, bay leaves, olives and raisins. Cook for 1 hour (simmer). Fix yellow rice according to package directions. Layer on a large platter or in a casserole dish, rice-meat mixture and top with cooked peas. Serve hot. Serves 10.

Marcia Freeman, Birmingham East Council

SICILIAN SUPPER

1 lb. ground beef
1/2 c. chopped onion
1 (6 oz.) can tomato paste
3/4 c. water
1 tsp. salt
1/8 tsp. garlic powder
1/2 c. chopped green
  pepper
1 Tbsp. margarine
1 (8 oz.) pkg. cream
  cheese, cubed
3/4 c. milk
1/3 c. grated Parmesan cheese
1/4 tsp. salt
2 c. noodles, cooked, drained

Brown meat; drain. Add onion; cook until tender. Stir

in tomato paste, water and seasonings; simmer 5 minutes.
Saute green pepper in margarine; add cream cheese and milk,
stirring until cream cheese melts. Stir in Parmesan cheese,
salt and noodles. In a 10x6 inch baking dish arrange alternate crosswise rows of meat mixture and noodles; bake at
350° for 20 minutes. Makes 6 to 8 servings.

Debbie Hearn, Birmingham East Council

STEAK, BEANS, ONIONS AND POTATOES CASSEROLE

1 lb. round steak or
  cubed, floured
1 can green beans, drained

Sliced onions
Potatoes (quantity depends
  on servings needed)

Layer potatoes (quartered), onion rings and green
beans in casserole. Brown floured steak in skillet. Remove
steak and place on top of vegetables. In skillet make brown
gravy and pour over all. Season to taste. Cover and bake
at 350° until done.

Margaret Boudreau, Huntsville Council

TACO CASSEROLE

2 lb. ground lean beef
1 onion, chopped
2 pkg. French's taco
  seasoning mix
Salt and pepper to taste
2 c. water
1 small can chopped
  black olives (optional)

1 small can whole kernel
  corn, drained (optional)
1 pkg. frozen El Chico's flour
  tortilla shells
1/2 of 8 oz. pkg. Monterey
  Jack cheese with jalapeno
  peppers, grated
1 (10 oz.) pkg. Cracker
  Barrel cheese, grated

Brown meat with salt, pepper and onions; drain. Add
French's taco mix and 2 cups water. Cook on medium heat
until mixture is hot. Let simmer on low heat, stirring when
needed until mixture is thick. Add drained corn and olives,
if desired; heat. Thaw and separate tortilla shells. Grate
each kind of cheese separately. Spray baking dish with Pam.
Fill each shell with a small amount of cheese (with peppers)
and meat. Roll filling into shell and lay in dish (side by side)
and pour rest of meat sauce over rolled shells. Cover the top
of shells with grated Cracker Barrel cheese; bake at 400° for
5 or 10 minutes until shells are hot and cheese has melted.
Serve with green salad.

Mrs. John R. Criswell, Mobile Council

TAMALE PIE

2 lb. ground beef
1 c. chopped onion
1/2 c. chopped green
 pepper
2 cloves garlic, minced
1 (16 oz.) can tomatoes

1 (16 oz.) can corn, drained
2 1/2 tsp. chili powder
1/2 tsp. oregano
1/4 tsp. pepper
Salt

Topping:

1 1/2 c. milk
2 Tbsp. butter
1 tsp. salt

1/2 c. corn meal
1 c. shredded cheese
2 eggs, beaten

Brown meat, onion, peppers and garlic; drain fat.
Add other ingredients and simmer 15 minutes. Turn into 3
quart casserole. Heat milk, butter and salt in saucepan; stir
in meat and cook about 5 minutes until thick. Remove from
heat. Stir in eggs and cheese; pour over meat mixture.
Bake in 375° oven for 35 minutes. Garnish with green pepper rings.

Debbie Tucker, Birmingham East Council

APPLE HAM CASSEROLE

3 c. cooked, diced ham
2 Tbsp. prepared mustard
2 apples, cored and sliced

2 Tbsp. lemon juice
1/2 c. brown sugar
1 tsp. grated orange rind
2 Tbsp. flour

Arrange cooked, diced ham in 1 1/2 quart casserole;
spread with mustard. Arrange the cored and sliced apples
over ham. Sprinkle with lemon juice. Combine brown sugar,
orange rind and flour and sprinkle over ham. Bake at 350°
for 30 to 35 minutes.

Sandra Miller, Anniston Council

CHUNKY HAM CASSEROLE

1 (7 oz.) pkg. elbow
 macaroni
1 (10 3/4 oz.) can cream
 of mushroom soup
2/3 c. Carnation milk
4 oz. shredded Cheddar
 cheese

6 oz. chunked ham
 (canned or fresh)
4 oz. sliced mushrooms
Salt (to taste)
1/2 c. cracker crumbs

Prepare macaroni according to package directions; drain.
Mix together soup, milk, cheese, salt, mushrooms and ham;

add macaroni and mix well. Pour into buttered 2 quart baking dish. Top with cracker crumbs. Bake uncovered for 45 minutes or until bubbly at 350°. Serves 4.

Rita Moore, Anniston Council

CREAMY CRUNCHY HAM AND ONION FRITTATA

2 Tbsp. margarine
5 eggs, slightly beaten
1/4 c. milk
1 (8 oz.) jar Cheez Whiz

1 c. chopped, cooked potatoes
1 c. chopped ham
1 (2.8 oz.) can Durkee's
  French fried onions

Melt margarine in 10 inch ovenproof skillet or omelet pan over low heat. Gradually add eggs and milk to process cheese spread; mix well. Stir in potatoes, ham and half of onion. Pour into skillet; bake at 350° for 20 minutes. Top with remaining onions; continue baking 5 minutes or until onions are lightly browned. Makes 4 to 6 servings.

Jane Courington, Montgomery Council

EASY BOILED HAM AND NOODLE CASSEROLE

8 slices oblong thin
  sliced boiled ham
1/4 inch wide egg noodles

1 can cream of mushroom
  soup
1/2 pt. sour cream

Cook egg noodles and drain. Place noodles on each ham slice and roll up. Place in baking dish. Mix soup and sour cream. Pour over ham. Top with grated Cheddar cheese; bake at 350° until bubbly.

Sara Lindsey, Riverchase Council

HAM-ASPARAGUS BAKE

1 (6 oz.) can (2/3 c.)
  evaporated milk
2 c. cubed, cooked ham
2 c. cooked rice
1/2 c. shredded process
  cheese

3 Tbsp. chopped onion
1 can cream of mushroom soup
1 (10 oz.) pkg. frozen
  asparagus spears, cooked
1/2 c. crushed corn flakes
3 Tbsp. butter

Add water to evaporated milk to make 3/4 cup. Combine ham, rice, cheese, soup and onion. Add juice from asparagus spears to ham mixture so it is very moist. Put half of ham mixture in baking dish, then arrange asparagus on top. Add remaining ham mixture; top with crumbs melted in butter and bake in 350° oven 25-30 minutes. Serves 6-8.

Hilda Hyche, Riverchase Council

1567-82

HAM CASSEROLE

2 c. chopped ham (add more ham if desired)
1 c. chopped celery
1 small carton sour cream
3 Tbsp. lemon juice
1 Tbsp. minced onion

3 hard boiled eggs, chopped
1 can cream of mushroom soup (undiluted)
1 pkg. (2 c. cooked) yellow rice (add more rice if desired)

Mix all ingredients and place in a large casserole. Top with 1 cup crushed corn flakes and 1/2 pack almonds. Bake at 350° for 30 minutes. Serves 12.

Bertha Capps, Birmingham East Council

HAM (OR SPAM) CASSEROLE

1 small green pepper, chopped
1 medium onion, chopped
1/4 c. margarine
1 (17 oz.) can whole kernel corn
2 Tbsp. flour

1 to 1 1/2 c. ham, chopped in bite size pieces, or 1 can Spam, chopped in bite size pieces
1 1/2 c. milk
Salt and pepper to taste
1 pkg. or box corn bread mix

Simmer chopped green pepper and onion in margarine; add corn and ham (or Spam). Sprinkle 2 tablespoons flour over these ingredients. Then add milk; stir and cook until slightly thickened. Salt and pepper to taste. Mix corn bread mix as directed on package or box. Drop in large tablespoons over top of mixture; bake in oven until bread is done according to package directions on corn bread mix (approximately 15 to 20 minutes at 400°).

Beverly McCoy, Montgomery Council

HAM CASSEROLE

Using ham hock left over from your Sunday dinner, place hock in boiler with water to cover and cook until meat comes off the bone. You will need at least 1 cup of ham when done. Using broth from ham, cook 1 cup or 6 ounce package of egg noodles until tender and they have absorbed most of the broth. Drain; add 1 can of mixed vegetables; add also 1 can of cream of chicken soup, undiluted. Let simmer for 15 minutes. This is one recipe that is really original.

Jamima Edney, Birmingham South Council

274

HAM CASSEROLE

Trim crusts from 16 slices of bread. Grease 9x13 inch pan. Butter 8 slices of the bread and place buttered side up. Place ham slices on bread, also grated cheese. Butter the other 8 slices; put in buttered side up. Beat 6 eggs with 3 cups milk, 1/2 teaspoon salt and 1/2 teaspoon dry mustard. Pour over the bread and ham slices and refrigerate overnight. Before cooking, add 1 cup crushed corn flakes on top and pour 1/2 cup melted butter on top. Bake at 350° for 1 hour.

Frances H. Lewis, Birmingham South Council

QUICK HAM-BROCCOLI CASSEROLE

1/4 c. chopped onion
1 (10 oz.) pkg. frozen
  chopped broccoli,
  thawed and drained
2 Tbsp. butter or
  margarine, melted
1 (10 3/4 oz.) can cream
  of chicken soup, undiluted

2 c. chopped, cooked ham
1 c. uncooked instant rice
1/2 c. process cheese
  spread
1/4 c. milk
1/2 tsp. Worcestershire
  sauce

Saute onion and broccoli in butter in a large skillet until onion is tender. Remove from heat; stir in remaining ingredients. Spoon mixture into a lightly greased 1 1/2 quart casserole. Bake at 350° for 25 to 30 minutes or until bubbly. Yield: 6 servings.

Regina Cash, Anniston Council

SAUCY HAM AND POTATO BAKE

2 Tbsp. chopped onion
1/4 c. margarine
1/4 c. flour
1 tsp. salt
1/2 tsp. dry mustard
Dash of pepper

1 1/2 c. milk
2 c. (8 oz.) shredded
  natural mild Cheddar
  cheese
1/2 lb. ham, cut into slices
6 c. cooked potato slices

Saute onion in margarine; blend in flour and seasonings. Gradually add milk and cook, stirring constantly, until thickened. Add 1 1/2 cups cheese; stir until melted. Toss potatoes in cheese sauce. Pour into 2 quart casserole, reserving 1 cup potato slices. Arrange ham and remaining potato slices on top of casserole; top with remaining cheese. Bake at 350° for 30 minutes. Makes 6 servings.

Martha Cantrell, Birmingham East Council

BATTER FRANKS

1 c. flour
1 1/2 tsp. baking powder
1/2 tsp. salt
2 tsp. corn meal

3 Tbsp. shortening
1 egg
3/4 c. milk
1 lb. frankfurters

Mix together in order given and dip franks into batter and fry in deep fat until brown. Drain on absorbent paper. Serve with mustard or catsup.

Jamima Edney, Birmingham South Council

CONEY ISLAND CASSEROLE

1 Tbsp. salad oil
1/2 lb. wieners,
   quartered crosswise
1 lb. hamburger meat
2 (15 oz.) cans herb sauce

1/2 c. sliced pimento-
   stuffed olives
8 oz. elbow macaroni
1/4 c. sharp Cheddar
   cheese

Brown wieners in salad oil and set aside. Brown hamburger meat in drippings. When meat is done, drain excess fat. Add cooked wieners, herb sauce and olives. Meanwhile, boil water and add macaroni slowly so water continues to boil constantly. After macaroni is tender, drain in colander and add to meat sauce. Pour into 4 quart casserole dish. Grate cheese and sprinkle around edges of casserole; cook at 375° about 40 minutes. Add slices of olives for garnish and serve

Mary M. Howell, Anniston Council

BAKED LASAGNA

Meat Balls:

1/2 lb. ground chuck
1/4 lb. ground veal
2 Tbsp. chopped onion
1 clove garlic, crushed
2 Tbsp. chopped parsley

1 tsp. dried oregano
3/4 tsp. salt
Dash of pepper
2 Tbsp. grated Parmesan
   cheese
1 egg

Tomato Sauce:

1/4 c. olive or salad oil
1/4 c. chopped onion
1 clove garlic, crushed
1 (1 lb. 12 oz.) can whole
   tomatoes, undrained
2 (6 oz.) cans tomato paste

2 tsp. dried oregano
1 tsp. dried basil
1 Tbsp. sugar
2 tsp. salt
1 tsp. garlic powder
1/4 tsp. pepper

276

Have ready:

1/2 pkg. (1 lb. size) lasagna	1 lb. Ricotta cheese
1 lb. Mozzarella cheese, diced	1 c. grated Parmesan cheese

1. Meat Balls: In medium bowl combine all ingredients; toss lightly to mix well. With teaspoon, shape mixture into 30 balls, each 3/4 inch in diameter. 2. Sauce: In hot oil in large heavy skillet, brown meat balls; remove. Add onions and garlic; saute 5 minutes. 3. Add rest of sauce ingredients with 1/2 cup water and meat balls; stir to mix. Bring to boiling; reduce heat and simmer, uncovered, 1 1/2 hours, stirring occasionally. 4. Heat oven to 350° F. Grease 13x9 x2 inch baking dish. Cook lasagna as label directs. Drain; rinse in water. 5. In baking dish layer half the ingredients: Lasagna, Mozzarella, Ricotta, tomato sauce with meat balls, Parmesan cheese. Repeat. Bake 30 to 35 minutes. Makes 6 servings.

Diane Lassiter, Huntsville Council

BAKED LASAGNA

2 lb. ground beef	8 oz. lasagna noodles
1 medium onion, chopped	2 eggs
2 tsp. parsley, chopped	1 lb. cottage cheese
2 (6 oz.) cans tomato paste	1 1/2 lb. Mozzarella cheese, grated
2 c. water	Grated Parmesan cheese
1/2 tsp. salt	
1/2 tsp. pepper	

In large heavy pan brown ground beef with onion and parsley; add tomato paste, water, salt and pepper. Simmer for 1 hour. Meanwhile, cook lasagna noodles as directed on package. Mix eggs and cottage cheese together. Using a 13x9x2 inch pan and an 11x7x2 inch pan, spread about 1/2 cup meat sauce in each. Then alternate layers of lasagna, meat sauce, cottage cheese mixture and Mozzarella cheese until pans are full. Top with meat sauce. Sprinkle generously with Parmesan cheese. Bake at 350° for 30-40 minutes until bubbly. Enjoyed immensely by this family, especially Brady!

Randy Wolfe, Birmingham South Council

EASY LASAGNE CASSEROLE

2 c. cooked egg noodles
1 lb. ground beef
1/4 c. chopped onion
1 (8 oz.) can tomato sauce
1/2 tsp. salt

1 (3 oz.) pkg. soft cream
  cheese
1 small (5.3 oz.) can
  evaporated milk
1/4 tsp. garlic salt
1/2 c. grated Mozzarella cheese

Cook noodles in boiling, salted water until tender. Cook beef and onion in skillet until beef is browned. Drain excess fat. Stir in tomato sauce and salt; simmer 5-10 minutes. Drain noodles. Place drained hot noodles back into saucepan; add cream cheese, evaporated milk and garlic salt. Stir until cheese melts and sauce thickens. Pour into 8 inch square pan. Spread meat mixture over top; bake 30 minutes at 325°. Remove and sprinkle grated cheese. Put back in oven 5 minutes or until cheese melts. Serves 2-4 people.

Bernadette B. McFerrin,
Birmingham Central Council

IMPOSSIBLE LASAGNE PIE

1 lb. ground beef
1 tsp. dried oregano
  leaves
1/2 tsp. dried basil leaves
1 (6 oz.) can tomato paste
1 c. shredded Mozzarella
  cheese

1/2 c. small curd creamed
  cottage cheese
1/4 c. grated Parmesan cheese
1 c. milk
2/3 c. Bisquick baking mix
2 eggs
1 tsp. salt
1/4 tsp. pepper

Heat oven to 400°. Grease pie plate (10 x 1 1/2 inches). Cook and stir beef over medium heat until brown; drain. Stir in oregano, basil, tomato paste and 1/2 cup of the Mozzarella cheese. Layer cottage cheese and Parmesan cheese in plate. Spoon beef mixture over top. Beat milk, baking mix, eggs, salt and pepper until smooth, 15 seconds in blender on high, or 1 minute with hand beater. Pour into plate. Bake until knife inserted between center and edge comes out clean, 30 to 35 minutes. Sprinkle with remaining cheese; cool 5 minutes. Makes 6 to 8 servings.

Pylman T. Patton, Mobile Council

ITALIAN LASAGNE

1 box lasagne noodles	3 Tbsp. grated
3 lb. Ricotta cheese	Parmesan cheese
2 Tbsp. dried parsley	1 1/2 tsp. salt
1/2 tsp. black pepper	9 eggs
	1/2 lb. Mozzarella cheese

In large mixing bowl beat at low speed all ingredients and set aside. Cook noodles as directed on box; drain and cool in cold water. Use a 9x13 inch deep casserole dish. Coat bottom with Italian sauce. Place 1 layer of noodles on bottom. Add some of the mix and build up layer of mix and noodles. On top layer of noodles sprinkle Parmesan cheese. Grate 1/2 pound of Mozzarella cheese and sprinkle on top; cover entire top with a generous amount of Italian sauce. Cover casserole dish tightly with aluminum foil; bake at 325° for 1 1/2 hours. (This Italian dish freezes very well.)

D. J. Del Guercio, Riverchase Council

LASAGNA

1 lb. ground chuck	2/3 c. grated Parmesan cheese
1/2 lb. lasagna noodles	1 can tomatoes
1/4 c. olive oil	1 tsp. basil
2 cloves garlic, minced	1 tsp. oregano
1 onion, chopped	1 1/2 tsp. salt
1 (16 oz.) can tomato	1/2 tsp. pepper
paste	1 lb. Mozzarella cheese

Brown meat lightly in olive oil with garlic and onion; add tomatoes, tomato paste, basil, oregano, salt and pepper. Bring to boil and simmer, covered, 2 or 3 hours. Cook noodles in salted, boiling water until tender. Drain noodles. In a shallow baking dish, put a layer of noodles and a layer of meat mixture and a layer of each kind of cheese. Repeat layers and top with Parmesan cheese; bake in a 350° oven for 45 minutes.

Sammie M. Jackson, Huntsville Council

BURRITOS

2 cans Bush's hot chili	3 Tbsp. salsa (hot sauce)
beans	jalapena
1/2 can green chilies,	1/2 c. sour cream
chopped	3/4 or 1 lb. hamburger meat
1 small onion, chopped	1 pkg. flour tortillas
1 c. grated Cheddar cheese	

1567-82

Mash beans and add other ingredients. Bring to a boil and simmer for 5 minutes; allow to cool and thicken. Spread over individual warmed tortillas and roll.

Judy Bejarano, Birmingham West Council

EASY CHICKEN ENCHILADAS

2 c. chopped, cooked chicken (canned chicken can be used)
2 (8 oz.) jars taco sauce
1 Tbsp. chicken-flavor instant bouillon
2 c. half & half
10 to 12 (8 inch) flour tortillas

2 c. (8 oz.) shredded Monterey Jack cheese
Fresh parsley sprigs (optional)
Jalapeno peppers (optional)
Flour tortillas with jalapeno peppers and/or Monterey Jack cheese with jalapeno peppers may be used for more spicier dish, if desired)

Combine chicken and taco sauce in a large saucepan; cook over low heat 15 minutes, stirring often. Dissolve bouillon in half & half in a large skillet over low heat (do not boil). Dip each tortilla into half & half mixture. Spoon 1 heaping tablespoon chicken mixture in center of each tortilla; roll up tightly, and place seam side down in a lightly greased 13x9x2 inch baking dish. Pour remaining half & half mixture over tortillas; sprinkle with cheese. Bake at 350° for 30 minutes. Garnish with parsley and jalapeno peppers, if desired. Yield: 8 servings.

Mary Ann Stanley, Mobile Council

ENCHILADAS

1 lb. ground beef
1 can refried beans
1 can enchilada sauce (hot)

8 oz. sour cream
8 oz. shredded Monterey Jack cheese
10-12 tortillas (flour or corn)

Brown ground beef; drain. Mix in refried beans and 1/2 can enchilada sauce. Simmer until hot. Roll into tortillas and place in baking dish. Top with sour cream, Monterey Jack and remaining enchilada sauce. Bake at 350° for 20 minutes.

Auretha Karrh, Decatur Council

GREEN CHILES ENCHILADA CASSEROLE

1 lb. ground beef
1 onion
1 can chopped green chiles

1 pkg. corn tortillas
1 can cream of mushroom soup
1 (8 oz.) pkg. Longhorn
   cheese

Brown ground beef; drain off excess fat. Add green chiles and onions to ground beef. Then add soup and a little of the cheese. Simmer on low heat about 15 minutes. Layer the bottom of casserole dish with tortillas, then add a layer of ground beef mixture. Top with cheese; continue to add layers. Top with cheese; bake at 350° for 30 minutes.

Margaret Turner, Tuscaloosa Council

IMPOSSIBLE TACO PIE

1 lb. ground beef
1/2 c. chopped onion
1 env. McCormick Schilling
   taco seasoning mix
1 (4 oz.) can chopped green
   chiles, drained

1 1/4 c. milk
3/4 c. Bisquick baking mix
3 eggs
2 tomatoes, sliced
1 c. shredded Monterey Jack
   or Cheddar cheese

Heat oven to 400°. Grease 10 x 1 1/2 inch pie plate. Cook and stir beef and onion until brown; drain. Stir in seasoning mix. Spread in plate; top with chiles. Beat milk, baking mix and eggs until smooth. Pour into plate. Bake 25 minutes. Top with tomatoes and cheese; bake (until knife comes out clean between center and edge) 8 to 10 minutes; cool 5 minutes. Top with sour cream, tomatoes, lettuce and cheese, if desired. Serves 6 to 8.

Jacqueline Adams, Tuscaloosa Council

MEXICAN BEANS

1 1/2 lb. ground beef
1 can pork and beans
1 can green limas
1 can kidney beans

1 small onion
1 Tbsp. mustard
1/2 c. ketchup
3 Tbsp. brown sugar
Chili powder (to suit taste)

Brown ground beef and onion; add all other ingredients and cook at 350° for 30 minutes.

Sandy Sprinkle, Anniston Council

MEXICAN PIE

1 lb. Cheddar cheese,
  grated
2 small cans green chiles

1 c. Bisquick
2 c. milk
4 eggs

Grease bottom and sides of pie pan and sprinkle grated cheese and chopped chiles on bottom. Mix the Bisquick, milk and eggs together and pour into pie shell. This pie will make its own crust. Bake pie in 425° oven for 30 minutes. Cool. Serve with sour cream topping.

Sharon Gallivan, Riverchase Council

MEXICAN SKILLET SUPPER

1 (8 oz.) pkg. chicken
  flavor Rice-A-Roni
1/4 c. sliced green
  onions, plus tops
2 cloves garlic, minced
2 1/2 c. cubed, cooked
  chicken

1 (4 oz.) diced green chiles
1/4 c. chopped parsley
1 c. shredded Monterey
  Jack cheese
2 to 3 California avocados,
  halved, pitted, peeled
1 (7 oz.) can chili salsa

Cook Rice-A-Roni according to package directions, adding onion and garlic with water. After cooking, stir in chicken, diced green chiles and parsley. Heat to serving temperature. Remove from heat; stir in cheese. Spoon 1 to 1 1/2 cups rice mixture over each avocado half. Top with chili salsa. Makes 4-6 servings.

Jacqueline Adams, Tuscaloosa Council

MEXICAN-STYLE CASSEROLE

1 lb. ground beef
1/2 c. coarsely chopped
  onion
1/2 c. coarsely chopped
  green pepper
1 pkg. Hamburger Helper
  mix for chili tomato

2 1/2 c. hot water
1 (16 oz.) can whole
  kernel corn, drained
1 (16 oz.) can whole tomatoes
1 c. sliced crushed corn
  chips

Heat oven to 375°. Cook ground beef, onions and green peppers in 10 inch skillet until beef is light brown; drain. Mix beef mixture, macaroni sauce mix, water, corn and tomatoes (with liquid) in 2 quart casserole dish. Bake uncovered until hot and bubbly, about 40 minutes. Sprinkle with crushed chips. Serves 5.

Freida Elkourie, Birmingham South Council

TACOS

1 lb. hamburger meat
1 can chili beans
1/2 can cumin powder
1 env. taco mix

1 jar hot sauce
1 jar mild sauce
1 head lettuce
Tomatoes

Fry hamburger meat; drain. Add 1 can chili beans, 1/2 can cumin powder, 1 small can tomato paste and 1 package taco mix. Cut up lettuce and tomatoes; put meat mixture in taco shells, then add lettuce, tomatoes and taco sauce in the shell. Heat shells with meat mixture in them before adding lettuce and tomatoes.

Dae Self, Birmingham West Council

TAMALE PIE

2 lb. lean ground beef
1 c. chopped onion
1/2 c. chopped green
  pepper
2 cloves garlic, minced
1 (16 oz.) can stewed
  tomatoes
1 (16 oz.) can whole
  kernel corn, drained
1 c. sliced pimiento-
  stuffed olives
2 1/2 tsp. chili powder

1/2 tsp. dried oregano,
  crushed
1/4 tsp. pepper
1 1/2 c. milk
2 Tbsp. butter or margarine
1 tsp. salt
1/2 c. corn meal
1 c. shredded Cheddar or
  Monterey Jack cheese
  (4 oz.)
2 slightly beaten eggs

In skillet cook meat, onion, chopped green pepper and garlic till meat is browned and vegetables are tender; drain off excess fat. Stir in tomatoes, corn, olives, chili powder, oregano, and pepper; simmer 10 minutes. Turn into un- greased 3 quart casserole.

In saucepan heat milk, butter or margarine and salt till butter melts. Slowly stir in corn meal; cook and stir about 5 minutes or till thickened. Remove from heat; stir in cheese and eggs. Pour over meat mixture; bake in 375° oven for 35 minutes.

Janet Stephens, Anniston Council

TAMALE PIE

1 jar tamales
1 can chili con carne
  (without beans)
2 cans Mexicorn

1 large can kidney beans
1 can enchilada sauce
2 lb. ground beef
1 medium onion

| 1 medium jar olives, | 2 c. grated cheese |
| chopped (green) | |

Brown meat and onions in skillet; add chili, corn, beans, enchilada sauce and olives. Heat over low heat until well blended. Remove husk from tamales and slice lengthwise. Place in oblong baking dish with meat side up. Pour mixture over tamales and top with cheese; bake at 350° for 30 minutes.

Denetiza Wilkes, Birmingham South Council

BETTER THAN PIZZA CASSEROLE

1 lb. ground beef	3/4 c. water
1/2 c. green peppers	1 can biscuits (10)
1 pkg. Kraft Italian style	1/3 c. Parmesan cheese
spaghetti sauce mix	1 (6 oz.) pkg. Mozzarella
1 (6 oz.) can tomato sauce	cheese

Using an 8x8 inch pan, line pan with biscuits. Brown ground beef in skillet with green peppers; add rest of ingredients (reserve cheese). Put into pan lined with biscuits. Sprinkle cheese on top; bake in 350° oven for 20 to 25 minutes.

Mrs. John Creel, Anniston Council

BREAKFAST PIZZA

1 lb. bulk pork sausage	3 eggs
1 pkg. crescent rolls	1/4 c. milk
1 c. frozen loose hash	1/2 tsp. salt
brown potatoes, thawed	1/8 tsp. pepper
1 c. shredded sharp	2 Tbsp. grated Parmesan
Cheddar (4 oz. pkg.)	cheese

Cook sausage until brown and crumbly; drain. Separate dough into 8 triangles. Place on ungreased 12 inch pizza pan with points toward center. Press over bottom and up sides, sealing to make crust. Spoon sausage on crust; sprinkle on potatoes. Top with Cheddar. Beat eggs with milk, salt and pepper; pour into crust. Sprinkle with Parmesan cheese; bake at 375° for 25-30 minutes.

Dee Mackey, Birmingham South Council

DEEP-DISH PIZZA

3 c. Bisquick mix
1 c. water
1 can tomato special
1 can herb sauce
1/2 tsp. salt
1/2 tsp. garlic salt
1 Tbsp. Italian
    seasoning
1 Tbsp. oregano leaves,
    crushed

1 Tbsp. grated Parmesan
    cheese
1 tsp. red pepper (optional)
1/2 lb. ground beef, browned
1/2 lb. sausage, browned
1/2 c. chopped onion
1/2 c. chopped green pepper
Italian sausage or pepperoni
    (optional)
2 c. shredded Mozzarella
    cheese

Preheat oven to 400°. Lightly grease cookie sheet. For crust: Mix Bisquick mix and water until soft dough forms with a fork. Gently smooth dough into ball on floured surface. Knead 20 times. Pat dough on bottom and sides of cookie sheet with floured hands. Sauce: Mix together tomato special, herb sauce, salt, garlic salt, Italian seasoning, oregano leaves, Parmesan cheese and red pepper (optional). Spread over dough evenly. Topping: Top with ground beef, onion, green pepper, Mozzarella cheese and Italian sausage or pepperoni (optional). Bake 20-25 minutes.

Carol Burns, Huntsville Council

EASY PIZZA

1 pkg. active dry yeast
1 c. very warm water
2 c. all-purpose flour
2 tsp. oil
1 tsp. sugar
1 tsp. salt
8 oz. Mozzarella cheese,
    shredded

1/2 lb. ground beef
    mixed with 1/2 lb. sausage
1 (8 oz.) can tomato sauce
1 tsp. Italian seasoning
Green peppers, onions,
    mushrooms, etc. for
    topping

In a small bowl add yeast to 1/4 cup warm water; stir and let dissolve 4-5 minutes. In a large bowl mix flour, oil, sugar and salt thoroughly; slowly add remaining water and stir to form a ball. Turn dough onto a floured surface and knead 8 turns. Place in greased bowl, coating entire surface and cover; let rise in a warm place about 1 hour. Grease a 12-15 inch pizza pan or a 10x15 inch shallow baking pan. Flour hands frequently and spread dough evenly, forming a lip around the edges. Spread tomato sauce; sprinkle meat, then Italian seasoning, toppings. Cover with cheese. Bake in preheated 400° oven 25 to 30 minutes. Crust will be light golden brown on bottom when pizza is fully cooked.

1567-82   Donna Wilson, Birmingham South Council   285

HOMEMADE PIZZA

1 box hot roll mix
1 pkg. cut pepperoni
Ground beef
1 Tbsp. minced onions
1 tsp. pizza seasoning
1 (8 oz.) pkg. Mozzarella
  cheese

4 slices American cheese
4 slices Cheddar cheese
1 small can tomato sauce
1/2 tsp. pepper
1/2 tsp. salt
1 bell pepper (if desired)
Mushrooms (if desired)

Go by directions on hot roll mix to make dough. Note: 1 box makes 2 crusts. Remaining can be refrigerated. Pour tomato sauce over crust. After ground beef has been cooked and grease drained off, add next. Add salt, pepper, minced onions, pizza seasoning. Next, add cheeses, then pepperoni; lastly, add bell pepper and mushrooms, if desired. Cook at 425° for 15-20 minutes until desired doneness.

Darlene Bradford, Decatur Council

MINIATURE PIZZAS

2 lb. sausage
1 lb. Velveeta cheese
1 jar Ragu spaghetti
  sauce
2 packs party rye bread

Parmesan cheese
1 Tbsp. oregano
1 Tbsp. catsup
1 Tbsp. A.1. Sauce
1 Tbsp. garlic salt

Cook sausage (crumbled) till done. In a separate saucepan melt the Velveeta cheese; add to cooked sausage catsup, A.1. Sauce, oregano and mix well. Add mixture to Velveeta cheese. Spread each piece of bread with mixture and top with 1 tablespoon of spaghetti sauce. Sprinkle with Parmesan cheese; bake at 450° for 10 minutes. May be frozen (before baking) for future use.

Debra Roberts, Birmingham South Council

ORIGINAL THICK CRUST ITALIAN PIZZA

Crust:

6 c. flour
2 c. water
2 pkg. yeast
3 tsp. salt

2 Tbsp. sugar
1 egg
3 Tbsp. melted butter or oil

Pizza Sauce:

1 (6 lb. 9 oz.) can
  tomato puree

1 1/2 c. olive oil or equivalent
3 Tbsp. salt
1 tsp. black pepper

2 tsp. crushed basil leaves	4 tsp. minced dried onion
4 tsp. oregano	2 tsp. garlic powder
	2 tsp. dehydrated green peppers

Pizza Sauce: Mix all ingredients together and simmer for 2 hours.

Crust: Add yeast to water per instructions on yeast package. Scramble egg and add other ingredients; slowly add flour and turn on floured board until elastic. Place in buttered dish and cover until double in size.

On floured board divide in two. Press and stretch dough to fit 15 inch round or large rectangular pan. Coat pan generously with oil. Place dough in pan; cover with pizza sauce. Sprinkle Parmesan cheese and shredded Mozzarella cheese. (Add slices of pepperoni - optional.) Bake at 375° for 27 minutes or until crust is brown on edges. (Pizza can be frozen and reheated for later use.)

D. J. Del Guercio, Riverchase Council

PORK CHOP AND BEAN CASSEROLE

6-8 pork chops, 1/2 inch thick	1 (1 lb.) can baked beans
Salt and pepper	1 (1 lb.) can baby lima beans, drained
1/4 c. minced onion	1/4 c. catsup
1 tsp. brown sugar	2 Tbsp. vinegar
1/2 tsp. prepared mustard	

Start heating oven to 350°. In a skillet brown chops slowly in 2 tablespoons oil until golden brown on each side. Sprinkle chops with salt and pepper. Place in covered casserole. In same skillet saute onion until tender; stir in brown sugar, mustard, beans, catsup and vinegar; mix well. Pour into casserole and mix with chops. Bake 45 minutes or until chops are fork tender.

Carole Carter, Montgomery Council

PORK CHOP CASSEROLE

6 pork chops	1/2 c. chopped onion
4 c. bread crumbs (corn bread and light bread, mixed)	Poultry seasoning as desired
	Salt and pepper to taste
1/2 c. chopped celery	1 can cream of celery soup

Salt and pepper pork chops and brown in hot skillet. Put pork chops aside. Put chopped celery and onion in

1567-82

skillet and cook until tender; add crumbled bread crumbs to this celery and onion mixture, adding water to make dressing the right consistency. Add poultry seasoning as desired. Put dressing mixture in bottom of baking dish and put pork chops on top. Pour the soup over top; soup should be diluted with 1/2 can water. Bake at 350° for 30 minutes or until brown. I keep my leftover corn bread in my freezer for use in making this casserole.

Jamima Edney, Birmingham South Council

PORK CHOP CASSEROLE

6 pork chops	1 can condensed celery soup
6 medium potatoes	(or cream of mushroom
1 large onion	soup can be substituted)
	Salt and pepper to taste

Flour and quickly brown pork chops in a skillet of Crisco. While browning pork chops, wash and peel potatoes and cut into medium size slices. Place potato slices in the bottom of a 2 quart casserole baking dish. Peel and cut onion into slices and place in a layer on top of potatoes; salt and pepper. Pour cream of celery soup on top and spread over entire casserole. Remove bones from pork chops and place them on top of casserole ingredients. Cover and bake for 45 minutes at 400°.

Janet Logsdon, Birmingham Central Council

PORK CHOP AND RICE CASSEROLE

1 c. rice	1 can beef consomme soup
4 pork chops	1 can onion soup

Pour rice in casserole dish. Brown pork chops on each side, not done, but brown. Place on rice. Cover rice and pork chops with beef consomme and onion soup. Bake at 350° for 1 hour.

Janet Stephens, Anniston Council

CHEESE/POTATO CASSEROLE

4 large potatoes	1 medium onion, chopped
2 c. grated cheese	1 c. milk
1/2 c. margarine	

Peel and cube potatoes; cook until tender in salted water; drain. Place layers of hot potatoes and cheese in casserole dish. Keep warm in oven. Melt margarine in skillet; add onion and saute until lightly browned. Add milk, stirring until heated. Pour over potatoes. Reheat, if necessary.

Melda H. Hicks, Anniston Council

HASH BROWN POTATO CASSEROLE

1 (2 lb.) bag hash brown
  potatoes
1/2 c. onions, chopped
1 (10 oz.) pkg. Cheddar
  cheese, grated

1 carton sour cream
1 can cream of chicken soup
1 tsp. salt
Pepper
1 stick melted oleo

Mix all together; put in greased 3 quart casserole. Cover top with bread crumbs and pour another stick of melted oleo over top. Bake at 350° for 1 hour 10 minutes. Serves about 30 people.

Bertha Capps, Birmingham East Council

LEFT-OVER MASHED POTATO CASSEROLE

About 4 servings (or
  1 lb.) cold leftover
  mashed potatoes

1 pt. sour cream
1 1/2 c. grated medium
  Cheddar cheese

Mix cold mashed potatoes and sour cream in a medium mixing bowl; set aside. Grate cheese; set aside. Spray covered baking dish with no-stick spray. Spread layer of mashed potato mixture, a layer of cheese; repeat, topping with remaining grated cheese. Cover and heat for 30 minutes in 350° oven. Goes with any meat. Can also be heated or reheated in microwave oven.

Jo Anne Gaskins, Birmingham South Council

PEPPERONI POTATO BAKE

5 large potatoes
1 (6 oz.) can tomato
  sauce
1 small onion

1 (6 oz.) pkg. Mozzarella
  cheese
1 (3 oz.) pkg. pepperoni
1 Tbsp. butter

Slice potatoes; arrange in bottom of baking dish. Salt and pepper. Cut butter in small pieces and add with slices of onion. Bake in 300° oven until potatoes are done. Top with cheese, half of tomato sauce, pepperoni, other half of tomato sauce. Put back in oven until cheese melts.

Ann Loree, Huntsville Council

1567-82

POTATO CASSEROLE (SOUTHERN LIVING)

4 medium potatoes,   2 tsp. finely chopped
  peeled and cooked   green onion tops
1 c. milk   1/2 tsp. salt
2 c. shredded Cheddar   5 slices bacon, cooked
  cheese, divided   and crumbled

Mash potatoes and set aside. Scald milk; add 1 cup cheese, onion and salt, stirring until cheese is melted. Add milk mixture and bacon to potatoes; blend well. Spoon mixture into a greased 1 quart casserole dish; sprinkle with remaining cheese. Bake at 350° for 10 minutes or until cheese melts. Makes 4 to 6 servings.

Debbie Hearn, Birmingham East Council

POTATO CASSEROLE

1 pkg. frozen shoestring   1 can cream of chicken soup
  fries   3/4 can water
1 medium onion, chopped 3/4 c. grated cheese
1 small pkg. cream cheese

Saute onion in small amount of margarine; add cream of chicken soup, water; stir till smooth. Chip in cream cheese and stir; cook about 5 minutes or till cheese has melted. Lightly butter 9x9 inch casserole; add layer of potatoes, sauce. Lightly sprinkle cheese, then potatoes, sauce and cheese. Bake at 350° for 45 minutes.

Hazel Campbell, Birmingham South Council

POTATO AND ONION CASSEROLE

4 onions   Butter or margarine
4 potatoes, washed   Salt
  and unpeeled   Pepper

Line a casserole dish with foil, leaving enough excess to wrap onions and potatoes with. Butter the bottom of foil. Line the bottom of foil in casserole dish with round slices of potatoes, then make layer of onion slices; top this with 3 pats of butter. Alternate to top of dish; salt and pepper top layer. Wrap the top with excess foil. Bake 1 hour at 350°.

Margaret Turner, Tuscaloosa Council

SAUSAGE TOPPED POTATO CASSEROLE

1 (10 1/2 oz.) can condensed cream of mushroom soup
1 c. (4 oz.) shredded Cheddar cheese
3/4 c. sour cream
1/3 c. milk
5 c. thinly sliced baking potatoes (approx. 4 large potatoes)
1 (12 oz.) pkg. link sausage

Combine soup, cheese, sour cream and milk. Place one-half of the potatoes in a buttered 2 quart baking dish. Cover with one-half of the soup mixture. Repeat layers; bake in preheated 375° oven for 45 minutes. Meanwhile, brown link sausages in skillet. Drain; cut each in half. Arrange sausage pieces on top of casserole and bake an additional 30 to 45 minutes, or until potatoes are done. Allow to stand 5 minutes before serving.

Bernice Henderson, Riverchase Council

MURPHIES CRABMEAT QUICHE

1 (9 inch) baked pie shell
3 eggs, slightly beaten
1 c. sour cream
1/2 tsp. Worcestershire sauce
3/4 tsp. salt
1 c. coarsely shredded Swiss cheese
1 (6 1/2 oz.) can crabmeat, drained and finely flaked
1 (3 1/2 oz.) can French fried onions

To the slightly beaten eggs add sour cream, Worcestershire sauce and salt; mix well. Then add shredded cheese, crabmeat and onions. Pour into baked pie shell. Bake 55 to 60 minutes at 300° or until custard is set and a knife inserted in center comes out clean. Serve hot.

Anne Spragins, Birmingham East Council

EASY QUICHE

4 eggs
1 1/2 c. plain yogurt
1 Tbsp. soy flour
1/2 tsp. salt
1/2 tsp. pepper
1/4 tsp. onion salt
1 medium onion, cut in chunks
1 1/2 c. Swiss cheese, cut in chunks
1 lb. sausage, browned until done
1 (9 inch) unbaked whole grain pie shell

Place first 6 ingredients in blender; process on low speed until blended thoroughly. Stop blender and add onions and cheese. Process on high speed long enough to chop and distribute ingredients evenly. Place sausage on the bottom of the pie crust and pour blended mixture over it. Bake in

1567-82

preheated 375° oven for 35 to 45 minutes, until a knife in-inserted in center comes out clean. Serves 4 to 6.
Kathleen Leggett, Huntsville Council

EGGPLANT QUICHE

1 small eggplant, pared and cubed (approx. 4 c.)	1 tsp. sugar
	1/2 tsp. salt
1/2 c. chopped bell pepper	1/4 tsp. black pepper
	1/8 tsp. oregano
3/4 c. chopped onion	1 c. grated sharp cheese
4 Tbsp. butter	4 beaten eggs
1 1/2 Tbsp. flour	1 peeled and chopped tomato
1 (10 1/2 oz.) can cream of chicken soup	2 frozen pie crusts
	Parmesan cheese

Partially bake crusts in preheated 450° oven for 6 minutes. Cook eggplant covered in boiling, salted water for 8 to 10 minutes; drain well. Cook onion and pepper in butter until tender. Blend in flour, soup, salt, sugar, oregano and black pepper. Heat until bubbly. Remove from heat; stir into beaten eggs. Fold in tomato, cheese and eggplant. Pour into pie shells; top with Parmesan cheese (sprinkle on top). Bake for 30 minutes at 350°.
Mary Norris, Birmingham Central Council

FRENCH ONION QUICHE

Prebake deep dish pie crust at 400° for 7 minutes. Do not prick crust. Cool. Sprinkle 1 3/4 cups grated Swiss cheese or Emmenthaler over crust and top with one 3 1/2 ounce can French fried onion rings. Beat 4 eggs, 2 cups light cream, 1/2 teaspoon nutmeg, dash of salt, pepper and paprika and 1/2 cup milk. Pour over crust; bake 30-45 minutes until set at 375°. Top each slice with sour cream or guacamole, if desired.
Debbie Tucker, Birmingham East Council

IMPOSSIBLE QUICHE

12 slices bacon (fry, drain and crumble)	2 c. milk
	1/2 c. Bisquick
1 c. shredded Swiss cheese	4 eggs
1/3 c. finely chopped onions	1/4 tsp. salt
	1/8 tsp. pepper

Heat oven to 350°. Grease 9 inch pie pan. Sprinkle

bacon, cheese and onion evenly over pie pan. Place remaining ingredients in blender on high speed for 1 minute. Pour over bacon, cheese and onion; bake until golden brown, 50-55 minutes. Let stand 10 minutes before cutting.

Mrs. Guy Pippin, Anniston Council

QUICHE

1 deep dish pie crust	1/2 can mushrooms
1 Tbsp. chives, chopped (approx.)	3 eggs
	1 1/2 c. half & half
6 oz. Swiss cheese, sliced	1/4 tsp. marjoram
2 slices ham	1/4 tsp. basil
2 strips bacon, cooked	1/4 tsp. summer savory
1/2 c. grated Mozzarella	Salt
1/4 onion, chopped	Pepper
1/4 bell pepper, chopped	Parmesan cheese

Saute onions and bell pepper. Cut cheese into strips. Chop ham into bite sized pieces. Sprinkle chives into bottom of pie crust. Layer cheeses, ham, crumbled bacon, onion, bell pepper and mushrooms. Sprinkle with Parmesan cheese. Make bottom and top layer Swiss cheese. Into small bowl beat eggs; add half & half. Sprinkle marjoram, basil, salt and pepper to taste; pour over layers in dish and bake at 350° for 1 hour to 1 hour 20 minutes.

Carol Donaldson, Birmingham South Council

QUICHE A LA MORRISON

1 pt. half & half	1 lb. sharp Cheddar cheese
1/2 pt. whipping cream	1 Tbsp. flour
1 medium size onion	Dash of cayenne and nutmeg
1 medium size green pepper	1/2 lb. fresh or canned
1/2 pkg. frozen spinach	mushrooms
1/2 pkg. frozen broccoli, chopped	4 large eggs
	Options: Shrimp, crabmeat,
2 pie shells	tuna, ham, bacon, celery

Thaw frozen vegetables. Grate cheese. Chop and saute peppers, onions and mushrooms in butter. Mix eggs, half & half and whipping cream, cayenne and nutmeg together. Mix flour and grated cheese. Line pie shells with cheese and add sauteed vegetables and thawed vegetables (if you use seafood, be sure to use chopped celery, too). Pour egg and cream batter over ingredients in pie shells; mix thoroughly. Bake at 325° for 35-50 minutes or until golden brown and fork comes out clean.

1567-82   Adrienne Morrison, Mobile Council

QUICHE OLE

Quiche:

2 c. shredded sharp
   Cheddar cheese
1/4 c. flour
4 eggs, slightly beaten

1 1/2 c. milk
1/2 tsp. salt
Dash of cayenne
1 (9 inch) unbaked pastry shell

Spanish Sauce:

1/2 c. chopped green
   pepper
1/2 c. celery slices

1/2 c. onion, chopped
1 c. catsup or chili sauce

Quiche: Toss cheese with flour; add eggs, milk and seasonings, and mix well. Pour into pastry shell and bake at 350° for 1 hour or until set. Cut into wedges and top with Spanish Sauce.

Sauce: Heat vegetables in catsup until crisp-tender. Makes 1 1/2 cups, 4 to 6 servings.

Fran Rhodis, Montgomery Council

QUICHE UNIQUE

3/4 c. shredded Swiss
   cheese
3/4 c. shredded
   Mozzarella cheese
1/2 c. chopped pepperoni
1 c. half & half

3 eggs, beaten
1/2 tsp. salt
1/4 tsp. oregano
1 unbaked 9 inch pie
   shell
Parsley

Combine cheese and pepperoni. Place in pie shell. Combine eggs, half & half, salt and oregano. Mix well and pour into pie shell; bake at 325° for 45 minutes. Allow to stand 10 minutes or more before cutting. Garnish with parsley.

Pam Gattis, Riverchase Council

SAUSAGE QUICHE

1 (9 inch) pie shell
1/2 lb. sausage
1 c. grated sharp
   Cheddar cheese

1 small grated onion
1 Tbsp. flour
1 large can Pet milk
2 eggs
Parsley

Brown sausage; drain. Place in pie shell. Sprinkle grated cheese, flour and onion on top. Beat eggs and milk; pour over mixture in pie shell. Sprinkle parsley on top; bake at 350° for 45 minutes or until set.

294   Julia Proffitt, Birmingham Central Council

SQUASH QUICHE

2 c. zucchini squash with peeling, sliced thin
2 c. yellow squash with peeling, sliced thin
1/2 c. chopped onion
1/4 c. chopped bell pepper

1/2 c. grated Cheddar cheese
2 eggs, well beaten
1/2 c. self-rising flour (if plain flour is used, add 1 tsp. baking powder)
1 Tbsp. oil
Salt and pepper to taste

Slice squash into thin rounds with peelings left on. Mix all ingredients. Butter a 9 inch pie pan. Pour in mixture. Top with crushed corn flakes. Preheat oven to 350°; bake 40 to 50 minutes or until knife inserted comes out clean. Remove from oven; let stand for 5 minutes. Slice as a pie. Serve while hot.

Velvo Chaney, Life Member, Mobile Council

ALMOND RICE

1 c. long grain rice
2 c. chicken broth
3/4 tsp. salt

1/4 c. butter or margarine
2 Tbsp. chopped scallions
1/4 c. chopped parsley
1/3 c. sliced almonds

Bring rice, broth and salt to a boil; reduce heat and cook 20 minutes. When the rice is cooked, add the remaining ingredients that have been sauteed in butter. Stir well and serve immediately. Serves 4-6.

Martha Cheney, Riverchase Council

BAKED ALMOND RICE

3 c. boiling chicken broth
1 1/2 c. regular rice, uncooked

1 1/4 tsp. salt
3/4 c. slivered almonds
3 Tbsp. butter or regular margarine

Mix broth, rice and salt in ungreased 3 quart casserole. Cover tightly. Bake in moderate 350° oven 25 to 30 minutes, until liquid is absorbed and rice is tender. Meanwhile, lightly brown almonds in butter. Add to hot cooked rice and toss to mix. Makes 6 to 8 servings.

Edwina Hicks, Montgomery Council

BACON FRIED RICE

1 bag (boil-in-bag) rice
6 slices bacon, cut in
  eighths
1 c. sliced fresh mushrooms

1 egg, slightly beaten
1/2 c. sliced water chestnuts
3 Tbsp. soy sauce
1/2 c. sliced green onion

Cook bag of rice according to package directions; drain. While rice is cooking, saute bacon in wok or 10 inch skillet until almost crisp. Remove bacon pieces and let drain on paper towel. Pour off all but 1/4 cup drippings. Stir mushrooms and onion into the hot fat. Stir fry 2-3 minutes or until mushrooms are limp. Add rice; continue to stir fry until rice is hot, about 3-5 minutes. Push rice to one side of skillet. Pour egg into other side and scramble. Add water chestnuts, soy sauce and reserved bacon pieces to skillet and mix well. Makes 4 servings (about 2/3 cup each), 319 calories per serving.

    Jane Horton, Birmingham Central Council

DIRTY RICE (RICE DRESSING)

1/2 lb. sausage
1/2 lb. hamburger
2 medium onions, chopped
1 small bell pepper,
  chopped
1 rib celery, chopped
2 cloves garlic

1 can chicken broth
Salt and pepper to taste
1/4 tsp. red pepper sauce
2 to 2 1/2 c. cooked rice
1/2 lb. chicken livers or
  gizzards
3 green onions, chopped

Saute meat till brown; add onion, celery, green pepper and garlic. Cook, stirring and scraping bottom of pan. Saute livers and green onions in butter till done. Finely chop livers. Stir liver mixture and chicken broth, salt, pepper and red pepper sauce into meat mixture. Reduce heat and simmer 40 minutes, covered. Simmer, uncovered, 20 minutes. Stir in rice as much as needed to make a moist dressing.

    Mary E. Gillis, Mobile Council

GREEN RICE

1 (8 oz.) jar Cheez Whiz
2 pkg. chopped broccoli
2 c. cooked rice
3/4 c. celery

1 stick margarine
3/4 c. onion
2 cans cream of
  mushroom soup

Chop onion and celery; saute in butter until clear. Cook broccoli as directed. Drain. Combine all ingredients with soup and cheese. Pour into greased casserole (1 large or 2 small); cook for 1 hour at 350° or until dry.

Lula Aycock, Life Member,
Birmingham Central Council

HOT RICE

1/3 c. butter
1 c. chopped onion
1/2 c. chopped celery
1 pkg. frozen chopped
  broccoli

1 1/2 c. cooked rice
1 can mushroom soup
1 small jar Cheez Whiz
  with jalapeno peppers

Cook broccoli and drain well. Combine cooked rice, mushroom soup, sauteed celery and onions, jalapeno Cheez Whiz and cooked broccoli. Bake in buttered Pyrex dish for 40 minutes at 350°.

Janet R. Williams, Mobile Council

RICE CASSEROLE

1 lb. good pork sausage
1 chopped green pepper
1 small chopped onion
2 stalks (1/2 c.) chopped
  celery

4 1/2 c. boiling water
2 pkg. dried Lipton chicken
  noodle soup mix
1/2 c. raw rice
1 pkg. slivered almonds
Sherry (optional)

Fry sausage, made into bite size pieces, until done and pour off grease. Take sausage out and in same pan cook peppers, onions and celery until tender. Add boiling water, soup mix and rice; cook 7 minutes. Add the sausage and almonds; bake 1 hour uncovered at 300°.

Optional: Just before serving, pour a little sherry on top.

Margaret Bunn, Birmingham Central Council

RED BEANS AND RICE

1/2 c. chopped onion
1/2 c. chopped green
  pepper
1 clove garlic
2 Tbsp. margarine

1 (16 oz.) can red kidney
  beans
2 c. cooked rice
1 tsp. salt
1/8 tsp. pepper

Saute the onion, pepper and garlic in the margarine until tender. Remove the garlic. Add remaining ingredients; simmer together 5 minutes to blend flavors. Serves 4 to 6.

1567-82   Flo Thompson, Montgomery Council

RICE CASSEROLE

1 c. rice
1/2 c. chopped onion

1/2 c. chopped celery
1 stick oleo

Brown rice, onions and celery in oleo. Pour into casserole and add 1 can onion soup and 1 can beef bouillon. Cover and cook at 375° for 1 hour.

Mrs. Guy Pippin, Anniston Council

RICE CASSEROLE

1 stick butter
1 c. rice (raw)
1 can sliced mushrooms

1 can water chestnuts
1 can onion soup and
1 can water

Brown rice in butter. Mix all together and bring to a boil. Bake in covered dish at 350° for 1 hour.

Janet Stephens, Anniston Council

RICE AND BROCCOLI CASSEROLE

2 c. cooked rice
1 pkg. frozen broccoli,
  cooked and drained
1/4 c. chopped onions
3 Tbsp. butter

1 can cream of chicken soup
1/3 c. milk
1 (5 oz.) can water chestnuts,
  drained and sliced
1 small jar Cheez Whiz

Mix all ingredients except the Cheez Whiz. Put in greased casserole dish and top with Cheez Whiz. Bake at 350° about 1 hour. May be made the day before, putting the Cheez Whiz on just before baking.

Marion Vann, Mobile Council

RICE CASSEROLE

1 pkg. yellow rice
1 can Mexicana corn
1 can cream of chicken soup

1/2 stick oleo or margarine
1 c. shredded sharp
  Cheddar cheese

Cook yellow rice according to directions on package. When rice is done, add 1 stick oleo, corn (with liquid from can included) and soup. Pour into a casserole dish; bake till done, approximately 20 minutes. Do not cover casserole dish. Bake at 350° F. Spread cheese over top and return to oven to melt. Serves 8 people.

Jane Courington, Montgomery Council

298

RICE MUSHROOM CASSEROLE

1 c. uncooked rice
2 cans consomme soup

1 can sliced mushrooms

Mix together and place in casserole dish; bake 1 hour at 350°.

Mrs. Vonda Cook, Riverchase Council

SAINT PAUL'S RICE

1 lb. hot sausage
1/2 c. onion
1/2 c. bell pepper
1/2 c. celery

1 c. cooked rice
2 pkg. chicken noodle
   Cup-a-Soup mix

Cook sausage and drain. Saute onion, bell pepper and celery in leftover sausage grease. Mix sausage, water, onion, bell pepper and celery; bring to a boil. Add rice and soup mix; cook on low heat until mushy. Serve with cracker crumbs on top.

Glenda Whitcomb, Birmingham East Council

SKILLET RICE CASSEROLE

1 can tomatoes
1 can tomato paste
2 tomato paste cans
   of water
1/2 c. raisins

1 c. rice, uncooked
2 Tbsp. seasoning salt
Salt and pepper to taste
Parmesan cheese

In skillet chop up tomatoes. Mix with tomato paste and water. When liquid is hot, add rice. Let simmer until rice is cooked (about 20 minutes). Add seasoning salt, salt, pepper and raisins; simmer about 5-7 minutes. Empty into serving bowl and top with cheese.

Judy Ivey, Birmingham South Council

SOUTH COAST HOMINY (CASSEROLE)

3 Tbsp. butter
1/2 c. green pepper,
   chopped
1/2 c. buttered bread
   crumbs
1 tsp. salt
1 1/2 c. sweet milk

1/2 c. pitted ripe olives,
   chopped
1/2 c. green stuffed
   olives, chopped
1 (1 lb. 13 oz.) can
   hominy, drained
1 small onion, minced

3 Tbsp. flour
1/2 tsp. dry mustard

1/4 tsp. black pepper
1 c. (1/4 lb.) Cheddar
  cheese, grated

Melt butter in saucepan; add onion and green pepper and saute 5 minutes. Blend in flour and seasonings. Add milk and cook and stir until mixture comes to a boil and thickens. Add grated cheese; stir until melted. Remove from heat; add olives and hominy. Pour into 1 1/2 quart casserole; sprinkle with buttered bread crumbs. Bake in preheated 375° oven for 30 minutes or until brown on top.

Billie G. Smith, Retired Life Member

SPANISH RICE

3/4 c. uncooked white rice
1 1/2 c. sliced, peeled
  onion
3 Tbsp. fat
1 (No. 2 1/2) can tomatoes
  (3 1/2 c.)

1 1/2 tsp. salt
4 Tbsp. diced green peppers
4 whole cloves (any size)
1 bay leaf

Cook rice and drain. Cook sliced onion in fat until tender. Add remaining ingredients and simmer 15 minutes. Remove bay leaf and clove; add rice. Turn in greased 1 1/2 quart casserole. Bake in moderate oven at 350° F. for 30 minutes.

Ruth Gregory, Montgomery Council

BREAKFAST CASSEROLE

1 lb. sausage, cooked
  and scrambled
6 slices white bread
1 c. grated Longhorn cheese

2 c. half & half
5 eggs
1 tsp. each salt and dry
  mustard, mixed together

Fry and scramble sausage; drain. Cut crust from bread and discard. Butter both sides of bread and cut in cubes. Spread buttered bread on bottom of 9x13x2 inch casserole dish. Top with sausage. Cover completely with grated cheese. Mix remaining ingredients together; beat well. Pour liquid over top of cheese, sausage and bread. Refrigerate for at least 8 hours; bake at 350° for 40 to 50 minutes or until browned slightly. Serve with bran muffins and peaches topped with cheese and sprinkled with coconut and broiled until cheese melts.

Joy Paschal, Birmingham East Council

BREAKFAST CASSEROLE

1 lb. mild sausage
6 eggs, beaten
2 c. milk
1 c. grated cheese

2 slices bread, cut into
  cubes (crusts too)
1 tsp. salt
1 tsp. dry mustard

Fry and drain sausage. Place bread and sausage in 10x13 inch baking dish. Blend all other ingredients and pour over sausage and bread cubes. Bake at 350° for 45 minutes. May be prepared and refrigerated uncooked overnight.

Becky Woo, Birmingham South Council

CORN SAUSAGE CASSEROLE

1/2 lb. pork sausage
1 small onion, chopped
1/2 green pepper,
  chopped
1/2 c. milk

2 (17 oz.) cans cream
  style corn
2 eggs, lightly beaten
Salt and pepper to taste
Buttered cracker crumbs

Break up sausage; cook until brown. Remove meat from skillet; cook onion and pepper in sausage drippings until browned. Remove from heat; drain off grease. Pour milk in skillet; loosen browned particles from skillet. Add corn, eggs, salt and pepper. Pour into buttered casserole; cover with bread crumbs. Bake in 375° oven until browned, about 30 minutes. Makes 4-6 servings.

Betty Chilton, Birmingham East Council

EGG-SAUSAGE CASSEROLE

8 slices bread, cubed
2 c. grated cheese
  (American or Cheddar)
2 lb. bulk sausage,
  browned and drained

4 eggs, beaten
2 1/2 c. milk
3/4 tsp. dry mustard
1 can cream of mushroom soup
1/2 c. milk

Place bread cubes in greased 9x13 inch pan. Sprinkle cheese over. Add browned sausage. Blend eggs, milk and mustard and pour over ingredients in pan. Refrigerate several hours or overnight. Blend soup and milk; pour over. Bake 1 1/2 hours at 300°.

A. M. Robertson, Huntsville Council

HUNGARIAN GOULASH

1 lb. sausage
2 cans kidney beans
1 large onion
1 large bell pepper
1 c. diced potatoes
1 or 2 cans tomatoes
  (or tomato juice)

1 tsp. garlic salt
1 1/2 tsp. seasoning salt
1 tsp. thyme
1 large bay leaf
1 qt. water

Brown sausage; drain. Add beans, onions, tomatoes or tomato juice, garlic salt, seasoning salt, thyme, bay leaf and water. Simmer 45 minutes to an hour. Add potatoes and bell pepper. Turn up heat and cook until potatoes are done.

Note: For larger servings, use 2 pounds sausage and 3 cans kidney beans.

Janice A. McKinney, Birmingham South Council

LAZY MAN'S SUPPER

1 pkg. Little Sizzler
  sausage links
1 large onion
1 large bell pepper

6 large potatoes
1 can tomato soup
1 can water

Brown sausage links and drain off grease. Slice onions, pepper and potatoes. Put all ingredients in pressure cooker. Pour 1 can tomato soup and 1 can of water and pressure for 8 minutes. Salt and pepper to taste.

Sandy Miller, Gadsden Council

SAUSAGE AND BROCCOLI CASSEROLE

1 lb. sausage links, cut
  in small pieces
1 (10 oz.) pkg. frozen
  chopped broccoli
1/4 c. shredded mild
  Cheddar cheese
3 Tbsp. chopped green
  pepper
2 Tbsp. grated onion

2 Tbsp. all-purpose flour
3 hard cooked eggs, sliced
1 (10 3/4 oz.) can cream of
  mushroom soup, undiluted
1/3 c. milk
1/2 c. dry bread crumbs
3 Tbsp. melted butter
Hot cooked rice
3 Tbsp. minced fresh parsley

Cook sausage until browned; drain. Cook broccoli according to package; drain well. Place broccoli in a lightly greased 1 1/2 quart casserole. Combine sausage, cheese, green pepper, onion, parsley and flour in a medium bowl; spoon half of sausage mixture over broccoli in casserole. Top sausage mixture with egg slices; spoon remaining
302

sausage mixture over eggs. Combine soup and milk; pour over casserole. Combine bread crumbs and butter; sprinkle over casserole. Bake at 375° for 30 minutes. Serve over hot cooked rice. Makes servings for 6.

Elaine Shelton, Huntsville Council

SPICY SAUSAGE CASSEROLE

1/2 lb. Zeigler's hot sausage (or mild)	1 c. uncooked macaroni (I use seashell)
1/4 c. chopped bell pepper	1/8 tsp. Italian seasoning
	1/2 tsp. salt
1/4 c. chopped onion	1/8 tsp. pepper
1 (16 oz.) can tomatoes, undrained	Dash of chili powder
3/4 can water	1/2 c. shredded Cheddar cheese

Brown sausage in skillet; pour off drippings. Reduce heat; add pepper, onion, tomatoes, water, macaroni and seasonings. Cover and simmer 25 minutes; uncover and simmer 10 minutes. Spoon into a lightly greased 1 quart casserole. Sprinkle with cheese. Place in 325° oven till cheese has melted.

Hazel Campbell, Birmingham South Council

SQUASH AND SAUSAGE CASSEROLE

1 lb. sausage, drained	1/2 c. Parmesan cheese
4 c. summer squash	1 tsp. salt
1/4 c. bell pepper	1/2 c. milk
1/4 c. diced onion	2 eggs, beaten
1 c. dry bread crumbs	

Brown and drain sausage; set aside. Steam squash until tender and drain. In large bowl combine squash and sausage; mix thoroughly. Add remaining ingredients. Pour into 8 1/2 x 11 x 2 inch baking pan; cook in preheated 325° oven 30 to 35 minutes.

Note: Try substituting hamburger or 2 cups diced, cooked ham for sausage in recipe.

Connie Herring, Anniston Council

SAUSAGE CASSEROLE

Brown 1 pound sausage and medium onion. Prepare 8 ounces egg noodles; reserve 1/2 cup broth. Mix:

1 can cream of
  mushroom soup
1 can Cheddar cheese
  soup

1 large can evaporated milk
1/2 c. noodle broth
Salt, pepper, garlic salt
  to taste

Combine sausage, noodles and soup together in casserole dish. Top with bread crumbs and butter. Bake at 350° until mixture bubbles or bread is brown. Can be frozen before being baked.

Peggy Hunter, Anniston Council

SAUSAGE CASSEROLE

1 lb. pork sausage,
  browned and drained
1 onion, chopped
1 bell pepper, chopped

2 stalks celery, chopped
2 pkg. chicken noodle
  dry soup mix
1/2 c. regular rice

Brown onion, bell pepper and celery in sausage drippings. Combine soup mix and rice in 4 cups boiling water; boil 7 minutes. Combine these 2 mixtures with sausage; bake in covered dish for 50 minutes at 350°. Uncover during last 10 minutes to brown.

Cindy Smith, Riverchase Council

CHICKEN-SHRIMP CASSEROLE

1 large can Pet evaporated
  milk plus enough
  homogenized milk to
  make 2 c. milk
3 Tbsp. butter or
  margarine
3 Tbsp. flour
1/4 c. cooking sherry

1/2 c. grated Cheddar cheese
2 c. cooked, diced chicken
2 c. boiled shrimp
1 c. cooked, diced mushrooms
1 hard boiled egg, sliced
Bread crumbs or cracker
  crumbs, to top
Large sprig of parsley

Melt the butter; add flour. Stir until smooth. Slowly add the milk, stirring with a wire whisk to make a thick white sauce. Add all of the other ingredients. Pour into a greased 8x10 inch casserole. Top with bread or cracker crumbs; bake in a 350° oven for 30 minutes, or until the casserole bubbles. Serves 6. Before serving, add a large sprig of parsley for decoration.

Martha Cheney, Riverchase Council

304

CRAB CASSEROLE

1 Tbsp. flour
1/2 c. butter, melted
1 c. milk

1 lb. crabmeat
1 c. bread crumbs
1 c. sharp grated cheese

Add flour to butter and gradually blend in milk until smooth. Combine sauce and crabmeat and season to taste. Put in casserole and sprinkle with bread crumbs and cheese. Bake at 350° until hot, crumbs brown and cheese melts.

Faith Kirby, Anniston Council

CRABMEAT CASSEROLE

1 lb. crabmeat (or 4 cans),
  drained
7 pieces bread (crust
  removed and cut into
  1/2 inch strips)
1/2 c. diced onion
1/2 c. diced bell pepper

1/2 c. diced celery
1/2 c. grated cheese
4 eggs
1 can cream of mushroom
  soup
1 c. grated sharp cheese

Line casserole with 1/2 bread strips. In bowl mix crabmeat, onion, bell pepper, celery and 1/2 cup cheese. Spoon over bread; add the rest of the bread to form another layer. Mix eggs with 1/2 of milk and pour over mixture. Mix soup with the rest of the milk and pour over. Top with sharp cheese. Bake 45-60 minutes at 350°. Serves 10.

Candy Bird, Birmingham South Council

CRUNCHY SHRIMP CASSEROLE

3 c. cooked shrimp
1 c. onions, diced
1 c. pimiento, diced
2 c. celery, diced
10 oz. sharp cheese,
  cubed

1 can water chestnuts,
  sliced
1 c. almonds, sliced
2 c. Hellmann's mayonnaise
Ritz cracker crumbs
  as topping

Combine all ingredients; mix well. Pour into large Pyrex dish and bake at 350° for 30-45 minutes. May substitute chicken or ham for shrimp. Makes 10 servings.

Jean Ivey, Riverchase Council

1567-82

SALMON PIE

1 1/2 c. flour
1/2 tsp. salt
1/2 c. (1 stick) margarine
4 to 5 Tbsp. cold water
2 (7 3/4 oz.) cans salmon,
  drained and flaked,
  reserving liquid
Milk
3/4 c. egg substitute

1 c. fresh bread crumbs
3 Tbsp. margarine
1 c. chopped celery
1/3 c. chopped onion
2 Tbsp. chopped parsley
2 Tbsp. lemon juice
1/2 tsp. lemon juice
1/2 tsp. salt
1/8 tsp. pepper

Combine flour and 1/2 teaspoon salt in a bowl; cut in 1/2 cup margarine with a pastry blender until mixture resembles coarse meal. Stir in cold water; mix well and shape into a ball. On a lightly floured board, roll out dough to fit a 9 inch pie plate. Transfer dough to a plate; trim and shape edges. Bake at 400° for 8 to 10 minutes. Drain salmon and add milk to salmon liquid to equal 1 cup. Combine egg substitute with milk mixture and beat slightly. Mix in bread crumbs; set aside. Melt remaining margarine and saute onion and celery until tender. Add salmon, celery and onion mixture, parsley, lemon juice, salt and pepper to egg mixture; mix carefully. Pour into prepared shell. Bake at 400° for 30 to 35 minutes or until set. Let stand 5-10 minutes before cutting. Makes 6 servings.

Mary C. Martin, Birmingham East Council

SEAFOOD CASSEROLE

2 pkg. wild and white
  rice, cooked
1 lb. crabmeat
1 pt. oysters
2 1/2 lb. cooked shrimp
3 cans cream of mushroom
  soup
1 (4 oz.) jar pimento

Paprika, garlic powder,
  parsley, salt and pepper
  to taste
1 c. sliced fresh mushrooms
1/3 c. chopped green onions
1 c. chopped bell pepper
1 c. chopped celery
2 Tbsp. lemon juice

Saute pepper, onions and mushrooms; add to rice and other ingredients. Mix well. Bake in 4 quart casserole at 325° for 1 hour.

Brenda Etheredge, Mobile Council

SEAFOOD CASSEROLE

1 c. rice, cooked
1 c. chopped celery
1/2 c. chopped green
  pepper
2 green onions, sliced

1 (6 1/2 oz.) can water
  chestnuts, sliced
1 (6 1/2 oz.) can crabmeat
1 (4 1/2 oz.) can shrimp
1 c. mayonnaise
3/4 c. tomato juice

Mix all ingredients together. Turn into greased casserole. Top with grated Parmesan cheese and bake in 350° oven for 25 minutes. Serves 4-6.

Verndale Bolton, Anniston Council

SHRIMP AND CRABMEAT CASSEROLE A LA HELTON

2 1/2 lb. shrimp, peeled
  and deveined
1 (6 oz.) can crabmeat, or
  1 1/2 lb. shrimp
1 (6 oz.) can crabmeat
  (claw)
1 (6 oz.) can crabmeat
  (lump)
1 large onion, chopped
1 large bell pepper,
  chopped

5 stalks celery, finely
  chopped
1 small jar pimiento
2 cans Campbell's golden
  cream of mushroom soup
4 cloves garlic, minced
1 stick margarine
1/2 c. parsley
1 bunch green peppers,
  chopped
Salt and pepper

Saute celery in melted butter, using heavy skillet with top. When celery is tender, add bell pepper, onion and garlic and cook until done. Add parsley and green peppers; add shrimp and cook until pink. Add soup and simmer 5 to 10 minutes (covered), stirring ingredients regularly. Add crabmeat and season to taste. Add pimiento; cook in covered pan for 20 minutes in preheated (350°) oven. While cooking on top of the stove, be careful not to let the mixture burn or stick to the skillet. Serve by folding into hot cooked rice; leftovers may be frozen for use at a later date.

Merv Helton, Birmingham Central Council

SHRIMP CASSEROLE

2 c. peeled, boiled shrimp
2 c. cooked rice
1 large can tomatoes,
  chopped up
5 slices bacon, fried

1 large onion, sliced thin
1 green pepper, sliced thin
2 stalks celery, sliced thin
1 small jar sliced mushrooms,
  drained

1567-82

Salt and pepper to taste. Prepare shrimp. Cook rice. Fry bacon and saute onion. Mix pepper and celery in bacon drippings and drain. Mix all ingredients and bake in greased dish at 400° for 45 minutes.

Shirley Downey, Mobile Council

SHRIMP CASSEROLE

2 lb. cooked shrimp
1 c. Minute rice (cook after measuring)
2 cans celery soup
1 can mushrooms
English peas
Parsley flakes
1/2 c. chopped onions, sauteed
1/2 c. chopped celery, sauteed

1/2 c. chopped bell peppers, sauteed
1 c. water
1/2 c. mayonnaise
Cracker crumbs (melt oleo and pour over crumbs)
2 tsp. Worcestershire sauce
2 boiled eggs
2 Tbsp. chopped pimento

Bake 20 minutes (or more) at 350°.

Patti Smith, Anniston Council

FAYE'S CHICKEN SPAGHETTI

1 can mushrooms (1 c.), chopped
1 medium onion, chopped
2 c. chopped celery
1 medium green pepper, chopped
3 cloves garlic
3 Tbsp. dry parsley

1 tsp. rubbed sage
1 small can pimiento
1/2 tsp. marjoram
1/2 tsp. ginger
2 tsp. salt
1 can mushroom soup
1 can tomato soup
3/4 lb. Velveeta cheese

Bake a 5 pound hen or 2 fryers; drain and cool broth and fat. Saute all the above chopped ingredients in 1/2 cup chicken fat until clear or lightly tender. Add seasonings. Add 1/2 cup cooking wine or 1/4 cup vinegar and 1 quart broth from chicken (or bouillon cubes). Add 1 can mushroom soup and 1 can tomato soup. Remove chicken skin; cube chicken. Add to above ingredients; stir well. Taste for flavor. Cook 1 pound spaghetti 5 minutes; drain. Add to chicken mixture; mix and bake at 250° for 1 hour. Cube 3/4 pound Velveeta cheese and add to chicken spaghetti. Stir lightly. Cook at 250° for 30 more minutes.

Cliff Cox, Birmingham Central Council

BOB'S SPAGHETTI

1 lb. ground chuck
2 (15 1/2 oz.) cans
   special sauce
1 pkg. spaghetti seasoning
   with mushrooms

1 (12 oz.) pkg. vermicelli
Garlic salt
Salt and pepper
Chopped onions, if desired

Brown ground chuck and pour off grease. Season and add the cans of Hunt's special sauce and spaghetti seasoning. Simmer about 10-15 minutes. Cook vermicelli and drain. Serve with sauce.

Joan Sims, Birmingham South Council

ITALIAN TOMATO SAUCE SUPREME
(With Italian Sausage, Meat Balls and Roast)

This recipe makes a large quantity of meat sauce and requires a 22 quart pot. The sauce can be frozen for future use. If a smaller amount is required, cut the amount proportionately.

2 large (6 lb. 9 oz.) cans
   tomato puree
1 (12 oz.) can tomato paste
1 large can water
1/2 c. oil
3 1/2 tsp. salt
1 tsp. black pepper
1 Tbsp. garlic powder
1 Tbsp. oregano

8 tsp. crushed basil leaves
1 large green pepper, diced
1 large onion, diced
2 tsp. fennel seeds
4 lb. ground beef
3 lb. mild Italian sausage
3-4 lb. chuck, butt or
   pork roast (optional)
3-4 lb. meat balls (optional)

Add ingredients to pot. Shred ground beef and stir in. Add sausage, meat balls and roast. Bring to boil, then lower to slow simmer. Cook for 6 to 7 hours, stirring gently on occasion to prevent bottom from burning.

Meat Balls:

4 lb. chopped meat
6 Tbsp. bread crumbs
5 eggs
1 1/2 tsp. black pepper
1 1/2 tsp. salt

1 Tbsp. garlic powder
2 1/2 Tbsp. minced onion
2 Tbsp. dried parsley flakes
4 Tbsp. grated Italian cheese
4 Tbsp. water

Mix all ingredients thoroughly and roll into 1 1/2 inch meat balls. (Makes approximately 25 meat balls.)

D. J. Del Guercio, Riverchase Council

1567-82

SOUPER SPAGHETTI CASSEROLE

2 lb. lean ground beef
1/2 c. chopped onion
1/4 chopped bell
  pepper
2 Tbsp. oleo
1 (10 1/2 oz.) can cream
  of mushroom soup

1 (10 1/2 oz.) can cream
  of tomato soup
1 soup can of water
1 clove garlic, minced
1 Tbsp. salt
1 (8 oz.) pkg. thin spaghetti
1 c. shredded cheese

Brown ground beef, onion and pepper in the oleo; stir often. Add soups, water and garlic. Cook spaghetti uncovered 8 minutes; add salt and drain well. Combine spaghetti with the meat mixture and 1/2 cup of the cheese. Mix well. Put in a large casserole (at least 3 quart) and top with 1/2 cup cheese. Bake at 350° for 30 minutes.

Evelyn Brock, Montgomery Council

SPAGHETTI CASSEROLE

1 1/2 lb. ground beef
1/2 c. chopped onion
1/4 c. chopped bell pepper
1/2 tsp. garlic salt or
  powder

1 can golden mushroom soup
1 can cream of tomato soup
1 pkg. spaghetti
Cheddar cheese, grated

Brown meat and drain; add onion, pepper and garlic salt. Add mushroom soup and tomato soup; turn heat on low and let simmer until flavors blend. Drain spaghetti and mix with meat sauce. In a large casserole dish, add a layer of the mixture of spaghetti and meat sauce, then a layer of grated cheese. Continue layers, ending with cheese on top. Bake at 300° until cheese has melted, approximately 10 minutes. (You can prepare ahead of time and freeze. Just allow 30 to 45 minutes when heating and cover top with foil so cheese won't burn.)

Freida Elkourie, Birmingham South Council

SPAGHETTI

1 lb. hamburger meat
1 tall can Pet milk
1 can tomato soup

1 can cream of mushroom soup
1/2 c. grated Cheddar
  cheese (sharp)
1 (12 oz.) pkg. vermicelli
  spaghetti

Cook spaghetti until done. Brown hamburger meat. Put

meat in large bowl; add cheese, soups, milk and spaghetti. Mix well and place in 13x9 inch pan. Cook until brown at 350°. Serve with salad, French fries and rolls.

Joyce Pollard, Opelika Pioneer Unit

SPINACH AND ARTICHOKES (CASSEROLE)

2 (10 oz.) pkg. frozen
  chopped spinach
1/2 c. chopped onion
2 Tbsp. butter
Salt and pepper to taste

1 (14 oz.) can artichoke
  hearts, well drained
1 pt. sour cream
3/4 c. grated Parmesan
  cheese (1/2 in dish,
  1/4 on top)

Preheat oven to 350°. Cook spinach and drain. Saute onion in butter. Combine all. Place in buttered 1 1/2 to 2 quart casserole dish. Bake 20-30 minutes.

Jeanie McCluskey, Riverchase Council

SPINACH BROCCOLI CASSEROLE

1 (10 oz.) pkg. frozen
  chopped spinach
1 (10 oz.) pkg. frozen
  chopped broccoli
5 oz. cream of mushroom
  soup, undiluted
1 (8 oz.) jar Cheez Whiz

1/4 lb. fresh mushrooms,
  sliced
2 Tbsp. butter
1/4 tsp. nutmeg
1/4 tsp. salt
1/8 tsp. pepper
2 Tbsp. Parmesan cheese,
  grated

Cook broccoli and spinach until barely tender; drain well. In double boiler combine soup and cheese, stirring until smooth. Saute mushrooms in butter. Combine all ingredients except Parmesan cheese and place in buttered 1 1/2 quart casserole. Top with Parmesan cheese; bake at 325° for 25 minutes. Serves 6.

Edwina Hicks, Montgomery Council

SPINACH CASSEROLE

3 (10 oz.) pkg. frozen
  spinach
1 (8 oz.) pkg. cream cheese

1 stick butter
2 Tbsp. lemon juice
Bread crumbs

Soften cheese and butter in casserole dish. Cook spinach enough to thaw and drain. Add hot spinach to cheese/butter. Add lemon juice and mix well. Clean edge of casserole dish. Cover top with bread crumbs. Bake uncovered at 350° until hot and bread crumbs brown (about 25-30 minutes).

Candy Bird, Birmingham South Council

SPINACH NOODLE CASSEROLE

6 oz. noodles (4 c.)
1 (10 oz.) pkg. frozen
  chopped spinach
1 env. Hollandaise
  sauce mix
1/2 tsp. dry mustard
1 c. dairy sour cream

1/4 c. grated Parmesan cheese
1/4 c. Italian seasoned bread
  crumbs
2 Tbsp. grated Parmesan
  cheese
1 Tbsp. butter or margarine,
  melted

Cook noodles and spinach separately according to package directions; drain and set aside. In saucepan combine Hollandaise sauce mix and mustard. Stir in 3/4 cup water; cook and stir till bubbly; stir in sour cream. Combine with noodles, spinach, the 1/4 cup Parmesan and 1/2 teaspoon salt. Turn into ungreased 1 1/2 quart casserole. Bake covered at 350° for 20 minutes. Combine bread crumbs, the 2 tablespoons Parmesan and butter or margarine. Sprinkle atop. Bake 10 minutes more. Place sliced tomatoes atop if desired. Makes 4-6 servings.

Dae Self, Birmingham West Council

BUTTERNUT SQUASH CASSEROLE

3 c. cooked, mashed
  butternut squash
1 c. sugar
1/2 c. butter

2 eggs, well beaten
1 tsp. vanilla
2 tsp. powdered milk

Combine ingredients and pour in baking dish.

2/3 c. brown sugar
1/3 c. flour

1/3 c. butter
1/2 c. nuts

Mix and spread on casserole and bake 45 minutes at 350°.

Colleen Dobbs, Decatur Council

312

BUTTERNUT SQUASH CASSEROLE

1 large butternut squash
2 Tbsp. butter
1/3 c. dark brown sugar

1/3 c. raisins
Marshmallows

Slice squash into quarters and boil; remove squash from water. Scrape contents from outer shells and throw away the shells. Put squash into casserole bowl with butter and brown sugar; blend with mixer until smooth like mashed potatoes. Add raisins to mixture. Top with miniature marshmallows and put in 400° oven until marshmallows are golden brown.

Judy Ivey, Birmingham South Council

GOLDEN SQUASH CASSEROLE

10 golden squash
6 pretty onions
Ample supply of black
   pepper (to your taste)

2 Tbsp. golden corn oil
1 large iron skillet
   with cover

Wash and cut squash and onions. Put corn oil in fryer. Put 1 layer of squash, 1 layer of onions. Sprinkle well with black pepper. Repeat method until all squash and onions are used. Put heat on medium for 25 minutes and then turn heat down low for 45 minutes. When cover is removed from fryer, you will have the tastiest "Golden Squash" ever put in your mouth.

Bettie Peyton Golden, Montgomery Council

CHEESY SQUASH CASSEROLE

1 lb. squash, chopped
1 small onion, chopped
3 Tbsp. butter
2 eggs, beaten

1 c. milk
1 c. grated cheese
1 c. cracker crumbs
Salt
Pepper

Combine squash, onion and butter; cook. Drain and mash. Add remaining ingredients, reserving 1/2 cup cheese to sprinkle over top. Pour into buttered casserole dish. Bake at 375° until firm. Sprinkle cheese on top after casserole is done.

Jane Courington, Montgomery Council

MARY'S SQUASH CASSEROLE

4 average size squash
  (yellow)*
3 or 4 Tbsp. grated
  onion*
1 stick margarine, melted
1/4 c. grated cheese*

1/4 c. Carnation milk
10 or 12 soda crackers,
  crumbled
Salt and pepper to taste
1 egg
1/2 small can Spam

*Grate as to use in cole slaw. Beat egg and add milk, then add to squash, onion, salt and pepper, cheese and crackers, Spam; mix well. Pour melted margarine over mixture and toss well. Then place into pan and bake in 400° oven for 20-25 minutes or until done to taste. Leftovers may be refrigerated and reheated with no loss of flavor.

Mrs. Ollie Scott, Anniston Council

YELLOW SQUASH CASSEROLE

1/4 c. melted butter
1 1/4 lb. yellow squash,
  thinly sliced
1/2 tsp. salt
1/4 tsp. pepper
1 egg, beaten

1/2 c. mayonnaise
1/2 c. sour cream
1/4 c. chopped onion
1 tsp. sugar
1/2 c. shredded sharp cheese

Pour melted butter into a 1 1/2 quart casserole; add squash and sprinkle with salt and pepper. Combine egg, mayonnaise, onion and sugar. Mix well and pour over squash. Sprinkle evenly with cheese; bake at 350° for 35 to 40 minutes. Yield: 4 to 5 servings.

Edwina Hicks, Montgomery Council

SQUASH CASSEROLE

3 c. squash (about 2 lb.)
2 eggs, beaten
1 c. evaporated milk
1 c. grated cheese
2 c. cracker crumbs

3/4 stick margarine
1 tsp. salt
1/2 tsp. celery salt
1/4 tsp. pepper
3/4 c. finely chopped onions

Cook squash and drain well before measuring. Add butter, salt, pepper, celery salt and milk. Mix all together. Then add beaten eggs, onions, cheese and cracker crumbs. Pour into greased casserole dish and bake at 375° for about 40 minutes. Makes 8 generous servings.

Nancy Williams, Life Member, Anniston Council

SQUASH CASSEROLE

2 c. yellow squash
1 can cream of chicken soup
1 c. sour cream
1 grated carrot
1 tsp. salt
1/2 tsp. pepper
1 small onion, chopped
Pepperidge Farm herb
   seasoned crumbs
Butter

Cook and mash squash; add soup, sour cream, grated carrot, onion, salt and pepper. Butter casserole; cover bottom with crumbs. Add squash mixture. Cover with additional crumbs and dot with chunks of butter; bake at 350° for 35 minutes.

Dorothy Franklin, Montgomery Council

ZUCCHINI AND YELLOW SQUASH CASSEROLE

3-4 medium zucchini
3-4 medium yellow squash
1 medium onion
1 Tbsp. butter
1 c. shredded Mozzarella
   cheese
1 c. crushed Triscuits
Salt and pepper to taste
2 eggs

Slice zucchini, yellow squash and onion; steam until tender in butter. Beat 2 eggs. Combine all ingredients except Triscuits in greased casserole. Top with Triscuits; bake at 350° for 30 minutes. Serves 4-6.

Beth Thomas, Birmingham East Council

ZUCCHINI SQUASH CASSEROLE

3 lb. zucchini squash,
   cubed
1/3 c. salad oil
3 medium onions
1 clove garlic
1 large can tomatoes
2 tsp. salt
2 tsp. oregano
1/8 tsp. pepper
1 Tbsp. wine vinegar
3 Tbsp. grated Parmesan
   cheese

Arrange squash in dish. Saute onions and garlic in the oil. Add tomatoes, seasonings and vinegar. Bring to boil, and simmer 1 minute. Pour tomatoes and onion mix over squash. Top with the cheese and bake in a 400° oven for 1 hour. Serves 8-10.

Judy Patterson, Huntsville Council

CRUNCHY SWEET POTATO CASSEROLE

2 c. mashed sweet potatoes
1 1/4 c. sugar
2 eggs, beaten
1/2 c. milk

6 Tbsp. melted butter
  or margarine
1/2 tsp. ground cinnamon
1/2 tsp. ground nutmeg

Topping:

3/4 c. crushed maple
  flavored wheat and
  buckwheat flake cereal
1/2 c. chopped nuts

1/2 c. firmly packed
  brown sugar
6 Tbsp. melted butter
  or margarine

Combine all ingredients except topping and mix well; spoon into a greased 2 quart casserole and bake at 400° for 20 minutes. Sprinkle with topping and bake an additional 10 minutes. Yield: 6 to 8 servings.

Topping: Combine ingredients and stir well. Yield: About 1 cup.

Eloise Brown, Tuscaloosa Pioneer Unit

PRALINE SWEET POTATO CASSEROLE

4 medium sweet potatoes,
  boiled, peeled, quartered
2 eggs
1/2 c. firmly packed
  dark brown sugar

1/3 c. butter or
  margarine, melted
1 tsp. salt
1/2 c. pecan halves

Mash sweet potatoes in large bowl; beat in eggs, 1/4 cup of the sugar, 2 tablespoons melted butter and salt. Turn into 1 quart casserole dish. Arrange pecan halves over top; sprinkle with remaining 1/4 cup sugar and drizzle with remaining melted butter. Bake uncovered at 375° for 20 minutes. Serve with warm Orange Sauce. Serves 6.

Orange Sauce: Blend 1/3 cup granulated sugar, 1 tablespoon cornstarch and 1/8 teaspoon salt in saucepan; add 1 teaspoon grated orange peel, 1 cup orange juice and 1 teaspoon lemon juice. Bring to boil over medium heat, stirring constantly until sauce thickens. Remove from heat; stir in 2 tablespoons margarine and 3 dashes of Angostura bitters.

Bobbie Robertson, Huntsville Council

SWEET POTATO CASSEROLE

3 c. mashed sweet potatoes
2 eggs, beaten
1/4 c. milk

1 c. sugar
1 tsp. vanilla
1/2 c. margarine

Topping:

1 c. brown sugar
1/3 c. flour

1 c. chopped pecans
1/3 c. butter, melted

Mix first 6 ingredients and place in baking dish. For topping, mix brown sugar, flour and chopped pecans. Spread on top of sweet potato mixture. Drizzle melted butter over topping; bake at 350° for 30 minutes.

Marilyn Aldridge, Birmingham South Council

SWEET POTATO CASSEROLE

3 large cooked sweet
    potatoes (can substitute
    with canned yams)
1 Tbsp. vanilla
1 c. pecans
1/4 c. white sugar

1 stick margarine
1 c. peanut butter
1 small bag miniature
    marshmallows
1/8 c. brown sugar
1/2 to 3/4 c. water

In 10 inch Pyrex dish sprayed with Pam, put sweet potatoes, cut in chunks. Dot margarine and peanut butter around potatoes. Sprinkle brown and white sugar over potatoes. Add enough water to casserole (do not cover potatoes). Spread peanut butter and marshmallows on top. Bake at 350° till liquid thickens and marshmallows are browned, about 30 minutes.

Andrea Dutton, Anniston Council

SWEET POTATO CREST

2 c. mashed sweet potatoes
1 c. sugar
1 c. milk
1 egg, beaten

1 tsp. vanilla flavoring
1/4 tsp. salt
1 small can coconut

Mix together and bake in buttered casserole dish 30 minutes in 350° oven. Makes 2 1/2 quarts. Set aside.

Topping:

1 small can crushed pineapple
    and juice
1 c. sugar

1/2 pt. maraschino cherries
    and juice
3 Tbsp. cornstarch

Cook over low heat until real thick; pour on top of potatoes.

1567-82   Eloise T. Cottrell, Mobile Council   317

MISS LOIS'S TUNA NOODLE CASSEROLE

1 pkg. wide flat noodles
1 can cream of chicken
  (or mushroom) soup

3/4 can water
2 cans tuna

Cook noodles in salted water and drain. Mix soup and water. Flake tuna into mixture. Layer in large casserole dish as follows: Noodles, soup/tuna mixture, black pepper. Repeat until caserole is full. Bake at 350° for 25 minutes.

Note: Crushed potato chips can be used for topping before baking if desired. Casserole freezes well, but topping should not be placed until just before placing in oven.

Anne Spragins, Birmingham East Council

CHEESE 'N TUNA CRESCENTS

1 (6 1/2 oz.) can tuna,
  drained
2 Tbsp. instant minced
  onion or 1/2 c.
  chopped onion
3/4 c. (3 oz.) shredded
  American or Cheddar
  cheese

1 (10 3/4 oz.) can condensed
  cream of mushroom soup
1 (8 oz.) can Pillsbury
  refrigerated quick crescent
  or Italian flavor crescent
  dinner rolls
1/2 c. milk

Preheat oven to 375°. In small bowl combine tuna, onion, 1/2 cup shredded cheese (reserve 1/4 cup) and 5 tablespoons soup. Separate crescent dough into 8 triangles. Place 2 tablespoons tuna mixture on the wide end of each triangle. Roll up; start at shortest side of each triangle and roll to opposite point. In small saucepan heat remaining soup, reserved shredded cheese and milk until bubbly. Pour 1/2 of soup mixture (3/4 cup) into ungreased 8 or 9 inch square pan. Arrange filled crescents over soup. Bake 25 to 30 minutes until golden brown. Serve with remaining sauce. Refrigerate any leftovers. Serves 4 to 6.

Fay King, Huntsville Council

SUPER QUICK CASSEROLE

3 c. cooked rice
1 1/2 c. drained tuna,
  or cooked, cubed
  chicken or turkey
1 1/4 c. (10 3/4 oz. can)
  cream of chicken soup
1 c. milk

1 c. cooked well drained
  green vegetables
1/2 c. celery
1/4 c. finely chopped onion
1 tsp. Worcestershire sauce
1/2 c. (2 oz.) shredded
  process American cheese

Combine all ingredients except cheese; mix thoroughly. Place in buttered 1 1/2 quart casserole. Top with cheese; bake in moderate oven (350° F.) for 35 to 40 minutes.
Chris Kirkley, Birmingham East Council

TUNA CASSEROLE

1 can tuna, drained	1 tsp. lemon juice
1 small can crushed	2 tsp. curry powder
pineapple	1/2 c. mayonnaise
1 c. cooked rice	1 small jar pimento
1 stalk celery, chopped	Green onions to taste
	1/4 c. chutney

Blend mayonnaise, chutney and curry powder. Then add other ingredients. Decorate with watercress or parsley.
Evelyn Hicks, Huntsville Council

TUNA CASSEROLE

1 can tuna, drained	2 green onions
1 c. chopped celery	1 small can asparagus tips
1/4 c. grated cheese	1 can chow mein noodles
1 can mushroom soup	1/2 c. water
1/2 c. mayonnaise	Dash of soy sauce

Mix well and bake at 350° for 20-25 minutes.
Mary C. Martin, Birmingham East Council

TUNA CASSEROLE

1 can English peas	1 can tuna
1 1/2 to 2 c. rice, cooked	2 slices cheese
	1 can cream of chicken soup

Halve all ingredients and make 2 layers in a 1 3/4 quart casserole dish, starting with peas, rice and tuna. Cut 1 slice of cheese in strips, placing over tuna, then add half of soup. Then repeat second layer. Cover with foil and cook 30 minutes at 450° or until soup and cheese are bubbling.
Willadean Cooley, Tuscaloosa Council

QUICK TURKEY-NOODLE CASSEROLE

3 c. diced, cooked turkey
1 (6 oz.) pkg. noodles
2 (10 oz.) pkg. frozen
  mixed vegetables
1/2 c. grated American
  cheese
1/2 tsp. salt
1 can condensed cream
  of mushroom soup
Dash of Worcestershire
  sauce
Dash of Tabasco sauce
1 chicken bouillon cube
1/2 c. boiling water

In a cup dissolve bouillon cube in boiling water. Cook noodles according to package directions; drain. In a casserole combine diced turkey, noodles and mixed vegetables. Mix well and sprinkle with cheese. In a bowl combine bouillon mixture, mushroom soup, salt, Worcestershire sauce and Tabasco sauce. Pour over cheese. Cover; bake at 350° for 20 to 25 minutes. Serves 6.

Mrs. Jeri Nuss, Decatur Council

TURKEY CRUNCH

3 c. chopped turkey
3/4 c. chopped celery
1 Tbsp. chopped onion
1 (4 oz.) can mushrooms,
  chopped
2 hard boiled eggs, chopped
1/2 c. slivered almonds
Chow mein noodles or
  crushed potato chips
1 can cream of chicken
  soup
3/4 c. mayonnaise

Combine first 6 ingredients. Mix mayonnaise and soup together and fold into turkey mixture. Put into 2 quart casserole; cover with noodles or chips. Bake in 350° oven for 30 minutes or until mixture bubbles.

Clealis Prestridge, Huntsville Council

TURKEY AND GREEN BEAN CASSEROLE

1 3/4 c. French style
  green beans
1 1/4 c. boiling water
2 1/2 c. diced, cooked
  turkey
1 (10 oz.) can condensed
  cream of mushroom soup
1/4 tsp. salt
1/2 tsp. pepper
Dash of Tabasco sauce
1 c. precooked rice
3 1/2 oz. French fried onion
  rings
6 tomato slices

Cook green beans in 1 1/4 cups of boiling water for 5 minutes. Add turkey, soup and seasonings to green beans. Cook slowly for 5 minutes; stir in the rice and half the onion rings. Pour into casserole. Top with remaining onion rings and tomato slices; bake at 400° for 20 to 25 minutes. Serves 6.

Mrs. Jeri Nuss, Decatur Council

BEAN AND CORN CASSEROLE

Layer:

2 cans green beans,
  well drained

2 cans whole kernel corn,
  drained
1 can water chestnuts

Mix:

1/2 pt. sour cream
1 can celery soup

1/3 c. chopped onion
1 c. grated cheese

Spread cheese mixture over vegetables. Melt 1/4 stick of butter and season with garlic salt, salt and pepper. Pour over 1 bag of crushed Ritz crackers. Pour over cheese mixture. Bake at 350° for 30-40 minutes. Put 1 can of onion rings on top and bake till brown.

Sara P. Mitchell, Montgomery Council

BRUSSELS SPROUTS - ARTICHOKE CASSEROLE

1 (10 oz.) pkg. frozen
  Brussels sprouts
1/2 c. water
1 (14 oz.) can artichoke
  hearts, drained
2/3 c. mayonnaise

1/2 tsp. celery salt
1/4 c. grated Parmesan
  cheese
1/4 c. margarine, melted
2 tsp. lemon juice
1/4 c. slivered almonds

Cook Brussels sprouts in 1/2 cup water just till tender. Drain. Arrange Brussels sprouts and artichokes in a greased 1 quart casserole. Combine remaining ingredients and spoon over vegetables. Bake uncovered at 425° for 8 to 10 minutes.

Lois Herlong, Birmingham South Council

CABBAGE DINNER

1 lb. ground beef
1 small onion
1 egg
1 tsp. salt
1/4 tsp. pepper
1/4 tsp. oregano
1/2 c. bread crumbs

2 Tbsp. margarine
4 c. shredded cabbage
1 bell pepper, sliced
4 medium raw potatoes, sliced
1 tomato, sliced
1/2 c. water

Mix first 7 ingredients and form into small meat balls. Brown meat balls on all sides. Drain on paper towel. In 6 quart saucepan melt margarine over low heat; add cabbage, bell pepper, salt and pepper. Next add potatoes; on top of potatoes slice the tomato. Add water, then arrange meat balls on top of vegetables. Cover tightly and steam over low heat about 30 minutes until potatoes are done. Do not stir! Serve directly from saucepan.

Sandy Sprinkle, Anniston Council

CABBAGE ROLLS (Microwave)

12 cabbage leaves
1 c. water
1/2 lb. ground beef
1/2 lb. ground pork sausage
1 egg
1/2 c. instant rice
1/4 c. finely chopped onion

1 tsp. garlic salt
1/4 tsp. pepper
Dash of hot pepper sauce
1 (8 oz.) can tomato sauce
1 (6 oz.) can tomato paste
1 Tbsp. sugar
1 tsp. basil
1 (1 lb.) can sauerkraut, rinsed and drained

1. Place cabbage and 1/2 cup water in a 3 quart casserole. Cover with a tight fitting lid or plastic wrap. Microwave on high (100% power) for 8 to 10 minutes or until leaves are pliable. Drain. Cut out thick core from each leaf. 2. Mix together ground beef, sausage, egg, rice, onion, garlic salt, pepper, hot pepper sauce and 1/4 cup tomato sauce. 3. Place about 1/4 cup of meat mixture in the center of each leaf. Fold in edges and roll up from core end. 4. Mix together remaining tomato sauce, tomato paste, remaining water, sugar and basil. 5. Place alternate layers of sauerkraut, cabbage rolls (seam side down) and sauce in an 11 3/4 x 7 1/2 x 1 3/4 inch baking dish. Cover with a tight fitting lid or plastic wrap. 6. Microwave on medium-high (70% power) for 20 to 25 minutes or until meat is no longer pink and rice is tender. Rearrange rolls halfway through cooking and baste with sauce. Makes 6 servings. Cooking time: 28 to 35 minutes.

Kathy Coats, Mobile Council

CARROT CASSEROLE

2 c. sliced raw carrots
4 oz. oleo
1/2 c. milk

3 eggs, beaten
2 c. grated Cheddar cheese

Cook carrots in salted water. Mash and add butter, milk and eggs. Fold in cheese and bake at 350° for 45 minutes.

Betty Hobbs, Riverchase Council

CELERY CASSEROLE

4 c. celery, cut (1 stalk)
1 whole pimiento, chopped
1 c. water
1 can undiluted cream of
  chicken soup

1 c. water chestnuts
  drained and sliced
  (8 1/2 oz. can)
1 c. sliced almonds

Cook celery in 1 cup salted water about 6 minutes; drain. Mix celery, pimiento and water chestnuts together in a 2 quart casserole dish. Add soup; sprinkle almonds on top. Bake, uncovered, at 450° for 15 minutes.

Nancy Williams, Life Member,
Anniston Council

CORN CASSEROLE

1 can French style
  green beans, drained
1 can cream of celery soup
1 can white shoe peg
  corn, drained

1 small carton sour cream
1 can water chestnuts, sliced
1/2 c. grated cheese
1 small onion, chopped
1/2 c. finely chopped celery

Mix all ingredients and put in buttered casserole dish. Crumble Ritz crackers over top of casserole and dot with butter. Bake at 325° for approximately 45 minutes.

Homer Jean Dunson, Montgomery Council

CORN/PEAS CASSEROLE

1 large can Niblets corn
1 can LeSueur English
  peas

1 small can water chestnuts,
  sliced
1 c. medium white sauce
1 small jar pimiento Cheez Whiz

Melt cheese in white sauce. Combine with other ingredients in greased casserole dish. Bake at 350° until bubbly.

Jean Ivey, Riverchase Council

CHINESE BEAN CASSEROLE

1 can Blue Lake French
  style green beans, drained
1 can Chinese bean sprouts,
  drained
1 can water chestnuts,
  chopped and drained

1 can cream of mushroom soup
1 can grated New York cheese
1 can French fried onion rings
Accent, salt, cayenne
  (just a pinch)
Slivered almonds

Mix together, making 2 layers, adding seasonings as you go. Sprinkle almonds on top. Dot with butter; bake 20 to 30 minutes at 350°. Add onion rings the last 5 minutes of baking. Bake covered until you add onion rings and then leave uncovered.

Debbie Hearn, Birmingham East Council

DEVILED PEA CASSEROLE

1 can English peas
1 c. grated cheese
1 c. chopped celery
1 can cream of tomato
  soup
1/2 c. chili sauce
1 can pimento
1 Tbsp. Worcestershire sauce
1 can mushroom soup (optional)
1 bell pepper (optional)
4 boiled eggs
1 1/2 c. white sauce

Mix first 9 ingredients. To make white sauce, use 2 tablespoons butter, 2 tablespoons flour and 1 cup milk. Make layers of mixture, then layer of sliced eggs. Bake 20 or 30 minutes at 350°.

Edwina Hicks, Montgomery Council

ENGLISH PEA CASSEROLE

1 head lettuce
1 can English peas (large
  crowd 2 cans)
4 stalks celery, chopped
1 red onion, chopped

In a large bowl place lettuce on bottom and around side. Make sure lettuce is not wet. Drain English peas, pour over lettuce. Put celery, bell pepper and onion on top of English peas. Cover with a lot of mayonnaise; sprinkle with Parmesan cheese. Use at least 1/2 of a small can or more. Put in refrigerator. Make 1 day ahead.

Barbara Spearman, Birmingham South Council

GARDEN SUPPER CASSEROLE

2 c. cubed soft bread
1/2 c. shredded sharp
  Cheddar cheese
  (about 2 oz.)
2 Tbsp. butter or
  margarine, melted
1 c. cooked peas or
  other vegetable
2 Tbsp. chopped onion
3 Tbsp. butter or margarine
3 Tbsp. flour
1 tsp. salt
1/8 tsp. pepper
1 1/2 c. milk
1 c. cut up cooked meat (beef,
  pork, lamb or chicken)
1 large tomato, sliced

Heat oven to 350°. Mix bread cubes, cheese and 2 tablespoons butter. Spread half the mixture in greased 1 quart casserole and top with peas. Cook and stir onion in 3 tablespoons butter until onion is tender. Blend in flour and seasonings. Cook over low heat, stirring until mixture is bubbly. Remove from heat. Stir in milk; heat to boiling, stirring constantly. Boil and stir 1 minute. Stir in meat; pour over peas. Arrange tomato slices on top and sprinkle with remaining bread mixture. Bake uncovered 25 minutes. Makes 4 servings.

Dorothy Darnell, Mobile Council

GREEN BEAN CASSEROLE

2 Tbsp. butter
2 Tbsp. flour
1 tsp. salt
1 carton sour cream
1 (6 oz.) pkg. Swiss
  cheese
2 Tbsp. melted butter

1/4 tsp. pepper
1 tsp. sugar
1/2 tsp. grated onion
2 cans French cut beans,
  drained
2 c. corn flakes, crushed

Melt butter and stir in flour, salt, pepper, sugar and onion; add sour cream and stir until thick. Add grated cheese; fold in beans. Pour in greased casserole. Add melted butter to crushed corn flakes and sprinkle on top. Bake at 400° for 20 minutes. Serves 6.

Mrs. P. A. Garrett, Huntsville Council

LAYERED VEGETABLE CASSEROLE

1 large can asparagus tips
1 can small green peas
1 can lima beans
1 can Niblets corn

1 small jar pimiento, chopped
1 c. shredded Cheddar cheese
1 can golden cream of
  mushroom soup
1 can French fried onion rings

Drain vegetables well. Layer each one evenly in large casserole dish. Dot each layer with a bit of butter; add salt and pepper to taste. Top with cheese, then spread evenly with undiluted soup to cover vegetables. Sprinkle with paprika and add onion rings. Cover with foil and bake 20 minutes at 350°. Remove foil and continue baking 15-20 minutes until onion rings are lightly browned. Serves 8-10.

Ken King, Birmingham Central Council

NOODLE AND VEGETABLE BAKE

1 pkg. Kraft egg noodle and chicken dinner	1 (10 oz.) pkg. frozen chopped broccoli
1/2 c. milk	1/4 c. onion, finely chopped
2 eggs, beaten	Salt and pepper to taste

Prepare dinner as directed on package. Add remaining ingredients and mix well. Pour into a 1 1/2 quart greased casserole. Cover and bake about 45 minutes on 350°. May sprinkle top with grated cheese.

Bobbie Bowles, Montgomery Council

STUFFED GREEN PEPPERS

6 large peppers, stems and seeds removed	1/2 or 10 oz. can condensed tomato soup
1/4 tsp. pepper	3/4 c. dry bread or cracker crumbs
1/2 lb. ground beef	
1 tsp. salt	1/2 chopped onion

Mix ground beef, bread crumbs, salt, pepper and onion and add tomato soup. Stuff peppers with meat mixture. Stand upright in small baking dish. Pour over remaining soup, diluted with 1/2 soup can water. Bake covered 45 minutes, uncovered 15 minutes longer.

Helen Mitchell, Huntsville Council

STUFFING CASSEROLE

1 stick margarine	1 egg
1/2 c. onion, minced	Milk (to make 1/2 c. with eggs)
1/2 c. celery stalks and leaves, chopped	2 Tbsp. salt
	1/2 tsp. pepper
4 c. plain white bread cubes	1 tsp. poultry seasoning (or more to taste if desired)

Melt margarine in large frying pan. Saute onions and celery until golden. Add half of the bread cubes to frying pan and heat. Beat egg slightly in measuring cup. Add milk to measure 1/2 cup. Mix well. Place remaining half of bread cubes in large mixing bowl. Sprinkle seasoning on dry bread cubes. Add egg mixture and contents of frying pan. Toss lightly. Put in large greased casserole; cover and bake in oven with turkey for the last hour. Serves 8 to 10.

Monica Burrough, Birmingham East Council

VEGETABLE CASSEROLE

1 can French green beans
1 can bean sprouts
2 cans mushroom soup
1 c. New York sharp
  Cheddar cheese, grated

1 can water chestnuts,
  thinly sliced
1 c. French fried onion
  rings

Place vegetables in layers in buttered casserole. Cover with mushroom soup. Bake at 350° for 30 minutes. Remove from oven. Sprinkle cheese on the top, then cover with onion rings. Return casserole to oven for 10 more minutes. Serves 6-8.

Martha Hastings, Birmingham South Council

VEGETABLE CASSEROLE

2 cans Veg-All, drained
1 c. chopped onion
1 c. chopped water
  chestnuts

1 c. grated Cheddar cheese
3/4 c. mayonnaise
1 roll Ritz crackers, crushed
1 stick oleo, melted

Mix first 5 ingredients. Pour into casserole. Then top with the crackers, mixed with melted oleo. Bake at 350° for 30 minutes.

Mary C. Martin, Birmingham East Council

ZIPPY VEGETABLE CASSEROLE

1 pkg. frozen limas
1 pkg. frozen English peas
1 pkg. frozen French beans
3/4 c. mayonnaise
2 boiled eggs

1/4 c. sour cream
3 Tbsp. lemon juice
Garlic and onion salt to taste
3 Tbsp. minced onion
1 tsp. prepared mustard

Cook limas, peas and beans separately in salted water, and drain. Mix mayonnaise, sour cream, lemon juice, garlic and onion salt, minced onion, mustard and boiled eggs. Add vegetables to mixture and heat.

Mae McFarland, Riverchase Council

** NOTES **

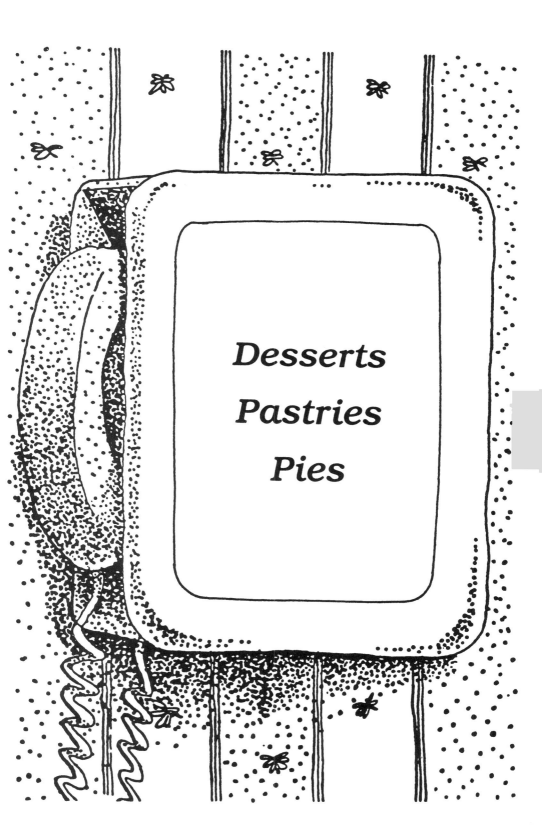

Desserts

Pastries

Pies

BAKING EQUIVALENTS

	When the recipe calls for:	Use:
Baking	½ cup butter 2 cups butter 4 cups all-purpose flour 2½ to 5 cups sifted cake flour 1 square chocolate 1 cup semisweet chocolate chips 4 cups marshmallows 2¼ cups packed brown sugar 4 cups confectioners' sugar 2 cups granulated sugar	4 ounces 1 pound 1 pound 1 pound 1 ounce 6 ounces 1 pound 1 pound 1 pound 1 pound
Cereal–Bread	1 cup fine dry bread crumbs 1 cup soft bread crumbs 1 cup small bread cubes 1 cup fine cracker crumbs 1 cup fine graham cracker crumbs 1 cup vanilla wafer crumbs 1 cup crushed cornflakes 4 cups cooked macaroni 3½ cups cooked rice	4 to 5 slices 2 slices 2 slices 28 saltines 15 crackers 22 wafers 3 cups uncrushed 8 ounces uncooked 1 cup uncooked
Dairy	1 cup shredded cheese 1 cup cottage cheese 1 cup sour cream 1 cup whipped cream ⅔ cup evaporated milk 1⅔ cups evaporated milk	4 ounces 8 ounces 8 ounces ½ cup heavy cream 1 small can 1 13-ounce can

Fruit	4 cups sliced or chopped apples
	1 cup mashed bananas
	2 cups pitted cherries
	3 cups shredded coconut
	4 cups cranberries
	1 cup pitted dates
	1 cup candied fruit
	3 to 4 tablespoons lemon juice plus
	    1 tablespoon grated lemon rind
	⅓ cup orange juice plus 2 teaspoons
	    grated orange rind
	4 cups sliced peaches
	2 cups pitted prunes
	3 cups raisins
		4 medium
		3 medium
		4 cups unpitted
		8 ounces
		1 pound
		1 8-ounce package
		1 8-ounce package
		1 lemon
		
		1 orange
		
		8 medium
		1 12-ounce package
		1 15-ounce package

DESSERTS, PASTRIES, PIES

APRICOT ICE

1 (No. 2) can apricots,
thoroughly mashed
(use juice too)

Juice of 1 lemon
Scant 1 1/2 c. sugar
2 c. milk

Mix well and freeze.

Jane Knox, Montgomery Council

ICE CREAM ALMOND BALL

Vanilla ice cream

Chopped almonds

Donna's recipe for Chocolate Sauce:

1 box chocolate icing mix
(any brand)

1 small can evaporated milk
1 stick margarine

Chocolate Sauce: Melt the margarine; add evaporated milk and the box of chocolate icing mix. Mix well; heat on low.

Scoop the ice cream in serving size balls and roll each in almonds. Place in individual ice cream dishes and pour on the chocolate sauce as desired.

Shirley Hunter, Tuscaloosa Council

BUTTER PECAN ICE CREAM

5 eggs, beaten
1 box dark brown sugar

1/2 c. white sugar

Beat together until thick and fluffy. Add:

1 1/2 c. toasted pecans
(toast in butter in oven)

1 pt. half & half
1/2 pt. whipping cream

Finish filling freezer with regular milk; freeze in freezer. Can make 1 gallon or 1 1/2 gallons.

Mary Ann Davis, Anniston Council

CHOCOLATE ICE CREAM

5 eggs
1 can condensed milk
(Dime Brand or Eagle
Brand)
2 cans Pet milk
1 pt. water

1/4 tsp. salt
1 Tbsp. vanilla
1 large can chocolate syrup
or 3 small cans
1 c. sugar

1567-82

Mix all ingredients with hand mixer. Mix well. Pour into freezer; fill to fill line with regular sweet milk. Put paddle in container. Swish back and forth to mix. Ready to freeze.

Dae Self, Birmingham West Council

HEAVENLY CHOCOLATE ICE CREAM

12 (1 3/4 oz.) Milky
  Way bars, cut into pieces
1 (14 oz.) can sweetened
  condensed milk
About 3 qt. milk
1 (5.5 oz.) can chocolate
  syrup

Combine candy and sweetened condensed milk in a large saucepan; cook over low heat, stirring constantly, until candy melts. Cool, stirring occasionally. Add about 1 quart milk to candy mixture; beat until well blended. Pour mixture into freezer can of 1 gallon hand turned or electric freezer; stir in chocolate syrup. Add enough milk to fill freezer container to within 4 inches from top. Freeze according to manufacturer's directions. Yield: 1 gallon.

Linda H. Austin, Tuscaloosa Council

CHOCOLATE ICE CREAM, PIE AND PARFAITS

1 tall (13 oz.) can Pet
  evaporated milk
3/4 c. Hershey's chocolate
  flavored syrup
1 Tbsp. sugar
1 tsp. vanilla
1/2 c. whipping cream

Pour Pet evaporated milk into large mixing bowl. Place bowl and beaters in freezer until ice crystals form around edges of evaporated milk. Whip until stiff peaks form. Fold in Hershey's syrup, vanilla, sugar and whipping cream. Freeze for 4-6 hours or overnight. Makes 8 generous 1 cup servings or approximately 2 quarts.

Pie and Parfaits: For the crust, crumble 10 Archway Dutch Cocoa, Fudge Nut Bar Cookies, or your favorite Archway variety and combine in bowl with 1/4 cup melted margarine or butter; press mixture onto bottom and sides of 9 inch pie plate. Refrigerate. Make the ice cream recipe to freezing stage. Pour half of mixture into prepared crust. Freeze several hours or overnight. Garnish as desired. Makes 6 servings. Pour remaining ice cream mixture into 8 inch square pan and freeze until firm for use in parfaits. Coarsely crumble 4 of your favorite Archway cookies. Fill 4 parfait glasses with alternate layers of ice cream and cookie crumbs. Reserve some crumbs for garnish. Freeze until firm. Makes 4 parfaits.

Brenda Stewart, Decatur Council

HOMEMADE ICE CREAM

1/2 gal. homogenized milk
3 large cans Carnation
2 cans water
3 c. sugar
6 eggs, salted slightly
1 Tbsp. vanilla

Beat eggs well and mix with other ingredients thorough-ly. Put in freezer (6 quart ice cream), electric or manual. Dee-licious. Makes 6 quarts, or can be mixed and divided for a smaller freezer. My original recipe.

Louise (Teske) Colvin, Retired

LAZY ICE CREAM

1 (15 oz.) can sweetened
   condensed milk
6 eggs
2 c. sugar
2 Tbsp. vanilla
1 pt. whipping cream
3/4 gal. milk (approx.)

Combine first 5 ingredients together in mixer until thoroughly blended. Pour into a gallon ice cream freezer, adding milk to within 1 inch of the top of the freezer. Makes 1 gallon of very smooth and delicious ice cream.

Elsie Fowler

EASY HOMEMADE ICE CREAM

5 eggs
2 (13 oz.) cans Pet milk
2 c. sugar
3 c. whole milk
1 Tbsp. vanilla
4 c. fresh fruit

Beat eggs. Mix Pet milk with sugar and add whole milk and vanilla. Mash fruit or put in a blender. Add to mix-ture. Freeze in crank or electric freezer.

Linda E. James, Tri-Cities Council

PAT'S HOMEMADE ICE CREAM

3/4 c. sugar
1/2 tsp. salt
1 Tbsp. flour
4 egg yolks
2 c. milk (canned milk)
1 tsp. vanilla extract
1 c. whipping cream
1 c. half & half

1567-82

Blend sugar, flour and salt together; add beaten egg yolks and milk. Cook in double boiler, stirring constantly, until mixture coats spoon. Cool custard by setting pan in cold water. Cover and let cool. After custard cools, add vanilla, whipping cream and half & half. Makes 1/2 gallon.

Pat Calhoun, Riverchase Council

LEMON ICE CREAM

4 lemons
3 c. sugar

3 large cans Pet skim milk
1 qt. whole milk

Slice 2 lemons paper thin. Add juice of 2 lemons; add rind of 1 lemon, grated. Sprinkle 3 cups of sugar over lemon mixture and let stand 1/2 hour. Add 3 cans of Pet skim milk and 1 quart of whole milk. Stir until dissolved. Put in 1 gallon freezer and turn until firm.

Bonnie Mayfield, Anniston Council

HOMEMADE SHERBET LEMON ICE CREAM

2 Tbsp. gelatin
1/4 c. cold water
1/3 c. lemon juice
1 1/2 c. milk

1/2 c. half & half
1/8 tsp. salt
1/3 c. sugar
1/3 c. light corn syrup

Soften gelatin in water and dissolve over hot water. Combine lemon juice, milk, half & half, salt, sugar and corn syrup; add dissolved gelatin. Chill 1 to 2 hours. Churn and freeze.

L. Whitt, Birmingham West Council

NO EGG ICE CREAM

5 qt. freezer
3 cans Eagle Brand
   condensed milk
Dash of salt

Peach or strawberry pie
   filling, if desired
2 Tbsp. vanilla flavoring
Milk (complete to fill line)

Place condensed milk, flavoring, salt and pie filling (if desired) in freezer pail. Add milk to full line and stir until mixed with other ingredients. Freeze and pack for 1 to 2 hours if desire firmer texture, or may be eaten as soon as frozen. Delicious!

Oris Bass

ORANGE SHERBET

1 (2 liter) orange drink
1 can Eagle Brand milk

1 small can crushed
   pineapple

Mix drink with milk well. Put in ice cream freezer and freeze until almost frozen. Add pineapple and freeze.

Camille Meggs, Tuscaloosa Council

PEACH ICE CREAM

1 can Eagle Brand milk
2 c. sugar
2 eggs

1 Tbsp. vanilla
6 peaches (very ripe),
   peeled and mashed
Milk

With electric mixer beat eggs; add sugar and beat until creamy. Add Eagle Brand and vanilla; beat well. Add peaches and milk. Freeze as usual for ice cream freezer.

Rachel Carroll, Decatur Council

JADIA'S HOMEMADE PEACH ICE CREAM

2 c. sugar
1 can Eagle Brand milk
1 large can Pet milk
1 can Nehi peach soda

6 peaches
1/2 gal. whole milk
1 Tbsp. vanilla

Cut peaches up very fine; add ingredients in ice cream freezer; freeze until hard.

Kim Freeman, Mobile Council

PEACHY PECAN ICE CREAM

4 c. fresh peaches, sliced
2 c. pecans, chopped
2 c. sugar
2 Tbsp. lemon juice

2 qt. half & half
   or 2 qt. whipping cream
2 tsp. vanilla
A dash of salt

Thoroughly mash peaches; add some of the sugar (about a cup). Add 1 tablespoon of the lemon juice. Let peach mixture stand for 30 minutes. After the peach mixture is ready, combine the rest of the ingredients and stir in the peach mixture. Place in a 4 quart ice cream freezer and freeze. Serves approximately 20 people.

Marsha P. Stevens, Mobile Council

STAN'S HOMEMADE PEANUT BUTTER ICE CREAM

2 c. sugar
1 1/2 c. chunky or plain
  peanut butter
2 large cans condensed milk

2 pt. heavy cream
1 qt. whole milk
6 eggs
2 Tbsp. vanilla

Combine sugar and eggs and beat until they turn white. Heat condensed milk, cream, whole milk and peanut butter for 5 minutes, then add to sugar and eggs and beat for 5 minutes. Add vanilla; stir and put in container for freezing.
Stan Self

RASPBERRY ICE CREAM

1 (10 oz.) pkg. frozen
  raspberries, thawed
1/2 c. sugar

2 1/2 c. milk
1 1/2 c. whipping cream
1 1/2 tsp. vanilla extract

Combine all ingredients; stir until sugar is dissolved. Pour mixture into freezer can of a 1 gallon freezer. Freeze according to manufacturer's instructions. Let ripen at least 1 hour. Yield: About 2 quarts.
Gloria H. Ramage, Birmingham South Council

STRAWBERRY SHERBET

1 egg, separated
1/2 c. dry instant
  nonfat milk
1/3 c. water

1/3 c. sugar
3 Tbsp. lemon juice
1 (10 or 12 oz.) box sliced
  frozen strawberries

In small bowl beat egg whites, milk and water till fluffy. Gradually add sugar and lemon juice, beating till stiff. Stir in egg yolk. Fold in berries with syrup. Pour into tray and freeze.
Jane Knox, Montgomery Council

SNOW ICE CREAM

3/4 c. sugar
2 eggs
1 tsp. vanilla

1 can condensed milk
3 c. sweet milk
Snow

Mix all but snow; add snow to thicken.
Lindie Rice, Tuscaloosa Council

TUTTI FRUTTI ICE CREAM

1 small can crushed
  pineapple
10 fresh peaches,
  mashed and ripe
1 large banana (ripe)

1 small jar cherries
  and juice, chopped
1 pt. whipping cream
1 can Eagle Brand milk
2 1/2 c. sugar
1/2 gal. milk

Mix everything together and freeze. (We put the fruit in the blender to chop.)

Rosemary Parker, Birmingham Central Council

RUTH'S VANILLA ICE CREAM

4 eggs, separated
2 1/2 c. sugar
1/2 tsp. salt

1 tsp. vanilla extract (pure)
4 cans evaporated milk
1 c. milk

In mixer cream egg yolks; add salt, sugar and vanilla. Then add evaporated milk and beat 2 or 3 minutes. Beat egg whites until stiff. Add to cream mixture and mix thoroughly. Pour into 1 gallon freezer and turn until frozen.

Mrs. Johnie Crittenden,
Birmingham East Council

WINNIE'S ICE CREAM

4 c. half & half (2 pt.)
2 1/4 c. sugar
4 c. milk (1 qt.)

1 c. (1/2 pt.) whipping cream
6 eggs
4 1/2 tsp. vanilla
1/2 tsp. salt

Optional:

Toffee - 12 Heath bars
  (chill, then crack)

Strawberries (crushed)
Peaches, sliced

Any of the above may be added prior to freezing. Mix all ingredients, beating eggs well. Follow instructions with home freezer to make this divine ice cream.

Betty W. Sanders, Birmingham Central Council

AMBROSIA

6 oranges, peeled
  and sectioned

1/2 c. sugar or to taste
1 coconut, grated

Place a layer of orange sections in a glass bowl; sprinkle

with sugar, and layer with coconut. Repeat layers, ending with coconut. Chill. Yield: About 6 servings.
Faith Kirby, Anniston Council

ORANGE AMBROSIA

2 c. hot water
1 pkg. lemon-flavored
  gelatin dessert
1/4 c. granulated sugar
Pinch of salt

1 Tbsp. lemon juice
2 Tbsp. grated orange rind
1 c. heavy cream, whipped
Orange segments

Pour hot water over gelatin dessert; stir until dissolved; add next 5 ingredients. Chill until small amount dropped from spoon mounds. Fold in whipped cream. Chill until set; turn into 1 1/2 quart mold; chill until set. Unmold. Serve in sherbet glasses with orange segments. Makes 6 servings.
Laura H. Smith, Tuscaloosa Council

ANGEL FOOD DESSERT

2 loaves bought angel
  food cake
1 can cherry pie filling
  (not canned cherries
  in syrup)
1 (8 oz.) pkg. cream
  cheese

2 c. whipped cream
  or substitute
1 c. confectioners sugar
  (but granulated will do)
1 tsp. almond flavoring
  (or vanilla)

Slice cake lengthwise into 2 layers. Make filling of cheese, cream, sugar and flavoring. Spread both bottom layers with filling, top with layer of pie filling, then top with remaining layer of cake, another layer of filling, lavishly thick this time, and the balance of the cherries. Do not try to ice sides of cake; this filling will not cling. Chill. (Sides can be iced with Cool Whip if desired.)
Betty Havard, Mobile Council

APPLE PANDOWDY

1 can apple pie filling
1 stick butter

1/2 box cake mix (can be yellow
  or white - any brand)
Cool Whip (optional)

Pour apples into 9x9 inch pan; sprinkle dry cake mix over apples. Melt butter; drizzle over top of dry cake mix. Bake 35 minutes at 350°. Delicious and quick anytime.
336   Vickie Knox, Birmingham East Council

APPLE MALLOW YAM BAKE

2 apples, sliced
1/3 c. pecans, chopped
1/2 c. brown sugar, packed
1/2 tsp. cinnamon

2 (17 oz.) cans yams, drained
1/2 c. margarine
2 c. miniature marshmallows

Toss apples and pecans with brown sugar and cinnamon. Alternate layers of apple mixture and yams in 1 1/2 quart casserole; dot with butter. Cover and bake at 350° for 35 to 40 minutes. Sprinkle marshmallows over yams and apples. Broil until lightly browned.

Judy Swindeld, Huntsville Council

TASTY FRIED APPLES

3 medium size tart
  cooking apples

3/4 c. sugar
1/3 c. margarine

Peel around the center of apples a strip about 1 1/2 inches wide. Cut apples in quarters, then slice each quarter in 3 or 4 sections. In heavy skillet, put apples; sprinkle sugar and add margarine. Cover and cook on medium heat. Cook 10-15 minutes; uncover and cook 10-15 minutes until apples are tender and transparent.

Rachel Carroll, Decatur Council

BAKED APPLES IN CARAMEL SAUCE

6-8 apples
Coconut or raisins
1/2 c. water
1/2 c. brown sugar

1/2 c. white sugar
1 Tbsp. lemon juice
1/4 tsp. cinnamon or cloves
2 Tbsp. butter

Wash and core apples; fill centers with coconut or raisins. Combine remaining ingredients in frypan. Set temperature control dial to 275° F. Bring mixture to boiling point. Add apples. Baste with syrup. Cover, with vent closed, and simmer until tender, approximately 15-25 minutes. Baste often with caramel sauce. Serves 6-8. For electric frypan.

Jamima Edney, Birmingham South Council

APPLE CRISP

6 large tart cooking apples, 1/2 tsp. cinnamon
   pared, cored and diced 3/4 c. flour
1/2 c. orange juice   1/4 tsp. salt
1 c. sugar   6 Tbsp. butter

    Place apples in a greased 11x7x2 inch baking dish. Pour orange juice over apples. Combine 1/2 cup sugar and cinnamon; sprinkle evenly over apples. Combine flour, remaining sugar and salt. Cut in butter until mixture is crumbly. Spoon over apples; bake at 350° for 45-60 minutes or until apples are tender and crust is brown. Serve warm or cold with cream or milk.
               Edgar McFarlen, Huntsville Council

APPLE DAPPLE

1 1/2 c. Wesson oil   3 c. sifted flour (all-purpose)
2 c. sugar   1 tsp. salt
3 eggs   1 tsp. soda
2 tsp. vanilla   3 c. apples in small pieces
                   1 c. pecans

Frosting:

1 c. brown sugar   1 stick oleo
1/4 c. sweet milk

    Mix all ingredients and put in greased tube pan. Put in cold oven (350°) for 1 hour or check with toothpick.
    Frosting: Cool for 3 minutes. I sift 1 cup flour and add salt and soda. Add nuts and apples before flour mixes.
        Elsie Thrasher, Birmingham South Council

APPLE FRITTERS

5 tart apples   1 pt. beer
1 c. sugar   1/4 c. oil
1 Tbsp. cinnamon   Powdered sugar
2 c. all-purpose flour Oil for deep frying

    Core apple; peel and slice crosswise. Mix sugar and cinnamon together; roll or shake apples in this mixture. Mix flour, beer and 1/4 cup oil; coat apples by dipping in this sauce. Heat oil in pan, depth to cover apples, to approximately 375° to 400°. Drop apples into oil until brown. Drain on paper towels. (Tastes like apple donuts and so easy.)
         R. R. Barfield, Decatur Council

APPLE SCRUNCH

3 sticks butter
2/3 box yellow cake mix

2 cans apple pie filling
1 1/2 c. pecans, chopped

Melt butter in 13x9 inch pan. Pour butter in bowl. Pour pie filling into pan; sprinkle dry cake over it, then the pecans. Drizzle the melted butter over all; bake 30 minutes in 400° preheated oven.

Louise McCormick, Retired

APRICOT CHEESE DELIGHT

1 (29 oz.) can crushed
  pineapple
1 (29 oz.) can apricots,
  finely cut
Water
2 pkg. orange jello
3/4 c. mini marshmallows

1/2 c. sugar
3 tsp. flour
1 egg, slightly beaten
2 Tbsp. butter
1 carton Cool Whip
3/4 c. grated Cheddar
  cheese

Drain pineapple and apricots, reserving syrup. Add water to syrup to equal 2 cups liquid. Dissolve jello in 2 cups boiling water. Add 1 cup fruit juice; chill until slightly congealed. Fold in fruit and marshmallows. Pour in an 11x7 x2 inch dish; chill until firm. Combine sugar and flour; blend in egg. Stir in remaining fruit liquid. Gradually cook over low heat until thickened, stirring constantly. Remove from heat; stir in butter. Cool and then fold in Cool Whip. Pour over jello mixture; sprinkle with cheese and chill. Serves 12.

Helen Bush, Birmingham West Council

APRICOT SQUARES

1 1/2 c. plain flour
1 tsp. baking powder
1 c. uncooked oats

1 c. brown sugar
1 1/2 sticks margarine
1 c. apricots

Mix flour, baking powder, oats and sugar. Add to this mixture the 1 1/2 sticks of margarine, melted. Place 1/2 of the mixture in the bottom of a baking dish; add the cup of apricots, forming a second layer. Add the remaining mixture as a third layer. Bake at 325° for 35 minutes.

Ed Wakefield, Birmingham Central Council

APRICOT WHIP

2 large cans apricots,
  peeled, drained and
  mashed

1 (10 oz.) box vanilla
  wafers, crushed
1 pt. whipping cream
2 c. broken nutmeats (optional)

Make a custard of 4 beaten eggs, 2 cups confectioners sugar, 1 cup butter or margarine. Cook in double boiler until thick; cool. Place 1/2 of vanilla wafer crumbs in Pyrex oblong baking dish, then all the cooled custard. Pour on 1/2 of whipped cream and 1/2 nuts, then pour all apricots. Next, the other half of cream and nuts. Cover with remaining crumbs. Let stand overnight in refrigerator. Cover with foil.

Faith Kirby, Anniston Council

BAKED FRUIT

1 (21 oz.) can cherry
  pie filling
1 (20 oz.) can pineapple
  chunks

1 (6 oz.) pkg. dried apricots
1 (12 oz.) pkg. dried prunes
2 (11 oz.) cans mandarin
  oranges

Place in large bowl; cover with foil and bake 1 hour at 350°.

Mary Ruth Kasulka, Birmingham South Council

BLUEBERRY DESSERT

1 c. flour
1 stick margarine
1 c. chopped nuts
Whipped cream

1 large pkg. Philadelphia
  cream cheese
1 c. sugar
1 can blueberry pie filling

Crust: Mix flour, margarine and nuts; press in baking dish. Bake for 20 minutes at 350°; let cool. Next layer: Mix cream cheese and sugar; put on top of crust. Next layer: Add blueberry pie filling; put whipped cream on top and sprinkle with nuts.

Cathy Porter, Tuscaloosa Council

340

BLUEBERRY TARTS

2 1/4 c. flour (plain)
3 sticks butter
2 Tbsp. sugar (heaping)
12 oz. cream cheese
9 oz. Cool Whip

1 c. sifted confectioners
  sugar
2 Tbsp. milk
1 can Comstock blueberry
  pie filling

Mix first 3 ingredients; spread on cookie sheet and bake 20 minutes at 350°; cool. Spread pie filling over crust. Mix cream cheese, confectioners sugar and milk well in blender. Fold in Cool Whip; spread over top of blueberries. Refrigerate. Cut in squares; top each with a cherry. May substitute cherry pie filling, drained crushed pineapple, homemade stewed apples.

M. Gray, Birmingham West Council

BLUEBERRY YUM YUM

Step 1:

1 (10 oz.) pkg. Lorna Doone
  cookies, crushed (reserve
  3/4 c. for topping)

1/4 c. butter

Cut butter into cookie crumbs and mix well. Press into large glass baking dish; bake in 350° oven for 5 minutes.

Step 2:

1 (8 oz.) pkg. cream cheese
1 c. powdered sugar
2 Tbsp. orange juice

1/2 c. softened butter
2 eggs, separated

In a medium bowl cream all ingredients except egg whites until mixture is smooth. Beat egg whites until stiff peaks form. Fold into cheese mixture and spread over cookie layers.

Step 3:

1 (21 oz.) can blueberry
  pie filling
1 c. chopped pecans

1 (12 oz.) carton non
  dairy whip (Cool Whip)
2 Tbsp. lemon juice
Remaining crushed cookie
  crumbs

Spread blueberry pie mix over cheese-egg mixture; cover with pecans and then spread non dairy whip over this. Sprinkle lemon juice over top and sprinkle cookie crumbs on top; chill.

Jamima Edney, Birmingham South Council

APPLE BROWNIES

1 stick margarine
1 c. sugar
1 egg
1 c. flour
1/2 tsp. baking powder

1/2 tsp. salt
1/2 tsp. cinnamon
1 c. cut up apples
1/2 c. walnuts or pecans

Cream margarine and sugar; add egg. Next add dry ingredients, then apples and nuts. Pour into greased 8 inch square pan; bake 40-50 minutes at 350°. Cool, then cut into squares.

Jeanne Anderson, Montgomery Council

BROWNIES

1 c. oleo
1 c. sugar
4 eggs

1 c. plus 1 Tbsp. flour (sift)
Large chocolate syrup
1 Tbsp. vanilla
1 c. pecans

Glaze:

6 Tbsp. oleo
6 Tbsp. cream
1 1/2 c. sugar

1 tsp. vanilla
1/2 c. chocolate chips

Combine all brownie ingredients; bake at 300° for 40-45 minutes. Glaze: Mix first 3 ingredients. Bring to boil; stir in chocolate chips and vanilla. Pour over brownies while hot.

Joyce Runyan, Huntsville Council

BLONDE BROWNIES

3/4 stick oleo (6 Tbsp.)
1 c. brown sugar, packed
1 egg
1 Tbsp. vanilla
1 c. flour

1/2 tsp. baking powder
1/8 tsp. soda
1/2 tsp. salt
1/2 c. chocolate chips
 (semi-sweet)

Melt oleo just until it is completely melted. Remove from heat; add sugar and egg and beat well. Add vanilla and beat well. Add flour and dry ingredients. Then add chocolate chips. Mix until distributed throughout batter. Pour in greased 8 inch square pan at 350° for 20 minutes. Cover with foil for 1/2 hour. This keeps brownies moist. Cut and store in airtight container.

Sandy Miller, Anniston Council

CARAMEL BROWNIES

1 box German chocolate
  cake mix
1/2 c. evaporated milk

3/4 c. soft butter or
  margarine
1 c. nuts

Mix together and grease pan; put 1/2 in pan and bake 6 minutes at 350°.

60 Kraft caramels

1/3 c. evaporated milk

Melt and mix together. Sprinkle 1 small package chocolate chips over cake, then drizzle caramels over, then put rest of cake on top and bake for 18-20 minutes at 350°. Do not remove from pan. Place in refrigerator for about 30 minutes and cut into squares.

Mary Thompson, Tri-Cities Council

CHOCOLATE PEANUT BUTTER BROWNIES

1 pkg. yellow cake mix
1 c. peanut butter
1/2 c. melted margarine
2 eggs
1 (12 oz.) pkg. semi-
  sweet chocolate chips

1 (15 oz.) can condensed
  milk
2 Tbsp. margarine
1/2 tsp. salt
1 c. chopped pecans
2 tsp. vanilla

Stir until holds together the cake mix, peanut butter, margarine and eggs; press 2/3 of batter in bottom of ungreased 9x13 inch pan. In heavy saucepan combine semi-sweet chocolate chips, condensed milk, margarine and salt. Melt over low heat, stirring constantly. Remove from heat and add pecans and vanilla; spread over batter. Crumble remaining 1/3 batter on top and press lightly. Bake at 325° for 20 to 25 minutes.

Sharon Crabtree, Tuscaloosa Council

DISAPPEARING MARSHMALLOW BROWNIES

1/2 c. butterscotch pieces

1/4 c. butter or margarine

Melt in heavy saucepan over medium heat and cool to lukewarm. Add:

3/4 c. plain flour
1/3 c. firmly packed
  brown sugar
1 tsp. baking powder

1/4 tsp. salt
1/2 tsp. vanilla
1 egg

Mix well and add:

1 c. miniature marshmallows   1 c. semi-sweet chocolate
1/4 c. chopped nuts   pieces

Fold in until just blended. Spread in a greased 9 inch square pan; bake at 350° for 20-25 minutes. Do not over-bake. Center will be soft, but will become firm when cool. Makes 12-18 bars.

Mrs. Howard D. Colegrove, Anniston Council

GERMAN CHOCOLATE BROWNIES

50 light caramels   1 (18.5 oz.) pkg. German
1 c. evaporated milk   chocolate cake mix
  (divide in half)   1 c. chopped nuts
3/4 c. margarine   1 c. chocolate chips

Combine caramels and 1/2 cup evaporated milk in top of double boiler; cook over low heat until caramels melt. Combine cake mix, margarine, remaining 1/2 cup milk and nuts. Lightly grease 9x13 inch pan. Spread 1/2 cake mixture in pan; bake in 350° oven for 6 minutes. Remove. Sprinkle chocolate chips over partially baked cake mixture. Then spread caramel mixture over chips. Drop remaining cake mixture by tiny spoonfuls over caramel mixture; bake 5 minutes. Remove from oven and spread to make a top layer. Return to oven and bake 13 minutes longer; cool before cutting.

Patricia Whitten, Tuscaloosa Council

BUTTERSCOTCH SURPRISE

1 (8 oz.) pkg.   1 small can Planters peanuts
  butterscotch morsels   1 small can chow mein noodles

Boil water in a double boiler. Take off heat when boils. Place morsels in top boiler; put over hot water just long enough to melt morsels. As soon as melted, remove from steam. Alternately add nuts and noodles (with spoon). Spoon out on waxed paper quickly. Makes about 24.

Barbara Davis, Decatur Council

CHEESE TARTS

2 (8 oz.) pkg. Philadelphia
  cream cheese
3/4 c. sugar
3 eggs
1 small carton sour cream

1 can cherry pie filling
1 pkg. finely crushed
  graham crackers
1 or 2 Tbsp. powdered sugar
1/4 tsp. vanilla

Mix cream cheese, sugar and eggs with beater or electric mixer until smooth. Put 1 package of finely crushed graham crackers in very small size muffin pan that has been well greased with margarine or shortening. Pour out excess crumbs. Pour cheese mixture into each cup. Bake at 300° for about 12-14 minutes, until they rise. Let cool. Mix sour cream, vanilla (1/4 teaspoon) and powdered sugar to taste in small bowl. Spoon small amount in center of each cup. Spoon cherry filling in center on top of sour cream mixture. May be served warm or chilled. May be frozen. Makes about 40.

Marcia Freeman, Birmingham East Council

APPLE WALNUT COBBLER

4 c. sliced apples
1 1/2 c. sugar, divided
1/2 tsp. ground cinnamon
1/2 c. coarsely chopped
  walnuts
1 c. all-purpose flour

1 tsp. baking powder
1/4 tsp. salt
1 egg, beaten
1/2 c. half & half
1/3 c. melted butter
  or margarine
1/4 c. finely chopped walnuts

Spread apples evenly in a greased 9 inch square baking dish. Combine 1/2 cup sugar, cinnamon and coarsely chopped walnuts; sprinkle over apples. Combine flour, 1 cup sugar, baking powder and salt; stir well and set aside. Combine egg, half & half and butter; mix well. Add flour mixture, beating until smooth. Pour over apples. Sprinkle with finely chopped walnuts; bake at 325° for 1 hour. Yield: 6 servings.

Margie Lavender, Riverchase Council

BLUEBERRY COBBLER

1 qt. frozen blueberries
  or 3 c. fresh blueberries
1 1/2 c. sugar

1 Tbsp. lemon juice
1 recipe Oil Pastry

Oil Pastry:

2 c. all-purpose flour, sifted	1/2 c. cooking oil
1 1/2 tsp. salt	4 or 5 Tbsp. ice water

Combine the flour and salt; add ice water to 1/2 cup oil. Then pour into flour mixture. Mix well; roll into pastry. Combine blueberries, sugar and lemon juice. Use a large shallow baking pan to bake the pie in. Put a layer of blueberries in the bottom, then a layer of thinly rolled pastry strips. Repeat. Then cover top with rolled pastry. Pour water into dish until it slightly covers pie; bake 1 hour at 350° or until light brown.

Flo Thompson, Montgomery Council

FRUIT COBBLER

1 stick or 1/2 c. butter	1 c. liquid, juice from fruit and water
1 can fruit or fresh fruit	1 c. self-rising flour
1/2 c. sugar (omit if fruit is already sweetened)	1 c. sugar
	2/3 c. milk

1. Put butter, fruit, sugar (if needed) and liquid from fruit in 8x8x2 inch pan. 2. Heat until butter is melted. 3. Mix flour and sugar; add milk and stir until smooth (in mixing bowl). 4. Pour batter evenly over fruit mixture. (Batter usually sinks to bottom of pan, but rises after cooking. 5. Bake at 375° for 25 minutes. (Serve hot or warm.) Suitable for freezing.

Thena B. Jenkins, Decatur Council

LAZY MAN'S COBBLER

3/4 stick margarine	1 c. self-rising flour
1 c. milk	1 can peach pie filling
1 c. sugar	

Preheat oven to 350°. Melt butter in dish. Mix sugar and flour and milk in bowl (separately), then pour batter over butter; do not stir. Spoon peach pie filling over batter. Bake at 350° for 1 hour or until brown.

Becky George, Mobile Council

CRUSTY PEACH COBBLER

3 c. sliced peaches
  (canned or fresh)
1/4 c. sugar
1 Tbsp. lemon juice
1 tsp. grated lemon peel
1 tsp. almond extract
1 1/2 c. flour

1/2 tsp. salt
3 tsp. baking powder
1 Tbsp. sugar
1/3 c. shortening
1/2 c. milk
1 well beaten egg
2 Tbsp. sugar

Arrange peaches in a greased 8 inch square pan. Sprinkle with mixture of 1/4 cup sugar, lemon juice, lemon peel and almond extract. Heat in oven while preparing shortcake. Sift together flour, salt, baking powder and sugar; cut in shortening until mixture is like coarse crumbs. Add milk and egg at once, and stir just until flour is moistened. Spread dough over hot peaches. Sprinkle with 2 tablespoons sugar. Bake at 375° F. for 40 minutes.

Mrs. Mildred Clayton, Birmingham South Council

OLD FASHIONED COBBLER

1 qt. fresh sliced peaches,
  strawberries or
  blackberries

1 c. sugar
2 Tbsp. oleo

Put half of fruit in deep pan or Corning Ware baking dish. Add 1 1/2 cups water, 1/2 cup sugar and dot with 1 tablespoon oleo. Make up biscuit dough or use canned biscuits. Roll out dough and cover fruit with strips of dough. Repeat same with rest of fruit, sugar and oleo, but omit water. I make up pie crust dough for top crust. Cover fruit with crust. Rub a little oleo over crust and sprinkle with a little sugar.

Marcia Freeman, Birmingham East Council

CARAMEL COCONUT SQUARES

1 stick margarine or butter
1 pkg. light brown sugar
2 eggs
1 tsp. vanilla

2 c. cake flour
1/4 tsp. salt
2 tsp. baking powder
1 can shredded coconut

Melt margarine or butter; add light brown sugar and cook over low heat until it bubbles once around edges. Add eggs, one at a time, and beat well with slotted spoon. Add vanilla. Mix together flour, salt and baking powder and add

to mixture. Add coconut. (Makes a stiff batter.) Spread
in 9x13 inch pan; bake 25 minutes in 350° oven. Cut in
squares when cool.

Earline Thornton, Tuscaloosa Council

CHOCOLATE CHERRY BARS

1 pkg. fudge cake mix	1 tsp. almond extract
1 (21 oz.) can cherry	2 eggs, beaten
fruit filling	

Frosting:

1 c. sugar	1/3 c. milk
5 Tbsp. butter or	1 (6 oz.) pkg. (1 c.)
margarine	semi-sweet chocolate pieces

Preheat oven to 350°. Using solid shortening or margarine (not oil), grease and flour 15x10 inch jelly roll or 13x9
inch pan. In large bowl combine first 4 ingredients. By
hand, stir until well mixed. Pour into prepared pan; bake
jelly roll pan 20 to 30 minutes or until toothpick inserted in
center comes out clean. While bars cool, prepare frosting.
In small saucepan combine sugar, butter and milk. Boil,
stirring constantly, 1 minute; remove from heat and stir in
chocolate pieces until smooth. Pour over partially cooled
bars. Makes about 3 dozen bars.

Elaine Shelton, Huntsville Council

CHOCOLATE DELIGHT

1 1/2 c. flour	1 1/4 c. Cool Whip
3/4 c. chopped pecans	3 small pkg. instant
1 1/2 sticks butter	chocolate pudding mix
or margarine	4 c. cold milk
8 oz. cream cheese	1 (9 oz.) Cool Whip
1 c. confectioners sugar	1/2 c. pecans, chopped

Mix flour and 3/4 cup pecans together. Melt butter
and pour over flour mixture; mix well. Press into 13x9x1
inch baking dish; bake at 350° until slightly browned; cool.
Blend cream cheese, confectioners sugar and 1 1/4 cups Cool
Whip; spread over crust. Mix instant pudding with 4 cups
milk. Spread for third layer. Top with 9 ounces Cool Whip
and garnish with chopped pecans. Store in refrigerator 4
hours or overnight before serving.

Helen Taylor, Mobile Council

CHOCOLATE QUAD DESSERT

First Layer:

1 stick oleo   1 c. finely chopped
1 c. flour   pecans

Mix together; press into 9x13x2 inch pan; bake at 350° for 15 minutes. Cool.

Second Layer:

8 oz. cream cheese   1 c. Cool Whip (from
1 c. powdered sugar   large size)

Mix together and carefully spread on cooled First Layer.

Third Layer: Mix 3 small packages instant chocolate pudding mix with only 3 cups whole milk; spread carefully on Second Layer.

Fourth Layer: Spread remaining Cool Whip on top and chill several hours before serving. Cut into small squares. Cover with lid or wrap.

Mrs. Jack E. Gentte, Sr., Montgomery Council

CHERRY COCONUT BARS

Pastry:

2 c. flour   1 c. butter
6 Tbsp. confectioners sugar

Filling:

2 c. sugar   2 tsp. vanilla
4 beaten eggs   1 c. coconut
1/2 c. flour   1 1/2 c. chopped pecans
1/2 tsp. salt   1 c. chopped maraschino
1 tsp. baking powder   cherries

Combine pastry ingredients and press firmly into an 8x16 inch pan. Bake at 350° for 25 minutes. Watch closely and do not brown. Mix ingredients for filling and pour on cooked pastry. Bake at 325° for 30 minutes; cut into squares.

Joella Bradford, Huntsville Council

CHERRY CRUNCH

1 can crushed pineapple
1 can pie filling
  (cherry, strawberry)

1 cake mix
1 stick butter

    Layer items in casserole. First: Crushed pineapple; second, pie filling; third, cake mix; fourth, cut butter and cover entire dish. Cook at 350° for approximately 40-45 minutes.

Donna Dunaway, Anniston Council

CHERRY DELIGHT

2 1/2 c. graham crackers
1 1/2 sticks margarine
1 can cherry or strawberry
  pie filling

1 box jello of same flavor
1 can Eagle Brand milk
1 carton Cool Whip
2 1/2 c. miniature marshmallows

    Crush up graham crackers and mix in melted butter. Spread in square cake pan or Pyrex dish. Mix jello with the water; cut in half. Pour in pie filling after the jello is mixed. Gradually stir in other ingredients. When all is mixed together, spread all over graham crackers.

Peggy Hunter, Anniston Council

CHERRY DELIGHT

    Crust:

1 c. butter
2 c. flour

1 c. pecans

    Filling:

1 lb. cream cheese (two
  8 oz. pkg.)
3 c. confectioners sugar

1 box Dream Whip (2 env.)*
3/4 c. pecans

    *Make Dream Whip by the directions on box.

    Crust: Mix together and mold into pan and bake 15-20 minutes at 350°. Let cool.

    Filling: Mix cream cheese and sugar, then add Dream Whip and pecans. Pour into the pan of crust and top with 2 cans of cherry pie filling. Let stand in refrigerator for about 24 hours or at least 12 hours.

Judy Luse, Mobile Council

CHERRY DUMP

2 cans cherry pie filling   1/2 c. sugar
1/2 can water

Pour the above in 9x12 inch pan. Use 1 box yellow Duncan Hines cake mix dry. Sprinkle over above. Slice up 2 sticks margarine on top. Bake at 350° for 45 minutes to 1 hour.

Dorothy Bishop, Huntsville Council

CHERRY SURPRIZE

1 pkg. cherry jello
1 can cherry pie filling
1 (8 oz.) pkg. cream
  cheese, softened

1 (6 oz.) can crushed
  pineapple
1/2 c. chopped pecans

Prepare jello, using only 1 cup of hot water; let cool. Fold in pie filling. Pour into large shallow dish; refrigerate until firm. Mix softened cream cheese and drained pineapple together till smooth. Gently spread mixture over cherries. Sprinkle with pecans. Keep refrigerated till time to serve.

A. M. Robertson, Huntsville Council

CHOCOLATE DELIGHT BARS

1/2 c. butter
1 egg yolk
2 Tbsp. water

1 1/4 c. flour (plain)
1 tsp. sugar
1 tsp. baking powder

    *Topping:

2 eggs
3/4 c. sugar

6 Tbsp. melted butter
2 c. chopped nuts

Mix butter, egg yolk and water. Sift flour, sugar, baking powder. Add to butter mixture. Press into greased pan and bake 10 minutes at 350°. Sprinkle one 12 ounce package chocolate over top. Bake for 1 minute, then spread.

    *Beat eggs till thick; add sugar, melted butter, nuts and vanilla. Spread on top; bake for 30-35 minutes.

Evelyn Howard, Decatur Council

CHOCOLATE MOCHA RUM TORTE

1 (15.5 oz.) box Duncan
  Hines double fudge
  brownie mix
1/4 c. water
1 egg
1/3 c. chopped walnuts

1/2 c. brown sugar
1/4 c. rum
Whole walnuts to decorate top
1 Tbsp. instant coffee,
  dissolved in 1 Tbsp. water
1 pt. cream

Mix batter as directed on package. Grease and flour 2 cake pans. Put wax paper, cut to fit the bottom of the round pans. Divide the batter equally in the pans; bake at 350° for 20 minutes or until cake will spring back when touched with finger; do not overcook. Turn cakes out on racks to cool and remove wax paper. Dip a tablespoon in rum and sprinkle the bottoms of the cake while hot. Whip the 2 half pint cartons of cream and just before it reaches stiffness, add the brown sugar. Then fold in the coffee. Spread between layers and on top and sides. Refrigerate overnight or at least 4 or 5 hours. Decorate top with whole walnuts. It is delicious, but serve small slices, as it is very rich.

Arnold L. Taylor, Retired

CHOCOMINT DESSERT

2 c. finely crushed
  chocolate wafers
1/2 c. butter or
  margarine, melted
1 (13 oz.) can
  evaporated milk
1 (3 oz.) pkg. lime
  flavored gelatin

1 (8 oz.) pkg. cream cheese
1 c. sugar
Several drops of green
  food coloring
1 (4 1/4 or 4 1/2 oz.) pkg.
  instant chocolate pudding mix
1 1/3 c. milk
1/4 c. finely crushed
  peppermint candies

Combine crumbs and margarine; reserve 1/3 cup for top. Press remainder over bottom of 13x9x2 inch pan. Freeze evaporated milk in freezer tray till crystals form around edges. Meanwhile, dissolve gelatin in 1 cup boiling water; let stand 30 minutes. Beat together cream cheese and sugar; gradually beat in gelatin and food coloring. Whip evaporated milk to soft peaks; fold in cheese mixture. Spread half over crust; chill 1 hour. (Keep remaining mixture at room temperature.) Beat together pudding mix and milk; stir in candy. Let stand 2 minutes; spoon over layer in pan. Top with remaining cheese mixture; add crumbs and chill. Makes 16 servings.

Jean Cater (Mrs. C. J.),
Birmingham South Council

CHURCH WINDOWS

1 (12 oz.) pkg. semi-sweet
  chocolate chips
1 stick margarine

1 bag colored miniature
  marshmallows
1 can coconut
1 c. chopped pecans

Melt chocolate chips and margarine; cool. Pour mixture over marshmallows and nuts. Use 4 pieces of wax paper. Divide mixture; with hands pat together. Make 4 rolls. Sprinkle coconut over rolls; roll in wax paper. Refrigerate 2 hours and slice.

Hazel Campbell, Birmingham South Council

CINNAMON ICEBOX ROLLS

2 pkg. active dry yeast
1/2 c. warm water
2 c. lukewarm milk,
  scalded, then cooled
1/3 c. sugar
1/3 c. vegetable oil
  or shortening

1 egg
5 to 6 c. self-rising flour
4 Tbsp. butter, softened
1/2 c. sugar
1 tsp. cinnamon
Powdered Sugar Frosting
  (below)

Dissolve yeast in warm water; stir in milk, 1/3 cup sugar, oil, egg and 2 to 3 cups flour. Beat until smooth. Mix in enough remaining flour to make dough easy to handle. Turn dough onto well floured board; knead until smooth and elastic, about 8 to 10 minutes. Place in greased bowl; turn greased side up. Cover and let rise until double, about 1 1/2 hours. (Dough is ready if an indentation remains when touched.) Grease 2 oblong 13x9x2 inch pans. Punch down dough and divide in halves. Roll one half into rectangular shape, about 12x10 inches. Spread with half of butter. Mix 1/2 cup sugar and the cinnamon; sprinkle half of this over rectangle. Roll up, beginning with widest side. Pinch edge of dough into roll to seal. Stretch roll to make even. Cut roll into 12 slices. Place slightly apart in one pan. Wrap pan tightly with aluminum foil; repeat with remaining dough. Refrigerate at least 12 hours, but no longer than 48 hours.

(To bake immediately, do not wrap with foil. Let rise in warm place until double, about 30 minutes.) Heat oven to 350°. Bake until golden, 30 to 35 minutes. Frost while warm.

Powdered Sugar Frosting:

1 c. powdered sugar
1 Tbsp. milk

1/2 tsp. vanilla

Mix until smooth and of spreading consistency. Frosts one pan of rolls.

Mattie Singleton, Retired,
Birmingham Central Council

COCOA FUDGE

4 Tbsp. cocoa
3/4 c. sweet milk
1 Tbsp. white Karo syrup
2 c. sugar
1/8 tsp. salt
2 Tbsp. butter
1 tsp. vanilla
1 c. pecans

Boil sugar, cocoa, milk, syrup and salt until it forms a soft ball in cold water; remove from heat and add butter, vanilla and pecans. Beat until creamy and pour on buttered pan; let set until firm before cutting into squares.

Glenda Whitcomb, Birmingham East Council

CONGO SQUARES

2 sticks butter, melted
2 3/4 c. self-rising flour
3 eggs
1 box brown sugar
1 c. pecans, chopped
1 (12 oz.) bag chocolate chips

Mix together melted butter and brown sugar; add flour and eggs alternately. Stir in pecans and chocolate chips. Pour into a 9x13 inch greased and floured baking pan and bake in 300° oven for 30-45 minutes.

Frances Mangum, Montgomery Council

CREAM CHEESE SQUARES

1 stick margarine
1 box cake mix
    (pudding in the mix)
1 (8 oz.) pkg. cream
    cheese (room temperature)
1 box confectioners sugar
3 eggs (room temperature)

Melt margarine and pour in a 9x13 inch pan. Combine 1 egg and cake mix together (will be dry) and spread over melted margarine. Combine 2 eggs, cream cheese and box of confectioners sugar; spread over cake. Bake in 350° oven for 30 minutes. Cool and cut into squares and serve.

Linda Norris, Montgomery Council

MINIATURE FILLED CREAM PUFFS

1 c. water
1/2 c. butter
1 c. plus 6 Tbsp. flour
6 eggs
1/2 c. sugar

1/2 tsp. salt
2 c. milk or cream
2 tsp. vanilla flavoring
    or other flavoring
Chocolate icing

Heat water and butter to boiling point in saucepan; stir in 1 cup flour. Stir constantly until mixture leaves side of pan and forms a ball, about 1 minute. Remove from heat; cool. Beat in 4 eggs, 1 at a time. Beat mixture until smooth and velvety. Drop from spoon onto ungreased baking sheet; bake until dry at 400° about 25 to 30 minutes. Allow to cool slowly. Mix sugar, salt and remaining flour; stir in milk. Cook over low heat; boil 1 minute. Remove from heat and stir a small amount of mixture into remaining beaten eggs. Blend into hot mixture in saucepan; bring to a boil. Cool and blend in flavoring. Fill puffs; frost with thin chocolate icing. Yield: 18 tiny puffs.
Virginia Mayo, Mobile Council

CURRIED BAKED FRUIT

1 (1 lb.) can pear halves
1 (1 lb.) can cling peaches
1 (1 lb.) can apricot halves
12 maraschino cherries

3/4 c. light brown sugar
2 tsp. curry powder
1/3 c. butter, melted
2/3 c. blanched almonds

Drain all fruit; add sugar and curry powder to butter. Arrange fruit and nuts in layers in casserole. Pour butter mixture; bake at 325° for 1 hour. May be refrigerated over-night and reheat at 350° before serving.
Frances H. Lewis, Birmingham South Council

CURRIED FRUIT BAKE

1 can mixed fruits
    (large pieces)
2 slices pineapple
1/4 c. brown sugar

1/2 tsp. curry powder
1/2 c. pecan halves
1/4 stick butter

Drain fruit; arrange in baking dish. Mix sugar and curry powder. Melt butter; pour over fruit. Sprinkle sugar and curry mixture over fruit. Spread pecan halves over fruit. Bake at 350° for 45 minutes. Serves 4.
Sarah Baker, Riverchase Council

DATE ROLL

2 c. brown sugar
1 c. granulated sugar
1 c. Pet milk (not
  diluted)

2 Tbsp. butter or margarine
2 tsp. vanilla
1 c. chopped dates
1 c. chopped pecans

Place sugar, milk and butter in a large saucepan; cook (stirring very little) until soft ball is formed. Add chopped dates. Cook until a little drop in cold water forms a hard ball. Place saucepan in cold water; let cool. Add vanilla and pecans; beat until stiff. Pour in wax paper box lined with foil; let stand for an hour. Remove and slice.

Mrs. W. L. Ankerson, Jr., Mobile Council

DELICIOUS DESSERT

1 c. flour
1 stick margarine
Pecans (optional)
8 oz. cream cheese
1 c. powdered sugar

3 c. milk
2 (3 oz.) pkg. instant pistachio
  pudding (or any other
  flavor)
1 (9 oz.) carton Cool Whip

Blend flour and margarine with fork; press in bottom of 9x13 inch glass dish. Bake 15 minutes at 350°. Beat cream cheese and powdered sugar; spread over cooled crust. Combine milk and pudding; beat until thick. Fold in 1/2 carton Cool Whip. Spread this over first layer. Top with remaining Cool Whip.

Steve Mackin, Birmingham South Council

EASY-DOES-IT DOUGHNUTS

1/3 c. sugar
1/2 c. milk
1 egg
2 Tbsp. melted shortening

1 1/2 c. sifted flour
2 tsp. baking powder
1/2 tsp. salt
Shortening for deep frying

Mix together sugar, milk, egg, melted shortening. Combine flour, baking powder and salt, then add to liquid mixture. Drop by teaspoons into shortening heated to 365°. Fry 3 to 4 minutes. Fry all doughnuts to same degree of brownness. Drain on paper towels.

Bea Windham, Montgomery Council

356

DUTCH APPLE DESSERT

1 1/2 c. finely ground
  graham crackers
1/4 c. melted margarine
1 (14 oz.) can Eagle Brand
  sweetened condensed milk

1 (8 oz.) carton sour cream
1/4 c. lemon juice
1 (21 oz.) can apple pie filling
1/4 c. chopped walnuts or
  pecans
1/4 tsp. ground cinnamon

Combine graham cracker crumbs and margarine; press evenly on bottom of ungreased 10x6x2 inch baking dish. Combine condensed milk, sour cream and lemon juice in small bowl; spread evenly over crumb crust. Spoon pie filling over top; bake at 350° for 30 minutes or until set. Sprinkle with nuts and cinnamon. Serve warm or cold.
    Note: Any pie filling may be substituted for apple.
          Linda Mason, Birmingham Central Council

FROZEN RAINBOW DESSERT

1 angel food cake
3 pkg. jello (orange,
  strawberry and lime)
1 can mandarin oranges

1 pkg. frozen strawberries,
  thawed
1 small can crushed pineapple
1/2 gal. vanilla ice cream,
  softened

Cut angel food cake into bite size pieces. Place 1/3 into 3 different bowls. Pour dry jello over cake, making a bowl of orange cake, strawberry cake and lime cake by tossing to cover cake with jello. In large tube pan place layer of orange cake; top with mandarin oranges. Top with layer of ice cream. Second layer is strawberry cake, then strawberries, then ice cream. Third layer is lime cake, then crushed pineapple and topped with ice cream. Place in freezer. When ready to serve, run knife around edge of pan to loosen. Press bottom of tube pan and lift out. Slice dessert and serve. Can be refrozen.
          Marian Turnipseed, Birmingham West Council

STAINED GLASS FRUIT CAKE MINIATURES

1 (14 oz.) can sweetened
  condensed milk
1 1/2 c. (12 oz.) whole red
  and green candied cherries
1 1/2 c. (12 oz.) cut up
  candied pineapple

1 1/2 c. (8 oz.) light raisins
1 1/3 c. (8 oz.) whole
  pitted dates
2 c. pecan halves
2 c. walnut halves

In large bowl combine all ingredients; mix well. Divide mixture and pack very firmly into buttered muffin pans (1 3/4 inch diameter), using 2 tablespoons batter for each miniature. Bake at 275° F. for 25-30 minutes; cool. Remove from pans. (Mixture makes approximately 10 cups batter.)

Carol Blackwood, Birmingham South Council

QUICK FRUIT DELIGHT

1 c. sliced bananas
1 c. raspberries
3/4 c. crushed
  pineapple

1 c. drained canned
  peach halves
1 c. sour cream
2 Tbsp. brown sugar
Dash of cinnamon

In large bowl combine fruit. Mix sour cream and sugar. Pour over fruit; chill 1 hour. Sprinkle with cinnamon.

Mattie Foster, Huntsville Council

HOT FRUIT

1 (No. 2) can chunk
  pineapple, drained
1 (No. 2) can pear
  halves, drained
1 (No. 2) can sliced
  peaches, drained
1 small bottle maraschino
  cherries

1 c. liquid reserved
  from mixed juices
1 c. white sugar
1 c. brown sugar
2 cinnamon sticks
1/2 tsp. nutmeg
2 Tbsp. ginger

Combine juices, sugars, cinnamon and nutmeg. Bring to a boil and let simmer 30 minutes. Pour over fruit (in a baking dish). Sprinkle with ginger and bake 25 minutes at 350°. Serve hot.

Sandra Herndon, Birmingham South Council

FUDGIE SCOTCH RING

1 (6 oz.) pkg. (1 c.)
  Nestle's semi-sweet
  chocolate morsels
1 (6 oz.) pkg. (1 c.)
  Nestle's butterscotch
  morsels

1 can Borden's Eagle Brand
  sweetened condensed milk
1 c. coarsely chopped walnuts
1/2 tsp. vanilla extract
1 c. walnut halves

Melt chocolate and butterscotch morsels with sweetened condensed milk in top of boiler over hot (not boiling) water. Stir occasionally till morsels melt and mixture begins to
358

thicken. Remove from heat; add chopped walnuts and vanilla. Blend well. Chill in refrigerator for about 1 hour till mixture thickens. Line bottom of 9 inch pie pan with a 12 inch square of foil. Place 3/4 cup walnut halves in bottom of pan, forming a 2 inch wide flat ring. Spoon chocolate mixture in small mounds on top of nuts to form ring. Decorate with remaining nuts. Add maraschino cherries, if desired. Chill in refrigerator until firm enough to slice. Cut into 1/2 inch slices. Makes about 36 slices.

Jean Reed, Anniston Council

QUICK GRAHAM CRACKER SQUARES

2 c. graham cracker
  crumbs
1 can Eagle Brand milk

1 c. chopped pecans
1 small pkg. chocolate chips
  (or butterscotch or
  peanut butter)

Mix and bake in greased 9x13 inch pan 30 minutes at 350°. Cut in squares.

Nancy Brown Tatum, Riverchase Council

JELLO AMBROSIA

1 large can fruit cocktail
1 large Cool Whip

1 small box peach jello
  (or any flavor)

Drain fruit cocktail. Pour dry jello over fruit cocktail mix. Combine mixture with Cool Whip, mixing well; chill.

Cheryl Connell, Riverchase Council

JELLO FRUIT DESSERT

1 small pkg. strawberry
  jello
1 (10 oz.) pkg. frozen
  strawberries, thawed
  and drained

1 c. peaches, drained, cubed
1 c. chunk pineapple, drained
1 1/2 medium bananas, cut up
1 small pkg. sour cream

Mix jello with 1/2 cup boiling water; add fruit. Divide mixture in half. Put 1/2 in loaf pan; chill. Add sour cream layer. Add last half of fruit mixture; chill.

Debbie Jarvis, Birmingham South Council

LEMON-BUTTER SNOWBARS

For Crust:

1/2 c. butter, softened

1 1/3 c. all-purpose flour
1/4 c. sugar

For Filling:

2 eggs
3/4 c. sugar
2 Tbsp. all-purpose flour

1/4 tsp. baking powder
3 Tbsp. lemon juice

You will need confectioners sugar (for the top).

Combine crust ingredients. Mix on low until blended (1 minute). Pat into ungreased 8 inch pan; bake at 350° for 15 to 20 minutes. Combine all filling ingredients; blend well. Pour over partially baked crust. Return to oven for 18 to 20 minutes or until set. Sprinkle with confectioners sugar. Cool; cut into 16 bars.

Lera Lee, Tuscaloosa Council

LEMON DELIGHT

1 large can evaporated milk, chilled in refrigerator at least 24 hours, preferably longer

1 c. sugar
1/2 c. lemon juice
Crushed vanilla wafers

Pour chilled evaporated milk into large mixing bowl; beat with electric mixer until the milk doubles in size. Gradually add the sugar while still beating and then pour in the lemon juice. The mixture will then thicken. Into a Pyrex dish (either square or rectangular) pour enough vanilla wafers to line or cover the bottom, then pour your mixture in. With remainder of vanilla wafers, sprinkle over the top of the mixture. Place in refrigerator for a few hours before serving.

Shirley Wood, Birmingham South Council

PERFECT MERINGUE

3 egg whites
1/2 tsp. vanilla

1/4 tsp. cream of tartar
6 Tbsp. sugar

In a deep bowl beat egg whites with vanilla and cream of tartar till soft peaks form. Don't overbeat the egg whites before adding the sugar, or the meringue will leak, making the top of the pie filling moist and slippery. Gradually add sugar, beating till stiff, glossy peaks form and sugar dissolves. Rub some meringue between your fingers; you shouldn't feel any sugar granules. Spread meringue over hot filling. To prevent the meringue from shrinking while baking, seal to edges of pastry. Bake in 350° oven for 12 to 15 minutes or till meringue is golden.

Emma Rousseau, Huntsville Council

MUD HENS (DESSERT)

1 1/2 sticks butter	1/4 tsp. salt
1 c. sugar	6 oz. semi-sweet chocolate bits
1 whole egg	2 eggs, separated
2 c. plain flour	1 c. mini marshmallows
1 tsp. baking powder	1 c. light brown sugar

Cream butter and sugar; beat in the whole egg and 2 egg yolks. Sift flour, baking powder and salt together. Combine the 2 mixtures and blend (will be stiff). Spread batter into a greased 9x13 inch pan. Sprinkle the chocolate bits and the marshmallows over batter. Beat the 2 egg whites till stiff and fold in brown sugar. Spread over the cake mixture. Bake 30 to 40 minutes at 350°. Cut in bars when cold.

Regina Tumblin, Birmingham South Council

NUTTY BANANAS

1 c. mayonnaise or	6 bananas
salad dressing	2 c. salted blanched
1/4 c. milk	peanuts (finely ground)
2-3 Tbsp. sugar	Cherries (optional)

Combine mayonnaise, milk and sugar; mix well. Slice 2 bananas and place in a 2 quart serving dish. Spread 1/3 of mayonnaise mixture evenly over bananas. Sprinke with 1/3 ground peanuts. Repeat layers.

Joyce Runyan, Huntsville Council

ORANGE ICEBOX DESSERT

1 can Eagle Brand	Dash of salt
condensed milk	2 egg whites, beaten
1/4 c. lemon juice (fresh)	stiff (fold in last)
1/4 c. orange juice	Vanilla wafers
Grated rind of 1/2 orange	Fresh orange sections
	(no membrane)

Combine first 6 ingredients into a mixture. In a square Pyrex dish put a layer of vanilla wafers (whole or crushed). Add a layer of 1/2 the mixture, a layer of orange sections, a layer of remaining 1/2 mixture. Top with crushed vanilla wafers. Refrigerate at least 6 hours; overnight is better.
Lois Herlong, Birmingham South Council

PEACH CRISP

1 (30 oz.) can peach
  halves, drained,
  reserving 2 Tbsp. syrup
1 3/4 c. Kellogg's Rice
  Krispies cereal, crushed
  to measure 1 c.
1/3 c. all-purpose flour

1/4 tsp. salt
1/2 c. firmly packed
  brown sugar
1/2 tsp. ground cinnamon
1/4 tsp. ground nutmeg
1/3 c. softened margarine
  or butter

Cut each peach half into 2 pieces. Combine with the 2 tablespoons peach syrup in 1 quart casserole. Combine remaining ingredients, mixing until crumbly. Sprinkle over peaches. Bake in 350° oven about 30 minutes or until topping is browned. Serve warm. Top with ice cream, if desired. Makes 6 servings.
Mary C. Martin, Birmingham East Council

PEACH DELIGHT

2 c. buttermilk
1 large box peach jello
1 large Cool Whip

1 can crushed pineapple
1 bottle maraschino cherries
Chopped nuts

Bring jello and pineapple to boil; set aside to cool. Add Cool Whip and buttermilk. Mix well. Add cherries and nuts.
Janet Stephens, Anniston Council

FRESH PEACH FRITTERS

1 c. flour
2 Tbsp. sugar
1 1/2 tsp. baking powder
1/2 tsp. salt
1/4 tsp. cinnamon, nutmeg
  and pinch of ginger
1 egg

1/4 c. milk
2 Tbsp. melted butter
2 Tbsp. drained crushed
  pineapple
1/4 Tbsp. vanilla
1/2 c. diced fresh peaches
Powdered sugar

Mix dry ingredients; stir in rest of ingredients except peaches and powdered sugar, just until smooth. Fold in

362

peaches. Drop from teaspoon into grease in a deep hot frying pan. Cook about 2 minutes; drain on paper towels. Roll in powdered sugar.

Margaret Hare, Anniston Council

PEACH SURPRISE

1 c. Eagle Brand milk	1 can sliced peaches
2 lemons (juice)	Graham cracker crust
1/2 pt. whipping cream	

Mix lemon juice in Eagle Brand milk; stir in peaches (sliced or mashed). Pour in graham cracker crust. Beat whipping cream and put on top. Garnish with peach slices. Refrigerate till time to serve.

Eloise Bennett, Decatur Council

PEANUT BUTTER BALLS

1 c. peanut butter	2 1/2 qt. popped popping corn
1 (14 oz.) can sweetened	1 (6 oz.) pkg. semi-sweet
condensed milk	chocolate pieces
1/2 c. coconut	

In a large bowl combine peanut butter, milk and coconut; add popcorn and toss until mixed. Form into 1 1/2 inch balls. Place on wax paper in large flat container. Refrigerate. Meanwhile, melt chocolate over hot water in double boiler. Spread over tops of balls in lacy pattern. Return to refrigerator to harden chocolate. Makes about 30 balls.

Flo Thompson, Montgomery Council

PEANUT BUTTER CRINKLES

1 c. margarine	2 1/2 c. unsifted flour
1 c. peanut butter	1 tsp. baking powder
1 c. sugar	1 tsp. baking soda
1 c. firmly packed	1 tsp. salt
brown sugar	Sugar
2 eggs	Nuts, chocolate kisses,
1 tsp. vanilla	jam or jelly

In bowl with mixer at medium speed beat first 6 ingredients until fluffy. At low speed beat in next 4 ingredients. Shape into 1 inch balls; roll in sugar. Place 2 inches apart on ungreased cookie sheets; bake in 350° oven 12 to 15 minutes or until browned. Immediately press nuts or candies into cookies, or press with thumb and fill with jam. Cool. Store in airtight container. Makes 6 dozen.

Flo Thompson, Montgomery Council

PEANUT BUTTER PETITS

1/2 c. brown sugar
1/2 c. sugar
1/2 c. softened margarine

1/2 c. peanut butter
1 egg
1 1/4 c. self-rising flour
1/4 tsp. vanilla

Preheat oven to 350°. Cream sugars and margarine until smooth. Add peanut butter, then egg; mix well. Add flour gradually and add vanilla last. Bake 9-11 minutes till light brown.

Donna Benford, Tuscaloosa Council

CLARA PAYNE MODERN PECAN ROLLS

1 (7 1/2 oz.) jar
  marshmallow cream
1 lb. sifted confectioners
  sugar

1 tsp. vanilla
1/4 tsp. almond extract
1 lb. caramels
Pecan halves or coarsely
  chopped pecans

Combine first 4 ingredients; knead in last of sugar gradually. Shape into 8 rolls 1 inch in diameter. Wrap in wax paper and freeze overnight or chill until quite hard. Melt caramels over hot water in double boiler; remove from heat, but keep over hot water. Keep some fresh hot water in double boiler ready for the last of the caramel mixture tends to harden when water cools. Dip marshmallow first in caramel to cover, then roll in nuts, pressing nuts firmly into caramel with fingertips. Cool. Store covered in cool dry place. Keeps at least a month. These rolls look quite professional. They make a very nice gift.

Patti Smith, Anniston Council

PECAN SURPRISE

1 c. sugar
3 egg whites
1 c. pecans, chopped

1 tsp. vanilla
1 tsp. cream of tartar
14 Ritz crackers, finely
  crushed

Beat egg whites stiff; add sugar, vanilla, cream of

tartar and beat. Add Ritz crackers and pecans; mix with spoon. Bake in greased pie pan 30 minutes at 350°. Cool; top with Cool Whip.

H. Paschal, Montgomery Council

PECAN TARTS

1 (3 oz.) pkg. cream cheese	1/2 c. butter 1 c. sifted all-purpose flour

Filling:

1 egg 3/4 c. brown sugar 1 Tbsp. butter, melted	1 tsp. vanilla extract 2/3 c. chopped pecans

Combine cream cheese and butter; blend in flour. Chill 1 hour. Shape into 1 inch balls and press into tiny ungreased muffin tins. Beat egg; add sugar, melted butter and vanilla; mix well and stir in pecans. Spoon into prepared shells and bake at 325° for about 25 minutes. Cool before removing from pans. Makes about 20. May be doubled. May be prepared ahead.

Mrs. G. W. Bates, Birmingham South Council

GLAZED PECANS

1 lb. pecans 2 egg whites	1 c. sugar Dash of salt

Beat egg whites, sugar and salt till firm. Fold in pecans. Melt 1 1/4 sticks butter in shallow pan. Spread pecans in pan; bake at 325° for 30 minutes. When done, drain on paper towel.

Mrs. Libby Pilling, Decatur Council

PECAN TASSIES

1 (3 oz.) pkg. cream cheese, softened Butter or margarine, softened 1 c. sifted flour	1 egg 3/4 c. brown sugar 1 tsp. vanilla 1/8 tsp. salt 2/3 c. coarsely chopped pecans

Blend cream cheese and 1/2 cup butter together well; add flour, blending well. Chill for 1 hour; shape into 24 balls. Press balls into small muffin pans, covering side and bottom of cups. Beat egg, brown sugar, 1 tablespoon butter,

vanilla and salt together just until smooth. Place half the
pecans in dough-lined cups; spoon filling over pecans. Top
with remaining pecans. Bake at 325° to 350° for about 30
minutes. Cool in pans. May be frozen. Yield: 24 servings.
Joyce Reavis, Decatur Council

PHILLY FRUIT

1 pkg. Philadelphia
  cream cheese

1 (No. 303) can fruit
  cockail (use juice also)
1 c. pecan pieces

Mix together all ingredients. Put in freezer tray. Let
set in freezer till very firm. Serve on lettuce leaf. This is
very rich and good.
Mildred Nelms, Birmingham West Council

PIE CRUST WITH PECANS

1 stick butter
1/4 c. brown sugar

1 c. sifted flour
1/2 c. chopped nuts

Mix together and spread in oblong pan. Bake 15
minutes at 350° till brown. Take out and stir with fork.
Press mixture while hot into greased pie pan. This crust
makes a plain lemon icebox pie something really special.
Faith Kirby, Anniston Council

PINEAPPLE SURPRISE

1 box Jiffy cake mix
  (yellow)
1 large box lemon
  instant pudding
1 large container Cool Whip
1 small jar cherries

1 c. pecans, chopped
2 1/2 c. homogenized milk
1 large can crushed pineapple
1 (8 oz.) pkg. Philadelphia
  cream cheese

Bake cake according to directions on box, in a long pan
or Pyrex pan. Let cool. With a toothpick prick holes in top
of cake; spread pineapple all over cake, pouring juice on it
too. In a bowl mix cream cheese, instant pudding and milk
until creamy, then spread this on top of pineapple. Then
spread Cool Whip on top of pudding mix. Now sprinkle cake
with your chopped nuts and line with cherries. Let chill
overnight or 3 to 4 hours. Makes a very pretty and delicious
cake.

Adrienna Cade, Birmingham South Council

366

PISTACHIO SALAD

1 box Jell-O instant
  pistachio pudding
1 (20 oz.) can crushed
  pineapple

1 c. small marshmallows
1 c. chopped nuts
1 carton Cool Whip
Few drops of green food
  coloring

Pour dry mix over undrained pineapple; add other ingredients and fold in Cool Whip last. Refrigerate 3-4 hours or overnight.

Mrs. Libby Pilling, Decatur Council

LAYERED PISTACHIO DESSERT

1 1/4 c. Bisquick mix
1 Tbsp. packed brown
  sugar
3 Tbsp. oleo
1/2 c. nuts, chopped fine
1 c. powdered sugar
  (confectioners)

1 (8 oz.) pkg. cream
  cheese, softened
2 (3 3/4 oz.) boxes pistachio
  pudding mix
2 1/2 c. cold milk
8 oz. whipping cream

Heat oven to 375°. Mix brown sugar, Bisquick mix and oleo till crumbly; stir in nuts. Press in ungreased pan. Bake till light brown. Beat cream cheese and confectioners sugar till smooth. Beat whipped cream in chilled bowl. Fold 1 cup whipped cream in cheese and sugar mixture. Spread this over baked layer of nuts, brown sugar and etc. Mix dry pudding and milk till thick (about 2 minutes). Pour over cream cheese mixture. Cover tight. Put in refrigerator till all set and firm. When ready to serve, put layer of whipped topping on top.

P.S. For a short cut I found out Cool Whip works well throughout recipe.

Marcia Freeman, Birmingham East Council

PORTUGUESE DOUGHNUTS

2 c. Bisquick mix
1 c. milk
1 egg

1/2 tsp. vanilla
4 slices bread
Sugar

Cut bread into 36 pieces. Heat cooking oil (2 to 3 inches) to 375° in deep fat fryer or kettle. Stir together baking mix, milk, egg and extract until smooth. Dip bread pieces into batter; fry in hot oil until golden brown; drain on paper towels. Roll in confectioners or granulated sugar. Serve hot with coffee or milk. Yield: 3 dozen.

Mrs. William H. Norris, Mobile Council

SAND TARTS

3/4 c. real butter
4 Tbsp. sugar
2 Tbsp. ice water
2 tsp. vanilla

1 c. chopped nuts
2 1/4 c. flour, sifted
   (or enough to make
   stiff dough)

Cream butter and sugar; add all other ingredients. Shape dough into small balls or crescents. Bake on greased cookie sheet 12 minutes at 400°. Sprinkle with confectioners sugar just before serving. These may be frozen.

Billie Bays, Decatur Council

STRAWBERRY-CREAM SQUARES

2 (3 oz.) pkg. strawberry
   flavored gelatin
2 (10 oz.) pkg. frozen
   strawberries

1 (13 1/2 oz.) can
   crushed pineapple
2 large ripe bananas,
   finely diced
1 c. dairy sour cream

Dissolve gelatin in 2 cups boiling water; add strawberries, stirring occasionally till thawed. Add pineapple and finely diced bananas. Pour half into 8x8x2 inch pan; chill till firm. Spread evenly with sour cream. Pour remaining gelatin atop; chill till firm. Cut in 9 squares. Top with about 1 teaspoon sour cream. Add a fresh strawberry, if desired.

Betty W. Sanders, Birmingham Central Council

STRAWBERRY FROZEN DESSERT

1 c. sugar
3 egg whites

1 (10 oz.) pkg. frozen
   strawberries

(Thaw strawberries a few minutes.) Mix all together in electric mixer on high speed. Beat 15 minutes by the clock; do not underbeat. Put above in crust; freeze. Serves 20 or more.

Crust:

1 c. chopped nuts
1 c. flour

1/4 c. brown sugar
1 stick softened oleo

Mix like pastry. Mix all together. Place on greased cookie sheet; bake 20 minutes at 325°. Save 1/3 of mixture for topping. Cool. Put in 9x13 inch pan. Use the rest of mixture over strawberries.

Ruth Moore, Montgomery Council

STRAWBERRY PIZZA

Crust:

2 c. flour
2 sticks margarine

1 c. nuts

First Layer:

1 (8 oz.) pkg. cream
  cheese

3 c. confectioners sugar
1 (12 oz.) Cool Whip

Top Layer:

1 c. sugar
1 c. water

3 Tbsp. cornstarch

Crust: Melt margarine with flour; press into pan and add nuts on top; press in. Bake at 350° until brown; cool completely.

First Layer: Blend cream cheese and sugar until smooth; fold in Cool Whip. Peak up on sides so top layer won't run off.

Top Layer: Mix in pan and bring to boil; cook till clear. Cool a little. Add 1 box strawberry jello; cool completely. Add 2 pints strawberries and spread on top.

Joyce Cater, Tuscaloosa Council

STRAWBERRY PRETZEL DESSERT

3 Tbsp. granulated sugar
1/2 c. powdered sugar
2 c. crushed pretzels
  (not too fine)
3/4 c. oleo, melted
1 (9 oz.) carton Cool Whip

1 (8 oz.) pkg. cream cheese
2 c. miniature marshmallows
1 (6 oz.) pkg. strawberry jello
2 1/2 c. boiling water
1 (10 oz.) pkg. frozen
  strawberries

Mix granulated sugar, pretzels and oleo in a 9x13 inch pan; bake 15 minutes in 350° oven. Set aside to cool. Cream softened cheese; add powdered sugar. Fold in Cool Whip; fold in marshmallows. Spread over baked layer. Dissolve gelatin; stir in berries and chill until thick. Spread over cream cheese layer and chill. Serves 16-20 people.

Louise Simpson Maze, Birmingham South Council

STRAWBERRY RIBBON

2 small boxes strawberry jello
1 small can crushed pineapple
1 1/2 c. sour cream
2 c. frozen or fresh (ripe) strawberries
1-2 bananas
1/2 c. pecans or walnuts (optional)

Prepare jello according to directions. While jello is slightly congealing, mash banana(s) and combine with pineapple, strawberries and nuts. Pour fruit and nut mixture into slightly congealed jello and stir. Place half of jello into a 9x11 inch dish and allow to congeal completely. Smooth a layer (approximately 1/2 inch) of sour cream over congealed jello over the sour cream and congeal. Cut in squares to serve.

Bernette Steptoe, Future Pioneer, Riverchase Council

SWEET POTATO CASSEROLE

3 c. mashed sweet potatoes
1/2 stick margarine
1 c. canned milk
1 1/2 c. sugar
2 eggs
1/2 tsp. nutmeg
1/2 tsp. cinnamon
1 tsp. vanilla

Mix all ingredients well and pour in baking dish; bake at 425° for 10 to 15 minutes.

Topping:

3/4 stick margarine
1/2 c. light brown sugar
1/2 c. chopped nuts
1/2 c. coconut
1 c. crushed corn flakes

Melt margarine; add sugar, nuts, coconut and corn flakes to margarine and mix well. Spread over top of potatoes and bake an additional 15 minutes at 400°.

Jane Paulk, Montgomery Council

SWEET POTATO CASSEROLE

3 c. mashed sweet potatoes
1 c. sugar
1/2 c. butter (oleo)
1/4 c. milk
2 eggs
1 tsp. vanilla

Mix real well. Pour in baking dish and add topping.

Topping:

1 c. brown sugar
1/2 c. flour
1 c. chopped pecans
1/3 c. butter (soft)

Mix together and sprinkle on top of potatoes. Bake at 350° for 25 minutes.

Kitty Maxey, Montgomery Council

RICH TART PASTRY

2 c. unsifted flour
3 Tbsp. sugar
3/4 c. butter

3 hard cooked egg yolks,
  mashed
2 raw egg whites
1/2 tsp. salt

Make a well in center of flour, working either on a table or in a bowl. Add all ingredients to the well. Butter should not be ice cold, nor so soft that it is oily. Using fingertips, make a paste of center ingredients, gradually incorporating flour to make a firm smooth ball of paste. Work as quickly as you can so the butter won't become greasy. When bowl or table top has been left clean, wrap the dough in waxed paper or aluminum foil and chill until firm enough to roll between sheets of waxed paper.

Note: To make pastry for quiche, hors d'oeuvres and meat pies, omit sugar and lemon rind from recipe.

Pastry can be made in a Kitchen Aide mixer by combining all ingredients together at once, using flat paddle. For a more brittle, less crumbly pastry, use only egg whites.

Nancy Brown Tatum, Riverchase Council

TEA TASSIES

1 (3 oz.) pkg. cream
  cheese
1/2 c. margarine
1 c. flour, sifted
Dash of salt

1 egg
2/3 c. pecans
3/4 c. brown sugar
1 Tbsp. soft margarine
1 tsp. vanilla

Cream cheese and 1/2 cup margarine; stir in flour. Chill 1 hour. Shape into 2 dozen 1 inch balls. Beat egg, brown sugar and 1 tablespoon margarine, vanilla and salt.

Anatalie Watson, Decatur Council

THREE LAYER DESSERT

1 stick butter
1 c. flour
1/2 c. chopped nuts
1 (8 oz.) pkg. cream cheese
1 c. confectioners sugar

1 large Cool Whip
2 pkg. instant chocolate
  pudding
3 1/2 c. milk
1 Tbsp. vanilla flavoring

1567-82

Mix first 3 ingredients; spread in 13x9 inch pan and bake in 350° oven for 15 minutes. Mix cream cheese, 1 cup confectioners sugar and 1 cup Cool Whip. Spread on top of crust layer. Mix together the chocolate pudding mix, milk and vanilla flavoring. Spread this on top of cream cheese mixture. Top with remaining Cool Whip.

Shirley Ward, Birmingham South Council

TORTONI SQUARES

1/3 c. chopped almonds	1 tsp. almond extract
3 Tbsp. butter or oleo	1 (10 or 12 oz.) jar
1 1/3 c. finely crushed	apricot preserves
vanilla wafers	3 pt. or 1/2 gal. vanilla
	ice cream

Toast almonds in butter or oleo. Combine with crushed vanilla wafers, adding almond flavoring. Use 9 inch square or 7x11 inch pan or Pyrex casserole (if using 1/2 gallon ice cream, use 9x13 inch pan). Layer crumbs, 1/2 ice cream. Spread apricot preserves, layer balance of ice cream. Top with remaining crumbs; freeze until firm. Serves 12 or more.

J. D. Kaylor, Mobile Council

WHITE CHOCOLATE DESSERT

3 egg whites	1 pt. whipping cream
Pinch of salt	Confectioners sugar
1 c. sugar	1/2 lb. grated white
1 tsp. vanilla	chocolate

Beat egg whites and salt until stiff; add sugar and vanilla. Crunch 23 Ritz crackers by hand. Fold into egg whites. Bake in buttered (greased) floured pan at 325° for 25 minutes. Whip cream, confectioners sugar and vanilla. Spread on top of cool cake. Sprinkle with 1/2 pound grated white chocolate.

Beverly Hearn, Riverchase Council

AGNUS SCOTT PIE

3 egg whites	1 c. pecans
1 c. sugar	1 large Cool Whip
23 Ritz crackers	3 Tbsp. instant cocoa
1 tsp. vanilla	

Beat sugar into eggs until stiff. Crumb crackers in blender. Fold in eggs, vanilla and nuts; cook 30-40 minutes. Cool. Mix cocoa and Cool Whip and cover pie; chill.

Cynthia Lee, Tuscaloosa Council

AMBER PIE

1 c. sugar	1/2 c. raisins
1/3 c. oleo	1/2 tsp. cinnamon
1 1/2 heaping Tbsp. flour	1/2 tsp. allspice
3 egg yolks	1/2 tsp. nutmeg
1 Tbsp. vinegar	1/2 tsp. cloves
	1 1/2 c. milk

Combine sugar, flour and spices in a saucepan and mix well; add other ingredients and mix well. Cook till it is very thick. Remove from heat and let get cold. Pour into baked pie shell. Cover with meringue.

Meringue: Beat 3 egg whites and 6 tablespoons sugar until they stand in stiff, dry peaks. After placing meringue on pie, put in oven (hot) or broiler about 2 minutes until meringue browns.

Sharon Solomon, Birmingham South Council

APPLE PIE

Crust:

2 c. flour	2/3 c. shortening or lard
3/4 tsp. salt	6-7 Tbsp. cold water

Filling:

1 c. sugar	1/8 tsp. nutmeg
2 Tbsp. flour	1/8 tsp. allspice
1/2 tsp. cinnamon	6 medium tart apples, peeled and thinly sliced

Crust: Sift flour and salt; cut in shortening. Add water; mix with a fork, cutting through mixture with each stroke. Roll out pastry, using plenty of flour on board and on rolling pin. Place one crust in pie pan.

Filling: Mix sugar, flour and spices; sprinkle half of mixture in pastry lined pan. Add apples; cover with remaining sugar mixture. Moisten edge of bottom crust with water; cover with top crust. Trim top pastry 1 inch from edge of pan. Tuck top pastry under bottom pastry; press edges together, then flute. Make large air hole in top pastry; bake at 400° for 45 minutes to 1 hour. Yield: 6 to 8 servings.

1567-82   Barbara Griffin, Birmingham West Council   373

DEEP DISH APPLE PIE

6 tart cooking apples
1 c. white sugar
1 stick butter

1/4 c. brown sugar
1 c. flour

Pack 6 tart cooking apples, which have been peeled and cut in eighths, into deep casserole dish. Cover with 1 cup white sugar. In separate dish blend together:

1 stick butter
1/4 c. brown sugar

1 c. flour

Blend until it looks like meal; spread over apples in casserole. Bake in 350° oven 1 hour.

Mary C. Martin, Birmingham East Council

APPLE PIE IN A BAG

Mix:
Apples, sliced (enough
  for 9 inch crust)

1/2 c. white sugar
2 Tbsp. flour

Put in crust and sprinkle with cinnamon. Mix:

1/2 c. white sugar

1/2 c. flour

Spread over top of apples; dot top with 1 stick margarine. Place in large paper bag; loosely clip or pin shut. Place on cookie sheet and bake 1 hour at 425°.

Eloise Bennett, Decatur Council

CRISPY APPLE PIE

5 medium apples
1 or 1 1/2 c. water
1/2 c. sugar

1 box dry yellow cake mix
1 1/2 sticks oleo
1 c. chopped nuts
Cinnamon

Peel, quarter and slice apples (thin). Place in sheath cake pan; add water. Sprinkle with cinnamon and sprinkle sugar on top. Spread dry cake mix evenly; top with chopped pecans. Slice oleo over mixture. Sprinkle cinnamon (to taste). Cook 45 minutes at 375°.

Rachel Carroll, Decatur Council

374

APPLE ANGEL PIE

Nut Crust:

1 egg white
1/4 c. sugar

1/8 tsp. salt
1 c. finely chopped nuts

Filling:

4-6 medium size apples
2 to 2 1/2 c. water
3/4 tsp. instant coffee

1/2 tsp. cinnamon
3 Tbsp. cornstarch
3 Tbsp. butter or oleo
1 3/4 c. sugar

Nut Crust: Beat egg whites; add sugar, salt and nuts. Blend. Press in bottom and sides of well greased pan with fork. Bake at 400° for 12 minutes and cool.

Filling: Cook and add to baked pie shell. Serve with sweetened whipping cream lightly sprinkled with instant coffee.

Emma Rousseau, Huntsville Council

APPLE PIE

3 c. grated apple (may
  be shredded)
1 1/4 c. sugar
3/4 stick margarine

1/4 tsp. salt
1 tsp. cinnamon
2 Tbsp. cornstarch
1 egg

Melt margarine; add other ingredients and mix well. Cook in unbaked pie shell at 350° for 1 hour and 15 minutes.

Mae B. Jordan, Birmingham Central Council

SOUR CREAM APPLE PIE

Crust:

1 c. self-rising flour
1/2 tsp. salt

1/3 c. shortening

Cut shortening into flour and salt mixture; roll and place in a 9 inch pie pan.

Filling:

1 egg
1 Tbsp. lemon juice
3/4 c. sugar
3 c. thinly sliced apples
  (not Delicious)

1/8 tsp. salt
3 Tbsp. flour
1 c. sour cream
1 Tbsp. sugar
1 tsp. cinnamon

1567-82

375

Beat together egg and lemon juice. Add flour, salt and 3/4 cup sugar. Mix well. Combine sour cream and apples and add to other mixture. Place in unbaked pie shell. Sprinkle with cinnamon and sugar; bake at 425° for 15 minutes, then lower heat to 350° for 35 minutes. Delicious.

Irene C. Bonner, Birmingham Central Council

MOCK APPLE PIE

Pastry for 2 crust
  9 inch pie
36 Ritz crackers
2 c. water
2 c. sugar

1 tsp. cream of tartar
2 tsp. lemon juice
Grated rind of 1 lemon
Butter or margarine
Cinnamon

Roll out bottom crust of pastry and fit into 9 inch pie plate. Break Ritz crackers coarsely into pastry lined plate. Combine water, sugar and cream of tartar in saucepan; boil gently for 15 minutes. Add lemon juice and rind; cool. Pour syrup over crackers; dot generously with butter or margarine and sprinkle with cinnamon. Cover with top crust. Trim and flute edges together. Cut slits in top crust to let steam escape. Bake in a hot oven (425°) for 30 to 35 minutes, until crust is crisp and golden. Serve warm. Cut into 6 to 8 slices.

Dianne McNutt, Anniston Council

FRESH APPLE PIE

4 or 5 Winesap apples
1/3 to 1/2 c. sugar
1/4 tsp. nutmeg
1/8 tsp. salt

1 tsp. lemon juice
2 Tbsp. butter
2 unbaked pie shells

Peel, core and cut apples. In glass pie plate grease with butter and line with pastry. Fill evenly with sliced apples. Mix sugar, nutmeg, salt and lemon juice and sprinkle over apples; dot with butter. Add top crust and dot with butter. Set oven at 425° F. Place pie in oven until butter has melted, then sprinkle with sugar. Bake 35 to 50 minutes until apples are soft and crust is brown.

Mrs. Annie Mims, Mobile Council

ENGLISH APPLE PIE

4 large apples
1 c. white sugar

1 tsp. cinnamon

Crust:

1 stick melted butter
1 c. flour
1 tsp. sugar

1/2 c. brown sugar
1/2 c. nuts

Slice apples and lay in pan. Sprinkle white sugar and cinnamon on top. Melt butter and mix with dry ingredients. Spread over apples and bake 45 minutes at 350°.

Margaret Hare, Anniston Council

BANANA CARAMEL PIE

Graham cracker shell
1 banana

1 can Eagle Brand
    condensed milk
Cool Whip

Cover unopened can of milk with water and boil for 3 hours on very low heat in pan with cover (this caramelizes the milk). Remove from pot and cool in refrigerator for 3 hours. Spoon milk into graham cracker pie shell. Slice banana and place on pie. Spread Cool Whip on top.

Mary Ann Fulmer, Tri-Cities Council

BANANA SPLIT PIE

(1):

1 box confectioners
  sugar

2 sticks margarine
2 eggs

(2):

2 c. graham cracker crumbs   1 stick margarine

(3) Sliced bananas

(4) Large can crushed pineapple, drained

(5) 1 jar strawberry glaze

(6) 1 large Cool Whip

Mix the ingredients in #1 and beat well. Let stand until you mix #2 and make crust. Then add #1 on top of crust. Add other ingredients as layers as they are listed.

Celia Stephens, Montgomery Council

BANANA SPLIT PIE

1 box graham cracker
crumbs
1 large can crushed
pineapple
4 large bananas
1 (8 oz.) pkg. Philadelphia
cream cheese

1 1/2 c. powdered
sugar
1/2 stick butter
(oleo)
1 (8 oz.) Cool Whip
1 (10 oz.) jar cherries
Pecans

1. Spread cracker crumbs in bottom of pie plate; add 1 heaping tablespoon of granulated sugar and melted butter. Mix real well and shape crust. 2. Place a layer of sliced bananas. Drain pineapple and reserve 1/3 cup of juice. Spread pineapple over bananas. 3. Mix cream cheese (softened) with powdered sugar; add pineapple juice and mix well. Spread over pineapple. 4. Spread Cool Whip over cream cheese mixture. 5. Top with cherries (halves) and pecans. This makes 2 (9 inch) pies or 1 (13x9 inch) rectangular pan pie.

Marguerite Hays, Birmingham West Council

BANANA SPLIT PIE

2 c. graham cracker
crumbs
1 stick margarine
2 1/2 c. confectioners
sugar
2 sticks margarine,
softened

1 can cherry pie filling
or strawberry
3 ripe bananas
1 medium can crushed
pineapple
1 large carton Cool Whip
Cherries (optional)
Nuts (optional)

In saucepan melt 1 stick margarine and combine with graham cracker crumbs in a 9x13 inch dish to form crust. Beat confectioners sugar and 2 sticks of softened margarine for 5 minutes or until spreadable so as to spread over crumb crust. (You may wish to add a little milk.) Add 1 can cherry pie filling over confectioners sugar mixture. Slice bananas over pie filling layer. Add can of crushed pine-apple (drained) over banana layer. Top with Cool Whip by spreading over entire pie and add cherries and nuts on top for decor.

Debbie Early, Birmingham South Council

OLD WORLD BAVARIAN PIE

2 c. finely chopped
  apples (tart)
3/4 c. sugar
2 Tbsp. all-purpose flour
1/3 tsp. salt
1 egg, beaten

1/2 tsp. vanilla
1 c. sour cream
1 unbaked 9 inch pie shell
  (use rich tart pastry or
  Johnston's butter flavored
  pie shell)

Topping:

1/3 c. all-purpose flour

1/4 c. butter or margarine
1/3 c. brown sugar

1. Peel and chop apples and set aside. 2. Combine sugar, flour and salt; add egg, vanilla and sour cream. 3. Beat until smooth. 4. Add apples and mix well. 5. Pour into pie shell. 6. Bake at 375° for 15 minutes; reduce heat to 325° and bake 30 minutes longer. 7. Remove from oven and sprinkle with topping.

Topping: 1. Combine ingredients and blend well. 2. Sprinkle over baked pie. 3. Return to oven and bake at 350° for 15-20 minutes or until topping is brown.

Nancy Tatum, Riverchase Council

BERRY PIE
(Blackberries, dewberries, etc.)

2/3 to 1 c. sugar
2 Tbsp. cornstarch
  (or 4 Tbsp. flour)
1/8 tsp. salt

3 c. fresh berries
1 recipe plain pastry (for
  8-9 inch double-crust pie)
1 Tbsp. butter

Mix sugar, cornstarch or flour and salt; sprinkle over fruit in 9 inch pastry lined pie pan; dot with butter and adjust top crust and cut in vents (or I prefer to lattice top crust). Bake in hot oven (450°) for 10 minutes, then in moderate oven (350°) about 30 minutes.

To prevent overcooking outer edge of crust, form 1 inch strips of aluminum foil over edge only. No need to remove until pie is done.

Note: Good warm with whipped cream or vanilla ice cream.

Ruth Apperson, Decatur Council

BLACK-BOTTOM PIE

1/2 c. sugar
1 Tbsp. cornstarch
2 c. milk, scalded
4 beaten egg yolks
1 tsp. vanilla
1 (6 oz.) pkg. semi-sweet
　　chocolate pieces

1 baked 9 inch pie shell
1 Tbsp. (1 env.)
　　unflavored gelatin
1/4 c. cold water
4 egg whites
1/2 c. sugar
1 c. heavy cream, whipped
Chocolate decorettes

Combine sugar and cornstarch; slowly add scalded milk to beaten egg yolks. Stir in sugar mixture; cook and stir in top of double boiler until the custard coats a spoon. Add vanilla. To 1 cup of the custard add the chocolate pieces; stir until chocolate is melted. Pour in bottom of cooled, baked pie shell. Chill. Soften gelatin in cold water; add to remaining hot custard; stir until dissolved. Chill until slightly thick. Beat egg whites, adding sugar gradually, until mixture stands in stiff peaks. Fold in custard-gelatin mixture. Pour over chocolate layer and chill until set. Garnish with whipped cream and chocolate decorettes.
Delora Clarke, Huntsville Council

BLACK RUSSIAN PIE

1 c. (14) Oreos, crumbled
2 Tbsp. butter, melted
24 large marshmallows
1/2 c. cold milk

1/8 tsp. salt
1/3 c. kahlua
1 c. whipping cream
Solid semi-sweet chocolate
　　for curls

Combine cookie crumbs (finely crushed) and butter in 8 inch pie pan; mix well and press firmly in an even layer over bottom and sides. Place in freezer till firm. Melt marshmallows with milk and salt over hot water (use double boiler). Cool until mixture will mound on a spoon; stir in kahlua. Beat cream stiff and fold into marshmallow mixture. Chill 30 minutes until mixture holds ripples when stirred lightly. Turn into chilled cookie shell and freeze. Put curls of chocolate on top.
Sheilah Miller, Birmingham East Council

BLUEBERRY CHERRY PIE

Crust:

1 c. oleo or butter, melted
2 c. flour (plain)

1 c. pecans, chopped real fine
1/2 c. brown sugar

Mix and pat into 9x13 inch pan; bake at 400° for 15 minutes and let cool. Mix together:

1 (8 oz.) pkg. (large)
  cream cheese

1 c. confectioners sugar
1 tsp. vanilla

Cream together well and set aside. Prepare 2 packages Dream Whip (regular size) as directed on package. Combine with cream cheese mixture and pour over crust. (Can use 1 large 11 ounce Cool Whip in place of Dream Whip.) Chill thoroughly (preferably overnight). Pour any flavor prepared pie filling over top and serve. (Best to place cans of pie filling in refrigerator overnight with other pie mixture everything is chilled). Return any unused portion of pie to refrigerator; the longer it sets the better. (Try half receipt for small family.) Can add fruit a few hours before serving. Be sure and let crust set up overnight before adding fruit. Serves about 20 to 24.

Earline Thornton, Tuscaloosa Council

BLUEBERRY PIE

1 can blueberry pie filling
1 large box instant
  vanilla pudding

1 (9 oz.) carton
  Cool Whip
Graham crackers

Mix instant pudding and Cool Whip together. Line large dish with graham crackers and spread pudding mixture on top. Then add layer of pie filling, then add another layer of crackers and repeat each step.

Peggy Hunter, Anniston Council

BUTTERMILK PIE

3 eggs
1 c. buttermilk
1 c. sugar

1 Tbsp. cornstarch or flour
1 tsp. nutmeg or lemon extract
2 Tbsp. butter

Beat egg yolks; add butter, sugar, cornstarch and milk. Place in uncooked pastry shell and bake in 350° oven until firm (45 minutes to 1 hour). Beat egg whites; add 1 tablespoon of sugar to each egg for meringue. Spread on top; place in 350° oven about 5 minutes or until meringue browns.

Mattie Singleton, Retired,
Birmingham Central Council

BUTTERNUT SQUASH PIE

2 eggs, well beaten
2/3 c. sugar
1 tsp. salt
1 Tbsp. pumpkin pie spice

1 3/4 c. canned or cooked
   mashed butternut squash
1 can condensed milk
2 unbaked 9 inch pie shells

Combine eggs, sugar, salt and spices; add squash and mix. Stir in milk. Pour into pie shells; bake in 425° oven about 40 minutes.

Imogene Davis, Birmingham Central Council

BUTTERSCOTCH PIE

3/4 c. brown sugar
1/4 c. granulated sugar
1/3 c. flour
2 c. scalded milk
1/8 tsp. salt

3 egg yolks, beaten
1 1/2 Tbsp. butter
1 tsp. vanilla
1 baked pastry shell
1 receipt meringue

Combine sugar with flour; add hot milk gradually, stirring constantly to make a smooth mixture. Add salt and cook in top of double boiler for 15 minutes, stirring occasionally, until thickened. Pour part of the hot mixture slowly onto egg yolks, stirring constantly. Pour back into double boiler and mix well; cook not more than 3 minutes, stirring almost constantly. Add butter; stir until melted. Cool; add vanilla; pour into pastry shell. Cover with meringue and proceed as directed. Makes one 9 inch pie.

Black Walnut Pie: Use all granulated sugar and only 2 tablespoons butter. Add 1 cup black walnut meats, chopped, to cooled filling.

Earlina Thornton, Tuscaloosa Council

CALYPSO PIE

18 crushed Oreo cookies
1/3 c. melted margarine
1 qt. vanilla ice cream,
   softened
1/2 c. peanuts or
   1/2 c. slivered almonds

1/2 c. sugar
1 1/2 squares unsweetened
   chocolate
2/3 c. Pet milk (small can)
1 large (9 oz.) Cool Whip
1 Tbsp. margarine

Combine crushed Oreos and melted margarine; pat into 13x9 inch pan. Spread ice cream on top. Put in freezer. Melt chocolate and margarine in saucepan; add sugar and milk. Cook till thick on medium heat. Cool, then spread on top of ice cream. Next spread large Cool Whip. Top with peanuts or slivered almonds; freeze overnight. Set out few minutes before serving.

Jeanne Anderson, Montgomery Council

CARROT CUSTARD PIE

3/4 c. sugar
3 Tbsp. margarine, softened
2 Tbsp. all-purpose flour
3 eggs

1 1/4 c. evaporated milk
1 1/4 c. grated carrots
1/4 tsp. ground cinnamon
1 unbaked 9 inch pastry shell

Combine sugar and butter; cream until light and fluffy. Stir in flour; add eggs, one at a time, beating well after each. Add milk, carrots and cinnamon. Spoon batter into pastry shell; bake at 425° for 15 minutes; reduce heat to 350° and bake 30 minutes or until firm.

Barbara Spivey, Mobile Council

CHEESE CAKE PIE

1 graham cracker crust (add about 1/4 tsp. cinnamon)
2 eggs

1 large pkg. cream cheese, softened
3/8 c. sugar

Cream together sugar and eggs; add cheese, mixing thoroughly. Pour in chilled crust. Bake 20 to 25 minutes at 350°.

Topping:

1/2 pt. sour cream
1/8 c. sugar

1/2 tsp. vanilla

Mix; pour over pie and bake another 5 minutes. Chill for approximately 1 hour before cutting.

Aileen Hardin, Riverchase Council

CHERRY PIE

1 Tbsp. sugar and 1 Tbsp. flour to sprinkle on bottom crust
1 can sour pitted cherries
1 c. sugar
1/4 c. plain flour

1/8 tsp. salt
1/4 tsp. almond extract
1 tsp. lemon juice
1 Tbsp. butter
Pie crust for top and bottom

1567-82

383

Drain cherries; save juice. Combine sugar, flour and salt. Gradually stir in cherry juice (not all of it, approximately 2/3). Add almond extract and lemon juice. Combine with cherries and pour into crust. Put butter on top and cover with second crust. Bake at 425° for 30-35 minutes.

Sandra Herndon, Birmingham South Council

CHERRY DELIGHT PIE

Crust:

1 1/2 c. graham cracker crumbs

6 Tbsp. melted margarine

Filling:

1 heaping c. powdered sugar
2 Tbsp. milk
1 (8 oz.) pkg. cream cheese

1 c. chopped pecans
1 pkg. whipped non-dairy topping
1 can cherry pie filling

Crust: Mix graham cracker crumbs and margarine to make crust. Press into a 9x12 inch pan; bake 10 minutes at 350°, then allow crust to cool. (Two prepared graham cracker pie crusts may be used.)

Filling: Mix powdered sugar, milk and cream cheese in a small bowl. Beat with mixer until creamy and smooth; spread over cool crust. Sprinkle pecans on top and refrigerate for 30 minutes. Mix whipped non-dairy topping and spread over nuts. Top with cherry pie filling. Strawberry filling can be substituted for the cherry, if desired.

Charlene Brown, Montgomery Council

CHERRY TOP CHEESE PIE

1 (8 oz.) pkg. cream cheese
1/4 c. sugar
1 Tbsp. almond extract

2 c. Cool Whip
1/2 can cherry pie filling
1 graham cracker crust

Beat cream cheese and sugar; add almond extract. Blend in 2 cups Cool Whip. Fold into graham cracker crust and top with 1/2 can cherry pie filling (chilled).

Nancy S. Black, Decatur Council

384

CHESS PIE

1 stick margarine
3 eggs
1 1/4 c. sugar

1 Tbsp. vinegar
1 Tbsp. self-rising flour
1 tsp. vanilla

Melt margarine and add other ingredients. Mix well. Bake in an unbaked pie shell at 350° for 50 minutes.
G. W. (Red) Webb, Life Member,
Birmingham Central Council

CHOCOLATE CHESS PIE

4 eggs
1 stick oleo
6 Tbsp. cocoa
3 c. sugar

6 Tbsp. cornstarch
1/2 c. evaporated milk
2 tsp. vanilla

Mix cocoa, sugar and cornstarch. Beat eggs, milk, oleo and vanilla. Add dry ingredients to egg mixture. Pour into 2 pie shells and bake 40 minutes at 325°.
Sue Shirley, Huntsville Council

GRANNY'S OLD FASHIONED CHOCOLATE PIE

2 egg yolks
1 c. sugar
1/4 c. self-rising flour
2 c. sweet milk

1/2 c. cocoa
1 tsp. vanilla flavoring
1-2 tsp. butter
Pinch of salt

Start with sugar and cocoa and flour; mix well. Beat in egg yolks. Add milk. Put into double boiler. Cook until thick. Add butter, flavoring and a pinch of salt. Pour into cooked pie shell.
Note: Use same basic recipe - substitute bananas, lemons or pineapple with vanilla wafers. Yum, yum.
Trudy B. McCann, Huntsville Council

CHOCOLATE CREAM PIE

1 1/4 c. sugar
3 Tbsp. cocoa
1/2 c. all-purpose flour
3 eggs, separated

1/2 stick butter or margarine
2 c. water
1 dash of salt
1 tsp. vanilla flavoring

Combine sugar, flour and cocoa in a medium size sauce-pan; add sufficient water to form paste. Beat in egg yolks well. Heat remaining water and add with butter and salt.

1567-82

Cook until thick; remove from heat and add vanilla. Cool and pour into prepared pie shell. Prepare meringue with the egg whites; place on pie and brown. Pie should cool before it is cut.

Emma Rousseau, Huntsville Council

CHOCOLATE PIE

1 1/4 c. sugar
1 1/2 c. water
1/2 stick butter
Dash of salt

1/2 c. flour
3 heaping Tbsp. cocoa
3 eggs, separated
6 Tbsp. sugar
1 tsp. vanilla

Mix sugar, flour and cocoa together; add enough water to make paste. Beat in egg yolks well; heat remaining water and add with butter and salt. Cook until thick; remove from heat and add vanilla. Cool and pour into 9 inch baked crust. Cover with meringue and brown.

Ernestine Gudgen, Birmingham South Council

HERSHEY CHOCOLATE BAR PIE

20 marshmallows
4 small Hershey's
almond bars

2/3 c. sweet milk
1 c. whipped cream

Melt Hershey's bars in top of double boiler; add marshmallows and milk. When melted, set aside to cool. Fold in whipped cream. Pour into vanilla wafer crust and top with whipped cream if desired.

Faith Kirby, Anniston Council

MAMA'S GERMAN SWEET CHOCOLATE PIE

2/3 pkg. German's
sweet chocolate
2/3 c. sugar
1 c. milk

4 eggs
2 Tbsp. butter
1 tsp. vanilla

Melt chocolate and butter together. Mix 1 whole egg, 3 yolks and sugar; beat gently. Add chocolate and butter and vanilla; beat gently. Add milk; mix. Pour into unbaked pie shell; bake at 375° approximately 20 minutes until thick. Beat egg whites; add 1/4 cup sugar. Spread over pie; return to oven and brown. Serve warm.

Betty Floyd Parker, Montgomery Council

EASY CHOCOLATE PIE

1 1/2 c. sugar
1/2 stick margarine
3 1/2 Tbsp. cocoa
2 eggs

1 small (5.33 oz.) can
   Pet milk
1 tsp. vanilla
Pinch of salt

Put all of the ingredients listed in a blender, and blend at low to medium speed (whip on some blenders) until smooth. Pour into an unbaked frozen pie shell. (Don't forget to prick pie shell with a fork!) Bake at 350° for 40-45 minutes. Allow to cool, then refrigerate for several hours. Tastes great with a scoop of vanilla ice cream!

Johnnie P. Walker, Birmingham Central Council

CHOCOLATE SILK PIE

This is so simple to make, but out of this world in taste.

1 (9 inch) baked pie shell
1 c. butter, softened
1 1/2 c. sugar
Whipped cream

4 squares baking chocolate,
   melted and cooled
4 eggs
1 tsp. vanilla

Cream butter and sugar; add chocolate and vanilla. Beat with electric mixer at low speed until well blended. Add eggs; beat 10 minutes. Pour into baked pie shell; chill for about 3 hours. Top with whipped cream if desired. May be frozen.

Faith Kirby, Anniston Council

COBBLER PIE

1 stick oleo
1 c. milk
1 c. sugar

1 c. self-rising flour
2 tsp. baking powder
2 c. fruit

Mix all ingredients; bake in 300° oven 45 minutes, until top is brown.

Frances Crenshaw, Birmingham East Council

COCONUT PIE

(This recipe is over 100 years old, as you can tell after reading.)

3 or 4 eggs (yellows)
4 c. water or milk

1 c. flour
1 square of butter

1 tsp. lemon flavoring   Thicken batter with
1 c. sugar   coconut

Mix sugar and flour together (dry). Beat egg yolks and add to sugar and flour with water or milk. Add butter and flavoring and cook until mixture begins to thicken; add coconut and put into pie shells. Beat egg whites stiff and put 2 tablespoons of sugar to the egg white. Put on pie and brown. Sprinkle with coconut.

Wilma N. Watson, Anniston Council

CREAMY COCONUT PIE

1 (3 oz.) pkg. cream   3 1/2 c. whipped topping
  cheese   1/2 tsp. almond extract
1 Tbsp. sugar   Graham cracker crust
1/2 c. milk   1 1/3 c. coconut

Beat cream cheese until softened in mixer bowl of electric mixer; beat in sugar. Gradually add milk and beat until smooth. Fold in coconut, whipped topping and extract. Spoon into crust. Garnish with toasted coconut.

Sue Waldrep, Anniston Council

OLD FASHIONED CARAMEL COCONUT PIE

1 1/3 c. sugar   3 eggs
2/3 c. boiling water   1 1/2 tsp. vanilla
1/2 tsp. salt   1 c. coconut
2 1/2 Tbsp. cornstarch   1 Tbsp. butter
1 Tbsp. flour   1 large pie crust or
3 c. milk   2 small ones

Meringue: Beat until fluffy 3 egg whites and 1/4 teaspoon cream of tartar; gradually beat in 6 tablespoons sugar. Continue beating until mixture is stiff and glossy. Brown in 350° oven about 15 minutes.

Melt sugar in heavy or iron skillet over moderate heat, stirring constantly to prevent sugar from scorching and getting too brown. Add boiling water, stirring constantly, until it forms a syrup. Set aside. Mix salt, cornstarch and flour. Stir in milk gradually and cook over moderate heat, stirring constantly until mixture is hot. Add the sugar syrup; cook mixture until thickens and boils; boil 1 minute and remove from heat. Stir 1 cup of hot mixture slowly into egg yolks, slightly beaten, then blend into hot mixture in saucepan; boil 1 minute, stirring constantly. Remove from heat; stir in butter, coconut and vanilla; cool,

stirring constantly. Pour into baked pie shell; chill thoroughly. Finish with meringue, whipped cream or Cool Whip.
Marcella James, Tri-Cities Council

COCONUT PIE
(Makes Its Own Crust)

4 eggs
1/2 c. self-rising flour
2 c. milk

1 1/2 c. coconut
1 tsp. vanilla
1 3/4 c. sugar

Combine all ingredients in order and mix well. Pour in well greased 10 inch glass pie pan and bake 45 minutes to 1 hour at 300°, until golden brown.
Rosemary Parker, Birmingham Central Council

COCONUT PIE

2 eggs
1 c. sugar
1 small can evaporated milk

1 Tbsp. vanilla
1/2 stick oleo or butter
1 can coconut

Cream eggs and sugar together; melt oleo. Mix with eggs and sugar. Add milk, vanilla and 3/4 can of coconut. Pour into unbaked 9 inch pie shell; sprinkle with remaining coconut. Cook at 350° for 30-45 minutes.
Ruby Webb, Mobile Council

FRENCH COCONUT PIE

3 eggs, beaten
1 1/2 c. sugar
1/2 c. butter, melted
1 tsp. vanilla

4 tsp. lemon juice
1 (3 1/2 oz.) can coconut
1 (9 inch) unbaked
 pie shell

Mix sugar and eggs well; add other ingredients. Pour in pie shell; bake at 350° for 45 minutes. Allow to cool completely to set before serving.
Gloria H. Ramage, Birmingham South Council

COCONUT ICE CREAM PIE

1/4 c. butter, melted
1 qt. strawberry ice cream
2 c. coconut

1 (4 1/2 oz.) container
 Cool Whip
Easy Chocolate Fudge Sauce

Add butter to coconut, mixing lightly. Press evenly into 8 inch pie pan; bake at 300° for 20 to 30 minutes or
1567-82

until golden. Cool. Alternate spoonfuls of ice cream and half of the sauce in crust for a ripple effect. Freeze until firm. Spread whipped topping over the top and freeze again. Sprinkle with toasted coconut and serve with remaining sauce, if desired.

Easy Chocolate Fudge Sauce: Combine one 4 ounce package German's sweet chocolate, 3/4 cup evaporated milk and 8 marshmallows in saucepan; cook and stir over low heat until chocolate and marshmallows are melted. Remove from heat; add 1/2 teaspoon vanilla and cool. Makes 1 1/2 cups.

Mary Ann Davis, Anniston Council

CRAZY CRUST PIE

1 stick margarine
1 c. flour
1 c. milk

1 c. sugar
1 can blackberries, peaches, or fruit of your choice

Put margarine in sheet pan and place in oven to melt. Mix flour, sugar and milk and pour into pan over butter. Spoon fruit over top of flour mixture; bake at 400° until crust is golden brown.

Joyce Reavis, Decatur Council

CREAM CHEESE PIE

1 (6 oz.) graham cracker
   pie crust
1 (8 oz.) pkg. cream
   cheese, softened
1 (14 oz.) can sweetened
   condensed milk

1/3 c. lemon juice
   (fresh or bottled)
1 tsp. vanilla
1 (21 oz.) can cherry or
   blueberry pie filling

Let cream cheese stand at room temperature until softened. In medium bowl beat cream cheese until light and fluffy. Slowly add sweetened condensed milk, beating until smooth. Stir in lemon juice and vanilla until well mixed. Pour into crust; chill 3 hours until firm and then top with pie filling. Makes 1 pie.

Patricia McDowell, Birmingham East Council

CREAM PIE

1 1/2 c. milk
1/4 c. sugar
1/4 tsp. salt
3 Tbsp. flour

1 egg yolk
1 Tbsp. margarine
1/2 tsp. vanilla extract
1 baked pastry shell
Whipped cream topping

390

Scald 1 cup milk over boiling water. Mix sugar, salt, flour and 1/2 cup milk; add to hot milk gradually, stirring constantly. Cook slowly until thickened, stirring. Cover and cook over boiling water 5 minutes, then add some of mixture slowly to egg yolk, before mixing yolk into pie filling. Cook 1 minute more; remove from heat and add margarine and vanilla. Cool slightly, then pour into pastry shell. Top with whipped cream before serving.

Variations: Banana - Add 4 sliced bananas. Chocolate: Add 1 ounce melted chocolate and 2 tablespoons sugar. Coconut: Add 1 1/2 cups shredded coconut.

Ruby Dickerson, Birmingham Central Council

DREAM PIE

First Layer:

1 c. flour	1 c. nuts
1 stick oleo	

Second Layer:

8 oz. cream cheese	1 tsp. vanilla
1 c. powdered sugar	1 c. Cool Whip

Third Layer:

2 (4 1/2 oz.) boxes instant chocolate pudding mix	3 c. milk

Mix flour and oleo with pastry blender; add nuts. Spread in a 9 1/2 x 13 inch pan and bake for 20 minutes at 350°. Let cool completely. For Second Layer, fold in Cool Whip and other ingredients and spread on top of First Layer. Next, mix pudding mix and milk and spread on top of other layer. Cover that layer with a layer of Cool Whip.

Barbara Speegle, Decatur Council

DREAM PIE

1 (16 oz.) can crushed pineapple (unsweetened)	1 (3 oz.) box orange jello
	Few drops of red cake coloring
1 (16 oz.) can sour cherries, drained	1 c. chopped pecans
	4 sliced bananas
1 1/2 c. sugar	2 graham cracker crusts
2 Tbsp. flour	

Mix together first 4 ingredients; cook until slightly thick. Add jello and cake coloring; let cool slightly. Add pecans and bananas. Pour into pie crust. Chill and top with Cool Whip.

1567-82   Frances Coleman, Huntsville Council   391

BOILED CUSTARD

1 qt. milk (half & half)	1 c. sugar
1 c. milk (canned)	2 tsp. vanilla
5 eggs, separated	

Scald 1 quart milk. Separate eggs. Beat egg yolks and add to 1 cup of milk. Into heated milk pour egg yolk and milk mixture; cook, stirring constantly, until thickened. Add vanilla; set aside. Beat egg whites stiff; add 1 cup sugar to beaten egg whites. Fold egg white mixture into cooled milk mixture. Cool and serve in chilled glasses - topped with nutmeg.

Kathleen Weldon (Mrs. George E.),
Montgomery Council

EGG CUSTARD MERINGUE PIE

4 eggs (3 egg whites for meringue)	1 tsp. cornstarch
	1 Tbsp. margarine
2/3 c. sugar, plus 6 Tbsp. for meringue	2 c. milk, scalded
	1 tsp. vanilla
2 Tbsp. flour	1 unbaked pie shell

Beat 3 egg yolks and 1 whole egg slightly; add 2/3 cup sugar, flour and cornstarch, sifted together; stir only to mix. Add hot milk; gradually add vanilla and margarine. Pour into uncooked pie shell; bake 30 minutes at 350°; do not preheat oven. Do not overcook. Beat egg whites until firm. Add 6 tablespoons sugar and beat well; add 1/2 teaspoon vanilla and pile on pie. Bake 15 minutes at 350°. Cool completely before cutting.

Edna Watters, Montgomery Council

MOM'S DEEP DISH PIE

2/3 stick oleo, melted in casserole dish	1 tsp. baking powder
	Pinch of salt
3/4 c. sugar	1 can fruit (cherries,
3/4 c. flour	peaches or apples)
3/4 c. milk	

Mix sugar, flour, milk and baking powder and salt. Pour this mixture over the melted butter. Over this pour 1 can of fruit. Bake in 350° oven for 40 minutes. Freeze leftovers. Reheat in 350° oven for about 30 minutes. Serves 5-6.

Libby Orenbaun, Tuscaloosa Council

EGG PIE

2 dozen hard boiled eggs	Pepper
Dumplings (as made for	Butter or margarine
chicken dumplings)	Sweet milk
Salt	

Place solid layer of dumpling dough to line bottom and sides of cobbler pie pan. Slice eggs and lay on bottom of pan. Add broth made from butter-milk-pepper and salt (measures according to taste). Alternate with layers of eggs, about 4 thin dumpling slices and broth until pan is filled 1 inch from top. Cover with solid dough topping and bake at 350° until brown and bottom crust is done.

Gladness Henderson, Montgomery Council

FOUR LAYER CHOCOLATE PIE

First Layer:

1 c. plain flour	1/2 c. nuts, chopped
1/2 c. butter, melted	

Second Layer:

8 oz. cream cheese	1 c. powdered sugar
(room temperature)	1 c. Cool Whip

Third Layer:

2 small pkg. instant	3 1/2 c. milk
chocolate pudding mix	1 tsp. vanilla

Fourth Layer: Cool Whip

Mix ingredients for First Layer in pan; mash over bottom and bake at 350° for 15 minutes. Cool. Mix ingredients for Second Layer with mixer and spread over First Layer. Beat ingredients for Third Layer with mixer until thick and spread over Second Layer. Spread remaining Cool Whip over Third Layer.

Note: Use 1 large Cool Whip for both layers.
Lula Aycock, Retired,
Birmingham Central Council

FRUIT PIE

1 stick butter	1 can pie filling (blueberry,
1 c. sugar	cherry, apple, peach
1 c. flour	or strawberry)
1/2 c. milk	

1567-82

393

Melt 3/4 stick butter; add 1/2 cup milk. Add 1/2 cup sugar, then add 1 cup flour and mix well. Take other 1/4 stick of butter and grease bowl well, then pour mixture into bowl. Then spoon out pie filling on top of mixture. Then sprinkle other 1/2 cup of sugar over pie filling and bake at 375° for 50 minutes or until brown.

Mrs. Buddy Gulledge, Anniston Council

QUICK FRUIT PIE

1 c. flour	1/4 tsp. salt
1 c. sugar	3/4 stick butter, melted
1 c. milk	1 c. fruit

Mix first 5 ingredients; pour into deep dish pie plate and pour fruit on top. Cook at 500° for 15 to 20 minutes.

Peggy Y. Hughes, Riverchase Council

JAPANESE FRUIT PIES
(2 Pies)

5 eggs	1 c. coconut
2 c. white sugar	1 tsp. vanilla
2 sticks margarine	1 tsp. vinegar
1 c. broken nuts	1 c. raisins

Melt margarine; cool slightly. Beat eggs; add sugar gradually. Beat until creamy (3 to 4 minutes). Beat in margarine and vinegar. Fold in remaining ingredients. Pour into 2 unbaked pie shells; bake at 350° for 35 to 45 minutes until light brown and pie doesn't wiggle when moved.

Georgia A. Krahn, Riverchase Council

SOUTHERN FRUIT PIE

1 stick butter, melted and cooled	1/2 c. chopped pecans
	1/2 c. coconut
1 c. sugar	1 unbaked pie shell
2 eggs, well beaten	Whipped cream
1 tsp. vanilla	1/2 c. raisins

Mix butter, sugar and eggs together. Add remaining ingredients and pour into pie shell. Bake at 300° for 40 to 50 minutes. Serve with whipped cream. Makes 8 to 10 servings.

Mary Griffin, Mobile Council

FRUIT FLUFF PIE

1 can condensed milk　　　　　1/2 c. lemon juice

Mix together. Drain well:

1 can mandarin orange　　　　1 (No. 2) can sliced peaches
　sections　　　　　　　　　　1 small can crushed pineapple

Mix fruit and condensed milk mixture; fold in one 9 ounce carton Cool Whip. Pour into 2 graham cracker crusts. Pies may be frozen for future use. Thaw several hours before serving.

Peggy Blevins, Anniston Council

FUDGE PIE

2 eggs, slightly beaten　　　　1 1/4 c. sugar
1/4 c. flour　　　　　　　　　1/4 c. cocoa
1 stick melted butter　　　　　1 tsp. vanilla
　　　　　　　　　　　　　　1 unbaked pie shell

Mix all ingredients together. Pour into an unbaked pie shell and bake at 350° about 30 minutes or until set.

R. W. Price, Huntsville Council

HOT FUDGE PIE

2 c. sugar　　　　　　　　　3/4 c. chopped pecans
1/2 c. flour　　　　　　　　　4 oz. chocolate (4 squares)
4 eggs, slightly beaten　　　　1 c. butter or margarine
2 tsp. vanilla

Set oven at 350°. Put chocolate and butter in top of double boiler over boiling water to melt. Blend flour and sugar; add eggs and beat only to blend. Add chocolate mixture and blend thoroughly. Add vanilla and pecans. Pour into buttered pie plates and bake for 30 minutes at 350°. Makes 2 pies.

Gay B. Harrison, Montgomery Council

GERMAN CHOCOLATE PIE

1 c. sugar　　　　　　　　　2 eggs, slightly beaten
1 Tbsp. cornstarch　　　　　3 Tbsp. margarine
2 Tbsp. flour　　　　　　　　3/4 c. coconut
2 Tbsp. cocoa　　　　　　　1/2 tsp. vanilla
Pinch of salt　　　　　　　　1/3 c. chopped pecans
2/3 c. milk　　　　　　　　　1 (9 inch) unbaked pie shell

Combine first 5 ingredients in mixing bowl; mix well. Add remaining ingredients except pecans and pie shell. Mix well. Stir in pecans. Pour into pie shell; bake in preheated 400° oven for 30 minutes or until set.

Fay King, Huntsville Council

HAWAIIAN PIE

1 prepared graham
  cracker crust
1 can Eagle Brand milk
1/3 c. lemon juice
2-3 medium bananas, fully
  ripened and sliced
1 medium can crushed
  pineapple (juice
  packed), drained

1 carton Cool Whip, thawed
1/2 c. coconut
1/2 c. pecans, chopped
Maraschino cherries to
  garnish
1 Hershey's bar, cut into
  chocolate curls or grated
  with grater

Combine Eagle Brand milk and lemon juice; stir well until thickened. Slice bananas and cover bottom of crust. Spread milk mixture over bananas and cover well to prevent bananas from darkening. Sprinkle drained pineapple over top of mixture. Sprinkle some pecans over pineapple. Spread with Cool Whip. Garnish with coconut, cherries, remaining pecans and chocolate. Chill several hours or overnight. This one won't last long!

Ken King, Birmingham Central Council

HEAVENLY PIE

1 (8 oz.) pkg. cream
  cheese, softened
1 (14 oz.) can sweetened
  condensed milk
1/3 c. lemon juice
1 (9 oz.) carton frozen
  whipped topping, thawed

1/2 c. chopped pecans
1 c. drained fruit (pineapple,
  peaches or fruit cocktail)
2 (9 inch) graham cracker
  pie shells

Combine cream cheese, condensed milk and lemon juice; beat until smooth. Fold in whipped topping; stir in pecans and fruit. Pour into pie shells and refrigerate for several hours. Yield: Two 9 inch pies.

Faith Kirby, Anniston Council

HERSHEY PIE

6 bars regular Hershey's bars with almonds

1 graham cracker pie crust
1 large container Cool Whip

Melt Hershey's bars in double boiler; remove from stove and cool about 3 or 4 minutes. Fold into Cool Whip and pour mixture into pie crust shell. Refrigerate several hours before serving.

Mary Ann McDowell, Riverchase Council

IMPOSSIBLE PIE

4 eggs
1/2 c. oleo, melted
  (1 stick)
1 3/4 c. sugar

1/2 c. self-rising flour
2 c. milk
1 tsp. vanilla
1 (4 oz.) can coconut

Beat eggs; add melted oleo, sugar, flour, milk and vanilla. Beat well. Add coconut and mix well. Pour into 2 ungreased 9 inch pie pans; bake at 350° for 30-35 minutes. (Makes its own crust.)

Mary Norris, Birmingham Central Council

KENTUCKY CHOCOLATE PIE

1 c. sugar
1/2 c. flour
2 eggs, well beaten
1 stick melted margarine

1 c. semi-sweet chocolate bits
3/4 c. pecans
1/2 c. coconut
Deep dish pie shell
1 tsp. vanilla

Blend together and pour into unbaked pie shell. Bake 30-35 minutes at 350° or until firm.

Dot Beadlescomb, Birmingham Central Council

KENTUCKY PIE

1 c. sugar
1/2 c. plain flour
1 stick butter or
  margarine

2 eggs, beaten
1/2 c. chocolate chips
1/2 c. pecan pieces
1 Tbsp. vanilla

Melt butter and pour into dry ingredients; add eggs and vanilla and stir well. Add pecans and chips. Pour into pie crust. Bake at 325° for 45 minutes.

Sandy Horn, Riverchase Council

KILLARNY FUDGE PIE

1 stick margarine (1/2 c.)
1 c. sugar
1/2 c. plain flour, sifted

1/2 c. chopped pecans
3 Tbsp. cocoa
2 eggs, beaten
1 tsp. vanilla

Melt margarine and cocoa together; add sugar and remaining ingredients. Pour into a well buttered pie plate; bake at 325° F. for 25 to 30 minutes. Serve warm. May top with ice cream, if desired.

Beverly McCoy, Montgomery Council

LAYER PIE

1 c. flour
1 stick margarine
  (soft)
1/2 c. nuts
1 c. Cool Whip

1 (8 oz.) pkg. cream cheese
  (soft)
1 c. sugar
1 pkg. chocolate instant
  pudding

First Layer: Mix margarine with flour with fork; press down in baking dish. Make crust, then add pecans. Sprinkle on top of crust. Bake at 325° for 20 to 25 minutes. Second Layer: Mix cream cheese and sugar till smooth, then add Cool Whip. Third Layer: Use 1 package chocolate instant pudding; use directions on package. Spread on top of Second Layer. Fourth Layer: Spread rest of Cool Whip, large container. Chill 2 hours.

Geraldine Strickland, Tuscaloosa Council

LAZY PIE

1 c. flour
1 c. milk
1 c. sugar

2 tsp. baking powder
1 can pie filling
  (apple, cherry, etc.)

Mix dry ingredients; add milk and pour into a greased 1 1/2 quart round baking dish. Empty can of pie filling in center (do not stir) and dot with butter. Bake in moderate oven (350°) about 40 minutes or until golden color on top.

Ruth Gregory, Montgomery Council

LEMONADE PIE

1 can condensed milk
1 small can frozen
  lemonade

1 large carton Cool Whip
Juice of 1/2 lemon
2 graham cracker pie crusts

Mix first 4 ingredients and pour into pie shells. Refrigerate at least 1 hour before serving.

Linda Sammons, Birmingham South Council

LEMON ANGEL PIE

3 eggs, separated
1/8 tsp. cream of tartar

3/4 c. sugar
1/2 c. chopped nuts

Filling:

1/2 c. sugar
1 Tbsp. grated lemon peel
3 Tbsp. lemon juice

Reserved 3 egg yolks, beaten
1 c. whipping cream,
  whipped

Preheat oven to 275°. Beat 3 egg whites with cream of tartar until fluffy. Gradually add 3/4 cup sugar, beating until stiff peaks form. Fold in nuts; spread over bottom and sides of greased 9 inch pie pan. Bake 60-65 minutes until light brown and crisp; cool.

In saucepan combine 1/2 cup sugar, lemon peel and lemon juice and egg yolks. Cook over low heat, stirring constantly until thickened. Cool. Fold in whipped cream. Pour into meringue shell, spreading to edge. Chill overnight. May top with more whipped cream and fresh strawberries.

Jeannie Riddles, Riverchase Council

LEMON CHESS PIE

2 c. sugar
1/4 c. margarine, melted
4 eggs, slightly beaten
1/4 c. milk
1/4 c. lemon juice

Grated lemon rind to taste
1 Tbsp. flour
1 Tbsp. corn meal
2 unbaked pie shells

Combine sugar, margarine, eggs, milk, lemon juice and rind in mixer bowl. Blend flour and corn meal together; add to lemon mixture. Beat at medium speed with electric mixer until blended. Spoon filling into pie shells. Bake at 400° for 10 minutes; reduce oven temperature to 300°. Bake for 50 minutes longer.

Jan Brady, Decatur Council

LEMON ICEBOX MERINGUE PIE

1 can Eagle Brand
  condensed milk
1/2 c. fresh lemon juice
2 large eggs, separated
Grated rind of 1 lemon

1/4 tsp. lemon extract
2 Tbsp. sugar
1/4 tsp. cream of tartar
1 (8 inch) graham
  cracker pie shell

Blend milk, juice, egg yolks, grated lemon rind and lemon extract until mixture thickens. Pour into pie shell. Beat egg whites and cream of tartar until stiff. Gradually add sugar. Cover pie with meringue and bake in 350° oven until meringue is golden brown. Chill before serving.

Shirley Ward, Birmingham South Council

LEMON MERINGUE PIE

Juice of 3 lemons
1/3 c. cornstarch
3 eggs

1 1/2 c. water
1 1/2 c. sugar
3 Tbsp. butter or margarine

Cream sugar and butter. Beat egg yolks well. Dissolve cornstarch, then add all ingredients and mix well; cook over low heat (stirring) until done, then pour in cooked pie shell and add meringue. Cook at 350° until golden brown.

For meringue, add 2 tablespoons sugar for each egg white and a dash of cream of tartar; beat until stiff.

Evelyn Gullett, Birmingham East Council

EASY LEMON PIE

1 graham cracker crust
1 large Cool Whip

1 small can frozen
  lemon concentrate
1 can sweetened condensed milk

Mix Cool Whip, lemonade and milk till creamy. Pour in pie shell and refrigerate.

Martha Hatcher, Montgomery Council

QUICK LIME PIE

2 cans Eagle Brand
  condensed milk
1 c. lime juice

1 large container Cool Whip
1 graham cracker pie crust

Combine milk and juice; pour into pie crust. Spread Cool Whip on top. Cut lime in small slices, quarter and decorate top. Nice for a summer afternoon, when there isn't any time for fancy pies.

400   Linda Mitchell, Decatur Council

LOUISIANA YAM PIE

1/2 c. sugar
1/4 tsp. cinnamon
1/2 tsp. salt
3 eggs, well beaten
9 inch pie shell, unbaked

1 1/2 c. mashed yams
2 Tbsp. margarine
1 c. Pet milk
1/2 tsp lemon extract

Mix sugar, salt, cinnamon and mix with eggs. Add margarine and mashed yams. Mix well and add lemon extract and milk, mixing well at all times. Bake at 400° for 15 minutes; reduce to 375° and cook 30 minutes.

Mrs. Libby Pilling, Decatur Council

MILLIONAIRE PIE

1 can condensed milk (Dime Brand or Eagle Brand)
1/3 c. lemon juice
1 medium can crushed pineapple

1 medium can sliced peaches
1 can mandarin oranges
1 small carton Cool Whip

Mix lemon juice with milk, then fold in Cool Whip and cut up fruits. Pour into cooked pie shell (Pet pie shell). Sprinkle cut up pecans on top. Place in refrigerator.

Bertha Capps, Birmingham East Council

MILLION DOLLAR PIE

1 c. crushed pineapple, drained
1 c. chopped nuts
1 c. Eagle Brand milk

1/2 c. chopped cherries
10 oz. Cool Whip
1/4 c. lemon juice

Mix Cool Whip, lemon juice and Eagle Brand milk; add nuts, pineapple, cherries. Pour in graham cracker crust. Makes 2 pies.

Frances Crenshaw, Birmingham East Council

MUD PIE

1 chocolate wafer crust
1 1/2 pt. ice cream, softened
1/3 c. cocoa
2/3 c. sugar

1 1/3 c. whipping cream
1 tsp. vanilla
2 squares semi-sweet chocolate (for garnish)

Carefully spoon ice cream into crust; freeze until firm (about 1 1/2 hours). Over medium heat cook cocoa, sugar, 1/3 cup cream and 3 tablespoons butter until smooth and
1567-82

boiling. Remove from heat; stir in vanilla. Cool mixture completely and pour over ice cream; freeze at least 1 hour.

Serving instructions: Beat remaining cream (1 cup) with 2 tablespoons sugar and 1 teaspoon vanilla until soft peaks form. Put on pie and garnish with chocolate shavings.
Pam Gattis, Riverchase Council

PASTRY FOR SMALL PIES

2 sticks margarine
  (room temperature)
2 small (3 1/2 oz.) pkg.
  cream cheese (room
  temperature)

2 c. plain flour
1/2 tsp. salt
1/2 tsp. vanilla flavoring
1 Tbsp. sugar

Mix with fork (mixed with my hands). You may store in refrigerator until needed. Pinch off in small balls and roll out. You may use peach preserves, your own cooked apple-sauce, cherry preserves.
Earline Thornton, Tuscaloosa Council

FRESH PEACH PIE

3/4 c. sugar
3 Tbsp. flour
1/4 tsp. nutmeg
  or cinnamon

Pinch of salt
2 Tbsp. butter or margarine
6 peaches, sliced
Cool Whip or whipped cream

Slice peaches; stir in flour, nutmeg, sugar and salt. Put in 9 inch pie shell. Dot with margarine or butter. Cook at 400° for 40 to 45 minutes. Serve with Cool Whip or whipped cream on slices.
Eloise Bennett, Decatur Council

PEACH JUBILEE PIE
(9 inch pie)

1 (1 lb. 5 oz.) can
  peach pie filling
2 Tbsp. sugar
1/2 tsp. cinnamon
1/4 tsp. nutmeg

1 env. whipped topping
  (2 to 2 1/2 c.)
1/4 c. sugar
1 c. (8 oz.) sour cream

Combine pie filling, 2 tablespoons sugar, cinnamon and nutmeg; set aside. Prepare whipped topping mix as directed on carton, except omit 2 tablespoons of the milk. Beat until stiff. Add 1/4 cup sugar at low speed. Gently fold in sour cream. Spoon about 1/2 the peach mixture into a baked and
402

cooled 9 inch pie shell. Spread about 2/3 of the whipped topping mixture over the peaches, then gently spoon the remaining peaches over the topping layer. With the remaining topping mixture, swirl a spoonful on each serving; top with a cherry, if desired, and chill until firm, about 2 hours. Store in refrigerator. Very good!

Mary C. Martin, Birmingham East Council

QUICK PEACH PIE

2 c. fresh peaches
 (sweetened and
 mashed)
1/2 c. sugar
1/2 c. flour

1/2 c. milk
1 rounded tsp. baking powder
 (if plain flour is used)
2/3 stick butter

Cut butter into small casserole. Mix sugar, flour, baking powder and milk to make a running batter. Pour batter over butter. Pour peaches over batter; bake at 350° until brown. Makes about 4 servings.

Florence Toney, Life Member,
Birmingham Central Council

PEANUT BUTTER PIE

1 (3 oz.) pkg. cream cheese
1/4 c. crunchy peanut
 butter

1 c. powdered sugar
1 (8 oz.) Cool Whip
1 graham cracker crust

In large mixer bowl blend together first 3 ingredients. Then fold in Cool Whip. Pour into crust; chill.

Nancy Williams, Anniston Council

PEANUT BUTTER PIE

1 baked pie shell
1 c. powdered sugar
1/2 c. peanut butter
1/4 c. cornstarch
2/3 c. granulated sugar
1/4 tsp. salt

2 c. scalded milk
3 egg yolks, beaten
1/2 tsp. vanilla
3 egg whites for meringue
1 Tbsp. butter

Combine powdered sugar and peanut butter until the appearance of biscuit mix. Spread half of this mixture over the pie shell. Combine cornstarch, sugar, salt and scalded milk. Pour small amount over the beaten egg yolks. Mix well, then return to the milk mixture. Cook in top half of a double boiler until mixture thickens. Add butter and vanilla;

pour into pie shell and top with meringue. Sprinkle remainder of peanut butter mix over meringue; bake at 325° until brown.

Bernice Henderson, Riverchase Council

KENTUCKY PECAN PIE

1 c. white corn syrup
1 c. dark brown sugar
1/3 tsp. salt
1/3 c. melted butter or
   margarine

1 tsp. vanilla
3 whole eggs, slightly
   beaten
1 heaping c. shelled
   whole pecans

Combine syrup, sugar, salt, butter and vanilla; mix well. Add slightly beaten eggs. Pour into 9 inch unbaked pie shell; sprinkle pecans all over. Bake in preheated 350° oven for approximately 45 minutes.

Rose Mary Beasley, Tuscaloosa Council

PECAN PIE

1 c. white corn syrup
1 c. dark brown sugar
1/2 tsp. salt
1/3 c. melted butter

3 whole eggs
1 heaping c. pecans
1 Tbsp. vanilla

Mix syrup, sugar, salt, butter and vanilla. Mix in slightly beaten eggs. Pour into 9 inch unbaked pie shell; sprinkle pecans over filling. Bake in 350° oven approximately 45 minutes.

Jewel Edney, Riverchase Council

PECAN CREOLE PIE

Cream Cheese Filling:

1 lb. cream cheese
1 egg

2 tsp. vanilla flavoring

Beat until real smooth.

Syrup Filling:

2 c. sugar
2 c. light Karo syrup

2 tsp. vanilla flavoring
7 eggs
2 c. pecans, cut into pieces

Beat eggs on low speed; do not overbeat. Eggs will foam. Add other ingredients and beat on low speed until blended well. Do not overbeat; eggs will still foam. Pour

404

Cream Cheese Filling into uncooked pie shell; add Syrup Filling and sprinkle with pecans. Cook at 325° until pie kind of cracks. Do not overcook; pie will dry out. Cream Cheese Filling will rise between pecans and syrup. Makes 2 deep dish pies.

Althorn Martin, Montgomery Council

CRACKER PECAN PIE

3 egg whites
1 c. sugar
1/4 tsp. cream of tartar
1 c. pecans

10 saltine crackers
1/4 c. Hershey's chocolate syrup
8 oz. Cool Whip

Beat 3 egg whites stiff; gradually fold in 1 cup sugar and 1/4 teaspoon cream of tartar. Add 1 cup pecans and 10 saltine crackers that have been rolled into crumbs; mix well. Bake in buttered 9 inch pie pan for 30 minutes at 325°.

While crust is cooling, mix together 1/4 cup Hershey's chocolate syrup with 8 ounces of Cool Whip. When crust is thoroughly cooled, pour Cool Whip mixture on top.

Rhonda Swann, Decatur Council

QUICK AND EASY PECAN PIE

1/2 c. melted butter
1 c. pecans
1 c. light brown sugar
1/2 c. white sugar

1 heaping Tbsp. flour
2 eggs
1/2 egg shell of milk
1 tsp. vanilla
1 unbaked pie crust

Combine all ingredients; pour into unbaked pie crust. Bake at 350° for 35 minutes; lower oven temperature to 250° and bake an additional 30 minutes.

Darlene Day, Decatur Council

PEPPERMINT PIE

1 tsp. vanilla
4 egg whites
1 tsp. vinegar
1 tsp. baking powder

1/2 pt. whipping cream, whipped
5 peppermint sticks, crushed
1 c. sugar

Whip together egg whites, vinegar, vanilla and baking powder. Add sugar slowly, continuing to whip. Line a pie plate with waxed paper. Pour whipped mixture in and bake at 275° for 1 hour or until it cracks on top. Allow to cool;

spread whipped cream on top of cooled pie. Top with crushed peppermint. Refrigerate overnight.

Chris Kirkley, Birmingham East Council

PINEAPPLE PIE

1 small can Pet milk,
  chilled and beaten

1 small can crushed pineapple
20 regular size marshmallows

Drain juice. Melt marshmallows in juice; cool. Whip can of Pet milk; gradually add pineapple and marshmallow syrup. Continue beating. Pour in baked cooled graham cracker crust and chill.

Faith Kirby, Anniston Council

QUICK PINEAPPLE PIE

2 graham cracker pie
  crusts
1 (20 oz.) can crushed
  pineapple, well drained
1 (14 oz.) can Eagle
  Brand condensed milk

1 (9 oz.) carton whipped
  topping
1/3 c. lemon juice concentrate
1 c. chopped nuts
Maraschino cherry halves for
  garnish or fresh strawberries

Combine pineapple, milk, lemon juice and nuts. Fold in whipped topping. Pour into pie shells and refrigerate for at least 2 to 3 hours. Garnish with cherries or strawberries before serving.

Eugenia Kite, Montgomery Council

PINEAPPLE COCONUT PIE

4 eggs
2 c. sugar
1 stick butter, melted

1 small can crushed
  pineapple
1 can coconut

Heat oven to 300°. Mix eggs and sugar together. Melt butter and add to eggs and sugar mixture. Add crushed pineapple and coconut; stir well. Pour into 2 unbaked pie shells. Bake about 40 minutes or until brown at 350°. Remove and let cool; serve.

Mary McCulley, Birmingham East Council

EASY PISTACHIO PIE

1 pkg. pistachio pudding,
  mixed according to
  directions

8 oz. Philadelphia
  cream cheese

Beat well. Mix 1 package Dream Whip. Blend with mixer and put in graham cracker crust. Refrigerate at least 1 hour before serving.

Carol Higdon, Riverchase Council

SHOO-FLY PIE

Crumb Part:

1/4 c. shortening
1 1/2 c. flour

1 c. brown sugar

Work the above ingredients together.

Liquid Part:

3/4 tsp. baking soda
1/8 tsp. nutmeg
A little ginger, cinnamon
  and cloves

1/4 tsp. salt
3/4 c. molasses
3/4 c. hot water

Mix well together and add hot water. Into an unbaked pie shell combine the crumbs and liquid in alternate layers with crumbs on bottom and top. Bake 15 minutes at 450°, then 20 minutes at 350°.

Irmadine Gibbons, Montgomery Council

PUMPKIN PIE

1 (9 inch) unbaked
  pie shell
1 c. sugar
1/4 tsp. salt
1 tsp. cinnamon
1/2 tsp. ginger

1/4 tsp. nutmeg
1/4 tsp. cloves
1 1/2 c. canned pumpkin
3 eggs, separated
1 c. sour cream

Combine sugar, salt, spices and pumpkin. Beat egg yolks well; stir into pumpkin mixture. Add sour cream. Beat egg whites until soft peaks form; fold into pumpkin mixture. Pour into unbaked pie shell. Bake 10 minutes at 450°, then lower oven temperature to 350°. Bake 1 1/2 hours longer; cool.

M. C. Arndt, Birmingham South Council

SOUTHERN PECAN PIE

1 c. white sugar
1/2 c. light brown sugar
1 c. dark Karo syrup
1/2 stick margarine
4 eggs

1 tsp. vanilla
1/4 tsp. salt
1 1/2 c. pecans
1 (9 of 10 inch) unbaked
   pie shell

Melt sugar and syrup over low heat; cut the margarine into small slices and add to the hot syrup. In a separate bowl beat 4 eggs and add salt and vanilla. Slowly add the hot syrup, beating all the time. Lastly, add the pecans. Pour into the pie shell and bake at 350° for 45 minutes or until the pie is almost firm.

Naomi H. Tucker, Birmingham East Council

ICE CREAMY PINEAPPLE PIE

1 graham cracker crust
3 3/4 oz. vanilla instant
   pudding
1 c. milk

1 (20 oz.) can crushed
   pineapple
1 Tbsp. cornstarch
1 pt. vanilla ice cream

Mix instant pudding, milk and vanilla ice cream. Pour into graham cracker crust. Place in refrigerator to set for about 20 minutes. In saucepan mix 1/2 cup of juice from pineapple and cornstarch. Stir until it becomes clear. Add pineapple and stir for about 5 minutes. Set aside until it completely cools. Then spread over pie and chill for 1 hour before cutting.

Vanessa Simpson, Birmingham South Council

PRALINE PIE

9 inch unbaked pie shell
1/4 c. margarine, melted
1/2 c. brown sugar
2/3 c. pecans, broken

2 pkg. butterscotch
   instant pie filling
2 c. milk
1 c. Cool Whip

Mix margarine, brown sugar and pecans together and pour into unbaked pie shell; bake at 400° until pie shell is golden brown and praline mixture is bubbly. Remove and set aside to cool. Add the butterscotch pie filling to 2 cups cold milk and mix until thick. Fold in Cool Whip and pour mixture into cooled pie shell. Refrigerate for 2-3 hours. Serve with another scoop of Cool Whip and enjoy.

Brenda McDaniel, Huntsville Council

RAISIN-CREAM PIE

1 3/4 c. milk
1 c. sugar
4 eggs
1/2 c. dark raisins
1 tsp. vanilla flavor
1/8 tsp. salt
1 heaping tsp. margarine
4 heaping tsp. cornstarch
1 (7 oz.) pkg. cocoanut
  macaroons for crust

Contents makes 1 pie in 9 inch pan. Soak raisins 5 minutes in hot water, then drain. Add milk (hold back 1/4 cup), sugar, vanilla flavor in saucepan and mix well. Beat eggs briskly; add to contents. Bring to boil; add margarine, salt and raisins (hold back handful raisins for top); continue to stir. Dissolve starch in remainder of milk. Make paste, then add to contents. Boil and stir until it thickens. This makes one 9 inch pie. Use one 7 ounce package cocoanut macaroons for crust. Pour over crust. Serve warm or refrigerate 20 minutes and serve with Cool Whip topping. "Very nutritious and delicious."

Mrs. Paul D. Dawson (Myra),
Birmingham Central Council

RAISIN PIE

9 inch unbaked pie shell
4 eggs, separated
2 Tbsp. soft butter
1 1/2 c. sugar
1 c. chopped nuts
1 c. dark raisins
1 Tbsp. cider vinegar
1 tsp. vanilla extract

Preheat oven to 325°. In medium bowl slightly beat egg yolks. Beat in butter until blended; add sugar. Beat until light and fluffy. Add pecans, raisins, vinegar and vanilla; mix well. In medium bowl beat egg whites until foamy and add to mixture. Stir until well blended; pour into pie shell and bake 50 minutes. This pie bakes its own little lace doily on top and is good eating!

Elsie B. Barton, Birmingham South Council

RITZ CRACKER PIE

3 egg whites
1 c. sugar
2 tsp. baking powder
16 Ritz crackers, crushed
1 tsp. vanilla
1 can black walnuts
Whipped cream

Beat egg whites until stiff; add sugar and baking powder gradually. Then add Ritz crackers, vanilla and black walnuts and mix. Bake in 320° oven for 20 to 25 minutes; cool. Then top with whipped cream.

1567-82   Faith Kirby, Anniston Council

STACKED PIE AND ICING

5 egg yolks
1 c. (scant) sugar

1 c. oleo/butter, melted
2 Tbsp. cream

Icing:

1 c. brown sugar
2 Tbsp. oleo

1/2 c. cream
1/2 tsp. vanilla

Mix egg yolks, sugar, oleo and cream together. Spread evenly in 4 or 5 unbaked pie shells and bake.

Icing: Cook brown sugar, oleo, cream and vanilla until very soft ball and spread between each pie and on top.

Janet Logsdon, Birmingham Central Council

STRAWBERRY PIES

1 1/2 c. sugar
4 Tbsp. cornstarch
2 c. water
1/2 pkg. strawberry jello

1 tsp. lemon juice
1/2 tsp. red food coloring
2 pt. fresh strawberries
2 baked pie shells

Mix together sugar, cornstarch, jello, food coloring, lemon juice and water; cook till clear. Take away from heat. Pour over strawberries placed in cooked pie shells. Let set and get cold. Top with Dover Farms topping.

Pauline Campbell, Retired,
Birmingham Central Council

GLAZED STRAWBERRY PIE

Baked 9 inch pie shell,
  cooled
1 qt. drained hulled
  strawberries

1 (3 oz.) pkg. white cream
  cheese, softened
1 1/2 c. juice
1 c. sugar
3 Tbsp. cornstarch

Spread softened cream cheese over bottom of pastry shell. Cover with half the berries (choicest). Mash and strain rest of berries until juice is extracted; add water, if needed, to make 1 1/2 cups juice. Bring juice to boil; stir in sugar and cornstarch. Cook over low heat, stirring constantly, until boiling; boil 1 minute. Pour over berries in pie shell. Chill 2 hours. Just before serving, decorate with whipped cream.

Mrs. C. L. Wood, Decatur Council

OLD FASHIONED SUGAR CREAM PIE

2 Tbsp. flour
1 Tbsp. cornstarch
3/4 c. sugar
1/4 tsp. nutmeg
2 Tbsp. butter

1 unbaked 8 inch pie shell
1/3 c. evaporated milk
3/4 c. half & half (about)
3/4 c. whole milk

Mix flour, cornstarch, sugar, nutmeg and butter together until it forms a crumbly mixture. Pour into pie shell. Pour evaporated milk over mixture. Pour equal amounts half & half and milk into pie shell until shell is full. Bake at 425° until brown crust forms over top, about 25-35 minutes. Gently break crust with a rubber spatula; reduce oven temperature to 350° and bake 20 minutes longer or until pie begins to thicken.

Helen Aker, Mobile Council

SWEET POTATO PIE

2 c. cooked sweet potatoes
1/4 c. butter
3 eggs
1 c. milk
1 1/4 c. sugar

1/4 tsp. salt
1/4 tsp. ground nutmeg
1 tsp. vanilla extract
1/4 c. bourbon
Unbaked 9 inch pie shell

Boil sweet potatoes in jackets until tender. Peel and cream potatoes until smooth. Then combine with other ingredients and place in unbaked pie shell. Bake at 425° F. for 15 minutes, then reduce heat to 350° F. and cook an additional 1 hour and 20 minutes. Yield: One 9 inch pie.

Mrs. Mildred Clayton, Birmingham South Council

VINEGAR PIE

4 eggs
1 1/2 c. sugar
1/4 c. butter or
  margarine, melted

1 1/2 Tbsp. cider or
  white vinegar
1 tsp. vanilla
9 inch frozen pie shell,
  defrosted

Preheat oven to 350°. In large mixing bowl combine eggs, sugar, butter, vinegar and vanilla; mix well. Pour in pie shell; bake until firm, about 50 minutes. Cool on a rack. Garnish with chopped nuts or whipped cream, if desired.

R. C. Hicks, Mobile Council

WHAT-CHA-MA-CALL-IT PIE

1 c. coconut
1 c. chopped nuts
1/2 c. self-rising
   flour (sifted)
1 c. sugar

6 Tbsp. butter
2 eggs
Dash of salt
1 tsp. vanilla

Beat eggs and set aside. Mix all other ingredients, then mix in eggs. Pour in well greased and floured pie pan; bake for 30-35 minutes at 325°.

Ruth Garrett, Anniston Council

BANANA PUDDING

2 large pkg. vanilla
   instant pudding
5 c. sweet milk
8 oz. sour cream

9 oz. Cool Whip
Vanilla wafers
Bananas

Beat instant pudding with milk; add sour cream and Cool Whip until mixture is folded together well. Place layers of wafers and bananas in large bowl. Pour pudding mixture over wafers and bananas. Let stand for 2 hours before serving.

Mrs. Bill Wheeler, Birmingham South Council

OLD FASHIONED BANANA PUDDING

3/4 c. sugar
2 Tbsp. flour (heaping)
1 c. milk
2 egg yolks

1/2 stick margarine
Pinch of salt
1 tsp. vanilla
1 box vanilla wafers
6 to 8 ripe bananas

Mix together dry ingredients. Separate egg yolks from whites; reserve whites for meringue. Beat egg yolks with milk (a fork will do nicely) and combine all ingredients in top of a double boiler. Cook until thick, stirring constantly. Remove from heat; cool and add vanilla. Line a dish with vanilla wafers, alternating with a layer of sliced bananas, then more wafers. Pour sauce over all. Beat egg whites for meringue. Brown in a 350° oven. Makes 8 servings.

Betty W. Sanders, Birmingham Central Council

QUICK BANANA PUDDING

8 oz. Cool Whip
1 (14 oz.) can Eagle
  Brand sweetened
  condensed milk

1 small box instant
  banana pudding
2 c. milk
1 box vanilla wafers
6 or 7 large bananas

Layer bananas and vanilla wafers in a large casserole dish. Combine pudding, Cool Whip, Eagle Brand milk and milk. Blend with mixer for 5 minutes, then pour mixture over bananas and wafers; chill.

Jan Davidson, Riverchase Council

BREAD PUDDING

2 c. dry bread crumbs
4 c. milk, scalded
2 eggs
1/2 c. sugar

1/4 tsp. salt
1/4 tsp. nutmeg
1 tsp. vanilla
1/2 c. raisins

Soak bread crumbs in milk until soft. Beat eggs until light; add sugar, salt, nutmeg, vanilla and raisins. Mix thoroughly with bread mixture. Pour into a greased baking dish and bake for 1 hour in 350° oven until a knife inserted in center comes out clean. Serve warm or cold with any desired sauce.

Peggy Hunter, Anniston Council

BREAD PUDDING WITH RUM SAUCE

1 dry loaf French bread
1 qt. milk
1 3/4 c. white sugar
2 sticks butter

6 eggs
1 1/2 tsp. vanilla
1 medium can fruit cocktail

Break bread into large pieces. Place in large shallow dish. Combine sugar, milk, eggs, vanilla and cocktail syrup. Pour fruit over bread, then top with liquid. Break up butter over top; bake at 350° for 1 3/4 hours. Serves 10.

Rum Sauce: Combine -

2 c. water
1 stick butter

2 tsp. rum extract
1 c. sugar

Boil slowly for 45 minutes. Serve hot over pudding.

Alvis Allinder, Birmingham South Council

CARAMEL PUDDING

Dough:

1 1/2 c. dark brown sugar, packed	1 3/4 c. flour
Butter size of walnut	1 tsp. soda
1/2 c. buttermilk	1/2 tsp. salt
	1 c. nuts
	1 c. raisins

Sauce:

3 c. boiling water	Butter size of egg
1 c. dark brown sugar, packed	1 tsp. vanilla

Mix sauce in 9x12 inch (approximately) pan. Drop dough mixture in sauce by spoonfuls. Bake 30 minutes at 350°. Serve topped with whipped cream and cherry.

Joyce Davis, Birmingham Central Council

CHERRY PUDDING DELIGHT

1 deep Pyrex dish	1 c. flour
1 can cherries (pie type)	1 1/2 tsp. baking powder
1 stick butter	with plain flour
1 1/2 c. sugar	1/2 tsp. salt
	3/4 c. milk

In a separate dish add 1/2 cup sugar to cherries and dissolve sugar. Melt butter in Pyrex dish. Mix together milk, 1 cup sugar and flour to make a thin batter. Add batter to center of butter. Don't stir. Add cherries on top of batter; bake 45 minutes to 1 hour at 350°. Crust will cook to the top.

Juanita Johnson, Birmingham South Council

CHOCOLATE PUDDING

2/3 c. sugar	2 c. milk
1/4 c. sugar	2 egg yolks
6 Tbsp. flour	2 Tbsp. butter or margarine
Dash of salt	1 tsp. vanilla extract

Combine sugar, cocoa, flour and salt in saucepan; add enough milk to make a smooth paste. Add egg yolks; beat well. Stir in remaining milk and butter. Bring to a slow boil over medium heat, stirring constantly; boil for 2 to 3 minutes. Remove from heat; stir in vanilla. Pour into serving dish; chill.

414   Fay King, Huntsville Council

DATE PUDDING

1 c. granulated sugar
2 c. flour
1 lb. dates, chopped

5 tsp. baking powder
Milk to make a stiff batter
1 c. chopped nutmeats

Sauce:

2 c. brown sugar
2 c. water

3 Tbsp. butter

Combine sugar, flour and baking powder; add chopped dates and nuts. Add milk to make batter as in cake and put in a well greased cake pan (approximately 9x9 inches). Mix sauce and boil for 5 minutes. Pour boiling sauce over batter and bake 35 minutes at 300° to 325°. Serve warm with whipped cream.

Helen Aker, Mobile Council

LEMON CAKETOP PUDDING

3 Tbsp. butter
4 egg yolks
2 tsp. grated lemon rind
3 Tbsp. flour
1 c. sugar

1/3 c. lemon juice
1/4 tsp. salt
1 c. milk
4 egg whites

Cream butter and sugar until light and fluffy; add egg yolks and beat well. Add flour, lemon juice and rind and salt and mix well. Stir in milk. Beat egg whites until stiff and fold into mixture. Pour in loaf pan and set in pan of hot water. Bake in slow oven at 325° for 40 minutes.

Faith Kirby, Anniston Council

LEMON PUDDING DESSERT

1 1/2 c. flour
1 c. chopped nuts

1 stick margarine

Mix and mash flat into a 9x13 inch pan; bake 20 minutes at 350°. Cool.

1 (8 oz.) pkg. cream cheese
1 c. powdered sugar

1 1/2 c. Cool Whip
(large size)

Mix together and spread over crust.

2 small boxes lemon
  instant pudding

3 c. milk
1 tsp. vanilla

Whip till thick; pour over last layer. Spread remainder of Cool Whip on top. This is good to use chocolate pudding.

1567-82   Hazel Campbell, Birmingham South Council   415

PEACH PUDDING

3 to 4 medium peaches,
  sliced
3/4 c. sugar
2 Tbsp. shortening
1/2 c. milk

1 c. flour
Pinch of salt
1 tsp. baking powder
1 tsp. vanilla

Butter a 9 inch glass pie plate. Fill with sliced peaches. Combine remaining ingredients and pour over peaches. Bake at 350° for 30 minutes.

Diane Dawkins, Birmingham South Council

PERSIMMON PUDDING

2 c. persimmon pulp
1 1/2 c. sugar
1/2 c. buttermilk
1/2 c. flour

1/2 tsp. cinnamon
1/4 tsp. nutmeg
Pinch of salt
2 eggs, slightly beaten

To get pulp, boil persimmons until tender; rub through sifter. Mix all ingredients. Bake at 350° approximately 45 minutes in ungreased loaf pan.

F. E. Hodges, Huntsville Council

PINEAPPLE BREAD PUDDING

1/4 c. butter or
  margarine, softened
1 (4 serving pkg.) instant
  vanilla pudding mix
1 tsp. ground cinnamon
3 eggs
3 c. milk

1 (8 oz.) can crushed
  pineapple in its own juice
2/3 c. flaked coconut
1/2 c. raisins
1 tsp. vanilla
8 slices day-old white bread,
  cut in 1/2 inch cubes

In a large mixer bowl cream together butter or margarine, vanilla pudding mix and cinnamon till fluffy. Add eggs, one at a time, beating well after each addition. In another bowl combine milk, undrained pineapple, coconut, raisins and vanilla. By hand blend milk mixture into creamed mixture (mixture will look curdled). Fold in bread cubes. Pour into an ungreased 2 quart casserole or 8x8x2 inch baking dish. Place casserole or baking dish in larger shallow pan on oven rack. Pour hot water into larger pan to a depth of 1 inch. Bake in 325° oven 1 1/4 hours for casserole (1 hour for baking dish) or till knife inserted off-center comes out clean. Serves 8.

Jamima Edney, Birmingham South Council

PINEAPPLE PUDDING

1 c. sugar
1 egg
1 stick oleo

1 large can crushed pineapple
1 c. pecans, chopped
1 (9 oz.) Cool Whip
1 (12 oz.) box vanilla wafers

Cream sugar, egg and oleo; add pineapple and nuts and Cool Whip. Starting with wafers, layer in 9x13 inch pan. Top with Cool Whip if desired. Refrigerate overnight.
Opal Kemp, Mobile Council

PUDDING DELIGHT

1 large box Jell-O
  instant pudding
  (vanilla)

1 large can sliced peaches
  (other fruits may be used)
1 c. shredded coconut
Vanilla wafers

Prepare vanilla pudding as directed on box; add all ingredients except the vanilla wafers. Mix well and place in individual dessert bowls or small glasses that have been lined with vanilla wafers. This may be garnished with a sliced peach or a strawberry with shredded coconut also.
Jean R. Jordan, Montgomery Council

RICE PUDDING

1 1/2 c. cooked rice
3/4 c. raisins
1/2 c. sugar
2 eggs, beaten
1/4 tsp. vanilla extract

1/2 tsp. ground cinnamon
Dash of ground nutmeg
2 c. milk, scalded
2 Tbsp. melted butter

Combine first 7 ingredients; add scalded milk and melted butter; mix well. Pour into 1 1/2 quart casserole. Bake at 350° F. about 1 hour or until mixture is firm. Yield: 6 servings.
Mrs. Mildred Clayton, Birmingham South Council

GRATED SWEET POTATO PUDDING

4 c. grated sweet
  potatoes (raw)
1 c. Georgia cane syrup
1/2 c. sugar
1 c. milk
1/2 c. butter

3 eggs
1/2 c. chopped nutmeats
1 c. raisins
1/2 tsp. cloves
1 tsp. allspice
1 tsp. cinnamon

Cream butter and sugar; add eggs and beat well. Add syrup and mix. Add other ingredients and mix well. Pour into large greased pan or bowl. Bake at 400°. Stir occasionally.

Mattie Singleton, Retired,
Birmingham Central Council

SWEET POTATO PUDDING

4 c. grated sweet potatoes	1/2 tsp. ground nutmeg
Grated rind of 1 lemon	1/2 tsp. ground cloves
Grated rind of 1/2 orange	1/2 c. molasses
2 eggs, beaten	2/3 c. milk
1/2 c. brown sugar	1/3 c. bourbon
1/2 tsp. ground cinnamon	1/2 c. melted butter

Mix sweet potatoes, lemon and orange peel. Beat eggs and sugar and stir into potato mixture, then add the spices, molasses, milk, bourbon and butter. Mix thoroughly and put in buttered 2 quart casserole. Bake at 325° F. for 1 hour. Yield: 8 servings.

Mrs. Mildred Clayton, Birmingham South Council

SUGAR PLUM PUDDING

2 c. flour	3/4 c. butter
1 1/2 c. sugar	1 c. buttermilk
1 tsp. cinnamon	1 1/4 tsp. soda (add
1 tsp. nutmeg	to buttermilk)
1 c. chopped prunes,	2 eggs, beaten
cooked	

Glaze:

3/4 c. sugar	1/2 c. butter
1/2 c. buttermilk	1 tsp. vanilla

Sift dry ingredients together. Cream sugar and butter; add eggs. Add dry ingredients alternately with buttermilk; fold in prunes. Bake at 325° until done, approximately 25 minutes. Melt butter in pan; add sugar and buttermilk; cook for 1 minute (boil). Remove and add vanilla. Pour over hot cake.

Elaine Pass, Birmingham West Council

418

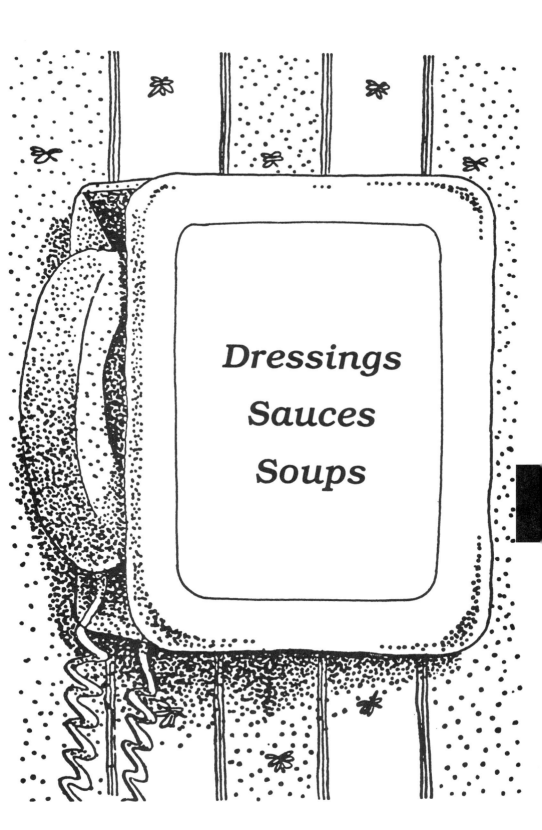

Dressings

Sauces

Soups

NO-SALT SEASONING

Salt is an acquired taste and can be drastically reduced in the diet by learning to use herbs and spices instead. When using fresh herbs, use three times the amount of dry herbs. Begin with small amounts to determine your favorite tastes. A dash of fresh lemon or lime juice can also wake up your taste buds.

Herb Blends to Replace Salt

Combine all ingredients in small airtight container. Add several grains of rice to prevent caking.

No-Salt Surprise Seasoning — 2 teaspoons garlic powder and 1 teaspoon each of dried basil, oregano and dehydrated lemon juice.

Pungent Salt Substitute — 3 teaspoons dried basil, 2 teaspoons each of summer savory, celery seed, cumin seed, sage and marjoram, and 1 teaspoon lemon thyme; crush with mortar and pestle.

Spicy No-Salt Seasoning — 1 teaspoon each cloves, pepper and coriander, 2 teaspoons paprika and 1 tablespoon dried rosemary; crush with mortar and pestle.

The Right Herb Complements

Beef	bay leaf, chives, cloves, cumin, garlic, hot pepper, marjoram, rosemary, savory
Pork	coriander, cumin, garlic, ginger, hot pepper, savory, thyme
Poultry	garlic, oregano, rosemary, savory, sage
Cheese	basil, chives, curry, dill, garlic, marjoram, oregano, parsley, sage, thyme
Fish	chives, coriander, dill, garlic, tarragon, thyme
Fruit	cinnamon, coriander, cloves, ginger, mint
Bread	caraway, marjoram, oregano, poppy seed, rosemary, thyme
Salads	basil, chives, tarragon, parsley, sorrel
Vegetables	basil, chives, dill, tarragon, marjoram, mint, parsley, pepper

Basic Herb Butter

Blend 1 stick unsalted butter, 1 to 3 tablespoons dried herbs or twice that amount of minced fresh herbs of choice, 1/2 teaspoon lemon juice and white pepper to taste. Let stand for 1 hour or longer before using.

Basic Herb Vinegar

Heat vinegar of choice in saucepan; do not boil. Pour into bottle; add 1 or more herbs of choice and seal bottle. Let stand for 2 weeks before using.

PAT COCHRAN'S HOMEMADE BUTTER

1 lb. margarine (solid)	1 c. buttermilk
1/2 c. Crisco oil	1/2 tsp. salt

After margarine has obtained room temperature, place in large pan; beat until creamy. Add oil, buttermilk and salt; beat until fluffy. Place in plastic containers and store in refrigerator.

Pat Cochran, Birmingham South Council

HONEY BUTTER

1/4 lb. each butter, margarine	1/4 c. each honey, half & half

Mix butter and margarine together in electric mixer at medium speed, until well blended. Beat in honey, a tablespoon at a time, until blended thoroughly. Beat in half & half, a tablespoon at a time, until smooth and fluffy. Makes about 1 1/2 cups.

Faith Kirby, Anniston Council

WILLA'S BUTTERY PEANUT BUTTER

2 c. granulated sugar	1 c. butter
1 c. light corn syrup	2 c. peanuts
1/2 c. water	1 tsp. soda

Combine sugar, corn syrup and water in 3 quart saucepan; cook and stir till sugar dissolves. When syrup boils, blend in butter. Stir frequently after mixture reaches the syrup stage (230°). Add nuts when temperature reaches soft crack stage (280°) and stir constantly till temperature reaches the hard crack stage (305°). Remove from heat. Quickly stir in soda, mixing thoroughly. Pour onto 2 cookie sheets or two 15 1/2 x 10 1/2 x 1 inch pans. As candy cools, stretch it out thin by lifting and pulling from edges with 2 forks. Loosen from pans as soon as possible; turn candy over. Break in pieces.

Jane Patterson, Riverchase Council

BAKED POTATO TOPPING

2 Tbsp. soft butter
1/2 c. sharp Cheddar
  cheese, grated
4 Tbsp. sour cream

1 1/2 tsp. chopped chives
  or parsley or green onions
1/8 tsp. salt

Cream all ingredients together and chill before serving.

Carolyn G. Blackburn,
Birmingham Central Council

BATTER FOR FRIED CHICKEN

2 eggs
Juice of 2 lemons
1 c. flour
2 c. milk

1/4 c. syrup
Salt
Pepper

Mix all ingredients. Salt chicken and dip into batter, then flour and fry.

Phillip McMillan, Montgomery Council

FISH BATTER

1 box saltine crackers
1 c. self-rising flour

1 tsp. all season salt

Crumble a few saltine crackers at a time in a blender until very fine. Add flour and all-season salt. Mix well. Soak fish in buttermilk, then roll in batter. Remaining batter can be saved and reused.

Helayne Ledbetter, Anniston Council

FISH FILET, SHRIMP OR OYSTER BATTER

1 egg yolk, beaten with
  fork
2 c. ice water
1 2/3 c. self-rising flour

1/8 tsp. baking soda
  (yes, soda)
Garlic or onion powder and
  more salt, if desired

Roll fish, shrimp or oysters in plain corn meal, coating well. Dip quickly into batter. Deep fry approximately 1 minute.

Bobbie Hayes, Mobile Council

420

SEASONED SALT FOR MEAT AND POULTRY

6 boxes salt
1/2 c. pepper
1/4 c. white pepper

1 Tbsp. cayenne pepper
1/4 c. ground ginger
1 c. chopped garlic

Combine all ingredients in large mixing bowl; let stand, uncovered, for at least 6 hours or overnight. Store in air-tight containers.

Fay King, Huntsville Council

MARINADE FOR ROAST BEEF

1/2 c. lemon juice
1/2 c. soy sauce
1/2 c. salad oil

1 clove garlic
1 bay leaf
Salt and pepper

Au Jus Sauce:

3 Tbsp. finely chopped
   scallions
2 Tbsp. butter

Pan drippings
1/2 c. or more red or
   white wine

Mix all ingredients and pour over a 5 pound roast, rolled rump or sirloin tip. Marinate in the refrigerator for 24 hours, turning the meat occasionally. Bake at 350° for about 1 1/2 hours for rare roast beef.

Sauce: Saute the onion in the butter until soft. Add the pan drippings and wine; cook until sauce reduces about half. Salt and pepper to taste. Pour over the sliced roast beef or serve in a bowl.

Flo Thompson, Montgomery Council

MARINADE FOR STEAK

1 1/6 c. pineapple juice
1/6 c. vinegar
1/2 c. sherry (optional)

1/3 c. soy sauce
1/4 c. sugar
3/4 Tbsp. salt or Accent
1/2 tsp. garlic powder

Blend well. Marinate steak for 2 or 3 hours. Can be refrigerated and re-used.

Linda Mason, Birmingham Central Council

KABOB MARINADE AND BASTING SAUCE

1/2 c. salad oil
1/2 c. soy sauce
2 Tbsp. vinegar
2 small onions, chopped

1 clove garlic, minced
3 Tbsp. chopped candied
  ginger
1/2 tsp. pepper
1/2 tsp. dry mustard

Mix together all ingredients. Marinate meat several hours or overnight in mixture. Brush meat with remaining marinade during cooking time.

O. W. Norton, Birmingham South Council

GIBLET GRAVY

Giblets from 1 turkey
  or chicken
2 c. chicken broth
  medium onion, chopped
1 c. chopped celery

1/2 tsp. poultry seasoning
2 Tbsp. flour
Salt and pepper to taste
2 hard cooked eggs, sliced

Cook giblets and neck in chicken broth until tender. Chop giblets into broth; discard neck. Add onion, celery, poultry seasoning; cook until vegetables are tender. Add salt and pepper to taste and egg slices. Yield: About 2 cups.

Note: Dissolve 2 tablespoons flour in a small amount of water before stirring into broth.

Peggy Y. Hughes, Riverchase Council

MILK GRAVY

1 1/2 c. milk
2 Tbsp. flour (rounding
  full)
Salt and pepper to taste

5 or 6 Tbsp. drippings from
  frying meat (chicken,
  sausage, bacon, pork
  chops, etc.)

Put flour in drippings and slightly brown (do not over-heat). Add salt and pepper; pour in milk and cook till thick. If gravy is too thick, add slowly a little more milk or a small amount of water to thin.

Marcia Freeman, Birmingham East Council

DRESSING

2 c. diced celery
1/2 c. diced bell pepper
2 c. white and green onions
6 boiled eggs

1 qt. diced, boiled chicken
1 can cream of celery soup
Corn bread
1 can cream of chicken soup
4 eggs

Boil chicken with pepper, onion and celery salt and pepper and water until comes off bone. Remove chicken; bone and dice (1 chicken should be enough). Return chicken to broth; add corn bread, soups and diced, boiled eggs. Mix. Add water or chicken broth until soupy. Beat 4 eggs and mix into mixture. Bake in 2 pans at 350° for 1 hour, then 500° for 15 minutes to brown top.

Shirley Downey, Mobile Council

EASY DRESSING

1/2 lb. ground meat
1 can cream of mushroom
  soup
1 can onion soup

1 c. raw rice
1/2 c. chopped celery
1 c. chopped bell pepper
3 onions

Salt and pepper to taste. Mix all ingredients thoroughly and place in a well greased casserole dish with cover. Bake at 350° for 1 1/2 hours. Do not uncover or stir. Be sure casserole is large enough for some expansion of ingredients.

Catherine F. Pittman, Mobile Council

CORN BREAD DRESSING

2 c. chopped onions
3 c. chopped celery
Butter or margarine
6 c. corn bread, crumbled
3 c. stale or toasted white
  bread, crumbled
2 Tbsp. poultry seasoning

1 tsp. celery seed
1 tsp. sage
1 tsp. salt
3 eggs, well beaten
2-3 c. broth (enough
  to moisten)

Saute onion in butter until tender, but not brown. Repeat for celery. Heat stock. Combine all other ingredients, then add stock and mix well. Place in greased casserole dishes and bake at 350° for 40 minutes or until nicely browned.

Ann Terry

CORN BREAD DRESSING

6 c. corn bread crumbs
1 small chopped onion
1 can cream of chicken soup
1 can water
1 tsp. + 1 Tbsp. sage
1/2 stick melted oleo
6 Tbsp. flour

Mix corn bread crumbs and onion. Brown flour and oleo; add chicken soup, sage and water. Pour over corn bread mixture. Bake 1 hour at 300°.

Billie Harrison, Decatur Council

HOT PEPPER DRESSING

1 pone corn bread,
  crumbled
4 slices light bread,
  broken into pieces
Pepper
1 large can deviled ham
Hot peppers (as desired, about 8)
1 large onion, chopped
1 heaping tsp. salt
5 strips bacon, chopped

Fry chopped bacon over low heat. When it starts browning, add onion and pepper. Saute; add corn bread and light bread crumbs. Add water, stirring all the time. Add deviled ham, salt and pepper. Add water as needed during cooking to keep moist.

Carol Arnold, Huntsville Council

CORN BREAD OYSTER DRESSING

2 c. Jim Dandy self-rising
  meal
1 c. buttermilk
4 stalks celery, chopped
2 large onions, chopped
1 can cream of chicken soup
1 large fryer
1 pt. oysters
1/4 c. oil
2 eggs

Boil chicken until it slips off bone; cool and remove from bone. Mix corn meal, buttermilk, chopped celery, chopped onions, eggs and oil. Cook at 450° until brown. Use chicken broth and cream of chicken soup to mix with cooked corn bread. Remove chicken from bone and mix with all ingredients and bake at 400° for about 1 hour. Add broth as needed to keep from being dry. Add oysters about 1/2 hour before done.

Harold Busby, Mobile Council

424

RICE DRESSING

1/2 c. cooking oil
1 c. rice, uncooked
1 c. chopped celery
1 c. chopped bell pepper
Salt and pepper to taste

1 c. chopped onion
1 can Niblets Green Giant
    corn
2 cubes beef bouillon
    and 2 c. water

Brown rice in oil; add other ingredients. Cook at low heat on top of stove for about 30 minutes, stirring occasionally.

A. M. Robertson, Huntsville Council

NANCY'S OYSTER DRESSING

1 pt. fresh oysters
1 pkg. Pepperidge Farm
    herb stuffing mix
    (not corn bread type)

1 egg
1 small onion
1 stalk celery
1 stick oleo
1 1/2 c. water (to taste)

Saute onion and celery in oleo until tender. Combine with stuffing mix; add water and egg and mix well. Add oysters and liquid; gently fold oysters in. Sprinkle lightly with pepper. Bake at 400° until top is browned and bubbly. (Don't remove liquid which may come to top.) Bake about 20 minutes.

Betty Floyd Parker, Montgomery Council

NEW TURKEY DRESSING

4 c. crushed dry bread
1/2 c. sage
1/4 c. onions
1/2 c. celery

1/2 c. uncooked popcorn
1 tsp. salt
5 c. broth

Mix well; stuff turkey. Cook 5 hours at 300° or until popcorn blows the ass off the turkey.

BACON VINEGAR DRESSING

4 slices bacon, cooked
    and quartered
1 small onion, chopped
1 Tbsp. cornstarch
1/4 c. brown sugar

Pepper
1/4 tsp. celery seed
2/3 c. water
1/4 c. cider vinegar

Mix all ingredients (except bacon). Place ingredients

1567-82

in the microwave oven on high power for 3 1/2 minutes. **Stir** twice while cooking. Add bacon. This is good over lettuce or fresh spinach. Serve warm.

Linda L. Unger, Riverchase Council

BLEU CHEESE DRESSING

2 c. sour cream
4 green onions,
  chopped fine
4 Tbsp. mayonnaise

4 Tbsp. lemon juice
1 c. crumbled Bleu cheese
Salt and pepper to taste

Combine ingredients, blending well. Refrigerate for several hours. Makes approximately 10 servings.

Voncile Wolf, Mobile Council

DIET DRESSING

1/2 c. salad oil
1/4 c. lemon juice
1/4 c. water
1/2 tsp. salt

1/4 c. ketchup
1 tsp. dry mustard
1/4 tsp. paprika
1/2 tsp. Worcestershire sauce

Combine salad oil, lemon juice, water, salt, ketchup, mustard, paprika and Worcestershire sauce. Beat with rotary beater until well mixed. Chill in tightly covered jar. Mix well before serving. Makes 1 1/4 cups.

Frances Harris, Birmingham South Council

HONEY FRUIT SALAD DRESSING

1/3 c. salad oil
3 tsp. lemon juice

1/2 tsp. salt
1/3 c. liquid honey

Combine salad oil, lemon juice and salt; chill in tightly covered jar. Mix well before serving. Makes 3/4 cup.

Frances Harris, Birmingham South Council

DRESSING FOR GREEN SALAD

1 c. mayonnaise
1/2 c. Wesson oil
1/4 c. chili sauce
1/4 c. catsup
1 tsp. Worcestershire sauce

1 tsp. prepared mustard
1 tsp. black pepper
1 dash of Tabasco sauce
Garlic salt to taste
Juice of 1 onion

Add 2 tablespoons of water last and stir well. This makes about 1 1/2 pints and will keep well if refrigerated.

Eleanor Cochran, Birmingham Central Council

$200 SALAD DRESSING

2 tsp. salt
2 tsp. celery salt
2 tsp. paprika
3 tsp. dry mustard

2 c. salad oil
1/2 c. sugar
1/2 c. vinegar
2 tsp. grated onion

Put all in double boiler and heat to 98° F. Remove from heat and beat while cooling until as thick as soft mustard. Makes 3/4 quart. Shake well when serving. (Do not put on ice.)

Ann Eberhart, Anniston Council

CALIFORNIA WALDORF DRESSING

1 Tbsp. granulated sugar
2 Tbsp. cider or wine vinegar
1 Tbsp. grated onion

1 tsp. salt
1/2 tsp. celery seed
1 c. sour cream

Combine sugar, onion, salt and vinegar. Let stand 15 or 20 minutes. Fold in well-chilled sour cream and celery seed. Makes 1 1/2 cups dressing.

Mary Edna Fife, Montgomery Council

SUNSHINE FRUIT DRESSING

1/3 c. sour cream
1/3 c. mayonnaise
2 bananas, peeled, mashed

1 Tbsp. honey
2 Tbsp. finely chopped toasted almonds

Combine sour cream with mayonnaise, mashed bananas, honey and nuts. Serve over fresh fruit salad.

Betty Parker, Montgomery Council

FRUIT SALAD DRESSING

1/2 c. sugar
4 tsp. cornstarch
1/4 tsp. salt
1 c. unsweetened pineapple juice

3/4 c. orange juice
1 Tbsp. lemon juice
2 eggs, beaten
2 (3 oz.) pkg. cream cheese

Combine dry ingredients in pan; blend in juices. Cook, stirring constantly, until clear. Remove from heat and slowly stir in eggs; return to low heat and cook 3 to 5 minutes until slightly thickened. Cool 5 minutes; beat in cream cheese. Makes a great topping for fresh fruit salad. Can also be frozen.

1567-82   Carol Johnston, Montgomery Council   427

HAM DRESSING

Corn Bread:

1 beaten egg	1/2 tsp. salt
Approx. 3/4 c. buttermilk	1/2 tsp. baking soda
	1 c. white corn meal

You will need:

1 recipe of Corn Bread	3/4 c. celery, chopped
Approx. 2 c. ham broth	3 or 4 eggs
6 slices of dry regular	2 tsp. rubbed sage
loaf bread	1/2 tsp. salt
1 medium sized onion,	1/2 tsp. pepper
chopped	

Beat egg slightly; add about half of the milk and mix. Sift meal with salt and soda into the egg and milk mixture; mix well. Add the rest of the milk. Bake in 450° oven in a small greased hot skillet or in a greased hot muffin pan (will make 6 corn bread muffins). Bake until bread is desired brownness on top. Cool for handling.

For ham broth, use drippings from a baked ham or boil trimmings from hams obtained from your supermarket meat department. (Boil in a small quantity of water to retain as much of the ham taste as possible.) Even by using the ham drippings, you may need some of the boiled trimmings broth to have the 2 cups needed. Boil the onion and celery in the 2 cups of broth until they're tender. While this is cooling slightly, crumble the 2 kinds of bread in a large mixing bowl. Beat the eggs well and add to the breads. Add sage, salt and pepper, then pour the broth with the onions and celery into the mixture. Mix well and bake at 450° in an ungreased 8x8 inch pan until top is a medium brown. (To have a dressing that isn't too dry, nor too soft when serving, use your own judgment when adding the broth. The mixture shouldn't absorb all of the broth when you've stirred it up just prior to pouring it into the pan, but only a small amount of the broth should be evident.) Good luck!

Jimmie Clark (Mrs. Charles R.),
Decatur Council

RUTH SPITZER'S ITALIAN DRESSING

1 c. Crisco oil	1/2 tsp. dry mustard
1/3 c. vinegar	1/2 tsp. oregano
2 Tbsp. lemon juice	1/4 tsp. basil
1 tsp. garlic salt	Freshly ground black pepper
1 tsp. sugar	

428

Combine all ingredients in a screw top jar; cover tightly and shake vigorously to blend well. Store covered in refrigerator. Shake well before using.

Patsy S. Dean, Mobile Council

KUM-BACK SALAD DRESSING

1 tsp. mustard
2 cloves garlic, minced
Dash of Tabasco sauce
1 lemon, juiced
1 pt. mayonnaise

1 Tbsp. Worcestershire sauce
Dash of paprika
1 bottle chili sauce
1 tsp. black pepper
1/4 onion, grated

Mix all ingredients together with electric mixer and chill. Serve over green tossed salad.

Susan Tucker, Huntsville Council

LEMON-SOUR CREAM DRESSING

1/4 c. dairy sour cream
1/4 c. mayonnaise

2 tsp. lemon juice
1/4 tsp. salt

Mix all ingredients. Goes well on cooked chicken or green salads.

Alice White, Mobile Council

OLIVE OIL SALAD DRESSING

1 (2 oz.) jar imported
  olive oil
3 oz. white vinegar

1/4 tsp. garlic salt
1/4 tsp. onion salt
1 head chopped lettuce

Combine all ingredients except lettuce and shake vigorously. Serve over chopped lettuce.

G. O. Cox, Jr., Tuscaloosa Council

POPPY SEED DRESSING

2/3 c. cider vinegar
1 1/2 c. sugar
2 tsp. dry mustard
2 tsp. salt

3 Tbsp. onion juice
2 c. Wesson oil
3 Tbsp. poppy seed

Mix sugar, mustard, salt and vinegar until sugar is well dissolved. Stir in onion juice. Continue mixing. Add oil slowly, beating constantly, until thick. Stir in poppy seeds. Beat for 2 minutes longer; refrigerate. This tends to separate if too cold or kept over a few days.

1567-82   Betty Parker, Montgomery Council   429

ROQUEFORT DRESSING

2 oz. Roquefort cheese
4 oz. Blue cheese
1/2 pt. sour cream
1 pt. mayonnaise
3 cloves garlic, grated
1 small onion, grated

1 whole hard cooked egg,
  plus 1 hard cooked egg
  yolk, grated
Juice of 1 lemon
Dash of salt, pepper, sugar,
  ketchup and Worcestershire

Cream or break up cheese as you prefer. Combine all ingredients, blending well. Store in refrigerator in a closed fruit jar and use as needed. Makes 1 quart.

Mrs. O. O. Prickett, Selma Council

ROQUEFORT DRESSING

1 pt. sour cream
2 Tbsp. vinegar
2 Tbsp. mayonnaise
1/2 tsp. salt

1/2 tsp. garlic salt
1/2 tsp. celery salt
1/2 tsp. black pepper
6 oz. Roquefort or Blue cheese

Mix all ingredients except cheese. Add chunks of cheese. Dressing will keep for weeks.

Alexine S. Becker, Montgomery Council

SALAD DRESSING

1 grated onion
1 Tbsp. celery seed
1/2 c. catsup
1 tsp. salt

Dash of red pepper
1/2 c. sugar
1/2 c. vinegar
1 tsp. Worcestershire
1 c. oil

Mix well and serve.

Opal Kemp, Mobile Council

HESTER'S SALAD DRESSING

1 c. mayonnaise
1/4 c. French dressing

1/4 c. grated Bleu cheese
4 or 5 cloves garlic, pressed

Combine all ingredients thoroughly and chill for several hours before serving. Delicious!

Johnnie P. Walker, Birmingham Central Council

SHRIMP DRESSING

2 medium bell peppers
2 onions
6 stalks celery

2 Tbsp. parsley
5 lb. shrimp
2 1/2 c. uncooked rice

Cook rice about half done; rinse and set aside. Saute chopped bell peppers, onions, celery and parsley in 2 sticks butter; set aside. Cook shrimp in salted and peppered water until done (peel shrimp before cooking); save water. If shrimp are large, cut into smaller pieces. Mix rice, sauteed vegetables and shrimp. Add water left over from cooked shrimp and bake for about 1 hour at 400°, covered. (Should be soupy.) Uncover; dot with butter and brown on top, if desired.

Linda Moss, Huntsville Council

SLAW DRESSING

2 c. sugar
2 c. vinegar
1 c. salad oil

2 tsp. salt
5 Tbsp. dehydrated green
   bell peppers
2 Tbsp. dehydrated onions

Mix all ingredients together. Let marinate 12 hours before using. Unused portion can be stored indefinitely in refrigerator. Makes 1 quart.

O. W. Norton, Birmingham South Council

DRESSING FOR COLD SLAW

1/2 c. vegetable oil
1/3 c. catsup
1/4 c. vinegar
1/3 c. sugar
1 Tbsp. salt

1 medium onion, chopped
   fine, onion flakes or
   powder to equal 1
   medium onion
1 Tbsp. Worcestershire sauce

Blend well; refrigerate 4 hours. Shred fresh chilled cabbage. Pour dressing over individual servings to taste.

Thelma Corbin, Birmingham East Council

SPINACH SALAD DRESSING

1 c. oil
5 Tbsp. red vinegar
1 1/2 tsp. salt
1/2 tsp. dry mustard

2 Tbsp. sugar
Coarsely ground black pepper
2 tsp. parsley
1/4 tsp. garlic powder

1567-82

Mix dressing and let set overnight before tossing onto salad. Toss just before serving. Top spinach greens with any of the following: Bacon bits, crumbled boiled eggs, fresh sliced mushrooms.

Mary C. Martin, Birmingham East Council

CREAMY SWEET 'N SOUR DRESSING

1/2 c. mayonnaise
2 Tbsp. white vinegar

4 tsp. sugar
1/4 tsp. garlic salt

In small mixing bowl stir all ingredients together. Makes enough for 6 servings when poured lightly over salads, like ham or chicken salad.

Wanda Lynch, Montgomery Council

SQUASH DRESSING

4 medium squash
1 large onion
1/2 stick butter
 or oleo

1/2 bag Pepperidge
 stuffing mix
1/2 (8 oz.) can Campbell's
 cheese soup
Salt and pepper to taste

Cook squash and onion until tender. To 1/2 cup of liquid from squash add melted butter, salt and pepper to taste in an ovenproof dish. Add stuffing mix and top with cheese soup; bake 15 minutes at 350°.

Lillian Weaver, Huntsville Council

THOUSAND ISLAND DRESSING

1/8 c. pimiento,
 chopped fine
1/4 c. bell pepper,
 chopped fine
2 Tbsp. mixed pickles,
 chopped fine

1/4 c. celery, chopped fine
1 Tbsp. olives, chopped fine
1 c. mayonnaise
1/2 c. catsup
1/4 c. chili sauce
1 tsp. sugar

Mix all ingredients well and store in covered jar.

Sammie M. Jackson, Huntsville Council

THOUSAND ISLAND DRESSING

2 Tbsp. catsup
2 Tbsp. chili sauce
1 Tbsp. mustard
2 Tbsp. grated onion,
   or juice

2 Tbsp. pimento, mashed
2 hard boiled eggs
   (mash while warm)
1/2 c. mayonnaise

Mix first 3 ingredients; add remaining ingredients. Stir well and refrigerate.

Bobbie Bowles, Montgomery Council

MURPHIE'S ALMOND CHEESE SAUCE

1 (11 oz.) can condensed
   Cheddar cheese soup
1/4 c. milk

1/4 c. slivered almonds
1/4 tsp. curry powder

Stir soup until smooth. Gradually blend in milk. Add remaining ingredients. Heat; stir often. Makes 1 1/2 cups sauce. Serve over cooked broccoli or cauliflower.

Anne Spragins, Birmingham East Council

MRS. SMITH'S GLORIFIED APPLESAUCE

1 c. cottage cheese
1/2 c. applesauce
3 Tbsp. sour cream
1 tsp. grated lemon rind

The juice of 1 lemon
3 Tbsp. sugar
Pulverized nutmeg

Combine the cottage cheese, applesauce, sour cream, rind, lemon juice and sugar in a bowl. Mix thoroughly. Sprinkle with nutmeg and chill for 1/2 hour before serving.

Alma Pitt, Decatur Council

BLUE CHEESE BASTING SAUCE

1 c. salad oil
1/3 c. lemon juice
1/3 c. Blue cheese
1/4 tsp. paprika

1 Tbsp. Worcestershire
   sauce (optional)
1 tsp. salt
1/4 tsp. pepper

Combine all ingredients in blender; blend thoroughly. Let stand several hours before using to allow flavors to blend. Especially good with chicken.

Anne Spragins, Birmingham East Council

1567-82

BUTTERSCOTCH SAUCE

1/3 c. butter (5 Tbsp.)   2 Tbsp. white Karo
1 c. brown sugar, packed   1/3 c. cream

Melt butter over low heat; add sugar, Karo and cream. Bring to boil. Serve over ice cream when cool.
Margie Judge, Mobile Council

MA PINSON'S CATSUP

1 gal. tomatoes, chopped   1 c. vinegar
1 large and 1 small   3 or 4 small hot peppers
  onion, chopped   1 tsp. salt
3 1/2 c. sugar

Mix all the ingredients; bring to a boil, reduce heat and cook until mixture is not quite as thick as applesauce. Pour into jars while mixture is still hot and seal. Yield: About 6 pints. This is delicious with meats or vegetables.
Hubert Pinson, Decatur Council

GREEN TOMATO CATSUP

3 qt. green tomatoes,   1 pt. chopped onions
  chopped fine   2 green hot peppers
1/2 c. salt   1/2 tsp. each cloves,
1 pt. vinegar   spice and horseradish
1 pt. sugar

Combine tomatoes and salt; let drip overnight. Next morning add vinegar, sugar, onions, peppers and spices. Do not cook or seal. Put in a jar. Make this in the fall and it will keep all winter.
Mary C. Martin, Birmingham East Council

CHEESE SAUCE

1/4 c. margarine   Dash of pepper
2 Tbsp. plain flour   1/4 c. milk
1/4 tsp. salt   1/2 c. Cheddar cheese, grated

Melt margarine in saucepan over medium heat; add flour, salt and pepper, stirring constantly to make a paste. Gradually add milk, stirring until smooth. Add grated cheese and stir until melted. Remove from heat. Serve over hot asparagus. Serves 4.
Fay Wann, Huntsville Council

"POT'S" CHILI SAUCE

1 gal. tomatoes
2 large onions
1 bell pepper
2 c. sugar
1 stalk celery

1/2 tsp. allspice
1 pinch of cloves
2 pinches of cinnamon
1 1/2 c. vinegar

Cook together tomatoes, onions, pepper and celery, until they cook down (about 2 hours). Add sugar; cook until contents thicken. Add spices and vinegar; cook 2 hours until thick.

"Pot" Harris, Tuscaloosa Council

CHILI SAUCE

5 c. sugar
6 c. vinegar
3 or 4 large onions
5 to 7 hot peppers

1 tsp. salt
1 tsp. cinnamon
1 tsp. cloves
1/2 bushel tomatoes

Peel and quarter tomatoes (drain as much juice as you can from tomatoes). Chop onions and peppers, then mix all ingredients and cook until mixture thickens. This will take approximately 3 hours before mixture is thick. (This recipe is very good to eat with dried beans or to bake with roast or pork chops.)

Mary Thompson, Tri-Cities Council

MISS KITTY'S CHILI SAUCE

50 ripe tomatoes
25 onions
12 green peppers
1 bunch celery, finely
    chopped
1/2 gal. vinegar
2 long hot peppers

1 Tbsp. each allspice,
    cloves, cinnamon and mace
2 Tbsp. salt
3 c. sugar
1 Tbsp. flour
2 tsp. vinegar

Grind tomatoes, onion and green peppers. Crush spices and put with hot peppers in a cloth bag and cook with mixture. Add all ingredients except sugar, flour and vinegar, and boil for 2 to 2 1/2 hours, stirring constantly. Add sugar. Make a smooth paste of the flour and vinegar; add paste to the sauce to thicken a few minutes before end of cooking time. Pour into hot sterile jars. Makes approximately 15 pints.

Larry Rogers, Huntsville Council

CRANBERRY SAUCE

2 c. sugar
2 c. water
1 lb. (4 c.) cranberries

Dash of ground cinnamon
1/2 tsp. vanilla flavoring

Combine sugar and water in saucepan; stir to dissolve sugar. Heat to boiling and boil 5 minutes. Add cranberries and cook until skins pop, about 5 minutes. Add cinnamon and vanilla. Serve warm or chilled. Makes 4 cups.

Joyce Hobbs, Huntsville Council

CREOLE SAUCE

1 medium onion, finely
    chopped
1 bell pepper, finely
    chopped
1 1/2 c. chopped celery
1 (16 oz.) can tomatoes
1 Tbsp. Worcestershire

1 Tbsp. lemon juice
Dash of Tabasco
Salt and pepper to taste
1 Tbsp. butter or
    margarine
1 bay leaf

Combine all ingredients; simmer for 20 minutes. Remove bay leaf before serving over fish.

Billie Bays, Decatur Council

MURPHIE'S COCKTAIL SAUCE FOR SEAFOOD

1 c. chili sauce
1/2 c. lemon juice
2 tsp. horseradish
1/4 medium onion

2 tsp. Worcestershire sauce
1/4 tsp. garlic sauce (juice)
4 drops of Tabasco sauce

Place all ingredients in blender; cover and process until onion is chopped and ingredients are combined. Refrigerate until serving. Makes 1 1/2 cups.

Anne Spragins, Birmingham East Council

FUDGE SAUCE

1 c. sugar
2 squares unsweetened
    chocolate

1 large can evaporated milk
1 tsp. vanilla

In top of double boiler add chocolate and sugar and melt; remove from heat and slowly add milk. Return to direct heat (medium low) and cook until thick; stir constantly.

Mrs. Vonda Cook, Riverchase Council

GOLDEN EMBER SAUCE

3/4 c. salad oil
1/4 c. melted butter
1/4 c. lemon juice
1 Tbsp. prepared mustard
2 Tbsp. brown sugar
1 Tbsp. salt
1 tsp. paprika

1/4 tsp. black pepper
2 tsp. grated onion
2 cloves garlic, cut in halves
1/2 tsp. Worcestershire
  sauce
1/4 tsp. Tabasco sauce
1/4 c. ketchup

Combine all ingredients in jar or bottle; shake thorough-ly. Let stand several hours before using. Good on charcoal broiled chicken; need to brush on chicken often while chicken is cooking.

Wanda Ange, Birmingham East Council

CAJUN BARBEQUE SAUCE

2 sticks oleo or butter
1 c. Worcestershire sauce
1 tsp. powdered yellow
  mustard
3 cloves crushed garlic
1 large diced onion

1 c. catsup
1 c. white vinegar
2 Tbsp. lemon juice
3 Tbsp. brown sugar
Tabasco sauce to taste

Mix all ingredients; bring to a boil. Cover and simmer 30 minutes.

Sandra Herndon, Birmingham South Council

WHITE BARBECUE SAUCE

1 pt. mayonnaise
2 Tbsp. pepper
2 Tbsp. salt

6 Tbsp. lemon juice
6 Tbsp. vinegar
4 Tbsp. sugar

Mix all ingredients until smooth; use to baste chicken, pork chops or ribs, as they cook on the grill. Any leftover sauce will keep in the refrigerator several weeks.

Nancy Morgan, Decatur Council

SWEET AND SOUR BAR-B-QUE SAUCE

1 c. ketchup
1 tsp. grated ginger
4 tsp. butter
2 Tbsp. Worcestershire
  sauce

3 Tbsp. lemon juice
1 tsp. minced garlic
2 Tbsp. honey
1 tsp. coriander (ground)

In a saucepan mix ingredients in, as in above order.
Bring to a boil; reduce heat and simmer 15 minutes. Coat
meat on both sides once before cooking and then after cooking as desired for your taste.

Anita J. Rooks, Riverchase Council

ORIGINAL "TWIX AND TWEEN" BAR-B-Q SAUCE

2 c. catsup	1 tsp. salt
1 c. dill pickle juice	1 tsp. lemon juice
3/4 c. mustard	3 Tbsp. Louisiana hot sauce
3 Tbsp. sugar	1 tsp. paprika
Pinch of garlic salt	2 tsp. Worcestershire

Mix well; let come to a boil. Take off stove and cool.
Use with Bar-B-Q pork or beef.

Lemmie Cochran, Montgomery Council

BARBECUE SAUCE - FOR SPARERIBS, STEAKS AND HAMBURGERS

2 Tbsp. butter	2 Tbsp. lemon juice
1 medium size onion, sliced	2 Tbsp. Worcestershire
1 clove garlic	sauce
1/2 c. chopped celery	2 Tbsp. brown sugar
3/4 c. water	1 tsp. dry mustard
1 c. ketchup	1 tsp. salt
2 Tbsp. vinegar	1/4 tsp. pepper

Melt butter; add onions and cook until browned. Add
remaining ingredients and cook 20 minutes. Makes about
2 1/4 cups, or enough for 3 pounds of meat.

Berniece Peterson, Birmingham South Council

FRANK REYNOLDS' BARBECUE SAUCE

Saute 2 large or 4 medium onions in 1/2 to 3/4 pound
butter.

1/4 to 1/2 c. honey or molasses	1/4 c. prepared mustard
	1/4 tsp. turmeric
2 whole fresh lemons, sliced and added with peelings	1 Tbsp. mustard seed
	1 tsp. basil
	2 or 3 whole bay leaves
1/4 c. lemon juice concentrate	2 or 3 whole cloves
	5 or 6 fresh tomatoes, or 1 can
2 or 3 Tbsp. black pepper	tomato sauce, 1 can tomato puree and 1 can tomato paste

1 to 1 1/2 c. vinegar
Water as needed

1 or 2 cayenne peppers,
if desired

Cook all of the above ingredients until thick and put on meat when 3/4 cooked. Cook over low fire. It may be helpful to blend mustard and honey with blender. Rub meat in salt before cooking.

Another helpful hint to keep meat moist is to apply a solution of salt, pepper, vinegar and water while cooking. Makes about 1 gallon.

Brenda B. McKinney, Birmingham South Council

BARBEQUE SAUCE

1 c. vinegar
1 Tbsp. butter
1 small onion, chopped
    fine
1/2 Tbsp. red pepper
    (crushed)
1/2 Tbsp. black pepper
1/2 Tbsp. salt

1/2 Tbsp. garlic
3 lemons, quartered
1 Tbsp. Worcestershire sauce
1 1/2 Tbsp. mustard
1/2 c. sugar
1 (32 oz.) bottle ketchup
1 c. vinegar (taste to see if
    all this c. is needed)

Bring 1 cup vinegar to boil. Stir in remaining ingredients, in succession, over a 10-15 minute period. Let boil for 15-20 minutes, stirring occasionally, to prevent sticking. Simmer 2-3 hours, stirring occasionally. Additional vinegar and/or sugar may be added for taste. However, bring to boil again and let simmer 15 minutes. Remove lemon peels the following day.

John Eppenger, Birmingham Central Council

BARBECUE SAUCE

3 sticks oleo
Juice of 3 lemons
1/2 c. vinegar

6 cloves garlic, grated
1 tsp. hot stuff
Salt and pepper

Makes enough for 5 chickens.
Anatalie Watson, Decatur Council

RED COCKTAIL SAUCE

1 c. chili sauce
1 c. catsup
1 Tbsp. lemon juice

2 Tbsp. prepared horseradish
1 tsp. Lea & Perrins
    Worcestershire

Combine all ingredients and refrigerate.
Betty Parker, Montgomery Council

HORSERADISH SAUCE

1/2 c. chilled whipping
  cream

3 Tbsp. horseradish
1/2 tsp. salt

Beat whipping cream in chilled bowl until stiff; fold in well drained prepared horseradish. Add salt.

Eleanor Gearhart, Montgomery Council

JEZEBEL SAUCE

1 (5 oz.) jar horseradish
1 (1.12 oz.) can dry
  mustard
1 (18 oz.) jar pineapple
  preserves

1 (18 oz.) jar apple
  jelly
2 Tbsp. coarsely ground
  pepper

Mix the horseradish and dry mustard well. Combine with remaining ingredients. Will keep in refrigerator for a long period of time. Especially good on sliced ham. Makes 4 cups.

Edwina Hicks (Mrs. Jimmy),
Montgomery Council

JEZEBEL SAUCE

1 c. pineapple preserves
1 c. apple jelly

1/2 tsp. dry mustard
2 Tbsp. prepared
  horseradish, drained

Combine ingredients in double boiler and heat, stirring until well blended. Very good with baked ham, Canadian bacon or pork chops.

Fran Rhodis, Montgomery Council

MARINARA SAUCE

1 clove garlic, minced
2 Tbsp. olive oil
6 finely chopped
  anchovies

1/2 tsp. oregano
1 Tbsp. chopped parsley
2 1/2 c. canned, pressed and
  drained whole tomatoes

Saute garlic in a mixture of olive oil and oil from anchovies. Slowly add tomatoes and stir. Bring to a boil; reduce heat and simmer, uncovered, for 15-20 minutes. Serve over spaghetti with grated Parmesan cheese. Can also omit the oregano and add 5 chopped artichoke hearts. Simmer 3-4 minutes longer.

Anne Spragins, Birmingham East Council

440

MARINADE SAUCE

1/2 c. soy sauce
1/2 c. water
2 Tbsp. Worcestershire

1 Tbsp. sugar
1/2 to 1 tsp. garlic salt

Mix well. Marinate meat at least 2 hours before cooking.

Billie Bays, Decatur Council

MORNAY SAUCE

1/4 c. margarine
1/4 c. flour
1/2 tsp. salt
Dash of pepper
2 c. milk

1 c. (4 oz.) shredded
  Swiss cheese
1/4 c. (1 oz.) grated
  Parmesan cheese

Melt margarine in saucepan over low heat; blend in flour and seasonings. Gradually add milk; cook, stirring constantly until thickened. Add cheeses; stir until melted. Serve over hot cooked broccoli, asparagus, sliced turkey or ham. Yield: 2 3/4 cups.

Nice to know: This sauce can be refrigerated and then reheated.

Fran Rhodis, Montgomery Council

MUSTARD SAUCE

1/4 tsp. salt
1 Tbsp. flour
2 Tbsp. dry mustard
1 c. light cream

4 Tbsp. sugar
1 egg yolk, beaten until
  thick and lemony
1/4 c. vinegar, heated

Combine the salt, flour, dry mustard and 1/4 cup light cream. In a heavy saucepan heat remaining 3/4 cream and sugar. Stir in mustard mixture; heat until almost boiling, stirring constantly; remove from heat. Slowly add 1/2 cup cream mixture to beaten egg and blend well. Slowly stir egg mixture into cream mixture; cook over low heat, stirring constantly until thick; do not allow to boil. When thickened, slowly stir in hot vinegar. This is delicious with ham or corned beef.

Fran Rhodis, Montgomery Council

RAISIN SAUCE FOR HAM

4 Tbsp. cornstarch
2 tsp. mustard
1 c. brown sugar,
  packed

1/2 c. apple cider vinegar
2 c. water
1 1/2 c. currant or apple
  jelly (optional)
1 c. raisins

Combine first 3 ingredients in saucepan; stir in vinegar, water and jelly. Cook on medium heat until thick and bubbly. Stir in raisins; spoon over ham.

Helen Reideler, Birmingham South Council

SEAFOOD SAUCE

2 c. chili sauce or catsup
  (or combination of both)
2 Tbsp. Worcestershire

3 Tbsp. prepared horseradish
Dash of Tabasco (optional)
1 Tbsp. vinegar
Juice of 2 lemons

Mix ingredients and chill. Good on shrimp and crabmeat.

Billie Bays, Decatur Council

SEAFOOD COCKTAIL SAUCE

3/4 c. chili sauce
3 Tbsp. lemon juice
3 Tbsp. horseradish

2 tsp. Worcestershire sauce
1 tsp. grated onion
Few drops of Tabasco sauce

Combine all ingredients; add salt to taste. Chill. Serve with seafood.

Nancy Morgan, Decatur Council

KATHY'S SHRIMP SAUCE

1 bottle chili sauce
3 Tbsp. Worcestershire
3 stalks celery, minced

Juice of 1 lemon
4-6 shakes of hot sauce
Horseradish to taste

Mix ingredients together for desired taste.

David Stewart, Mobile Council

ITALIAN SPAGHETTI SAUCE

Fry 2 chopped onions in a small amount of shortening. Add 1 pound hamburger and 3 cloves of garlic; cook until brown. Add 2 cans tomatoes, 1 can tomato paste, 1 can tomato sauce and salt to taste. Add desired amount of Italian seasoning. Cook in crock pot all day on low or simmer on stove as long as possible.

Donna Campbell, Anniston Council

ITALIAN SAUCE

1 (8 oz.) can tomato sauce with cheese	1/2 tsp. oregano
	1/2 tsp. garlic salt
1/4 tsp. black pepper	

Combine all ingredients; simmer 15 minutes, stirring often. Keep hot. Makes about 1 cup.

Becky Cook, Huntsville Council

SKILLET SPAGHETTI SAUCE

1 lb. ground beef	1 garlic pod
1 medium onion	2 tsp. mixed Italian seasonings
1 medium can whole tomatoes	
1 small can tomato sauce	1 tsp. sugar
1/2 tsp. salt	2 dashes of cinnamon
2 dashes of pepper	1/2 c. water

In a large skillet or pot saute onion and garlic, then add ground beef; cook until brown. Then add whole tomatoes (cut into pieces), tomato sauce, water and seasonings. Cover and simmer for about 30 to 40 minutes or until thick. Remove from heat; pour over cooked spaghetti and top with Romano cheese.

Marian R. D'Anna, Future Pioneer, Birmingham East Council

ALL PURPOSE MEAT SAUCE

2 lb. lean hamburger	5 c. water
3 medium onions, diced	Garlic, salt and sugar (to taste)
2 (8 oz.) cans tomatoes	
1 (4 oz.) can tomato paste	1/2 c. red wine (if desired)
	Dash of red pepper (more if desired)

Brown onions, meat and garlic; add all other ingredients. Bring to a boil, stirring well. Let simmer 45 minutes to 1 hour. May be stored in freezer or refrigerator for an applicable period of time.

Eleanor Gearhart, Montgomery Council

SPAGHETTI SAUCE

2 1/2 lb. lean hamburger
  meat
2 small cans tomato soup
1 small can tomato paste
  (not puree)
1 small can mushrooms
2 large onions

1 large can tomatoes
1/2 tsp. garlic powder
  or juice
1 or 2 tsp. basil
1 or 2 tsp. oregano
1 bay leaf (optional)

Make as many meat balls as desired. Heat large pan medium hot. Brown meat balls. Take out meat balls; add chopped onions and any hamburger you have left; stir while cooking, until meat is no longer pink and onions begin to turn translucent. Add 1 can tomato paste, 1 can mushrooms and mix. Add water if necessary to make sauce consistency. Add bay leaf, garlic powder or juice, basil, oregano. Add tomatoes, squashed in small pieces. Simmer 1 or more hours in large pot. Serve with Mozzarella cheese on top.

Viola Vines, Huntsville Council

SPAGHETTI SAUCE

1 lb. hamburger
1 medium onion
1 bell pepper

1 (6 oz.) can tomato paste
1 (10 3/4 oz.) can tomato puree
1 (15 oz.) can tomato sauce

Brown 1 pound hamburger meat; add onion and bell pepper. Simmer about 5 minutes. Add paste, puree and sauce. Simmer 10 to 15 minutes; salt to taste.

Donna Dunaway, Anniston Council

VEGETARIAN SPAGHETTI SAUCE

2 cans tomatoes, chopped
1 can tomato paste
1 c. chopped mushrooms
1/2 c. red bell pepper
1/2 c. green bell pepper

1/2 c. butter
1 large onion, chopped
2 Tbsp. seasoning salt
1 Tbsp. pepper
1 Tbsp. basil leaves, crushed
1 Tbsp. oregano

In skillet melt butter; add onions and bell peppers and mushrooms. Saute until onions are clear. Add other

444

ingredients and simmer until sauce is smooth. You may need to add a little water to get desired consistency.

Judy Ivey, Birmingham South Council

GENERAL KROESSEN'S STEAK SAUCE

1 c. Italian sweet vermouth
1/2 c. soy sauce
1/4 c. Worcestershire
   sauce
1/2 c. catsup

1 tsp. garlic salt
1 tsp. onion salt
2 Tbsp. dry mustard
Juice of 1 lemon

Combine all ingredients. Store in jar in the refrigerator. This is a great marinade for steaks to be cooked on the grill.

Debbie Tucker, Birmingham East Council

SWEET AND SOUR SAUCE

1/2 c. vinegar
1/2 c. water
1/4 c. brown sugar
1/4 c. granulated sugar

1/4 c. cornstarch
1/2 c. pineapple juice (or
   half lemon and half
   pineapple)

Bring vinegar, water and sugars to boil. Combine cornstarch and pineapple juice; add to hot mixture and cook until thickened. Yield: 2 1/4 cups.

Mary C. Martin, Birmingham East Council

SWEET AND SOUR SAUCE

3/4 c. finely chopped onion
2 Tbsp. vegetable oil
1/2 c. water
2 Tbsp. orange marmalade
1/2 tsp. powdered ginger

1/4 c. finely chopped
   green pepper
1 Tbsp. cornstarch
1 (8 oz.) can tomato sauce
2 Tbsp. vinegar

Cook onion and green pepper in oil over medium heat until tender. Blend cornstarch with water; add with remaining ingredients. Simmer 5 to 10 minutes. Keep hot. Serve with pork, ham, lamb or chicken fondue. Makes about 1 3/4 cups.

Becky Cook, Huntsville Council

SWEET AND SOUR SAUCE FOR CHICKEN

12 oz. pineapple preserves   2 oz. mustard
2 oz. horseradish

Stir all ingredients in saucepan; bring to a boil. Serve with chicken fingers.

Marcia Freeman, Birmingham East Council

TARTAR SAUCE

1 c. mayonnaise
1 small sour pickle,
   finely minced

1 Tbsp. finely minced parsley
2 stuffed olives, finely chopped
1 small onion, finely chopped

Mix all ingredients and serve with sliced lemon on fish, oysters or clams.

Billie Bays, Decatur Council

TARTAR SAUCE

1 c. sour cream
1 c. mayonnaise
2/3 c. chopped sweet
   pickles

1/4 c. chopped olives
Juice of 1/2 lemon
1 small onion, grated

Mix all ingredients; chill for several hours.

Flo Thompson, Montgomery Council

TOMATO SAUCE

2 qt. tomatoes
2 c. sweet pepper
2 pods hot pepper
1/2 c. onions
1 Tbsp. salt

1/2 c. sugar
1 Tbsp. black pepper
1 c. vinegar
1 Tbsp. pickling spice,
   tied in cloth

Cook until thick; remove spice and seal.

Judy Burnett, Decatur Council

WINE-MUSHROOM SAUCE
(To be served with meat, fondue, etc.)

1/4 c. butter
1 c. fresh mushrooms,
   sliced or chopped
1/4 c. chopped onion
2 Tbsp. flour

2 tsp. instant beef bouillon
1/2 tsp. salt
1 Tbsp. chopped parsley
Dash of pepper
1 c. burgundy wine
1/2 c. water

Saute mushrooms and onions in butter; blend in flour and seasonings. Add wine and water gradually while stirring. Cook until smooth and thickened. Serve hot.

Carol Higdon, Riverchase Council

CHILI

1 1/2 to 2 lb. ground beef, browned and drained
1 large red onion, chopped
1 bell pepper, chopped
1 (2 1/2 oz.) jar "Mr. Mushroom" chopped mushrooms with liquid
1 (28 oz.) can tomatoes
2 (8 oz.) cans tomato sauce
1 (30 oz.) can "Joan of Arc" kidney beans, drained
1 tsp. black pepper
1 clove garlic, minced
2 Tbsp. chili powder
1 c. water

Put all ingredients in slow cooker; stir thoroughly. Cover and cook on automatic 5-6 hours, on slow 10-12 hours, on high 3-4 hours.

Mary C. Martin, Birmingham East Council

"CHARLIE'S CHILI"

1 Tbsp. cooking oil
2 medium size onions, chopped fine
1 bell pepper, chopped fine
1 large celery stalk, chopped fine
2 garlic cloves, chopped fine
4 lb. coarse ground round steak or lean chuck
1 (No. 2) can tomato sauce
1 (No. 2) can stewed tomatoes
1 pt. water as needed
1 (6 oz.) can tomato paste
2 oz. chili salsa
1 (3 inch) green hot pepper, chopped fine
1 (3 oz.) can chili powder
2 oz. green diced chilies
Dash of oregano
Salt and garlic salt to taste
Black coarsely ground pepper to taste

Put oil into 8-10 quart pot; add onions, bell pepper, celery and garlic cloves. Cook until onion is transparent. Add meat slowly and stir until redness disappears. Add remaining ingredients, stirring after each addition. Lower heat and simmer 2 1/2 to 3 hours; stir to keep from scorching. Makes about 1 1/2 gallons. You can put it in the freezer - to age - the better it will taste.

C. M. Cunningham, Montgomery Council

DAD'S OLD COUNTRY CHILI

3/4 c. green pepper,
  chopped
3/4 c. onion, chopped
1 1/2 lb. ground beef
3 (15 oz.) cans kidney
  beans

2 (46 oz.) cans tomato juice
1 (46 oz.) can water
3 Tbsp. butter
Lawry's seasoning salt
Chili powder

Brown meat, onion and pepper in skillet. Blend seasoning salt and garlic powder; season to taste. Drain off grease, leaving just a little for moisture. Pour contents into 8 or 10 quart pot; add kidney beans, tomato juice and water. Stir and heat; bring to a boil. Once chili starts to boil, turn heat down to simmer; add butter and chili powder. Let simmer 3 hours; stir occasionally. Serve hot with cold hard rolls. Refrigerate or freeze for future meals.

Note: Add chili powder sparingly. Take taste and hold in mouth, swallowing slowly to get real after taste. Too much too soon will not be enjoyable to eat.

Jim South, Selma Council

SPEEDY'S CHILI

1 lb. hamburger
2 medium size onions,
  chopped

3 small cans tomato sauce
1 pkg. Chili-O mix
1 large and 1 small can
  kidney beans

Scramble hamburger in skillet over medium heat until half done and add chopped onions. Continue cooking until hamburger and onions are done. Put hamburger and onions with all other ingredients in boiler pan and cook on slow simmer for 30 minutes. Can also be cooked in crock pot on low setting for 3-4 hours.

R. D. Chilton, Birmingham East Council

MY CHILI

2 cans tomatoes, blended
2 cans tomato sauce
2 cans tomato paste
4 cans red kidney beans
2 lb. ground beef

1 medium onion, chopped
1 bell pepper, chopped
1/2 chili brick or con carne
1 tsp. chili powder
Salt
Pepper

Chop and saute onion and bell pepper; brown ground beef with onions and bell pepper. Drain off juices; add tomatoes, tomato paste, tomato sauce and beans; mix well. Add salt, pepper and chili powder. Cook on low. When chili is hot cut in chili brick. Cook with lid on pot, cocked open to allow steam to escape. Serve alone or over cooked elbow macaroni for chili mac.

Art Fleet, Birmingham South Council

CHILI CON CARNE

1 1/2 lb. venison, trimmed	1/2 tsp. cayenne pepper
1/4 c. beef suet	1 tsp. crushed oregano
2 cans kidney beans	1/4 tsp. garlic powder
1 1/2 (15 oz.) cans	(optional)
tomato sauce	1 tsp. fresh ground pepper
3 Tbsp. chili powder	1/2 c. minced dehydrated
1/2 c. water (if needed)	onions

Chop the venison into small pieces; saute the beef suet in a heavy frying pan, and when the fat is hot, add the venison pieces and saute until brown. Combine all remaining ingredients except water in a large saucepan; add the venison, and simmer for 2 hours, stirring occasionally. Taste after 1 hour, and if the sauce is not hot enough, add more cayenne. If the sauce is too thick, add the water. Serve very hot with lots of crackers and butter. Beef may be used in place of the venison. I do not use ground meat, as it tends to cook all to pieces. Also, the thicker the sauce, the better the chili.

T. H. Broach, Phenix City

CHILI CON CARNE

1 large onion	2 c. canned tomatoes
1 green pepper	2 Tbsp. chili powder
1 lb. ground beef	1 1/2 tsp. salt
3/4 c. tomato sauce	4 c. cooked pinto beans

Chop onion and green pepper. Crumble ground beef into heated frypan; add onion and pepper and cook until tender. Drain off fat. Stir in rest of ingredients; boil gently about 45 minutes until thickened. Makes 6 servings, 1 cup each.

Sammie M. Jackson, Huntsville Council

RON'S CHILI

1 lb. ground beef
1 medium onion, chopped
2 medium cloves garlic,
  minced
1 beef bouillon cube,
  dissolved in about
  10 oz. water
1 (14 1/2 oz.) can tomatoes

1 (6 oz.) can tomato paste
2 Tbsp. chili powder
2 Tbsp. vinegar
1/2 tsp. each of cayenne,
  cumin and salt
2 c. dried kidney
  (or pinto) beans
1/2 to 1 c. liquid from beans

Cook beans until tender, reserving the 1/2 to 1 cup liquid. Brown the ground beef with onion and garlic; drain off the fat from the browned beef and add the bouillon in water, canned tomatoes, tomato paste, seasonings, vinegar, beans and liquid. Simmer on top of the stove for at least 1 hour. Add more and/or other seasonings as desired.

Ron May, Riverchase Council

CHOW TIME CHOWDER

1 (5 1/2 oz.) pkg.
  scalloped potato mix
5 c. water
1 1/2 c. milk

1 chicken bouillon cube
1 Tbsp. dried chives
1 can salmon (bones and
  skin removed)

In large saucepot combine scalloped potatoes, sauce mix, water, milk, bouillon cubes and chives. Mix well. Bring to boiling; cover and simmer 30 minutes or until potatoes are tender, stirring occasionally. Add salmon. Heat 5 minutes. Makes 6 servings.

Debbie Owen, Birmingham East Council

GOLDEN CHEESE CHOWDER

1 c. butter or margarine
1/2 c. all-purpose flour
4 c. milk
4 c. (1 lb.) shredded
  sharp cheese
3 c. water
4 medium potatoes,
  peeled and diced

1 c. chopped celery
1 c. diced carrots
1/2 c. diced onion
3/4 tsp. salt
1/4 tsp. pepper
2 c. diced, cooked ham
Hot sauce (to taste)

Melt butter in a heavy 2 quart saucepan over low heat and add flour, stirring until smooth. Cook 1 minute; stir constantly. Gradually stir in milk; cook over medium heat, stirring constantly, until thick and bubbly. Add cheese, stirring until cheese is melted. Remove from heat and set aside. Combine water, vegetables, salt and pepper in a 5 quart Dutch oven; heat to boiling. Reduce heat and cover; simmer 10 minutes or until vegetables are tender. Stir in all other ingredients. Cook over low heat until thoroughly heated (do not boil). Makes 12 to 14 servings.

Betty Floyd Parker, Montgomery Council

NEW ENGLAND CLAM CHOWDER

1 large onion, chopped	2 c. clam juice
2 cloves garlic, minced	3/4 c. diced pork
6 Tbsp. butter	2 medium potatoes, cubed
3 (8 oz.) cans minced	2 c. half & half
clams, drained	Salt and pepper to taste

Saute onion and garlic in 2 tablespoons butter 5 minutes. Add clams and clam juice; cover and cook over low heat 10-15 minutes. Fry pork until brown; drain on paper towel. Cook potatoes in boiling, salted water until barely done; drain. Add pork and potatoes to clams. Gradually stir in half & half; heat, but do not boil. Add salt and pepper. Serve, dotted with remaining butter.

Jane Patterson, Riverchase Council

GUMBO

1 lb. bacon	6 c. fresh peeled and
4 c. diced celery	diced tomatoes
(include leaves)	1 can cream of chicken soup
2 c. diced bell pepper	6 beef bouillon cubes
2 c. chopped green onions	2 c. flour
2 c. diced white onion	4 qt. peeled fresh shrimp
3 c. thinly sliced okra	1 qt. crabmeat

Fry bacon crisp; remove and crumble. Saute pepper, onion and celery in bacon drippings until clear. Saute okra until tender. Remove all from bacon drippings; drain. Put in big pot and add 6 quarts water. Add salt and pepper, beef cubes, dissolved, and soup. Simmer 1 hour. Brown flour (very slowly - do not burn) in 1 cup bacon drippings until dark brown (takes about 30-45 minutes). Add to pot; cook 30 minutes. Add crabmeat and cook 15 minutes. Add shrimp; simmer 1 hour. Add water if needed to thin down, up to 4 quarts. Serve 1/2 cup rice and 2 cups gumbo. Serves 20.

Shirley Downey, Mobile Council

OKRA SEAFOOD GUMBO

6 hardshell crabs
2 lb. okra
2 Tbsp. bacon fat
2 Tbsp. flour
1 c. onion, chopped
1/2 c. green onions, chopped
1 clove garlic, finely chopped
1 green pepper, chopped

1 (11 oz.) can tomatoes
2 lb. raw shrimp
6 c. water
1 tsp. salt
Pinch of pepper
5 dashes of Tabasco
1 bay leaf
1/2 tsp. thyme
1 c. cooked ham, diced

Boil crabs until they turn red (about 20 minutes); set aside and reserve water. Wash okra and cut into 1/4 inch rounds. Put 2 tablespoons of fat in an iron skillet and fry okra, stirring often, to prevent burning, until it is browned and dried out, with all trace of sliminess gone.

In a deep pot melt remaining 2 tablespoons fat and blend in flour to make a roux, cooking and stirring until deep brown. Add chopped onion, garlic and green pepper; stir and cook a few minutes, then add ham. Add tomatoes and peeled raw shrimp. After cooking a few minutes, add cooked okra and 6 cups of crab-boiling water or water. Add seasoning and let boil slowly about 2 hours, adding more water if necessary.

During this time, remove shell from crabs; crack claws with a nutcracker so they will pull apart easily, and either break bodies in halves, or remove meat from them, depending on which way you prefer to serve them. During the last half hour of cooking, add crab claws and halved bodies or meat to gumbo. Serve gumbo in a bowl over a mound of hot rice. Serves 8.

Gumbo: Choctaw Indian's word for sassafras is Kombo from which we get the word "gumbo".

Linda Unger, Riverchase Council

SAUSAGE GUMBO

1 pkg. smoked sausage or any sausage links
2 cans Veg-All
2 cans whole kernel corn

1 pkg. okra (optional)
1 can whole stewed tomatoes
1 medium sized onion
Gumbo file (1/2 tsp.)

Drain off liquid from cans of Veg-All and corn; do not drain liquid from tomatoes. Place all ingredients in large size pot. Add gumbo file after 5 minutes. Cook until onions are soft. Season to taste. Serves 4.

Brenda J. Love, Birmingham Central Council

SHRIMP CREOLE

1/4 c. butter
2 Tbsp. instant minced onion
1 c. chopped celery
1/2 c. chopped green
  pepper
2 Tbsp. flour
1 Tbsp. Season-All

1 bay leaf
1/8 tsp. red pepper
2 tsp. parsley flakes
3 1/2 c. tomatoes
  (No. 2 1/2 can)
1/2 c. water
1 lb. cooked, cleaned shrimp

Melt butter in large skillet. Saute onion, celery and green pepper in butter until onion is lightly browned. Blend in flour. Add remaining ingredients except shrimp; mix well. Cover and simmer 30 minutes. Stir in shrimp and continue simmering just until shrimp is heated through. Serve over hot steamed rice. Serves 4.

Bertha Capps, Birmingham East Council

SHRIMP CREOLE

2 onions, chopped
3 ribs celery, chopped
1/2 bell pepper,
  chopped
2 Tbsp. butter
2 Tbsp. bacon grease
2 Tbsp. ham or salt
  pork, chopped

1 large can tomatoes, cut
  into small pieces
Pinch of thyme
Parsley, chopped
Bay leaf
Salt and pepper
1/2 c. white wine
1-2 lb. boiled shrimp
Tabasco

Melt butter and bacon grease together in skillet. Saute onion, celery and pepper until soft. Add tomatoes, ham, seasonings and wine. Cover. Allow mixture to cook 30 minutes to 1 hour. Add water if it gets too thick. Add shrimp; cook slowly for 15 minutes. Serve over rice.

Debbie Tucker, Birmingham East Council

ARTICHOKE SOUP

1/4 lb. butter (1 stick)
2 medium onions, chopped
1 c. celery, chopped
1/2 c. green onions,
  chopped (white)
2 garlic toes, chopped
2 cans cream of celery soup

2 cans artichoke hearts
  (reserve 1/2 can liquid)
1 can water
2 Tbsp. parsley, chopped
1/2 c. Parmesan cheese
1/3 c. Italian bread crumbs

Saute the chopped onion, celery, green onions and garlic in butter till onions are tender. Add the celery soup,

1567-82

artichoke hearts (chopped), parsley, liquids and simmer for 30 minutes. Add Parmesan cheese and Italian bread crumbs to thicken. If too thick, add more water, but consistency should be thick rather than clear. Delicious with oysters. You may add 1 pint of oysters and some of the liquid.

Hilda A. Powe, Birmingham Central Council

AUTUMN SOUP

1 lb. cooked ground beef	1/4 tsp. pepper
1 c. chopped onion	1 bay leaf
4 c. water	1/8 tsp. basil
1 c. diced celery	1 (28 oz.) can tomatoes
1 c. cut up potatoes	(or you may use 2 cans
2 tsp. salt	Campbell's tomato soup)
1 tsp. Banquet sauce	1 c. cut up carrots

Cook and stir the onions with ground beef until onions are tender, about 5 minutes. Stir in remaining ingredients except tomatoes and heat to boiling. Reduce heat; cover and simmer 20 minutes. Add tomatoes; cover and simmer until vegetables are tender.

Mary Scott, Anniston Council

14 BEAN SOUP

Ham bone or ham hocks	1 clove garlic
1 1/2 c. Bean Mixture*	1 Tbsp. onion juice
1 can tomatoes	1 green pepper, chopped
1 large onion, chopped	Salt and pepper

Wash beans; cover with water. Add salt; soak 3 hours and drain. Place beans in large pot; add rest of ingredients and enough water to cook (about 2 to 3 quarts). Simmer 3 hours.

*Bean Mixture consists of the following 14 beans, plus barley, mixed together: Pinto, navy, red kidney, Great Northern, black, lima, speckled butter bean, lentil, white, garbanzo or chick pea, black-eyed pea, green and yellow split pea and barley.

Jean Piecki, Montgomery Council

GARBANZO BEAN SOUP

2 cans garbanzo beans
1 link Polish sausage
Water

2 medium onions, chopped
5 medium potatoes, diced

Mix beans and chopped onions in a large kettle; add 2-3 cans water and cook over medium heat until liquid becomes creamy, approximately 45 minutes. Cut sausage into bite size pieces and add to mixture. Add potatoes; cook until potatoes are tender. Salt and pepper to taste. Yield: Approximately 6 servings.

Melissa Burnthall, Decatur Council

QUICK BEEF-AND-VEGETABLE SOUP

1 1/2 lb. ground beef
1 medium onion, sliced
1 (16 oz.) can stewed
   tomatoes
2 beef flavor bouillon cubes
7 c. water
1/2 c. regular long grain
   rice

2 tsp. salt
1/2 tsp. basil
1/4 tsp. pepper
1 (16 oz.) pkg. frozen
   mixed vegetables
   (broccoli, carrots and
   cauliflower)

In a 5 quart Dutch oven, over high heat, cook ground beef and onion until all pan juices evaporate and meat is well browned, stirring frequently. (Drain meat if needed.) Add stewed tomatoes and next 6 ingredients; heat to boiling. Reduce heat to low; cover and simmer 15 minutes, stirring occasionally. Add frozen mixed vegetables; over high heat, heat to boiling. Reduce heat to low; cover and simmer 10 minutes longer or until vegetables are tender, stirring occasionally. Makes about 12 cups or 6 main dish servings.

Libby McDowell, Montgomery Council

BEEF-VEGETABLE SOUP

1 lb. ground beef
1 Tbsp. butter
1 small can whole
   kernel corn
1 small can English peas

1 small can tomato paste
   plus 2 cans water
1 large can tomatoes
3 small potatoes, diced
1 large onion, chopped

Brown meat in butter; add canned ingredients. Season with salt and pepper to taste. Simmer for 1 1/2 to 2 hours. Stir occasionally and check seasonings. Serve piping hot with crackers.

Frances Crenshaw, Birmingham East Council

1567-82

CABBAGE SOUP

1 large cabbage, chopped
2 large onions, chopped
2 green peppers, chopped
2 stalks celery, chopped

6 to 7 tomatoes or 3 (16 oz.)
   cans stewed tomatoes
1 onion soup mix

(Add herbs and spices you like.) Put all ingredients in a large pot and cook on medium to low until all vegetables are tender.

Mike Murray, Birmingham West Council

SOUPER BOWL BEER CHEESE SOUP

1 pkg. celery soup mix
1 pkg. leek soup mix
1/2 pkg. French onion
  soup mix
8 c. cold water

1 lb. Hickory Farms Ohio
  sharp cold pack Cheddar
  cheese food
1/2 can (6 oz.) beer
  (room temperature)

Mix soups with cold water; bring to boil. Reduce heat and simmer until thick. Slowly add cheese food, stirring constantly, until melted and smooth. Add 1/2 can beer. Heat thoroughly. Makes 12 cups or 6 hearty bowls of soup.

Aileen Hardin, Riverchase Council

HOMEMADE CHICKEN SOUP

2 stalks celery, cut into
  3 inch pieces
1 large carrot, cut into
  3 inch pieces
1 large leek, cut into
  3 inch pieces
6 sprigs fresh parsley
1 bay leaf
2 cloves
1 large onion
9 c. water
1 (5 to 6 lb.) baking hen

1 Tbsp. salt
8 whole peppercorns
1 c. diced carrots
1/2 c. diced celery
1/2 c. diced onion
1/2 c. uncooked regular rice
1 (10 oz.) pkg. frozen green
  peas
1/2 tsp. salt
1/4 tsp. pepper
Chopped fresh parsley
  (optional)

Combine first 5 ingredients in a cheesecloth bag. Insert cloves into onion. Combine water, baking hen, vegetable bag, clove-studded onion, 1 tablespoon salt and peppercorns in a large Dutch oven; cover and simmer 2 to 2 1/2 hours or until hen is tender. Remove chicken from broth; remove meat from bones and chop. Set aside 3 to 4 cups chopped chicken, and reserve remaining chicken for use in other recipes. Strain broth and discard vegetables. Skim

456

off excess fat. Stir in diced carrots, celery, onion and rice; simmer 10 minutes. Add 3 to 4 cups chicken, peas, 1/2 teaspoon salt and pepper; continue to cook 10 minutes or until rice is tender. Sprinkle with parsley, if desired. Yield: About 14 cups.

Regina Cash, Anniston Council

YELLOW CHICKEN SOUP

2 lb. chicken (after bone
   is removed) (use backs,
   ribs and bony pieces)
2 medium onions
4 sticks celery
1 bay leaf
1 tsp. red pepper

4 chicken cubes
3 Tbsp. butter
3 1/2 qt. water
2 Tbsp. turmeric
2 Tbsp. parsley
1/2 c. rice, uncooked

Boil chicken pieces until tender and remove bone; add water and pieces of chicken and cook for 45 minutes. Add all spices, onions, celery, butter, chicken cubes and rice. Cook for 45 minutes on low speed. Soup will be thick; add water if for thinner soup. Salt and pepper to taste.

Louise Berrey, Montgomery Council

CHICKEN VELVET SOUP

1/3 c. chicken fat
3/4 c. flour
1 1/2 qt. chicken
   stock, heated
1 pt. warm milk

2 c. diced, cooked chicken
1 tsp. Accent
Salt and pepper
   to taste
Chopped pimento

Melt chicken fat; add flour and cook over medium heat, stirring constantly. Cook until thick. Add remaining milk, stock and chicken. Heat thoroughly. Add Accent. Season to taste with salt and pepper. Garnish with diced pimento, well drained.

Note: You may use 1/2 light cream and 1/2 milk.

Betty Parker, Montgomery Council

SHE CRAB SOUP

2 c. crabmeat (fresh)
2 Tbsp. butter
1 small onion, grated
Salt and pepper to taste
1/8 tsp. mace
3 stalks celery, chopped fine

1 c. milk
1/4 c. half & half cream
1/2 Tbsp. Worcestershire sauce
1 tsp. flour
1 Tbsp. water
4 Tbsp. sherry

1567-82

Put crabmeat in double boiler; add butter, salt, pepper, mace, onion and celery; let simmer 5 minutes. Heat milk and add to above. Stir; add cream and Worcestershire sauce. Thicken with flour and water. Add sherry; cook over low heat for 30 minutes. Serve with a wisp of lemon and pass a small pitcher of warm sherry. Serves 4-6.

Elizabeth Yeilding, Riverchase Council

MEAT AND VEGETABLE SOUP

2 c. meat (chicken, turkey, pork, beef) (may be used in any combination as available)
2 c. broth (from above)

1 medium onion, chopped
2 carrots, sliced
1 celery stalk, chopped
1 c. cooked tomatoes (may be canned)
1 c. whole kernel corn

Any other vegetables may be added, such as peas, beans, okra, in 1 cup measures. Add all ingredients. Bring to boil and simmer for 45-60 minutes, until done; add water as necessary. Salt and pepper to taste.

James Andress, Montgomery Council

FRENCH ONION SOUP

4 large onions, sliced thin
1/2 stick butter
1/2 tsp. paprika

1 Tbsp. flour
1 1/2 qt. beef bouillon
2 tsp. Worcestershire sauce

Saute onions slowly in butter in heavy stock pot until transparent. Sprinkle flour, paprika and Worcestershire over onions and cook another 3 minutes, stirring frequently. Slowly add bouillon, stirring constantly until soup begins to boil. Lower heat; cover and simmer for 20 minutes. Serve with croutons and grated Parmesan cheese.

Betty Parker, Montgomery Council

OYSTER SOUP

1 (12 oz.) can fresh oysters
4 Tbsp. butter
1/4 c. chopped onions
4 Tbsp. plain flour

1 1/8 c. milk
1 small can evaporated milk
Salt and white pepper to taste

Saute onions in butter until soft; add seasoning and flour. Stir constantly over low heat until mixture thickens. Poach oysters in own liquid until curly; do not overcook.

Add to flour mixture and cook until bubbly. Add milk, stirring constantly until steaming; do not boil. Serve with oyster crackers. Serves two.

Rita Moore, Anniston Council

COLD CELERY POTATO SOUP

3 c. celery, sliced	1/2 tsp. dried tarragon
1 c. onion, sliced	1/2 tsp. chervil
2 Tbsp. butter	1/2 tsp. summer savory
3 c. chicken broth	3 c. potatoes, diced
2 c. water	and peeled
1 tsp. salt	1/2 c. milk or cream

Saute celery and onions in butter for 10 minutes; add chicken broth and water, salt and seasonings. Allow to simmer a few minutes. Add potatoes and simmer 25 minutes or until potatoes are soft. Blend in blender, then puree for 30 seconds. Pour into bowl and stir in milk. Let cool, then chill. Serve in chilled bowls. Sprinkle each serving with chopped fresh tarragon. Makes 8-10 servings.

M. Jewel Posey, Life Member,
Tri-Cities Council

ALMOST "HOMEMADE" CREAM OF POTATO SOUP
(Also called "Monday Night Football Soup")

Saute in a squirt of Squeeze Parkay:

2 or 3 Tbsp. minced onion, or 2 or 3 green onions (include some green)	1 garlic clove (mince or press in garlic press)

Add:

1 can Campbell's cream of potato soup	1/2 or 1 soup can half & half or coffee cream or milk, or whatever
1 soup can water	Black pepper

Stir in leftover mashed potatoes (if you have them). Heat until bubbly. Ladle into soup bowls and sprinkle with a bit of dill weed (if you like dill) or parsley flakes, or nothing, etc. Serve alone or with grilled cheese sandwiches. Makes generous servings for working wife and hungry husband.

Julie Young, Riverchase Council

POTATO-TOMATO SOUP

2 c. sliced onions
1/4 c. butter
2 c. sliced potatoes
6 c. boiling water
3 c. canned tomatoes

2 tsp. sugar
1 tsp. salt
1/8 tsp. paprika
1 c. cream

Saute onions until translucent in butter; add potatoes and water. Simmer 30 minutes. Add tomatoes, sugar, salt and paprika and simmer 20 minutes longer. Put soup through blender or strainer. Season to taste. Scald cream; stir into tomato mixture.

Dorothy Franklin, Montgomery Council

SHRIMP SOUP

1 medium onion, sliced
1 clove garlic, sliced
1 medium carrot,
  scraped and sliced
5 c. water

1 stalk celery with leaves,
  sliced
1 qt. (2 lb.) raw shrimp
  (in shell)
1 tsp. salt

Bring water to a boil with all ingredients except shrimp. Add shrimp and cook until tender; drain, reserving liquid. Peel shrimp; place in blender with 2 cups of the liquid. Blend until shrimp are finely chopped; add to remaining liquid in a saucepan. Taste for seasoning. Serve hot with thin slice of lemon for garnish.

AUNT B'S SPINACH SOUP

1 pkg. chopped frozen
  spinach, cooked
  according to pkg.
  directions and drained
1 onion, chopped

2 chicken bouillon cubes
1 stick butter
2 Tbsp. flour
3 1/2 c. milk

Melt butter in skillet; add onion and saute until tender. Add flour and cook until slightly thick. Add chicken bouillon cubes, then pour in milk. Cook until slightly thick. Add spinach and cook a few minutes more. To serve, sprinkle with Parmesan cheese.

Mrs. William O. McCoy,
Birmingham Central Council

SQUASH SOUP

3 lb. yellow squash
1 large onion
2 cloves garlic
4 c. chicken broth (or
  2 cans chicken soup
  and 2 c. water)

1 carton half & half
1/2 c. butter or margarine
1/2 c. vegetable oil
2 tsp. salt
1 tsp. white pepper

Cook squash, garlic and onion in small amount of water until tender. Place in blender with small amount of chicken broth. Add other ingredients; stir until smooth. Refrigerate until ready to heat, then add half & half. Do not boil.

Mrs. R. E. Brinton, Birmingham East Council

JELLIED TOMATO SOUP

2 Tbsp. gelatin (unflavored)
2 1/4 c. tomato juice
3 chicken bouillon cubes
2 c. boiling water

1/2 tsp. grated onion
  (flakes may be used)
1/8 tsp. salt
Dash of pepper

Mix tomato juice slowly with gelatin to soften. Dissolve bouillon cubes in water; stir into gelatin and tomato juice mixture until gelatin is dissolved. Stir in onion, salt and pepper. Refrigerate until set. Serve in small bowl placed in larger bowl of crushed ice.

Eleanor Gearhart, Montgomery Council

VEGETABLE SOUP

1/2 gal. tomatoes,
  peeled and chopped
1 large onion, sliced thin
6 or 8 pods of okra, sliced
  (more if small)

1 c. butter beans
1 c. cream corn
1 c. carrots, sliced
1 hot pepper (optional)

Cook butter beans about 30 to 45 minutes; drain. Cook cream corn as you do to eat (omit seasoning) for about 30 minutes. Cook carrots for about 20 minutes; drain. Mix all together. Cook till other ingredients are done. Season with salt and 1/2 stick oleo. This can be canned, but only mix together all ingredients, pack in quart jars, add 1 teaspoon salt and pressure for 20 minutes at 10 pounds pressure.

P.S. No butter if canned.

Marcia Freeman, Birmingham East Council

HOMEMADE VEGETABLE SOUP

2 lb. ground beef
2 pkg. frozen vegetables
1 can tomatoes
3 c. water
Salt and pepper

3 c. potatoes, diced
1 medium onion, chopped
1 small can tomato sauce
1-2 Tbsp. Worcestershire
   sauce

Brown ground beef in skillet; drain well. In a large saucepan combine beef and all remaining ingredients and cook until vegetables are tender. Serve with hot corn bread.
Shirley Ward, Birmingham South Council

VEGETABLE SOUP

6 medium size potatoes,
   cubed
4 carrots, sliced

2 medium onions, chopped
4 bouillon cubes (beef)
1 1/2 c. water

Place above in pressure cooker and cook about 8 minutes after weight starts to jiggle. Remove from heat. When top can be removed, add:

Salt to taste
1 can whole kernel corn

1 can green limas or peas
2 cans tomatoes

Cook about 5-8 minutes more after weight starts to jiggle. When cool enough to remove top, stir and serve.
Melda H. Hicks, Anniston Council

QUICK VEGETABLE BEEF SOUP

1 lb. ground beef
1 large (46 oz.) can
   V-8 juice
2 cans Veg-All or other
   mixed vegetables
2 cans tomatoes

1 or 2 beef bouillon cubes,
   dissolved in 1 c. boiling
   water
2 or 3 bay leaves
Oregano flakes to taste
1 Tbsp. parsley flakes
Salt and pepper to taste

Brown ground beef; drain off all grease. Drain mixed vegetables. In Dutch oven or other large pot, mix V-8 juice, tomatoes, cup of water in which beef bouillon cube dissolved, bay leaves, oregano and parsley flakes. Add ground beef and drained mixed vegetables. Salt and pepper to taste. Cook over low to medium heat about 1 hour. Remove bay leaves before serving.
Jane Knox, Montgomery Council

462

VEGETABLE BEEF SOUP

1 pkg. short ribs of beef
2 carrots, diced
2 medium white potatoes, diced
2 stalks celery, diced
2 medium onions, diced
1 medium jar chopped mushrooms
1 small can butter beans
1 small can English peas
1 small can whole kernel corn
1 small can okra and tomatoes
1 or 2 medium cans stewed tomatoes
1/2 c. Heinz tomato catsup
1 small can green beans

Cut beef across and lengthwise to bone; cover with water. Boil while preparing vegetables until bone can be removed. Cut meat into bite size pieces; return to boiling juice. Heat vegetables in separate container, part at the time if necessary. Do not add cold vegetables to meat. When vegetables begin to boil, add them to meat and simmer until vegetables are done. Catsup may be added at any time or omitted. An extra piece of beef fat helps to season. Salt to taste and, if you think necessary, add a little margarine.
Pearl Reynolds, Montgomery Council

CAJUN VEGETABLE BEEF SOUP

2 (46 oz.) cans tomato juice
1 (32 oz.) can whole peeled tomatoes
2 (10 1/2 oz.) cans beef broth
3 1/2 lb. beef cubes (stew meat, chuck or round)
1 medium head cabbage, coarsely chopped
1 large onion, chopped
1/2 bell pepper, sliced
3 cloves garlic
3 bay leaves
4 large carrots, sliced
4 large stalks celery, chopped
1 (1 lb.) bag frozen corn
1 (1 lb.) bag frozen English peas
1 (1 lb.) bag frozen lima beans
1 (1 lb.) bag cut green beans
2 Tbsp. Tony's Creole Seasoning (if Tony's seasoning is unavailable, salt and pepper to taste)

In 10 quart pot pour tomato juice, cut up tomatoes and beef broth; add beef cubes and the remainder of the ingredients. Bring to a boil and simmer on low 3 to 4 hours, or until vegetables are done. Tastes great the first day, but even better the second! Freezes very well!
Johnnie P. Walker, Birmingham Central Council

VICHYSSOISE

4 leeks with tops
3 c. peeled, sliced
   potatoes
3 c. boiling water
4 chicken bouillon cubes
3 Tbsp. butter

1 c. half & half
1 c. milk
1 tsp. salt
1/4 tsp. pepper
2 Tbsp. minced chives
1/4 tsp. paprika

Finely chop leeks and green tops. Cook potatoes and leeks in boiling water (uncovered) about 10 minutes or until tender. Do not drain. Press mixture through a sieve into a double boiler. Add next 6 ingredients. Mix well; reheat. Chill thoroughly. Serve very cold. Top with chives and paprika. Also very good topped with chopped fresh spinach.

Sandra Herndon, Birmingham South Council

BEEF STEW

2 lb. beef stew
2 c. potatoes
2 c. onions
2 c. celery
2 c. carrots
1 large can mushrooms
   (liquid)

1 Tbsp. sugar
2 Tbsp. salt
1 tsp. pepper
1/2 tsp. basil
5 Tbsp. tapioca
3 c. V-8 juice

Mix V-8 juice and tapioca together and set aside. Put other ingredients in heavy pot and pour V-8 mixture over, stirring well. Cover pot and cook on stove or bake in 250° oven for 5 hours.

Mrs. W. T. Harbuck

BEEF STEW WITH RED WINE

18 to 20 small white onions
1 lb. lean salt pork, cut
   in strips about 1 1/2
   inches long, 1/4 inch
   thick
3/4 lb. sliced or whole
   small mushrooms
3 Tbsp. butter
3 lb. boneless beef (chuck
   or rump), cut in bite
   size pieces, and patted
   dry before cooking

1 bay leaf
2 Tbsp. chopped shallots
1 finely chopped carrot
3 Tbsp. flour
1 c. hot beef stock
2 c. dry red wine
1 Tbsp. tomato paste
1 garlic clove
1 tsp. dried thyme
Salt and pepper
4 parsley sprigs

Step 1: Blanch the salt pork in 1 quart simmering water for 5 minutes; drain and dry on paper towels. Put in skillet and brown over moderate heat until crisp and golden. Remove strips and drain on paper towel. In the rendered fat, brown 18 to 20 small white onions. Shake the pan and roll onions around so they brown evenly. Set pan aside.
Step 2: Melt 3 tablespoons butter and cook 3/4 pound sliced or whole small mushrooms; add to onions and set aside.
Step 3: Brown beef in any leftover fat from onions, plus added fat if needed. When brown, put into casserole; add bouquet garni made of 4 parsley sprigs and 1 bay leaf. To pan in which beef was browned, add 2 tablespoons chopped shallots and 1 finely chopped carrot and cook until lightly colored. Stir in 3 tablespoons flour. If mixture looks dry, add butter or pork fat. When flour begins to brown slightly, remove from heat and add 1 cup hot beef stock. Blend with wire whisk. Stir in 2 cups dry red wine and 1 tablespoon tomato paste. Stir until sauce thickens. Mix in 1 garlic clove (crushed), 1 teaspoon dried thyme, salt and pepper. Pour sauce over beef; add pork strips and let simmer in 350° oven for 2 to 3 hours until meat is tender. Gently stir in onions and mushrooms and their juices; skim off all fat on surface and let cook few minutes more. If too thin, remove meat and vegetables with slotted spoon and boil it down rapidly, then return meat and vegetables. Serve in casserole. Much better if made a day in advance.

Bobbie Robertson

GROUND BEEF STEW

1 lb. ground beef
1 can cream of mushroom
  soup
1 can Veg-All

1 c. water
Salt and pepper to taste
1 (5 oz.) pkg. egg noodles

Brown ground beef and drain excess fat. Add soup, Veg-All, water, salt and pepper; simmer 10-15 minutes. Serve over cooked noodles.

Ann Perry, Birmingham South Council

BRUNSWICK STEW

2 1/2 lb. chicken
3 (No. 2) cans tomatoes
2 (No. 2) cans okra
  (canned or frozen)

3 lb. potatoes, mashed
  or creamed
1 stick butter or margarine
Dash of Worcestershire sauce

1567-82

2 1/2 lb. pork roast
1 (8 oz.) can tomato paste
2 (No. 2) cans yellow
  corn (cream style)

3 large onions
Red pepper and salt to taste
Small amount of garlic
  (optional)

(For increasing stew, add 1 can lima beans.)

Stew chicken and pork roast until tender; save broths. Separate meat from bones. Add meats, tomatoes, tomato paste, onions (cut fine), salt and pepper. Cover and simmer in large heavy pot for 3 hours. Add creamed potatoes, corn, okra, butter, Worcestershire sauce (garlic and lima, optional). Simmer an extra 30 minutes, stirring continually, butter will stick. Serves 8 to 12. (Can be frozen.)

Becky Cook, Huntsville Council

BRUNSWICK STEW

1 (4 or 5 lb.) hen
3 to 5 lb. pork roast
1 c. onion, chopped
2 c. chicken broth
1 c. pork broth

2 or 3 cans corn (half grain
  or cream)
Juice of 1 lemon
1 (14 oz.) bottle catsup
1 (5 oz.) bottle Worcestershire
1 or 2 Tbsp. vinegar

Cook meat until tender and falls off bone; add all ingredients together and simmer for 1 hour.

Louie Spear, Montgomery Council

HOMEMADE BRUNSWICK STEW

1 (16 oz.) can cream
  style corn
1 (10 3/4 oz.) can cream
  of chicken soup
1 (16 oz.) can tomatoes
1 c. chopped celery

1 medium onion, chopped
1/2 green pepper, chopped
1 1/2 Tbsp. chili powder
1 lb. hamburger meat (ground
  beef)
Dash of Worcestershire sauce

Brown ground beef and drain. In large pot or saucepan mix all ingredients and ground beef. Cook for 30-40 minutes or until celery is tender. It's delicious!

Ruth Gregory, Montgomery Council

HYRB'S BRUNSWICK STEW

1 c. sliced onions
3 Tbsp. oil
2 (16 oz.) cans tomatoes
1/4 c. each water and
   sherry (or 1 c. water)
1 env. French's beef
   stew seasoning mix
1 (10 oz.) pkg. frozen
   whole kernel corn

1 (10 oz.) pkg. frozen
   lima beans
1 Tbsp. French's
   Worcestershire sauce
1/2 tsp. salt
3 1/2 to 4 c. cubed, cooked
   chicken or turkey
1 (10 oz.) pkg. frozen okra
1 small zucchini, sliced

Cook onions in oil in large pan until tender; add tomatoes, water, sherry, seasoning mix, corn, beans, Worcestershire sauce and salt. Simmer, covered, 15 minutes. Add chicken, okra and zucchini; simmer 10 minutes. Makes 6 servings.

Jacqueline Adams, Tuscaloosa Council

CROCK POT STEW

Beef roast
Carrots
Celery

White onions
Potatoes (optional)
Lawry's seasoned salt

Dice vegetables and place in crock pot. Trim most of the fat from the beef. Season with seasoned salt, regular table salt and pepper. Place beef in crock pot on top of the vegetables (it takes vegetables longer to cook than the beef). Do not add any liquids (the natural juices from the vegetables will be enough). Cook on low setting for approximately 8 hours or until done.

Note: For a good diet recipe, leave potatoes out of recipe.

Carol Y. Smith, Birmingham Central Council

GREEN BEAN AND ROAST STEW

4 lb. chuck roast
2 lb. green beans
1 medium can tomato
   juice

5 medium potatoes
1 medium onion
1 tsp. sweet basil
Salt and pepper

Cut meat into stew pieces. Brown in pan (on medium) with oil; cut potatoes in fourths and brown in same pan. Cut onion and brown. Place each ingredient in Dutch oven as it finishes browning. Place well drained beans in frypan in small amount of oil and fry for about 5 minutes. Place beans in Dutch oven. Pour tomato juice in pan and cook about 5

1567-82

minutes, then pour into Dutch oven and rinse frypan with small amount of water and pour this into Dutch oven. Sprinkle sweet basil and salt and pepper. Cook on low for 3 hours or until meat is tender.

Dorothy Hayes, Birmingham Central Council

HOBO STEW

4 hamburger patties
4 potatoes, unpeeled
4 carrots

4 pats of butter
Tiny pinch of sea salt for
    each patty
4 large pieces of foil

Place foil pieces on table. Use 1 potato, sliced thin, for each piece of foil. Put patty on top of potato slices. Divide onion slices evenly. Slice 1 carrot for each pack. Add a little butter and a pinch of salt on top. Fold foil up and place packets on baking sheet; bake in preheated 400° oven for 30 minutes or until the carrots and potatoes are done. Serve in foil. Serves 4.

Kathleen Leggett, Huntsville Council

INDIAN STEW

2 medium onions,
    chopped fine
1/2 green pepper,
    chopped fine
2 Tbsp. butter
1 lb. ground beef

1 (No. 2) can whole kernel
    corn (2 c.)
1 can tomato soup
1 tsp. sugar
1 tsp. salt
2 Tbsp. flour blended with
    2 Tbsp. water

Cook onions and green pepper in frying pan with butter for 5 minutes. Add meat and allow to brown well, stirring frequently. Add corn, soup, sugar and salt; simmer about 15 minutes. Stir in blended flour and water. Cook for a few minutes and then serve. (Use more flour to make stew thicker.)

Vinnie Mae Lyon, Birmingham Central Council

OYSTER STEW

1 qt. oysters
1 stick butter
4 Tbsp. green onion,
    chopped

1 tsp. Worcestershire
1 qt. milk, heated
Salt and pepper to taste

468

Drain oysters; reserve liquor. Saute onions in butter until tender; remove. Heat oysters in remaining butter until edges curl. Combine all ingredients, including oyster liquor. Season to taste. For a richer stew, use 1/2 light cream and 1/2 milk.

Betty Parker, Montgomery Council

OYSTER STEW

2 green onions, chopped	1 qt. half & half
2 Tbsp. butter	Salt to taste
1 pt. oysters, undrained	Pepper to taste

Saute onions in butter; add oysters and their liquid. Cook over low heat 3 or 4 minutes or until edges of oysters curl. Add half & half, salt and pepper and heat thoroughly. Serve with crackers. Serves 8.

Carol York, Montgomery Council

** NOTES **

** NOTES **

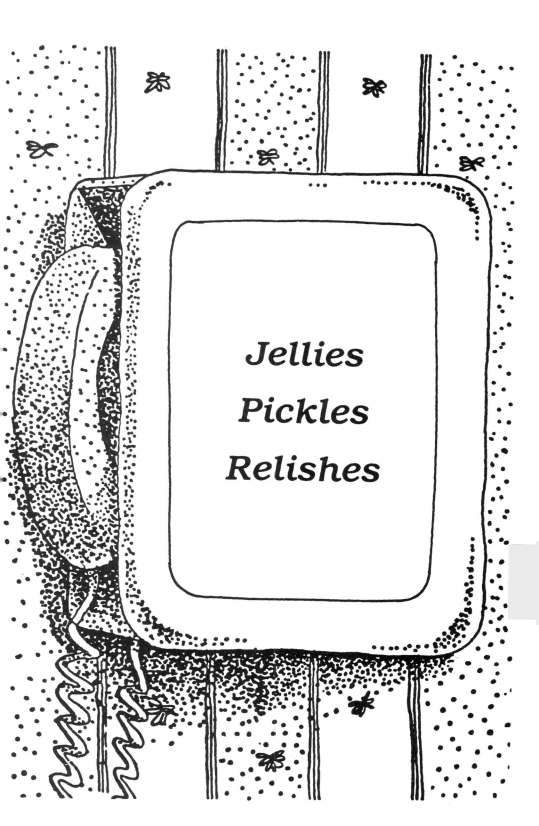

Jellies

Pickles

Relishes

QUANTITIES TO SERVE 100

Baked beans . . . . .5 gallons
Beef . . . . .40 pounds
Beets . . . . .30 pounds
Bread . . . . 10 loaves
Butter . . . . .3 pounds
Cabbage for slaw . . . . .20 pounds
Cakes . . . . 8 cakes
Carrots . . . . .33 pounds
Cauliflower . . . . .18 pounds
Cheese . . . . .18 pounds
Chicken for chicken pie . . . . .40 pounds
Coffee . . . . .3 pounds
Cream . . . . 3 quarts
Fruit cocktail . . . . 1 gallon
Fruit juice . . . . 4 (No. 10) cans
Fruit salad . . . . 20 quarts
Ground beef . . . . .30 to 36 pounds
Ham . . . . .40 pounds
Ice cream . . . . .4 gallons
Lettuce . . . . .20 heads
Meat loaf . . . . .24 pounds
Milk . . . . .6 gallons
Nuts . . . . .3 pounds
Olives . . . . 1¾ pounds
Oysters . . . . 18 quarts
Pickles . . . . 2 quarts
Pies . . . . .18 pies
Potatoes . . . . .35 pounds
Roast pork . . . . .40 pounds
Rolls . . . . 200 rolls
Salad dressing . . . . 3 quarts
Scalloped potatoes . . . . .5 gallons
Soup . . . . .5 gallons
Sugar cubes . . . . .3 pounds
Tomato juice . . . . 4 (No. 10) cans
Vegetables . . . . 4 (No. 20) cans
Vegetable salad . . . . 20 quarts
Whipping cream . . . . 4 pints
Wieners . . . . .25 pounds

JELLIES, PICKLES, RELISHES

SHERRIED APPLE BUTTER

4 lb. tart cooking apples,
  cored and quartered
  (about 16 medium apples)
4 c. apple cider
1 c. cider vinegar
5 c. sugar

1 c. sweet sherry
1 whole lemon, seeded
  and finely ground
1 1/2 tsp. ground cinnamon
1/2 tsp. cloves
1/2 tsp. allspice

In a 6 quart Dutch oven put apples, cider and vinegar. Bring mixture to boil; reduce heat and simmer covered for 1 hour. Puree mixture (should have about 10 cups). Stir in sugar, sherry, lemon, cinnamon, cloves and allspice. Bring mixture to boil; reduce heat and boil gently for 1 1/2 hours or until very thick. Stir frequently. Ladle hot apple butter into clean pint jars, leaving 1/2 inch headspace. Adjust lids; process in boiling water. Boil 10 minutes (start counting when water is boiling). When processing time is up, transfer hot jars to rack to cool. Makes 4 pints.

Vickie Knox, Birmingham East Council

APPLE-PEACH CONSERVE

2 c. chopped, unpared
  tart apples
2 c. chopped, peeled
  peaches

1/2 c. lemon juice
  (fresh, frozen or canned)
3 c. sugar

Combine ingredients; cook slowly until apples are transparent, about 20 minutes. Pour into hot sterilized glasses; seal immediately. Makes seven 6 ounce glasses.

Dot Mastin, Mobile Council

DRIED APPLE (MOCK)

2 gal. thinly sliced
  apples

4 c. sugar
1/4 c. dark vinegar

Mix sugar and vinegar; pour over apples and let stand overnight. Cook until tender. Can be canned or frozen. Yield: About 7 pints.

Judy Burnett, Decatur Council

RUTH SPITZER'S APPLE JELLY

6 lb. apples, stemmed and coarsely chopped
6 c. water

3 c. sugar
2 Tbsp. lemon juice

Combine apples and water in large Dutch oven; bring to boil. Cover; reduce heat and simmer 20-25 minutes. Strain apples through a jelly bag or 4 layer cheesecloth, reserving 4 cups juice; discard pulp. Combine 4 cups juice, sugar and lemon juice in Dutch oven; bring to boil, stirring frequently. Boil until mixture reaches 220° on candy thermometer. Skim off foam. Quickly pour jelly into hot sterilized jars, leaving 1/2 inch headspace. Seal with 1/8 inch layer of paraffin and cover with lids. Yield: About 4 pints.

Patsy S. Dean, Mobile Council

APRICOT JAM

1/2 lb. dried apricots
1 whole orange (grind all except seeds)

1 (8 oz.) can crushed pineapple
3 c. sugar

Soak apricots overnight in water to cover. Cook apricots in this soaking water until tender. Mash thoroughly; add orange and pineapple and bring to a boil. Stir in sugar and continue cooking, stirring constantly until thick. Put into 4 sterile half pint jars and seal.

Joyce Hobbs, Huntsville Council

RUTH SPITZER'S BLACKBERRY JELLY

4 to 6 qt. blackberries
7 1/2 c. sugar

2 (3 oz.) pkg. liquid fruit pectin

Press enough berries through a sieve to extract 4 cups juice. Combine 4 cups juice and sugar in Dutch oven; bring to rolling boil. Cook 1 minute, stirring frequently and add fruit pectin; bring to boil. Continue boiling 1 minute, stirring frequently. Remove from heat and skim off foam. Pour into jars. Yield: 7 half pints.

Patsy S. Dean, Mobile Council

RUTH SPITZER'S FIG PRESERVES

2 qt. (about 4 1/2 lb.) figs
7 c. sugar
1/2 c. lemon juice

1 1/2 qt. water
2 lemons, thinly sliced

Cook figs 15-20 minutes in enough boiling water to cover; drain figs and set aside. Combine sugar, lemon juice and 1 1/2 quarts water in a large Dutch oven; cook over medium heat, stirring constantly, until sugar dissolves. Add figs; return to a boil and cook 10 minutes, stirring occasionally. Add lemon slices and boil 15 minutes or until figs are tender and clear. Carefully remove figs from syrup with a slotted spoon; boil syrup additional 10 minutes or until desired thickness. Return figs to syrup; skim off foam. Quickly ladle preserves in hot sterilized jars, leaving 1/4 inch headspace. Cover with lids; process in boiling water bath 30 minutes. Yield: 5 half pints.

Patsy S. Dean, Mobile Council

PEELED FIG PRESERVES

4 qt. peeled figs
3 qt. sugar
1 orange, sliced

1 lemon, sliced
1 c. water

Peel figs, removing stems, and rinse well to remove small portions of skin. Make a syrup of sugar and water; add sliced orange and lemon. Cook until syrup spins a good thread. Remove orange and lemon and add figs. Cook until figs are clear and tender, and syrup is thickness desired.

Betty Parker, Montgomery Council

FIG-STRAWBERRY PRESERVES

3 c. mashed figs
3 c. sugar

2 small boxes strawberry jello
(or 1 large family box)

Cook mashed figs and sugar 20 or 25 minutes. When ready, add 2 small boxes jello; cook until dissolved (a few minutes). Pour into jars; seal.

Betty Havard, Mobile Council

TROPICAL FRUIT MARMALADE

2 c. frozen peaches	1 1/2 Tbsp. lemon juice
1/2 c. canned pineapple	2 c. sugar
1 small orange	2 Tbsp. rum

Drain and slice peaches; drain and chunk pineapple, quarter and seed orange. Mix all ingredients except rum. Simmer and stir over low heat until thick (approximately 30-40 minutes). Just before sealing in sterilized jar, stir in rum.

Carol York, Montgomery Council

MUSCADINE PRESERVES

Wash fruit and mash inside into a pan, being careful to get all seeds out of hulls. Place hulls in another pan and put water up to 1 inch from top of hulls. Cook pulp until seeds can be removed by running through a strainer. When hulls are tender, combine with pulp after removing seeds. Measure into large pan 1 cup fruit and 3/4 cup sugar. Cook until done and can immediately.

Faith Kirby, Anniston Council

ORANGE MARMALADE

4 medium oranges	6 c. water
3 lemons	Sugar

Lightly grate outer edge of oranges and lemons. Remove peel and cut into thin slivers; measure peel. To 2 cups orange peel and 1 1/2 cups lemon peel add 6 cups water; let stand overnight. Next day, cook until peel is tender. Let stand overnight. On third day, add 2 cups sugar for each 2 cups of cooked peel and liquid. Cook to jelly stage (10 minutes). Let stand until slightly cool; stir occasionally. Pour into sterilized jars and seal. Yield: 2 pints.

Peggy Autry, Birmingham South Council

NO COOK PEACH JAM

2 1/4 lb. ripe peaches	1 tsp. ascorbic acid crystals
5 1/2 c. sugar	2 pouches liquid fruit pectin
1 c. Karo syrup	1/3 c. lemon juice

Wash, peel and thinly slice 2 1/4 pounds ripe peaches. Fully crush, one layer at a time. Measure 2 3/4 cups. In 4 quart bowl stir together fruit, 5 1/2 cups sugar, 1 cup Karo syrup and 1 teaspoon ascorbic acid crystals until well

474

blended. Let stand 10 minutes. In small bowl mix two 3
ounce packages liquid fruit pectin and 1/3 cup lemon juice.
Stir into fruit mixture; stir vigorously 3 minutes. Ladle into
clean 1/2 pint freezer containers. Cover and let stand at
room temperature until set (24 hours).
Wanda Lynch, Montgomery Council

DRIED PEACHES (MOCK)

1/2 bushel peaches   5 lb. sugar
  (do not peel)   1 c. vinegar

Cook until thick. Can or freeze.
Judy Burnett, Decatur Council

PEAR CONSERVE

1 orange   5 c. peeled, chopped pears
2 lemons   2 c. raisins
                            5 c. sugar

Run the orange and lemons through food grinder, using
coarse knife. Combine ground fruit, chopped pears, raisins
and sugar. Cook slowly until thick. Pour into hot sterilized
jars and seal. Yield: 3-4 pints.
Peggy Autry, Birmingham South Council

PEAR HONEY

1 lb. ground pears   1/4 c. canned crushed
  (1 1/2 c.)   pineapple
1 1/2 c. sugar   1 tsp. lemon juice

Wash, peel and core fruit. Put pears through a food
chopper, using coarse blade. Mix all ingredients and heat
mixture, stirring thoroughly until sugar is dissolved. Boil
mixture until it is thick and clear. Pack in hot standard
canning jars. Adjust jar lids and bands. Process in boiling
water bath canner (212° F.) for 10 minutes.
Mildred Albright, Life Member,
Birmingham Council

PEAR PRESERVES

Wash, peel and cut fruit into good size chunks. Cook with 1/2 cup sugar to 1 cup fruit. Wash and cut ends from 1 lemon, cut in half, and juice. Remove all seeds and put lemon hull and all in with fruit mixture. Cook over medium heat until fruit is transparent. Can immediately.

Faith Kirby, Anniston Council

PEAR-PINEAPPLE-PEACH CURRY

1 (16 oz.) can Bartlett
  pears
1 (20 oz.) can pineapple
  slices or chunks
1 (16 oz.) can peach halves
2 c. combined syrups
  from fruit
2 Tbsp. onion, minced

1 Tbsp. margarine
1 Tbsp. cornstarch
2 tsp. curry powder
1/8 tsp. cardamon
1/8 tsp. ginger
2 Tbsp. lemon juice
1 tsp. grated lemon peel

Drain fruit. Combine syrups and measure 2 cups; set aside for sauce. Saute onion in margarine until tender; add cornstarch, curry powder, cardamon and ginger. Gradually add combined syrups, cooking and stirring until smooth and thickened. Add lemon juice and peel, then fruits. Fruit may be left in halves or quartered. Simmer gently about 5 minutes or until fruit is heated through. Serve hot with meat or poultry. Serves 10 to 12.

Evelyn Hannigan, Birmingham Central Council

HOT PEPPER JELLY

2/3 c. green hot peppers
1 bell pepper
1 1/2 c. vinegar

6 c. sugar
1 bottle Certo
1 tsp. food coloring (red
  or green)

Chop peppers and put in blender with vinegar; add sugar and mix well. Bring mixture to a rolling boil, 1 minute. Strain; return to stove and bring to boil again, 5 minutes. Remove from heat, and at once add Certo and food coloring. Put into six 1/2 pint jars and seal.

Mary C. Martin, Birmingham East Council

MOCK PINEAPPLE

3 c. sugar
1 1/2 c. lemon juice
1 (46 oz.) can pineapple juice

1 gal. coarsely grated
  zucchini, peeled and
  seeded

Simmer for 20 minutes. Pack in pint jars or freeze. (Pint jars must be pressured at 10 pounds for 10 minutes.)
Sara Lindsey, Riverchase Council

QUICK-AND-EASY STRAWBERRY JAM

1 3/4 c. prepared fruit
  (about 1 qt. fully ripe
  strawberries)

4 c. (1 3/4 lb.) sugar
2 Tbsp. lemon juice
1 pouch Certo fruit pectin

Use any containers 1 pint or smaller that have tight fitting lids. Wash, scald and drain containers and lids, or use automatic dishwasher with really hot (150° F. or higher) rinse water. Stem and thoroughly crush strawberries, 1 layer at a time. Measure exactly 1 3/4 cups fruit. Place in a large bowl or pan. Thoroughly mix sugar into fruit; let stand 10 minutes. Combine lemon juice and fruit pectin; stir into fruit. Continue stirring about 3 minutes. (A few sugar crystals will remain.) Ladle quickly into containers. Cover at once and let stand at room temperature for 24 hours to set. Then store in freezer. If jam is to be used within 2 or 3 weeks, it may be stored in refrigerator. Makes about 5 cups of jam.
Betty Floyd Parker, Montgomery Council

FROZEN STRAWBERRY PRESERVES

3 1/2 c. crushed berries
6 1/2 c. granulated sugar

1 c. cold water
1 box Sure-Jell

Clean berries; wash and drain. Crush with potato masher. Add 1 cup water to 1 box Sure-Jell. Bring to a boil and boil 1 minute. Pour over berries and sugar; stir until sugar is dissolved. Pack into container and place in deep freeze after chilling in refrigerator.
Nell French, Decatur Council

WATERMELON GRANITA

Use 5 cups cubed watermelon pulp (about 6 pounds with the rind), seeded, 1/3 cup superfine granulated sugar, 1/4 cup fresh lime juice and 1 tablespoon grated lime rind. In a food processor fitted with the steel blade or in a blender in

1567-82

batches puree the watermelon and transfer the puree to a bowl. In a stainless steel or enameled saucepan combine the sugar, the lime juice, the lime rind and 2/3 cup water and bring the liquid to a boil, stirring to dissolve the sugar. Simmer the syrup for 5 minutes and let it cool. Stir the syrup into the puree; pour the mixture into an 8 inch square baking dish and freeze it in the freezing compartment of the refrigerator until it is firm but not frozen hard. In a food processor fitted with the steel blade or in a chilled bowl beat the mixture until it is smooth. Return the mixture to the pan and freeze it for 3 hours, or until it is firm. To serve, let the granita stand at room temperature for 5 minutes, or until it is soft enough to scoop. Serves 4 to 6.

Katherine Creamer, Mobile Council

WATERMELON HONEY

Use the pulp from 5 pounds watermelon, seeded and cut into pieces, 1 to 2 tablespoons honey, or to taste, and 1 tablespoon fresh lime juice.

In a heavy stainless steel or enameled saucepan cook the watermelon over low heat, stirring occasionally, and being careful not to let it scorch, for 1 hour and 30 minutes and puree it through the fine disk of a food mill into a bowl. Stir in the honey and the lime juice; pour the mixture into sterilized Mason-type jars, filling the jars to within 1/2 inch of the top, and seal the jars with the lids. Serve the honey over sherbets and fruit compotes. The watermelon honey keeps, chilled, for up to 3 months. Makes about 1 1/2 cups.

Katherine Creamer, Mobile Council

BREAD AND BUTTER PICKLES

4 qt. sliced medium cucumbers	1 1/2 tsp. turmeric
6 medium white onions	1 1/2 tsp. celery seed
2 bell peppers	2 Tbsp. mustard seed
1/3 c. salt	3 c. vinegar
	5 c. sugar

Slice cucumber thin, onion and peppers; add salt and mix thoroughly. Cover with ice and let stand 3 hours. Drain thoroughly. Combine remaining ingredints. Pour over cucumbers and heat to a boil; put in jars and seal.

Jean Ethridge, Riverchase Council

478

BREAD AND BUTTER PICKLES

Use 2 gallons of cut or sliced cucumbers, 1 1/2 cups of salt and enough water to cover cucumber pieces. Let stand 3 days. Drain and put in weak vinegar and water solution with 1 ounce of alum. Let stand for 2 days; drain. Boil together the following:

6 c. vinegar	4 tsp. mustard seed
5 lb. sugar	1 tsp. celery seed
1 Tbsp. cinnamon	12 cloves

Pour over cucumbers. Let stand overnight; boil for 10 minutes and put in jars and seal. Sugar may be reduced to suit taste.

Betty Godwin, Tri-Cities Council

CUCUMBER PICKLES

8 lb. cucumbers	2 qt. vinegar
2 c. household lime	9 c. sugar
2 gal. water	2 Tbsp. salt

Slice cucumbers crosswise. Place in a mixture of lime and water in enameled or pottery container. Let stand overnight. Remove from lime water. Wash cucumbers through 3 changes of fresh cold water. Mix vinegar, sugar and salt and place drained cucumber slices in mixture. Let stand in sugar mixture for 3 hours; bring to a boil and boil for 30 minutes. Place in hot sterilized jars.

Virginia Mayo, Mobile Council

DILLED CUCUMBERS

2 large thinly sliced	1 c. granulated sugar
cucumbers	1/2 c. water
1 c. white vinegar	2 tsp. fresh dill

In a pot combine vinegar, sugar, water, salt and dill. Bring to a boil. Pour hot mixture over slices in a quart jar; close tightly. Refrigerate; chill for 3 hours. May be topped with sour cream. Serves 6.

Mrs. Jeri Nuss, Decatur Council

CANDIED DILL PICKLES

Slice 1 gallon whole dill pickles and cover with ice; when it melts (about 5 hours), drain. Mix 4 pounds sugar, 2 cups vinegar and 3 tablespoons pickling spices. Pour over pickles. Let stand for 3 days, stirring every day. (Do not cover.) Put in jars on the third day.

Ernestine Gudgen, Birmingham South Council

COLD WATER DILL PICKLES

Brine:

8 c. cold water
3/4 c. pickling salt (scant)

2 c. 4% to 6% cider vinegar

To each quart:

4 large sprays fresh dill
1/4 tsp. cream of tartar

1/4 tsp. powdered alum
or 2 lumps solid alum

Rinse pickles off (important - never soak in water). Put 2 dill sprays in clean jar; add pickles, alum, cream of tartar and 2 dill sprays on top. Now add the brine to cover. Put lid on tight; keep at room temperature 6 days. Pickles must work in jars; they won't spoil. Store in cool dark place. Ready to use in 8 weeks.

Tony Kelly, Wetona Kelly, Life Member,
Birmingham Central Council

DILL PICKLES

1 qt. vinegar
2 qt. water
1 c. salt

Dill (to taste)
Garlic (to taste)

Wash cucumbers thoroughly and place them in very hot water. In a large pot boil vinegar, water and salt for 2 minutes. Drain hot water from cucumbers and put in sterile jars with dill and garlic. Pour boiling solution over cucumbers and seal immediately. Open in 3 to 4 weeks.

Norma Wilson, Tri-Cities

HOT DILL PICKLES

Pour the following into jars:

1 gal. cucumbers
1 1/2 Tbsp. mustard seed
1 1/2 tsp. alum

1 small onion
2 garlic cloves
3 hot peppers
1 dill head

480

Bring to a boil:

1 qt. vinegar   1 c. salt
3 qt. water

Pour in jars and seal.

Becky Russell, Decatur Council

FREEZER CUCUMBERS

3 medium cucumbers   2 Tbsp. salt

Syrup:

2 c. sugar   12 whole cloves
12 whole allspice   12 whole peppercorns
3 bay leaves   1 c. vinegar
3/4 c. water

Cover first 2 ingredients with water and let stand 1 hour or more and drain. Boil syrup 15 minutes; let cool. Pour syrup over cucumbers. Add a few pieces of onion, if desired. Pack in plastic container and freeze.

Mrs. J. H. (Sandy) Grace, Tri-Cities Council

MARINATED REFRIGERATOR PICKLES

2 c. sugar   9 medium sized cucumbers
1 c. vinegar   1 medium sized onion
1 tsp. celery seed   1 bell pepper

Wash and slice cucumbers paper thin. Add chopped onion and chopped bell pepper. Mix sugar, vinegar and celery seeds. Pour over vegetables; mix well. Place in jars with tight fitting lids and refrigerate. The flavor of these pickles improves with age.

Regina Pollock, Huntsville Council

MILLION DOLLAR PICKLES

4 qt. sliced cucumbers   4 c. sugar
8 to 10 small onions   1/2 tsp. celery seed
2 small green peppers   1 tsp. turmeric powder
2 small red peppers   2 Tbsp. white mustard seed
1/2 c. salt   1 tsp. mixed pickling spices
1/2 qt. cider vinegar

Slice cucumbers, onions and peppers. Put in large crock. Sprinkle salt over them and cover with water. Soak overnight. Drain. Combine vinegar, sugar, celery seed,

1567-82

turmeric powder, mustard seed and spices in large kettle; bring to boil. Put drained cucumbers in syrup and cook 20 minutes or until tender. Do not overcook, or pickles will become mushy. Pack in hot sterilized jars; seal. Yield: 6 pints.

W. H. Long, Huntsville Council

MIXED PICKLES

1 c. green tomatoes, chopped	1 c. carrot, chopped
	1 c. green beans, chopped
1 c. bell peppers, chopped	2 tsp. mustard seeds
1 c. cabbage, chopped	2 tsp. celery seed
1 c. onions, chopped	2 c. vinegar
1 whole cucumber, chopped	2 c. sugar

Soak tomatoes, pepper, cucumber, onions overnight in 2 quarts water, 1/4 cup salt. Drain. Cook carrots and green beans for 10 minutes and drain. Mix all ingredients. Heat to a boil. Pack in jars and seal.

Marcia Freeman, Birmingham East Council

STRIP PICKLES

7 lb. cucumbers	2 tsp. green cake coloring
Pickling lime	(if desired)
4 1/2 lb. sugar	1 tsp. whole cloves
2 qt. white vinegar	2 tsp. pickling spices
1 tsp. salt	1 tsp. celery seed

Use large size cukes, as all seed pockets have to be removed. Cut in strips as for French fries. Do not use metal. To 1 gallon water add 1 cup lime (pickling lime). Let set 24 hours. Wash through several waters until clear. Cover with clear water; let set 24 hours. Wash again until water is clear. Spices may be put in a cloth bag or added directly to other ingredients to make syrup. Bring to a rolling boil; add cukes. Remove from heat; let set overnight. Bring to a boil; boil 40 minutes or until clear. Can. If spices are added directly to syrup, syrup should be strained before canning. Also, food coloring may be added right before canning. That way, pickles can be colored green, red or some left white. They are quite colorful at Christmas time. The removed seed pockets may be used to make relish.

Emma Arnold, Decatur Council

CRISP SWEET PICKLES

1 (46 oz.) jar Polish or
  kosher dill pickles,
  or 12 pickles
3 c. sugar

1/2 c. vinegar
1 tsp. celery seed
1 tsp. mustard seed
16 to 20 whole cloves

Cut in 1/4 inch slices or sticks. Add ingredients and stir. Stir later to dissolve sugar. Let stand 24 hours. Put in jars and keep in refrigerator.

Mrs. C. S. Bigbee, Montgomery Council

SWEET 'N SOUR CUCUMBERS

2 medium peeled
  cucumbers, thinly sliced
1/4 c. sugar
1/2 c. vinegar

1/2 tsp. salt
1 Tbsp. minced parsley
1/4 c. water
Lemon juice

Dry cucumber slices well on absorbent paper. In a bowl combine all ingredients except cucumber and lemon juice. Cover; chill for 10 minutes. Pour chilled mixture over cucumber; sprinkle with juice. Serves 6.

Mrs. Jeri Nuss, Decatur Council

PICKLED BEETS

12 medium to large beets
1 1/2 c. sugar
4 c. cider vinegar

2 tsp. cloves
4 Tbsp. allspice
2 pt. size canning jars

Scrub beets clean, using cold water. Place beets in a large saucepan and cover with water. Cover pan; place over high heat and bring to a boil; cook 30 minutes or until tender. Drain and cool under running water; peel and slice. Combine sugar, vinegar and spices in saucepan. Bring to a boil; add beets and bring to a boil again; simmer for 5 minutes. Sterilize jars in very hot water. Spoon hot beets into hot jars, leaving 1/2 inch air space at top. Pour vinegar mixture over beets. Place lids on jars and tighten to seal. Makes about 2 pints.

Joyce Hobbs, Huntsville Council

PICKLED BEETS

1 (1 lb.) can sliced
  beets, drained
1 small onion, sliced thinly

3/4 c. apple cider vinegar
1/4 c. water
1 Tbsp. brown sugar

1567-82

1/2 tsp. caraway seed   1/4 tsp. cloves
1/2 tsp. cinnamon   1/4 tsp. salt

In a 3/4 to 1 quart glass dish layer beets and onions which have been separated into rings. Stir remaining ingredients together in an enamel saucepan and heat to full rolling boil. Pour over beets and onion rings immediately. Cover and refrigerate overnight. If onions are omitted, beets will pickle in 6 hours.

For a zippy variation of this recipe, substitute 1/2 teaspoon celery seed and 1/4 teaspoon dry mustard for cinnamon and clove.

Julie Baeder, Huntsville Council

PICKLED EGGS

1 dozen medium eggs   1/2 tsp. salt
1 1/2 c. white vinegar   6 whole cloves
1/2 c. water   1 bay leaf
1 c. sugar   1 large onion, sliced
                               2 pods hot pepper

1. Cover eggs with cold water; bring to boil, reduce heat and simmer 15 to 18 minutes. 2. Drain and immediately run cold water over eggs in pan for several minutes. Peel eggs and place in narrow deep jar. 3. In medium saucepan combine vinegar, water, sugar, salt, cloves and bay leaf. Bring to a boil; reduce heat and simmer for 5 minutes. 4. Pour hot vinegar solution over eggs, making sure eggs are completely covered with the liquid. 5. Place pepper and onion slices on top of eggs. Cover tightly. Place in refrigerator and let stand several days. 6. Eggs may be served whole, halved or sliced, or in sandwiches or salads.

G. O. Cox, Jr., Tuscaloosa Council

PICKLED OKRA

For each pint:

Fresh okra   1 hot green pepper
1 tsp. dill seed   2 cloves garlic
1 hot red pepper

Liquid mixture for 5 pints:

1 qt. vinegar   1/2 c. salt (not iodized)
1 c. water

Place 1/2 teaspoon dill seed in bottom of sterilized jar. Pack washed okra tightly in jar, being careful not to bruise;

add 1/2 teaspoon dill seeds, peppers and garlic. Combine vinegar, water, salt and bring to boil. Cover okra with liquid mixture; seal jars and allow to stand for 2 weeks. Serve icy cold.

Margaret Welch Keith, Huntsville Council

DILL ONION RINGS

1 large Bermuda onion	1/2 c. white vinegar
1/4 c. water	2 tsp. salt
1/4 tsp. dill weed	Liquid no-calorie sweetener
(or dill seed)	(6 tsp.) or 1/2 c. sugar

Peel and cut onion into thin crosswise slices. Separate into rings; place in small bowl. Combine vinegar, water, salt, dill weed and sugar in saucepan; heat to boiling. Pour over onion rings; cover tightly and chill at least 1 hour to blend flavors. The liquid can be reheated and used on another onion. Also, we find that cucumbers, pared and sliced, are delicious fixed in this same solution, with onions.

Mary C. Martin, Birmingham East Council

PICKLED PEACHES

2 lb. brown sugar	4 qt. peaches, peeled
2 c. dark vinegar	1 oz. stick cinnamon
1/2 oz. whole cloves	

Boil sugar, vinegar and spices 20 minutes. Place a few peaches at a time in syrup and cook until tender. Pack into sterilized jars. When jars are full, fill with juice to cover. Seal jar immediately.

Betty Parker, Montgomery Council

YELLOW SQUASH PICKLE

8 c. squash, sliced thin	2 tsp. celery seed
2 c. onions, sliced thin	2 tsp. mustard seed
2 c. vinegar	3 c. sugar
4 bell peppers, sliced thin	Salt to sprinkle

Combine the squash and onions; sprinkle with salt. Set aside for 1 hour; drain liquid off. Combine vinegar, sugar, celery seed, mustard seed and peppers in a pan; bring to a hard boil. Add squash and onions; mix well. Pack in jars and seal. Process in boiling water bath canner for 10 minutes.

Camille Meggs, Tuscaloosa Council

1567-82

GREEN TOMATO PICKLES

Lime Water:

7 lb. small green tomatoes	3 c. lime 2 gal. water

Syrup:

5 lb. sugar	1 tsp. whole cloves
2 qt. vinegar	1 tsp. whole allspice
1 cinnamon stick	1 tsp. mace
1 tsp. celery seeds	1 tsp. ginger

1. Soak tomatoes in the lime water for about 24 hours; remove from lime water and soak in clear water 4 hours. Change the water hourly. 2. Soak overnight in syrup. 3. Boil 45 minutes; put in hot jars and seal. Makes 10-12 pints.

Alexine S. Becker, Montgomery Council

WATERMELON RIND PICKLES

7 lb. melon rinds (real thick) (peel off all red and green and soak in slaked lime overnight)	3 1/2 lb. sugar 1 pt. vinegar 1/2 tsp. oil of cloves 1/2 tsp. oil of cinnamon

Cut rinds into about 1 inch pieces and cook until tender. Drain. Make syrup of sugar, vinegar and spices. Pour over cooked rinds and let stand overnight. Drain syrup; heat and pour back over rinds. Next morning, set rinds and syrup on stove and let come to a good boil for about 1 minute. Put in jars and seal. When ready to serve, refrigerate overnight.

Faith Kirby, Anniston Council

PINK PICKLED WATERMELON RIND

Rind from 5 lb. watermelon	1 tsp. whole cloves
1 c. cider vinegar	2 slices ginger root, each
1 c. sugar	the size of a quarter,
1/4 c. grenadine	peeled and flattened
3 inch cinnamon stick	slightly

Remove the thin green peel from the watermelon rind with a vegetable peeler and cut the rind into 1 x 1/2 inch pieces. In a kettle of boiling water, boil the rind for 15 to 18 minutes, or until it is just tender; drain it, and transfer it to a heatproof ceramic or glass bowl. In a stainless steel or enameled saucepan combine the vinegar, the sugar, the grenadine, the cinnamon, the cloves and the ginger root; bring the liquid to a boil, stirring to dissolve the sugar, and simmer the syrup for 3 minutes. Pour the syrup over the rind and let the rind stand, covered, at room temperature overnight. Drain the syrup into another stainless steel or enameled saucepan and bring it to a boil. Pour the syrup over the rind and let the rind stand, covered, at room temperature overnight. Transfer the rind and the syrup to another stainless steel or enameled saucepan; bring the syrup to a boil and pack the mixture into sterilized Mason-type jars, filling the jars to within 1/2 inch of the top. Wipe the rims with a dampened cloth and seal the jars with the lids. Put the jars in a water bath canner or on a rack in a deep kettle and add enough hot water to the canner to cover the jars by 2 inches. Bring the water to a boil and process the jars, covered, for 10 minutes. Transfer the jars with canning tongs to a folded cloth and let them cool. Store the pickles in a cool, dark place. Makes about 4 cups.

Katherine Creamer, Mobile Council

CABBAGE RELISH

3 large heads cabbage	3 Tbsp. salt
2 qt. grated onion	6 Tbsp. mustard
2 qt. sugar	3 Tbsp. turmeric
2 qt. vinegar	1 c. flour

Cook first 7 ingredients 1 1/2 hours till tender. Mix flour with water to make paste. Add flour paste to other ingredients; stir and cook 10 minutes. Put in hot jars and seal. Good with hot dogs and hamburgers.

Mrs. Libby Pilling, Decatur Council

SWEET CABBAGE RELISH

7 lb. cabbage	8 onions
8 bell peppers	1/2 box celery seed
8 c. sugar	1 small box mustard seed
8 c. white vinegar	1 c. salt

Grind cabbage, onions and bell pepper; put in crock. Sprinkle with salt; let stand 1 1/2 hours. Pour in 3 cups water; squeeze with hands to remove brine. As you squeeze out, place in another crock. Combine sugar, vinegar, celery seed and mustard seeds; pour over and let stand 3 days before serving. Put a jar in refrigerator and store the rest in jars for winter.

Charlotte Adair Smith, Birmingham Council

CARROT RELISH

4 large carrots
1 lemon, thinly sliced

1/2 c. sugar
1/2 tsp. salt

Grind carrots and lemon together; add sugar and salt. Mix well and refrigerate. Relish will keep for several days. Serve with fish or meat.

Virginia Mayo, Mobile Council

CHOW CHOW

10 green tomatoes
10 green bell peppers
3 red bell peppers, if desired
10 medium onions
1 medium cabbage
1/2 c. salt
4 c. apple cider vinegar

6 c. sugar (part brown, if desired)
1 Tbsp. celery seed
1 Tbsp. mustard seed
2 Tbsp. whole cloves
2 Tbsp. allspice berries
1 oz. cinnamon stick

Chop and mix vegetables. Sprinkle salt over mixture and let stand overnight in glass or pottery container. Do not put in tin or aluminum container. In the morning, cover with cold water and squeeze out. Mix other ingredients to boiling vinegar; cook 20 or 30 minutes or until tender. Makes 8 pints Chow Chow.

Mary Edna Fife, Montgomery Council

CORN RELISH

1 c. vinegar
1/2 c. sugar
1 1/2 tsp. mustard seeds
1/2 tsp. salt
3 1/2 c. cooked fresh corn, cut from cob

1/2 c. chopped green pepper
1/2 c. diced pimiento
1/4 c. chopped celery
1/4 c. chopped onion
1 small clove garlic, minced

Combine first 4 ingredients in a Dutch oven; boil 2 minutes, stirring to dissolve sugar. Add remaining ingredients to sugar mixture and boil 3 minutes; cool. Store in refrigerator in an airtight container. Yield: 3 1/2 to 4 cups.

Linda Mitchell, Decatur Council

CORN RELISH

20 ears corn
1 c. chopped green peppers
1 c. chopped red peppers
1 c. chopped onions
1 c. chopped cucumbers
1 c. chopped green tomatoes

1 1/2 c. sugar
2 1/2 Tbsp. mustard seeds
1 tsp. celery seed
1/2 tsp. turmeric
3 c. vinegar
2 c. water

Drop corn in boiling water; boil 15 minutes. Remove and put in cold water. Drain and cut from cob. Combine corn with all other ingredients; boil 15 minutes, stirring constantly. Keep mixture hot while packing in jars. Fill jars within 1/4 of top; seal jars. Process in boiling water bath canner; cover tips for 15 minutes. Remove jars and cool. Yield: 5 or 6 pints.

Geraldine Strickland, Tuscaloosa Council

CRANBERRY-ORANGE RELISH

2 c. cranberries
1 orange

3/4 c. sugar

Wash cranberries and orange. Put orange and cranberries through food chopper; add sugar. Mix well; let stand for 30 minutes before serving.

Bea Windham, Montgomery Council
Suzanne Beaty, Riverchase Council

GREEN TOMATO RELISH

4 qt. green tomatoes
1 pt. finely chopped onions

1 pt. chopped green or
   red peppers

Cover with water; add 1 cup salt. Boil 1 hour, then drain. Add equal parts water and vinegar. Add these spices:

1 Tbsp. paprika
1 oz. celery seed

1 oz. mustard
1 Tbsp. ground cloves
2 c. brown sugar

Cook 1 hour; put in sterilized jars. Seal and store in cool dry place.

Virginia Mayo, Mobile Council

HOT GARLIC RELISHES

4 pt. green tomatoes
1 pt. garlic
1 pt. green hot peppers
  (red can be used too)
1 qt. red vinegar wine

1 pt. onions (use green
  tops), with bottoms
2 pt. cabbage or 1 small
  cabbage
Salt
3 qt. apple cider vinegar

Use food chopper or blender to chop all ingredients; pack in 1/2 pint jars and add 1 teaspoon salt to each jar. Heat vinegar to boiling and pour over packed vegetables and seal. May be used in 2 weeks. Makes 9-10 pints.

Louise Berrey, Montgomery Council

PEAR RELISH

8 qt. peeled, cored pears
5 green peppers
5 red peppers
3 hot peppers

5 large onions
5 c. cider vinegar
5 c. sugar
1 tsp. salt

Grind pears through coarse food chopper and drip until excess juice is removed. Grind peppers and onions. Combine all ingredients; bring to a boil and boil 20 minutes. Fill containers and seal. Process in a water bath canner (212° F.) for 10 minutes.

Mildred Albright, Life Member,
Birmingham Council

HOT PEPPER RELISH

100 hot peppers
40 small onions
1 Tbsp. salt

8 c. sugar
1 qt. vinegar

Grind peppers and onions in food mill; bring to boil and boil slowly for 30 minutes. Put in jars and seal. Have a towel handy to wipe the tears. You will cry a lot!

Eileen Bevis, Tri-Cities Council

PEPPER RELISH

4 qt. chopped hot or
  sweet peppers
12 onions, chopped
5 c. sugar

3 c. red vinegar
1/3 c. salt
1 tsp. cinnamon

Cook on medium. After the relish strikes a boil, boil about 20 minutes. Put in sterilized jars and seal. Makes 3-4 pints.

Granny Bishop, Huntsville Council

SWEET 'N SPICY PICKLE RELISH

24 medium cucumbers	Ice water
10 medium onions	3 Tbsp. salt
2 c. sugar	3 c. white vinegar
1 Tbsp. turmeric	1 Tbsp. celery seed
1 Tbsp. ground ginger	

Wash cucumbers and cover with ice water. Let stand for 3 hours. Slice cucumbers and onions; sprinkle with salt. Drain. (Reserve 1 cup of juice that has been released by vegetables.) Add juice to remaining ingredients in a kettle. Add vegetables; bring to a slow boil and cook until vegetables are clear and transparent (about 30 or 40 minutes). Pack hot relish into hot sterilized jars; adjust lids and process in water bath canner for 5 minutes. Makes about 5 pints.

Mildred Albright, Life Member,
Birmingham Council

GREEN TOMATO RELISH

24 medium green tomatoes	1 cucumber, peeled
12 medium onions	1/2 c. salt
1 cabbage	6 c. sugar
6 bell peppers	2 Tbsp. mustard seed
12 hot red peppers	2 Tbsp. turmeric

Chop vegetables; add salt and let stand overnight. Wash and drain in colander. Heat sugar, mustard seed and turmeric to a boil; pour over mixture and simmer 10 minutes. Put in jar and seal.

Jean Wharton, Birmingham South Council

TOMATO RELISH

1 peck tomatoes, peeled	4 1/2 c. sugar
12 large onions, chopped	2 c. red vinegar
4 sweet peppers, chopped	Dash of salt
4 hot peppers, chopped	1 tsp. cinnamon

Put peeled tomatoes, onions, pepper, sugar, vinegar

and salt in dish pan. Cook all of this until thick, about 1 1/2 to 2 hours on medium/low heat. Put in sterilized jars and seal. Makes 3-4 pints.

Granny Bishop, Huntsville Council

TOMATO RELISH (UNCOOKED)

1 peck or 8 qt. ripe
  tomatoes
2 c. chopped onions
2 c. chopped celery
2 qt. cider vinegar
4 large peppers,
  chopped fine

1 small hot red pepper,
  chopped fine
2 c. granulated sugar
1/2 c. mustard seed
2 Tbsp. celery seed
1/2 c. salt
1 tsp. black pepper
1 tsp. paprika

Peel and chop tomatoes and put in colander to drain; add above ingredients and mix well. Boil sugar and vinegar and add to the tomato mixture. Put in pint Mason jars and seal tightly. Ready for use in 6 weeks.

Mary C. Martin, Birmingham East Council

ZUCCHINI RELISH

12 c. chopped zucchini
4 c. chopped onion
2 1/4 c. white vinegar
3 Tbsp. celery seed

1 tsp. black pepper
1 tsp. turmeric
1 tsp. nutmeg
1 tsp. cornstarch
3 c. sugar

Grind or grate zucchini and onion; sprinkle with salt and let stand overnight. Drain; rinse with cold water; drain again. Mix all other ingredients and pour over zucchini and onion. Bring to a boil and boil 5 minutes. Pack in sterilized jars and seal.

Patsy Mitchell, Birmingham East Council

*   *   *   *   *

Courtesy is to business what oil is to machinery.

*   *   *   *   *

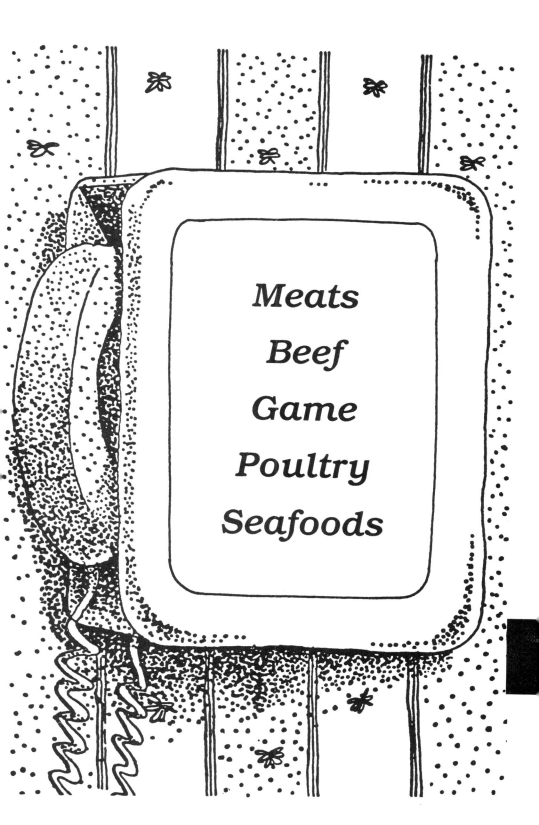

Meats

Beef

Game

Poultry

Seafoods

COOKING MEAT AND POULTRY

ROASTING
- Use tender cuts of beef, veal, pork or lamb and young birds.
- Place meat fat side up, or poultry breast side up, on rack in foil-lined shallow roasting pan. Do not add water; do not cover.
- Insert meat thermometer in center of thickest part of meat, being careful that end does not touch bone, fat or gristle.
- Roast at 300 to 350 degrees to desired degree of doneness.

BROILING
- Use tender beef steaks, lamb chops, sliced ham, ground meats and poultry quarters or halves. Fresh pork should be broiled slowly to insure complete cooking in center. Steaks and chops should be at least ½ inch thick.
- Preheat oven to "broil". Place meat on rack in foil-lined broiler pan.
- Place meat on oven rack 2 to 5 inches from the heat source, with thicker meat placed the greater distance. Brush poultry with butter.
- Broil until top side is browned; season with salt and pepper.
- Turn; brown second side. Season and serve at once.

PANBROILING
- Use the same cuts suitable for broiling.
- Place skillet or griddle over medium-high heat. Preheat until a drop of water dances on the surface.
- Place meat in skillet; reduce heat to medium. Do not add water or cover. The cold meat will stick at first, but as it browns it will loosen. If juices start to cook out of the meat, increase heat slightly.
- When meat is brown on one side, turn and brown second side.

PANFRYING
- Use comparatively thin pieces of meat, meat that has been tenderized by pounding or scoring, meat that is breaded and chicken parts.
- Place skillet over medium-high heat. Add a small amount of shortening—2 tablespoons will usually be sufficient.
- When shortening is hot, add meat or poultry. Cook as in panbroiling.

BRAISING
- Use for less tender cuts of meat or older birds. You can also braise pork chops, steaks and cutlets; veal chops, steaks and cutlets; and chicken legs and thighs.
- Brown meat on all sides as in panfrying. Season with salt and pepper.
- Add a small amount of water—or none if sufficient juices have already cooked out of the meat. Cover tightly.
- Reduce heat to low. Cook until tender, turning occasionally. Meats will cook in their own juices.

COOKING IN LIQUID
- Use less tender cuts of meat and stewing chickens. Browning of large cuts or whole birds is optional, but it does develop flavor and improve the color.
- Brown meat on all sides in hot shortening in saucepan.
- Add water or stock to cover meat. Simmer, covered, until tender.
- Add vegetables to allow time to cook without becoming mushy.

FRANKS AND BACON

8 frankfurters, partially
  split
8 strips Cheddar cheese

4 strips bacon, cut in
  halves to make 8 short
  strips

Fill each frankfurter with cheese strip. Place on bacon strip and wrap bacon around frankfurter, securing with a toothpick. Place on ungreased cookie sheet, cheese side up. Bake at 375° for 15 minutes or until bacon is done. Makes 8 servings.

Melda H. Hicks, Anniston Council

FRANKS AND CRESCENTS

8 frankfurters, partially
  split
8 strips of Cheddar cheese

1 (8 oz.) can refrigerator
  crescent rolls

Fill each wiener with cheese strip. Separate crescent dough into 8 triangles. Place wiener on wide end of triangle; roll up. Place on greased cookie sheet, cheese side up. Bake at 375° for 15 minutes, or until rolls are golden brown. Makes 8 servings.

Melda H. Hicks, Anniston Council

GRILLED STUFFED FRANKS

1 (8 oz.) can tomato sauce
1 Tbsp. sugar
2 Tbsp. spicy brown
  mustard
1/2 tsp. garlic powder

8 frankfurters
6 small green onions,
  chopped
8 slices bacon
8 hot dog buns

Combine tomato sauce, sugar, mustard and garlic powder; stir well. Slice frankfurters lengthwise to make a pocket. Brush inside each pocket with sauce; sprinkle with onion. Wrap each frankfurter with bacon, securing with a wooden pick. Cook frankfurters over hot coals 10 to 15 minutes or until bacon is crisp, turning often and basting with remaining sauce. Serve in hot dog buns. Yield: 8 servings.

R. Cash, Anniston Council

SWEET-SOUR FRANKFURTERS

1 (8 oz.) can tomato sauce
3 Tbsp. cider vinegar
1/3 c. packed light brown
  sugar

1 tsp. chili powder
1 small onion, sliced thin
1 clove garlic, crushed
1 lb. cocktail wieners

    Mix all ingredients and simmer 10 minutes or until franks are hot and onions are soft.

                   Sandra Herndon, Birmingham South Council

BEEF GOULASH

1 1/2 lb. chuck or stew
  meat
1 pkg. onion soup mix

1 Tbsp. oil
1/5 to 1/2 can tomato paste
2 c. water

    Cut meat into 1/2 inch cubes. Brown in large pan or Dutch oven in 1 tablespoon oil. Mix tomato paste, onion soup mix and water together. Pour in pan with meat. Cover and simmer for 1 1/2 hours. Serve over large egg noodles or rice.

              Becky Cook, Huntsville Council

HAMBURGER GOULASH

1 lb. ground meat
1 large onion, chopped
1 can whole grain corn

1 can cream of mushroom soup
1 can mushrooms
Salt and pepper to taste

    Brown ground meat; add onion and brown. Pour off grease. Add whole grain corn, cream of mushroom soup, mushrooms, salt and pepper. Put in casserole; bake in 350° oven for 30 minutes. Cover with grated cheese before baking, if desired. Yield: 8 servings.

              Teddy Mears, Mobile Council

HUNGARIAN GOULASH ALA ANNA

1/2 c. chopped green
  pepper
1/2 c. chopped onions
1 1/2 lb. ground beef
1 (8 oz.) pkg. noodles
  (elbow, twist or shell)
Light or dark brown sugar

Lawry's seasoning salt
Garlic powder
Oregano
Sweet basil leaves
1 (8 oz.) can tomato sauce
1 (3 oz.) can tomato paste
2 Tbsp. butter

    Saute onions and pepper in butter. Brown ground beef over medium heat in large skillet and season to personal

494

taste. Continue to brown meat and add onions and green pepper. Taste and add more seasoning to personal taste. Drain grease from meat, leaving enough to keep moist. Fix noodles to package directions. Add tomato sauce and paste to browned meat over low heat and stir; stir in noodles and 2 tablespoons brown sugar thoroughly; taste. Add more brown sugar, being careful not to make too sweet. Cook for 10 minutes, stirring continuously. Serve with tossed salad, tea and garlic bread. Refrigerate leftovers for future meals. Reheat over low heat, adding a little water to thin sauce.

Jim South, Selma Council

BROILED LIVER

1 1/2 lb. calf liver	1/4 tsp. salt
2 Tbsp. salad oil	1/4 tsp. celery salt
1 Tbsp. vinegar	1 Tbsp. grated onion

Cut liver into slices about 1/2 inch thick. Mix remaining ingredients; add liver slices, turning until thoroughly coated. Cover and refrigerate 30 minutes. Drain excess liquid. Place liver on greased broiler and broil 4 inches from heat, about 5 minutes, turning to brown both sides. Makes about 4 to 6 servings.

Kay Boyett, Montgomery Council

SMOTHERED LIVER

Use medium thick slices calves liver; dip in flour and brown in oil. Drain off excess oil and add small amount of water and 1 large onion in rings, separated. Sprinkle into this mushroom powder, Worcestershire, dried parsley, dried celery, salt and pepper. Cover and simmer for 5 minutes or until good and hot. Add not more than 1/4 cup red wine. Cover and simmer until tender.

Eleanor Gearhart, Montgomery Council

BACON-WRAPPED BEEF PATTIES

1 lb. ground beef	1 Tbsp. Parmesan cheese
1/2 c. shredded	1 Tbsp. Worcestershire sauce
Cheddar cheese	1/2 tsp. salt
1/3 c. finely chopped onion	1/8 tsp. pepper
1/4 c. catsup	6 strips bacon
	1 egg

Combine ground beef, Cheddar cheese, onions, catsup,

Parmesan cheese, Worcestershire sauce, salt, pepper and egg. Mix well. Shape into six 11 inch rolls. Place 6 strips of bacon on a piece of waxed paper. Place each roll on a piece of bacon; roll up. Secure each roll with toothpicks. Broil 7 inches from top, approximately 6-10 minutes on each side, or, for best results, charcoal outside on the grill. If outside grill is used, 2 pieces of bacon may be used for each roll.

Shirley Crocker, Riverchase Council

BARBECUE CUPS

1 lb. ground beef	1 1/2 Tbsp. brown sugar
1/2 c. barbecue sauce	1 can refrigerator biscuits
1 Tbsp. minced onion	3/4 c. grated sharp Cheddar cheese

Brown the meat in a frying pan until crumbly and drain off the grease. Stir in the barbecue sauce, onion and brown sugar. Grease a muffin pan with shortening, and press each biscuit into a cup in the muffin pan (you can stretch a 10-biscuit can to fill 12 cups). Spoon the meat mixture into the cups and sprinkle with the grated cheese. Preheat the oven to 400° and bake 10 to 12 minutes until brown.

Jack C. Ferguson, Riverchase Council

BEAN BURGERS

1 1/2 lb. ground chuck	1 1/2 tsp. salt
1 medium onion, chopped	Pepper to taste
1/2 medium bell pepper, minced (optional)	1 1/2 tsp. prepared mustard
	1 large can pork 'n beans
2 Tbsp. oleo	Sliced cheese (optional)
1/2 c. catsup	Hamburger buns

Saute onions and bell pepper in oleo; add ground chuck, salt and pepper and brown. Drain fat and add catsup, beans and mustard. Simmer for 10 to 15 minutes. Serve open-faced on hamburger buns with cheese on top.

Phyllis Painter, Riverchase Council

496

BEEF AND BEAN BARBEQUE CASSEROLE

1 lb. ground beef
1 tsp. salt
1 (16 oz.) can pork
   and beans

3/4 c. barbeque sauce
1 small onion, chopped
1 (9.5 oz.) can biscuits
1 c. shredded Cheddar cheese

Preheat oven to 375°. Brown ground beef and onion; drain. Add salt, pork and beans, barbeque sauce and stir until blended; heat until bubbly. Pour into a 2 quart casserole. Cut biscuits in halves to form 20 half circles. Place cut side down around edge of casserole. Sprinkle with cheese; bake at 375° for 25 to 30 minutes, until biscuits are golden brown. Refrigerate any leftovers.

Nancy S. Black, Decatur Council

BEEF AND CHEESE CRESCENTS

1 lb. ground beef
1/2 c. chopped onions
3/4 c. barbeque sauce

2 tsp. toasted sesame seeds
6 slices American cheese
2 (8 oz.) cans crescent rolls

Brown ground beef and onion; drain. Add barbeque sauce and set aside. Place crescent rolls in 4 rectangles. Press middles together to form 1 rectangle. Put meat mixture in center of crescents to within 1 inch of shorter ends. Put cheese slices on top. Fold short ends up and then fold sides to meet in middle. Sprinkle sesame seeds on top; bake at 375° for 25 minutes. Serves 6.

Sherry Lonnergan, Anniston Council

BEEF BISCUIT ROLL

1 lb. ground beef
1/2 c. onion, chopped fine
2 Tbsp. green pepper,
   chopped fine
2 Tbsp. mayonnaise
2 Tbsp. catsup

3/4 tsp. salt
1/8 tsp. pepper
1/4 tsp. celery salt
1 egg
3 1/4 c. prepared biscuit mix
1 c. milk

To the beef add onion, green pepper, mayonnaise, catsup, salt, pepper, celery salt and egg; stir until blended. Measure biscuit mix into 2 quart bowl; add milk and mix thoroughly with fork. Turn out on lightly floured board; roll or pat dough into rectangular shape about 12x18 inches. Spread beef mixture evenly over surface; roll as for jelly roll and cut into 12 slices about 1 1/2 inches thick. Place in a greased baking pan; bake in hot oven about 25 minutes. Combine 1 can of cream of celery or mushroom soup with 2/3 cup milk in a saucepan; bring to boil over medium heat; stir often. Use over rolls.

Jamima Edney, Birmingham South Council

BEEF ORIENTAL

2 medium onions, finely
  chopped
3 Tbsp. butter (margarine)
1/2 c. regular uncooked
  rice
1/4 c. soy sauce
1 can bean sprouts
1/4 tsp. black pepper

1 c. diced celery
1 lb. ground beef
1 can each cream of mushroom,
  cream of chicken and cream
  of celery soup
1 1/2 c. water
Chinese noodles

Brown onion and celery in butter; remove from pan. Brown rice and ground beef. Put aside in a buttered 2 1/2 quart casserole dish. Combine soups, water, soy sauce and black pepper (salt to taste at table). Add browned onion and celery. Put this mixture in with the ground beef and rice; stir in bean sprouts lightly. Bake covered in moderate oven (350°) for 30 minutes; uncover and bake 30 minutes longer; be sure rice is tender. Serve with warm crunchy Chinese noodles. Serves 8 to 10.

Elsie Fowler, Retired

CHEESE-STUFFED BURGERS

1 1/2 c. mixture of Edam,
  Cheddar and Romano
  cheese, finely grated
1 lb. ground beef

1/4 tsp. pepper
1 tsp. salt
A few drops of Worcestershire
  sauce

In a bowl mix the ground beef, salt, pepper and Worcestershire sauce; roll into 8 patties. Top 4 of the patties with the cheese mixture and top them with the other 4 patties. Seal the edges tightly and broil.

Brenda Stewart, Decatur Council

CREAMY FLORENTINE SKILLET

1 lb. ground chuck
1 1/4 c. (10 oz.) thawed
  frozen chopped spinach
1 c. sliced onion

1 3/4 c. (14 1/2 oz.)
  stewed tomatoes and juice
1 tsp. salt
1/2 tsp. garlic salt

498

1/4 tsp. pepper
1 c. water
2 c. noodles (4 oz.)

1 thinly sliced large
   green pepper
1 c. evaporated milk
2 Tbsp. flour

Brown chuck in large skillet; drain off excess fat. Add spinach, onion, tomatoes, marjoram, salts, pepper, water and noodles. Stir gently. Cover and simmer 5 minutes, stirring occasionally. Add green pepper; cook 15 minutes. Add small amount of evaporated milk to flour, stirring to make a paste. Add remaining evaporated milk gradually, stirring until blended. Add to skillet; cook over low heat, stirring constantly, until thickened. Makes about 7 cups.

Dorothy Hayes, Birmingham Central Council

GROUND BEEF DINNER

2 lb. ground beef
3 or 4 medium sized onions
7 or 8 medium sized potatoes

1 can either cream of
   mushroom soup or cream
   of chicken soup
Salt and pepper to taste

Make ground beef into patties and line in casserole on bottom and alternate with a layer of potatoes, onions and meat. Pour soup over casserole and 1 can water or less and salt and pepper to taste. Bake at 350° for about 1 hour until done.

Annette Turner, Birmingham East Council

GROUND CHUCK PATTIES

4 lb. ground chuck
4 Tbsp. chopped bell pepper
2 tsp. thyme

2 tsp. garlic salt
4 eggs
2 lb. thin sliced bacon

Mix all ingredients (except bacon) well; make a roll. Wrap in bacon, then foil. Freeze, then slice. Broil or grill.

W. W. Hall, Montgomery Council

HAMBURGER AND POTATOES

Number of hamburgers
   desired per person,
   patted out 1/2 inch thick
Number of potatoes per
   person, sliced thin

Salt (to taste)
Pepper (to taste)
Garlic salt (to taste)
Tabasco (to taste)
Worcestershire (to taste)

Place patties on foil and have enough foil to cover to steam potatoes. Sprinkle spices over potatoes to taste. Cook

1567-82

at about 350° until potatoes are tender, about 1 1/2 hours, then uncover and brown top of potatoes.

Sharon Simpson, Decatur Council

HAMBURGER NOODLE BAKE

2 Tbsp. shortening
1 lb. ground beef
1 clove garlic
Salt and pepper to taste
1 c. sour cream

1 tsp. sugar
2 c. tomato sauce
1 (8 oz.) pkg. noodles
6 green onions
1 (3 oz.) pkg. cream cheese

Saute ground beef in shortening; add garlic, salt, pepper, sugar and tomato sauce. Cover; cook slowly for 15 minutes. Cook noodles according to directions; drain. Add onion tops to cream cheese and sour cream; put layer of noodles about 1/3; use 1/3 cream mixture; cover with meat sauce. Sprinkle with cheese and bake 20 minutes.

Mary C. Martin, Birmingham East Council

HAMBURGER PIE

1 lb. ground beef
1 small onion, diced
1 jar Ragu spaghetti
  sauce

1 can (8) crescent rolls
1 jar mushrooms, sliced
  and drained
1 small pkg. Mozzarella
  cheese (4 slices)

Preheat oven to 350°. Take crescent rolls and press into a 9 inch pie plate to make a crust. In a skillet brown ground beef; saute onions and drain. Stir in mushrooms and Ragu sauce. Pour onto crescent rolls. Place cheese over meat mixture; put into oven and bake 10-15 minutes or until crust is golden brown and cheese is melted.

Debbie Lindley, Birmingham East Council

HAMBURGER SURPRISE

1 lb. ground beef
1 c. scrambled sausage,
  cooked

4 fresh mushrooms, sliced
Optional: Sliced cheese

Make very thin medium size hamburger patties. Top 1/2 of the patties with 2 tablespoons scrambled sausage; add a few mushrooms. (Optional: Add a slice of cheese on each.) Top patties with remaining patties; press edges together, forming a sandwich. Either fry slowly in covered skillet or broil.

Cheryl Williams, Birmingham South Council

500

IMPOSSIBLE TACO PIE

The pie that does the impossible by making its own crust.

1 lb. ground beef
1/2 c. chopped onion
1 env. (1 1/4 oz.) taco
   seasoning mix
1 (4 oz.) can chopped
   green chilies, drained

1 1/4 c. milk
3/4 c. Bisquick baking mix
3 eggs
2 tomatoes, sliced
1 c. shredded Monterey Jack
   or Cheddar cheese

Heat oven to 400°. Grease pie plate (10 x 1 1/2 inches). Cook and stir beef and onion until brown; drain. Stir in seasoning mix. Spread in plate; top with chilies. Beat milk, baking mix and eggs until smooth, 15 seconds in blender on high or 1 minute with hand beater. Pour into plate; bake 25 minutes. Top with tomatoes and cheese; bake until knife inserted in center comes out clean, 8 to 10 minutes longer. Cool 5 minutes. Serve with sour cream, chopped tomatoes, shredded lettuce and shredded cheese, if desired. Makes 6 to 8 servings.

Brenda Stewart, Decatur Council

JULIE'S BEEF 'N RICE

4 ground beef patties
1/2 c. water

1 pkg. Birds Eye French
   style rice mix

Brown beef patties quickly in heavy skillet; drain well. Bring water to boil; add contents of rice package to water. Mix well. Spread over patties; cover and simmer 15 minutes. Serves 4.

Juelene Humphrey, Huntsville Council

LUAU HAMBURGER

3/4 lb. hamburger meat
2 tsp. cornstarch
3/4 c. water

2 Tbsp. ketchup
1 pkg. Birds Eye
   Hawaiian veggies

Brown hamburger well in skillet, leaving meat in large chunks. Blend cornstarch with water; add ketchup and pour into skillet. Add veggies and bring to full boil over medium heat. Separate veggies and stir until sauce cubes are blended. Reduce heat, cover and simmer for 3 minutes. Serve over rice. Makes 3 servings.

Bonnie Summers, Huntsville Council

1567-82

MEXICAN FESTIVE MEAL

3 lb. ground beef
2 cans stewed tomatoes
1 pkg. Chili-O mix
2 lb. rice
1 bottle favorite steak
  sauce
3 c. cracker crumbs
1 can taco sauce

2 c. chopped pecans
1 small jar stuffed olives,
  split in halves
2 onions, shredded
3 fresh tomatoes, cubed
1 head lettuce, shredded
3 lb. Hoop cheese, grated
1 c. sweet milk
2 cans Cheddar cheese soup

Cook ground beef, tomatoes and Chili-O. Mix on medium high until boiling; cook on low 1 hour. Cook rice until tender. Mix milk, Cheddar cheese soup and heat. Arrange as follows on serving dishes for help yourself: Cracker crumbs, lettuce, rice, meat, steak sauce, taco sauce, grated cheese, tomatoes, onions, Cheddar cheese soup, olives, pecans.
Donna Clements Hamner, Tuscaloosa Council

ORIENTAL BEEF

2 onions, finely chopped
1 c. diced celery
3 Tbsp. butter
1/2 c. rice, uncooked
1 lb. ground beef
1 can cream of chicken soup

1 can cream of mushroom soup
1 1/2 c. water
1/4 c. soy sauce
1/4 tsp. pepper
1 can bean sprouts
1 can Chinese noodles

Brown onions and celery in butter; remove from pan. Brown rice and beef; put aside. Mix all other ingredients except Chinese noodles. Add onions, celery and ground beef; bake in casserole at 350° for 30 minutes, covered, and uncovered 30 minutes. Serve over toasted Chinese noodles.
Dorothy Franklin, Montgomery Council

PIGS IN A BLANKET

1 lb. lean ground beef
3/4 c. dry bread crumbs
  or cracker crumbs
1 egg

1/4 c. chopped onions
1/4 c. chopped bell pepper
Salt and pepper
1 small to medium cabbage
  (outer leaves)

Mix together first 6 ingredients; shape into 4 individual meat loaves. Gently separate cabbage leaves and place in large pan. Add 1 cup of water; bring to boil, reduce to simmer for 10 minutes. Gently remove cabbage leaves from pan and let cool till cool enough to handle. Wrap cabbage leaves around meat loaves and place in baking pan; bake at 350° for 40 minutes.

M. P. Langston, Huntsville Council

SKILLET SUPPER

1 lb. ground beef	4 or 5 large potatoes, diced
1 large onion, chopped	Garlic salt
	Pepper

Brown ground beef, salt and pepper to taste. Remove from skillet. Fry potatoes. Just before browned, add onion and beef; mix and serve.

Theresa Elkourie, Birmingham East Council

SMOTHERED HAMBURGER STEAKS

2 lb. ground beef	4 Tbsp. A.1. Steak Sauce
3 large onions	Salt and pepper to taste
	1/4 c. water

Combine meat, salt, pepper and steak sauce. In broiler pan slice 2 onions into rings. Pat meat into large patties and place on top of onions; slice other onion on top of steaks. Broil in oven until slightly brown; turn patties over, onions and all. Cook until tender. Pour 1/4 cup water in pan; turn oven off, close door and simmer 5 or 10 minutes.

Rachel Carroll, Decatur Council

SPAGHETTI

2 cans tomato paste	3 cloves garlic (1/2 tsp. garlic powder each clove)
2 cans tomato sauce	
2 c. water	1 bell pepper, chopped
1 1/2 lb. ground chuck	1 tsp. sugar
1 large onion, chopped	1 tsp. garlic salt
1 tsp. chili powder	1 tsp. celery salt
2 Tbsp. Worcestershire sauce	1 tsp. paprika
2 bay leaves	1/4 c. oil (I just pour a little in a pan)

Cook bell pepper and garlic powder or garlic cloves, chopped, in oil for 5 minutes; add ground chuck and cook until red disappears. Add onion; cook till tender. Add all other ingredients and cook uncovered 1 1/2 hours. Serves 8 to 10.

Anatalie Watson, Decatur Council

1567-82

STUFFED HAMBURGER CUPS

1 1/2 lb. ground chuck	1 Tbsp. Worcestershire sauce
1/2 tsp. salt	1 egg
1/2 tsp. black pepper	1 c. bread crumbs
	1/2 c. cream

Dressing for Hamburger Cups:

6 c. corn bread	1/2 c. chopped bell pepper
3 c. crumbled dry-like	2 tsp. sage
bread	1/2 tsp. black pepper
1 c. chopped onions	3 boiled chopped eggs
1 c. chopped celery	

Hamburger Cups: Mix ingredients well together and divide into 8 balls, forming each ball into a cup. Place on baking sheet and fill with dressing or stuffing.

Dressing: Cook onions and celery in skillet, using 1 tablespoon butter until tender. Then add to other ingredients. Mix well, using your favorite broth (chicken, beef, etc.). Fill hamburger cups. Bake at 350° until meat is done. Serve with gravy. Serves 8.

Renee Willis

TACO PIE

1 lb. ground beef	1 1/4 c. milk
1/2 c. chopped onion	3/4 c. Bisquick baking mix
1 env. (1 1/4 oz.) taco	3 eggs
seasoning mix	2 tomatoes, sliced
1 (4 oz.) can chopped	1 c. shredded Monterey Jack
green chilies, drained	or Cheddar cheese

Heat oven to 400°. Grease 10 inch quiche dish or pie plate (10 x 1 1/2 inches). Cook and stir beef and onion over medium heat until beef is brown; drain. Stir in seasoning mix; spread in plate. Sprinkle with chilies. Beat milk, baking mix and eggs until smooth, 15 seconds in blender on high or 1 minute with hand beater. Pour into plate; bake 25 minutes. Top with tomatoes; sprinkle with cheese. Bake until knife inserted between center and edge comes out clean, 8 to 10 minutes longer. Cool 5 minutes. Serve with sour cream, chopped tomatoes and shredded lettuce.

Nancy S. Black, Decatur Council

INDIAN MEAT BALLS

1 1/2 lb. ground chuck
1/4 c. instant minced
  onions
2 Tbsp. ground coriander
1 3/4 tsp. salt

1/4 tsp. ground red pepper
1/8 tsp. ground black pepper
1/4 tsp. ground cumin
1/4 tsp. ground ginger
6 Tbsp. soft bread crumbs

Combine all ingredients; mix well. Shape into 1 1/2 inch balls. Place in baking pan; bake in preheated 350° oven for 15 minutes. Turn; bake 15 minutes longer. Yield: 8 servings.

Donna L. Daniel, Montgomery Council

MEAT BALLS

4 lb. ground beef
1 egg, slightly beaten
1 large onion, chopped

Salt and pepper to taste
4 c. bread crumbs

Roll into small balls; brown in skillet until done. Add:

2 cans golden mushroom
  soup

1 Tbsp. Worcestershire sauce
Dash of Tabasco sauce

Cook in crock pot or covered pan until desired doneness.

Jo Cook, Birmingham South Council

MEAT BALLS AND SAUCE

Meat Balls:

1 lb. hamburger
2 bread crusts, moistened
1/2 grated onion

1 egg
1 tsp. salt
1/2 tsp. pepper

Sauce:

1 (15 oz.) can tomato sauce
1 (12 oz.) can tomato paste
  (fill paste can 2 times
  with water)
1 tsp. dried basil leaves
2 tsp. dried oregano leaves

1 Tbsp. salt
1/4 tsp. pepper
1 Tbsp. sugar
Dash of crushed red
  pepper (optional)
1 small onion (whole)

Combine meat, moistened bread and remaining Meat Ball ingredients; form into balls. Brown in oil; drain off oil and grease. Add Sauce ingredients; cook with lid partially covered for 1 hour. Remove onion before serving.

Kathy Leggett, Huntsville Council

1567-82

505

MEAT BALLS AND SAUCE SUPERB

1 lb. ground beef
1/3 c. dry bread crumbs
1 egg, beaten
2 Tbsp. chopped onion
1 tsp. salt
1/2 tsp. Worcestershire
  sauce
Dash of pepper
2 Tbsp. chopped parsley

Oil
1 Tbsp. margarine
3/4 c. milk
1 (8 oz.) pkg. cream cheese,
  cubed
1 (2 1/2 oz.) jar mushrooms,
  drained
1/4 c. grated Parmesan cheese
Hot parslied rice

Combine meat, bread crumbs, egg, onion and seasonings; mix lightly. Form into meat balls; brown in oil. Cook 10 to 15 minutes or until done. Saute onion in margarine; add milk and cream cheese. Stir over low heat until cream cheese melts; stir in mushrooms, Parmesan cheese and parsley; heat. Arrange meat balls over rice; cover with sauce. Makes 6 to 8 servings.

Debbie Hearn, Birmingham East Council

MEAT BALLS, HOT SAUSAGE AND SPAGHETTI SAUCE

1 lb. ground chuck
1 large grated onion
1 egg (beat slightly)

Tomato catsup (enough
  to moisten well)
Approx. 1/2 c. bread
  crumbs, flavored

Form meat balls and brown in skillet.

Sauce:

1 large jar marinara sauce
1 large can tomato sauce

1 large can tomato paste

Simmer until well mixed. Place meat balls in sauce. Cut up 1 green pepper and 1 onion. Put in sauce. Add hot sausage with meat balls, pepper and onion; cook slowly for approximately 1 1/2 to 2 hours. Cook and serve over spaghetti.

Kathy Ward, Montgomery Council

PORCUPINE MEAT BALLS

2 lb. hamburger meat
1 1/2 c. rice, uncooked
1 medium onion, chopped
1 egg

1/2 tsp. salt
Pepper
1/2 tsp. garlic salt
1 can tomatoes
1 small can tomato paste

506

Combine all ingredients except tomatoes and tomato paste; shape into small meat balls and place in pressure cooker. Add tomatoes and tomato paste; fill with water till meat balls are covered. Cook at 10 pounds pressure approximately 40 to 45 minutes.

Bea Windham, Montgomery Council

HINT FOR BAKING A MEAT LOAF

When baking a meat loaf, lay strips of bacon lengthwise in bottom of the pan. This flavors the loaf and prevents sticking.

"BEST EVER" MEAT LOAF

2 lb. ground beef	2 eggs
1 env. onion soup mix	1/3 c. catsup
1 1/2 c. soft bread crumbs	3/4 c. water

Preheat oven to 375°. Combine all ingredients. Form into a loaf. Bake 45 to 50 minutes. Drain off fat. Top with additional catsup and bake another 5 minutes if desired.

Nancy Morgan, Decatur Council

BUTTERMILK MEAT LOAF

1 lb. ground beef	Pepper to taste
1 egg, slightly beaten	1/4 c. chopped onion
1/2 c. catsup	1/2 c. dry bread crumbs
1/2 c. buttermilk	1 tsp. prepared mustard
3/4 tsp. salt	Flour

Mix ground beef with egg; add remaining ingredients, except flour, in order listed. Mix well; form into loaf and place in baking pan. Rub small amount of flour on top of loaf. Bake in preheated 350° oven for about 45 minutes or until done. Yield: 6 servings.

Marguerite Hancock, Birmingham West Council

FROSTED MEAT LOAF PIE

1 (9 inch) pie shell	4 crackers
1 lb. ground beef	3/4 c. catsup
1/4 c. green pepper, chopped	3 c. mashed potatoes
	Cheese
1/4 c. onion, chopped	1 egg

1567-82

507

Mix ground beef, pepper, onion, egg, crackers, catsup (and salt and pepper to taste) as for meat loaf. Spread in pie shell. Add a little catsup on top; bake at 350° for 35-45 minutes. "Frost" with creamed potatoes and cheese; bake 10-15 minutes until cheese melts.

Cathy Lee, Birmingham Central Council

LILLIAN'S MEAT LOAF

Meat Loaf:

2 lb. ground meat	1 small green pepper, chopped
4 slices white bread,	1 small onion, chopped
soaked in 1 c. milk	Salt and pepper to taste
2 eggs	

Sauce:

2 Tbsp. oleo	2 Tbsp. brown sugar
2 Tbsp. vinegar	1 c. water
3 Tbsp. Worcestershire	1/2 c. catsup
4 Tbsp. lemon juice	1 onion, chopped

Meat Loaf: Mix together and make into loaf. Bake for 1 1/3 hours at 350°.

Sauce: Mix and simmer 5 minutes; pour over meat loaf. Baste about every 30 minutes.

Eloise Brown, Tuscaloosa Council

QUICK AND EASY MEAT LOAF

1 1/2 lb. ground beef	1/2 c. catsup, or if preferred,
1 or 2 large crackers,	use Bar-B-Q sauce
crumbled	1 pkg. dry onion soup mix
	1 egg

Mix all ingredients and bake in 350° oven for approximately 30 minutes or until done. If desired, pour small amount of catsup or Bar-B-Q sauce on top of meat loaf before cooking.

Mary Martin, Birmingham East Council

RIBBON MEAT LOAF

2 lb. lean ground beef	1/2 c. milk
1 tsp. salt	1 (8 oz.) pkg. herb-flavored
Few grains of pepper	bread stuffing
1 small onion, minced	

Grease 9x5x3 inch loaf pan. Combine beef, salt, pepper, onion and milk; mix thoroughly. Prepare stuffing mix as directed on package. Fill pan with 3 layers of meat and 2 layers of stuffing, beginning and ending with meat. Bake at 350° for 1 hour and 15 minutes. Serve hot or cold. Makes 6 servings.

Mae Jordan, Life Member,
Birmingham Central Council

SELF-GLAZING MEAT LOAF

1 c. V-8 vegetable
  juice cocktail
3 slices bread (fresh, soft)
3 eggs
1 tsp. salt
1/4 tsp. pepper
1 Tbsp. minced onion
1 lb. ground chuck

1/2 lb. ground ham
1/2 lb. ground veal
4 Tbsp. dark brown sugar
4 Tbsp. cider vinegar
1/4 tsp. dry mustard
Dash of cayenne
2 Tbsp. Worcestershire sauce
2 Tbsp. water

Put the V-8 juice into a small saucepan; heat thoroughly. Place the bread, well broken up, into a medium-sized mixing bowl. Pour the vegetable cocktail over it. With the beaters of your mixer at low speed, beat until the bread and juice are thoroughly mixed and cooled. Then turn your mixer to its highest speed and add the eggs, one at a time. Add the salt, pepper and onion. Now stir in the ground meat by hand. Be sure that all is thoroughly mixed. Mix the sugar, vinegar, dry mustard, cayenne, Worcestershire sauce and water together. Pour this into the bottom of a loaf tin. Form the meat mixture into a loaf and place in the tin. Bake in a 375° F. oven for 1 hour. At the end of this time, invert the loaf on an ovenproof platter and continue to bake for 30 minutes longer. The glaze which was at the bottom of the loaf will now glaze the top. If you wish, spoon the glaze over the top and sides from time to time.

Joyce Reavis, Decatur Council

BARBECUE BEEF

5 lb. stew meat or chuck
  roast, cut into cubes
1/4 c. liquid smoke
1 Tbsp. chili powder
1 Tbsp. paprika (optional)
1/2 tsp. red pepper

1/2 tsp. salt
1/2 tsp. black pepper
1/4 c. vinegar
1/4 c. Worcestershire sauce
2 c. catsup

Cover meat with water; add liquid smoke, chili powder, paprika, red pepper, black pepper and salt. Simmer on top of stove for 1 1/2 hours. Then add vinegar, Worcestershire and catsup. Simmer 30 more minutes. Serve as is or on buns.

Ginger Seaman, Mobile Council

BEEF BOURGUIGNONNE

2 lb. lean beef (chuck or round), cut in 1 1/2 inch pieces
1/3 c. flour
2 tsp. salt
1/4 tsp. pepper
1/3 c. vegetable oil
1/4 lb. bacon, diced
1 onion, chopped
2 carrots, chopped
1 clove garlic, minced
1 (6 oz.) can tomato paste
2 c. water
1 c. burgundy wine
1/4 c. minced parsley
1 bay leaf
1 tsp. thyme
1 lb. small white onions
1/2 lb. fresh mushrooms

Coat beef with mixture of flour, salt and pepper. Brown meat in oil in large skillet; pour off fat. Transfer meat to large casserole. Add bacon to skillet; brown lightly. Add chopped onion, carrots and garlic; cook about 5 minutes. Add onion mixture to meat along with tomato paste, water, wine, parsley, bay leaf and thyme. Bake, covered, at 350° for 2 hours or until meat is tender. Remove bay leaf and skim off fat if necessary. Stir onions and mushrooms into meat; cover and bake 30 minutes longer. Makes 6 servings.

Faith Kirby, Anniston Council

BEEF BURGUNDY

5 medium onions, sliced thin
2 Tbsp. bacon drippings
2 lb. beef chuck, cut in 1 1/2 inch cubes
2 Tbsp. flour
Salt and pepper
Thyme, marjoram
1/2 c. beef broth
1 c. dry red wine
1/2 lb. fresh mushrooms, sliced

In heavy skillet cook onions in bacon drippings until brown. Remove from pan. Add beef and more drippings; brown on all sides. Sprinkle beef with flour and seasonings. Stir broth and wine. Simmer slowly for 2 1/2 to 3 hours. (If necessary, add more broth and wine.) Return onions to pan and add mushrooms; cook 30 minutes. Serve over rice.

Marie Rogers, Birmingham Central Council

BEEF IN WINE

3 lb. lean stew beef
1 can onion soup

1 can cream of mushroom soup
3/4 c. red wine
1/4 c. brandy

Preheat oven to 350°. Place all ingredients except brandy in 3 quart casserole; cover tightly. Bake 3 hours and 30 minutes; stir in brandy, cover and cook 30 minutes more. Serve over rice or noodles.

Linda Crear, Riverchase Council

BEEF STROGANOFF

1/2 stick butter or oleo
1/2 c. chopped onion
1 1/2 lb. ground chuck
1 tsp. salt
1/2 tsp. black pepper
3 Tbsp. flour

1 small can water chestnuts, drained and thinly sliced
1 small can sliced mushrooms
1 can cream of mushroom soup
1 c. commercial sour cream
Cooked rice or Chinese noodles

Melt butter in skillet; add onion and saute until transparent, but not brown. Add meat and brown. Stir in the salt, pepper and flour; blend well. Add the water chestnuts, mushrooms with liquid, and chicken soup. Cook and stir for 5 minutes. Turn off heat and add sour cream. Serve over rice or Chinese noodles.

Sara P. Mitchell, Montgomery Council

BEEF STROGANOFF

1 lb. ground beef
1 c. dairy sour cream
1 can mushrooms (stems and pieces), or 1/4 lb. fresh mushrooms, sliced

1 Tbsp. ketchup
2 tsp. Worcestershire sauce
1/2 to 3/4 tsp. salt (optional)
1 can condensed cream of mushroom or chicken soup
Egg noodles

Brown beef; pour off excess fat. Add soup and other ingredients except sour cream; heat through. Just before serving, stir in sour cream. Serve over cooked noodles. Serves 4.

Mae B. Jordan, Life Member, Retired, Birmingham Central Council

BURGUNDY BEEF

4 lb. round steak, cut
  in small cubes
1/4 c. shortening
5 large onions, sliced
1 lb. fresh mushrooms,
  sliced

3 Tbsp. flour
2 tsp. salt
1/4 tsp. each marjoram,
  thyme and pepper
1 c. beef bouillon (Campbell's)
2 c. burgundy wine

Roll meat in flour and brown; remove meat and saute onions and mushrooms until tender. Add all ingredients and simmer for 1 1/2 hours. Serve over rice.

Mary Ann Davis, Anniston Council

CHINESE SWEET AND SOUR BEEF

2 lb. boneless stew beef,
  cut into bite size pieces
5 Tbsp. vegetable oil
1 large onion, chopped
1 (8 1/2 oz.) can water
  chestnuts, drained
  and sliced
1 green pepper, cut
  into squares

1 (13 1/4 oz.) can pineapple
  tidbits or chunks, undrained
2 Tbsp. catsup
1 Tbsp. wine vinegar
2 Tbsp. soy sauce
1 Tbsp. cornstarch
1/2 tsp. sugar
3 Tbsp. cold water
2 firm ripe tomatoes

Prepare meat with tenderizer. Heat 3 tablespoons vegetable oil to hot, but not smoking. Quickly brown beef over high heat. Remove to platter. Heat remaining 2 tablespoons oil in same skillet. Add onion, water chestnuts and green pepper. Stir-fry until tender-crisp, about 3 minutes. Add undrained pineapple, catsup, vinegar, soy sauce and sugar. Heat to boiling. Mix cornstarch with cold water; add to sauce, stirring until sauce clears and thickens. Return meat to skillet; add tomatoes and heat through. Serve over chow mein noodles.

Emma Eastman, Montgomery Council

CHOP SUEY

2 slices bacon, diced
1/2 lb. pork loin in
  1/2 inch cubes
1/2 lb. sirloin in
  1/2 inch cubes
1 onion, diced
4 or 5 stems celery
  with leaves

1 small head cabbage, shredded
1/2 c. water
1 1/2 tsp. salt
1 can mushrooms
1 can bean sprouts
2 Tbsp. soy sauce
1 Tbsp. Worcestershire
  sauce

512

In skillet fry bacon until fat is fried out; add meat and brown quickly on all sides. Add onion, celery and cabbage; brown these quickly in hot fat, adding more bacon fat if necessary. When vegetables are thoroughly browned, add water and salt, put on cover and steam slowly until all ingredients are tender. Mushrooms and bean sprouts are added now; also both sauces may be added. Gravy may be made by stirring in 2 tablespoons flour, moistened with cold water. Serve with rice, salad and dessert for complete meal.

Jamima Edney, Birmingham South Council

CORNED BEEF SQUARES AND CABBAGE

2 (12 oz.) cans corned
  beef, crumbled
1 c. milk
1 c. cracker crumbs
2 eggs, beaten
1/2 c. onion, coarsely
  chopped
1 Tbsp. horseradish

1 tsp. prepared mustard
1 medium head cabbage
1 (10 3/4 oz.) can cream of
  mushroom soup, undiluted
2/3 c. milk
1 tsp. dill seeds
1 tsp. mustard seeds

Combine first 7 ingredients, mixing well; spoon into a greased 9 inch square pan; bake at 350° for 30 minutes. Cut cabbage into 9 wedges; cover and cook 10 minutes in a small amount of boiling, salted water. Drain cabbage well. Combine soup, milk, dill seeds and mustard seeds in a small saucepan; cook over medium heat, stirring constantly, until mixture comes to a boil. Remove from heat. Cut corned beef mixture into 9 squares. Carefully arrange the cabbage wedges and corned beef squares on a serving platter, then pour soup mixture over top. Yield: 9 servings.

R. Cash, Anniston Council

CREAMED CHIPPED BEEF ON TOAST POINTS

1 (4 oz.) jar dried beef
4 Tbsp. butter
3 Tbsp. flour

2 c. half & half
Pepper and salt to taste
Minced parsley (optional)

Rinse beef under running water; drain and snip into small pieces. Heat butter in skillet; add the beef. Cook over low heat, stirring constantly, for 3 to 5 minutes. Stir in flour and cook, stirring all the time, for 3 or 4 minutes longer. Stir in half & half; cook until sauce is thickened. Season with salt and pepper. If desired, sprinkle with parsley. Serve over crisp toast points or biscuits.

Nancy Morgan, Decatur Council

CROCK POT BEEF BURGUNDY

2 to 2 1/2 lb. beef (good stew meat or round steak)
1 pkg. Lipton onion soup flakes
1 can golden mushroom soup
1 soup can burgundy
2 cans mushrooms

Trim meat and flour; simmer in skillet to brown, then put in crock pot. Saute mushrooms and add to crock pot. Add onion soup flakes, mushroom soup and burgundy. Cook all day if possible. Serve over noodles or rice. Serves 8 or 10.

Jane Knox, Montgomery Council

HAMBURGER BEEF STROGANOFF

1/2 c. finely chopped onion
1 clove garlic, minced
1/4 c. butter (1/2 stick)
1 lb. ground chuck or beef
2 Tbsp. flour
1 tsp. salt
1/4 tsp. pepper
1 can sliced mushrooms
1 can cream of chicken soup, undiluted
1 c. sour cream
Paprika to garnish

Cook onion and garlic in butter until transparent on medium heat; add meat and cook and stir until color is gone. Add flour, salt, pepper and mushrooms; cook 5 minutes. Add soup; stir in well. Add sour cream. Stir and simmer 15 minutes. Serve over hot rice. Garnish with paprika, if desired.

Note: Also good with noodles. If any left, reheat and serve over toast.

Theresa Elkourie, Birmingham East Council

HAMBURGER STROGANOFF

1 1/2 lb. ground beef
1 can mushroom soup
2 Tbsp. dry onion soup mix
1 (8 oz.) carton sour cream
1 small can mushrooms
Salt
Pepper
Parsley flakes

Brown meat with salt and pepper; drain. Stir in mushroom soup, sour cream, onion soup mix and mushrooms. Simmer for 10 minutes. Serve garnished with parsley flakes. Serve on hot buttered noodles or rice.

Carolyn Benson, Montgomery Council

MARINATED BEEF KABOBS

1/2 c. lemon juice
1/4 c. Worcestershire sauce
1 c. vegetable oil
3/4 c. soy sauce
1/4 c. prepared mustard
2 cloves garlic, minced
3 lb. sirloin tip, cut
  into 1 1/2 inch cubes

2 large green peppers, cut
  into 1 1/2 inch pieces
1/2 lb. fresh mushroom caps
12 cherry tomatoes
12 small onions
Hot cooked rice (optional)

Combine first 6 ingredients; stir well. Add meat. Cover and marinate 12 hours in refrigerator; turn meat occasionally. Remove meat from marinade, reserving marinade. Alternate meat and vegetables on skewers. Grill over medium coals 15 to 20 minutes or until desired degree of doneness, basting with marinade. Serve with rice, if desired. Yield: 12 servings.

Regina Cash, Anniston Council

MARINATED SIRLOIN KABOBS

1/4 c. lemon-lime
  carbonated beverage
1/4 c. dry sherry
1/4 c. soy sauce
3 Tbsp. sugar
3 Tbsp. vinegar
1/2 tsp. garlic powder
1/4 tsp. salt
1/4 tsp. pepper

2 lb. (1 1/2 inch thick)
  boneless sirloin steak,
  cut into 1 inch chunks
1/2 lb. fresh medium
  mushroom caps
1 pt. cherry tomatoes
2 onions, cut into eighths
2 green peppers, cut into
  1 inch pieces
1 small fresh pineapple,
  cut into 1 inch pieces

Combine first 8 ingredients, mixing well; pour into a large shallow dish. Add meat; cover and marinate at least 2 hours in the refrigerator, turning occasionally. Remove meat from marinade, reserving marinade. Alternate meat, vegetables and pineapple on skewers. Grill over medium-hot coals 10 to 15 minutes or until desired degree of doneness, basting frequently with marinade. Yield: 4 to 5 servings.

Regina Cash, Anniston Council

OVEN CHOP SUEY

2 lb. beef steak, cubed	2 c. water
1 onion	1 can mushrooms
1 c. celery	1 can cream of chicken
1/2 c. rice	soup
1 c. peas	3 Tbsp. soy sauce

Brown beef steak and add the rest of the ingredients to Dutch oven; bake at 350° for 1 1/2 hours.

Thelma D. Hodgson, Birmingham West Council

"POLLY'S BEEF TIPS AND RICE"

1 pkg. beef tips	1 can golden mushroom soup
	1 can onion soup

Brown beef tips (roll in flour and place in cooking oil). After beef tips are good and brown, place in crock pot. Pour mushroom and onion soup over beef tips and cook 6-8 hours on low temperature. Serve on rice.

Ann Sellers, Tuscaloosa Council

SHISH KABOB

1 c. wine vinegar	1 (5 lb.) leg of lamb, cut
1/2 c. olive or salad oil	in 1 1/2 inch cubes
1/4 c. lemon juice	4 tomatoes, quartered
1/2 tsp. each salt,	2 green peppers, cut in
pepper, monosodium	1 1/2 inch squares
glutamate	4 onions, quartered and
1 clove garlic, crushed	separated

Mix first 5 ingredients; add lamb. Refrigerate at least 24 hours before skewering. Remove lamb from marinade, reserving marinade. Skewer lamb alternately with vegetables to form colorful rod. Broil over coals for 10 to 30 minutes until done, basting with reserved marinade and turning occasionally for even browning. Place ingredients on skewer loosely for well done state or tightly for rare. Yield: 8 servings.

Virginia Mayo, Mobile Council

516

VEAL PARMIGIANA

1/2 c. freshly grated
  Parmesan cheese
3 oz. sliced Mozzarella
  cheese
2 beaten eggs
2 lb. boneless veal cutlets
2 cans tomato sauce

1 1/4 c. crumbled bread
  crumbs
1/4 lb. fresh sliced mushrooms
1 Tbsp. water
1 tsp. salt
1/3 c. olive oil
1/4 tsp. pepper
1/2 tsp. rosemary

With a meat hammer, pound the veal until it is extremely thin and then cut it into 6 equal pieces. Heat the olive oil and saute the mushrooms. Remove from the oil. Mix together the Parmesan and the bread crumbs. Place the water, eggs, salt and pepper in a bowl; mix well. Dip the veal first in the egg mix and then the bread crumbs. Brown the cutlets in the olive oil and then add the tomato sauce, mushrooms and sliced Mozzarella over the veal. Reduce heat; cover and allow to simmer 7-10 minutes. Remove and serve.
Brenda Stewart, Decatur Council

BEEF PARMIGIANA

1/4 c. finely grated
  Parmesan cheese
4 slices of American cheese
4 slices of Mozzarella cheese
8 slices of thin roast beef
1 beaten egg

1/3 c. fine bread crumbs
1/4 c. butter
3/4 c. tomato paste
2 Tbsp. milk
1 tsp. salt
1/8 tsp. black pepper

Mix the egg, pepper, salt and milk together. Heat the butter in a skillet. Dip the roast beef into the egg mixture and let soak. Mix the Parmesan and crumbs together. Remove the beef and dip in the crumbs. Brown in the butter over a low flame. Drain. Cover the beef with the 2 remaining cheeses and top with tomato paste. Over a low flame, cook 20 more minutes.
Alma Pitt, Decatur Council

BEEF OR VENISON HASH

2 Tbsp. bacon fat
1 large chopped onion
3 c. cooked, chopped
  beef or venison roast
2 medium potatoes, cut
  in about 16 pieces each

2 Tbsp. flour
1 clove garlic, minced
3 c. beef broth from roast
1/4 Tbsp. seasoned salt
  and black pepper
1/2 Tbsp. chili powder

1567-82

Brown onion and potatoes in bacon fat; add flour and brown. Add broth and other ingredients. Let simmer until tender.

Virgil E. Cobb, Birmingham West Council

KID'S POT ROAST

3 to 4 lb. pot roast
1/4 medium lemon
2 medium onions, sliced thin
2 tsp. onion powder
1 small green pepper, cut
1 tsp. dry mustard
4 stalks celery with
  leaves, sliced

6 small whole carrots
1/8 tsp. garlic powder
2 tsp. safflower oil
1/4 lb. mushrooms, sliced
2 medium potatoes, unpeeled
1 tsp. ground ginger
2 c. salt-free tomato or
  V-8 juice

The night before, squeeze lemon juice over entire roast. Pierce with a fork and rub the lemon juice in. Put roast in glass container; cover tightly, and refrigerate overnight. This tenderizes the meat and is all that needs to be done to it the night before. Wash the vegetables and set out the seasonings for the next day. About 3 hours before dinner, put the roast in a Dutch oven or electric skillet. Slice vegetables. Pour tomato juice over roast; sprinkle the seasonings on the meat. Put the onion, green pepper and tomato on the roast and the other vegetables around it. Cover and let simmer until done; check occasionally. Add more juice if necessary. Cook at 275° to 300° if using an electric skillet. Serve with horseradish. Serves 6.

Kathleen Leggett, Huntsville Council

ONE POT POT ROAST

1 (2 or 3 lb.) roast
  (any cut)
1 can cream of mushroom
  soup

1 pkg. onion soup mix
8 potatoes, peeled
8 carrots, peeled

Brown roast on both sides in large pan; add enough water to almost cover. Add soup and mix. Let cook until inside is pink. Add potatoes and carrots; cook until tender. Serve with salad and tea.

Debbie Owen, Birmingham East Council

POT ROAST WITH SOUR CREAM GRAVY

1 (3-4 lb.) sirloin roast (or
   your favorite cut of
   beef roast)
2 bay leaves
3/4 c. red wine

2 onions, chopped
1 small garlic clove, minced
8 oz. sour cream
3 Tbsp. flour

Dredge roast in flour; sprinkle with salt and pepper. Heat small amount of olive oil in Dutch oven. Brown roast well on all sides with garlic and onions in pan. When browned well, lower heat to simmer and add red wine, bay leaves and 3/4 cup of water. Simmer roast, covered, for approximately 2 hours, turning every 15 minutes. Add 1/4 cup more water as necessary, if not enough liquid remains to keep roast from sticking in pan. When meat is done, remove to warm serving platter. Strain drippings in pan to remove onion and bay leaves. Turn drippings into measuring cup and add water if necessary to make 1 1/2 cups. Return to pan and bring to a boil, stirring in the 3 tablespoons of flour to thicken. Stirring constantly, add the sour cream and allow to thicken. Season as necessary with salt, pepper and paprika. Serve with finished roast. The meat will be really tender and the gravy is delicious with it!

Ken King, Birmingham Central Council

ROAST BEEF AU JUS

1 beef roast (lean cut
   like sirloin tip)
4-6 Tbsp. soy sauce

1/4 to 1/2 c. Worcestershire
   sauce
1/2 onion (optional)
Salt and pepper

Place roast in ovenproof dish; salt and pepper to taste. Pour soy sauce and Worcestershire sauce over roast; it will drip down to bottom of dish. Use enough sauce to have 1/4 to 1/2 inch liquid in dish. Place cut up onion on roast. Cover and cook at 350° to desired doneness. The natural juices will blend with the sauces to form a thin gravy for serving over meat and potatoes.

Margaret Watkins, Tuscaloosa Council

ROAST SUPREME

5-6 lb. chuck roast
1 can cream of mushroom
  soup
Salt and pepper to taste

1 pkg. frozen stew vegetables
   (fresh vegetables may be
   used, such as potatoes,
   carrots, celery and onions)

Preheat oven to 350°. In a large Dutch oven or broiler, brown the meat on both sides. Arrange the vegetables over the meat along with the salt and pepper. Mix the cream of mushroom soup with 1 1/2 cans of hot water and pour over meat and vegetables. Bake covered in the oven for about 2 1/2 to 3 hours.

Note: This can also be cooked in a crock pot, either low or high speed.

Jean R. Jordan, Montgomery Council

ROULADEN

4 to 8 slices breakfast beef or any thin slices good roast
Spicy mustard or hot

1/2 lb. ground chuck or round (approx.)
Dill pickles
Garlic salt
Pepper

Salt and pepper beef; spread with mustard. Put thin layer of ground beef on top of mustard. Salt and pepper. If using small pickle, use whole; if large pickles, slice and use 1/4 or half, depending on size. Put pickle on meat and roll up; tie or use toothpicks to secure roll. Brown in fat and make brown gravy. Simmer about 1 hour or till done. Serve with rice, potatoes or noodles. Other things may be added, such as mushrooms, onions, etc., if desired.

Theresa B. Elkourie, Birmingham East Council

BAKED ROUND STEAK

2 to 3 lb. round steak
1 pkg. dry Lipton onion soup mix

6 Tbsp. Worcestershire sauce
Salt
Pepper
Meat tenderizer

Salt and pepper steak; add tenderizer. Top with onion soup mix. Sprinkle Worcestershire sauce. Bake in aluminum foil at 350° for about 45 minutes or until tender.

Rachel Carroll, Decatur Council

CHICKEN-FRIED ROUND STEAK

1 1/2 to 2 lb. round steak, 1/2 inch thick
2 beaten eggs
2 Tbsp. milk

1 to 1 1/2 c. fine cracker crumbs
1/4 c. cooking oil
Salt and pepper

Pound steak thoroughly; cut into serving pieces. Season. Mix eggs and milk. Dip meat into mixture, then into cracker crumbs. Brown on both sides in hot oil. Cover and cook over very low heat 45 to 60 minutes.

Betty Jo Lubert, Montgomery Council

COUNTRY-STYLE CUBE STEAK

1 lb. cube steak
1/4 c. flour
1/2 tsp. salt
1/8 tsp. pepper
3 Tbsp. oil
1 medium onion,
  chopped

1 medium green pepper,
  cut in strips
1 Tbsp. brown sugar
1/2 tsp. dry mustard
1/2 c. catsup
1/4 c. water
2 Tbsp. vinegar
2 Tbsp. Worcestershire

Coat meat with mixture of flour, salt and pepper; brown in oil with onion and green pepper. Stir in brown sugar, mustard, catsup, water, vinegar and Worcestershire. Cover and simmer 15 minutes or until meat is tender. Serves 4.

Sheila Brothers, Anniston Council

DEVILED SWISS STEAK

1 (3 lb.) beef round steak
1 1/2 tsp. salt
1 1/2 tsp. dry mustard
1/4 tsp. pepper

2 Tbsp. cooking oil
1 (6 oz.) can mushrooms
1 Tbsp. Worcestershire
  sauce

Trim fat from meat. Combine salt, dry mustard and pepper. Sprinkle over meat and pound with mallet. In heavy skillet, brown steak slowly on both sides in hot oil. Drain off excess fat. Drain mushrooms, reserving 1/2 cup liquid. Add mushroom liquid and Worcestershire to skillet. Cover tightly and cook over very low heat for 1 3/4 to 2 hours or until tender. Last few minutes add mushrooms and heat through. Skim fat from sauce before serving. Makes 8 servings.

Betty C. Gray, Montgomery Council

GRANDMOTHER'S DISH

(Usually served on Thursday night at Grandmother's house.)

1 to 1 1/2 lb. cubed steak	Flour
1 jar canned carrots	Salt
1 can whole tomatoes	Pepper
Spaghetti	Milk
	Oil

Salt and pepper steak; flour steak. Brown steak on both sides in oil; remove steak. Add to drippings milk and flour to make gravy. Pour carrots in bottom of baking dish. Put a little raw spaghetti on top of carrots. Place meat on spaghetti, then tomatoes, chopped up; cover almost to top of dish with gravy. Bake at 350° for 1 hour.

Teri Griswold, Birmingham South Council

GREEN PEPPER STEAK

1 lb. steak, cut into 1/2 x 1 inch strips	2 c. water
1 Tbsp. oil	1 large green pepper, cut into strips
1 pkg. Lipton onion soup mix	2 Tbsp. cornstarch, mixed with 1/2 c. water

Fry steak in oil until brown; do not flour. Add onion soup mix and water; mix well. Simmer about 30 minutes until done. Add strips of green pepper; cook until tender. Mix cornstarch and 1/2 cup water; add to mixture. Stir until thick.

For a variation, you can add frozen Chinese vegetables and serve over rice. Serves 4.

Dorothy Roebuck, Mobile Council

LIPTON PEPPER STEAK

1 1/2 lb. boneless chuck steak	2 c. water
2 Tbsp. shortening	1 medium green pepper, chopped
1 env. Lipton onion soup mix	1 1/2 Tbsp. cornstarch

Cut meat into thin strips about 2 inches long. In large skillet heat shortening and brown meat, turning often. Stir in Lipton soup mix and 2 cups water. Cover; simmer 30 minutes. Add peppers; cover and simmer 10 minutes or until meat is tender. Blend cornstarch with 1/2 cup water; stir into skillet. Cook; stir constantly, until thickened. Serve over rice. Makes 4 to 6 servings.

Melda H. Hicks, Anniston Council

MARINATED BLUE CHEESE STEAK

1/4 c. finely crumbled
  Blue cheese
1 1/2 lb. flank steak
1 small clove garlic

1/3 c. white wine vinegar
1/3 c. lightly salted water
1 1/2 Tbsp. soy sauce
Freshly ground pepper to taste

Begin a day before you plan to serve the steak. To marinate the steak, mix the soy sauce, vinegar, water, garlic, onion and pepper in a shallow dish. Score your steak intermittently with a sharp knife and allow to soak uncovered in the refrigerator overnight. When broiling the steak, begin by grilling on one side for 7-9 minutes and then turning. Spread the Blue cheese on the broiled side; allow the other side to cook, remove and serve.

Brenda Stewart, Decatur Council

MEXICAN STYLE STEAK

1 lb. round steak
1/2 tsp. salt
2 tsp. chili powder
1/2 c. flour

4 Tbsp. melted fat
1/2 clove garlic, minced
1 onion, chopped fine
1 c. tomatoes

Mix salt, chili powder and flour; beat into steak. Fry garlic and onion in fat until tender; add steak and brown on both sides. Add tomatoes and enough water to cover. Cover with lid and simmer 45 minutes until meat is tender.

Jamima Edney, Birmingham South Council

MOCK SALISBURY STEAKS - MICROWAVE

2 Tbsp. cornstarch
1 (10 3/4 oz.) can beef
  consomme
1 (4 oz.) can sliced
  mushrooms, drained
2 tsp. Worcestershire
  sauce
1/4 tsp. basil

1 1/2 lb. ground beef
1/2 c. cooked rice
  (or soft bread crumbs)
1 medium onion, chopped
1 egg
1 tsp. seasoned salt
1/4 tsp. pepper
Parsley

Power level: High (100%). 1. Mix together cornstarch and consomme. Stir in mushrooms, Worcestershire sauce and basil; set aside. 2. Mix together beef, rice, onion, egg, salt and pepper. Shape into 6 patties. Place in a baking dish; cover with waxed paper. 3. Microwave on high (100%) for 6 minutes; drain off excess fat. Turn and re-arrange patties. Pour sauce over steaks; cover. 4. Micro-wave on high (100%) for 10 to 12 minutes or until no longer pink. Allow to stand 5 minutes before serving. Garnish with parsley. Makes 6 servings.

Kathy Coats, Mobile Council

OLIVE-ROUND STEAK-ROAST

Round Steak Delight: Pound until thin 2 round steaks, totaling 3 pounds; rub in salt, pepper, plenty of paprika. Overlap steaks on meat board, making 1 large steak. Spread steaks with a 1/4 pound layer of sliced mushrooms. Blanket with a layer of thinly sliced onions; add pimento. Cover with finely rolled bread crumbs.

With beater, combine 1/2 cup of melted butter or back drippings, tablespoon boiling water, whole raw egg. Imme-diately dribble this mixture over bread crumbs. Arrange stuffed olives in a row on long side of steak. Begin the roll of the meat around olives. Tie roll firmly. Flour the outside and brown in 1/4 cup butter or bacon drippings, in roaster or deep earthenware baker.

Place 6 whole mushrooms, 3 small onions into roaster and sprinkle all lightly with salt, pepper and paprika. Add 1 cup red wine. Roast meat in 350° oven for about 2 hours. Serve hot or cold. Serves 6.

Ernestine Gudgen (Mrs. Raymond),
Birmingham South Council

PEPPER STEAK

1/4 c. all-purpose flour	1 (8 oz.) can tomatoes
1/2 tsp. salt	1 3/4 c. water
1/8 tsp. pepper	1/2 c. chopped onion
1 1/2 to 2 lb. round	1 small clove garlic, minced
steak, cut 1/2 inch	2 1/2 tsp. Worcestershire
thick	sauce
1/4 c. cooking oil	1 large green pepper,
or shortening	cut in strips
	1 c. long grain rice

Combine flour, salt and pepper; dredge meat strips in flour mixture. Cook meat in hot oil in large skillet until browned on all sides. Drain tomatoes, reserving liquid; add tomato liquid, water, onion, garlic and Worcestershire sauce to meat in skillet. Bake in 250° oven for 2 hours. Add tomatoes and pepper strips. Return to oven; continue cooking for 15 minutes at 400°. Serve over hot rice. Yield: 6 servings.

Mary Ann Goodson, Birmingham South Council

PEPPER STEAK

1 lb. round steak, 1/4 inch thick (pound to tenderize if desired)	1 beef bouillon cube
	1 c. boiling water
	1 (1 lb.) can tomatoes
2 Tbsp. oil	(2 c.)
1/4 c. chopped onion	1 bell pepper, sliced thin
1 clove garlic, minced	3 Tbsp. flour
1 tsp. salt	1/4 c. cold water
1 tsp. pepper	2 Tbsp. soy sauce

Cut steak in slices and brown in oil 10-15 minutes; add onion, garlic, salt and pepper. Dissolve bouillon cube in boiling water, then add to meat. Cover and simmer 25 minutes; add tomatoes and bell pepper and simmer 15 minutes more. Mix flour, cold water and add to soy sauce. Add to meat and stir slowly until thickened, and cook 30 minutes more. Can be prepared early and reheated. Good over rice.

Auretha Karrh, Decatur Council

PEPPER STEAK AND PEA PODS

About 1/2 lb. tender steak	1 green and 1 red pepper, seeded and cut into 1 inch chunks
1 Tbsp. each soy sauce and sherry	
1/4 tsp. ground ginger	1/2 c. fresh or frozen pea pods
1 tsp. each brown sugar and cornstarch	
	1/2 tsp. salt
1 Tbsp. oil	1/8 tsp. pepper
1 medium onion, sliced	1/4 c. beef bouillon or water
	1 c. cooked brown or white rice

Trim fat and bone away from steak; slice into thin strips. (This is easier if the steak is partially frozen.) Pound these strips flat. Combine soy sauce, sherry, ginger, sugar and cornstarch into a smooth mixture; add steak strips and toss to coat well. Heat oil in wok; stir-fry steak strips for several minutes. Add onion, peppers, pea pods, salt and pepper. Stir-fry 2 minutes, then add bouillon and soy liquid. Cover and cook 5 minutes more. Serve over hot

1567-82

rice. Makes 2 low-cal delicious servings! To stretch this recipe, mushrooms, celery, water chestnuts, bean sprouts, etc. could be added, along with more bouillon, cornstarch and seasonings.

> Betty Darr (Mrs. E. M.),
> Birmingham Central Council

ROUND STEAK ROLL-UPS

1 1/2 lb. round steak, 1/2 inch thick	1/4 tsp. sage
1/2 c. chopped celery	1/4 tsp. poultry seasoning
1/4 c. chopped onion	1 Tbsp. parsley (optional)
2 c. bread crumbs	3 Tbsp. margarine
1/2 tsp. salt	1 can cream of mushroom soup
1/4 tsp. pepper	1 c. water

Pound steak to tenderizer; cut into 4 strips. Combine celery, onion, crumbs and seasonings. Fill steak strips with dressing; roll up and secure with toothpicks. Brown on all sides in margarine. Blend soup and water; pour over steak rolls. Cook slowly for 1 hour and 30 minutes or until tender and baste frequently.

> Jamima Edney, Birmingham South Council

STEAK AND RICE

1 1/2 lb. tenderized round steak	1 (10 3/4 oz.) cans condensed cream of mushroom soup
1 1/2 Tbsp. vegetable oil	1/2 c. dry sherry
2 large onions, cut 1/2 inch and in rings	1 1/2 tsp. garlic salt
1 (4 oz.) can sliced mushrooms (drain, reserve liquid)	3 c. cooked rice

Cut steak into thin strips. In a large skillet brown meat in oil, using high heat. Add onions. Saute until tender crisp. Blend soup, sherry, liquid from mushrooms and garlic salt. Pour over steak; add mushrooms. Reduce heat; cover and simmer 1 hour or until steak is tender. Serve over rice.

> Jane Pridmore, Decatur Council

STEAK STICKS OR FRENCH-FRIED STEAK

2 lb. round steak, sliced
  1 inch thick (should be
  a good cut or tenderized)

Flour
Cooking oil

Trim outer edge, fat and bone, leaving only lean meat. If frozen steak is used just before it is completely thawed, cut into strips 1 inch wide and 2 inches long. Place enough flour in paper sack to cover steak and shake until steak is well floured. Have vegetable oil in deep fryer at least 2 inches deep to cover steak heated to 375° to 400°. Drop pieces of steak in hot fat and cook until brown and floating in top of oil. Remove from oil; drain on paper towels.

Note: This is an excellent way to serve beef to a large group of cattlemen. It is easily prepared and is good hot or cold as long as it lasts. Serves 8.

Mrs. C. Y. Linder, Life Member Partner,
Anniston Council

SWEET-SOUR BEEF AND VEGETABLES
FOR SLOW COOKER

2 lb. round steak, cut
  in 1 inch cubes
2 Tbsp. vegetable oil
2 (8 oz.) cans tomato
  sauce
2 tsp. chili powder
2 tsp. paprika
1/4 c. sugar

1 tsp. salt
1/2 c. vinegar
1/2 c. light molasses
2 c. carrots, sliced 1/4
  inch thick
2 c. small white onions, peeled
1 large green pepper, cut in
  1 inch squares

Brown meat in hot oil in skillet; transfer to cooker. Add all remaining ingredients; mix well. Cook 6 to 7 hours on low setting or 4 hours on high setting. Serve with shell macaroni or rice (we prefer rice). Makes 6 servings.

Charlotte Johnson, Huntsville Council

SWISS STEAK

2 Tbsp. butter or
  margarine
2 Tbsp. all-purpose flour
1 tsp. salt
1/4 tsp. pepper
1/4 tsp. dry mustard

1 1/2 to 2 lb. boneless beef
  round steak, cut into
  serving pieces
1 medium onion, sliced
1/4 c. packed brown sugar
1/2 c. catsup

1. Place butter in 2 quart (12x7 inch) glass baking dish. 2. Microwave on roast for 1 minute or until melted.
1567-82

Combine flour, salt, pepper and mustard in plate. Coat meat in seasoned flour. Arrange seasoned meat in melted butter. Cover with glass lid or plastic wrap. 3. Microwave on high for about 5 minutes or until no longer pink. Turn meat over. Place onion rings on top. Combine catsup and brown sugar in 2-cup measure. Pour over meat. Cover with plastic wrap. 4. Microwave on simmer for 20 minutes. Rearrange meat; recover and continue cooking on simmer for 20 to 25 minutes or until fork tender. Let stand, covered, 5 minutes before serving. Makes about 4 servings.

Becky Cook, Huntsville Council

SWISS STEAK

1/2 c. flour
2 lb. round cubed steak
1/4 c. fat
1/2 onion, chopped

1/2 bell pepper, chopped
Salt and pepper
2 c. tomato juice

Pound flour in steak. Saute steak in hot fat until browned. Put steak in baking dish; add onions, pepper, tomato juice. Cook covered on low heat for 1 1/2 to 2 hours at about 300°. Serve with yellow rice.

Bobbie Bowles, Montgomery Council

SWISS STEAK ON RICE

Round steak
Seasoning salt
1 can stewed tomatoes
1/2 onion, chopped
1 tsp. Worcestershire sauce

Dash of garlic salt
Flour
Salt and pepper
Rice

Have steak cubed at grocery store; cut in strips and season with seasoning salt, garlic salt and salt and pepper. Batter in flour and brown in cooking oil until brown on both sides. Add canned tomatoes, onion and Worcestershire sauce. Cover and let simmer for about 30 minutes. Serve on rice.

Gay B. Harrison, Montgomery Council

TENDERIZED FLANK STEAK

1 (2 lb.) flank steak
1/4 c. vegetable oil
1/4 c. red wine vinegar
1/4 c. lemon juice

1/2 tsp. sugar
1/2 tsp. salt
1/2 tsp. dried whole thyme
1/2 tsp. pepper

Score surface of steak with a knife. Place steak in a shallow baking dish. Combine remaining ingredients, stirring well. Pour over steak; cover and marinate about 12 hours in the refrigerator, turning steak occasionally. Remove steak from marinade; grill 5 inches from hot coals about 8 minutes on each side. To serve, slice across grain into thin slices. Yield: 6 servings.

Regina Cash, Anniston Council

TERIYAKI STEAKS

1/2 c. soy sauce
1 small piece ginger root
  (fresh), crushed
  (or grated)

2 buds garlic (crushed or
  minced)
2 Tbsp. sugar

Mix well. Pour over beef; marinate at least 3 hours (overnight is better). This sauce is for 3 pounds of beef (sirloin, T-Bone, etc.). Meat can be broiled on charcoals, in oven or in an iron skillet. Skillet should be very hot. Do not use shortening or oil. Juice from marinated beef can be strained to remove garlic and ginger; add about 1/2 to 1 cup water and thicken with cornstarch. Makes gravy for rice or potatoes. If juice tastes bland, add more soy sauce; if too salty, add more sugar.

Estelle Green, Birmingham Central Council

BARBECUED RABBIT

1 Tbsp. vinegar
2 Tbsp. Worcestershire
  sauce
4 Tbsp. water
2 Tbsp. melted oleo
  or butter
3 Tbsp. brown sugar

3 Tbsp. ketchup
1 tsp. salt
1 tsp. mustard (in jar
  like used on hot dogs)
1 tsp. chili powder
1 tsp. paprika (optional)
1 tsp. red pepper

Mix well; beat with egg beater until well blended. Melt lard and grease inside of brown paper bag. Cut rabbit into pieces like chicken. Salt each piece and dip in sauce and place in bag. Pour remaining sauce over rabbit in bag. Twist and tie bag securely. Place bag in dry roaster in oven and cook at 500° for 15 minutes. Place lid on roaster and reduce heat to 350° and cook for 1 hour and 15 minutes. Remove roaster cover and lift off bag. Leave rabbit in the roaster and baste with sauce left in roaster until brown.

George Burns, Huntsville Council

1567-82

FRIED DOVE

12 medium doves, cleaned
1/2 tsp. seasoned salt
1/2 tsp. salt
1/4 tsp. black pepper
1 c. water, divided

1/2 c. melted butter
2 Tbsp. lemon juice
1 Tbsp. all-purpose flour
Cooked wild rice

Place doves in a large iron skillet; sprinkle with salt and pepper. Pour 1/2 cup water into skillet; cover tightly and steam over medium heat 20 minutes. Remove lid and continue cooking until all water is gone.

Peggy Y. Hughes, Riverchase Council

BARBECUE VENISON

10 lb. venison roast
2 garlic buttons
1 fifth red Claret wine
 (dry)
2 1/2 c. Worcestershire
1 can mushroom steak sauce

2 jars whole mushrooms
1 c. Mazola oil
1 large bell pepper
1 Tbsp. black pepper
Lawry's seasoned salt
 (to taste)

Put all ingredients in a roasting pan and cover. Venison roast may be in several pieces. Cook at 350° until meat is very tender. Baste venison hourly if possible.

Note: Remove all fat from venison before cooking.

Luke Chastain, Montgomery Council

COUNTRY-FRIED VENISON AND GRAVY

Venison
Salt and pepper
All-purpose flour

Shortening
Water

Thinly slice venison steaks. Tenderizer with mallet or saucer edge. Salt and pepper to taste. Shake in bag containing flour to dredge well. Fry in skillet in shortening until brown. Remove to paper towel or rack to drain. Pour off all shortening except 2 tablespoons. Add several tablespoons flour to drippings and brown. Add water to desired consistency; bring to boil and simmer at least 15 minutes.

Mrs. G. W. Bates, Birmingham South Council

CROCK POT VENISON

1 1/2 lb. venison, cut in strips	1 large onion, sliced 1 (1 lb.) can tomatoes
1/4 tsp. pepper	3 Tbsp. soy sauce
1 tsp. salt	1 green pepper, sliced
1/3 c. flour	1 (4 oz.) can mushrooms

Put venison strips, pepper and salt in crock pot; stir well to coat meat. Add remaining ingredients. Cover and cook on low setting 8 hours (high for 4 hours). Serve over rice.

G. W. Bates, Birmingham South Council

CROCK POT VENISON

Venison, cut into pieces	Garlic salt to taste
1 medium onion	Salt and pepper as desired
1 stalk celery	1 can cream of mushroom soup

Chop venison into pieces. Salt and pepper meat as desired. Brown venison in olive oil; set aside and cool. Chop 1 medium onion and 1 stalk celery and fry in olive oil. Add venison and seasoning, 1 cup cream of mushroom soup. Low cook or simmer for 8 hours.

Virgil E. Cobb, Birmingham West Council

VENISON A LA MUSHROOM

1 to 2 lb. sliced venison	Meat tenderizer
Flour	2 jars Heinz mushroom gravy
Salt, pepper to taste	Cooking oil

Venison should be sliced approximately 1/2 inch thick. Mix flour, salt, pepper and meat tenderizer; coat venison slices with flour mixture. Fry venison in oil till done. Place cooked venison in casserole dish with cover. Pour gravy over venison. Heat in 150° oven for about 2 hours. This gives the gravy a chance to soak into the meat.

Jim Meeks, Birmingham South Council

VENISON CUTLETS

1 egg	Oil
1/2 c. milk	1 lemon
1 (4 oz.) pkg. soda crackers, crushed	Salt and pepper Venison (any cut)
1/2 c. flour	

Cut meat into slices about 1/4 inch thick; pound with tenderizing hammer. Mix egg and milk in bowl and dip meat roll in cracker and flour mixture. Fry in hot oil until golden brown. Remove and place on paper towel to drain. Squeeze lemon on meat immediately.

Peggy Y. Hughes, Riverchase Council

UNBELIEVABLE VENISON

Venison tenderloin
  (allow 1/4 lb. per person)
Bacon strips (to match
  venison)
2 shakes meat tenderizer
  per slice

1/4 c. lemon juice
Garlic powder, as desired
  to taste
1 or 2 toothpicks per roll
Pastry brush for lemon juice

The key to this recipe, as to any venison recipe, is proper treatment of the meat. Mistakes in field dressing, aging, butchering, packaging and storage cannot be corrected in the kitchen. Slice tenderloin in strips 6 inches long, 2-3 inches wide and 3/8 to 1/4 inch thick. Brush lightly with lemon juice. Sprinkle with meat tenderizer and garlic powder. Cut the bacon strips in halves crosswise and lay them out side by side. Lay a piece of prepared venison on a bacon strip and match up one end. Roll the venison and bacon from the unmatched end, bacon on the outside. Secure with toothpicks. Place on gas or charcoal grill at medium heat for 8-10 minutes, turning occasionally to brown all over. Enjoy! These may be successfully frozen and reheated in the microwave, so fix extras!

Llewelyn Labriola, Birmingham Central Council

FARM BREAKFAST

1/2 c. shredded American
  cheese
5 whole eggs
4 slices lean bacon
1 Tbsp. onion, chopped

1/2 tomato, chopped
3 boiled small potatoes,
  cubed
1/2 tsp. salt
A generous dash of pepper

Cut the bacon into bits and drain, returning about 1 tablespoon of fat. Add the onions, salt, pepper, tomatoes and potatoes. Saute until potatoes start to brown. Add the cheese. Drop in the eggs and stir the mixture. Serve on toast.

Alma Pitt, Decatur Council

BOSTON BUTT A LA CROCK POT

3 to 4 lb. Boston Butt   6 to 8 oz. hickory smoked
  pork roast   Bar-B-Q sauce
                          Garlic salt to taste

Trim off excess fat prior to washing meat and placing in your crock pot; cook 8 hours on the low setting of your crock pot. Pour off grease and separate from the cooked lean meat. Add more Bar-B-Q sauce and serve.

John I. Wood, Jr. Birmingham South Council

BOSTON-STYLE BUTT

2 to 3 lb. smoked   Whole cloves
  shoulder butt   1/3 c. brown sugar
Prepared mustard

Place meat in deep kettle; cover with water. Simmer (do not boil) 60 minutes per pound or till tender. Remove from water. Place in shallow baking pan. Spread meat with prepared mustard and stud with whole cloves. Sprinkle with brown sugar. Bake in moderate oven (350°) about 30 minutes or till meat is glazed. Makes 8 servings.

Boney "Suzanne" Summers, Huntsville Council

BAKED HAM SUPREME

1 slice center cut ham,   A sprinkle of allspice
  1 inch thick   A sprinkle of clove powder
1/4 c. brown sugar   A sprinkle of cinnamon
1 small can crushed   A sprinkle of ginger
  pineapple in heavy syrup A sprinkle of nutmeg

Preheat oven to 400°. Coat ham slices generously with brown sugar. Sprinkle with allspice, clove powder, cinnamon, ginger and nutmeg. Cover with crushed pineapple; bake at 400° for 30 to 40 minutes.

Sharon Cox. Tuscaloosa Council

HAM-AND-CORN CHOWDER

2 c. diced, cooked ham   3 (10 oz.) pkg. frozen
1 c. chopped celery   cream style corn, thawed
1/2 c. chopped onion   1 c. milk
1/2 c. butter or   1/2 tsp. onion salt
  margarine, melted   1/2 tsp. celery salt

1/2 tsp. pepper   Chopped fresh parsley
                                         (optional)

Saute ham, celery and onion in butter in a Dutch oven.
Stir in next 5 ingredients, and bring to a boil. Reduce heat
and simmer 20 minutes. Garnish with parsley, if desired.
Yield: About 6 cups.

                 Regina Cash, Anniston Council

HAM BALLS

1 1/2 lb. ground ham   1 c. milk
1 lb. ground pork   2 c. bread crumbs
2 eggs

     Sauce:

1/2 c. vinegar   1 c. brown sugar
1/2 c. water   1 Tbsp. mustard

Mix ingredients together; form into meat balls. Place
in oblong baking dish. Mix sauce; pour over meat balls.
Bake at 325° for 1 hour; turn over and bake 1/2 hour or
longer.

                 Joyce Runyan, Huntsville Council

HAM ROLLS

2 pkg. long Danish ham   2 boxes frozen stalk broccoli,
3 pkg. long Swiss cheese   cooked according to pkg.
                                  directions

Roll ham and cheese around broccoli. Put in long dish.
Make 2 cups white sauce. Use about 1/4 cup sauterne
instead of all milk. Saute in small amount of butter:

1/2 c. onion   1 can mushrooms,
1/2 c. bell pepper   drained

Add to white sauce and pour over ham; cover and bake
at 350° for about 30 minutes. Serves 6.

                 Peggy Daniels, Montgomery Council

HAM CROQUETTES

2 c. ground ham   1 egg, beaten
1/2 c. soft bread   1 (16 oz.) can sliced
  crumbs   peaches, drained
1/4 c. milk   1 Tbsp. brown sugar

Combine first 4 ingredients; mix well. Shape ham mixture into 4 rolls. Place rolls in a lightly greased 12x8x2 inch baking dish. Bake at 350° for 40 minutes. Remove from oven. Arrange peaches around rolls; sprinkle peaches with brown sugar. Bake an additional 10 minutes. Yield: 4 servings.

Regina Cash, Anniston Council

HAM JAMBALAYA

1 onion, chopped
1 bell pepper, chopped
3 Tbsp. Wesson oil
1-2 c. chopped ham

1 can beef bouillon
1 c. water
3/4 c. rice, uncooked

Saute onion and bell pepper in oil until tender; add bouillon diluted with 1 soup can water, rice and ham. Cover and cook slowly 30 minutes. A good quick skillet meal the whole family will like.

Mrs. O. O. Prickett, Selma Council

HAM VIENNESE WITH RICE

(Ideal for the working gal - quick and easy.)

3 c. hot cooked rice
12 oz. fully cooked ham,
   cut in thin strips
   (can use canned)
1 1/2 Tbsp. margarine
1/2 c. chopped onion
2 c. thinly sliced celery

1 (10 3/4 oz.) can condensed
   cream of chicken soup
2 Tbsp. dry white wine
   (optional)
1 1/2 tsp. prepared mustard
1/4 tsp. dill weed
3/4 c. sour cream
1/3 c. chopped pimentos

While rice is cooking, saute ham in margarine about 2 minutes (use large skillet). Add onions and celery; continue cooking until vegetables are tender crisp; stir in soup, wine, mustard and dill weed. Heat thoroughly. Add sour cream and pimentos; heat, but do not boil. Serve over hot rice. Makes 6 servings.

Note: Add a salad and you have a complete meal.

Mildred Parker, Huntsville Council

*   *   *   *   *

It's too bad we can't forget our troubles as easily as we forget our blessings.

LAYERED HAM LOAF

2 potatoes, boiled, diced
Salt and freshly ground
  pepper
1 c. cubed, cooked
  ham

1/2 c. whipping cream,
  whipped
1/2 c. shredded sharp
  Cheddar cheese
1 1/2 tsp. prepared
  horseradish

Heat oven to 350°. Place diced potatoes in a well buttered 8 1/2 x 4 1/2 x 2 1/2 inch loaf pan. Lightly sprinkle with salt and pepper. Layer the cubed ham over the potatoes. Blend the whipped cream with the cheese and horseradish. Spread over ham. Bake for 30 minutes or until hot and bubbly. Serves 3 to 4.
Dee Dozier, Anniston Council

SCALLOPED POTATOES AND HAM

6 to 8 potatoes, according
  to size
2 Tbsp. minced onion
2 Tbsp. butter or
  margarine

Leftover ham, as desired
2 Tbsp. flour
1 qt. milk
1/2 tsp. salt
Cracker crumbs or substitute

Peel potatoes and slice thin. Place a layer of potatoes in a flat baking dish. Sprinkle lightly with flour; add a layer of diced ham, sprinkle with minced onion. Alternate layers of potatoes and ham until all is used. Scald the milk; add the butter, salt and pour over top. Put a ring of cracker crumbs around inside of pan. This prevents it from boiling over. Bake in 350° oven 1 hour or until potatoes are done and top lightly browned.
Jamima Edney, Birmingham South Council

TRUCK DRIVER SPECIALS

1 1/2 c. precooked ham
  (approx. 2 slices)
1 medium onion

1 tsp. margarine
2 tsp. water
4 slices white bread

Dice onions and thick sliced ham. Melt margarine in large frying pan and saute onion. Add diced ham and cook until hot. Add 2 teaspoons water. Lay 4 slices of white bread on top of ingredients. Cover frying pan and simmer for 1 minute or until bread is steamed and soft, but not soggy. Spoon ham and onions onto bread and serve as sandwiches. Yield: 2 quick and easy sandwiches.
Art Lipski, Birmingham Central Council

APPLE-CRUMB STUFFED PORK CHOPS

4 (1 inch thick) pork chops, cut with pockets
Apple-Crumb Stuffing

Salt and pepper to taste
1 Tbsp. butter or margarine
3 Tbsp. water

Stuff pockets of pork chops with Apple-Crumb Stuffing and secure with toothpicks. Sprinkle pork chops with salt and pepper. Melt butter in a large heavy skillet; brown pork chops on both sides. Add water; reduce heat. Cover and simmer 50 to 55 minutes or until pork chops are tender. Yield: 4 servings.

Apple-Crumb Stuffing:

1 c. soft bread crumbs
1/2 c. diced apple
3 Tbsp. minced onion
3 Tbsp. raisins, chopped
1/2 tsp. salt

1/2 tsp. sugar
Pinch of pepper
Pinch of ground sage
1 1/2 Tbsp. butter or margarine, melted

Combine all ingredients; mix well. Yield: About 1 3/4 cups.

Faith Kirby, Anniston Council

ATLANTA PORK CHOPS AND RICE

4 pork chops
2 Tbsp. Wesson oil
1/4 c. sliced celery
2 (8 oz.) cans Hunt's tomato sauce with onions

1 1/2 c. water
2 Tbsp. brown sugar
1 tsp. salt
1/2 tsp. basil
1 c. uncooked regular rice

In large skillet brown chops in hot oil (375°); remove chops. Add celery; cook lightly. Drain fat. Stir in remaining ingredients; add chops. Bring to boil. Simmer covered 30 minutes. Makes 4 servings.

Jane Courington, Montgomery Council

BAKED PORK CHOPS

6 loin pork chops, 1 inch thick
3 Tbsp. brown sugar

3/4 c. ketchup or chili sauce
6 onion slices
6 lemon slices

Place chops in baking pan in single layer; salt and pepper to taste. Spread 2 teaspoons brown sugar and 2 tablespoons ketchup on each chop. Top with slice of onion and slice of lemon. Add enough water to reach a level halfway up on chops. Bake, covered, at 350° for 2 1/2 to 3 hours. Uncover last half hour of cooking. Serves 6.

Edwina Hicks (Mrs. Jimmy),
Montgomery Council

BAKED PORK CHOPS

1/4 c. butter	1/8 tsp. pepper
1 c. Ritz cracker crumbs	1 egg
3 Tbsp. Parmesan cheese	2 Tbsp. milk
1/2 tsp. salt	6 pork chops

Place butter in shallow baking dish and melt in oven. Combine cracker crumbs, cheese, salt and pepper; set aside. Blend egg and milk in a shallow bowl. Coat chops in crumb mixture; dip in egg mixture and again in crumb mix. Place in dish with melted butter; bake at 350° for 30 minutes. Carefully turn chops and bake an additional 30 minutes or until done.

Becky Woo, Birmingham South Council

GRILLED PORK CHOPS

6 pork loin chops, cut 1 1/2 inches thick	1 Tbsp. orange juice
	Sweet basil to taste
2 c. cider vinegar	1 1/2 tsp. sugar
2 1/2 Tbsp. Worcestershire	2 Tbsp. celery leaves
	1/4 tsp. paprika
1 Tbsp. steak sauce	2 dashes of hot pepper sauce
1 tsp. salt	1/4 tsp. white pepper
	1 Tbsp. lemon juice

In glass dish combine all ingredients except pork chops. Add chops; cover and marinate at least 6 hours. Remove chops from marinade. Place on grill 4 to 6 inches from coals. Cook 24 to 30 minutes per side or until done, turning and brushing frequently with marinade.

Tom George, Birmingham South Council

ORANGE-GLAZED PORK CHOPS

4 (3/4 inch thick) pork chops	1/2 c. orange juice
	2 Tbsp. orange marmalade
Salt and pepper to taste	2 Tbsp. brown sugar
All-purpose flour	1 Tbsp. vinegar
1 Tbsp. vegetable oil	

Sprinkle pork chops lightly with salt and pepper; dredge in flour. Heat oil in a heavy skillet; brown pork chops on both sides. Combine remaining ingredients, mixing well; pour over pork chops. Reduce heat; cover and simmer 40 to 45 minutes. Yield: 4 servings.

Faith Kirby, Anniston Council

PORK CHOP DINNER

4 pork chops
1 Tbsp. vegetable oil
4 to 6 potatoes, quartered
4 large carrots, cut into
  1 inch thick slices
1/4 c. chopped onion
1/4 c chopped celery

1 chicken-flavored
  bouillon cube
1 c. boiling water
1 tsp. salt
1/8 tsp. pepper
2 Tbsp. all-purpose flour
1 c. water

Saute pork chops in hot oil in an electric skillet set at 300° for 15 minutes, turning once; drain. Top pork chops with vegetables. Dissolve bouillon cube in boiling water; pour over vegetables and sprinkle with salt and pepper. Reduce heat to 220°; cover and cook 30 minutes or until vegetables are tender. Remove meat and vegetables to serving platter, reserving drippings in skillet. Combine flour and 1 cup water, mixing until smooth. Gradually add mixture to drippings; cook over medium heat until thickened and bubbly, stirring constantly. Serve sauce with meat and vegetables. Yield: 4 servings.

Nancy Williams, Life Member, Anniston Council

PORK CHOPS PARMESAN

2 Tbsp. butter or
  margarine
4 pork chops, 1/2 inch
  thick
1/3 c. evaporated milk
2 Tbsp. grated Parmesan
  cheese

1/4 c. flour
1/2 tsp. salt
Few grains of pepper
1/3 c. evaporated milk
1/2 c. grated Parmesan
  cheese
1 (8 oz.) can tomato sauce

Turn oven on 350°. Melt the butter in a 12x8 inch pan. Dip the pork chops in the 1/3 cup milk, then roll in mixture of cheese, flour, salt and pepper. Put into pan and bake uncovered 30 minutes. Meantime, mix 1/3 cup milk and 1/2 cup cheese. Pour tomato sauce around pork chops after taking from oven, and put cheese and milk mixture over them and return to oven for 20 to 25 minutes more or until meat is tender. Cutlets or round steak could be used instead of pork chops.

Jamima Edney, Birmingham South Council

PORK CHOP POCKETS

2 Tbsp. butter or
  margarine, softened
1 (5.5 oz.) pkg. au
  gratin potatoes
2 c. water

1 (16 oz.) can sliced
  carrots, drained
4 or 5 pork chops
1 (5.33 oz.) can evaporated
  milk (2/3 c.)

Tear off 4 or 5 pieces heavy-duty foil about 24 inches long. Fold in half, shiny sides in. Lightly butter center of foil. Place some of the potato slices and carrots on each piece; top with chops. Wrap loosely around meat and vegetables, using tight double or triple folds. Seal one end, again using tight folds. Leave other end open. Combine water, milk and seasoning mix; pour into open end of pockets and seal with tight double folds. Place on grill over hot coals; grill 40 to 50 minutes, turning frequently until chops are cooked and potatoes are tender. Makes 4 to 5 servings.

Brenda Stewart, Decatur Council

PORK CHOPS AND POTATO SCALLOP

1 (10 3/4 oz.) can cream
  of mushroom soup,
  undiluted
1/2 c. commercial sour
  cream
1/4 c. water

1/2 tsp. dried dill weed
4 c. thinly sliced potatoes
4 pork chops
Salt and pepper to taste
Vegetable oil
Parsley (optional)

Combine mushroom soup, sour cream, water and dill weed in a small bowl; blend well. Alternate layers of potatoes and soup mixture in a lightly greased 2 quart casserole. Cover and bake at 375° for 45 minutes. Sprinkle pork chops with salt and pepper; brown on both sides in a small amount of oil in a large skillet. Drain on paper towels. Place chops on top of potatoes; cover and bake an additional 30 minutes. Garnish with parsley, if desired. Yield: 4 servings.

Regina Cash, Anniston Council

PORK CHOPS AND RICE

6 to 8 pork chops
6 to 8 Tbsp. rice
6 to 8 slices onion

6 to 8 slices tomato
6 to 8 slices bell pepper
1 can chicken broth

Brown pork chops on both sides. Grease casserole well. Place 1 tablespoon rice for each pork chop in bottom. Place chops on rice. Place slice of onion, tomáto and pepper on each chop. Cover with chicken broth; bake for 1 hour at 350°. Yield: 6-8 servings.

Mattie Foster, Huntsville Council

PORK CHOP SKILLET DINNER

6 lean pork chops
2 Tbsp shortening
Salt and pepper
1 c. tomato juice

3 medium onions
3 medium potatoes
6 wedges of cabbage
6 carrots
Paprika

Brown pork chops lightly in shortening; salt and pepper to taste and savory, if desired. Add tomato juice; cover tightly and simmer 45 minutes. Prepare the vegetables and add; sprinkle with paprika and additional salt. Cover and cook until vegetables are tender, about 30 minutes. Add additional juice while cooking, if needed. There should be very little liquid remaining in the pan when ready to serve. Meal for 6.

Brenda Cantrell, Birmingham South Council

PORK CHOP SUPREME

4 thick pork chops,
  seasoned and browned
4 thin onion slices

4 thin lemon slices
4 Tbsp. brown sugar
4 Tbsp. catsup
1/4 c. water

Top each browned pork chop with 1 slice onion, 1 slice lemon, 1 tablespoon brown sugar and 1 tablespoon catsup. Add water; cover and bake 1 1/2 hours at 350°.

Note: The granulated brown sugar doesn't give as much flavor as the other type.

Mrs. Rudy Jackson, Montgomery Council

PORK CHOPS AND WILD RICE

4 pork chops
1/2 c. chopped onion
1 (6 oz.) pkg. long grain
  and wild rice mix (do not
  use quick rice)

2 2/3 c. water
2 beef bouillon cubes
1 medium tomato, sliced
  (optional)

Slowly brown pork chops on both sides in a 10 inch skillet; remove chops. Cook onion in pan drippings until tender but not brown. Add rice, water and bouillon cubes. Place chops on top of rice mixture. Cover; reduce heat to simmer. Cook until chops are tender and rice has absorbed all the liquid, about 50 to 60 minutes. If desired, place tomato slices on chops and heat through.

Chris Williams, Riverchase Council

PORK WITH WILD RICE

1 (6 oz.) box long grain
  and wild rice
1 can cream of mushroom
  soup
1 1/4 c. water

1 (4 oz.) can sliced
  mushrooms*
6 lean pork chops*
Salt
Paprika

Mix contents of box, soup, water in shallow 10 inch casserole. Add mushrooms; arrange pork chops on top. Sprinkle with salt and paprika; bake, covered, for 1 hour and 20 minutes at 350°.

*Mushrooms are optional. You can substitute chicken for the pork chops.

Joan Sims, Birmingham South Council

QUICK B-B-Q PORK CHOPS

8 pork chops
1 1/2 c. catsup
1 king size Coke

1/4 c. Worcestershire
  sauce
Dash of salt and pepper

Mix all ingredients and bake in covered dish at 400° about 1 hour.

Note: Other meats may be used besides pork chops.

Charlotte Johnson, Huntsville Council

SKILLET PORK CHOPS AND RICE

4 loin or rib pork chops,
   cut 1 inch thick and
   trimmed of excess fat
1 tsp. cooking oil
2 tsp. salt

1/4 tsp. pepper
1 c. uncooked rice
1 (10 1/2 oz.) can condensed
   onion soup
1 c. hot water

Brown chops well on each side, about 8-10 minutes over moderately high heat in a skillet brushed with oil. Pour off all but 1 tablespoon drippings; sprinkle chops with half the salt and pepper. Scatter rice over chops and sprinkle with remaining salt and pepper. Add soup and water; cover and simmer 50 to 60 minutes until chops are tender.

Sandra Tutt, Montgomery Council

SOUR CREAM PORK CHOPS

Pork chops
Salt and pepper
Flour
2 Tbsp. margarine
Whole cloves

1 Tbsp. sugar
1/2 c. water
1/2 c. sour cream
1 bay leaf
2 Tbsp. vinegar

Season pork chops with salt and pepper; dredge with flour. Brown in 2 tablespoons butter. Insert a clove in each pork chop and place in baking dish. In same pan where pork chops were browned, put sugar, water, sour cream, bay leaf and vinegar. Bring to boil; pour over chops. Tightly cover and bake in 350° oven for 1 1/2 hours.

Mary Scott, Anniston Council

SPANISH PORK CHOPS

6 pork chops, 1 inch thick
6 bell pepper rings
6 onion slices (round)

2 small cans tomato sauce
2 1/2 c. Rice Stuffing

Salt and pepper chops and brown chops on both sides. Arrange in baking dish. Lay pepper rings on top of each pork chop and fill ring with 1 to 2 tablespoons Rice Stuffing (made as below). Lay slice of onion on top of Rice Stuffing, and cover the 6 pork chops with 1 can of tomato sauce. Place in oven for 1 hour or until pork chops are tender at 250°.

Rice Stuffing:

1 1/2 c. rice
1 can tomato sauce

1/2 c. chopped bell pepper
1/2 c. chopped onion

1567-82

1/3 c. celery   Salt and pepper to taste

Mix thoroughly and place in pepper rings on top of chops.

Willie Mae Crews, Birmingham East Council

SWEET AND SOUR PORK CHOPS

1 tsp. ginger
1 tsp. salt
1/2 tsp. pepper
1 tsp. paprika
1/4 c. flour

6 pork chops (loin or
   shoulder)
1 Tbsp. shortening
1 c. orange juice
2 Tbsp. vinegar
3 Tbsp. brown sugar

Mix ginger, salt, pepper, paprika and flour together. Coat both sides of chops in this mixture. Melt shortening in skillet; add chops and cook over low heat until brown on both sides. Pour in orange juice and vinegar; sprinkle with sugar. Cook over a low heat for 40 minutes or until chops are tender when tested with a fork. Serves 4-6. (May substitute pineapple juice.)

Bonnie Summers, Huntsville Council

SWEET AND SOUR PORK CHOPS

4 pork chops, 3/4 inch thick
1 white onion, sliced in rings
3 Tbsp. vinegar
3 Tbsp. maple syrup

1 bell pepper, sliced in rings
1 small can mushrooms
   and juice
2 Tbsp. soy sauce
1 c. water

Salt, pepper and flour chops; fry in 2 tablespoons oil until golden brown. Pour off grease and add water, vinegar, syrup, soy sauce and mushrooms. Cover tne chops with onion and pepper rings. Put top on pan and bring to a boil. Lower heat and cook slowly for 1 hour. Check at about 30 minutes to be sure all of the gravy has not cooked out. Serve with rice and put onion and pepper rings on chops.

Arnold L. Taylor, Opelika Council

VERSATILE PORK CHOPS

1 (6 oz.) pkg. long
   grain and wild rice
1 Tbsp. soy sauce
1 tsp. grated orange peel
6 lean loin pork chops

1 (8 oz.) can tomato sauce
Juice of 1 orange
1 Tbsp. brown sugar
1 tsp. nutmeg

Prepare rice mix according to package directions; stir in soy sauce and orange peel, then set aside. In skillet brown chops on both sides; pour off fat. Combine tomato sauce, orange juice, brown sugar and nutmeg; pour 1/2 over chops. Spoon rice around chops, then pour on remaining tomato sauce. Simmer covered for 1 hour or until chops are tender. Makes 6 servings.

Bobbie Bowles, Montgomery Council

CHERRY-GLAZED ROAST LOIN OF PORK

Salt
1 (5 lb.) pork loin roast
1 (No. 2) can sour red
   cherries
2 Tbsp. flour

1/4 tsp. dry mustard
1/4 c. brown sugar
1 clove garlic, minced
10 whole cloves
3 Tbsp. vinegar

Rub salt into pork. Drain cherries, reserving juice. Pour juice into roasting pan. Mix flour, mustard and 1/2 teaspoon salt, brown sugar, garlic and cloves; add vinegar. Add to cherry juice in pan; mix until smooth. Place roast, fat side up, in pan with sauce. Roast in 325° oven until well done; baste frequently with sauce. Add reserved cherries during last 30 minutes to heat through and glaze. Remove meat to platter; slice and pour sauce over slices. Yield: 10-12 servings.

Irene Whiddon

MARINATED PORK KABOBS

3 lb. boneless pork
   shoulder, cut into
   2 inch cubes
1/2 c. vegetable oil
1/3 c. dry sherry
2 Tbsp. soy sauce
2 Tbsp. honey
2 Tbsp. fresh lemon juice
2 garlic cloves, minced

1 Tbsp. minced fresh sage
   leaves or 1 tsp. dried
1 1/2 tsp. fresh thyme or 1/2
   tsp. dried
1 bay leaf, crumbled
Additional bay leaves, halved,
   and fresh sage leaves for
   threading on the kabobs
Grilled peppers and onions
   as an accompaniment

In a shallow dish let six 10 inch wooden skewers soak in water to cover for 2 hours and let them drain on paper towels. Or have ready six 10 inch metal skewers. In a ceramic or glass bowl toss the pork with the oil, the sherry, the soy sauce, the honey, the lemon juice, the garlic, the minced sage, the thyme, the crumbled bay leaf, and pepper to taste and let it marinate, covered and chilled, for 2 hours. Drain the pork, reserving the marinade.

Thread the pork and the additional bay leaves and sage leaves on the skewers, threading a halved bay leaf and a sage leaf on either side of each piece of pork, and brush the kabobs with the reserved marinade. Grill the kabobs over glowing coals or broil them under a preheated broiler about 4 inches from the heat, turning them frequently, for 20 to 25 minutes, or until the juices run clear when the meat is pierced. Divide the grilled peppers and onions among 6 plates and top each serving with a kabob. Serve the kabobs with summer rice salad. Serves 6.

Katherine Creamer, Mobile Council

SWEET AND SOUR PORK

1/4 c. flour
2 tsp. ginger
1 lb. pork, cut in
   1/2 inch cubes
1 1/2 tsp. Worcestershire
   sauce
1/3 c. sugar
1 1/2 tsp. salt
1 Tbsp. chili sauce
16 oz. bean sprouts

13 1/4 oz. crushed pineapple
   (reserve liquid)
1 green pepper, cut
   into 1/4 inch strips
1/4 c. oil
1/4 c. vinegar
1/4 c. soy sauce
1/4 tsp. pepper
8 oz. water chestnuts

Mix 2 tablespoons flour and ginger; coat pork and fry in oil. Remove pork from skillet; add water to pineapple juice to make 1 cup. Shake rest of flour and syrup in covered container. Stir flour mixture, vinegar, soy sauce and Worcestershire into oil left in skillet. Boil 1 minute; reduce heat. Stir in sugar, salt, pepper and pork. Cover and simmer until pork is tender (about 45 minutes). Add pineapple, and green pepper; cook uncovered for 10 minutes. Stir in sprouts, chestnuts and chili sauce. Cook 5 minutes. Serve over rice.

Debbie Tucker, Birmingham East Council

SWEET AND SOUR PORK ROAST

5 to 6 lb. loin pork roast
1 Tbsp. flour
1/2 tsp. salt
1 Tbsp. sugar
2 tsp. ginger

1 Tbsp. garlic salt
1/2 c. orange juice
1/4 c. lemon juice
1/4 c. soy sauce
1 Tbsp. ketchup
1 large Reynolds Brown 'N Bag

Trim excess fat from roast. Put flour in bottom of Brown 'N Bag and shake bag well to coat bag. Add all other ingredients in bag and shake well. Put roast in bag; seal and store in refrigerator overnight (or until ready to cook). Place bag in broiler pan; cut six 1/2 inch slits up top of bag to near twist tie. Cook in preheated 325° oven for 3 hours.

Rachel Carroll, Decatur Council

APPLES ON SAUSAGE PATTIES

1 (16 oz.) pkg. bulk
  pork sausage
2 medium cooking apples
3 Tbsp. sugar

1/4 tsp. ground cinnamon
2 Tbsp. butter or margarine
2 Tbsp. chopped fresh
  parsley (optional)

Shape sausage into 6 patties 3 1/2 inches in diameter and about 1/2 inch thick. Cook patties over medium heat until done, turning once. Place on serving dish and keep warm. Core apples; remove a 1/4 inch slice from both ends and discard. Cut remainder of each apple into 3 rings. Combine sugar and cinnamon; mix well. Dredge apple rings in cinnamon mixture. Melt butter in a skillet; add apple rings, and cook over medium heat until browned, turning often. Sprinkle any remaining cinnamon mixture over apples as they cook. Place an apple ring on top of each sausage patty; sprinkle with chopped parsley, if desired. Serve immediately. Yield: 6 servings.

Regina Cash, Anniston Council

BEANS AND SAUSAGE

1 lb. beans (large white
  butter beans or pintos)
1 lb. link sausage
1 bunch of green onions or
  1/2 large onion

1 tsp. garlic salt
4 beef bouillon cubes
3/4 tsp. Tabasco sauce
6 c. cold water

Cut sausage into 1/2 pieces. Mix ingredients. Cook in slow cooker, all night or all day.

Elizebelle Scott, Huntsville Council

SWEET SOUR SAUSAGE

1 green pepper, sliced
1 medium onion, sliced
1 lb. Eckrich smoked
   sausage, cut into
   3/4 inch pieces
1 Tbsp. butter
1 Tbsp. cornstarch

1/2 tsp. ground ginger
  (can be omitted)
1 Tbsp. vinegar
1 Tbsp. soy sauce
1/2 c. apricot preserves
1 c. pineapple chunks
Hot cooked rice

Cook green pepper, onion and sausage in butter for 5 minutes. Combine cornstarch and ginger; stir in vinegar. Add soy sauce and preserves. Stir into sausage mixture. Heat over low heat until sauce thickens. Stir in pineapple. Heat until hot. Serve over rice. Makes 6 servings.

Louise C. Bonds, Retired,
Birmingham Central Council

OVEN BAKED BARBECUE RIBS

4 to 5 lb. pork ribs
1 large bottle Kraft
  barbecue sauce

1 large onion
Salt and pepper
1 1/2 c. water

Cut and brown ribs in skillet. Place meaty side up in broiler pan. Sprinkle lightly with salt and pepper; top with sliced onion rings. Mix barbecue sauce and water and pour over ribs. Bake 4 hours at 300°.

Rachel L. Carroll, Decatur Council

SAUERKRAUT AND SPARERIBS

3 lb. spareribs

1 (No. 2 1/2) can sauerkraut
1 1/2 tsp. salt

Cut ribs into serving size portions. Pack into pot and cover with water. Add salt; cook until tender, about 1 hour. Add kraut, pushing down into meat stock. Cook 30 minutes longer or until most of liquid is evaporated. Makes 5 servings.

Gene Gorff

TANGY BARBECUED SPARERIBS

3 lb. spareribs
1 large onion, finely
  chopped
2 cloves garlic, finely
  chopped

2 Tbsp. vegetable oil
1 (12 oz.) bottle chili sauce
1/2 c. lemon juice
1/4 c. molasses

1/4 c. dark rum
3 Tbsp. Dijon mustard

1 Tbsp. Worcestershire
sauce

Cut ribs into serving size pieces (3 to 4 ribs per person); place in a large Dutch oven. Add enough water to cover ribs; cover and simmer 40 minutes. Drain ribs, and place in a shallow baking dish. Set ribs aside. Saute onion and garlic in oil in a medium saucepan until onion is tender. Stir in next 6 ingredients; reduce heat and simmer 25 minutes. Pour barbecue sauce over ribs; cover and marinate overnight in refrigerator. Place ribs, bone side down, on grill over slow coals. Grill 20 minutes; turn meaty side down, and cook 10 to 15 minutes. Brush ribs with sauce, and let cook 5 to 10 additional minutes on each side. Yield: 4 to 5 servings.

Regina Cash, Anniston Council

APRICOT CHICKEN

3 whole chicken breasts,
  cut in halves lengthwise
  and with skin removed
Salt and pepper (to taste)
1 (21 oz.) can apricot
  pie filling

1 Tbsp. lemon juice
1/2 tsp. salt
1/2 tsp. ground nutmeg
1/2 c. pecan halves
Hot cooked rice

Arrange in 13x9x2 inch baking dish; sprinkle chicken with a little salt and pepper. In bowl combine apricot pie filling, lemon juice and 1/2 teaspoon salt and nutmeg; stir in pecans. Pour over chicken pieces; cover and bake in 375° oven 55 to 60 minutes. Arrange chicken on hot cooked rice and spoon mixture atop chicken. Makes 6 servings. (This recipe is also delicious using peach, pineapple or cherry pie filling.)

Sandra Burnette, Birmingham East Council

AUSTRIAN CHICKEN DUMPLINGS

Boil chicken; bone and skin. Return to broth. Add:

2 stalks celery, chopped
2 carrots, cut in slices

4 Tbsp. chives
Salt and pepper to taste

Melt 3 tablespoons of butter in stainless steel bowl; beat and add 2 large eggs. Add 9 tablespoons of Cream of Wheat (dry) to butter mixture. Mix well; cover bowl with plate and soak for 30 minutes. Bring broth to boil. Drop in dumpling mixture 1/2 teaspoon at a time. Cover; turn heat to low and cook covered for 20 minutes (don't lift lid).

1567-82   Marie Rogers, Birmingham Central Council   549

BAKED CHICKEN AND RICE

2 c. uncooked rice
2 c. clear chicken broth
8 chicken breasts
1 pkg. dry onion soup mix

2 c. cream of mushroom
  soup
Few grains of paprika
1 Tbsp. dry parsley

Spread rice on bottom of buttered 9 1/2 x 11 1/2 x 2 inch pan; add chicken broth. Place pieces of unseasoned chicken on top; sprinkle with onion soup mix. Spread with mushroom soup (plus 2 cups water). Sprinkle with paprika and parsley. Bake uncovered at 325° for 1 hour and 30 minutes. Cover and bake 30 minutes longer. Yield: 8 servings. This baking time is very accurate. This helps when a meal is needed right on time. Excellent for luncheons.

Alexine S. Becker, Montgomery Council

BAKED CHICKEN BREASTS

6 chicken breasts, halved
1/2 tsp. pepper
12 bacon slices
1 pkg. dried beef

2 cans cream of chicken soup
1 1/2 c. sour cream
3 oz. cream cheese
4 c. hot rice

Add pepper to chicken breasts. Wrap slice of bacon around each halved chicken breast. Place layer of dried beef (not corned beef) in bottom of baking dish. Arrange bacon wrapped chicken on beef slices. Cover with mixture of chicken soup, sour cream and cream cheese. Cover pan tightly with foil; place in 325° oven for 2 hours. When tender, remove foil and let brown slightly. Serve on bed of hot rice. Suitable for freezing.

Emma Arnold, Decatur Council

BAKED CHICKEN - MUSHROOMS

6 chicken breasts
2 cans cream of
  mushroom soup
1/2 tsp. salt

1/2 tsp. pepper
1 tsp. parsley flakes
1 tsp. celery flakes
1/2 tsp. celery salt

Wash pieces of chicken and drain. Pour soup in casserole dish or pan in which the chicken is to be baked and add 1 1/2 cans of water. Warm soup on stove, stirring slowly. Add salt, pepper, celery flakes, parsley flakes and celery salt. Stir well. Lightly salt and pepper pieces of chicken. Place in heated soup mixture and spoon soup mixture over any pieces not completely covered. Cover dish or pan

550

tightly with foil and bake at 325° to 350° for about 2 hours. Do not uncover casserole (or pan) while baking. Serves 6.

Vivian L. Cole, Montgomery Council

BARBECUE CHICKEN

1 chicken	1 tsp. brown or white sugar
1/2 c. ketchup	1 (10 oz.) Coke

Bring ketchup, sugar and Coke to a boil. Skin chicken and add salt and pepper. Place chicken in above mixture and cook until chicken is done over medium heat.

Imogene Davis, Birmingham Central Council
Variation submitted by Hester Thompson

BARBECUED "CROCK POT" CHICKEN

1 (4 lb.) chicken, cut up	1 medium onion, chopped
1 small bottle catsup	1 (10 oz.) bottle Coca-Cola
	Salt and pepper

1. Place the above ingredients in 3 1/2 quart crock pot in order listed. 2. Stir once. 3. Turn pot to low setting and cook overnight. 4. Remove bones from chicken and serve meat and sauce over hot rice. Makes 6 servings.

Bonnie Mayfield, Anniston Council
Nathalie H. Brooks, Birmingham South Council

CHEESE FILLED CHICKEN CUTLETS

3 whole medium chicken breasts	1/8 tsp. pepper
1/4 tsp. salt	1/2 c. water
All-purpose flour	1/2 c. milk
Butter or margarine	1/4 c. cooking or dry white wine
1 (8 oz.) pkg. Mozzarella cheese, thinly sliced	1 chicken flavor bouillon cube or env.
1/2 lb. mushrooms, thinly sliced	Parsley sprigs for garnish

About 45 minutes before serving: 1. Cut chicken breasts into cutlets. On cutting board cut each chicken breast in half. Working with one half at a time, place it skin side up. With tip of sharp knife, starting parallel and close to large end of rib bone, cut and scrape meat away from bone and rib cage, gently pulling back meat in one piece as you cut. Discard bones and skin and cut off white tendon. Holding knife parallel to work surface, slice each piece of

1567-82

boneless chicken breast horizontally to make 2 cutlets. 2. With meat mallet or dull edge of French knife, pound each chicken cutlet to about 1/8 inch thickness. On waxed paper, mix salt with 3 tablespoons flour. Coat chicken cutlets with flour mixture. 3. In 12 inch skillet over medium heat, melt 3 tablespoons butter or margarine; add cutlets, a few at a time, and cook until lightly browned on both sides, adding more butter or margarine if necessary. Remove cutlets from skillet. Arrange cheese slices on 6 cutlets; top with remaining cutlets. Skewer cutlets together with toothpicks; set aside. 4. In drippings remaining in skillet, over medium heat, melt 2 more tablespoons butter or margarine. Add mushrooms; cook until tender, stirring occasionally. 5. To mushroom mixture, stir in pepper and 1 tablespoon flour until blended. Gradually stir in water, milk, wine and bouillon; heat to boiling, stirring to loosen brown bits from bottom of skillet. Return cutlets to skillet; heat to boiling. Reduce heat to low; cover and simmer 5 minutes or until cheese is melted. Discard toothpicks. Spoon cutlets and sauce onto large platter and garnish with parsley sprigs. Makes 6 servings.

Dorothy Hayes, Birmingham Central Council

CHICKANA

3 whole broiler-fryer
  chicken breasts
1 lemon, quartered
1/2 orange, quartered

2 cloves garlic, split
2 whole cloves
1 bay leaf
1/2 c. Mazola corn oil

Cook lemon, orange, garlic, cloves and bay leaf in corn oil over medium heat in heavy small saucepan about 20 minutes or until skin of fruit is brown. Pour mixture over chicken and marinate 2 hours or overnight. Heat large heavy skillet, over medium heat. Remove chicken pieces from marinade. Place chicken breasts in hot skillet; cook, uncovered, over medium heat about 20 minutes on each side until brown and tender. Add marinade, if necessary, to prevent sticking.

Linda Byrd, Montgomery Council

552

CHICKEN ALMOND

2 c. cubed raw breast
  of chicken
2 c. sliced celery
1/2 c. sliced mushrooms
2 Tbsp. soy sauce
1/4 to 1/2 c. cornstarch

1/4 c. peanut or salad oil
1 can drained bean sprouts
1/2 c. blanched almonds
2 1/2 to 3 c. chicken broth
1/2 c. cold water

Fry chicken in oil in a preheated heavy large pan. Add remaining ingredients, except cornstarch and water. Mix thoroughly; cover and steam 5 minutes. Blend cornstarch and water; add to chicken and cook, stirring constantly until mixture thickens. Garnish with extra almonds. Serve with rice.

Note: High heat and quick stirring are essential. The secret is to avoid overcooking.

Becky Cook, Huntsville Council

CHICKEN AND DRESSING

1 large fryer or small hen
Celery
Onions

Salt
Pepper

Scrub and clean chicken well. Place in large pot and cover with water. Add about 1/2 cup diced celery, 1/4 cup diced onion, about 1 teaspoon salt and 1/2 teaspoon pepper. Boil till chicken is tender. Add a little water as it boils just so you end up with about a quart of broth. Cool chicken and remove from bone.

Dressing: Cook a pan of corn bread. Cool and crumble up bread. Add about 2 slices of loaf bread or 1 cup dry bread crumbs. Beat 2 whole eggs and 1/2 cup milk together. Add 1 tablespoon sage, 1/4 cup diced celery, 1/4 cup diced onion. Mix all together with broth. Add 1/2 stick melted margarine. Make dressing slightly thin. Grease pan. Pour in half of dressing; add chicken (deboned). Pour in rest of dressing. Bake till set and a little brown on top.

P.S. Try not to overbake.

Gravy:

1 can Campbell's cream
  of chicken soup
2 boiled eggs, chopped

1 tsp. margarine
Little black pepper
1/8 tsp. salt

Mix all together; bring to boil.

Marcia Freeman, Birmingham East Council

1567-82

CHICKEN AND DRIED BEEF

8 chicken breasts, boned
3/4 lb. dry chipped beef
8 strips lean bacon

1 (10 1/2 oz.) can cream
  of mushroom soup
1 (8 oz.) carton sour cream

Chop the chipped beef and sprinkle on bottom of large baking dish. Wrap each piece of chicken with 1/2 strip of bacon and secure with toothpick. Place chicken over beef. Blend soup and sour cream until smooth; pour over chicken. Bake at 300° for 2 hours, covered, and 350° for 30 minutes, uncovered.

Mrs. Lowell Hobbs, Riverchase Council
Mary P. Caddell

CHICKEN AND DUMPLINGS

1 large fryer
1 large can flaky biscuits

1 can cream of chicken soup
1 c. flour

Cook chicken until it slips off bone easily. Place chicken broth, boned chicken and soup in large cooking pan. Bring to a boil. Peel biscuits off in layers and roll in flour. Cut in strips and place in boiling broth. Cook fast for about 10 minutes, then turn heat to low and cook for about 30 to 40 minutes.

Harold Busby, Mobile Council

CHICKEN AND OKRA OVER RICE

1 fryer, cut up, deboned
1/2 c. cooking oil
2 lb. small okra, sliced
2 medium onions, chopped

1 small can tomatoes
1 can tomato sauce
4 c. water
Rice, cooked separately

Brown chicken in oil; remove and brown okra. Remove okra and brown onions. Add to onions the other ingredients and simmer for a few minutes, then add chicken and okra. Serve over rice.

Eleanor Gearhart, Montgomery Council

CHICKEN AND RICE

1 fryer, cut up, or
  4 chicken breasts
1 1/4 c. uncooked rice
1 can cream of chicken soup

1 can cream of mushroom
  soup
1 can cream of celery soup
Sliced almonds

Mix together soups and rice and put in baking dish;

save 2 or 3 spoonfuls to spread over top of chicken. Push chicken down in mixture and spoon remaining rice mixture over top. Sprinkle with sliced almonds, if desired. Some water may need to be added to soup mixture to keep from getting dry. Cover with foil and bake 1 1/2 to 2 hours at 350°. Serves 4.

Charlene Brown, Montgomery Council

CHICKEN AND VEGETABLES TARRAGON

4 boneless skinless
   chicken breast halves
No-stick cooking spray
1 tsp. finely chopped
   shallots or green onions
3/4 c. white wine
1/2 tsp. salt

1/2 tsp. tarragon
3/4 lb. asparagus
4 medium carrots, cut into
   matchstick pieces
1 1/2 tsp. cornstarch
2 Tbsp. cold water
1 Tbsp. chopped fresh
   parsley

Spray skillet with no-stick cooking spray. Over medium-low heat, brown chicken on both sides. Remove to platter; stir shallots into skillet and cook until wilted, about 3 minutes, stirring constantly. Stir in wine, salt and tarragon; heat to boiling. Return chicken and add asparagus and carrots. Reduce heat to medium, cover and simmer 10-15 minutes, until chicken is done and vegetables are tender-crisp. Remove chicken and vegetables to platter. Stir cornstarch into cold water until completely dissolved. Stir into boiling liquid in skillet and cook until sauce thickens. Serve sauce with chicken and vegetables. Serves 4. Low calorie - 197 calories per serving.

V. M. Chandler, Riverchase Council

CHICKEN AND WILD RICE

1 (3 lb.) chicken
1 c. sherry
1 can mushrooms
2 (6 oz.) pkg. long grain
   and wild rice

Seasonings
1 (10 1/2 oz.) can
   mushroom soup
1 c. diced celery
1/4 tsp. curry powder
1 c. sour cream

Place chicken in deep kettle. Add water, sherry, salt, curry powder and celery. Cover and bring to boil. Put on simmer for 1 hour. Remove chicken; strain broth and refrigerate broth at once. When cold, remove meat from bone. Discard skin and cut into bite sized pieces. Measure broth and use as part of liquid to cook rice (following instructions on box). Combine chicken, mushrooms and rice. Blend sour cream and soup. Toss with chicken and rice mixture. Pour into casserole and bake at 350° for 1 hour. Freezes well.

Sara P. Mitchell, Montgomery Council

CHICKEN ANNIVERSARY

1 (3 to 4 lb.) chicken, cut up
8 oz. Mozzarella cheese, grated
2 (15 oz.) cans Hunt's special tomato sauce
2 (4 oz.) cans sliced mushrooms
1/2 tsp. garlic salt
1/2 tsp. oregano
Salt and pepper
1 (8 oz.) pkg. spaghetti

Place chicken in baking dish, making only 1 layer. Sprinkle with cheese, salt and pepper. Combine remaining ingredients and pour over chicken. Bake covered at 450° for 1 hour. Serve over spaghetti. Serves 4-6.

Rita Moore, Anniston Council

CHICKEN BREASTS IN SOUR CREAM

6 chicken breasts, skinned
4 Tbsp. melted butter or margarine
1/2 c. chopped onion
1/2 c. chopped celery
1 green pepper, chopped
1 (4 oz.) can sliced mushrooms, undrained
1 c. commercial sour cream
1/2 tsp. salt
1/4 tsp. pepper

Saute chicken in butter; arrange chicken in a lightly greased 13x9x2 inch pan; set aside. Saute onion, celery and green pepper in pan drippings until tender. Remove from heat, and let cool slightly. Combine vegetables, mushrooms, sour cream, salt and pepper. Spoon mixture over chicken. Cover and bake at 350° for 45 to 55 minutes or until chicken tests done. Yield: 6 servings.

Note: This may be prepared and refrigerated up to 24 hours before needed.

Mary C. Martin, Birmingham East Council

CHICKEN BREASTS IN WINE SAUCE

4 deboned chicken breasts
  (8 halves)
1 (3 oz.) can sliced
  mushrooms

1 can cream of mushroom soup
1/2 soup can of sherry
  (cooking or otherwise)
1 c. sour cream
Paprika

Arrange chicken breasts in shallow pan so pieces do not overlap. Cover with mushrooms. Combine soup, sherry and sour cream; stir until blended. Pour over chicken, completely covering it. Dust with paprika; bake uncovered at 350° for 1 1/2 hours. Place each chicken breast on a bed of rice on each plate and spoon wine sauce over all.

Mary C. Martin, Birmingham East Council

CHICKEN CACCIATORE

2 fryers, skinned, cut up
1/4 c. olive oil
3 cloves minced garlic
1 large can tomatoes
1 (8 oz.) can tomato paste
2 Tbsp. margarine
1/2 c. onion, chopped
1/2 c. water

1 tsp. salt and pepper
1/4 tsp. thyme
2 bay leaves
1/4 tsp. oregano
1 Tbsp. parsley flakes
1 (4 oz.) can mushrooms
1 Tbsp. flour (heaping)
Small thin vermicelli noodles

Brown chicken in olive oil for 25 minutes; drain. Melt margarine and saute all vegetables. Add seasonings. Add flour and cook until slightly brown, stirring constantly. Add tomatoes (break up with potato masher), tomato paste and water. Add pieces of chicken and cook slowly for 1 1/2 hours. Cook spaghetti noodles and serve chicken and sauce over the noodles. Add garlic bread and green salad to complete your meal. Best served in winter.

Charlotte Adair Smith, Birmingham East Council

CHICKEN CASSEROLE

1 fryer, cut up
1 can cream of celery soup

1 can cream of asparagus soup
5 c. cooked rice

Fry chicken in light batter until golden brown. Place cooked rice in bottom of baking dish with chicken on top. Cover with soup; bake 30 minutes at 350°.

Voncile Wolfe, Mobile Council

1567-82

CHICKEN CONTINENTAL

3 lb. chicken pieces
1/3 c. seasoned flour
1/4 c. butter
1 (10 1/2 oz.) can cream
  of chicken soup
2 1/2 Tbsp. grated
  onions

1 tsp. salt
Dash of pepper
1 tsp. chopped parsley
1/2 tsp. thyme
1 1/3 c. water
1 1/3 c. rice, uncooked
  (Minute rice)

Roll chicken in flour; brown in butter. Remove chicken. Stir in flour and onions; brown. Add soup and water and bring to a boil. Spread rice in a 1 1/2 quart shallow casserole. Pour all but 1/3 cup of soup mixture over rice and stir. Top with chicken and rest of soup mixture. Bake covered at 375° for 30 minutes or until chicken is done.

Mary Griffin, Mobile Council

CHICKEN CORDON BLEU

2 thin slices cooked ham,
  finely chopped
1 oz. triangle process
  Gruyere cheese or
  Swiss cheese, finely
  chopped
2 slivers fresh garlic,
  crushed, or powdered
  garlic
1/4 tsp. black pepper

1/4 tsp. thyme leaves
  or powder
1 egg, beaten
2 large halves chicken breast,
  skinned and boned
1 Tbsp. flour
4 Tbsp. bread crumbs
2 tsp. butter
2 tsp. vegetable oil

Mix chopped ham, cheese, garlic, pepper and thyme. Use to stuff 2 large halves chicken breasts in packet left from boning. (Make a pocket if necessary with sharp knife in breast of chicken.) Fold ends over to make roll. Roll chicken in flour, then in beaten egg and then in bread crumbs, coating well. In a proper size skillet heat butter and oil and brown chicken on all sides. Place in a foil lined baking pan or casserole and bake 20 to 25 minutes in a pre-heated 375° oven or until done. Chicken will feel firm to the touch. Pour any pan drippings over chicken. Enjoy. Serves 2 people.

Ruth C. Rice, Life Member, Tri-Cities Council

558

CHICKEN CRUNCH

1/2 c. chicken broth
2 cans cream of
  mushroom soup
4 c. diced, cooked
  chicken
1/4 c. onion, minced

1 can water chestnuts, sliced
1 c. celery, diced
1 (3 oz.) can chow mein
  noodles
1/3 c. toasted almonds

Blend broth into soup in a 2 quart casserole. Mix in remaining ingredients except almonds. Bake at 325° for 40 minutes. Before serving, sprinkle with almonds.
Note: Instead of chestnuts, you may substitute 1 1/2 cups chopped celery. I also use a little more liquid in my mixture.

Frank Marcus, Mobile Council

EASY CHICKEN DIVAN

2 (10 oz.) pkg. frozen
  broccoli
4 chicken breasts,
  cooked and boned
2 cans cream of
  chicken soup

1 c. mayonnaise
1 tsp. lemon juice
1/2 tsp. curry powder
1/2 c. shredded sharp cheese
1/2 c. bread crumbs
1 Tbsp. melted butter

Cook broccoli in boiling, salted water until tender; drain. Arrange stalks in greased 10x10 inch baking dish. Place chicken on top. Combine soup, mayonnaise, lemon juice and curry powder; pour over chicken. Sprinkle with cheese. Combine crumbs and butter; sprinkle over all. Bake at 350° for 25-30 minutes. Serves 6-8.

Pauline Woodham, Mobile Council

CHICKEN DIVAN

2 pkg. frozen broccoli
2 c. sliced, cooked chicken
  (or 3 chicken breasts)
2 cans cream of chicken
  soup
1 c. mayonnaise

1 tsp. lemon juice
1/2 tsp. curry powder
1/2 c. shredded sharp cheese
1/2 c. bread crumbs (soft) or
  Pepperidge Farm stuffing
1 Tbsp. melted butter

Cook broccoli in boiling salt water until tender; drain. Arrange stalks in greased baking dish. Place chicken on top. Combine soup, lemon juice, mayonnaise, curry powder; pour over chicken. Sprinkle with cheese. Combine bread crumbs and butter; sprinkle over top. Bake at 350° for 25 to 30 minutes. Serves 4.

1567-82   Sarah Baker, Riverchase Council

CHICKEN IN WINE

1 chicken or 8 breast halves
1 c. white wine
1 c. chicken broth
Salt and pepper to season
Olive oil
1 c. sherry
1 clove garlic

Roll seasoned chicken pieces in flour. Brown in olive oil. Remove browned chicken; add 1 clove garlic, wine, sherry and broth to pan; simmer a few minutes. Remove garlic. Place chicken in casserole; pour sauce over it and bake at 350° for 50 minutes.

A. M. Robertson, Huntsville Council

CHICKEN KIEV

1 c. butter, softened
2 Tbsp. chopped parsley
1 tsp. rosemary
3/4 tsp. salt
1/8 tsp. pepper
6 whole chicken breasts, split, boned and skinned
3/4 c. all-purpose flour
3 eggs, well beaten
1 1/2 to 2 c. bread crumbs
Salad oil

Combine butter and seasonings in a small bowl; blend thoroughly. Shape butter mixture into 2 sticks; cover and put in freezer about 45 minutes or until firm. Place each half of chicken breast on a sheet of waxed paper; flatten to 1/4 inch thickness, using a meat mallet or rolling pin. Cut each stick of butter mixture into 6 pats; place a pat in center of each half of chicken breast. Fold long sides of chicken over butter; fold ends over and secure with toothpick. Dredge each piece of chicken in flour; dip in egg, and coat with bread crumbs. Cover and refrigerate about 1 hour. Fry chicken in salad oil heated to 350°. Cook 5 minutes on each side or until browned, turning with tongs. Place in warm oven until all chicken is fried. Yield: 12 servings.

Faith Kirby, Anniston Council

CHICKEN LICKIN'

2/3 c. milk
1/3 c. creamy peanut butter
1 tsp. salt
1 tsp. Accent flavor
  enhancer
6 Tbsp. flour
6 Tbsp. cornstarch
1 tsp. paprika
6 broiler-fryer drumsticks
6 broiler-fryer thighs
1/4 c. Mazola corn oil

Mix milk and peanut butter together until smooth; stir

560

in salt and Accent. In separate bowl mix flour, corn meal and paprika together. Dip chicken in peanut butter mixture, then coat with flour mixture. Pour oil into foil-lined shallow baking pan; place chicken in single layer, skin side up, in oil. Bake in 425° oven uncovered 20 minutes. Turn chicken and bake about 20 minutes longer or until fork can be inserted into it with ease. Makes 6 servings.

Melba McSwain, Decatur Council

CHICKEN LOAF

2 fryers or large hen
5 c. broth
10 slices bread or 2 c.
   bread crumbs
1/2 bell pepper
1 large onion, chopped

1 c. slivered blanched
   almonds
1 small can mushrooms,
   chopped and drained
1 1/2 tsp. salt (if chicken was
   not salted when cooked)
4 eggs

Sauce for Chicken Loaf:

3/4 c. plain flour
2 c. chicken broth
1/2 c. sweet milk

1 c. mushroom soup
1 stick oleo

Butter 9x13 inch casserole dish. Heat oven to 325°. Cook and debone fryer or large hen; leave in rather large bite size pieces. Saute in oleo bell pepper and onion. Combine chicken, sauteed vegetables and crumbs, almonds, mushrooms and salt, if needed. Add 3 cups broth; add eggs last; beat in well. Pour into long pan and bake for 1 hour. Serve with hot sauce on squares.

Sauce for Loaf: Brown flour in oleo; add chicken broth, milk and soup; bring to boil and cook until thick. Refrigerate if not used immediately. Then reheat and serve over chicken loaf.

Jim Chaffin, Tuscaloosa Council

CHICKEN NUGGETS

6-8 chicken breasts,
   boned and skinned
1 c. flour
1 tsp. salt

1 c. water
2 eggs
4 Tbsp. sesame seeds
Hot oil

Cut chicken breasts in bite size pieces. Mix flour, salt, water, eggs and sesame seeds. Beat together until smooth. Dip chicken in batter and drop in hot oil. Oil should cover

1567-82

chicken. Cook each piece about 5 to 7 minutes or until golden brown. Drain. Serve with sweet and sour sauce, if desired.

Becky Russell, Decatur Council

CHICKEN PARMESAN

2 fryers, cut into pieces
1/2 c. Parmesan cheese
2 c. dry bread crumbs
1/4 c. chopped parsley
2 sticks margarine

1 tsp. paprika (or oregano)
1/4 tsp. basil
2 tsp. salt
1 tsp. Accent
Dash of pepper

Wash and dry fryers; set aside. Combine remaining ingredients except margarine. Melt margarine. Dip chicken pieces in margarine; roll in crumb mixture. Arrange pieces skin side up in shallow baking pan; pour remaining margarine over chicken. Bake in 350° oven for 1 hour or until tender. (Baste with drippings. Do not turn chicken.)

Darlene Neely, Birmingham East Council

CHICKEN PIE

3-4 c. cooked, diced
    chicken
1 large can Veg-All, drained

2 cans cream of chicken soup
1 1/2 cans chicken broth
Salt and pepper to taste

Pastry:

1 1/2 c. plain flour
1/2 c. Crisco

Ice water

Prepare pastry dough; roll out 1/3 of dough. Cut in strips and place in bottom of greased baking dish. Bake until done at 400°. Add chicken, Veg-All, soup and broth (blended together), salt and pepper. Add a layer of pastry to top of pie. Bake uncovered at 400° until pastry is brown.

Virginia H. Green, Birmingham Central Council

CHICKEN-SHRIMP SUPREME

1/4 c. butter
1/2 lb. sliced fresh
    mushrooms
2 Tbsp. sliced green onions
2 cans cream of chicken soup
1/2 c. sherry
Hot buttered rice

1 c. (4 oz.) shredded
    Cheddar cheese
2 c. cut up cooked chicken
2 c. cooked shrimp
2 Tbsp. chopped parsley
1/2 c. light cream or
    half & half

562

In 3 quart saucepan melt butter; add mushrooms and onion and saute 5 minutes. Add soup; gradually stir in sherry and light cream. Add cheese and heat over low heat; stir occasionally until cheese is melted. Add chicken and shrimp; heat to serving temperature (do not boil). Just before serving, add parsley. Serve over rice. Makes 8 servings. May be prepared ahead. Refrigerate; reheat.

Marion Vann, Mobile Council

CHICKEN SPECTACULAR

1 large chicken, deboned and cut up
1 can French green beans (seasoned), drained
1 small (6 oz.) box Uncle Ben's curried rice
1 (8 oz.) can water chestnuts, sliced

1 small onion or 3 Tbsp., chopped very fine
1 (10 1/2 oz.) can cream of celery soup
1 c. mayonnaise
1 small jar pimientos (optional), for color
Salt to taste

In a covered boiler cook rice in 2 1/2 cups plus 2 tablespoons of chicken broth for 20 minutes. Then add onion and cook for 5 minutes more. Stir rice occasionally. Add all other ingredients in rice and pour in large pan. Bake 50 minutes at 350°. Serves 12-14.

Ernestine Gudgen, Birmingham South Council

CHICKEN SOUFFLE

1 large hen, cooked and removed from bone
12 slices bread
8 eggs, beaten
1 qt. milk

2 c. broth
2 sticks oleo
2 Tbsp. onion powder
1 can mushroom soup
1 can cream of celery soup

Gravy:

1 can cream of mushroom soup
1 can cream of celery soup

1 c. water
1/2 stick oleo
1 small jar pimentos

Place chicken in large buttered flat pan. Heat soup, milk, broth and oleo. Add bread and let set for a few minutes. Mash bread real well. Add onion powder and eggs; salt and pepper to taste. Pour over chicken and bake until light brown at 400° (approximately 45 minutes to 1 hour).

Gravy: Heat and serve over chicken. (Use as individual serving - do not pour over chicken.)

Joyce Runyan, Huntsville Council

CHICKEN TETRAZZINI

1 medium onion, chopped
1/4 c. chopped celery
3 Tbsp. butter
2 c. cooked chicken, diced
6 oz. (about 1 1/2 c.) spaghetti, uncooked and broken in pieces

1 (10 1/2 oz.) can cream of chicken soup, undiluted
2 1/2 c. chicken broth or bouillon
1 tsp. lemon juice
1/4 tsp. pepper
Pinch of nutmeg
1 (3 oz.) can sliced mushrooms, drained

Saute onion and celery in butter in Dutch oven until crisp-tender. Arrange chicken in layer over vegetables; add spaghetti in layer. Combine soup, broth, lemon juice, pepper and nutmeg and pour over spaghetti, making certain all of spaghetti is moistened. Sprinkle mushrooms over top. Cover and bring to a boil; reduce heat and simmer, stirring constantly (15 to 20 minutes), until spaghetti is tender. Garnish with Parmesan cheese and paprika.

N. Shanks, Anniston Council

CHICKEN TETRAZZINI

1 hen (you can use canned chicken)
8 oz. vermicelli (spaghetti)
1/2 c. chopped bell pepper
1 large chopped onion

2 cans mushroom soup
1/4 tsp. celery salt
1/2 tsp. black pepper
1 Tbsp. Worcestershire sauce
3/4 lb. Cheddar cheese, grated

Remove chicken from bone and cut in bite size pieces. Cook bell pepper and onion in 1 cup chicken broth. Cook vermicelli in remainder of broth real slow. Mix all ingredients. Heat 25 minutes at 350°.

Eulene Miller, Mobile Council

CHICKEN WELLINGTON

2 chicken breasts, halved, skinned, boned
1/4 c. mayonnaise
1 tsp. rosemary leaves, crushed
2 tsp. chopped chives
1 tsp. salt

1/2 tsp. white pepper
1 egg, beaten
1 tsp. flour
1 (4 oz.) can mushrooms (save liquid)
3 Tbsp. cream
1 1/2 tsp. white wine

In frypan place mayonnaise and melt over heat. Add rosemary and chives. Sprinkle salt and pepper on both sides of chicken and place in frying pan. Cook uncovered over medium heat 3 minutes, turn over and cook 3 minutes longer until tender. Separate dough in triangles. Put chicken in middle and place another triangle on top. Pinch all sides to cover and brush with beaten egg. Bake uncovered at 375° for 15 minutes on cookie sheet. Sauce: Add flour to drippings; stir and boil over medium heat. Add wine and liquid from mushrooms, cream and stir constantly and add mushrooms. Pour over chicken and serve.

Ruth Garvin, Montgomery Council

CHICKEN WIGGLE

1 baking hen or 1 pkg. breasts and 1 pkg. legs or thighs	1/2 lb. butter or margarine
	1 lb. egg noodles
2 onions, chopped	1 small can pimento and juice
1 can English peas, drained	1 small can undiluted mushroom soup
2 big shakes Worcestershire sauce	1 small can sliced mushrooms
	2 bell peppers, chopped
Salt and pepper to taste	Dash of Tabasco

Boil hen until tender; cool and cut into bite sized pieces. Cook noodles in chicken broth until tender. Cook butter, onions, Worcestershire, peppers, pimento, mushrooms and soup on simmer 30 minutes. Add hot sauce and peas. Mix all with noodles; mixture should be moist, but not soupy. Heat in 350° oven until hot.

Melba McSwain, Decatur Council

CHICKEN WITH PINEAPPLE GLAZE

2 broiler chickens, quartered	1 (9 oz.) can crushed pineapple
Butter	1 c. brown sugar
Salt	2 Tbsp. lemon juice
Pepper	2 Tbsp. prepared mustard
Paprika	Dash of salt

Rub chicken with butter, salt, pepper and paprika. Grill chicken, skin side up, over flame at medium low setting, 30-45 minutes. Turn once while cooking to give skin time to brown. Blend pineapple, brown sugar, lemon juice, prepared mustard and dash of salt. Baste chicken with this mixture frequently during the last 10-15 minutes cooking time. Makes 4-6 servings.

Mary C. Martin, Birmingham East Council

CHICKEN WITH SHERRY

8 to 10 pieces chicken
Salt and pepper
1 can cream of chicken soup
1 can cream of celery soup
1/2 c. cooking sherry

Arrange chicken in a long glass baking dish. Salt and pepper to taste. In a pan mix thoroughly the soups and sherry. Bring to boil; pour over chicken. Bake at 325°, uncovered, for 2 hours.

Cora Nelson, Decatur Council

CORNISH CROCK POT

2 Cornish game hens
1 pkg. pecan rice
1 1/2 c. water
Salt and pepper to taste

Place rice and water in crock pot; stir well. Place Cornish hens on top of rice; add salt and pepper. Cook on low setting 6 hours. (Can be cooked all day if you go to work.)

Voncile Wolf, Mobile Council

COUNTRY CAPTAIN CHICKEN

1 broiler-fryer chicken,
  cut in serving pieces
1 tsp. flavor enhancer
1/2 c. flour
1 1/2 tsp. salt
1/2 tsp. pepper
1/4 c. corn oil
1 medium onion, chopped
1 medium pepper. chopped
1/2 c. celery, chopped
1 clove garlic, minced
2 tsp. curry powder
1/4 tsp. dried leaf thyme
1 (1 lb.) can tomatoes
2 Tbsp. currants or raisins,
  chopped
2 Tbsp. toasted slivered
  almonds
3 c. hot cooked rice

Sprinkle chicken with flavor enhancer on aluminum foil. Mix flour, salt and pepper. Coat chicken with seasoned flour mixture. Heat corn oil in a 10 inch frypan over medium heat. Add chicken; brown on all sides, turning as needed. Remove chicken; add onion, green pepper, celery and garlic to remaining oil in skillet; saute until tender. Mix in 1 teaspoon salt, curry powder, 1/4 teaspoon pepper and thyme. Add tomatoes; bring to boil. Return chicken pieces in sauce in frypan; reduce heat and simmer covered about 30 minutes or until chicken is tender. Just before serving, sprinkle with currants and nuts. Serve over rice.

Suzette Alison, Montgomery Council

CRESCENT CHICKEN SQUARES

1 (5 oz.) can boneless
  chicken
1 (3 oz.) pkg. cream cheese
1/4 c. milk
Salt
Pepper
Onion salt
Butter or margarine
1 (8 count) pkg. crescent
  rolls

Mix chicken, cream cheese (softened), milk and seasonings to taste. Divide crescent rolls into triangles; fill with mixture. Fold tops over to form squares. Brush tops with butter; bake in 400° oven for 20 minutes or until golden brown.

Jennie F. Kerley, Birmingham South Council

DOWN HOME FRIED CHICKEN

8 pieces of chicken
  (about 1 3/4 lb.)
2/3 c. buttermilk
3/4 c. all-purpose flour
1 1/2 tsp. salt
1 tsp. onion powder
1/4 tsp. pepper
1 c. vegetable shortening

Put chicken in bowl and pour on buttermilk. Turn to coat each piece. Marinate in refrigerator at least 1 hour. Combine dry ingredients in paper or plastic bag. Add chicken and shake until well coated. Meanwhile, melt shortening in heavy skillet on medium heat. Add chicken and cook, turning frequently until lightly browned. Reduce heat to low; cover and cook for 20 minutes, turning occasionally. Remove cover; cook over medium high 3 more minutes to allow chicken to be crisp. Drain on paper towel. Makes 4 servings.

Muriel P. Hayes, Montgomery Council

FRIED CHICKEN WITH SWEET/SOUR SAUCE

4 chicken breasts (halves)
2 eggs
4 Tbsp. flour
1 tsp. salt
1/2 tsp. pepper
1/2 small box sesame seed
1 small bottle Wesson oil

Sweet/Sour Sauce: Bring mixture to a boil -

12 oz. pineapple preserves
2 Tbsp. horseradish
2 Tbsp. mustard

Cook chicken in boiling water 7-8 minutes or until done; cool and cut into finger lengths. Combine eggs, flour, salt, pepper and sesame seed; mix well. Dip chicken in batter and

drop in hot oil. Cook until brown; drain on paper towels.
Serve with Sweet/Sour Sauce or Dijon mustard.

Virginia H. Green, Birmingham Central Council

GREEK STYLE ROASTED CHICKEN

4 to 6 chicken breasts, or Whole fresh lemon
   your favorite pieces   Black pepper
Wesson oil   Oregano
                          Sweet basil

Preheat oven to 350° to 375°. Rinse chicken pieces
and put them in a shallow roasting pan. Coat liberally with
Wesson oil. Squeeze some juice from a few lemon slices over
the pieces, then put the slices of lemon into the pan. Sprinkle the chicken with pepper, oregano and sweet basil. Roast
for 30 minutes. Remove from oven; turn over pieces and
add more lemon juice and spices. Roast another 30 minutes
and repeat this process. Roast about another 30 minutes
and enjoy.

Tim E. Cuthbertson, Riverchase Council

GRILLED BAR-B-QUE CHICKEN

Marinade:

1 c. salad oil   1 tsp. paprika
1/3 c. distilled white   1/4 tsp. oregano
   vinegar   1 minced garlic clove
1 tsp. salt

Marinate with the pieces of chicken; let stand overnight.
Cook on grill and brush repeatedly with sauce below:

1/2 c. butter   1 tsp. Tabasco
1/2 c. lemon juice   1 tsp. salt
1 tsp. Worcestershire

Sandra Herndon, Birmingham South Council

HAWAIIAN STYLE CHICKEN

2 chickens, cut in eighths   1 c. pineapple juice and
2 Tbsp. lemon juice   pineapple slices (1 medium
2 Tbsp. soy sauce   can sliced pineapple)

Cut chicken; toss lightly in flour seasoned with salt and
pepper. Brown in skillet. Mix lemon juice, soy sauce and

pineapple juice; pour over chicken. Cover and bake at 350°
for 45 minutes. Place pineapple over chicken and cook for
15 minutes. Serve hot over rice.

Frances H. Lewis, Birmingham South Council

HERBED BAKED CHICKEN

6 chicken breasts, skinned
1 stick oleo, melted
1 c. fine dried bread crumbs
1 tsp. salt

1/2 tsp. onion powder
1/4 tsp. poultry seasoning
1/4 tsp. sage
1 Tbsp. dried parsley

Combine seasonings and herbs. Sprinkle chicken with
herb mixture; dip in crumbs and dip in melted oleo. Bake at
400° for approximately 1 hour. Baste several times with
herbs and oleo drippings during baking. Serves 4-6.

Suggestion: Serve with Rice Loaf (with mushroom
sauce). This recipe is also submitted, on page 699.

Elaine Rindt, Riverchase Council

ITALIAN CHICKEN

1 (2 /12 lb.) fryer, cut up
1 tsp. salt
1/2 tsp. pepper
1/2 tsp. garlic powder
1 tsp. poultry seasoning
2 tsp. paprika
14 1/2 oz. canned tomatoes
   and 8 oz. juice

1 clove garlic, crushed
3 Tbsp. onion flakes
1/2 medium green pepper,
   diced
1 c. fresh sliced
   mushrooms
1/2 tsp. oregano

Place fryer in ovenproof casserole dish. Combine next 5
ingredients and sprinkle on all sides of chicken. Combine all
other ingredients (except mushrooms and oregano) and pour
over chicken. Cover and bake at 400° for 1 hour or until
chicken is tender. Baste chicken several times during baking with pan juices. Remove chicken to hot platter and keep
warm. Bring to boil and allow to reduce and thicken. Add
mushrooms and oregano; cook slowly another 5 minutes or
until mushrooms are tender.

Delores Champion Dugger, Decatur Council

JAMBALAYA

3 Tbsp. flour
1 (15 oz.) can chicken broth
1 (8 oz.) can tomato paste
2 onions, cut fairly large
2 bell peppers, cut fairly
   large
.1 can tomato wedges
Dash of salt, pepper,
   Worcestershire, garlic
   powder and oregano

1 lb. smoked sausage or
   kielbasa, cut in small
   slices, fried and drained
2 cooked chicken breasts,
   shredded (or you may use
   canned Swanson white meat)
10-15 pepperoni slices
1 (8 oz.) can mushroom
   slices, drained
2-3 c. cooked rice

In a 3-4 quart pot brown flour by itself on medium heat till milky brown color. Add next 5 ingredients; simmer until thickened. Add rest of the ingredients except rice. Leave simmering about 45 minutes. Serve over cooked rice.

            Donna Benford, Tuscaloosa Council

JAMBALAYA

4 chicken breasts
4 c. water
4 Tbsp. oil
2 c. chopped onions
2 c. chopped green
   peppers
1 c. ham, diced
16 small pork sausages,
   cut into 3/4 inch pieces

3 cloves garlic
2 (No. 2) cans tomatoes (5 c.)
2 c. raw rice
3 c. chicken broth
1 tsp. thyme
2 tsp. parsley
1/2 tsp. chili powder
2 tsp. salt

Day before: Cook chicken in water; remove from bones. Preheat oven to 350°. Heat oil in skillet; add onion, green pepper and garlic. Cook slowly until onion and green pepper are soft. Add chicken, ham and sausage; cook 5 minutes. Add tomatoes with liquid, rice, broth and spices. Put in casserole dish and bake 1 hour. Refrigerate overnight. Next day, reheat at 350° until rice is tender.

            Debbie Tucker, Birmingham East Council

JESSICA'S CHICKEN

8 slices bacon, partially
   cooked
4 whole chicken breasts,
   halved, skinned and
   boned (or thighs)
1 (2 1/2 oz.) jar dried
   beef, chopped

2 cans undiluted cream of
   mushroom soup
1 c. sour cream
Mushrooms, sliced and sauteed
Parsley sprigs (optional)
Hot cooked rice

Wrap 1 slice bacon around each piece of chicken. Place side by side in greased 12x8x2 inch baking dish. Sprinkle with beef. Mix soup and sour cream; pour over chicken. Bake in 225° oven 3 1/2 hours. Garnish with mushrooms and parsley. Serve with rice. Makes 8 servings.

Jean Carter (Mrs. C. J.),
Birmingham Central Council

LEMON CHICKEN

Chicken breasts
Meat tenderizer
Garlic salt
Lemon and pepper seasoning
Lemon juice
Margarine

Sprinkle chicken breasts with meat tenderizer, garlic salt and lemon and pepper seasoning to taste. Marinate in 1 cup lemon juice for 3-4 hours. Turn chicken after 1/2 marinating time. Remove chicken from marinade and place in baking dish with a pat of margarine on each piece. Bake at 350° for 1 hour. Delicious with rice and dill weed!

Bobbie DeGaris, Riverchase Council

LEMON CHICKEN

1/4 c. butter
2 (2 1/2 lb.) chickens, cut
  into serving pieces
2 Tbsp. flour
2 c. sour cream
1 1/2 tsp. salt
2 Tbsp. parsley
4 chopped green onions
2 Tbsp. grated lemon rind
1/2 lb. sliced mushrooms
3 Tbsp. fresh lemon juice
1/4 tsp. pepper

Melt butter and brown chicken in 6 quart casserole. Remove chicken and stir flour into pan juices. Add sour cream and salt and pepper; mix well. Stir in all ingredients except lemon juice. Add chicken and spoon sauce over it. Bake, covered, at 350° for 1 hour. Remove chicken and place on a platter. Stir lemon juice and pour over chicken and serve.

Debbie Tucker, Birmingham East Council

LOUISIANA CHICKEN

1 fryer, boiled and boned
1 large onion
1 can green chilies
1 pkg. tortilla chips
  (regular flavor)
1 can cream of chicken soup
1 can cream of mushroom soup
2 c. broth from boiled fryer
Grated cheese

1567-82

Cook onion and chilies in small amount of margarine until onion is tender. Add your soups and the broth a little at a time, so that your soup won't be lumpy. Bring to a simmer and let simmer while preparing in a casserole dish 1 layer of chicken, a layer of tortilla chips. Then pour on some of the hot soup mixture. Repeat until all is gone. Cover with cheese; bake at 350° until cheese is melted.

Carol Burns, Huntsville Council

MAGNIFIQUE BREASTS OF CHICKEN

4 whole chicken breasts, split
Salt to taste
1/4 c. melted margarine
2 c. sliced mushrooms
2 (10 3/4 oz.) cans cream of chicken soup, undiluted

Dash of ground thyme
1 clove garlic, minced
1/8 tsp. rosemary
2/3 c. half & half
Hot cooked rice
Toasted slivered almonds

Sprinkle chicken with salt and brown in margarine. Remove chicken from skillet, and set aside. Saute mushrooms in drippings. Add chicken, soup, thyme, garlic and rosemary; cover and cook over low heat 45 minutes. Stir in half & half; heat well. Serve over rice; sprinkle with almonds. Yield: 8 servings.

Faith Kirby, Anniston Council

MEXICAN CHICKEN

1 (2 1/2 to 3 lb.) chicken
1 medium onion, chopped
1 (8 oz.) pkg. tortilla chips, broken
1 1/2 c. shredded Cheddar cheese

1 can cream of mushroom soup, undiluted
1 can cream of chicken soup, undiluted
1 (10 oz.) can tomatoes with hot peppers
3/4 c. chicken broth

Cook chicken in salted water; remove from broth, reserving broth. Cool. Bone chicken and cut into small pieces. Place chicken in bottom of a lightly greased 2 quart shallow casserole. On top of chicken put a layer of onion, half of the chips and cheese. Top with remaining chips. Combine soups, tomatoes and chicken broth; blend well. Pour over casserole and bake at 350° for 30 minutes.

Kathryn Robertson, Tuscaloosa Council

MEXICAN CHICKEN

1 large chicken or 4 large chicken breasts	1 pkg. taco Doritos
1 medium onion	1 can cream of chicken soup
1/2 lb. Velveeta cheese	1 can cream of mushroom soup
	1 can Ro-Tel tomatoes

Boil and bone chicken. Cut up and place in bottom of casserole dish. Slice onion and place onion rings over chicken. Dice Velveeta cheese and place on top of onion rings. Crush up Doritos and put half on top of cheese. Mix together in a bowl tomatoes and soups. Pour on top of Doritos. Put the other half of crushed Doritos on top; bake at 400° for 45 minutes.

Sharon Crabtree, Tuscaloosa Council

MURPHIE'S BREAST OF CHICKEN SCALA

3 whole chicken breasts, boned, halved and skin removed (approx. 2 1/4 lb.)	1/2 c. dairy sour cream
	1 tsp. salt
	1/4 tsp. black pepper
	1 Tbsp. grated Parmesan cheese
2 Tbsp. flour	2-3 onions
1/4 c. butter or margarine	1/2 lb. fresh mushrooms
1 (10 1/2 oz.) can condensed beef consomme (undiluted)	1 c. white wine

Wipe chicken with damp paper towel; sprinkle with flour. In hot butter in large Dutch oven, saute chicken until golden brown on each side (takes about 15 minutes in all). Saute chopped onion in with chicken. Saute mushrooms in butter and add to chicken; add consomme and wine. Simmer, covered, for about 45 minutes. Stir in sour cream, salt and pepper; simmer 10 minutes longer. (Good to let stand a couple of days.) Remove chicken breasts to heat-proof serving dish; stir sauce in pan to mix well. (Add cornstarch to thicken if desired.) Pour over chicken. To serve: Sprinkle cheese over top; run under broiler a few minutes until golden brown. Serve at once.

Anne Spragins, Birmingham East Council

MURPHIE'S STUFFED CHICKEN BREASTS

6 whole small boned chicken breasts	2 Tbsp. salad oil
	2 Tbsp. butter
1 1/2 tsp. salt	1/2 c. chopped onion
1/2 tsp. pepper	1 clove garlic, crushed
1 pkg. Uncle Ben's wild rice	3 Tbsp. flour

1 (13 1/4 oz.) can	1/2 tsp. liquid gravy
chicken broth	seasoning (such as
1 c. dry white wine	Kitchen Bouquet)

Rinse chicken in cold water and pat dry with paper towels. Remove fat and trim edges. Sprinkle with 1 1/2 teaspoons salt and 1/2 teaspoon pepper. Prepare 1 package Uncle Ben's wild rice by directions on package. Place about 1/3 cup of rice on one-half of each breast. Fold remaining half over and fasten with wooden picks. On medium heat brown stuffed chicken breasts, one at a time, in a mixture of oil and butter. Remove to ovenproof baking dish.

Sauce: Stir onions and garlic into remaining oil and butter mixture in skillet. Saute on low heat until golden brown (about 5 minutes). Blend in flour and cook 1 minute. Remove from heat; stir in chicken broth, wine, gravy seasoning and 1/4 teaspoon pepper. Cook until mixture comes to a boil, stirring constantly; boil for 1 minute. Pour over chicken breasts and bake at 350° until tender (about 50 minutes), basting occasionally.

Anne Spragins, Birmingham East Council

NO PEEK CHICKEN

1 chicken, cut up	1 can cream of celery soup
2 c. Minute rice, uncooked	1 can cream of mushroom soup
1 pkg. Lipton dry onion	1 c. water
soup mix	

Mix soups and rice; set aside. Grease casserole. Place chicken in it. Pour soup mixture over chicken. Cover tightly with foil; bake in 350° oven for 2 hours; do not peek. Can serve 4 to 5.

Dorothy M. Gauger, Life Member

NOT THE SAME OLD CHICKEN

This golden glazed chicken is named for the comments it elicits. It really does taste special. Power level: High. Microwave time: 18 to 22 minutes total.

Use 1 chicken (2 1/2 to 3 1/2 pounds), cut up. In 12x8x2 inch dish arrange chicken with thickest, meaty pieces to outside edges of dish.

1/4 c. mayonnaise	1/2 c. bottled Russian dressing
1 pkg. (1/2 of 2 3/4 oz.	1 c. apricot-pineapple
box) dry onion soup mix	preserves

In small bowl stir together mayonnaise, onion soup mix, dressing and preserves; spread over chicken, coating each piece. Cover with wax paper. Microwave at high 18 to 22 minutes, rotating dish 1/2 turn after 10 minutes. Allow to stand 5 to 10 minutes before serving, so chicken absorbs flavor of sauce. Serve with rice, if desired. Makes about 4 servings.

Mary C. Martin, Birmingham East Council

OVEN FRIED CHICKEN

1 c. Bisquick	1 small can evaporated milk
1 tsp. paprika	2 to 4 skinned chicken pieces
1 1/2 tsp. poultry seasoning	Butter
1 1/2 tsp. salt	

Mix dry ingredients in medium bowl. Put evaporated milk in another medium bowl. Dip chicken pieces in milk; roll in dry mixture. Place in casserole dish. Pour melted butter over each piece. Bake at 375° for 1 hour.

Royce Tyree, Riverchase Council

OVEN FRIED CHICKEN

1 packet crispy coating for chicken	1 egg
	1 Tbsp. water
1/4 c. oil or melted margarine	2 1/2 lb. chicken pieces

Preheat oven to 400°. Empty packet of coating onto a sheet of waxed paper. Spread oil in a 15x10x1 inch jelly roll pan. In a large bowl beat egg with a fork; add water and blend. Add all the chicken pieces and toss gently to moisten each piece on all sides. Starting with large pieces, place chicken in coating, then press firmly on all sides until chicken is thickly and evenly coated. Place in pan skin side down; fry in oven 25 minutes, then turn and fry an additional 25 minutes until tender. Remove from pan immediately. Makes 4 servings.

Mary C. Martin, Birmingham East Council

OVEN-FRIED PARMESAN CHICKEN

1 c. round buttery cracker crumbs	2 Tbsp. chopped fresh parsley
	1 (2 1/2 to 3 lb.) broiler-fryer, cut up
1/2 c. grated Parmesan cheese	1/2 c. butter or margarine, melted

Combine first 3 ingredients; mix well. Dip chicken in butter; dredge in cracker crumb mixture. Place chicken in a lightly greased 13x9x2 inch baking dish; bake, uncovered, at 350° for 1 hour. Yield: 4 servings.

Regina Cash, Anniston Council

PAELLA

2 c. cooked chicken,
  cut in 1 inch pieces
4 c. hot chicken or
  beef broth
1/4 c. olive oil
1/4 c. thinly sliced onion
2 c. rice
Dash of saffron

2 slices sweet red pepper
1 tsp. paprika
1/4 tsp. oregano
Thin slices of Spanish sausage
Raw shrimp
Raw scallops
2 cloves garlic

Use large lidded casserole. Heat olive oil and sliced onions until golden; add rice and brown lightly. Add hot broth and saffron; add garlic, pepper, paprika, oregano and sausage; season to taste. Add chicken and leave on top of mixture. Cover and bake at 350° for 15 minutes. Add, arranging them attractively on top, raw shrimp and scallops. Cover and steam 10 minutes longer. Serve at once.

Dorothy Franklin, Montgomery Council

PAPRIKASH (BEEF OR CHICKEN)

2 Tbsp. instant minced
  onion
2 lb. boneless beef stew
  meat or 2 1/2 lb.
  boneless chicken breasts
1/4 tsp. pepper
1 tsp. butter

1 Tbsp. flour
Water
1/4 c. flour
1 tsp. salt
1/4 c. oil
2 Tbsp. paprika, divided
1/2 c. milk
1 c. sour cream

Rehydrate minced onion in 2 tablespoons water; let stand 10 minutes to soften. Cut beef into 1 inch cubes or cut chicken into serving pieces. Dredge meat in flour mixed with salt and pepper. Heat oil in a large skillet. Add meat, onion and 1 tablespoon paprika. Brown meat well on all sides. Add 1/2 cup water; cover tightly and simmer until tender, about 1 1/2 hours for beef or 45 minutes for chicken, turning occasionally and adding more water if needed.

Sauce: In a small saucepan melt butter; blend in flour and remaining 1 tablespoon paprika. Cook and stir until mixture bubbles. Blend in milk; cook and stir until thickened. Gradually stir in sour cream, beating vigorously. Pour sauce over cooked meat in skillet and heat thoroughly, but do not boil. Serve hot with cooked broad noodles.

Andrea Dutton, Anniston Council

PARMESAN CHICKEN

4 chicken breasts, deboned
Green onion tops, chopped
Monterey Jack cheese, chopped
1/3 c. melted butter
1 Tbsp. Worcestershire sauce

2 cloves, pressed (or powder)
3/4 c. bread crumbs
1/4 c. Parmesan cheese
1/2 tsp. salt and pepper
3 or 4 Tbsp. parsley
1/4 tsp. garlic

Pound chicken breasts flat. Place small pieces of cheese and onion in center. Roll up and secure with toothpicks. Melt butter; add Worcestershire and garlic. Mix crumbs with parsley, salt and pepper, garlic and Parmesan cheese. Dip chicken rolls in butter sauce and roll in crumbs. Pour remaining butter over chicken. Place in baking pan and bake at 350° for 40 minutes.

Mildred Breedlove, Retired, Life Member, Montgomery Council

PARTY CHICKEN

8 chicken breasts
1 can cream of chicken soup
3/4 c. mayonnaise
1 tsp. grated onion

1 Tbsp. lemon juice
1/2 c. slivered almonds
1 c. crushed potato chips

Boil 8 chicken breasts until tender. Cool and bone. Mix chicken soup, mayonnaise, onion and lemon juice; spread over chicken and sprinkle with almonds and potato chips. Bake at 375° for 20 minutes.

Evelyn Lloyd, Birmingham South Council

PARTY CHICKEN

1 small jar Armour dried sliced beef
6-8 chicken breasts, deboned

1 (8 oz.) carton sour cream
1 (10 3/4 oz.) can mushroom soup

(Do not salt chicken.) Line Pyrex dish with dried beef. Lay 1/2 slice bacon over each chicken breast (optional) and place them in dish on top of beef slices. Mix sour cream and soup thoroughly and pour over chicken breasts. Cook 3 hours in 250° oven (or can bake covered with foil at 300° for 2 hours, increase heat to 350° and bake uncovered 20 to 30 minutes longer, basting several times).

Nancy Williams, Life Member, Anniston Council

POPPY SEED CHICKEN

6 chicken breasts, deboned
2 cans cream of chicken
  soup
Butter
1 pkg. Ritz crackers, crushed
Poppy seeds
1 or 2 small cartons sour cream

Cook chicken and drain and debone. Put chicken into bottom of casserole. Next pour mixed sour cream and soup over chicken. Crush crackers; dab a little butter on top and sprinkle with poppy seed. Bake in oven until it bubbles.

Gladys Whitman, Montgomery Council

ROMANO CHICKEN

Boneless chicken breasts
Parmesan cheese
Romano cheese
White wine (1/2 to 1 c.)
Seasoned bread crumbs

Roll chicken in bread crumbs and Parmesan cheese. Fry chicken, then put in casserole dish. Saute mushrooms in wine. Put mushrooms on chicken, Romano on top. Bake in oven until cheese melts.

Janet Stephens, Anniston Council

SESAME CHICKEN

1 egg, beaten
1/4 c. milk
1/2 c. fine dry bread
  crumbs
1/4 c. sesame seeds
3/4 tsp. salt
3 whole chicken breasts,
  split, skinned and boned
1/2 c. all-purpose flour
Vegetable oil
1/4 tsp. pepper

Combine egg and milk; stir well. Combine bread crumbs, sesame seeds, salt and pepper, stirring well. Dredge chicken in flour; dip in egg mixture, and dredge in bread crumb mixture. Heat 1 inch of oil in a large skillet to 325°; add chicken and fry 5 minutes on each side; drain on paper towels. Yield: 6 servings.

578   Regina Cash, Anniston Council

SESAME CHICKEN KABOBS

2 whole chicken breasts,
  skinned and boned
1/4 c. soy sauce
1/4 c. Russian reduced-
  calorie salad dressing
1 Tbsp. sesame seeds
2 Tbsp. lemon juice
1/4 tsp. ground ginger
1/4 tsp. garlic powder

1 large green pepper,
  cut into 1 inch pieces
2 medium onions, cut
  into eighths
3 small zucchini, cut into
  3/4 inch pieces
1 pt. cherry tomatoes
Vegetable cooking spray

Cut chicken breasts into 1 inch pieces; place chicken in a shallow container, and set aside. Combine next 6 ingredients in a jar; cover tightly and shake vigorously. Pour over chicken; cover and marinate in the refrigerator at least 2 hours. Remove chicken from marinade, reserving marinade. Alternate chicken and vegetables on skewers. Spray grill with cooking spray. Grill kabobs about 6 inches from medium-hot coals for 15 to 20 minutes or until done, turning and basting often with marinade. Yield: 6 servings (about 156 calories per serving).

Regina Cash, Anniston Council

SESAME SEED CHICKEN

1 tsp. salt
1/2 tsp. pepper
3/4 c. all-purpose
  flour, divided
4 whole chicken breasts,
  split and boned

4 eggs, beaten
4 Tbsp. milk
6 Tbsp. sesame seeds
Hot salad oil
Supreme Sauce

Combine salt, pepper and 1/4 cup flour in a bag. Add chicken and shake to coat. Combine eggs and milk in a small bowl; set aside. Combine remaining flour and sesame seeds in a small bowl. Dip each chicken breast in egg mixture, then coat with sesame seed mixture. Heat salad oil to 350°. Add chicken and saute about 15 minutes or until golden brown. Serve with Supreme Sauce. Yield: 8 servings.

Supreme Sauce:

6 Tbsp. butter or margarine
4 Tbsp. all-purpose flour

3 c. chicken broth
2 egg yolks, beaten

Melt butter in a small saucepan over low heat; add flour, blending until smooth. Gradually add chicken broth; cook, stirring constantly, until slightly thickened. Gradually add about 1/2 cup hot mixture into remaining hot mixture. Cook over low heat, stirring constantly, until sauce is thickened and smooth. Yield: About 2 cups.

Candice Akers, Birmingham South Council

SHERRY CHICKEN

3/4 stick oleo	1 chicken bouillon cube
1/2 c. cooking sherry	1 c. boiling water
1 1/2 Tbsp. flour	Almonds (optional)

Brown chicken in butter. Warm sherry. Light sherry while pouring over chicken. Take chicken out and add bouillon, water and flour for gravy. Put chicken back in and simmer until done, about 1 1/2 to 2 hours. (Add more water if needed.)

Angela S. Henderson, Huntsville Council

SODA POP BARBEQUE'D CHICKEN

1 fryer, skinned	Kraft Barbeque sauce
1 can Dr. Pepper	1/4 tsp. salt (optional)

Skin raw fryer; place in large pot. Pour can of Dr. Pepper and an equal amount of barbeque sauce over chicken. Add 1/4 teaspoon salt (optional). Simmer covered slowly for 1 hour or until chicken is tender. Turn chicken several times while simmering to make sure barbeque sauce covers all the chicken. Ready to serve.

Naomi H. Johnson, Birmingham Central Council

SOUTH GEORGIA BAR-B-Q CHICKEN

1 fryer, cut in half	1/4 to 1/2 c. butter, melted

Sauce:

1 lemon (juice only)	6 Tbsp. mayonnaise
1/4 tsp. black pepper	1 tsp. salt
	1 Tbsp. vinegar

Butter fryer well and wrap in foil. Cook for 1 hour or more at 350° in preheated oven. Baste with sauce several times while cooking. Reserve remaining sauce to serve over chicken when serving.

Bobbie D. Thompson, Decatur Council

SPANISH CHICKEN

1/4 c. margarine
3 whole chicken
  breasts, split
2 1/2 c. water
3 chicken bouillon cubes
1/2 c. chopped green pepper
1 medium garlic clove,
  minced

1 c. regular white rice,
  uncooked
1/4 c. pimento strips
Paprika
1 c. sliced onion
1 bay leaf
2 tsp. salt
1/4 tsp. pepper

Fry chicken in margarine, sprinkled with paprika, until brown. Drain fat; add water, bouillon cubes, onion, green pepper, garlic, bay leaf, salt and pepper. Reduce heat to simmer. Cover and cook. Stir rice into liquid; cover and continue cooking 10-15 minutes or until all liquid is absorbed and chicken is tender. Remove bay leaf and serve from skillet.

Donna Campbell, Anniston Council

TRADITIONAL FRIED CHICKEN

2 c. milk
2 eggs, beaten
2 Tbsp. butter or
  margarine, melted
2 tsp. paprika
1 1/2 tsp. salt
1 tsp. pepper

1 (2 1/2 to 3 lb.) broiler-
  fryer, cut up and skinned
Additional pepper
All-purpose flour
Vegetable oil

Combine first 6 ingredients; mix well. Place chicken in a shallow pan and pour milk mixture over top. Refrigerate at least 15 minutes. Remove chicken from liquid. Sprinkle lightly with additional pepper, and dredge in flour. Let stand 5 minutes. Heat 1 inch of oil in a large skillet to 325°. Add chicken and fry 30 minutes or until golden brown, turning once. Drain on paper towels. Yield: 4 servings.

Regina Cash, Anniston Council

"YUMMY CHICKEN"

1 fryer, cut up
1 (6 oz.) bottle Coke

1 c. ketchup
Worcestershire sauce, to taste

Coat fryer pieces with flour. Place in casserole. Mix Coke, ketchup, Worcestershire sauce and pour over chicken. Bake in 350° oven for 1 1/2 hours or till done.

Jimmie N. Smith, Mobile Council

HOW TO BAKE A TURKEY

Baste with melted oleo inside and out real well. Salt inside and out real well. Put turkey in roaster, 1 whole unpeeled apple (large cooking kind), 1 whole large peeled onion, several ribs of celery. For turkey 12 pounds and under, put 1 pint of water (16 pounds and up, use 1 quart water). Preheat oven to 475°. Put turkey in oven; cook 1 hour, then turn oven off. Do not open oven door until next morning.

Kitty Logan, Anniston Council

BAKED TURKEY

Rub turkey inside and outside with salt. Put in roasting pan with cover. Add:

1 1/2 qt. water	1 whole onion
1 whole apple, cored	2 stalks celery

Put cover on roaster and cook at 500° for 1 hour. Turn oven off and leave overnight.

Bonnie Mayfield, Anniston Council

SMOKED TURKEY BREAST - OUTSIDE GRILL

Smoke on grill with rotisserie at 100° to 150° for approximately 5 hours with cover closed - weight 6-7 pounds. Approximately 30 minutes after beginning, sprinkle heavy application of garlic salt. This should be done twice more, generally at 1 hour and 1 1/2 hours. All during cooking process, baste every 10-15 minutes with pure water in order to retain moisture.

The smoking process is done by using hickory nuts and hickory nut hulls which have been soaked in water 24 hours prior to using. Start the smoking process approximately 3 hours from beginning. Put the nuts and hulls on charcoal fire several times during last 2 hours. The breast will turn out a dark golden brown outside with pure white meat inside. Slice after complete cooking.

Guy Pippin, Anniston Council

SMOKED TURKEY - COVERED GRILL

1 turkey breast	1 bag hickory chips
1 small bottle vinegar	Charcoal lighter
Handful of salt	1 match
1 bag charcoal	1 bucket of water

Rub turkey all over with salt. Pour vinegar over entire turkey breast. Cover for about 1 hour. Light fire, using only a handful of charcoal. (Put charcoal in tiny pile in corner of covered grill.) Soak chips in water to be added as you cook. Put turkey on grill on its back with cavity filled with vinegar. Turn every 2 hours. Cook 5-7 hours. Add few lumps of charcoal occasionally. Add chips to keep smoke going.

Florence Cole, Birmingham South Council

TURKEY PIE

1 (9 inch) pie shell, baked	1/4 tsp. pepper
2 c. cooked, cubed turkey	1/2 tsp. salt
1 c. chopped celery	1 Tbsp. lemon juice
1/3 c. chopped green pepper	1/2 c. mayonnaise
2 Tbsp. finely chopped onions	1 (10 3/4 oz.) can condensed cream of chicken soup
1/2 c. coarsely chopped pecans	1/2 c. shredded Swiss or Cheddar cheese
	3 Tbsp. snipped fresh parsley

Combine turkey, celery, green pepper, onion, pecans, pepper, salt, lemon juice, mayonnaise and soup. Spoon into pie shell. Sprinkle cheese and parsley over top; bake in 350° oven for 30 minutes, or until heated through. If desired, sprinkle with chopped pecans. (I use chicken at times instead of turkey.)

Bertha Ross, Decatur Council

TURKEY ROLL WITH STUFFING CASSEROLE

1 boned turkey roll (5 to 7 lb.)	1/4 c. Chinese style spareribs or duck sauce

Place turkey roll in small roasting pan and roast according to package directions. One hour before turkey is finished, baste with Chinese style sauce. Serve with stuffing casserole. Serves 8 to 10.

Monica Burroughs, Birmingham East Council

BAKED BASS

2 lb. bass filets
2 Tbsp. butter, melted
1 lime, thinly sliced

1 lemon, thinly sliced
1 small orange, thinly sliced
1 finely chopped bell pepper

Place filets skin side down in a greased baking dish; brush with butter. Arrange slices over filets in alternating pattern and sprinkle on bell pepper. Bake at 350° for 30 minutes or until fish flakes with a fork easily. Serves 4 persons.

George Ponder, Decatur Council

RIVER BISQUE

2 carrots, diced
3 stalks celery, diced
1 bell pepper, diced
1/2 onion, diced
6 Tbsp. butter
1/8 c. flour

1 tsp. Worcestershire sauce
4 c. milk
1/4 tsp. pepper
1/2 tsp. salt
1 qt. small fillets (bass
    or bream)

Cook diced vegetables in 2 tablespoons butter until tender; add 2 tablespoons butter, flour, 1/2 salt and pepper. Cook to bubble; slowly add milk and heat to just below boiling.

In separate pan melt 2 tablespoons butter; add fish. Sprinkle remaining salt and pepper; add Worcestershire sauce. Cook until fish is done; add fish to milk and vegetable mixture. Simmer for 5 minutes and serve.

Jean Ponder, Decatur Council

BAKED BLUEFISH WITH SESAME SEEDS

Rind of 1 lemon, cut into
    fine strips
2 Tbsp. sesame seed
1 Tbsp. peeled and
    minced ginger root
1 stick (1/2 c.)
    unsalted butter
3 Tbsp. fresh lemon juice

1 tsp. Oriental sesame oil
    (available at Oriental markets
    and specialty foods shops)
1 tsp. Dijon style mustard
1/2 tsp. soy sauce
1/4 tsp. cayenne
2 (1/2 lb.) bluefish filets
4 scallions, sliced thin on
    the diagonal

In a saucepan of boiling water blanch the lemon rind for 5 minutes; drain it in a sieve, and refresh it under running cold water. Pat the rind dry. In a dry heavy skillet toast the sesame seed over moderately high heat, stirring, until it is golden brown. In a stainless steel or enameled skillet cook the ginger root in 2 tablespoons of the butter over moderately high heat, stirring, until it is golden. Add the remaining 6 tablespoons butter, cut into bits, and the lemon juice, and cook the mixture over low heat, stirring, until the butter is melted. Stir in the sesame oil, the mustard, the soy sauce, the cayenne, and salt and pepper to taste and remove the skillet from the heat.

Pat the fillets dry and arrange them skin side down in a buttered baking dish just large enough to hold them in one layer. Pour the sauce over the fillets; sprinkle the fillets with the lemon rind and the scallion, and bake them, covered with foil, in a preheated hot oven (425° F.) for 8 to 10 minutes, or until they just flake when tested with a fork. Sprinkle the fillets with the sesame seed. Serves 2.

Katherine Creamer, Mobile Council

BLUEFISH EN PAPILLOTE

2 Tbsp. minced shallot
3 Tbsp. unsalted butter
1 Tbsp. Dijon style
   mustard

2 Tbsp. minced fresh
   parsley leaves
1 tsp. fresh lemon juice
2 (1/2 lb.) bluefish fillets
8 lemon slices

In a small skillet cook the shallot in the butter over moderate heat, stirring, for 3 minutes, or until it is just softened; add the mustard, the parsley, and the lemon juice, and combine the mixture. Arrange each fillet skin side down on a double thickness of foil large enough to enclose it; pour half the sauce over it, and top each fillet with 4 lemon slices. Enclose the fillets in the foil, crimp the edges of the foil together to seal the packets well, and bake the packets on a jelly roll pan in a preheated very hot oven (450° F.) for 10 minutes. Transfer the packets to a heated platter. Serves 2.

Katherine Creamer, Mobile Council

BLUEFISH WITH GREEN CHILI SAUCE

1 onion, chopped
Enough fresh green semi-
   hot chili peppers, seeded
   and chopped, wearing
   rubber gloves, to
   measure 1/2 c.
2 garlic cloves, minced

2 Tbsp. vegetable oil
1/2 c. peeled, seeded
   and chopped tomato
1 Tbsp. white wine vinegar
4 (1/2 lb.) bluefish fillets
2 Tbsp. softened unsalted
   butter

1567-82

For the garnish: Use lime wedges, sprigs of fresh coriander.

In a food processor fitted with the steel blade, or in a blender puree the onion, the chili pepper and the garlic with 1/2 cup water. In a stainless steel or enameled skillet heat the oil over moderate heat until it is hot; add the puree carefully, and cook it, stirring, for 5 minutes, or until it begins to thicken. Add the tomato, the vinegar and salt and pepper to taste; cook the sauce over low heat, stirring, for 10 minutes, and keep it warm.

Pat the fillets dry and arrange them skin side down on the oiled rack of a broiler pan. Spread the butter on the fillets; sprinkle the fillets with salt and pepper, and broil them under a preheated broiler about 4 inches from the heat for 6 to 8 minutes, or until they just flake when tested with a fork. Transfer the fillets with a large spatula to heated plates, nap them with the sauce, and garnish them with the lime and the coriander. Serves 4.

Katherine Creamer, Mobile Council

BLUEFISH WITH ONIONS AND PARMESAN

3 small onions, sliced
thin crosswise and
separated into rings
2 Tbsp. unsalted butter

4 (1/2 lb.) bluefish fillets
1/2 c. mayonnaise
1/2 c. freshly grated Parmesan
combined with 1/2 c. fine
fresh bread crumbs

In a skillet saute the onions in the butter over moderately high heat until they are brown and tender. Pat the fillets dry; arrange them skin side down on the oiled rack of a broiler pan, and season them with salt and pepper. Spread each filet with 1 tablespoon of the mayonnaise and broil the fillets under a preheated broiler about 4 inches from the heat for 3 minutes. Divide the onions among the fillets; spread the remaining 1/4 cup mayonnaise over them, and sprinkle the fillets with the Parmesan mixture. Broil fillets for 2 to 3 minutes more, or until they just flake when tested with a fork and the topping is golden brown. Transfer the fillets with a large spatula to heated plates. Serves 4.

Katherine Creamer, Mobile Council

BLUEFISH WITH ORANGE MUSTARD SAUCE

Rind of 1/2 orange, cut
   into fine strips
4 (1/2 lb.) bluefish fillets
1/4 c. fresh lemon juice
   plus additional lemon
   juice to taste
3/4 c. fresh orange juice

3/4 stick (6 Tbsp.)
   unsalted butter
2 Tbsp. minced fresh
   parsley leaves
1 Tbsp. minced fresh chervil
   or 1 tsp. dried
1 tsp. Dijon style mustard
1 large egg yolk

In a saucepan of boiling water blanch the orange rind for 3 minutes; drain it in a sieve and refresh it under running cold water. Pat the rind dry. Arrange the fillets in a shallow glass dish just large enough to hold them in one layer; add 1/4 cup of the lemon juice combined with 1/4 cup of the orange juice, and let the fillets marinate, turning them frequently, for 1 hour.

In a stainless steel or enameled saucepan melt the butter; add the remaining 1/2 cup orange juice, the parsley, the chervil, the mustard and the orange rind, and simmer the sauce for 2 minutes. In a small bowl whisk a little of the sauce into the egg yolk; stir the mixture into the sauce, and cook the sauce over moderately low heat, stirring, until it is thickened slightly. Add the additional lemon juice and salt and pepper to taste and keep the sauce warm. Drain the fillets and sprinkle them with salt and pepper. Arrange the fillets skin side down on the oiled rack of a broiler pan and broil them under a preheated broiler about 4 inches from the heat for 6 to 8 minutes, or until they just flake when tested with a fork. Transfer the filets with a large spatula to heated plates and nap them with the sauce. Serves 4.

Katherine Creamer, Mobile Council

CUCUMBER-STUFFED BLUEFISH

2 slices bacon, chopped
1 onion, chopped
2 cucumbers, peeled,
   seeded and sliced
   1/4 inch thick
1 Tbsp. unsalted butter
1 c. coarse stale bread
   crumbs

1 large egg, beaten lightly
1 Tbsp. minced fresh parsley
   leaves
1 tsp. fresh lemon juice plus
   additional lemon juice to
   taste
2 to 3 lb. whole bluefish,
   cleaned and boned, leaving
   the head and tail intact

In a skillet cook the bacon and the onion over moderate heat, stirring, until the bacon is just crisp. Add the cucumber and the butter and cook the mixture, stirring, for 3 minutes. Let the mixture cool for 5 minutes and fold in the bread crumbs, the egg, the parsley, 1 teaspoon of the lemon juice, and salt and pepper to taste. Arrange the bluefish on a doubled and buttered sheet of foil large enough to enclose it; pat the cavity dry, and sprinkle it with the additional lemon juice and salt and pepper to taste. Spoon the stuffing into the fish, re-form the fish, and skewer the openings closed. Enclose the fish in the foil; crimp the edges of the foil together to seal the packet well, and bake the packet on a jelly roll pan in a preheated moderate oven (350° F.) for 30 minutes. Slit open the packet and transfer the bluefish carefully with spatulas to a heated platter. Serves 2 or 3.

Katherine Creamer, Mobile Council

GRILLED MARINATED BLUEFISH

1 c. white wine vinegar	1 tsp. salt
1 c. dry white wine	1/4 tsp. cayenne
4 garlic cloves, minced	4 (1/2 lb.) bluefish fillets,
1 small onion, minced	skin side slashed in
1 tsp. ground cumin	several places

In a stainless steel or enameled saucepan combine the vinegar, the wine, the garlic, the onion, the cumin, the salt and the cayenne; bring the liquid to a boil, and simmer the mixture for 15 minutes. Let the marinade cool. Arrange the fillets in a shallow ceramic or glass dish just large enough to hold them in one layer. Pour the marinade over them, and let the fillets marinate, covered and chilled, turning them frequently, for at least 3 hours or overnight. Drain the fillets, reserving the marinade.

Grill the fillets skin side down over glowing coals about 4 inches from the heat, basting them with the reserved marinade, for 6 to 8 minutes, or until they just flake when tested with a fork. Transfer the fillets with a large spatula to heated plates. Serves 4.

Katherine Creamer, Mobile Council

GRILLED SWEET AND SOUR BLUEFISH

1 onion, minced	1 Tbsp. Worcestershire sauce
1 red pepper, minced	2 tsp. pepper, or to taste
1/2 stick (1/4 c.) unsalted butter	2 tsp. sweet paprika
	2 tsp. chili powder
1/4 c. white wine vinegar	1 tsp. minced garlic
1 Tbsp. dark brown sugar	1 tsp. salt
	6 (1/2 lb.) bluefish fillets

In a stainless steel or enameled saucepan combine 1 cup water, the onion, the red pepper, the butter, the vinegar, the sugar, the Worcestershire sauce, the pepper, the paprika, the chili powder, the salt and the garlic; bring the liquid to a boil and simmer the mixture for 15 minutes. Keep the sauce warm.

Grill the fillets skin side down over glowing coals about 4 inches from the heat, basting them with the sauce, for 6 to 8 minutes, or until they just flake when tested with a fork. Transfer the fillets with a large spatula to heated plates and serve the remaining sauce in a heated sauceboat. Serves 6.

Katherine Creamer, Mobile Council

YOGURT MARINATED BLUEFISH

1/2 c. fresh lemon juice	1 c. plain yogurt
2 Tbsp. peeled and	1/4 c. peanut oil
chopped ginger root	4 (1/2 lb.) bluefish fillets,
2 Tbsp. minced garlic	skin side slashed in
1 Tbsp. salt	several places
2 tsp. coriander seed	Sweet paprika
1 tsp. cumin seed	Lemon wedges for garnish

In a blender blend the lemon juice, the ginger root, the garlic, the salt, the coriander seed and the cumin seed until the mixture is well combined. Transfer the mixture to a bowl and combine it with the yogurt and the oil.. Arrange the fillets in a shallow ceramic or glass dish just large enough to hold them in 1 layer. Pour the marinade over them, and let the fillets marinate, covered and chilled, turning them occasionally, overnight. Drain the fillets, reserving the marinade.

Grill the fillets skin side down over glowing coals about 4 inches from the heat, basting them occasionally with the reserved marinade, for 6 to 8 minutes, or until they just flake when tested with a fork. Sprinkle the fillets with the paprika; transfer them with a large spatula to heated plates, and garnish them with the lemon wedges. Serves 4.

Katherine Creamer, Mobile Council

BAKED CRABS

1 lb. crabmeat	4 or 5 sprigs celery,
1 medium green pepper,	finely chopped
finely chopped	4 sprigs parsley

1 onion
4 hard boiled eggs

8 slices brown toast
1 c. mayonnaise

White Sauce:

2 Tbsp. butter
2 Tbsp. flour

1 c. milk

Combine all ingredients and mix well with white sauce. Fill crab shells and sprinkle with crumbs. Bake at 350° for 20 minutes or until brown.

Brenda Etheredge, Mobile Council

BAKED CRAB AND WILD RICE

1 box Uncle Ben's long
   grain and wild rice
2 sticks butter
1 clove garlic, minced

1 lb. crabmeat
1 medium onion, chopped
1/2 lb. fresh mushrooms,
   sliced

1. Cook rice according to package directions. 2. Saute onions, garlic and sliced mushrooms in 1 stick of butter (do not use margarine) and add to cooked rice. 3. Add 1 stick melted butter. 4. Add crabmeat and stir with fork until blended. 5. Place mixture in a 10 inch casserole dish and heat thoroughly at 350° for 20 minutes.

Barbara S. Mason, Mobile Council

CRAB BISQUE

1 1/2 Tbsp. butter
1 1/2 Tbsp. flour
3 c. half & half
1/2 c. whipping cream
2 Tbsp. diced celery

1 (6 1/2 oz.) frozen crab
1/2 tsp. salt
2 Tbsp. sherry (optional)
Paprika

Melt butter in heavy saucepan; blend in flour and cook until bubbly. Gradually stir in half & half; cook over low heat, stirring constantly until thick. Add whipping cream, celery, crab, salt and sherry. Heat thoroughly, stirring constantly. Garnish with paprika. Makes 4 servings.

Jeannie Riddles, Riverchase Council

* * * * *

Patience is the ability to idle your motor when you feel like stripping your gears.

FISH PARMESAN (MICROWAVE STYLE)

1 lb. mild white fish
1/4 tsp. seasoned salt
2 Tbsp. butter

1/2 c. grated Parmesan cheese
2 Tbsp. chopped green onions
1/2 c. mayonnaise
Paprika

Microwave fish, salt and butter covered with wax paper on high for 2 minutes. Mix Parmesan cheese, onions and mayonnaise together and spread over cooked fish and microwave on high for 2-3 minutes or until done. Sprinkle paprika over when done.

Dina Johnson, Birmingham South Council

FRIED FROGS' LEGS

6 frogs' legs
Salt and pepper
Lemon juice

1 egg
Cracker crumbs

Skin frogs' legs, wash in cold water, then dry legs. Season with salt and pepper and lemon juice. Beat the eggs; add seasonings and dip the legs in beaten egg. Roll legs in cracker crumbs and fry in deep fat (390° F.) for 2 to 3 minutes.

Ruby Dickerson, Birmingham Central Council

LOBSTER NEWBERG

6 Tbsp. butter
2 Tbsp. all-purpose flour
1 1/2 c. light cream
3 beaten egg yolks

1 c. lobster, cooked
3 Tbsp. dry white wine
2 tsp. lemon juice

Melt butter; blend in flour and cream. Cook until thickens. Add egg yolks in small amounts and stir until thick. Add lobster and heat. Add wine and lemon juice. Serve over toast or rice.

Anna Lee Hickman, Tri-Cities Council

HERB-BAKED OYSTERS

1/3 c. butter
1 large clove garlic,
  crushed in a press
1 1/2 c. toasted unseasoned
  bread crumbs
3 Tbsp. minced parsley

1 1/2 tsp. oregano
1/2 tsp. thyme
1/2 tsp. salt
5 Tbsp. dry sherry
32 oysters

Melt butter over low heat; do not let it brown. When melted, add crushed garlic and bread crumbs. Stir until crumbs have absorbed all butter. Mix in parsley, oregano and thyme. Season with salt and sherry. Oysters may be baked on the half shell or in a baking dish, or in individual ramekins. To bake them on the half shell, top each oyster with a tablespoonful of the bread crumb mixture. Place a layer of rock salt in a pie plate and top with oysters. You will need three 11 inch pie plates to bake 32 oysters. To bake them in caseroles or ramekins, butter the inside of the baking dish, and arrange oysters in a single layer, allowing them to overlap slightly. Add a little of their liquor. Top with a layer of bread crumbs; bake in 425° oven for about 15 minutes, or until crumbs form a brown crust. Serve hot with lemon wedges. Makes 8 servings.

Linda Unger, Riverchase Council

OYSTER JAMBALAYA

1 1/4 lb. lean spareribs
1 can tomatoes
1 pkg. spaghetti

1 large onion
1 pt. oysters
Salt, pepper and water

To water add spareribs, tomatoes, salt, pepper and bring to slow boil. Brown onion and add to mixture. Boil until spareribs are done. Add spaghetti and cook until done and add oysters and boil 2 minutes more. Serve with catsup, etc.

Jamima Edney, Birmingham South Council

SALMON CORN PUFFS

1 (7 3/4 oz.) can salmon	Milk
1 c. flour	1 (8 3/4 oz.) can whole
1 tsp. baking powder	kernel corn, well drained
1 tsp. salt	1 egg, separated
1/8 tsp. white pepper	Oil for deep fat frying

Drain and flake salmon, reserving liquid. Combine flour, baking powder, salt and pepper; add milk to reserved salmon liquid to equal 2/3 cup. Combine milk and egg yolk. Stir into dry ingredients. Beat egg white until stiff. Fold into batter along with salmon and corn. Drop by heaping tablespoonfuls into oil heated to 375°. Fry until golden brown on both sides, turning once. Drain on paper towels. Serve hot. Great served with scrambled eggs or with cole slaw.

Betty Chilton, Birmingham East Council

SALMON CROQUETTES

1 large can pink or	1/4 c. flour
red salmon	1 egg

Put salmon in large bowl; remove bones. Stir in already mixed up egg. Then pour in flour and roll into balls; put them in hot frying oil, in deep fryer. Remove when brown.

Bobbie Traywick, Birmingham South Council

SALMON CROQUETTE

1 can salmon (do not drain -	1 onion, diced fine
pull skin off)	1 c. crushed corn flakes,
1 egg	not frosted

Mix together real well; cook in deep fat fryer or shortening in skillet.

Dae B. Self, Birmingham West Council

SALMON LOAF

1 large (15 oz.) can salmon	Dash of salt
1/2 bell pepper, chopped	Dash of pepper
2 eggs, beaten	2 Tbsp. corn meal
1 small can Carnation milk	1 Tbsp. shortening or butter
1/2 medium onion, chopped	1 c. bread crumbs or
	cracker crumbs

1567-82

Mix all ingredients well together. Then pour into a greased baking or casserole dish. Bake in 350° oven for 35 to 45 minutes or until golden brown. This should slice well. Can be rewarmed so none will be wasted. It can also be frozen in freezer before you cook it.

Sharon T. Allen, Tuscaloosa Council

SALMON LOAF

1 (15 1/2 or 16 oz.) can salmon	1 or 2 tsp. prepared horseradish
8 oz. cream cheese	1/4 tsp. salt
1 Tbsp. lemon juice	1/2 c. chopped pecans
1 Tbsp. grated onion	Stuffed olives

Drain salmon; remove skin and bone. Combine all and roll in wax paper. Chill several hours or overnight. Garnish with sliced stuffed olives.

Jane Knox, Montgomery Council

SALMON LOG

1 (1 lb.) can salmon	1 tsp. horseradish
1 (8 oz.) pkg. cream cheese, softened	1/4 tsp. salt
	1/2 tsp. liquid smoke
1 Tbsp. lemon juice	1/2 c. chopped pecans
2 tsp. grated onion	3 Tbsp. snipped parsley

Drain and flake salmon. Remove skin and bones. Combine salmon with next 6 ingredients; mix thoroughly. Chill several hours. Combine nuts and parsley. Shape mixture into 8x2 inch log. Roll in nut and parsley mixture. Chill well.

Verlan Harden, Montgomery Council

SALMON MOUSSE

1 env. unflavored gelatin	1 tsp. dried dill weed
2 Tbsp. lemon juice	1 lb. canned salmon
1 small onion, sliced	(drain and remove bones)
1/2 c. boiling water	1 c. whipping cream
1/2 c. mayonnaise	Cucumber sauce is optional
1/4 tsp. paprika	

Put the first 4 ingredients into a blender or food processor for 30 seconds on high speed. Add next 4 ingredients; blend for 30 seconds. With blender or food processor turned on high speed, add the cream very slowly. Pour into a greased mold and chill. Serves 4-6.

If desired, the mousse may be served with a cucumber sauce: Blend together 1 cup sour cream, 1/2 cup grated cucumber, 1/2 teaspoon salt, 2 teaspoons finely chopped chives, 1 teaspoon dill weed and 1/4 teaspoon coarsely ground black pepper. Allow to chill in the refrigerator 2 hours before serving. Serve with salmon mousse.

Martha Cheney, Riverchase Council

LIZ HUFFMAN'S SEAFOOD GUMBO

2 c. chopped onions
 (or more)
2 c. chopped celery
1/2 large chopped bell
 pepper (or whole small)
1 or 2 cloves minced garlic
1 c. okra (fresh or frozen)
2 large cans tomatoes
Salt and pepper to taste
1/2 to 3/4 c. flour and oil
 (roux - gravy)

2 cans Swanson chicken broth
2 cans Swanson beef broth
 (add 1 can water per
 can broth)
2 or 3 bay leaves
1 Tbsp. gumbo file
1 lb. crabmeat (or more)
5 lb. shrimp (or more),
 peeled and deveined
3 white chicken breasts,
 cooked, chopped (optional)

Put all liquids in large pot. Saute onions, celery, bell pepper and minced garlic in little oil or bacon grease. Add to liquid; add okra and bay leaf. Cook 1 to 2 hours on medium heat. Mix roux, 1/2 to 3/4 cup flour in little oil. Stir constantly while browning, no lumps. When golden brown, add to mixture. Add shrimp and crabmeat (cooked chicken also if desired). Salt and pepper to taste; cook about 20 minutes more. Take off heat. Take out bay leaves. Add gumbo file.

Wanda Kanaday, Mobile Council

STUFFED FILET OF SOLE

1 pkg. frozen chopped
 spinach
2 c. cooked rice
4 hard cooked eggs,
 chopped
4 green onions, chopped
1/4 c. chopped parsley

2 Tbsp. mayonnaise
6 medium sized sole filets
1 can cream of celery soup
1/2 c. white wine
1/2 c. milk
1/2 tsp. dill weed

Thaw spinach and squeeze out most of the moisture. Combine spinach and rice and arrange in the bottom of a 9x13 inch baking dish. In small bowl combine eggs, onion,

1567-82

parsley and mayonnaise. Divide equally among the sole filets and roll each filet over to enclose. Set rolls, seam side down over rice mixture. Stir together soup, wine, milk and dill and pour over fish. Cover with foil and bake at 350° until fish flakes easily (about 35 minutes).

Debbie Tucker, Birmingham East Council

BAR-B-QUED SHRIMP

1 lb. shrimp	Tabasco
Olive oil	Lea & Perrins Worcestershire
Cracked black pepper	sauce
(or ground)	Butter
Salt	Water (according to
Lemon juice	desired thickness)

Place whole shrimp; keep shells on, in single layer in ovenproof dish. Drizzle olive oil on top of shrimp. Pepper shrimp until they are black - when you think you have enough, add more! Add lots of salt, lemon juice, Tabasco and Lea & Perrins. Remember, you are seasoning through the shells. Cut up butter on top of shrimp and broil until shrimp cooked, 15 to 20 minutes. Be sure and taste to see if they are done. Good served with French bread. Base the amount of shrimp on the number of guests.

Dianne Bledsoe, Birmingham Central Council

BARBECUE SHRIMP

3 sticks butter	McCormick's barbecue
Juice of 4 lemons	seasoning or spice
1 Tbsp. pepper	(approx. 2 tsp.)
2 toes diced garlic	1 large onion, diced
(as desired)	5 lb. shrimp

Mix all ingredients; add shrimp in shells. Simmer in frypan with lid approximately 35 minutes or until tender. Put in oven in same pan (preheated to 400°) for additional 5-10 minutes without lid. Use leftover sauce for dipping French bread.

Betty Havard, Mobile Council

BECKY'S FAMOUS SHRIMP CREOLE

1/4 c. flour
1/4 c. bacon grease
1 1/2 c. chopped onions
1 c. chopped green onions
1 c. chopped celery with
   leaves
1 c. chopped bell pepper
2 cloves minced garlic
1 tsp. Worcestershire sauce
1 Tbsp. lemon juice
4 lb. shrimp

6 oz. tomato paste
1 (16 oz.) can tomatoes
   with liquid
8 oz. tomato sauce
1 c. water
5 tsp. salt
1 tsp. pepper
1 tsp. Tabasco
2 or 3 bay leaves
1 tsp. sugar

In a large roaster make dark roux of flour and grease. Add onions, green onions, celery, bell pepper and garlic; saute till soft. Add tomatoes, water, salt, pepper, Tabasco, bay leaves, sugar, Worcestershire sauce and lemon juice. Simmer 1 hour covered. Add (cooked and peeled) shrimp and cook 15 more minutes. Serve over rice.

Becky Chastang, Mobile Council

BOB'S SHRIMP

1 pkg. frozen shrimp
Lemon pepper (to taste)

Garlic salt (to taste)
1/2 stick melted butter

Combine all ingredients in baking dish. Cover and let cook in oven until piping hot.

Betty W. Sanders, Birmingham Central Council

DAUPHIN ISLAND DELIGHT

2 lb. boiled shrimp
5 c. small elbow
   macaroni, cooked
6 hard cooked eggs,
   chopped

1 small onion, chopped fine
1 c. mayonnaise
Dash of garlic powder
2 ripe tomatoes
6 lettuce leaves

Combine all ingredients, using salt and pepper to taste. Place on lettuce leaves and garnish with tomato wedges.

Voncile Wolf, Mobile Council

1567-82   597

EXOTIC SHRIMP

2 cloves garlic
1/2 c. butter or margarine
2 lb. fresh shrimp,
  uncooked in shell

1/2 c. white wine or dry sherry
1 Tbsp. Worcestershire
Salt
Fresh ground pepper

Crush garlic in skillet and add butter. Saute raw unpeeled shrimp in this mixture until they are red. Add wine, salt, pepper, Worcestershire and simmer about 5 minutes. Drain and serve in the shells. May be used as entree with green salad and bread.
    Mattie Foster, Huntsville Council

FISHERMAN'S WHARF JAMBALAYA

Brown:
2 Tbsp. margarine

1 pkg. chicken Rice-A-Roni
2 3/4 c. water

Stir:
1/4 tsp. pepper
Chicken packet

1/4 tsp. Tabasco
1 Tbsp. minced onion

Stir:
1/4 c. celery
1/4 c. bell pepper

2 c. diced, cooked ham
1 can shrimp

Cover and simmer for 15 minutes.
    O. W. Norton, Birmingham South Council

GOLDEN FRIED SHRIMP

1/4 c. all-purpose flour
1/4 c. cornstarch
1/8 tsp. salt
1/4 c. beer
1 egg yolk

2 Tbsp. melted butter
  or margarine
1 lb. large shrimp, peeled
  and deveined
Vegetable oil

Combine flour, cornstarch and salt in a small bowl. Add beer, egg yolk and butter; beat until smooth. Dip shrimp into batter; deep fry in hot vegetable oil (375°) until golden brown. Yield: 4 servings.
    Regina Cash, Anniston Council

LEMON-GARLIC BROILED SHRIMP

2 lb. medium shrimp,
  peeled and deveined
2 cloves garlic, halved
1/4 c. butter or
  margarine, melted
3 Tbsp. lemon juice

1/2 tsp. salt
Coarsely ground black pepper
3 drops of hot sauce
1 Tbsp. Worcestershire sauce
3 Tbsp. chopped fresh
  parsley

Place shrimp in a single layer in a 15x10x1 inch jelly roll pan; set aside. Saute garlic in butter until garlic is brown; remove and discard garlic. Add next 5 ingredients, stirring well. Pour mixture over shrimp. Broil shrimp 4 inches from heat for 8 to 10 minutes, basting once. Sprinkle with parsley; serve immediately. Yield: 6 servings.

Regina Cash, Anniston Council

MOBILE SHRIMP GUMBO

2 lb. medium peeled shrimp
2 cans chicken and rice soup
1 c. chopped onion
1 c. chopped celery
1 c. chopped okra

4 Tbsp. flour
2 Tbsp. oil
1 1/2 qt. water
1 Tbsp. Worcestershire sauce
2 Tbsp. file

Brown flour in oil; add onion and celery, and saute lightly. Add soup, water, okra and shrimp, salt and pepper to taste. Add Worcestershire sauce and simmer for 1 hour. Turn off heat; add file after boiling stops. Serve over rice with garlic bread.

Voncile Wolf, Mobile Council

MURPHIE'S SHRIMP SCAMPI

1 or 2 lb. medium or
  small shrimp, peeled
2 Tbsp. butter or
  margarine
Juice of 1 lemon

Salt and pepper to taste
Dash of Tabasco sauce
Finely chopped onions or onion
  flakes (season to taste)
Toasted bread, cut into 1 inch
  squares

Melt butter; do not brown. Add shrimp, lemon juice, salt, pepper, Tabasco and onions. Cook on medium for 7 to 10 minutes, stirring occasionally. Place cooked scampi on platter or in bowl. Arrange squares of toast around scampi. Dip shrimp out of sauce to eat and use the sauce as a dip for toast

Anne Spragins, Birmingham East Council

OKRA SHRIMP CREOLE

3/4 c. chopped pepper
1 c. diced celery
1 large onion, chopped
1/3 c. melted butter or
  margarine
1/2 tsp. sugar
2 tsp. salt
1/4 tsp. hot sauce
  (Tabasco)
1/4 tsp. black pepper
1/4 tsp. cayenne
  pepper

2 tsp. Worcestershire
  sauce
2 Tbsp. plain flour
1 c. water
1 c. tomato sauce
1 (12 oz.) can cocktail
  vegetable juice
1 (16 oz.) can okra and
  tomatoes
1 (8 oz.) can tomatoes, pureed
1/2 c. sliced water chestnuts
2 lb. shrimp

Saute pepper, celery, onion and margarine; add other ingredients except shrimp and water chestnuts. Simmer 20 minutes. Add shrimp and chestnuts, and simmer 10-15 minutes longer. Serve over rice.

Auretha Karrh, Decatur Council

SHRIMP RATATOUILLE

Ratatouille - a classic French vegetable stew is a delightful and handsome dish to set before guests. Don't let the fancy name frighten you away. Shrimp Ratatouille easily fills the bill for taking a little shrimp a long way. Simply saute all the vegetables together until the shrimp meat is white and tender, taking care not to overcook.

1 lb. raw peeled and
  deveined shrimp
  (fresh or frozen)
1/4 c. olive oil or salad oil
2 small zucchini, unpared
  and thinly sliced
1 small eggplant, peeled
  and cut into 1 inch cubes
1 medium onion, thinly
  sliced

1 medium green pepper,
  seeded and cut into
  1 inch pieces
1 c. sliced fresh mushrooms
1 (1 lb.) can tomato wedges
1 1/2 tsp. garlic salt
1 tsp. crushed basil
1 tsp. dried parsley
1/4 tsp. pepper

Thaw shrimp if frozen. Cut shrimp in half lengthwise. In large frypan saute zucchini, eggplant, onion, green pepper and mushrooms in oil for 10 minutes or until crisp-tender and add shrimp, stirring frquently for 2 minutes. Add tomatoes, garlic salt, basil, parsley and pepper. Cover and simmer about 5 minutes or until shrimp are tender. Serve with rice or noodles.

Marie Rogers, Birmingham Central Council

SHRIMP AND RICE A LA SUISSE

1 c. long grain rice
3 Tbsp. butter, melted
1 medium onion, chopped
1 green pepper,
  chopped
1 clove garlic, minced

1 1/2 tsp. salt
2 1/2 c. hot water
2 lb. raw shrimp, peeled
  and deveined
1/2 lb. Swiss cheese,
  shredded
1/3 c. evaporated milk

Brown rice in the melted butter; add onion, pepper and garlic and cook until onion is golden. Add salt and hot water. Place shrimp on top and cover. Cook over low heat 30 to 40 minutes or until the rice is done. Check that water does not cook away. Combine the Swiss cheese and the evaporated milk in a saucepan and cook, stirring constantly, over low heat until the cheese melts and the mixture is hot. Serve the cheese mixture in a separate sauce dish. Serves 6-8.

Debra Askew, Birmingham East Council

"SHRIMP CREOLE"

1 Tbsp. minced parsley
1/2 c. chopped onions
1/2 c. chopped green
  pepper (bell)
1 c. diced celery
1/4 c. melted butter

1/2 c. all-purpose flour
2 tsp. chili powder
2 1/2 Tbsp. salt
4 c. canned tomatoes
1 1/2 or 2 lb. shrimp
  (remove hulls)

Saute minced parsley, chopped onions, chopped green pepper and diced celery in melted butter. Blend in all-purpose flour, chili powder and table salt. Add canned tomatoes, stirring constantly until mixture thickens. Then reduce heat and simmer, uncovered, for 30 minutes. Stir in shrimp and bring to a boil. Reduce heat and simmer for about 25 minutes more. It is now ready to serve over hot rice.

Mike Akridge, Retired, Mobile Council

SHRIMP CREOLE (MOBILE STYLE)

1 lb. shrimp, chopped
1 lb. diced okra
1 c. diced celery
1/2 c. diced onions
1/2 c. diced bell pepper
1 pt. tomato juice

1 Tbsp. prepared mustard
1 qt. hot water
4 bouillon cubes
1 Tbsp. Heinz 57
1 Tbsp. Worcestershire sauce
Salt and pepper to taste

1567-82

Saute okra in bacon grease, then add celery, onions, bell pepper and saute till tender. Add shrimp, tomato juice, hot water, mustard, bouillon cubes, Heinz 57 sauce, Worcestershire, salt and pepper. Simmer until shrimp are cooked, about 45 minutes 1 hour. Serve over rice, white or yellow.

Margaret L. Gibson, Retired,
Mobile Council

SHRIMP CREOLE AND RICE

3 onions
1 bell pepper
5 stalks celery
1 pkg. cut okra
1 can tomatoes
3 (8 oz.) cans tomato sauce

1 can cream of mushroom soup
1 c. rice, cooked
1 pkg. spaghetti sauce
1 Tbsp. liquid crab boil
2 lb. peeled, boiled shrimp

Dice onion, bell pepper and celery; saute in 3/4 stick of oleo. Add tomatoes, tomato sauce and cook for 30 minutes. Add okra, cooked rice, shrimp and simmer for 30 minutes. Serves 6.

Harold Busby, Mobile Council

SHRIMP DESTIN

1/4 c. chopped scallions
  or green onion
2 tsp. minced garlic
1 c. butter or margarine,
  melted
2 lb. large shrimp, peeled
  and deveined
1 tsp. lemon juice

1 Tbsp. white wine
1/2 tsp. salt
Coarsely ground black pepper
1 tsp. dried whole dill weed
1 tsp. chopped fresh parsley
3 French rolls, split
  lengthwise and toasted

Saute scallions and garlic in butter until scallions are tender. Add shrimp, lemon juice, white wine, salt and pepper; cook over medium heat about 5 minutes, stirring occasionally. Stir in dill weed and parsley. Spoon shrimp mixture over the toasted rolls and serve immediately. Yield: 6 servings.

Regina Cash, Anniston Council

SHRIMP GUMBO

5 lb. shrimp	1 can tomatoes
2 c. flour	1 pkg. cut okra
3 bay leaves	1 tsp. onion salt
1 tsp. gumbo file	1/2 c. shrimp boil

Put shrimp boil in bag and boil shrimp 30 minutes at a slow boil. Brown flour and roll boiled shrimp in flour; add rest of ingredients with 1 quart water and boil 30 minutes.

Jamima Edney, Birmingham South Council

SHRIMP IN SOUR CREAM

1 1/2 to 2 lb. shrimp	2 Tbsp. flour
1/2 c. onion, minced	1 tsp. salt
1/2 c. butter, melted	2-3 c. sour cream
1/2 to 1 lb. sliced	1/4 c. sherry
fresh mushrooms	

Saute shrimp with onions in butter for 5 minutes, or until shrimp are pink. Add mushrooms and cook 5 minutes longer. Blend in flour, salt and pepper; add sour cream gradually. Cook gently, stirring constantly, until mixture is thick. Remove from heat and stir in sherry. Serve over rice.

Debbie Tucker, Birmingham East Council

SHRIMP JEAN LAFITTE

3 lb. large shrimp	1 large clove garlic, minced
1/4 c. chopped parsley	1 Tbsp. chopped pimento
1/4 c. chopped green	1/2 tsp. Worcestershire sauce
onions	2 sticks butter
2 Tbsp. chopped green	1/4 tsp. salt
pepper	1/4 c. dry white wine
1/2 c. chopped mushrooms	1 Tbsp. lemon juice
2 slices bacon, chopped	1/2 c. bread crumbs,
	unseasoned

Peel shrimp and place in baking dish in single layer. Combine remaining ingredients in food processor. With steel blade in processor, turn on and off several times. Scrape down sides until mixture is smooth. Spread evenly over shrimp. Place in 350° oven just until shrimp turns pink (about 10 minutes). Serves 6.

Marie Rogers, Birmingham Central Council

SHRIMP MOLD

1 can cream of mushroom
  soup
1 (6 oz.) pkg. cream
  cheese
1 Tbsp. gelatin
2 Tbsp. cold water
2-3 green onions, chopped

1 c. mayonnaise
1/2 c. chopped celery
  (optional)
6-10 oz. shrimp, cooked
  and mashed
Dash of Tabasco
Dash of lemon juice

Melt cheese and soup over low heat and remove from heat. Dissolve gelatin in water and add mayonnaise to soup mix. Stir in remaining ingredients. Pour into mold and refrigerate. Best prepared day before and chilled overnight. Serve with crackers.

Ann Smith, Tuscaloosa Council

SHRIMP ROMANOFF

1 pkg. Betty Crocker
  noodles Romanoff
1/2 lb. or more shrimp,
  cut in two

1 c. shredded Swiss cheese
1 Tbsp. chopped chives
  or green onions

Heat oven to 350°. Prepare noodles Romanoff as directed on package (except increase milk to 1/2 cup). In 1 1/2 quart casserole layer half the noodles, the shrimp and the cup of Swiss cheese. Top with remaining noodles. Sprinkle with chives. Cover and bake for 20 or 25 minutes. Makes 4 servings. One 6 1/2 ounce can of tuna may be substituted for shrimp.

Dot Mastin, Mobile Council

SHRIMP SCAMPI

2 lb. peeled and
  deveined shrimp
1/3 c. olive oil
1/2 c. vermouth wine
2 cloves garlic, crushed

3/4 tsp. salt
1/2 tsp. pepper
3 Tbsp. chopped parsley
3 Tbsp. lemon juice

Saute shrimp in hot olive oil; add vermouth, garlic, salt and pepper. Simmer until liquid is almost absorbed. Sprinkle with parsley and lemon juice. Stir gently to mix.

Marie Rogers, Birmingham Central Council

SNAPPER JOHN

3-5 snapper
3/4 c. olive oil
3/4 c. salad oil
4 lemons (3 juiced,
   1 sliced)
2 onions, sliced

2 tomatoes, sliced
2 c. small mushrooms
2 bell peppers, sliced
Parsley
1 tsp. salt
Garlic powder (to taste)

Create marinade. In a medium bowl combine olive oil, salad oil, juice of 3 lemons, salt and garlic powder. Place fish in a large shallow baking dish and top with onion slices, pepper slices and lemon slices. Pour marinade over all; cover and refrigerate 6-8 hours. To cook: Use BBQ grill with cover and medium hot coals. Place aluminum foil on grill and turn edges up to hold marinade. Brush some marinade on foil. Place fish on foil and top with onion slices (from marinade), pepper slices (from marinade) and tomato slices. Pour remaining marinade over fish; cover and cook 15 minutes. Add mushrooms and cook 15-20 more minutes, covered (until fish flakes). Remove from heat; top with parsley. Everything is edible and delicious.

Rick Johnson, Birmingham South Council

BROILED TROUT

6-8 trout (6 inch length)
1/2 c. water
2 oz. lemon juice
1/2 tsp. salt
1/2 tsp. pepper

3 Tbsp. minced chives (or 3
   Tbsp. finely chopped
   onions)
2 Tbsp. chopped parsley
2/3 c. heavy cream
1 c. bread crumbs

Arrange a half dozen or more trout in a shallow, greased baking dish. Add the water, the lemon juice, salt, pepper, minced chives and parsley; bake the trout uncovered at 400° F. for 15 to 20 minutes or until the fish flakes easily.

Meanwhile, heat the heavy cream to boiling and pour over the trout when it is done. Over this sprinkle the bread crumbs. Then broil the whole dish until the bread crumbs are a golden brown. Serve.

Mattie Foster, Huntsville Council

CREAMY TUNA TWIST

1 c. Hellmann's real
  mayonnaise
2 Tbsp. cider vinegar
Dash of pepper
4 oz. twist macaroni, cooked
1 (7 oz.) can tuna,
  drained, flaked

1 c. cooked peas
1 c. sliced celery
1/2 c. chopped red onion
1/4 c. snipped dill
  or 1 Tbsp. dried
  dill weed

In large bowl stir together first 3 ingredients until smooth. Add remaining ingredients; toss to coat well. Cover and chill. Makes 4 servings.

      Brenda Stewart, Decatur Council

TUNA AND CHEESE CASSEROLE (FOR SIX)

3/4 lb. thinly sliced
  Swiss cheese
1 large can tuna, packed
  in spring water
2 c. cooked noodles

1/2 c. bread crumbs
2 Tbsp. melted butter
2 Tbsp. finely diced olives
1/4 c. grated Parmesan
  cheese

Flake and drain the tuna. Lay down alternate layers of tuna, noodles and Swiss cheese in a buttered casserole. Cover with olives, bread crumbs, butter and Parmesan cheese. Bake at 350° for 20-30 minutes.

      Alma Pitt, Decatur Council

TUNA FISH DELIGHT

1 can all white good tuna
1 can Campbell's cream
  of mushroom soup,
  undiluted
1 small jar chopped
  mushrooms

1 (4 oz.) jar chopped pimentos
1/2 stick margarine
4 slices whole wheat bread,
  toasted, not too brown

Mix all ingredients except toast in cooking container. Heat thoroughly, but do not overcook. Add crumbled toast. Pour into favorite baking dish to keep warm in oven until ready to serve.

      Pearl Reynolds, Montgomery Council

TUNA OVER RICE

1 can breast of chicken tuna
Lemon juice
1 can cream of mushroom
  soup

Almonds (if on hand)
Chopped pimiento
Chopped boiled egg

Drain tuna on Scot towel. Sprinkle with lemon juice.
Mix all ingredients together and cook in top of double boiler.
Serve over rice.

              Nancy Williams, Life Member, Anniston Council

TUNA PATE

1 (8 oz.) pkg. cream
  cheese
2 Tbsp. chili sauce
2 Tbsp. chopped parsley

1 tsp. instant minced onion
1/2 tsp. hot sauce
2 cans tuna fish, drained

    Blend all together; mold overnight.
             Bonnie Summers, Huntsville Council

TUNA POTATO PIE

4 Tbsp. margarine
4 Tbsp. flour
1/2 c. chopped onions
2 c. milk
1/2 tsp. salt

1/4 tsp. pepper
2 (6 oz.) cans tuna, drained
1 can green peas, drained
2 c. mashed potatoes
1 Tbsp. margarine (optional)

    Melt 4 tablespoons margarine; add onions, blend in
flour until smooth. Add milk slowly, stirring constantly,
until bubbling. Reduce heat and cook about 3 minutes until
thickened. Add tuna, green peas, salt and pepper. Cook
until onions soften. Put in baking dish and top with mashed
potatoes. Dot with margarine and bake in 450° oven until
browned, about 15 minutes. Serves 6.

          Ruby Dickerson, Birmingham Central Council

TUNA TWIST

2 (6 1/2 oz.) cans tuna,
  drained
1 can sliced ripe olives,
  drained
1/2 c. chopped celery
1/2 c. chopped green
  pepper

1/4 c. chopped onions
1 can cream of mushroom
  soup
2 c. Bisquick
1/2 c. cold water
1/4 c. milk
1 egg

1 1/2 c. Cheddar   1 Tbsp. water
    cheese, shredded

Heat oven to 425°. Lightly grease cookie sheet. Mix
tuna, olives, celery, green peppers, onions and 1/4 cup
soup. Mix baking mix and 1/2 cup cold water until soft
dough forms; beat vigorously 20 strokes. Gently smooth
dough into ball on floured cloth-covered board. Knead 5
times. Roll dough into rectangle (14x11 inches); place on
cookie sheet. Spoon tuna mixture lengthwise down center
of rectangle. Sprinkle with 1 cup of cheese. Make cuts
2 1/2 inches long, at 1 inch intervals on both sides of rectangle. Fold strips over filling. Mix egg and 1 tablespoon
water; brush over dough and bake until light brown, 15 to
20 minutes. Mix remaining soup, remaining 1/2 cup cheese
and the milk over medium heat, stirring occasionally, until
hot. Serve over slices of twist. Makes 6 servings.
Denetiza Wilkes, Riverchase Council

**   NOTES   **

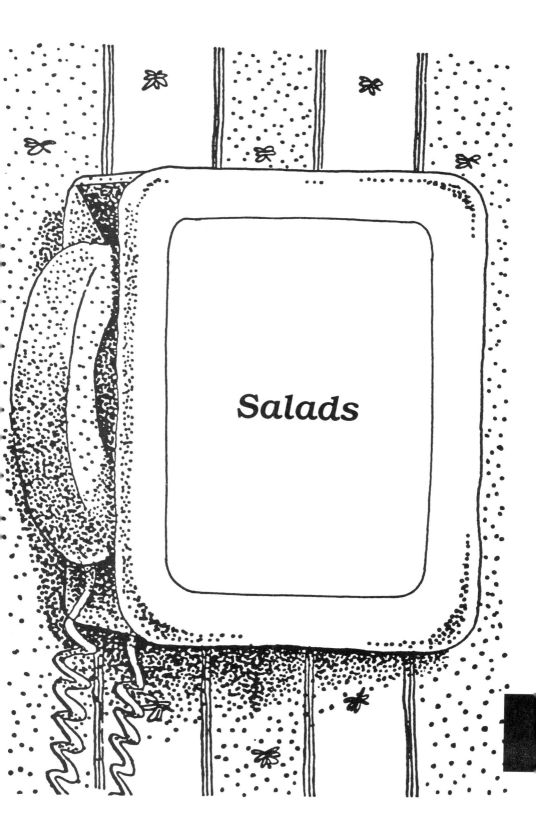

Salads

REFRIGERATION STORAGE

Food	Refrigerate	Freeze
Beef steaks	1-2 days	6-12 months
Beef roasts	1-2 days	6-12 months
Corned beef	7 days	2 weeks
Pork chops	1-2 days	3-4 months
Pork roasts	1-2 days	4-8 months
Fresh sausage	1-2 days	1-2 months
Smoked sausage	7 days	Not recommended
Cured ham	5-7 days	1-2 months
Canned ham	1 year	Not recommended
Ham slice	3 days	1-2 months
Baçon	7 days	2-4 months
Veal cutlets	1-2 days	6-9 months
Stew meat	1-2 days	3-4 months
Ground meat	1-2 days	3-4 months
Luncheon meats	3-5 days	Not recommended
Frankfurters	7 days	1 month
Whole chicken	1-2 days	12 months
Chicken pieces	1-2 days	9 months
Whole turkeys	1-2 days	6 months

Freezing Tips

- Date all items when you put them in the freezer.
- Frozen canned hams become watery and soft when thawed. Processed meats have a high salt content which speeds rancidity when thawed.
- Do not freeze stuffed chickens or turkeys. The stuffing may suffer bacterial contamination during the lenghty thawing process.
- Partially thawed food which still has ice crystals in the package can be safely refrozen. A safer test is to determine if the surface temperature is 40° F. or lower.

SALADS

HUSBAND'S HOMECOMING

I scrubbed the kitchen floor today,
And washed the woodwork, too,
I refereed the children's play
Until I'm black and blue.
I washed the clothes
And baked a cake
And cleaned the linen closet,
And now I'll just lie down
And take a little teeny rest --
That's just when you
Walk in and say
"So this is what you do all day!"

AMBROSIA

1 can fruit cocktail,
  strained
5 or 6 oranges, cut up
1 apple, cut up
1 small can pineapple,
  strained
1/2 c. sugar
1 c. miniature marshmallows
1 c. pecans
1 c. coconut
1/2 c. sour cream

Mix together and chill.

Barbara Davis, Decatur Council

AMBROSIA CONGEALED SALAD

1 (3 oz.) pkg. orange jello
1/2 c. sugar
1 c. boiling water
8 oz. sour cream
1 (8 oz.) can crushed
  pineapple
1 c. Angel Flake coconut
1 c. chopped pecans
3 oranges, cut up

Mix jello and sugar in boiling water. Pour into 13x9 inch container. Set in refrigerator for a little while (syrup consistency, not gelled). Add remaining ingredients, then refrigerate.

Jeanne Anderson, Montgomery Council
Lula Aycock, Life Member

1567-82

APPLE SALAD

1/2 c. sliced maraschino
  cherries
1 carton whipping cream
1/3 c. plain flour
4 large apples

1 large can crushed
  pineapple
1/2 stick margarine
3/4 c. sugar
1 c. chopped nuts

Mix flour and sugar well; stir into whipping cream (not whipped). Add pineapple. Cook in double boiler until thick. Remove and add margarine and let cool. Peel and dice apples. Add apples and nuts to cooked mixture and mix. Use cherries on top as dressing.

Laura St. Cyr

APRICOT SALAD

2 boxes apricot Jell-O
2 c. boiling water
2 c. cold water
1 c. miniature
  marshmallows
1/2 c. sugar
2 Tbsp. butter (oleo)
1 large pkg. cream cheese

1 c. (No. 2 can) crushed
  pineapple, drained
4 bananas, diced
1/2 c. pineapple juice
2 Tbsp. flour
1 egg
1/2 pt. whipping cream

Dissolve gelatin; add cold water and marshmallows. Let cool. Add pineapple and bananas; let jell. Take pineapple juice, sugar, flour, butter and eggs; cook until thick. Beat well and add cream cheese and chill by itself. Whip the whipping cream and fold into thickened sauce. Spread over Jell-O and let stand.

Mary Hargrove, Montgomery Council

APRICOT CONGEALED SALAD

1 large pkg. apricot jello
2 large bananas
2 c. boiling water
2 c. cold water

1 c. marshmallows
1 large can crushed
  pineapple (drain and
  save juice)

Mix and put in refrigerator to congeal.

Topping: Cook in double boiler until thick -

2 Tbsp. margarine
1/2 c. sugar

1/2 c. pineapple juice
2 Tbsp. flour

610

Mix:

1 pkg. Dream Whip, mixed as directed   1 large pkg. cream cheese

Beat about 2 minutes on high, until creamy and mix with cooled topping and spread over congealed jello. Top with crushed pecans.

Ilean Moore, Decatur Council

FROSTED BERRY MOLD

2 c. boiling water
6 oz. cherry jello
1 (10 oz.) pkg. frozen
  strawberries, undrained

1 (16 oz.) can cranberry
  sauce
1 c. pecans, chopped
3/4 c. mayonnaise
3/4 c. dairy sour cream

Combine water and jello, stirring until jello is dissolved. Add strawberries, cranberry sauce and pecans. Place in 7x11 inch glass dish and chill. Combine mayonnaise and sour cream and spread over top. Chill until set. Serves 12.

Edwina Hicks, Montgomery Council

BLACKBERRY SALAD

1 large can crushed
  pineapple
1 large pkg. blackberry
  jello
1 large can blackberries,
  drained

2 c. hot water
1 oz. cream cheese
1 1/2 c. sour cream
1/2 c. sugar
1 tsp. vanilla
1 tsp. lemon juice

Dissolve jello in water; add pineapple and the blackberries. Let set overnight. Next day add remaining ingredients together and place on top of other ingredients. Keep refrigerated.

Martha Thompson, Gadsden Council

BLUEBERRY SALAD

1 (16 oz.) can blueberries
  with juice
1 (8 1/2 oz.) can crushed
  pineapple with juice

1 (3 oz.) pkg. black
  cherry gelatin
1 (3 oz.) pkg. raspberry
  gelatin
2 c. boiling water

Topping:

1 (8 oz.) pkg. cream cheese   1/2 c. sugar

1567-82

1 pt. sour cream   1/2 c. pecans, chopped
1/2 tsp. vanilla

Drain blueberries and pineapple, reserving juice. Dissolve gelatin in boiling water. Add 1 cup pineapple and blueberry juice combined to gelatin. Stir in drained fruit and pour into 13x9x2 inch dish. Refrigerate to congeal.

Topping: To be spread over congealed salad. Soften cream cheese and fold in sugar, sour cream, vanilla and pecans. (To make salad prettier, save a few pecans to sprinkle on top of finished salad.)

R. R. Barfield, Decatur Council

BRIDE'S SALAD

1 pkg. lime gelatin   1 c. nuts
1 c. crushed pineapple   3/4 c. mayonnaise
1 c. Cheddar cheese

Prepare gelatin. When partly congealed, add pineapple, cheese, nuts and mayonnaise; mix well. Pour into molds. Chill to firm. Top with whipped cream.

Sandra Surrett, Anniston Council

BUTTERMILK SALAD

1 large can crushed   1 large Cool Whip
  pineapple   2 c. buttermilk
1 large pkg. strawberry   1 c. chopped pecans
  Jell-O

Bring pineapple with juice to a boil; add Jell-O; stir until Jell-O is melted. Add Cool Whip and buttermilk. Mix well; add nuts. Chill before serving.

Julia Rains, Huntsville Council
Leola H. Payne, Life Member

CALIFORNIA SALAD

1 (13 1/2 oz.) can   1 c. shredded coconut
  pineapple chunks   1/2 c. miniature
1 (11 oz.) can mandarin   marshmallows
  oranges   1 c. sour cream

Drain fruit. Combine with coconut and sour cream; chill for 12 hours. Serve with baked ham. Serves 8.

Pauline Woodham, Mobile Council

POLLY'S CARROT-APPLE SALAD

In a large serving dish, mix together:

2 c. shredded carrots
1 c. chopped apple
1/2 c. raisins

1/2 c. chopped pecans
Mayonnaise, just enough to
    lightly coat the ingredients

A real advantage of this recipe is that measurements don't have to be exact. And you can change the ratio of carrots to apples to suit your taste. Try pineapple instead of apples for a variation.

Rubie Nelson, Montgomery Council

BLACK CHERRY SALAD

1 pkg. black cherry jello
1 c. hot water

1 can black cherries
    and juice

Congeal the above ingredients.

Dressing:

1 (6 or 8 oz.) pkg.
    cream cheese
1 Tbsp. canned milk
10 large marshmallows, diced

1/3 c. mayonnaise
1/2 c. chopped nuts
1 small c. Cool Whip (add
    1 tsp. vanilla)

Fold Cool Whip into rest of ingredients and spread on salad. Serves approximately 8 to 10.

Jewel Edney, Riverchase Council

CHERRY CONGEALED SALAD

1 can cherry pie filling
1 can crushed pineapple

1 can Eagle Brand
    condensed milk
1 carton Cool Whip

Mix together well and set aside to congeal. Refrigerate.

Peggy Hunter, Anniston Council

BING CHERRY SALAD

1 large can pitted Bing
    cherries
1 c. sugar
2 pkg. plain gelatin
2 c. orange juice

2 Tbsp. lemon juice
1 small can sliced pineapple
2 (3 oz.) pkg. cream cheese
1 c. pecans

Drain 1 large can pitted Bing cherries. To this juice add 1 cup sugar. Let come to boil. Take 2 packages of

1567-82

gelatin and dissolve with 1/2 cup orange juice. Pour boiled cherry juice over gelatin mixture. Add 1 1/2 cups orange juice, 2 tablespoons lemon juice, part of the juice from pineapple, put in refrigerator and let start congealing. Then add whole Bing cherries and cubed pineapple. Take 2 packages cream cheese and 1 cup finely chopped pecans and make into small balls and put in center of each salad (use individual molds). Keep in refrigerator until ready to serve.

Note: Frozen orange juice can be used instead of pure oranges. Serves 8.

Irene Whiddon

COCA-COLA SALAD

1 (No. 2 1/2) can black
  pitted cherries
1 (No. 2) can crushed
  pineapple
1 pkg. black cherry jello
1 pkg. strawberry jello

1 c. chopped pecans
  (or other nuts)
3 (3 oz.) pkg. cream cheese
  (or one 8 oz. pkg.)
2 (6 oz.) bottles Coca-Cola

Cream cheese and nuts first and set aside. (Nuts and cheese are optional.) Drain juice from cherries and pineapple; bring to boil. Pour over jello and dissolve. Let cool and add Cokes. Cut up nuts and cream with cheese. Combine all ingredients and refrigerate.

Instead of cheese you might like to top with sour cream. If you cut this recipe or increase it, measure Coke and juices to be sure you have 1 cup of hot liquid (juices) and 1 cup of cold (Cokes) for each small package of jello. Check instructions on jello package. Serves 24.

Mattie Singleton, Retired, Life Member,
Birmingham Central Council

CONGEALED SALAD

1 pt. Cool Whip
1 pt. cottage cheese

1 (3 oz.) pkg. jello (any flavor)
1 can fruit cocktail (or any
    fruit)

Drain fruit; add Cool Whip, cottage cheese and jello. Mix all ingredients very well. Put in covered dish and let set in refrigerator several hours before serving.

Jim Chaffin, Tuscaloosa Council

CONGEALED SALAD

2 small pkg. strawberry jello
2 c. hot water
1 small pkg. cream cheese
1/2 c. chopped nuts
1/2 pt. vanilla ice cream
1 (10 oz.) pkg. frozen
  strawberries
1 (4 1/2 oz.) pkg. Cool Whip

Mix jello in hot water; add cream cheese and beat until smooth. Add strawberries (still frozen), cut up. Let congeal. Fold in Cool Whip and ice cream.

Melba McSwain, Decatur Council

CONGEALED SALAD

2 small boxes strawberry
  banana jello
2 diced bananas (thin)
1 can crushed pineapple,
  drained (small can)
1 pt. sour cream
1 pt. strawberries, sliced

Put 2 cups boiling water in jello; dissolve. Add strawberries. Let dissolve. Add pineapple and bananas. Take half and put in bowl and put in refrigerator. Let rest set out covered. When jells in refrigerator, add sour cream (in layer) and pour rest of jello on top. (Better if sets overnight.)

Dorothy Bishop, Huntsville Council

CRANBERRY SALAD

1 large box strawberry jello
2 env. plain gelatin
1 orange
1 c. sugar
1 box fresh cranberries
1 small flat can drained
  crushed pineapple
1 1/2 c. hot water
1/2 c. cold water
1/2 c. pineapple juice

Put through blender orange (ground), 1 cup sugar, 1 box cranberries (ground), crushed pineapple, 1/2 cup pineapple juice, 1/2 cup cold water. Dissolve jello in 1 cup of hot water; dissolve gelatin in 1/2 cup of hot water. Mix jello and gelatin. After it begins to jell, blend all ingredients together. Oil mold and fill.

Frank Marcus, Mobile Council

FROZEN CRANBERRY SALAD

1 (8 oz.) pkg. cream
  cheese (leave out
  overnight)
2 Tbsp. mayonnaise
1/4 c. sugar

1 large container Cool Whip
1 can whole cranberry sauce
1 large can drained
  pineapple
1/4 c. pecans, cut fine

Mix all above together well with spoon. Place in cup-cake papers into muffin rings and freeze. Keeps for months.

Bertha Ross, Decatur Council

CRANBERRY CHUTNEY

1 lb. fresh cranberries
1 c. sugar
1/2 c. brown sugar
1/2 c. golden raisins
2 tsp. cinnamon

1 1/2 tsp. ginger
1/2 tsp. cloves
1/4 tsp. allspice
1 c. water
1 c. chopped apple
1/2 c. chopped celery

Simmer cranberries, sugars, spices and water in a saucepan over medium heat, stirring frequently until the juice is released from the berries, about 15 minutes. Reduce heat and stir in apple and celery. Simmer uncovered until thick, about 15 minutes. Serve with meats, curries, or pour over cream cheese and serve on party crackers as an hors d'oeuvre. Keeps in refrigerator for up to 2 weeks.

Betty Chilton, Birmingham East Council

CLARA'S CRANBERRY SALAD

2 c. hot water
2 pkg. raspberry gelatin
1 large can whole
  cranberry sauce

1 small can crushed
  pineapple, drained
1/2 pt. sour cream
1/2 c. chopped nuts

Dissolve gelatin in hot water; add cranberry sauce and chill until syrupy. Fold in sour cream and nuts; chill until firm.

Patti Smith, Anniston Council

616

CREAM CHEESE SALAD

1 large pkg. lemon jello
1 large can crushed
  pineapple
1 large pkg. cream cheese

1 c. whipped cream
1/2 c. celery
1/2 c. pecans
1/2 c. cherries

Drain juice from pineapple and add enough water to make a cup. Bring to boil; add jello and let cool. Add cream cheese and let it thicken in refrigerator. After it sets and thickens, add all other ingredients, then fold in whipped cream. Let set in refrigerator about 4 hours. Ready to eat.

Doris Holder, Decatur Council

PHILADELPHIA CREAM CHEESE SALAD

4 slices pineapple
1 bottle cherries
12 marshmallows

2 small pkg. cream
  cheese
1 pt. whipping cream

Cut pineapple, cherries and marshmallows fine. Cream cheese and add fruit and marshmallows. Add whipped cream and cherry juice. Mix well and chill in refrigerator.

Sherry A. Liles, Future Pioneer,
Tri-Cities Council

FLUFFY PINK SALAD

1 can cherry pie filling
1 can Eagle Brand milk
1 medium size can crushed
  pineapple, drained

1 (8 oz.) carton sour cream
1 large carton Cool Whip
1 Tbsp. lemon juice
1 c. chopped nuts

Mix together and chill.

Margaret Hare, Anniston Council

FROSTED SALAD

2 regular size pkg.
  lemon jello
2 c. hot water
2 c. 7-Up

20 oz. crushed pineapple,
  drained (save juice)
1 c. small marshmallows
2 bananas, sliced

Topping:

1/2 c. sugar
1 c. pineapple juice (saved
  from crushed pineapple)
2 Tbsp. flour

1 egg, beaten
2 Tbsp. butter
2 c. whipping cream

1567-82

Dissolve gelatin in 2 cups boiling water; add 7-Up. Let partially set. Add marshmallows, pineapple and bananas; chill solid.

Topping: Cook until thick the sugar, flour, pineapple juice and egg. Add butter and cool. When cool, add whipped cream and spread over gelatin that has set. Sprinkle with grated cheese and cherries. Use 9x13 inch dish.

Joy James, Birmingham South Council

FRUIT SALAD

1 can peach pie mix
1 large can chunk
  pineapple

1 can mandarin oranges
1 can grapes

Mix together above ingredients and add in 2 packages frozen strawberries and 4 bananas.

Marilyn Smith, Mobile Council

FRUIT SALAD

1 large pkg. cream cheese
1/2 c. mayonnaise
1 large can fruit cocktail

1/2 c. chopped cherries
2 1/2 c. small marshmallows
1 large Cool Whip
Pecans

Cream together cream cheese and mayonnaise at room temperature. Add all other ingredients; mix well and chill.

Frances Coleman, Huntsville Council

FROZEN FRUIT SALAD

1 box lime jello
1 c. hot water
2 c. crushed pineapple,
  drained
12 large marshmallows

3 bananas, sliced
1/2 c. chopped nuts
2 stalks celery
2/3 c. cream cheese
1/3 c. chopped cherries

Mix all ingredients together while hot. Freeze in molds. Defrost about 10 minutes before serving.

Gem Beaty, Riverchase Council

618

FROZEN DESSERT OR SALAD

1 can cherry pie filling
1 (20 oz.) can crushed
  pineapple, undrained

1 large Cool Whip
1 can condensed milk
1 c. chopped pecans

Fold all ingredients together in large bowl; pour into Pyrex dish (large) and freeze. This takes 3 or 4 hours to freeze. It also makes a good salad on lettuce leaves. Very easy to make.

Mrs. J. A. Smelley

SUPER FRUIT

1 large can sliced peaches,
  cut into bite sizes
1 large can fruit cocktail
1 large can pineapple
  chunks
5 bananas, sliced

1 small jar maraschino
  cherries, drained and
  cut in halves
1 (3 1/2 oz.) pkg. lemon
  instant pudding and pie
  filling
1 (3 1/2 oz.) pkg. vanilla instant pudding and pie filling

Dump fruit and syrup (omit cherry syrup) into large mixing bowl; add dry pudding mixes and stir. Chill and serve. Refreshing as a breakfast fruit. Ideal with plain cake or cookies as dessert. Super sauce for topping ice cream.

Geneva Montgomery, Tuscaloosa Council

GOLDEN GLOW SALAD

1 pkg. lemon Jell-O
1 c. boiling water
1 c. canned pineapple juice
1 Tbsp. vinegar

1 c. pineapple, diced, drained
1 c. grated raw carrots
1/3 c. pecans, cut fine
1/2 tsp. salt

Dissolve Jell-O in boiling water; add pineapple juice. Chill. When slightly thickened, add vinegar, pineapple, carrots, pecans and salt. Turn into individual molds. Chill until firm. Serve on lettuce with mayonnaise dressing. Serves 8.

Rachel Key, Montgomery Council

GRAPE-BLUEBERRY SALAD

1 can blueberry pie filling
2 small boxes grape jello

2 c. boiling water
1 small can crushed pineapple

Mix together and congeal.

Topping:

8 oz. cream cheese
8 oz. sour cream
1/2 tsp. vanilla

1/2 c. sugar
1/2 c. pecans

Mix and spread over top.
Ann Terry

HEAVENLY HASH SALAD

1/2 pkg. miniature
  marshmallows
1 large can pineapple
  chunks, drained
1 small can crushed
  pineapple, drained

Chopped pecans (optional)
1 carton whipping cream
4-6 Tbsp. sugar
1/2 c. milk
2 Tbsp. flour
2 tsp. vinegar

Whip cream, adding sugar gradually; set aside. Cook over stove milk and flour, stirring constantly on low heat. Add vinegar; add marshmallows, pineapple and nuts to whipping cream mixture. Add milk mixture; chill for several hours.
David Stewart, Mobile Council

DRY JELLO SALAD

Pour 1 package orange jello (dry) over:

1 pt. cottage cheese
1 can mandarin oranges

1 pt. Cool Whip
1 c. crushed pineapple,
  drained

Stir well and chill.
Ivy Clemons, Decatur Council

JELLO SUPREME

1 large box black
  cherry jello
1 c. hot water
1 (16 oz.) can
  blueberries, sweetened

1 (8 oz.) can crushed
  pineapple
1 c. pecans
1 (16 oz.) Cool Whip

620

Mix jello with hot water. Drain blueberries and pineapple. Add this liquid to jello. Next add blueberries, pineapple and pecans; chill about 1/2 hour. Add Cool Whip and mix well. Store in refrigerator overnight.

Sue Hodges, Huntsville Council

LEMON-LIME SALAD MOLD

1 pkg. lemon flavored
   gelatin
1 pkg. lime flavored gelatin
24 full-sized marshmallows
3 c. boiling water

2 small pkg. cream cheese
2 Tbsp. vinegar
1 (No. 2) can crushed
   pineapple
1 c. finely chopped nuts

Pour boiling water over gelatins and marshmallows. Stir until marshmallows are melted and gelatin is dissolved. Chill. Blend cream cheese with vinegar until smooth. Add pineapple and juice; blend thoroughly, adding chopped pecans to this mixture. Chill. When gelatin mixture is ready to thicken, combine the 2 mixtures and mold as desired. One large ring mold makes a pretty platter when circled with crisp lettuce and centered with mayonnaise.

Mablean Patterson, Montgomery Council

HEAVENLY LIME SALAD

2 small or 1 large pkg.
   lime-flavored gelatin
2 c. boiling water
1 (8 oz.) pkg. cream
   cheese, softened
18 large marshmallows

1/4 c. boiling water
1 1/2 c. cold water
1/2 c. whipping cream,
   whipped
1 (No. 2) can crushed
   pineapple
1 c. chopped pecans or
   English walnuts

Dissolve the gelatin in 2 cups boiling water in large mixing bowl. Mash cream cheese in small bowl; add hot gelatin mixture and stir until dissolved. Melt marshmallows in 1/4 cup boiling water in top of double boiler and add gelatin mixture. Add 1 1/2 cups cold water; add whipped cream and beat mixture until it is smooth. Add pineapple and nuts. Pour into greased mold, large baking dish, or individual molds. Yield: 18 to 20 servings.

Mrs. Mildred Clayton,
Birmingham South Council

CREAMY LIME SALAD

1 pkg. lime jello
1 can Pet milk
1 (9 oz.) can crushed
   pineapple (do not drain)
1 tsp. lemon juice

1 container cream style
   cottage cheese
1/2 c. chopped pecans
1/2 c. finely chopped celery
1/2 c. mayonnaise

Dissolve jello in 3/4 cup boiling water; cool slightly and add Pet milk. Chill until mixture is thick, but not set. Add remaining ingredients. Pour into an 8 inch square pan or 5 cup mold. Chill until firm. Serve in lettuce. Serves 8.

Mary Ann Aycock, Riverchase Council

LIME ICE CREAM SALAD

3 oz. lime jello
1 c. water
1 pt. vanilla ice cream
1/2 c. mandarin oranges,
   drained and halved

1/2 c. banana, sliced
1/2 c. pecans, chopped
1 (8 oz.) can crushed
   pineapple, drained

Dissolve jello in boiling water; add ice cream and stir until melted. Add remaining ingredients; refrigerate in 9x9 inch pan. Serves 9.

Edwina Hicks, Montgomery Council

MANDARIN SALAD

1 pkg. orange gelatin
1 c. boiling water
1 (6 oz.) can orange
   juice concentrate
3/4 orange juice can
   cold water

2 Tbsp. lemon juice
1 (9 oz.) can crushed
   pineapple, undrained
1 (11 oz.) can mandarin
   oranges, drained

Dissolve gelatin in boiling water; add orange concentrate, water, lemon juice and pineapple. Let stand until mixture begins to thicken. Add oranges. Chill until firm.

Alexine S. Becker, Montgomery Council

ORANGE-APRICOT RING

2 (16 oz.) cans apricot
   halves
2 (3 oz.) pkg. orange
   gelatin
2 Tbsp. lemon juice

1 (6 oz.) can frozen orange
   juice concentrate
1 (7 oz.) bottle (about 1 c.)
   lemon-lime carbonated
   beverage, chilled

Drain apricots, reserving 1 1/2 cups syrup. Puree apricots in blender or mash well. Heat reserved syrup to boiling. Dissolve gelatin and dash of salt in syrup. Add puree, juice concentrate and lemon juice. Stir until concentrate is dissolved. Slowly pour carbonated beverage down side of pan and mix gently. Pour mixture into 6 1/2 cup ring mold. Chill. Makes 10 or 12 servings.

Dressing for Orange-Apricot Ring: Cook until thick, about 5 minutes -

1 egg, beaten	2 tsp. lemon peel
1/2 c. sugar	2 Tbsp. lemon juice
1 Tbsp. orange peel	

Cool mixture and fold in 1 to 1 1/2 cups Cool Whip.
Jane Knox, Montgomery Council

ORANGE DELIGHT SALAD

1 large box orange jello	1 (8 oz.) pkg. cream cheese
1 large can crushed	3/4 c. sugar
pineapple (save juice -	2 Tbsp. flour
1 c.)	2 egg yolks, well beaten
1 box Dream Whip	2 Tbsp. lemon juice

First layer: Mix jello as directed; chill in 9x13x2 inch glass dish until slightly thickened. Drain pineapple (save juice). Stir pineapple into jello; chill until firm. Second Layer: Mix Dream Whip as directed. Beat cream cheese; add Dream Whip and blend until smooth. Third layer: Mix 1 cup pineapple juice, 3/4 cup sugar and 2 tablespoons flour; add 2 egg yolks, well beaten, and 2 tablespoons lemon juice. Mix well and cook over low heat until thickened. Let cool. Add 1 cup chopped pecans.
Evelyn E. Hathcock, Mobile Council

POLLYE'S ORANGE SALAD

1 large box orange jello	1 (8 oz.) carton sour cream
1 can mandarin oranges	Chopped pecans (if desired)
1 small can fruit cocktail	

Drain juice from oranges and fruit cocktail; add 1 cup water. Bring to a boil and add jello; let cool. Combine fruit, sour cream and, if desired, chopped pecans. Beat together, then fold into the jello mixture.
Ann Smith, Tuscaloosa Council

1567-82

ORANGE CONGEALED SALAD

1 large Cool Whip
1 medium cottage cheese
1 box orange jello

2 small cans mandarin oranges
1 medium can crushed
   pineapple
1 c. chopped nuts

Drain well mandarin oranges, pineapple. Chip oranges in small pieces. Mix dry jello, Cool Whip and cottage cheese well. Add well drained oranges, pineapple and nuts; mix well. Pour in salad bowl and chill before serving. Serve with baked ham or dressing. Very good.
Edith Dixon, Birmingham South Council

ORANGE CONGEALED SALAD

1 large pkg. orange jello
1 c. hot water
1 small can crushed
   pineapple

8 oz. sour cream
1 small can coconut
1 small can mandarin
   oranges, drained
1 c. pecans

Dissolve jello with hot water; add sour cream, blending well, then add pineapple, coconut, mandarin oranges and pecans. Refrigerate until congealed.
Margie Judge, Mobile Council

ORANGE TAPIOCA FRUIT SALAD

1 pkg. orange or vanilla
   tapioca pudding
1 (No. 2) can pineapple
   chunks

1 can mandarin oranges
1 small bottle cherries,
   cut in halves
1 banana

Drain all juices and save 1 1/4 cups. Add juice to pudding and cook until it boils, stirring constantly. Boil 1 minute while stirring. Cool until steam stops. Pour over fruit. Just before serving, add sliced banana.
Louise Cox. Montgomery Council

PEACH SALAD

1 can peach pie filling
1 large can crushed
   pineapple, drained

1 medium size bowl Cool Whip
1 can Eagle Brand milk

Mix all ingredients together and freeze in a 9x13 inch pan. This can be used as a dessert.

Margaret Medders, Tuscaloosa Council

SPICED PEACHES

2 large cans peaches
1 1/3 c. sugar
1 c. cider vinegar

4 pieces stick cinnamon,
  3 inches long
2 tsp. whole cloves

Drain syrup from peaches into large saucepan. Put peaches in large bowl. Add sugar, vinegar, cinnamon and cloves to juice. Bring to boil; lower heat and simmer gently for 10 minutes. Pour hot syrup over peaches. Cover and cool thoroughly. Refrigerate several hours or overnight. Will keep 1 week in refrigerator. Leftover syrup may be used in jello salad.

Lillie Clary, Tuscaloosa Council

BLUE-PEAR SALAD

2 oz. Roquefort cheese
4 ripe pears
4 Tbsp. cream cheese

1/2 c. cream
1 oz. butter
Pinch of salt
Paprika

Peel and split the pears, removing the cores. Allow the Roquefort and butter to soften to room temperature and then mix them to a creamy texture. Fill the hollow pears. Mix enough cream into the cream cheese with a light whisk until it will pour, adding a pinch of salt Place the pears on a bed of lettuce and pour the mixture over them. Sprinkle lightly with the paprika. Chill 1/2 hour before serving.

Alma Pitt, Decatur Council

PINEAPPLE AND CHEESE SALAD

2 cans pineapple, cubed
1/2 lb. cheese, cubed
1/2 c. pecans, chopped
1 c. marshmallows

1 heaping Tbsp. flour
1 c. sugar
2 eggs, beaten
1/2 c. milk
Pinch of salt

Drain pineapple juice and mix with sugar, flour, eggs, milk and salt. Cook until thickened (best in double boiler)*. Pour over pineapple, cheese, marshmallows and nuts.

*I use thick boiler and stir constantly.

Marilyn Smith, Mobile Council

PINEAPPLE-CHERRY SALAD

1 c. boiling water
1 (3 oz.) pkg. cherry
  gelatin (or your favorite)
Cold water

1 (8 1/4 oz.) can sliced
  pineapple, drained
  (reserve juice)

Combine:
3 oz. cream cheese,
  softened
1 tsp. powdered sugar

1/3 c. chopped maraschino
  cherries
1/3 c. chopped pecans

Melt gelatin in 1 cup hot water. To pineapple juice, add cold water to make 1 cup. Put 1/2 cup gelatin in shallow container; chill until firm. Chill other gelatin until consistency of egg whites. Place pineapple slices over firm gelatin. Fill centers with cream cheese mixture (will be somewhat mounded). Add rest of gelatin to cover all. Makes 4 servings.
    Note: Filling can be stretched for 6 pineapple slices.
        Ruth Apperson, Decatur Council

PISTACHIO SALAD

1 can pineapple (crushed)
1 can fruit cocktail
1 pkg. pistachio pudding

1 c. miniature marshmallows
1 (9 oz.) container Cool Whip
1 carton cottage cheese

Drain pineapple and fruit cocktail well. Then add pistachio pudding and mix thoroughly. Add marshmallows, Cool Whip and cottage cheese. Mix well and place in refrigerator until ready to eat.
        Mattie Singleton, Life Member,
        Birmingham Central Council

PISTACHIO SALAD

1 small box (dry) instant
  pistacho pudding
1 (8 oz.) can crushed
  pineapple and juice

1 c. miniature marshmallows
2 c. Cool Whip or Dream
  Whip

Mix all ingredients; chill several hours before serving.
        Connie Mudd, Birmingham Central Council

SPICY PLUM SALAD RING

2 env. plain gelatin
1 (6 oz.) can frozen orange
  juice concentrate, thawed
2 c. boiling water
1/2 tsp. salt

1/2 tsp. pumpkin pie spice
1 (1 lb. 15 oz.) can
  purple plums
3 Tbsp. lemon juice
2 c. sour cream

Mix gelatin with orange juice. Dissolve in boiling water and add salt, spice, sugar and lemon juice. Fold in sour cream. Pit 6 plums and arrange in bottom of 1 1/2 quart ring mold. Dice remaining plums and fold into partially congealed gelatin mixture. Turn into mold over plums; chill until firm. Unmold onto salad greens. Serves 6.

        Martha Hastings (J. C. Hastings),
        Birmingham South Council

PRETZEL JELLO SALAD

2 1/2 c. pretzels,
  coarsely crushed
1/3 c. margarine
3 Tbsp. sugar
8 oz. cream cheese
2 c. boiling water

1 c. sugar
1 large container Cool Whip
2 (3 oz.) pkg. strawberry
  jello
2 (10 oz.) pkg. frozen
  strawberries

Mix well pretzels, margarine and 3 tablespoons sugar and bake in a 9x13 inch pan at 350° for 10 minutes; cool completely. Cream the cheese and blend in 1 cup sugar. Add the Cool Whip, mixing well. Spread over the cooled pretzels. Dissolve the jello in the boiling water; add frozen strawberries, breaking up with a fork as you stir. Chill until slightly thickened. Pour over Cool Whip layer; chill until set.

        Barbara Seegmiller, Decatur Council

RASPBERRY SALAD

1 large pkg. raspberry jello
1 (8 oz.) pkg. cream
  cheese

1 can whole cranberry sauce
1 large can crushed pineapple
1 pkg. Dream Whip

Use 1/2 water called for in package jello. Dissolve. Add softened cream cheese, cranberry sauce and pineapple. Chill 30 minutes. Spoon in whipped Dream Whip. Stir, then congeal.

        Etta Lowe Wilson (Ernest Wilson),
        Birmingham Council

RASPBERRY OR STRAWBERRY BUTTERMILK SALAD

1 large (6 oz.) pkg. jello   1 (20 oz.) can crushed
  (raspberry or strawberry)   pineapple

Heat over medium heat until jello is dissolved. Cool.
Add:

2 c. buttermilk   1 c. chopped nuts

Stir well and refrigerate until it begins to thicken.
Then add 9 ounces Cool Whip.
Peggy Hunter, Anniston Council

RIBBON CHRISTMAS SALAD

1 box strawberry jello   1 pkg. marshmallows
1 box lime jello   1 small pkg. cream cheese
1 box lemon jello   1 small carton whipping cream

Congeal strawberry jello in large square bowl for
several hours. Prepare lemon jello, but omit cold water.
Allow to partially congeal. Melt 20 marshmallows in double
boiler. Add cream cheese and melt. Whip cream. Add
lemon jello and marshmallow mixture to whipping cream and
mix well. Pour this mixture slowly into strawberry mold.
Put into freezing unit to congeal rapidly. Mix lime jello
according to directions and pour over congealed lemon mixture. Congeal.
Wanda Lynch, Montgomery Council

RIBBON SALAD

2 (3 oz.) pkg. lime-   1 (8 oz.) pkg. cream cheese
  flavored gelatin   1 (1 lb. 4 oz.) can crushed
2 c. boiling water   pineapple, drained
1 1/2 c. cold water   1 c. pineapple juice
2 (3 oz.) pkg. lemon-   1/2 pt. cream, whipped
  flavored gelatin   2 (3 oz.) pkg. raspberry-
1 c. boiling water   flavored gelatin
2 c. miniature   2 c. boiling water
  marshmallows   1 1/2 c. cold water

Dissolve lime gelatin in 2 cups boiling water; add 1 1/2
cups cold water. Pour into pan; chill until set. Dissolve
lemon gelatin in 1 cup boiling water in top of double boiler.
Add marshmallows and cream cheese, which has been cut
into small pieces; beat until well blended. Remove from heat
and stir in pineapple and pineapple juice. Cool, then fold in

whipped cream; spoon over top of chilled lime gelatin. Chill until lemon layer is firm. Dissolve raspberry gelatin in 2 cups boiling water. Add 1 1/2 cups cold water. Cool, then pour over chilled lemon layer. Chill until firm.

Sallie Curry, Tuscaloosa Council

STRAWBERRY SALAD

1 large or 2 small pkg. strawberry jello

1 c. boiling water

Mix these two ingredients together. Add:

2 (10 oz.) pkg. strawberries and juice
3 large bananas, mashed

1 large can crushed pineapple, drained
1 1/2 c. chopped nuts
2 cartons sour cream

Mix everything together except sour cream. Pour 1/2 of mixture in large Pyrex and let chill. Then spread sour cream and pour remainder on top. Chill.

Eulene Miller, Mobile Council

STRAWBERRY NUT SALAD

2 pkg. strawberry gelatin
1 c. boiling water
2 (10 oz.) pkg. frozen sliced strawberries

1 (1 lb.) can crushed pineapple, drained
3 medium bananas, mashed
1 c. chopped nuts
1 pt. sour cream

Dissolve gelatin in boiling water; fold in strawberries. Mix pineapple, bananas and nuts; add to gelatin. Pour half of mixture into a 12x8 inch dish; chill until firm. Spread over sour cream. Gently pour remaining mixture over sour cream. Refrigerate until congealed and ready to serve.

Edgar McFarlen, Huntsville Council

STRAWBERRY SALAD

1 (10 oz.) pkg. frozen strawberries
1 (6 oz.) pkg. strawberry jello
1 small can crushed pineapple (do not drain)

1 c. boiling water
1 (8 oz.) pkg. cream cheese
2 c. confectioners sugar
1 (8 oz.) pkg. Cool Whip
1 c. pecan pieces
2 bananas, mashed

First step: Mix strawberry jello with boiling water;

reserve 1/4 cup jello. Pour into 13x9 inch Pyrex dish. Add frozen strawberries, pineapple and bananas. Stir until strawberries melt. Put in refrigerator to jell. Second step: Soften cream cheese at room temperature. Cream with confectioners sugar, 1 cup at a time. Add 1/4 reserved jello and stir. Add Cool Whip and stir well. Fold in nuts. Pour over jello mixture. Garnish with pecans or fresh strawberries.

Katrina White, Huntsville Council

STRAWBERRY DELIGHT SALAD

1 large carton Cool Whip
1 large can crushed
  pineapple
1 can Eagle Brand milk

1 (8 oz.) carton sour cream
1 can strawberry or cherry
  pie mix
1 c. chopped pecans

Just pour everything in the bowl and stir until thoroughly mixed, then refrigerate for about an hour or freeze, depending on which firmness you prefer.

Sandy Scott, Birmingham Central Council

SUNSHINE SALAD

2 c. grated carrots
1/2 c. raisins
1 can mandarin oranges,
  drained

1 c. coconut
1 c. pineapple chunks
1 (8 oz.) carton sour cream

Mix all ingredients and refrigerate.

Kathy Ward, Montgomery Council

TOOTIE FRUITIE SALAD

1 can sliced peaches
1 can pineapple chunks
1 pt. strawberries
2 large bananas

1 can fruit cocktail
1 pkg. instant lemon pudding
1 pkg. instant vanilla pudding

In large mixing bowl place peaches, pineapple and fruit cocktail if used with all juices, slice strawberries and add to other fruit and then add pudding mixes. Do not prepare puddings; just dump in bowl with fruit and mix. Add bananas, sliced or chunk sizes. Mix all and refrigerate.

Thelma Holmes, Birmingham East Council

WATERGATE SALAD

1 large can crushed
  pineapple

1 box pistachio instant
  pudding mix

Stir together, then add:

1 large Cool Whip
Nuts, if desired

1/2 sack or 1 c.
  miniature marshmallows

Refrigerate and enjoy.

Nancy Carter, Montgomery Council

WALDORF SALAD RING

1 pkg. lemon jello
1 c. hot water
2 tsp. vinegar
1 c. diced apples

3/4 c. diced celery
1 c. cold water
1/4 tsp. salt
1/4 c. broken walnuts

Dissolve jello in hot water; add cold water, vinegar and the salt. Chill until slightly thickened. Fold in apples, nuts and celery. Turn into 1 quart mold; chill until firm. Unmold on crisp salad greens. Garnish with wedges of apple and mayonnaise.

David Stewart, Mobile Council

MURPHIE'S ARTICHOKE RICE SALAD

1 pkg. chicken flavored
  rice mix
4 green onions, sliced thin
1/2 green pepper, seeded
  and chopped

12 pimiento-stuffed
  olives, sliced
2 (6 oz.) jars marinated
  artichoke hearts
3/4 tsp. curry powder
1/3 c. mayonnaise

Cook rice as directed on package, omitting butter. Cool rice in a large bowl. Add the green onions, green pepper and olives. Drain artichokes, reserving the liquid. Add curry powder and mayonnaise to the liquid. Add the hearts to the rice; toss with the dressing and chill.

Anne Spragins, Birmingham East Council

3 BEAN SALAD

1 (1 lb.) can cut green beans	2/3 c. vinegar
1 (1 lb.) can yellow wax beans	Juice of 1 garlic clove
	3/4 c. sugar
	1 tsp. salt
1 (1 lb.) can red kidney beans	1/2 tsp. pepper
1 small onion	1/3 c. salad oil or
1 small bell pepper	Italian dressing

Drain all beans and put in large mixing bowl with cover. Mix all other ingredients and pour over beans. Refrigerate overnight. Drain and serve cold. Makes 10-12 servings.

Sherry A. Liles, Future Pioneer, Tri-Cities Council, Dae Self, Birmingham West Council

HOT BEAN SALAD

1 1/3 c. fine cracker crumbs, buttered, divided	3 green onions, chopped
	1 c. (4 oz.) shredded Cheddar cheese
1 (16 oz.) can kidney beans, drained	1/2 c. mayonnaise
	1/3 c. chopped sweet pickle

Combine all ingredients except 1/3 cup cracker crumbs. Toss lightly and spoon into a greased 1 quart casserole dish. Sprinkle with crumbs and bake at 450° for 10 minutes. Makes 4 servings.

Flo Thompson, Montgomery Council

24 HOUR BEAN SALAD

1 large can French cut green beans	1 large onion, chopped
	2 pimentos, chopped
1 large can medium size green peas	1 stalk celery, chopped

Mix the above ingredients, then salt and let stand until you pour your seasoning over it.

1/2 c. Wesson oil	1/2 tsp. paprika
1 c. vinegar	2 Tbsp. water
1 1/2 c. sugar	

Mix well and pour over vegetables. Mix and let stand 24 hours.

Marie Walden, Birmingham Central Council

GREEN BEAN SALAD

1 (No. 2) can green beans (French style)
1 (No. 2) can English peas (small)
1 small jar diced pimiento

4 pieces of celery, chopped
1 bell pepper, chopped
2 or 3 small onions (rings)

Marinade:

1/2 c. salad oil (corn oil)
1 c. vinegar

1 c. sugar
Salt and pepper to taste

Mix vegetables and pour marinade over. Let stand 24 hours. Drain and serve. This can be made days before and keeps well. Marinade can be used again.

Mrs. O. O. Prickett, Selma Council

BEET SALAD

2 c. chopped beets
1 c. small peas
1 c. chopped celery

1 boiled egg, chopped
3 Tbsp. pickle relish
Mayonnaise as desired

Mrs. Wallace Mintz, Anniston Council

BREAD SALAD

1 large loaf white bread
Butter
1 small onion, finely diced
6 hard boiled eggs, grated

2 cans small shrimp (or tuna)
1 can King crab (or salmon)
2 c. celery, finely diced
1 1/2 scant c. mayonnaise

Remove crusts from bread; butter lightly. Cut each slice into 25 small squares. Put in large bowl. Add onion and egg. Toss lightly; cover and refrigerate overnight. Next morning, add shrimp and crab, drained. Add celery. Toss and add mayonnaise. Cover and let stand 8 hours in refrigerator. Garnish with cherry tomatoes and cucumber slices. Serves 10 very generously or 12 average.

Evelyn Hannigan, Birmingham Central Council

BROCCOLI SALAD

2 stalks broccoli (use just the flowerets and cut them up into bite size pieces

1 bell pepper, finely chopped
1 peeled tomato, cut into small wedges

1567-82

Sauce:

1 c. sour cream
1 c. mayonnaise
1 c. Parmesan cheese

1 finely chopped onion
1 good dash of garlic salt

Combine all ingredients of sauce; toss with vegetables. Chill and serve.

Edwina Hicks, Montgomery Council

BROCCOLI AND CAULIFLOWER SALAD

1 pkg. fresh broccoli
1 head cauliflower
1 jar mushrooms

Radishes
1 pkg. Good Seasons Italian
   salad dressing

Make up Good Seasons according to package directions. Chop up cauliflower into bite size pieces. Take broccoli and cut off tops into bite size pieces. Slice mushrooms and radishes. Pour Good Seasons Italian dressing over salad. Marinate several hours before serving.

Sheilah Miller, Birmingham East Council

CALICO SALAD

1 1/2 c. finely shredded
   red cabbage
1 1/2 c. finely shredded
   green cabbage
1/4 c. minced onions

1/3 c. mayonnaise or
   salad dressing
1 Tbsp. vinegar
2 tsp. sugar
1/2 tsp. salt
1/2 tsp. celery seeds

Combine chilled vegetables. Combine remaining ingredients, stirring to dissolve sugar. Pour dressing over vegetables.

Bertha Ross, Decatur Council

YUMMY CARROT SALAD

4 or 5 large carrots,
   scraped and washed
1 (8 oz.) can crushed
   pineapple, drained

4 Tbsp. sugar
1/2 c. raisins
1/3 c. mayonnaise
   (more or less)

Use fine grater and grate carrots. (If your blender has a grate button, you may use it to grate them.) Put into medium sized salad bowl, adding the sugar, pineapple, raisins and mayonnaise; toss well. Refrigerate until ready to serve. (Bananas and apples may be added also.)

634   Billie Bays, Decatur Council

CREAMY CAULIFLOWER SALAD

1 medium head cauliflower, broken into flowerets
1 bunch green onions, sliced
1 c. sliced radishes
1 c. mayonnaise
1 (0.7 oz.) pkg. garlic cheese dressing
2 tsp. caraway seed

Combine first 3 ingredients in a medium bowl. Combine remaining ingredients and pour over vegetables. Toss lightly to coat. Cover; refrigerate overnight. Yield: 6 to 8 servings.

Regina Cash, Anniston Council

CAULIFLOWER SALAD

1 head lettuce
1 head cauliflower
1 pkg. frozen green peas, uncooked
1/2 to 1 lb. bacon, fried crisp and crushed
1 pkg. Good Seasons Italian dressing (dry - not mixed)
1 1/2 c. mayonnaise
1 large onion, chopped
8 oz. to 1 lb. grated Cheddar cheese

Tear lettuce in bite size pieces; slice and dice cauliflowerets. Sprinkle with frozen uncooked peas. Toss. Sprinkle with crushed bacon and onion, then sprinkle with Good Seasons. Spread the mayonnaise, then top with grated cheese. Mix all together when ready to serve. Serves about 16 people. Keep in layers in refrigerator and dip out if serving a smaller group.

Wanda Ange, Birmingham East Council

CAULIFLOWER-LETTUCE-BACON SALAD

1 head lettuce
1 head raw cauliflower
1 big red onion, sliced
1 lb. bacon, cooked, crumbled

Dressing:

3 Tbsp. sugar
4 Tbsp. Parmesan cheese
1 c. mayonnaise
Salt and pepper to taste

Layer vegetables and bacon in bowl. Spread mixed dressing over all and set in refrigerator overnight.

Denetiza Wilkes, Riverchase Council

CHEESE SALAD

Dressing:

1/4 tsp. dry English
  mustard
6 Tbsp. olive oil

A dash of black pepper
2 Tbsp. vinegar
1/4 tsp. salt

Salad:

2 c. diced Swiss cheese
4 diced hard boiled eggs
3 slices cooked,
  crumbled bacon
3 Tbsp. minced shallots

5 small red potatoes
1/2 c. diced celery
1/2 c. mayonnaise
3 Tbsp. minced parsley
A dash of salt and a
  dash of black pepper

Scrub potatoes, dice and boil in salted water until tender. Drain and sprinkle with dressing lightly. When cool, mix lightly with cheese, onion, most of the parsley, celery, most of the eggs, and the bacon. Mix mayonnaise with the dressing and pour onto the salad. Sprinkle the remaining egg and parsley on top; chill for 7 minutes approximately and serve.

Joyce Reavis, Decatur Council

BAKED CHICKEN SALAD

4 c. chopped chicken
  (I use chicken breast)
2 c. chopped celery
2/3 c. cream of chicken
  soup
1/2 c. bell pepper,
  chopped
2/3 c. mayonnaise

2 Tbsp. lemon juice
1/2 c. chopped onion
2 pimentos, chopped
Salt to taste
4 boiled eggs, sliced
1 small can water chestnuts
Mushrooms (optional)

Mix the above ingredients. Top with:

1 c. cheese, grated
1/2 c. almonds

1 c. crushed potato chips

Bake at 350° for 25-30 minutes.

Anatalie Watson, Decatur Council

EXOTIC CHICKEN SALAD

2 qt. coarsely chopped
  chicken
1 lb. fresh or canned
  seedless grapes
2 (12 oz.) cans water
  chestnuts, drained
  and chopped
2 c. finely chopped celery

3 c. toasted almonds
  or pecans
3 c. mayonnaise
2 Tbsp. lemon juice
1 Tbsp. curry powder
2 Tbsp. soy sauce
1 (20 oz.) can chunk
  pineapple

Blend mayonnaise, lemon juice, curry powder and soy sauce. Mix with all other ingredients.

Brenda Etheredge, Mobile Council

FAYE'S CHICKEN SALAD

3-5 cooked, deboned
  chicken breasts, salted
1 bunch of green grapes

1-2 pkg. sliced almonds,
  toasted
Mayonnaise

Cut the chicken into bite size pieces. Slice the grapes in halves and add to the chopped chicken. Place almonds and enough mayonnaise to make the mixture creamy, in with the chicken and grapes; stir just until well mixed.

Sandra Herndon, Birmingham South Council

CHICKEN SALAD MOLD

1 whole chicken, boiled
  (2 to 3 lb.)
2 eggs, boiled and
  chopped fine
1/8 c. onions, chopped fine

1/2 c. celery, chopped fine
4 oz. sweet salad cube
  pickles
4 oz. mayonnaise

Remove bones and cut chicken into very small pieces. Add eggs, pickles, onions, celery and mayonnaise. Mix well, adding salt and pepper to taste. Place in a covered dish overnight in refrigerator to form a mold. When ready to serve, pour salad on a serving tray with party rye bread or crackers.

Mary H. Bolton, Anniston Council

HOT CHICKEN SALAD

1 whole fryer, cooked,
  cut in bite size
2 c. diced celery
3 hard cooked eggs,
  chopped
1/2 c. mayonnaise

1 Tbsp. lemon juice
2 Tbsp. minced onions
1 can water chestnuts,
  sliced thin
1 can cream of chicken soup
Potato chips

Mix all ingredients except potato chips. Put in 2 quart ovenware bowl. Crush potato chips over casserole; bake at 350° for 20 to 25 minutes, or until bubbly hot. Serves 12.

Ludie Lunsford, Birmingham West Council

MANDARIN CHICKEN SALAD

2 c. cooked rice
1/2 c. sliced or
  chopped celery
1/4 c. finely chopped
  onions
1/4 c. chopped green
  pepper
1/4 c. sliced water chestnuts

Mandarin orange sections
2 (5 oz.) cans boned
  chicken with broth
1/2 c. French dressing
  (or Catalina)
1 Tbsp. soy sauce
1/4 tsp. ginger

In bowl combine rice, celery, onion, pepper and water chestnuts; lightly toss in chicken. Combine French dressing, soy sauce and ginger. Toss with rice mixture until well coated. Garnish with mandarin orange sections. Makes 4 servings. Chill for 1 hour (better if made several hours or the day before).

Carolyn Benson, Montgomery Council

CHICKEN-FRUIT SALAD

1 (16 oz.) can pineapple
  chunks
1 apple, cored and sliced
1 c. seedless grapes

3 c. diced, cooked chicken
Whipped Cream Fruit Dressing
Lettuce
1/3 c. toasted slivered almonds

Drain pineapple chunks, reserving juice. Dip apple slices in pineapple juice. Combine fruit and chicken; chill. Add Whipped Cream Fruit Dressing, and toss lightly. Serve on lettuce and top with almonds. Yield: 6 to 8 servings.

Whipped Cream Fruit Dressing:

3 Tbsp. butter or margarine 3 Tbsp. all-purpose flour

638

1/4 c. sugar
1 tsp. salt
1/3 c. lemon juice

1/3 c. pineapple juice
2 egg yolks, slightly beaten
1/2 c. whipping cream, whipped

Faith Kirby, Anniston Council

NUTTY CHICKEN SALAD BY MRS. ELLIOTT

2 c. cooked chicken, chopped
1 small onion, chopped

2 stalks celery, chopped
2 tsp. lemon juice
3/4 c. toasted almond slivers

Mix all ingredients; chill before serving. Makes 4 servings.

Catherine Pittman, Mobile Council

CHINESE 24 HOUR SALAD

1 can Chinese vegetables, drained
1 can water chestnuts, sliced
1 can French cut green beans, drained
1 can LeSueur peas, drained

1 small (4 oz.) can mushroom stems and pieces
1 c. diced onions
1 1/2 c. diced celery
3/4 c. white vinegar
1 1/2 c. sugar
Salt and pepper to taste

Marinate 24 hours.

Cynthia Lee, Tuscaloosa Council

CORN SALAD

1 can shoe peg white corn, drained
2 or 3 green onions with tops, sliced
1 small green pepper, chopped

1 c. chopped celery
1/2 c. mayonnaise
1 Tbsp. prepared horseradish mustard
1 Tbsp. lemon juice
Salt and pepper

Mix together the first 4 ingredients. Combine mayonnaise, mustard and lemon juice; add to corn mixture. Season with salt and pepper to taste. Refrigerate overnight.

Pauline Corbin, Montgomery Council

CORN SALAD

1 (12 or 15 oz.) can whole
  kernel Niblet corn
1 (12 oz.) can whole kernel
  white shoe peg corn

1/2 c. chopped bell pepper
1/2 c. chopped celery
1 small onion, chopped fine
1 (2 oz.) jar chopped pimientos

Mix above with mayonnaise; cover and refrigerate overnight, if possible.

Bonnie Mayfield, Anniston Council

SHOE PEG CORN SALAD

1 (12 oz.) can shoe peg
  corn, drained
1/4 c. diced green
  pepper
2 Tbsp. pimento,
  chopped
1/2 c. finely chopped celery

1/2 c. sliced red onion,
  separated into rings
1 c. diced cucumber
1/3 c. oil
3 Tbsp. sugar
1 1/2 tsp. salt
3 Tbsp. red wine vinegar

Combine all vegetables. Mix oil, sugar, vinegar and salt. Stir until sugar dissolves. Pour over vegetables and toss gently; chill 8-10 hours. Drain before serving. Makes 4-6 servings.

Mrs. Howard D. Colegrove, Anniston Council

CRABMEAT SALAD

1 c. flaked crabmeat
  (16 1/2 oz. can or
  one 6 oz. frozen pkg.)
2 large canned artichoke
  hearts, chopped
2 hard boiled eggs,
  chopped

1/4 c. thinly sliced
  small mushrooms
1/4 c. sliced black olives
1/4 c. mayonnaise
2 Tbsp. wine or vinegar
Snipped chives
Salt
Pepper

Combine all ingredients, adding chives. Salt and pepper to taste. Refrigerate until serving time. Serve on lettuce leaf with lemon wedges. Serves two.

W. C. Hershberger, Birmingham South Council

CRISP WINTRY SALAD

1 (6 oz.) or 2 (3 oz.)
  pkg. lemon gelatin
2 c. boiling water
1 1/2 c. cold water
3 Tbsp. vinegar
2 tsp. salt

1/8 tsp. black pepper
1/4 c. grated onion
1/2 c. cut green bell pepper
1/2 c. diced pimento
2 1/2 c. very small pieces
  cauliflower

Dissolve lemon gelatin in boiling water; add cold water. Chill until slightly thickened. Mix remaining ingredients; let stand. After gelatin thickens slightly, fold in mixture. Serves 8 to 10. Garnish with lettuce. Top off with mayonnaise.

J. D. Kaylor, Mobile Council

CUCUMBER SALAD

3 medium cucumbers,
  sliced thin
1/2 c. sour cream

1/4 c. vinegar
1 medium onion, sliced

Cover cucumbers in salt; let stand 1 hour. Squeeze all juice from cucumbers. Add onion, sour cream and vinegar; add pepper if desired.

Helen Gorff, Birmingham West Council

GREEN PEA RELISH SALAD

1 can French cut
  green beans
1 can English peas
1 large onion, chopped

1 cucumber, chopped
3 stalks celery, chopped
1 bell pepper, chopped

Put in dish in layers. Mix together:

1 c. vinegar
1/2 c. Wesson oil

1 c. sugar
1 tsp. salt

Pour over vegetables and let marinate in refrigerator 48 hours. Makes 2 quarts (approximately). Great with fowl.

Wanda Ange, Birmingham East Council

OVERNIGHT TOSSED GREEN SALAD

This is a large salad - great for patio or large groups. You can add or subtract to suit your crowd.

1 pkg. fresh spinach, uncooked
1 head iceberg lettuce
1 bunch leaf lettuce
1 box cherry tomatoes

1 pkg. uncooked frozen green peas (always thaw out)
1 small bunch green fresh onions
1/2 lb. chopped, drained bacon

Dressing:

2 c. mayonnaise
1 carton sour cream

1/2 tsp. sugar
Salt and pepper to taste

After the salad is all mixed, put it into the serving bowl you wish to use. Take the dressing and "frost" the top of the salad. This will seal all ingredients. Cover with Saran Wrap. Refrigerate all night or until you are ready to serve the next day. Just before serving, mix frosting (dressing) all through the salad. Serve immediately.

Faith Kirby, Anniston Council

HEARTY HAM SALAD

3 c. diced, cooked ham
1 1/2 c. (6 oz.) shredded Cheddar cheese
2 c. diced apples, unpeeled

1 c. diced celery
1/2 tsp. lemon-pepper seasoning
3/4 to 1 c. mayonnaise
Lettuce leaves (optional)

Combine all ingredients except lettuce; mix well. Chill 2 to 3 hours before serving. Serve on lettuce leaves, if desired. Yield: 6 to 8 servings.

Regina Cash, Anniston Council

HAM AND CHEESE POTATO SALAD

1/4 c. chopped green pepper
1/4 c. chopped onion
1 Tbsp. margarine
1/2 lb. Velveeta cheese

1/4 c. milk
3 c. chopped, cooked potatoes
3/4 c. chopped ham
1/4 tsp. salt

Saute green pepper and onions in margarine; add Velveeta cheese and milk; stir until melted. Add remaining ingredients. Mix well. Serve hot. Makes 4 to 6 servings.

Jackie O'Dell

642

HAWAIIAN SALAD

1/2 head medium sized
  cabbage
1/2 c. sweet shredded
  coconut

1/2 c. golden raisins
2 Tbsp. sesame seed
1/4 to 1/2 c. mayonnaise
1 Tbsp. tarragon vinegar

Shred cabbage finely. Soak raisins until swollen. Mix raisins, coconut and heated sesame seeds. Mix mayonnaise and vinegar in separate cup and blend in.

Peggy Blevins, Anniston Council

KRAUT SALAD

1 large (No. 2 1/2)
  can kraut
1 can bean sprouts
1 3/4 c. sugar
1 c. white vinegar

1 c. chopped onions
1 c. chopped celery
1 c. chopped bell pepper
1 c. stuffed olives,
  chopped

Bring sugar and vinegar to boil and cool. Mix onion, celery, bell pepper and olives in Pyrex bowl with kraut and bean sprouts. Pour vinegar and sugar mixture over it and mix well. Keep refrigerated.

Polly Greenhill, Birmingham Central Council

LAYERED SALAD

1/2 head of lettuce
  (or 1 small head)
1/2 medium onion, sliced
1 can sliced water chestnuts
4 stalks celery, sliced

1 small can peas
1 pt. Hellmann's mayonnaise
2 Tbsp. sugar
4-5 Tbsp. Mozzarella cheese
2 Tbsp. Parmesan cheese

Arrange all ingredients in the order given in a bowl or oblong dish. Cover this and chill overnight. Before serving, top with any of following: Hard boiled eggs, crisp bacon pieces, tomato wedges, parsley.

Jane Drake, Birmingham West Council

LAYERED LETTUCE SALAD

1 head lettuce
1 c. diced celery
4 boiled eggs
1 can English peas

1/2 c. bell pepper
1 small onion
Bacon bits

Topping:

2 c. mayonnaise   Shredded Cheddar cheese
2 Tbsp. sugar

Place in large bowl in layers as listed above; repeat until all ingredients are used. Spread mayonnaise over top and sprinkle with sugar and cheese. Set overnight.

Connie Mudd, Birmingham Central Council

CRUNCHY MACARONI SALAD

1 (8 oz.) pkg. elbow   1 (2 oz.) jar diced
  macaroni   pimiento, drained
1 c. chopped celery   1/2 c. mayonnaise
1/4 c. chopped fresh   1/2 c. commercial sour cream
  parsley   1 Tbsp. red wine vinegar
1/3 c. chopped green   1/4 to 1/2 tsp. seasoned salt
  pepper   1/4 tsp. pepper
6 green onions, sliced   Lettuce leaves
2/3 c. diced Cheddar cheese

Cook macaroni according to package directions; drain and let cool. Add next 6 ingredients and stir gently. Combine next 5 ingredients; mix well. Pour the dressing over macaroni mixture and stir gently. Cover and chill at least 2 hours; serve salad on lettuce leaves. Yield: 12 servings.

Regina Cash, Anniston Council

MACARONI SALAD

1 (8 oz.) pkg. macaroni   1/4 c. sweet pickles,
1 tomato   finely chopped
1/2 green pepper, finely   6 stuffed olives, finely
  chopped   chopped
1/2 small onion, finely   1 c. mayonnaise
  chopped   2 Tbsp. vinegar
1/2 c. celery, finely   2 Tbsp. sugar
  chopped   Paprika
                             3 boiled eggs

Cook macaroni in 4 cups boiling water with 2 teaspoons salt and 1 teaspoon black pepper and 1 tablespoon oil for 8 minutes. Drain; rinse with cold water. Drain. Add 2 tablespoons margarine. Chop tomatoes, pepper, onion and celery and eggs and olives. Mix with macaroni. Mix 1 cup mayonnaise, sugar and vinegar; mix with all ingredients. Sprinkle top with paprika.

Brenda Etheredge, Mobile Council

644

MACARONI SALAD

2 c. macaroni, cooked
1 c. celery, chopped
2 green onions, chopped
1 carrot, grated

1 small can English peas,
  drained
Grated sharp Cheddar cheese
Bell pepper, chopped

    Mix together:
1 c. mayonnaise
1 tsp. dry mustard
  (no substitute)
1 tsp. sugar

3 Tbsp. vinegar or
  lemon juice
Dash of Bac-Os
Salt and pepper to taste

Add mayonnaise mixture to above ingredients; mix well. Leave in refrigerator overnight, or make early in the morning before using at night. This is important!
              Betty C. Gray, Montgomery Council

MACARONI SALAD

1 (1 lb.) bag macaroni,
  cooked
1/2 large bell pepper,
  diced
Green onion (use bottom
  and part of top)
1 small jar olives
1/2 c. grated sharp
  cheese

3 to 4 heaping Tbsp.
  mayonnaise
1/2 c. sweet relish or sweet
  pickle, diced
2 sticks celery, cut up
2 boiled eggs (optional)
Pimento
Lemon pepper
Salt

Mix all ingredients thoroughly and season to taste with salt and lemon pepper. Garnish with pimento. Chill. Yield: 1 large salad bowl. Add additional portions of ingredients and make as much as you like.
              Rosa Stoudemire, Montgomery Council

MACARONI AND SHRIMP SALAD

8 oz. macaroni, cooked
6 hard boiled eggs,
  chopped
1/2 c. celery, chopped fine

1 c. carrots, grated
1 1/2 lb. cold cooked shrimp
Enough mayonnaise to make
  quite moist

Mix all ingredients together and refrigerate several hours.
              Evelyn E. Hathcock, Mobile Council

SHRIMP AND MACARONI SALAD

4 lb. shrimp
2 (12 or 14 oz.) pkg. shell
  macaroni (not quick
  cooking)
3 small cucumbers
3 hearts of celery
8 eggs (4 to garnish)
1 large bottle broken
  olives, drained

1 large bottle whole
  olives (garnish)
4 small bell peppers
5 small red onions
1 qt. mayonnaise
Season salt
Pepper

Boil shrimp in lemon slices and salt. Clean, devein and cut up. Boil macaroni and drain. Cut up celery, onions, peppers, eggs, cucumbers. Mix thoroughly all ingredients, including olive pieces and shrimp, one at a time. Season to taste; add mayonnaise and mix well. Line bowls with lettuce and garnish top of salad with remaining eggs and olives. Makes 3 serving bowls. Make 1 day ahead for best flavor.

Barbara J. Wood, Birmingham Central Council

MARINATED SALAD

1 small can English peas,
  drained
1 (17 oz.) can white shoe
  peg corn, drained
1 (15 oz.) can French style
  green beans, drained
1 (2 oz.) jar diced
  pimento, drained

1/2 c. diced celery
1 c. diced onion
1/2 c. diced green peppers
1/2 c. sugar
1/2 tsp. pepper
1 tsp. salt
1/2 c. vegetable oil
3/4 c. vinegar

Mix in bowl. Take sugar, pepper, salt, oil and vinegar and combine; bring to a boil and pour over vegetables. Cover and chill 24 hours. Marinate for 8 hours.

Marian Browne, Birmingham Central Council
Joella Bradford, Huntsville Council

MARINATED VEGETABLE SALAD

Flowerets from 2 bunches
  of broccoli
Flowerets from 1 bunch
  of cauliflower
1 c. sliced celery

1 c. black olives, sliced
2 small cans mushrooms
1 can water chestnuts, sliced
1 c. Italian Wish-Bone
  dressing
1 Tbsp. Italian seasoning

Marinate 24 hours. Add fresh cherry tomatoes or sliced just before serving.

Edgar McFarlen, Huntsville Council

MARINATED VEGETABLE SALAD

1 head cauliflower
1 bunch broccoli
Several small squash, sliced
Several radishes, sliced
1 cucumber, sliced (optional)

1 onion, sliced (optional)
1 bottle Marie's Italian cheese dressing (or any cheesy Italian dressing)
1 carton sour cream

Break up cauliflower and broccoli into flowerets. Mix with other vegetables, and marinate overnight in Italian dressing and sour cream mixture.

Jane Knox, Montgomery Council

NACHO CHIP SALAD

Lettuce
Cabbage
Celery

Raw onions
Fresh tomatoes

Chop and add together the above ingredients. Grate carrots and mix with enough mayonnaise to hold together, salt, pepper, sugar. Add crushed nacho chips and grated cheese. Saute ground beef if desired. Mix all together and sprinkle with Catalina Dressing.

Dorothy Franklin, Montgomery Council

ORIENTAL SALAD

1 (16 oz.) can small green English peas, drained
1 (16 oz.) can bean sprouts, drained
1 (12 oz.) can whole kernel white corn, drained
2 (6 oz.) cans water chestnuts, drained and sliced
1 (6 oz.) can sliced mushrooms, drained

1 (4 oz.) jar pimento, drained and chopped
1 large green pepper, thinly sliced, or may be diced
1 large onion, thinly sliced, or may be diced
1 c. celery, diced
1 c. salad oil
1 c. water
1 c. sugar
1/2 c. vinegar
Seasoned salt and pepper

Combine vegetables in a large bowl, stirring gently.
Combine remaining ingredients and pour over vegetables.
Cover and chill 24 hours; drain before serving.

Pat Prestridge, Birmingham Central Council

ENGLISH PEA SALAD

2 large cans Green Giant
   early peas (small
   tender peas)
4 hard boiled eggs
Kraft salad dressing

Pimentos, diced
2 stalks celery
1 small bell pepper
1 Tbsp. sugar
Salt and pepper

Drain peas off; place in medium sized bowl. Chop up
eggs, celery and bell pepper. Add to peas. Mix with about
4 large tablespoons of salad dressing (more or less for individual taste and texture). Add 1 tablespoon of pimento.
Add sugar and salt and pepper to each individual taste.
Chill in refrigerator covered for about 1 hour. Great with
barbeque ribs, chicken, etc.

L. M. Davis, Birmingham West Council

ENGLISH PEA SALAD

1 can English peas
1 boiled egg, shredded
1/2 c. chopped pecans

1 tsp. seasoning salt
1 tsp. pickle relish
2 Tbsp. mayonnaise

Mix all ingredients. Chill before serving.

Judy Ivey, Birmingham South Council

AUNT SADIE'S POTATO SALAD

10 potatoes, boiled in
   jackets, peeled and
   sliced
1 head cabbage (green
   or red or mixed),
   shredded
1 qt. mayonnaise or
   salad dressing

About 3 green bell peppers,
   sliced in rings
4 or 6 hard boiled eggs, sliced
Celery seed, salt and pepper
   (on each layer of potatoes)
Paprika on top of salad
   to decorate
About 3 onions, sliced in
   rings

Begin with layer of shredded cabbage in bowl; add
layer of sliced potatoes. Salt and pepper, and sprinkle with
celery seed. Add onion rings and pepper rings (your own

preference for onion and pepper will determine how much to use). Add sliced eggs and then spread mayonnaise over all. Be sure to use enough to cover mixture. Now start all over and add as many layers as needed, ending with mayonnaise and eggs. The above amount will serve about 10. This mixture must be refrigerated at least 24 hours before serving.

Kitty Logan, Anniston Council

COVERED BRIDGE POTATO SALAD

10 potatoes	2 heaping Tbsp. flour
2 small onions	1 c. sugar
1 carrot	4 eggs, beaten
3 stalks celery	1 heaping Tbsp. dry mustard
18 olives	1 c. vinegar
8 hard cooked eggs	1 tsp. salt
4 slices bacon	1/4 tsp. pepper

Cook potatoes in jackets until tender; peel and dice. Mince onions; dice carrot and celery. Chop olives; slice hard cooked eggs. Combine potatoes, onions, carrot, celery, olives and sliced eggs; set aside. Dice bacon; fry until crisp. Stir in flour to make a smooth paste. Combine sugar, eggs, mustard, 1 cup water, vinegar, salt and pepper; mix well. Add to flour paste. Place over low heat; cook until thick, stirring constantly. Pour over potato mixture; mix lightly. Let stand in cold place for several hours. Yield: 12 servings.

Joyce Reavis, Decatur Council

MILDRED COOK'S POTATO SALAD

3 large potatoes, boiled whole, then peeled and diced	3 or 4 medium sweet pickles, diced
1 onion, diced	3 large eggs, boiled hard and diced
2 stalks celery, diced	1 small jar pimento peppers, chopped and drained
1 bell pepper, diced	
Miracle Whip salad dressing	Salt and pepper
	Paprika

Combine all above with enough salad dressing to make it cling together; salt and pepper to taste. Sprinkle paprika on top. Chill.

Diane Cook, Montgomery Council

1567-82

MAMA'S SOUTHERN POTATO SALAD

5 medium potatoes
8 c. water
1 Tbsp. salt (optional)
6 hard cooked eggs,
    cooled and peeled

1 Tbsp. sugar
1/8 tsp. prepared mustard
1/2 c. chopped onion
1 c. mayonnaise
Paprika

Place potatoes, water and salt in large Dutch oven; bring to a boil. Cook until cool; peel. Chop potatoes and 5 eggs; reserve remaining egg for garnish. Combine sugar, salt, pepper, mustard, pickles, onion and mayonnaise* in large bowl. Quarter or slice reserved egg; garnish top of salad. Sprinkle with paprika. Makes 7 servings.
    *Note: If picnicking, remember to carry mayonnaise in separate container, and add it to salad just before serving.
        L. Whitt, Birmingham West Council

POTATO SALAD

4 medium potatoes,
    cooked in skin
1/2 c. French dressing
1 tsp. salt
Pepper to taste
3/4 c. chopped celery

1/4 c. chopped onion
2 or 3 hard cooked eggs, diced
1/4 c. sweet pickle relish
1/2 c. mayonnaise
1/2 tsp. curry
Paprika

Peel cooked potatoes while still warm; cut into cubes. Pour French dressing over potatoes. Add salt and pepper and let stand for several hours. Add celery, onion, eggs, relish. Mix thoroughly; add mayonnaise and mix until well blended. Sprinkle with paprika.
        Flo Thompson, Montgomery Council

GERMAN HOT POTATO SALAD

8 medium potatoes
1 pt. sour cream
1/3 c. chopped green
    onions (tops too)

1 c. grated cheese
1 stick margarine
1 can cream of chicken soup
Corn flakes

Boil 8 medium potatoes in jacket; cool and peel. Grate potatoes into large bowl; add 1 pint sour cream, 1/3 cup chopped green onions, using tops, too, and 1 cup grated Cheddar cheese. Mix all together. Melt in saucepan 1 stick margarine, 1 can cream of chicken soup and add to potato mixture. Mix well; put in casserole dish. Top with crushed

corn flakes mixed in small amount of margarine. Bake at 350°
until bubbly. Best when made a day ahead of time. Add
topping just before baking.

Denetiza Wilkes, Riverchase Council

HOT GERMAN POTATO SALAD

10 medium potatoes, boiled in their skins	2 eggs, beaten
8 slices bacon, diced	3/4 c. vinegar
2 medium onions, diced	Salt to taste
3/4 c. sugar	Pepper to taste
2 tsp. dry mustard	4 eggs (hard cooked), sliced
	2 Tbsp. parsley, chopped

Peel and cube the potatoes and put in an ovenware bowl
or casserole. Fry bacon. Remove bacon from pan and reserve. Fry onions in bacon fat until tender, but not
browned. Mix sugar and mustard together. Add to onions
in frying pan; add the beaten eggs and vinegar to onion mixture, and cook until thickened, stirring constantly. Pour
over the potatoes; add salt and pepper to taste. Add reserved bacon and egg slices. Mix lightly. Heat in a 250° F.
oven for 30 minutes or until ready to serve. Sprinkle parsley on top. Serves 8 to 10.

Joyce Reavis, Decatur Council

PRETZEL SALAD

2 c. pretzels	8 oz. cream cheese
1 c. pecans	2 Tbsp. lemon juice
1 stick oleo	1 large pkg. strawberry jello
1 c. + 3 Tbsp. sugar	2 c. strawberries
8 oz. Cool Whip	2 c. boiling water

Mix pretzels, pecans, oleo and 3 tablespoons sugar,
then press in an oblong Pyrex dish. Bake 10 minutes at 350°
and let cool. Mix cream cheese with 1 cup sugar and lemon
juice. Fold in Cool Whip; spread over bottom layer. Mix
jello with water. Cool, then add strawberries. Pour over
center. Place in refrigerator until jello sets up.

Sharon Crabtree, Tuscaloosa Council

SHRIMP MOLD

1 (10 oz.) can tomato soup
3 (3 oz.) pkg. cream
  cheese (room temperature)
1 env. unflavored gelatin
1/4 c. cold water
2 1/2 c. boiled shrimp,
  seasoned and shredded

1 c. mayonnaise
1 small onion, grated
1/2 c. finely chopped celery
1 Tbsp. lemon juice
Dash of garlic powder
Salt, pepper and red
  pepper to taste

Heat soup and dissolve cream cheese in it. Soak gelatin in cold water and add to soup mixture. Let cool to room temperature (about 1 1/2 hours). Add all other ingredients; pour into oiled molds. Chill overnight.

Brenda Etheredge, Mobile Council

SHRIMP SALAD

1 c. diced, cooked shrimp
1 c. chopped celery
1 1/2 Tbsp. lemon juice

3/4 c. mayonnaise
1 Tbsp. grated onion
Cooked rice (1 1/2 c. after
  cooked)

Combine shrimp and celery in a bowl; stir in mayonnaise mixed with lemon juice and onion. Then add rice (cool) and mix with a fork; chill. This is very good second day. Serve on lettuce and garnish with tomato wedges. Serves 4 or 5.

Louie Spear, Montgomery Council

SOUR CREAM SALAD

1 (11 oz.) can mandarin
  oranges
1 c. pineapple chunks
1 c. mini marshmallows

1 c. sour cream
1 c. coconut
1/3 c. heavy cream, whipped
1/2 tsp. vanilla

Mix sour cream and marshmallows and coconut; add well drained fruits. Blend whipped cream with vanilla and whip. Fold into salad. Add a handful of broken nuts, if desired. Chill overnight. Garnish with maraschino cherries.

Martha Hatcher, Montgomery Council

CABBAGE SLAW

1 medium head cabbage	1 tsp. sugar
2 medium onions	1 c. vinegar
3/4 c. sugar	3/4 c. oil
1 tsp. celery seed	1 1/2 tsp. salt
1 tsp. prepared mustard	

Shred cabbage; slice onions. Take bowl. Use layer of cabbage and layer of onions to fill bowl. Top with 3/4 cup sugar. Put in boiler vinegar, salt, mustard, celery seed, teaspoon sugar. Bring to boil; stir in oil. Pour over cabbage and onions. Cover and refrigerate overnight, then stir up.

Elizabeth Cornwell,
Birmingham Central Council

CABBAGE SALAD

In a large container arrange the following ingredients in layers:

1 large head cabbage, shredded	2 medium onions, thinly sliced (separate the onion rings)
1 green pepper, sliced paper thin	1 medium can or jar pimento, drained

Do not stir! For the dressing, mix together the following ingredients and boil for 2 minutes:

1 c. salad oil	1 1/2 tsp. salt
1 c. sugar	1 tsp. celery seed
3/4 c. white vinegar	

Pour the hot dressing over the vegetables; cover tightly and refrigerate at least 4 hours before serving. Makes about 15 servings.

Jewel Edney, Riverchase Council;
Brenda McKinney and Karen Jones, Birmingham South Council

GERMAN SLAW

1 large head cabbage, shredded	1/2 c. vinegar
1 large purple onion	2 Tbsp. sugar
1 bell pepper, sliced thin	1 tsp. salt
1/2 c. sugar	1 tsp. celery seed
3/4 c. oil	1 tsp. dry mustard

Alternate cabbage and onions in glass bowl. Sprinkle with 1/2 cup sugar; do not stir. Bring remaining ingredients to a boil. Pour over cabbage. Refrigerate for 4 hours or more. Toss when ready to serve.

Bobbie Bowles, Montgomery Council

HOLIDAY SLAW

1 medium cabbage	3/4 c. salad oil
1 small onion	2 Tbsp. sugar
3/4 c. sugar	1 tsp. salt
1 c. red vinegar	1 tsp. celery seeds

Shred cabbage and slice onion thinly. Separate the onion slices and place in a bowl with the shredded cabbage. Pour 3/4 cup of sugar over the cabbage and onions. In a saucepan combine vinegar, salad oil, 2 tablespoons sugar, salt and celery seeds. Bring this mixture to a boil and pour it over the cabbage and onions. Do not stir this in with the onions and cabbage! Refrigerate the slaw for 12 hours. Drain and toss lightly before serving. Serves 6-8 people.

Martha Swartz, Birmingham South Council

MARINATED COLE SLAW

1 medium cabbage, shredded	3/4 c. white vinegar
1 bell pepper, chopped	3/4 c. Crisco oil
1 red pepper or pimento, chopped	1 tsp. salt
	1/2 tsp. turmeric
1 c. sugar	1 medium onion, chopped

Combine cabbage, red and green peppers and onion. Set aside. Combine sugar, vinegar, oil, salt and turmeric and boil for 1 minute. Pour over cabbage. Keep refrigerated. (Best if made at least a day before serving.)

Ann Ensor, Retired, Life Member

MARINATED (GERMAN) SLAW

#1 ingredients:

1 1/2 c. vinegar	1 tsp. salt
1 c. salad oil	1 tsp. dry mustard
1/4 c. sugar	

#2 ingredients:

1 large hard head cabbage, thinly shredded

2 large onions, thinly sliced and separated
1 tsp. celery seed

Bring to boil #1 ingredients; remove from heat. Toss together #2 ingredients. Pour cooled #1 ingredients over #2 ingredients. Toss together. Cover tightly and let set in refrigerator several hours before serving. Will keep in refrigerator for a week.

Alberta Ray (Mrs. E. E.),
Birmingham West Council

REFRIGERATOR SLAW

1 head cabbage, chopped fine

2 medium onions, sliced

Arrange in alternate layers in a deep covered dish. Add 7/8 cup sugar to top. Bring to boil:

1 c. vinegar
3/4 c. oil
2 Tbsp. sugar

1 tsp. dry mustard
1 tsp. celery seed
   or celery salt
1 tsp. salt

Pour over cabbage and onion mixture; cool. Cover and store in refrigerator. Keep at least 24 hours before serving and this may be kept for a week or two. (One pound cabbage makes 6 servings.)

Mary C. Martin, Birmingham East Council

WALDORF SLAW

1 c. Hellmann's mayonnaise
1/2 c. Karo light corn
   syrup
1 Tbsp. lemon juice
1/4 tsp. salt
2 qt. shredded cabbage

1 (8 oz.) can pineapple
   chunks, drained
1 (11 oz.) can mandarin
   orange segments, drained
2 c. diced red apple
1/2 c. dark seedless raisins
1/4 c. chopped walnuts

Mix together first 4 ingredients; chill. Toss with next 5 ingredients. Garnish with walnuts. Makes 2 quarts.

Cynthia Lee, Tuscaloosa Council

COLD SPAGHETTI SALAD

16 oz. Viva salad dressing
1/4 container McCormick's
  "Salad Supreme"
1 chopped tomato

1 chopped red onion
1 chopped green pepper
1 lb. pkg. (#8) spaghetti
1 chopped cucumber

Cook spaghetti; cool. Add the rest of the ingredients and toss (should set at least 12 hours in the refrigerator).
Sue Fehrenbach, Birmingham Central Council

SPINACH SALAD

Salad:

Raw spinach, torn up
Raw mushrooms, sliced

1 can bean sprouts,
  drained and rinsed
Crumbled crisp bacon

Dressing:

1 c. oil
1/2 c. brown sugar
1/4 c. vinegar

1/3 c. catsup
1 Tbsp. Worcestershire
  sauce

Shake dressing ingredients in a jar. Pour as desired over salad ingredients. Dressing keeps well in refrigerator.
Barbara Munson, Birmingham South Council

LAYERED SALAD

1 medium head lettuce,
  torn into small pieces
1/2 c. chopped celery
1/2 c. chopped bell
  pepper

1 red onion, sliced, separated
1 can tiny English peas (small)
6 or 8 strips crisp bacon,
  crumbled
1 Tbsp. sugar

All in layers. Spread over top with mayonnaise (approximately 1 pint). Seal all sides and corners. Cover with Saran Wrap and foil. Refrigerate for 24 hours.
Mary Sue Andrews, Montgomery Council

SEVEN LAYER SALAD

Lettuce 2/3 full
  (broken small)
1/2 c. bell pepper
1/2 c. celery

1/2 c. sweet onions
  (or green onions)
1 small can water
  chestnuts, sliced
1 pkg. frozen English peas

Place in oblong 9x13 inch pan in the order listed. Mix 2 cups mayonnaise with 1 tablespoon of sugar. Spread over salad (this seals the moisture in). Refrigerate overnight. Before serving, spread with 1/2 cup of grated cheese. (Bacon bits optional.)

Frances H. Lewis, Birmingham South Council

TACO SALAD

Lettuce
1/2 c. shredded
  Cheddar cheese
Tomato slices
10 olives
1 lb. hamburger

1/2 pkg. dried onion
  soup mix
Fritos or Doritos
1/2 bottle French dressing
1/2 bottle taco sauce
1/4 onion, cut in rings

Prepare lettuce and refrigerate. Cook hamburger with onion soup mix and drain well (otherwise it will taste greasy when cool). Put lettuce in bottom of large bowl. Then put the hamburger on top of lettuce. Put the next in layers, tomatoes, olives, onion rings and cheese. Crush the Doritos and put on top. Mix the taco sauce and French dressing together and pour over top; refrigerate overnight.

Barbara Seegmiller, Decatur Council

TOMATO, ONION AND CUCUMBER
IN ITALIAN DRESSING

6 tomatoes, peeled
  and sliced
1 onion, sliced

2 cucumbers, sliced
1/4 c. commercial Italian
  dressing

Combine all vegetables in salad bowl; add Italian dressing. Refrigerate until ready to serve. Makes 4 to 6 servings.

Barbara Hall, Huntsville Council

TOMATO SOUP SALAD

1 can tomato soup
  (Campbell's)
2 env. plain gelatin
1 c. mayonnaise
1 (8 oz.) pkg. cream cheese

1 small bottle stuffed olives
1 can shrimp (can use 2)
1 1/2 c. chopped bell pepper
Celery and onion salt to taste

Heat soup and gelatin which has been dissolved in 1/4 cup cold water. Mix mayonnaise with cream cheese; gradually

add cooled soup seasoned with red pepper and Worcestershire sauce. Add bell pepper, celery, shrimp and olives.
Refrigerate in mold. Serves 10 to 12 or more. Be careful
about salt. Seems to go over well at luncheon.
Maggie Sivley, Decatur Council

EVELYN'S TOMATO SOUP SALAD

1 can tomato soup
2 env. gelatin

1/2 pt. cottage cheese, drained
1/2 c. diced celery
1/2 c. diced cucumbers

Sprinkle gelatin over soup and let stand 5 minutes.
Add other ingredients and pour into molds and chill.
Mildred J. Norton, Riverchase Council

CREAMY TUNA SALAD

6 hard cooked eggs
2 (8 oz.) pkg. cream
   cheese
2 (7 oz.) cans tuna,
   drained

1/4 c. minced green onions
2 Tbsp. minced parsley
2 tsp. Worcestershire sauce
2 tsp. lemon juice
1/2 tsp. salt

Reserve 8 center egg slices for garnish. Chop remaining eggs. Stir cream cheese until softened; add chopped
eggs, tuna, green onions, 2 tablespoons parsley, Worcestershire sauce, lemon juice and salt. Mix until blended. Chill
at least 2 hours. Divide mixture in half; shape into 2 balls.
Roll in parsley. Garnish bottom edge with egg slices.
Sue Quarles, Tuscaloosa Council

TUNA TOSSED SALAD

2 c. or 2 (7 oz.) cans
   solid packed tuna
1 c. pineapple chunks

3 c. grated raw carrots
1 c. celery, chopped fine
1 c. mayonnaise
1 c. raisins

Toss well. Serve on lettuce. Garnish with parsley,
ripe or green olives. Can use grapes or apples in place of
pineapple.
Mary C. Martin, Birmingham East Council

VEGETABLE SALAD

3/4 c. apple cider vinegar
3/4 c. Mazola oil
1/2 c. sugar

1 tsp. salt
1 tsp. pepper

Mix together and bring to boil and cool. Take vegetables, drain and mix:

1 (10 oz.) can white
shoe peg corn
1 small can French
style green beans
1 small can LeSueur
English peas (small)

1 c. chopped bell
pepper
1 c. chopped celery
2 bunches green onions,
chopped
1 small jar chopped pimentos

Add vegetables and liquid mixture; allow to marinate overnight. Will keep for long time; the longer it marinates, the better it tastes.

Billie Ellsworth, Mobile Council

VEGETABLE VINAIGRETTE

1 pkg. frozen whole
cooked green beans
1 c. sliced carrots,
cooked 5 minutes
1 cucumber, sliced thin
18 cherry tomatoes,
peeled
3 green onions, minced

1 c. olive oil or salad oil
1/3 c. wine vinegar
2 garlic cloves, crushed
1/4 tsp. oregano
1 tsp. salt
1/2 tsp. pepper
1/2 tsp. dry mustard

In tightly covered jar shake oil, vinegar, oregano, salt, pepper, mustard and garlic; pour over vegetables. Cover; chill 2-3 hours. Just before serving, arrange vegetables on lettuce. Sprinkle with green onion. Drizzle dressing over the top.

Jeannie Riddles, Riverchase Council

WEST INDIES SALAD

1 lb. lump crabmeat

1 medium onion, chopped

Layer these ingredients in a bowl with a lid.

4 oz. Wesson oil
6 oz. white vinegar

4 oz. ice water

Pour the oil, vinegar and ice water over the crabmeat

and onion. Salt and pepper to taste. Do not stir. Chill 12
hours in covered bowl. Makes 4 large bowls.

Virginia H. Greene,
Birmingham Central Council

** NOTES **

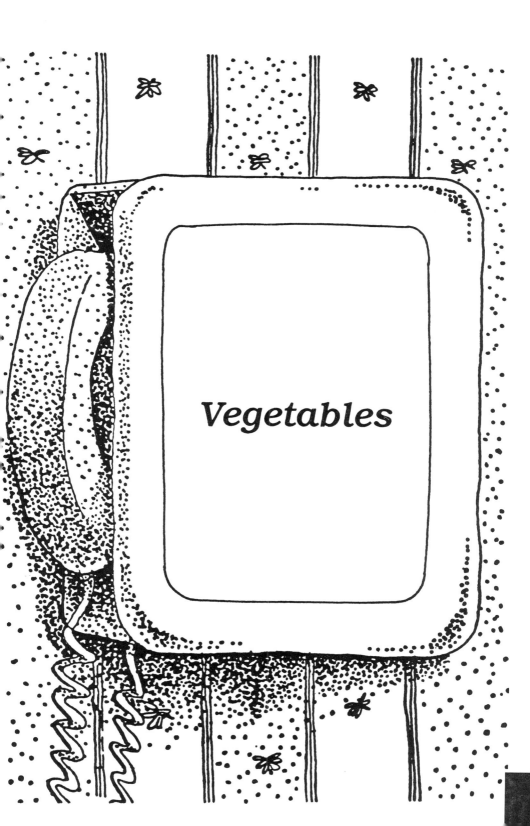

Vegetables

CALORIE CHART OF VEGETABLES

Artichoke:
  1 lg 88
  hearts, frozen, 3½ oz 26
Asparagus, 1 cup 35
Beans:
  green, fresh, 1 cup 35
  kidney, dried, 1 cup 635
  limas, dried, 1 cup 656
  navy, dried, 1 cup 697
  soy, dried ½ cup 95
  wax, fresh, 1 cup 30
Beets, 1 cup 58
Broccoli, 2 lg stalks 145
Brussels sprouts, 1 cup 55
Cabbage:
  green, 1 cup 36
  red, 1 cup 28
Carrots:
  raw, 1 whole 30
  cooked, 1 cup 50
Cauliflower:
  fresh, cooked, 1 cup 30
  raw, chopped, 1 cup 31
Celery, 1 lg stalk 7
Chard, 1 lb 113
Chestnuts, 1 cup 310
Collards, cooked, 1 cup 65
Corn:
  cream-style, ½ cup 100
  fresh, 1 ear 70
  whole kernel, ½ cup 85
Cucumber, 1 lg 45
Dandelion greens, 1 lb 204
Eggplant, boiled, 1 cup 38
Endive:
  Belgian, 1 head 8
  curly, 1 cup 10
Kale, fresh, cooked, 1 cup . . . 45
Kohlrabi, fresh, 1 cup 41
Lentils, dried, 1 cup 646
Lettuce:
  Bibb, 1 cup 8
  iceberg, 1 cup 7
  romaine, 1 cup 10
Mushrooms:
  canned, 1 cup 40
  fresh, 1 lb 125

Mustard greens:
  cooked, 1 cup 30
  fresh, 1 lb 141
Okra, fresh, 1 cup 36
Onions, fresh, 1 cup 65
Parsley, fresh, 1 cup 26
Parsnips, cooked, 1 cup 82
Peas:
  black-eyed, fresh, 1 cup . . 184
  green, fresh, 1 cup 122
Peppers:
  hot chili, ½ cup 18
  sweet green, 1 med 14
  sweet red, 1 med 19
Potatoes, sweet:
  baked, 1 med 155
  candied, 1 med 295
  canned, ½ cup 110
Potatoes, white:
  baked, 1 sm 93
  boiled, 1 sm 70
  French-fried, 10 pieces . . 175
  hashed brown, ½ cup . . . 177
  mashed, ½ cup 90
  scalloped, ½ cup 120
Pumpkin, canned, 1 cup 81
Radishes, 10 whole 14
Rutabagas, fresh, 1 cup 87
Spinach:
  cooked, 1 cup 40
  fresh, 1 cup 15
Sprouts:
  alfalfa, 1 cup 10
  Mung bean, fresh, 1 cup . . 37
Squash:
  summer, fresh, 1 cup 25
  winter, mashed, 1 cup . . . 129
Tomatoes:
  canned, 1 cup 50
  green, fresh, 1 lb 99
  ripe, fresh, 1 lb 88
Turnip greens
  fresh, cooked, 1 cup 30
Turnips, fresh, 1 cup 39
Watercress, 1 bunch 20
Water chestnuts, 1 cup 70
Zucchini, fresh, 1 cup 22

CINNAMON-APPLE WEDGES

1/2 c. sugar
2 (1 3/4 oz.) bottles
   red cinnamon candies

6 c. thickly sliced, pared
   cored apples (2 lb.)
1 c. water

Combine sugar, candies and water in a 2 1/2 quart saucepan; stir over high heat to dissolve sugar and candies. Reduce heat; add apple slices. Simmer covered and stirring occasionally, until apples are just tender, not mushy (about 10 minutes). With slotted spoon, remove apples to large bowl. Bring cinnamon syrup to boiling; boil uncovered until thick; pour syrup over apples. Refrigerate.

Sharon Crabtree, Tuscaloosa Council

ASPARAGUS AU GRATIN

1 lb. cooked asparagus
   or 1 box frozen
   asparagus or 1 (No. 2)
   can asparagus
2 Tbsp. margarine or
   butter
2 Tbsp. flour
1/2 tsp. salt

Liquid from asparagus and
   enough milk to make
   1 1/2 c.
1 c. Cheddar cheese, grated
4 hard cooked eggs, sliced
1/2 c. soft bread crumbs
Paprika

Save liquid from asparagus. Melt butter or margarine and blend in flour and salt. Add liquid and cook until thickened, stirring frequently. Remove from heat. Add cheese; stir until cheese is melted. Alternate layers of hard cooked eggs, asparagus and cheese sauce. Cover with bread crumbs in greased 2 quart casserole. Sprinkle paprika over crumbs. Bake in preheated 350° oven for 30 minutes. Serves 4.

Mary Norris, Birmingham Central Council

APPLE-YAM BAKE

6 medium sized tart
   apples, peeled and
   sliced to make 6 c.
1 (1 lb.) can yams, halved
1 Tbsp. grated orange peel

1/3 c. packed brown sugar
1/2 tsp. salt
1/2 tsp. cinnamon
6 Tbsp. melted butter
1 1/2 c. Wheaties

Combine apples and yams and orange peel. Sprinkle 1/2 of the sugar, salt, cinnamon mixture over apples and

yams, Drizzle 1/2 of the butter over mixture. Bake at
350° for 1 hour, covered. Toss cereal with rest of sugar
mixture. Stir in melted butter. Sprinkle cereal mixture
over casserole; bake 15 minutes or until top is crisp.

LaDon S. Young, Birmingham Central Council

DRY LIMAS OR PEAS

Place about 1/2 pound of dry beans into pan; cover
with water. Add at least 2 cups or more (room temperature
water). Let soak overnight if you plan to cook at noon
meal next day, or soak all day if you cook at night (supper).
Wash beans; cover with water in pot. Add 3 tablespoons
bacon fat drippings or fat meat, or you can use a ham hock.
Cook beans or peas on medium heat for at least 1 hour.
Check to see if you need to add a little water along. Test
beans to see if tender (cook till done). Salt to taste.

Marcia Freeman, Birmingham East Council

BUNDLE OF BEANS

2 (No. 303) cans whole   2 tsp. dry mustard
   green beans   Bacon to wrap
1 c. brown sugar

Drain juice from beans. Mix brown sugar and dry
mustard; pour over beans in a bowl and toss well. Divide
beans into bundles and wrap 1/2 slice of bacon around each
bundle and secure with toothpick. Bake 30 minutes in 350°
oven.

Nancy Murray, Birmingham South Council

BAKED BEANS

3 onions, chopped   4 Tbsp. butter
1/2 c. catsup   1 tsp. mustard
2 c. brown sugar   1/2 tsp. pepper
1/4 c. vinegar   1 can kidney beans, drained
1 can pork and beans   1 can lima beans, drained

Cook onions in butter until tender. Mix all ingredients.
Bake 45 minutes at 350°. Also good cooked in crock pot on
low setting for 4 hours.

Barbara Hampton, Birmingham South Council

BEANS ACROSS THE BORDER

2 lb. dry Mexican pinto
  beans
Salt pork (several chunks)

6 pods garlic, cut fine
2 tsp. oregano
3 jalapenos, mashed up
2 Tbsp. salt

Wash beans. Combine all ingredients. Fill pot about half full of water. Bring to boil on medium flame, stirring occasionally. Turn down as low as you can barely simmer beans. Keep water covering beans; when adding water add hot water so beans won't cool. Cook about 4 hours or until done.

Note: If you soak beans overnight or several hours, it reduces cooking time some.

Charlotte Johnson, Huntsville Council

BOSTON BAKED BEANS

1 (12 oz.) pkg. white
  Great Northern beans
1 medium yellow onion, diced
1/2 c. tomato ketchup
1/2 c. brown sugar
1/4 c. honey or molasses

2 cloves garlic, minced
2 Tbsp. white wine vinegar
1 tsp. mustard
1 tsp. lemon juice
2 oz. salt pork
1 Tbsp. salt

Soak dried beans overnight; add salt pork and cover with water (2 inches) and boil in a covered saucepan 1 1/2 hours. Remove from heat. Pour beans and remaining water in large deep baking dish; stir in remaining ingredients and bake uncovered 1 1/4 hours in 350° oven.

George B. Reed, Riverchase Council

PICNIC BAKED BEANS

1 large onion
1 bell pepper
1 can chili
1 can whole kernel
  corn and peppers

1/4 c. tomato catsup
1 can pork and beans
1 can kidney beans
1 Tbsp. Worcestershire
  sauce

Chop onion and brown; add remaining ingredients. Season with salt and pepper. Place in well greased casserole and bake 1 hour at 325° or longer.

Jean Wharton, Birmingham South Council

BAR-B-Q BEANS - MEXICAN STYLE

1 can pork 'n beans
1 can red kidney beans
1 can pinto beans
1 large onion, chopped
1 large bell pepper,
  chopped

1 large can tomatoes, cut up
1/2 c. Bar-B-Q sauce
1 to 2 Tbsp. Worcestershire
  sauce
1 tsp. mustard

Combine all ingredients. Can be cooked on top of stove, slow cooker or can be baked in oven until onions and bell pepper are tender.

Marilyn Pharr, Selma Council

OLD FASHIONED BAKED BEANS

2 lb. navy beans
2 qt. cold water
1 medium onion, sliced
1 Tbsp. salt
4 tsp. cider vinegar
1 tsp. prepared mustard

3 Tbsp. brown sugar
1/2 c. molasses
1/4 c. catsup
Black pepper
Hot water, if needed
1/2 lb. salt pork, diced

Add cold water to beans; cover, heat to boiling and simmer for 30 minutes. Drain, but do not discard the liquid. Place onion slices in bottom of bean pot or 10 cup casserole. Combine salt, vinegar, mustard, brown sugar, molasses, catsup and pepper; turn into bean pot. Add beans and enough hot drained liquid or water to cover. Arrange salt pork slices on top; cover and bake at 250° for 7 or 8 hours. Add additional liquid as needed. Remove cover last hour of cooking so salt meat can brown.

Brenda Etheredge, Mobile Council

GREAT NORTHERN DELIGHT

1 (1 lb.) pkg. Great
  Northern beans
1 medium bell pepper
1 medium onion

4 Tbsp. red Karo syrup
4 Tbsp. sugar
1 ham hock
Salt and pepper

Soak beans overnight. Place in crock pot. Cover well with water; add chopped pepper, chopped onion. Add all other ingredients. Cook on high for 8 hours.

Rachel Carroll, Decatur Council

664

GREEN BEANS AMANDINE

2 lb. fresh green beans	2/3 c. slivered almonds
1 small ham hock	3 Tbsp. melted butter
1 c. water	or margarine
1/3 c. minced onion	1 tsp. salt

Remove strings from green beans; cut beans into 1 1/2 inch pieces, and wash thoroughly. Place in a 5 quart Dutch oven; add ham hock and water. Bring to a boil, then reduce heat. Cover and simmer for 1 hour. Drain off excess liquid. Saute onion and almonds in butter until onion is tender. Add to beans, along with salt; toss lightly. Yield: 8 servings.

Rita Finley, Huntsville Council

EASY GREEN BEANS

1 lb. green beans	1/2 c. sliced onions
(young tender beans)	Salt
Bacon drippings	Water

Cut only tips off each end of bean. You are using "first fruits" of bean crop, not fully matured and filled out. Wash beans and place them in large saucepan in enough water to coat bottom of pan about 1/2 inch along with other ingredients. Do not stir. Turn over with spatulas once or shake pan to coat all beans with liquid. Cook until tender.

Chris Morgan, Riverchase Council

PEACHY GINGER BAKED BEANS

1 lb. fully ripened peaches	2 Tbsp. finely chopped
2 (1 lb.) cans baked beans	onions
1/4 c. dark corn syrup	1 tsp. ginger

Peel, pit and slice peaches. Measure 2 cups peaches in 2 quart casserole. Stir together with beans, syrup, onion and ginger. Top with remainder peaches. Bake for 1 to 1 1/2 hours, basting frequently, or until peaches are well glazed in a 400° oven.

Claudelle Mayo, Birmingham South Council

*   *   *   *   *

If we don't enjoy what we have, how could we possibly be happier with more?

SWEET BAKED BEANS

1 (28 or 31 oz.) can pork
  and beans, well drained
1/4 c. plus 2 Tbsp. apple
  jelly
1/4 c. plus 2 Tbsp.
  pineapple preserves

2 Tbsp. butter or
  margarine, melted
1 tsp. vanilla extract
1 tsp. lemon juice
1/2 tsp. ground cinnamon

Preheat oven to 350°. In medium bowl combine ingredients; mix well. Turn into 1 quart baking dish; bake uncovered 45 minutes or until hot. Refrigerate leftovers. Makes 4 servings.

Linda L. Unger, Riverchase Council

GRECIAN STYLE STRING BEANS

3 lb. string beans
5 scallions, chopped
1 c. water
1 green pepper, chopped
2 large carrots, sliced thin
2 Tbsp. olive oil

2 large potatoes,
  quartered and sliced
3 Tbsp. parsley, chopped fine
1/2 c. tomatoes
2 Tbsp. butter
1/2 tsp. salt
1/8 tsp. pepper

Clean and cut string beans in halves; wash and drain. Place all vegetables in medium saucepan. Top with parsley. Add butter, oil, 1 cup water, salt and pepper to taste. Cover and cook on high flame till boiling point, lower flame to medium and continue cooking for 45 minutes until vegetables are tender. Serves 4 or 5.

Joan M. Beiers, Huntsville Council

SWEET AND SOUR GREEN BEANS

3 strips bacon
1 small onion
1 can water chestnuts,
  sliced
1 (16 oz.) can French
  style green beans
2 tsp. cornstarch

1/2 tsp. salt
1/4 tsp. dry mustard
1 Tbsp. brown sugar
1 Tbsp. vinegar
3 Tbsp. chopped
  pimento

Fry bacon until crisp; remove and drain and crumble. Add onion and water chestnuts to bacon fat. Saute until onion is golden, stirring frequently. Drain green beans, reserving 1/2 cup liquid. Combine bean liquid, cornstarch, salt, mustard, brown sugar and vinegar; add to skillet; cook,

stirring constantly until mixture thickens. Add green beans and pimento; heat through. Serve garnished with crumbled bacon. Makes four 1 cup servings.
Sonja Shell, Montgomery Council

SUPER LIMA BEANS

4 slices bacon	1 (10 3/4 oz.) can tomato soup
1 large onion, chopped	2 Tbsp. melted butter
4 c. cooked, drained	or margarine
lima beans	1/2 c. soft bread crumbs

Cook bacon until crisp; remove from skillet, crumble and set aside. Saute onions in bacon drippings until tender; add beans, soup and bacon, mixing well. Spoon into a greased 1 1/2 quart casserole. Combine butter and bread crumbs; sprinkle over top. Bake at 375° for 30 minutes. Yield: 5 to 6 servings.
Betty Floyd Parker, Montgomery Council

LIMA BEANS IN SOUR CREAM

3 c. lima beans, cooked	1 small jar pimento peppers,
3 Tbsp. butter	chopped
1/2 c. onion	1/2 c. sour cream

Saute onions in butter; add pimento and beans and heat through. Stir in sour cream. Serve immediately.
Diane M. Cook, Montgomery Council

MERV'S NEW ORLEANS STYLE RED BEANS

1 lb. red kidney beans, dried	1 large onion, diced
1 Tbsp. garlic salt	2 stalks celery, diced
5 bay leaves	1/2 bell pepper, diced
2 Tbsp. sugar	Salt
1 1/2 lb. seasoning meat (ham, ham hocks, sausage, etc.)	Pepper
	Fresh or dried parsley (4 Tbsp.)

Place beans in refrigerator a day or two before cooking. Cull beans, then wash and soak them in water for a few hours prior to cooking. Cover beans with water and bring to a rapid boil in a heavy pot with lid. Stir beans occasionally and maintain just enough water to keep them covered. When the beans start to get soft, add all the seasoning except salt, pepper and smoked sausage if it is used for seasoning. After

1567-82

beans really begin to get tender, salt and pepper to taste; add smoked sausage at this time and lower heat. Simmer for 20 minutes, stirring often. During this time, mash a few of the beans and continue cooking until the liquid becomes creamy. Serve hot over rice. The seasoning is the key; adjust it to suit your taste. Serves 6 to 8 people.

Merv Helton, Birmingham Central Council

RED BEANS AND RICE

1 whole ham hock
1/4 c. bacon drippings
1 pkg. large red kidney
  beans
1 bay leaf

2 large onions, chopped
1 Tbsp. flour
4 c. cooked rice
Salt and pepper

Put ham hock and beans in large pot; cover with water. Season with salt and pepper and bay leaf. Cover over low fire 4 to 5 hours, or until meat falls off bone and beans are done. Saute onions in bacon drippings. Add flour; add this mixture to bean pot and cook until mixture thickens. Takes about 1 hour. Salt and pepper to taste. Serve over rice. Serves 8-10.

Anne Spragins, Birmingham East Council

RED BEANS AND RICE

1/2 c. onion, finely
  chopped
1/2 c. celery, chopped
1 clove garlic
2 Tbsp. butter

1 (16 oz.) can kidney beans
  (may substitute pinto beans)
2 c. cooked rice
1 tsp. parsley, chopped
Salt and pepper to taste

Brown onion, celery and garlic in stew pot. Add all other ingredients. Cook at a low boil for 15-20 minutes.

James Andress, Montgomery Council

BEETS IN RAISIN SAUCE

1 (16 oz.) can diced beets
1 (8 1/4 oz.) can crushed
  pineapple
2 Tbsp. butter or
  margarine

1/2 c. firmly packed
  brown sugar
2 to 3 Tbsp. all-purpose flour
1/4 tsp. salt
1/3 c. vinegar
1/2 c. seedless raisins

Drain beets and pineapple, reserving juices. Put beets and pineapple in separate dishes; set aside. Combine butter, sugar, flour and salt in a saucepan. Gradually stir vinegar and reserved juices into saucepan mixture. Cook, stirring constantly, until mixture thickens. Add raisins and pineapple; pour over beets. You may let stand for several hours for flavors to blend, if desired. You may heat before serving or serve cold. Yield: 6 servings.

Beverly McCoy, Montgomery Council

HARVARD BEETS

1 (1 lb.) can beets	1/2 c. sugar
1/4 c. vinegar	1/2 tsp. salt
1 Tbsp. flour or cornstarch	1 Tbsp. margarine

Drain liquid from beets into saucepan; boil down to half. Shake together vinegar and flour; stir into boiling mixture. Add sugar and salt; bring to a boil. Add beets and margarine; heat through.

Catherine Pittman, Mobile Council

SWEET BEETS

5 large beets, sliced	1/2 c. sugar
1 qt. water	1 tsp. celery seed
1 c. vinegar	1 Tbsp. ground allspice

Cook beets whole in 1 quart water until tender; remove from heat. Run cold water over beets to cool enough to skin and slice. Let vinegar, sugar and spices cook together. Pour beets into spice; cook for 3 more minutes. Remove from heat and cool. Good with meat or vegetable.

Susan Tucker, Huntsville Council

SARRAH'S ROASTED BELL PEPPERS

4 bell peppers	2 or 3 cloves garlic
2 Tbsp. oil	1 c. tomatoes

Roast 4 bell peppers over open flame (or in oven on broil) until skin is charred. Place peppers while hot in a brown paper bag and seal for 5 or 10 minutes. (Flesh is softened and skin will peel off easily.) Peel and seed peppers and cut in thin strips. In about 2 tablespoons of oil, lightly cook 2 or 3 garlic cloves (cubed). Add 1 cup tomatoes and cook until almost dry. Add peppers and cook until tender.

Ann Spragins, Birmingham East Council

1567-82

STUFFED BELL PEPPERS

4 extra large bell peppers
  or 8 small ones
2 lb. ground beef
2 eggs
1 Tbsp. onion flakes

2 Tbsp. soy sauce
5 Tbsp. catsup
1 can cream of mushroom
  soup (undiluted)
1 c. cooked rice

Cut large pepper in half and remove seeds (small peppers cut off tops). Place in roasting pan. Mix 3 table-spoons catsup and 3 tablespoons mushroom soup in a small bowl. Mix all other ingredients in large bowl. Mix with hands until well blended. Fill peppers until all mixture is used (heap if necessary), use mixture in small bowl to spread over top. Fill roasting pan 1/4 full with water. Cook in 325° oven for 1 1/2 hours. Freeze leftover cooked peppers in foil for later use.

Note: Soy sauce and soup will add the salt - more salt may be added if you like.

Louise G. Kellum, Life Member,
Birmingham Central Council

STUFFED GREEN PEPPERS

1 lb. ground beef
1 1/2 c. rice, uncooked
1 large onion
1 Tbsp. Worcestershire
  sauce

1 can tomatoes
1 can tomato sauce
1 Tbsp. paprika
Salt and pepper

Mix above. Stuff in peppers and wrap in foil. Bake at 350° for 1 1/2 hours.

Ellen Johnston

CHEESY BROCCOLI BAKE

1 (10 oz.) pkg. frozen
  broccoli, chopped
1 (10 3/4 oz.) can
  Cheddar cheese soup
1/2 c. sour cream

1 can Tender Chunk ham,
  chicken or turkey,
  flaked with fork
1 c. cooked rice
1/2 c. buttered bread crumbs

Preheat oven to 350°. Cook broccoli until barely tender. Drain well. Stir soup and sour cream together. Add remaining ingredients to soup and sour cream mixture. Spoon into 1 1/2 quart casserole. Sprinkle with bread crumbs. Bake 30-35 minutes. Serves 4-6.

Catherine F. Pittman, Mobile Council

BROCCOLI ITALIAN

3 pkg. frozen broccoli
  spears
2 Tbsp. olive oil

4 Tbsp. butter
1 clove garlic
3/4 c. grated Parmesan cheese

Partly defrost broccoli. In a large skillet heat the olive oil and butter. Cut garlic in half and saute until golden. Remove the garlic and spread the broccoli in a single layer in the pan. Saute, turning gently, for 10 minutes, or until tender. Arrange in a flameproof serving dish. Sprinkle with cheese and place under broiler for about 1 minute. Serves 6 to 8.

Minerva B. Boston, Birmingham East Council

BROCCOLI PARMESAN

3 Tbsp. butter
2 Tbsp. minced onion
2 Tbsp. flour
1 tsp. salt
1 tsp. dry mustard
1/2 tsp. marjoram

Dash of pepper
2 c. milk
1 chicken bouillon cube
1/2 c. grated Parmesan cheese
2 pkg. frozen chopped
  broccoli
Paprika

Saute onion in butter until brown; blend in flour, salt, mustard, marjoram and pepper. Gradually add milk, then bouillon cube. Cook, stirring constantly, until smooth. Stir in cheese, reserving 2 tablespoons. Cook broccoli until tender. Drain; arrange in shallow 1 1/2 quart casserole. Pour sauce over. Sprinkle with reserved cheese and paprika. Place under broiler and brown lightly.

Debbie Tucker, Birmingham East Council

COMPANY CABBAGE

5 c. finely shredded
  cabbage
1 c. finely shredded
  carrots
1/2 c. chopped green
  onion
1/2 tsp. salt
1 c. hot chicken broth

1/8 tsp. pepper
1/4 c. butter or
  margarine
Boiling water
1 tsp. prepared mustard
1/3 c. chopped pecans
1/4 tsp. paprika

Put cabbage, carrots, onion, salt and pepper into slow pot. Pour in chicken broth and enough boiling water to cover vegetables. Cover and cook on high 3 to 4 hours. Melt butter in small skillet; stir in mustard and pecans. Toss to coat. Transfer vegetables to serving dish. Top with butter and pecan mixture and sprinkle with paprika. Makes about 6 servings.

Mattie Foster, Huntsville Council

CABBAGE CREOLE

2 Tbsp. butter or oleo
1/2 c. chopped onion
1 c. chopped bell pepper
1 c. thinly chopped
  celery

2 c. diced tomatoes
  (fresh or canned)
1 qt. shredded cabbage
1 1/2 tsp. salt
1 tsp. sugar
1/2 tsp. pepper

Melt butter in 10 or 12 inch skillet; add all ingredients and mix well. Cover and cook until vegetables are tender (approximately 10 minutes), stirring occasionally. Do not overcook. Serves 8.

Bertha Capps, Birmingham East Council

SPICY CABBAGE

1 head cabbage
1 1/2 lb. ground beef
Salt and pepper to taste

1 can Ro-Tel (tomatoes
  and green chiles)

Brown ground beef in Dutch oven; drain off fat. Add Ro-Tel, chopped cabbage on top of beef and simmer until tender.

Bobbie Bowles, Montgomery Council

SWEET AND SOUR CABBAGE

1/2 c. water
1/2 c. vinegar
1/2 to 3/8 c. sugar
1 tsp. salt

2 Tbsp. butter
1 apple, sliced
Up to 3 lb. cabbage, cut
  up as in slaw

Cook all ingredients together over low heat approximately 20 minutes or until tender. Make day before you serve.

Bonnie Summers, Huntsville Council

672

CARROTS AU GRATIN

3 c. diced carrots
6 crackers, crushed (1/4 c.)
1 tsp. onion salt
1/4 c. chopped green pepper

1/8 tsp. pepper
2 Tbsp. melted butter
1/2 c. grated sharp cheese

Heat oven to 425°. Cook carrots in 1/2 inch boiling, salted water 10 minutes. Combine crackers, onion salt, green pepper and pepper. Alternate layers of carrots and crumb mixture in greased 1 quart baking dish. If any carrot liquid is left, spoon over top. Pour batter over and sprinkle with cheese. Bake 15 to 20 minutes, or until cheese melts. Makes 6 servings.

Linda L. Unger, Riverchase Council

CANDIED CARROTS

1 bunch or 1 lb. carrots
1 c. water
1/2 tsp. nutmeg or
  cinnamon (optional)

1/2 c. brown or white sugar
1/2 stick butter
Dash of salt

Cut carrots in 2 inch lengths or in thick slices. Mix all ingredients together. Place in medium size boiler. Cover; cook for 10 or 15 minutes or until carrots are tender. Uncover and cook until heavy syrup is formed. Be careful not to burn.

To oven cook, boil the carrots until tender; drain. Make a syrup by boiling together the sugar and water. Cut each carrot in half or in thick slices. Dip each piece into syrup and lay in a greased baking dish. Season with salt, nutmeg and butter. Pour over carrots any syrup that remains. Bake in 400° to 450° oven until carrots are brown. They will brown quickly. Makes 6 to 8 servings.

Mrs. Edith Johnson, Life Member,
Birmingham Central Council

STIR FRIED CARROTS AND CELERY
(MICROWAVE STYLE)

1 c. sliced carrots
1 c. sliced celery

2 Tbsp. margarine,
  melted

Preheat browning grill for 1-2 minutes on high. Microwave 3 1/2 to 5 minutes on high. Stir 1/2 way through. Pour butter on grill, then pour on vegetables.

Dina Johnson, Birmingham South Council

MARINATED CARROTS

2 small pkg. carrots
1/2 c. vinegar
1/2 c. sugar

1/2 c. vegetable oil
1 can cream of tomato soup
Onion and bell pepper

Cut up and cook 2 small packages of carrots. Marinate overnight in vinegar, sugar, vegetable oil and cream of tomato soup. Ring an onion and bell pepper on top. Serves 6 to 8 people.

Myrtle Parks, Montgomery Council
Agatha Peevy, Mobile Council

PINEAPPLE GLAZED CARROTS

Cooking time: 15 minutes. Set out a 1 1/2 quart saucepan. Drain, reserving liquids, contents of one Number 2 can sliced carrots (2 cups drained). Use one 9 ounce can pineapple tidbits (or 2/3 cup drained). Combine in the saucepan:

2 tsp. cornstarch

1/2 tsp. salt

Mix and add gradually to cornstarch mixture, stirring constantly:

2/3 c. reserved carrot
    liquid

1/3 c. reserved pineapple
    syrup

Bring to boiling, stirring constantly; cook about 3 minutes, or until the liquid is thick and clear. Stir in 1 tablespoon butter or margarine. Add carrots and pineapple. Heat thoroughly. Makes 4 or 5 servings.

Willie J. Harris, Riverchase Council

CARROT SOUFFLE

3 Tbsp. butter or
    margarine, melted
3 Tbsp. flour
1 c. milk, heated
1/4 tsp. salt

3 eggs
2 c. cooked carrots, mashed
1 tsp. vanilla
3 tsp. sugar
1/2 tsp. nutmeg

In a mixing bowl blend the butter and flour; add the milk and remaining ingredients. Mix thoroughly. Pour into greased 1 1/2 quart baking dish. Bake at 350 for 40 minutes. Makes 6 servings.

Wanda Lynch, Montgomery Council

SHREDDED CARROTS

6 c. shredded carrots   Butter
2 c. green onions, sliced   Salt
Chicken broth   Parsley

Prepare 6 cups shredded carrots. Cook, over lowest flame, with 2 cups finely sliced onions and enough chicken broth to cover until liquid is reduced to nothing, stirring occasionally. Add 4 tablespoons of butter and salt to taste and sprinkle with parsley.

Carol York, Montgomery Council

VEGETABLE-TOASTED CARROTS

6 carrots
2 Tbsp. mayonnaise
1/4 tsp. salt
1/16 tsp. pepper

1 1/4 c. toasted wheat
    flakes or fine bread crumbs
Dash of paprika

Roll whole cooked carrots in mayonnaise, then in crushed wheat flakes seasoned with salt, pepper and paprika. Place under broiler with moderately low temperature (350°) for 10 minutes, turning carrots several times.

Dot Gray, Montgomery Council

WAR EAGLE CARROTS

4 c. sliced carrots
3 Tbsp. melted butter
1/3 c. apricot preserves
1/4 tsp. salt

1/4 tsp. grated orange rind
1/2 tsp. ground nutmeg
2 tsp. lemon juice

Cook carrots until tender in enough salted water to cover (about 20 minutes). Drain. Combine remaining ingredients, stirring until well blended. Spoon over carrots and toss well. Serve at once. Makes 6 to 8 servings.

Betty Floyd Parker, Montgomery Council

CHEESE FROSTED CAULIFLOWER

1 head cauliflower
1/2 c. mayonnaise

2 tsp. prepared mustard
3/4 c. shredded sharp cheese

Cook cauliflower, leaving whole; drain well. Place it in a shallow pan and frost with mayonnaise, mixed with mustard. Sprinkle on cheese; bake at 350° until cheese melts, about 10 minutes.

Nancy S. Black, Decatur Council

1567-82

BAKED CORN ON THE COB

1 Tbsp. mustard
1 tsp. salt
1 tsp. horseradish

Dash of pepper
1 stick softened oleo

Mix all ingredients and spread on corn. Wrap each piece loosely in aluminum foil. Bake at 450° for 25 minutes. Does approximately 6 ears.

Emma Rousseau, Huntsville Council

BOSTON BAKED CORN

2 large cans white
   or yellow corn
3/4 c. brown sugar
3/4 c. ketchup
1/2 tsp. dry mustard
1/2 tsp. garlic salt

1/4 tsp. pepper
1 small onion, chopped
1/2 bell pepper, chopped
3-4 bacon strips, cut in
   small pieces

Drain corn. Mix all ingredients. Pour mixture into greased casserole and bake for 1 hour at 350°. May also leave bacon in strips and lay across casserole.

Bobbie Bowles, Montgomery Council

GRILLED CORN-ON-THE-COB

6 ears fresh corn
Melted butter

Salt and pepper

Husk corn right before cooking. Brush with melted butter and sprinkle with salt and pepper. Wrap each ear tightly in aluminum foil. Roast on grill 10 to 20 minutes, turning frequently.

Billie Bays, Decatur Council

BARBECUED CORN

6 ears fresh corn
1/2 c. butter or
   margarine, melted

1/2 (3 oz.) pkg. instant
   tomato soup mix (2 env.)
1/2 c. water
1 medium onion, finely chopped

Remove husks and silks from corn just before cooking. Combine remaining ingredients, stirring well. Place each ear on a piece of aluminum foil, and spoon 2 tablespoons sauce over each. Wrap foil tightly around corn. Bake at 425° for 12 to 15 minutes. Yield: 6 servings.

Linda Mitchell, Decatur Council

676

CREAM CORN

Clip and scrape about 4 to 6 ears corn. Add a little water (not too much). Melt 2 tablespoons oleo in pan; add corn, salt to taste plus 1 teaspoon sugar. Cook for 45 minutes on medium to low heat. You may have to add a little water. Cook till creamy and thick.

Marcia Freeman, Birmingham East Council

FRIED CORN

1 qt. frozen corn
3/4 stick margarine
2 Tbsp. sugar
Salt to taste
Some water

Put frozen corn and above ingredients in covered thick pan and cook for 1 hour.

Mrs. Barbara Stewart, Decatur Council

CORN PUDDING

4 large eggs, beaten
1/2 tsp. salt
1/3 c. sugar
2 Tbsp. flour
1 1/3 c. milk
3 Tbsp. butter
2 c. white or yellow corn
  (fresh or frozen)

Mix flour, salt and sugar with corn; add beaten eggs. Stir in milk and butter. (Be sure eggs are mixed well with other ingredients.) Bake at 325° for 45 minutes or until you have a good firm custard look to your dish.

Janet Logsdon, Birmingham Central Council

SCALLOPED CORN

1/4 c. chopped onion
2 Tbsp. melted butter
2 Tbsp. all-purpose flour
1 tsp. salt
1/2 tsp. paprika
1/4 tsp. dry mustard
Dash of pepper
3/4 c. milk
1 (17 oz.) can whole
  kernel corn, drained
1 egg, beaten
1/2 c. cracker crumbs
3 Tbsp. melted butter

Saute onion in 2 tablespoons butter till lightly browned; stir in flour and seasonings. Remove from heat and gradually stir in milk. Return to heat; boil 1 minute, stirring constantly. Remove from heat; stir in corn and egg. Pour into greased 1 quart baking dish. Combine cracker crumbs and 3 tablespoons butter. Stir till moist; sprinkle over casserole. Bake at 350° for 20 to 30 minutes.

Debbie Hearn, Birmingham East Council

CREAMY-CHEESY-CORN

3 oz. cream cheese, softened
1/4 c. milk
1 Tbsp. margarine

1/2 tsp. onion salt
16 oz. whole kernel shoe peg corn, drained

Mix all ingredients except corn; cook over low heat until cheese melts, stirring often. Add corn and heat thoroughly.

Mildred Parker, Huntsville Council

ROASTED CORN WITH BOUILLON BUTTER

4 ears sweet corn
1/4 c. butter or margarine

1 or 2 tsp. chicken-flavor instant bouillon or 1 or 2 chicken-flavor bouillon cubes

Remove husks and silk from corn; rinse and pat dry. In small saucepan, over low heat, dissolve bouillon in butter. Brush corn with butter. Wrap each ear securely in aluminum foil. Grill over hot coals 15 to 20 minutes, turning frequently. Remove from grill; brush with additional butter. Serve immediately.

Tip: Corn can be boiled, then brushed with bouillon butter.

Flo Thompson, Montgomery Council

BAKED DEVILED EGGS

9 hard boiled eggs
1/3 c. each green onions, bell pepper and celery
1 small jar pimento

1 can cream of mushroom soup
1 c. sour cream
1/2 c. chopped mushrooms
1 c. Cheddar cheese

Filling for Egg Whites:

2 Tbsp. mayonnaise
1 tsp. mustard
1/2 tsp. sugar

1/4 tsp. salt
Dash of pepper
1 tsp. sweet pickle juice

Boil until done 9 eggs. Mix egg yolks and the previous filling and put into egg whites. Place filled eggs into baking dish. Saute 1/3 cup each of green onions, bell pepper and celery. Pour over filled eggs. Then pour this mixture over the eggs, also 1 small jar pimento, cream of mushroom soup, 1 cup sour cream, 1/2 cup chopped mushrooms. Sprinkle top with grated cheese. Bake for 20 minutes in 350° oven.

James T. Gurley, Decatur Council

SCALLOPED EGGPLANT

1 large eggplant	2 tsp. salt
2 tsp. butter	Black pepper
1 green pepper,	1 c. buttered bread
chopped fine	crumbs
1 small onion, chopped fine	1 can tomatoes

Salt sliced eggplant; drain 15 to 30 minutes. Cook in water and drain. Mash. Add other ingredients except bread crumbs. Put in casserole dish; top with bread crumbs and bake 10 to 15 minutes. Serve.

Theresa Elkourie, Birmingham East Council

FRIED EGGPLANT ROUNDS

1 medium eggplant, peeled,	1 tsp. salt
sliced 1/4 inch thick	1/2 tsp. pepper
2 c. ice water	1/2 tsp. paprika
2 Tbsp. salt	1/2 c. flour
1 c. fine dry bread	2 eggs, beaten
crumbs	2 Tbsp. milk

Add 2 tablespoons salt to 2 cups water; soak eggplant for 30 minutes. Drain eggplant well. Combine bread crumbs, 1 teaspoon salt, pepper and paprika. Combine eggs and milk; strain. Season eggplant with salt and pepper; dredge in flour. Dip in egg mixture; roll in seasoned bread crumbs. Fry in deep fat at 375° until golden. Drain on absorbent paper.

Betty Parker, Montgomery Council

FRIED EGGPLANT

1 eggplant	Flour or meal
1 egg, beaten	

Peel eggplant; cut into thin slices. Soak eggplant for 10

minutes in salted water. Dip eggplant in egg; roll in flour. Fry in hot fat in skillet until browned. Drain on absorbent paper. Serve.

Joyce Reavis, Decatur Council

FRIED EGGPLANT STICKS

1 large or 2 small eggplants
3/4 c. fine bread crumbs
    or flour
6 Tbsp. grated Parmesan
    cheese

2 eggs
2 Tbsp. milk
Salt
Pepper

Peel and cut eggplant into strips (approximately 1/2 inch). Soak in water for approximately 15 minutes. Combine other ingredients (except crumbs or flour). Dip eggplant strips into mixture, then roll in crumbs (or flour). Fry in deep fat or oil (375°). Sprinkle with salt and pepper. Drain and serve.

Eleanor Gearhart, Montgomery Council

EGGPLANT QUICHE

1 small eggplant, pared
    and cubed (approx. 4 c.)
1/2 c. chopped bell
    pepper
3/4 c. chopped onion
4 Tbsp. butter
1 1/2 Tbsp. flour
1 (10 1/2 oz.) can cream
    of chicken soup

1 tsp. sugar
1/2 tsp. salt
1/4 tsp. black pepper
1/8 tsp. oregano
1 c. grated sharp cheese
4 eggs, beaten
1 tomato, peeled and chopped
2 frozen pie crusts
Parmesan cheese

Partially bake crusts in preheated 450° oven for 6 minutes. Cook eggplant covered in boiling, salted water for 8 to 10 minutes; drain well. Cook onion and pepper in butter until tender. Blend in flour, soup, salt, sugar, oregano and black pepper. Heat until bubbly. Remove from heat. Stir into beaten eggs. Fold in tomato, cheese and eggplant. Pour into pie shells. Top with Parmesan cheese (sprinkle on top); bake for 30 minutes at 350°. Freezes well.

Mary Norris, Birmingham Central Council

EGGPLANT PARMESAN

1 medium eggplant
2 eggs
1/4 c. water
1/3 c. all-purpose flour

1 c. fine dry bread crumbs
Cooking oil
1 recipe Italian Sauce
8 oz. sliced Mozzarella cheese
1/4 c. grated Parmesan cheese

Cut unpeeled eggplant crosswise into 1/4 inch slices. In medium bowl beat together eggs and water. Coat eggplant slices in flour; dip in egg mixture, then coat with bread crumbs. In large skillet cook eggplant slices in a small amount of hot oil till lightly browned, turning once. Drain on paper towel. In bottom of 10x6x2 inch baking dish spread 1/2 cup of the Italian Sauce. Layer half the eggplant slices, half the cheese and half the remaining Italian Sauce. Repeat layers. Sprinkle with Parmesan cheese. Bake uncovered in 350° oven for 20 to 30 minutes. Serves 6 to 8.

To make Italian Sauce: In large saucepan cook 1 medium onion, sliced, and 1 1/2 cups sliced fresh mushrooms in 2 tablespoons cooking or olive oil till tender, but not brown. Stir in one 8 ounce can undrained tomatoes, cut up, one 8 ounce can tomato sauce, 1/2 of a 6 ounce can (1/3 cup) tomato paste, 2 tablespoons dry red wine, 1 small clove garlic, minced, 2 teaspoons dried oregano, crushed, and 1/4 teaspoon salt. Bring to boil. Reduce heat; simmer, uncovered, 30 minutes. Makes 2 1/3 cups.

M. Hatcher, Montgomery Council

ENGLISH PEAS AND ALMONDS

24 oz. frozen English peas
1 stick butter

1/2 c. slivered almonds
Mushrooms (optional)
Salt

Saute peas, almonds and mushrooms in butter approximately 10 minutes until done. Salt and serve.

Carol York, Montgomery Council

COLLARD GREENS

1 1/2 to 2 lb. fresh
  collard greens or 2
  (10 oz.) pkg. frozen
  chopped collard greens

3 c. water
1 1/2 tsp. salt
1/2 c. diced salt pork

Check leaves of collards carefully; remove pulpy stems and discolored spots on leaves. Wash leaves thoroughly; drain well and chop. Combine collards, water and salt in a

1567-82

Dutch oven. Bring to a boil; reduce heat to low. Simmer, uncovered, for 25 minutes or until tender. Drain well. Saute salt pork in a skillet until golden brown; do not drain. Add collards, stirring lightly. Cook over low heat 5 minutes. Yield: 6 to 8 servings.

Billie Bays, Decatur Council

WILTED GREENS

4 or 5 slices bacon
2 Tbsp. butter
1/4 c. mild vinegar
1 tsp. grated onion

1 tsp. sugar
1 head lettuce, separated
Shredded cabbage
2 hard cooked eggs, sliced

Saute bacon until crisp; remove from pan. Drain; crumble into small pieces. Melt butter in skillet; stir in vinegar, bacon, onion and sugar. Combine lettuce and cabbage in bowl. Pour hot dressing over greens; toss to coat evenly. Arrange servings on warm plates. Garnish with eggs. Dandelion greens or young spinach leaves may be substituted for cabbage, if desired. Yield: 4 servings.

Joyce Reavis, Decatur Council

GREEN CHILI PIE

1 can green chilies,
  chopped

4 eggs, well beaten
1 (10 oz.) pkg. Cheddar
  cheese, grated

Lightly grease a 9 inch pie pan with butter. Spread chilies evenly over bottom of pan. Layer cheese evenly. Drizzle beaten eggs over cheese. Bake at 275° for 1 hour. Cut into bite sized pieces. To make a hotter pie, use 2 cans of green chilies or 1 or 2 finely chopped jalapeno peppers. Serve with crackers.

Jan Thomas, Birmingham East Council

BEER BATTER MUSHROOMS

Small fresh mushrooms
1/2 tsp. salt
2 Tbsp. butter
2/3 c. beer

1/4 c. flour
1/4 tsp. pepper
2 eggs

Wash and dry mushrooms. Heat oil in deep fat fryer (2 to 3 inches) at 375°. Beat egg whites until stiff. Combine melted butter, egg yolks and remaining ingredients; beat until smooth. Fold egg whites into mixture. Dip each mushroom into batter, letting excess drip into bowl. Fry a few mushrooms at a time in hot oil until golden brown.

Margie Popwell, Decatur Council

BAKED MUSHROOMS

Mushrooms
Butter
Onions

Wine
Monterey Jack cheese
Cheddar cheese

Saute mushrooms and onions in the butter and wine. Pour off excess liquid and place in baking dish alternating layers of mushrooms and cheeses. Bake in 350° oven until cheese is bubbly and brown.

Sandra Herndon, Birmingham South Council

MUSHROOMS BURGUNDY

1/3 c. butter
2 small green onions, chopped
1 clove garlic, crushed
1 lb. fresh mushrooms, sliced

1 c. burgundy wine
1/2 tsp. salt
Freshly ground pepper to taste
2 Tbsp. fresh parsley

Melt butter in saucepan and add chopped onion, garlic and mushrooms. Saute until tender; add other ingredients. Simmer until the wine is reduced by half. Great served with charcoal broiled steak. Serves 4.

Flo Thompson, Montgomery Council

FRENCH-FRIED MUSHROOMS

1 egg
1/2 c. milk
1/3 c. all-purpose flour
1/2 tsp. salt

20 medium size fresh mushrooms
1 c. corn flake crumbs
Vegetable oil
Seasoned salt

Combine egg and milk, beating well. Stir together flour and salt. Dredge mushrooms in flour mixture, and dip in egg mixture; roll in corn flake crumbs. Deep fry in hot oil (375°) until golden brown. Drain on paper towels and sprinkle with salt. Serve immediately. Yield: 20 appetizer servings.

Regina Cash, Anniston Council

MARINATED MUSHROOMS

2 (4 oz.) cans button
  mushrooms
1/2 tsp. salt
Pepper to taste
1 tsp. tarragon vinegar

1/2 bottle McCormick
  vegetable flakes
1 tsp. garlic powder
1/2 c. vegetable oil
2 Tbsp. lemon juice

Place mushrooms in bowl; add all the ingredients and mix well. Refrigerate at least 12 hours. Drain before serving. When using 16 ounces of mushrooms, I add 1/2 bottle Italian oil and herb dressing to regular recipe.

Anne Spragins, Birmingham East Council

PICKLED MUSHROOMS

2 lb. fresh mushrooms
  (small - stems may be
  cut out or left on)
1/2 c. lemon juice
1/2 c. white wine
  (vermouth is good)

1/2 c. olive oil
4 bay leaves
1 tsp. oregano
2 cloves crushed garlic
1/2 small onion, finely minced
1 Tbsp. salt
1 tsp. black pepper

Bring all ingredients to a boil, except the mushrooms. Wash mushrooms and put them into liquid, then simmer for 10 minutes with lid on. Serve cold. Serves 8 people and will keep a week to 10 days in a closed container in the refrigerator. They need to set overnight to really absorb the flavor. (One large can of asparagus may be substituted for the mushrooms. This makes a delicious cold salad plate.)

Aileen Hardin, Riverchase Council

MUSHROOMS STUFFED WITH CRABMEAT

1/2 lb. cooked King
  crabmeat (thawed and
  drained if frozen),
  chopped
1/4 c. minced pimiento
1/4 c. minced celery

1/4 c. mayonnaise
1 Tbsp. snipped fresh chives
1/3 c. fresh lemon juice
30 mushrooms, 1 1/4 to
  1 1/2 inches in diameter

In a bowl combine well the crabmeat, the pimiento, the celery, the mayonnaise, the chives, some of the lemon juice to taste, and salt and pepper to taste and chill the mixture, covered, for at least 2 hours or overnight. Remove the stems from the mushrooms carefully, reserving them for another use. Wipe the caps with a damp cloth, and brush them all over with the remaining lemon juice. Mound about 1 tablespoon of the crabmeat mixture in each mushroom. The mushrooms may be assembled 2 hours in advance and stored, covered and chilled. Arrange the mushrooms on a serving tray and serve them at room temperature. Makes 30 hors d'oeuvres.

Katherine Creamer, Mobile Council

STUFFED MUSHROOMS

1 lb. medium or large
  mushrooms
Sausage (amount equal
  to about 2 patties
1/4 c. finely chopped green
  onions (include some of
  the tops)

1/4 c. finely chopped celery
1/4 c. finely chopped
  mushroom stems
1/4 c. seasoned bread crumbs
  finely crumbled

Remove stems from mushrooms; wash caps and place on paper towel to dry. While caps are drying, fry sausage, stirring frequently, so sausage will be finely crumbled. Remove sausage and saute onions and celery in drippings. When onions and celery are clear (do not let them brown), remove from pan and saute chopped mushroom stems. Combine all cooked ingredients in a bowl with bread crumbs. Brush each mushroom cap inside and out with olive oil and then stuff firmly with mixture. Place stuffed mushrooms in a shallow greased baking dish and bake for 25 minutes at 350°.
(For variety, you may wish to add a pinch of grated Parmesan cheese on top of each stuffed mushroom.)

William M. Johnson, Jr.,
Birmingham Central Council

MUSHROOM RICE

3/4 stick margarine
1 c. raw rice (regular)
1 can onion soup

1 can beef bouillon soup
1 can Dawn mushroom
  steak sauce

Use part of margarine to grease casserole dish. Place all ingredients in dish and bake uncovered for 1 hour at 350°.

Cordelia Grigsby, Riverchase Council

MUSHROOMS AND ZUCCHINI

1/4 c. (1/2 stick)
  butter or margarine
3/4 c. chopped onion
1/4 lb. mushrooms,
  sliced, or 14 oz. can
  sliced mushrooms,
  drained

1 zucchini, shredded
  (do not peel)
1/4 c. chopped parsley
1/2 tsp. dried leaf basil
1 tsp. salt
1/8 tsp. pepper

In a medium saucepan melt the butter; add the onion and cook until tender. Add the remaining ingredients; cook about 5 minutes, until the mushrooms and zucchini are tender. Makes 4 servings.

Wanda Lynch, Montgomery Council

FRIED ONION RINGS

4 to 5 large onions
1 egg
1 c. milk
1 c. flour

1 tsp. garlic and
  parsley salt
1 c. Wesson oil

Slice onions and separate into rings. Make a batter of the beaten egg and milk. Sift together flour and seasoned salt; dip onions in flour and then in batter. Drop onion rings into hot Wesson oil and cook until golden brown. Serve hot.

M. Hopkins, Huntsville Council

OKRA FRITTERS

1 c. thinly sliced okra
1/2 tsp. salt
1/3 c. chopped tomatoes
1/4 c. all-purpose flour

1/4 c. corn meal
1/2 tsp. curry powder
1 egg, beaten
1/4 tsp. pepper

Combine all ingredients; stir well. Drop by tablespoons into hot oil; cook until golden brown, turning once.

Glenda Hassey, Montgomery Council

OKRA HASH

Okra
1 ripe tomato
1 green tomato

Onion
Potatoes, cut in small cubes
Corn meal (enough to cover)

Slice okra. Cube tomatoes, chop onion and cube

686

potatoes. Mix together and cover in corn meal. Place in skillet with cooking oil and fry long enough to heat thoroughly and only slightly brown. Remove from skillet and place in a covered casserole dish and place in 350° oven and steam for 30 minutes, so that potatoes will be completely done.

Linda S. Vick, Birmingham South Council

GRANNY GREENES' OKRA AND TOMATO
1930'S DEPRESSION DISH

2 large onions, chopped
2 lb. fresh okra, cut up

5 or 6 large tomatoes,
cut up

Saute chopped onions and add the cut okra. Cook okra and onions until okra seems well blended (about 10 minutes). Add tomatoes; add more or less, according to desired amount, or two 28 ounce cans Hunt's tomatoes. Stir in the tomatoes and simmer until okra is done. A very small amount of plain flour may be added for extra thickness if desired. Either flour okra before adding to onions or add flour while okra and tomatoes are simmering. Serve with pone of hot corn bread.

Jim Chaffin, Tuscaloosa Council

FRENCH FRIED OKRA

Cut into 1/4 inch slices about 12 (more or less) pods of okra. Do not use too young pods or too old; use about 4 inch long pods. Beat 1 egg with 1/2 cup milk. In meantime, bring your cooking oil to hot temperature (as for French fried potatoes). Sift about 1 cup flour in pan. Dip 5 or 6 slices at a time in milk and egg mixture. Drop in flour and roll, then drop into hot oil. Work fast and put most or all in at once. Fry till light brown. Drain on paper towel; salt. Serve warm.

Marcia Freeman, Birmingham East Council

ONION-CHIP PATTIES

1 1/2 c. finely chopped
  onions
2 c. crushed potato chips
2 eggs
1/2 tsp. oregano

1/4 tsp. chervil
1/4 tsp. celery salt
1/8 tsp. garlic powder
2 Tbsp. chopped parsley
2 Tbsp. vegetable oil

Combine onion, potato chips, eggs and seasonings, blending well. Allow to stand 10 to 15 minutes. Shape into patties about 2 inches in diameter. Heat oil in skillet over medium heat. Saute onion. Chop patties in hot oil until golden brown on each side.

Frances Crenshaw, Birmingham East Council

NEW YEAR'S BLACK-EYED PEAS

2 c. dried black-eyed peas	2 tsp. butter or margarine
1/2 lb. ham	1/2 to 1 tsp. Italian
2 qt. water	seasoning
1 c. uncooked regular rice	1 tsp. sugar
1 c. chopped onion	1 1/2 to 2 tsp. salt
1 c. chopped celery	1/4 tsp. pepper

Sort and wash peas; place in a heavy saucepan. Cover with water and bring to a boil; cook 2 minutes. Remove from heat; cover and let soak 1 hour. Drain. Combine ham and 2 quarts water in a large Dutch oven; bring to a boil. Reduce heat; cover and simmer 15 minutes. Add peas; bring to a boil. Reduce heat; cover and simmer 45 minutes. Add remaining ingredients; bring to a boil. Reduce heat; cover and simmer an additional 30 minutes or until black-eyed peas are done. Remove ham; cut into small pieces. Stir ham into pea mixture. Yield: 10 to 12 servings.

Linda Mitchell, Decatur Council

STRIKE SURVIVAL

1 c. dried black-eyed peas, cooked	1/3 c. onions, finely chopped
	1 Tbsp. bread crumbs
2 eggs	1 Tbsp. flour

Mash peas and eggs well until fluffy; add other ingredients. Shape into croquettes and fry in deep fat until brown.

Louise Berrey, Montgomery Council

POT LIKKER

Into 3 quarts of cold water put a 1/2 pound piece of salt pork and place on fire to boil for 45 minutes. Wash young turnip greens in several waters and clean them well. Put them into the pot along with the pork and let boil for another hour. Drain the water from the greens and meat; chop the greens rather fine and season well with salt and pepper. Place the greens on a hot dish and on top arrange slices of the pork; pour over the greens and meat about 1 1/2 cups of the water in which the greens were cooked (pot likker). Corn Meal Dodgers are frequently served along with this dish and are arranged around the greens.

Corn Meal Dodger for Pot Likker:

1/2 pt. white corn meal	2 Tbsp. melted butter
1/2 tsp. salt	or other shortening
	Cold water

Add salt to corn meal and stir in the melted butter. Add sufficient cold water so dough will hold shape. Mold dough into biscuit size pieces and drop into boiling pot likker. Cook in closely covered pot for 20 minutes. Serve garnished with the greens from the "pot likker".

Mary Wilkerson, Mobile Council

AU GRATIN POTATOES

1 stick butter	Cheddar cheese (mild)
1 onion	6-8 potatoes
2 c. milk	Flour
American sliced cheese	

Heat oven to 350° to 375°. Slice potatoes 1/8 inch wide lengthwise. Place 1 layer of potatoes in clear casserole dish. Sprinkle 1 large tablespoon flour in layer of potatoes. Take 5 or 6 slices of butter on first layer of potatoes. Sprinkle onions. Slice American cheese; put on top of potatoes (approximately 1 1/2 slices). Then fill in open spaces with Cheddar cheese. Lay second layer of potatoes and repeat process. When complete, fill the dish 1/2 full with milk, cover and put in oven for approximately 1 1/2 hours. Serves 6.

Cindy Morris, Montgomery Council

POTATOES AU GRATIN

3 lb. potatoes	3 oz. grated cheese
1 1/2 c. milk	1 stick butter or margarine

Boil potatoes in skin, not soft; cool and peel. Grate potatoes. Put butter and milk in saucepan; add 1/2 of cheese and heat. Salt and pepper potatoes; pour mixture over potatoes. Put remaining cheese on top and bake in 350° oven from 45 minutes to an hour.

Auretha Karrh, Decatur Council

LEFTOVER POTATO PATTY FRY

Leftover mashed potatoes
1/3 c. chopped onion
1/2 tsp. seasoned salt
1/2 tsp. pepper
1/2 tsp. parsley flakes
1/3 c. flour
1/4 c. margarine or
    bacon grease

    Combine mashed potatoes, onion, salt, pepper and parsley flakes. Shape into patties and coat both sides in flour. Melt margarine in skillet over medium high heat. Brown patties in margarine on both sides. Serve for breakfast with scrambled eggs.

        Julie Baeder, Huntsville Council

POTATOES AND GRAVY

    Cover potatoes with water; bring to boil. Pour water off and cover with water a second time and salt to taste; cook until tender. Make flour and milk paste and pour into potatoes and water. Let simmer for about 3 minutes and add margarine.

        Billie Bays, Decatur Council

BAKED STUFFED POTATOES

8 baking potatoes
1 stick butter
Milk
1 Tbsp. grated onion
Cheddar cheese slices
Salt and pepper

    Bake the potatoes for 1 hour at 350° until you press them and they are soft. Cut a slice off the top (do not halve) and scoop out the inside with a spoon and reserve the shells. Put the potato pulp in an electric beater. Add the butter, onion and enough milk to make mixture the consistency of mashed potatoes. Add salt and pepper to taste. Fill the potato shells with mixture. Bake for 15 minutes at 350°. Put a cheese slice on top of each one and bake for 15 minutes more.

        Flo Thompson, Montgomery Council

BUTTERED POTATO WEDGES (MICROWAVE)

1 c. butter or oleo
1/8 tsp. pepper
2 lb. baking potatoes
3 Tbsp. grated Parmesan cheese
3/4 c. cut up green onions
    in 1/2 to 3/4 inch pieces

    Place butter in 1 cup measuring cup; microwave at high 45 to 60 seconds or until melted. Stir in pepper. Cut

690

each potato into quarters. Arrange potato wedges on 12 inch plate or large microwave baking sheet. Brush with half of butter. Cover with plastic wrap. Microwave at high 5 minutes; rearrange potatoes and brush with remaining butter. Sprinkle with cheese and green onion; cover. Microwave at high 7 to 13 minutes or until potatoes are just fork tender. Let stand, covered, 5 to 6 minutes.

Advance preparation: Cover with foil during standing time. Potatoes will hold temperature for 30 minutes before serving when covered with foil. Cook on high 2 medium potatoes, sliced 1/8 to 1/4 inch thick, for 3 minutes*, then add 1 to 3 tablespoons butter, 1/2 medium onion, sliced 1/4 to 3/8 inch thick and broken into rings, 3 1/2 to 4 1/2 minutes.

*Stir after 1 1/2 minutes to prevent sticking.

Terry Dillard, Riverchase Council

TWICE BAKED POTATOES

4 large baked potatoes	1 1/2 c. shredded sharp
2 Tbsp. milk	natural Cheddar cheese
1/4 c. margarine	1/2 tsp. salt
4 crisply cooked bacon	Dash of pepper
slices, crumbled	2 Tbsp. chopped chives

Slice each potato in half lengthwise; scoop out centers to form a shell. Mash potatoes; combine with 1 cup cheese, milk, margarine and seasonings. Beat until fluffy. If potatoes are too dry, beat in small amounts of additional milk. Stir in 1 tablespoon chives and half of bacon. Fill shells. Bake at 350° for 20 minutes. Toss remaining cheese, chives and bacon together; sprinkle over potatoes. Continue baking 10 minutes. Serves 8.

June Crowe, Anniston Council

TWICE-BAKED POTATOES

Cut baked potatoes in halves; scoop out potato. Whip until fluffy with butter, milk, salt and pepper. Mound back into shells. Sprinkle with paprika or grated cheese. Bake at 400° for 20 to 25 minutes.

Lynn Gray, Montgomery Council

CHEESE POTATOES

5 large potatoes, sliced thin
1 medium onion, chopped
5 slices bacon, cooked

1 c. Cheddar cheese
1 stick butter
Salt and pepper

Spray 13x9 inch Pyrex dish with Pam. Arrange potatoes; add onion. Crumble bacon. Sprinkle with cheese; top with sliced butter. Salt and pepper. Cover with foil and bake 45 minutes to 1 hour or until done at 350°.

Susie Conway, Birmingham East Council
Miriam Stokes, Montgomery Council

GLORIFIED POTATOES

5 medium potatoes, cooked with skins
2 medium onions, diced
3 bell peppers, diced large
2 sticks margarine

1 small can button mushrooms
1 medium jar pimento
1/2 c. sharp cheese, cut in 1 inch pieces

Saute onions and peppers in butter until tender; add 1/4 cup flour (enough to make a good paste for gravy). Then add 1 1/2 cups milk. Mix diced potatoes into sauce in baking dish. Add mushrooms and cheese. Arrange for pretty appearance. Bake at 350° until bubbly.

Camille Meggs, Tuscaloosa Council

BAKED HASH BROWN POTATOES

2 lb. frozen hash browns
1 tsp. salt
1 tsp. pepper
1 can cream of chicken soup
1 small onion

1 c. sour cream
1 (8 oz.) block Cheddar cheese
1 1/2 c. crushed corn flakes
1 stick margarine

Put hash browns in a 9x13 inch casserole dish; sprinkle salt and pepper on potatoes. Pour can of soup on potatoes. Saute chopped onions in margarine and pour onto potato mixture and stir in well. Spread sour cream on top. Grate cheese and sprinkle on top. Sprinkle corn flake crumbs over top; bake 1 hour 15 minutes at 300°.

Barbara S. Mason, Mobile Council

JALAPENO POTATOES

5-6 medium Irish potatoes
1 small bell pepper,
  chopped
1 small can pimientos
Salt and pepper to taste
1/2 stick butter

1 1/2 Tbsp. flour
1 1/4 c. milk
2 c. shredded cheese
1 Tbsp. parsley
1 tsp. garlic
1 jalapeno pepper, chopped
  (or to taste)

Prepare potatoes as for potato salad. Pour into oblong baking dish. In medium saucepan saute bell and jalapeno peppers in butter until almost tender. Add flour and all other ingredients except cheese; stir until mixture thickens slightly and pour over potatoes. Sprinkle cheese evenly over potatoes; bake 20-30 minutes at 375°. If potatoes become too dry, additional small amounts of milk may be added. This is a never-fail recipe and always a favorite!

Jan Williams, Birmingham South Council

POTATO KUGEL

6 to 8 large potatoes
1/4 small onion
1 c. milk

3 eggs, well beaten
6 Tbsp. melted butter
2 tsp. salt

Pare and cut into French fry size. Combine with remaining ingredients. Mix well and pour into shallow baking pan; bake uncovered approximately 1 hour 15 minutes in 350° oven.

Mamie E. Smith, Mobile Council

MICROWAVE SCALLOPED POTATOES

4 medium potatoes
1 Tbsp. all-purpose flour
1 tsp. salt

1/4 c. chopped onions
1 1/2 c. sweet milk
1/2 stick butter or margarine

Peel and thinly slice potatoes; arrange in 3 quart glass casserole. Sprinkle on flour, salt and chopped onion. Pour milk over all. Dot with butter or margarine. Cover with glass lid or plastic wrap. Microwave on high for 10 minutes. Stir. Recover, and continue cooking on high for 8 to 10 minutes or until potatoes are tender. Let stand. If necessary, reheat potatoes, covered, or reheat for 3 to 4 minutes, or until hot.

Nancy Wyatt, Tuscaloosa Council

SCALLOPED POTATOES

1 can Campbell's cream	1/2 c. thinly sliced onion
of celery soup	1 c. shredded sharp
1/3 c. milk	Cheddar cheese
4 c. thinly sliced potatoes	1 Tbsp. butter or margarine

Blend soup, milk, dash of pepper. In buttered 1 1/2 quart casserole, arrange alternate layers of potatoes, onions, soup mixture and cheese. Dot top with butter; sprinkle with paprika. Cover; bake at 375° F. for 1 hour. Uncover; bake 15 minutes more or until done. Makes about 4 cups.

Jane Courington, Montgomery Council

SCALLOPED POTATOES SUPREME

8 medium Irish potatoes	1/8 tsp. pepper
1/4 c. chopped green	1 can cream of mushroom soup
pepper	1 c. milk
2 tsp. salt	1/4 c. chopped onion

Place alternate layers of thinly sliced potatoes, green pepper and onion in buttered baking dish. Season each layer with salt and pepper. Mix soup and milk; pour over potatoes and bake 1 1/2 hours at 350°.

Marcella James, Tri-Cities Council

SOUR CREAM AND CREAM CHEESE POTATOES

8 large potatoes	1 (8 oz.) c. sour cream
1 (8 oz.) pkg. cream	Salt
cheese	

Cook potatoes; drain and add cream cheese and sour cream. Mix well; add salt to taste. If mixture is too thick, add hot water, never milk or cream. Put in baking dish. Dot with butter and seasoning if desired. Bake at 350° for 30 or 35 minutes until slightly brown on top. This may be prepared a day before and kept in refrigerator.

Mrs. R.F. Holliday, Montgomery Council

TASTY STUFFED POTATOES

1 (1 lb.) box instant
  mashed potatoes
1 can smoked oysters,
  chopped
1 carton French onion dip

6 slices bacon, broiled
  and crumbled
Parsley to taste
American cheese slices

Prepare instant potatoes as directed on box. Pour potatoes into large mixing bowl. Add smoked oysters, French onion dip, bacon crumbles and parsley. Put in potato shells; top with cheese and heat until melted. Freezes well, but not to be reheated. Make sure mixture isn't dry before freezing.

Mrs. Michael J. Maher,
Birmingham Central Council

OVEN-FRIED POTATOES

3 medium potatoes
1/4 c. vegetable oil
1 Tbsp. grated Parmesan
  cheese

1/2 tsp. salt
1/4 tsp. garlic powder
1/4 tsp. paprika
1/4 tsp. pepper

Scrub potatoes and cut each into 1/8 inch wedges. Place wedges, slightly overlapping, in a single layer in a 13x9x2 inch baking pan. Combine remaining ingredients, stirring well. Brush potatoes with half of oil mixture; bake uncovered at 375° for 45 minutes, basting occasionally with remaining seasoned oil mixture. Yield: 4 to 6 servings.

Regina Cash, Anniston Council

SOUTHERN-FRIED POTATOES

1 small onion, chopped
1/2 c. vegetable oil
1/2 tsp. salt
1/8 tsp. pepper

3 medium potatoes, peeled
  and cut into 1 1/2 inch
  cubes

Saute onion in oil in a heavy 10 inch cast-iron skillet until transparent; add potatoes. Fry until potatoes are tender and golden, turning as necessary. Sprinkle with salt and pepper. Yield: 4 servings.

Regina Cash, Anniston Council

LEMONY NEW POTATOES

2 lb. new potatoes
2 Tbsp. lemon juice
2 Tbsp. chopped parsley

2 Tbsp. butter or margarine, melted
1 3/4 tsp. grated lemon rind

Wash potatoes; peel a thin strip around center. Cook potatoes, covered, in boiling, salted water 10 minutes. Add lemon juice, and cook an additinal 5 to 10 minutes or until tender; drain.

Combine butter, parsley and rind; spoon over hot potatoes, and stir gently until coated. Yield: 6 to 8 servings.

Regina Cash, Anniston Council

CANDIED SWEET POTATOES

1 c. Karo dark corn syrup
1/2 c. firmly packed
  dark brown sugar

2 Tbsp. Mazola margarine
12 medium sweet potatoes, cooked, peeled and halved lengthwise

Bring first 3 ingredients to boil; reduce heat and simmer 5 minutes. Pour half into shallow baking dish; add potatoes. Top with remaining syrup. Bake at 350°, basting often, for 20 minutes. Makes 12 servings.

Kitty Logan, Anniston Council

SWEET POTATO CROQUETTES

4 medium sweet potatoes
1 c. bread crumbs
1 egg

1 Tbsp. sugar
Dash of salt
Oil, enough to fry

Steam potatoes or boil in their jackets until tender. Peel, mash and add egg yolk, salt, sugar and 1/2 bread crumbs. Beat white of egg until stiff; stir into mixture. Form croquettes. Roll in bread crumbs and fry slowly in oil. Turn and brown on both sides. Serves 6.

"Pot" Harris, Tuscaloosa Council

SWEET POTATO BALLS

1 c. cooked yams
1/4 c. butter
3/4 c. brown sugar
2 Tbsp. milk
1/4 tsp. salt

1/2 tsp. grated lemon peel
8 to 10 large marshmallows
1/2 c. crushed corn flakes
1/2 c. chopped pecans

696

Combine all ingredients except corn flakes and marshmallows. Take approximately 1/4 cup potato mixture and form around marshmallows, making a ball. Roll in crushed corn flakes. Cook on buttered dish in warm oven until marshmallows "ooze". You can fix these ahead of time and freeze until needed. It's great for Thanksgiving and Christmas.

Bobbie Bowles, Montgomery Council

ORANGE SWEET POTATOES

6 large sweet potatoes	3/4 c. orange juice
1/2 lb. butter	1 c. chopped pecans
1 1/2 c. sugar	1 bag miniature marshmallows

Peel and slice potatoes; cook until tender and drain. Whip until fluffy. Add other ingredients, reserving a few marshmallows for topping. Put in 2 quart casserole and top with marshmallows. Bake at 350° until bubbly and marshmallows browned. May be made ahead and refrigerated until time to bake and serve. Serves 8. May use canned sweet potatoes.

Edgar McFarlen, Huntsville Council

SWEET POTATO CASSEROLE

3 c. cooked sweet potatoes	2 eggs, beaten
3/4 c. sugar	1 tsp. vanilla
1/2 c. butter	1/3 c. Pet milk

Topping:

1 box light brown sugar	1 c. chopped pecans
1/2 c. self-rising flour	1/3 c. melted butter

Mix first 6 ingredients together and put in casserole dish. Mix Topping ingredients till crumbly and put on top of sweet potato mixture. May be too much topping. This can be saved until later. Store in jar in refrigerator. Bake 25 to 30 minutes at 325°.

Eloise Bennett, Decatur Council

SWEET POTATO SOUFFLE

3 c. cooked sweet potatoes	2 eggs
1 c. sugar	1/3 c. milk
1 stick oleo	1 tsp. vanilla flavoring

Mix oleo until creamy. Add remaining ingredients; mix well. Place in 9x13 inch pan.

Topping:

1 c. brown sugar	1/3 c. melted oleo
1/2 c. plain flour	1 c. pecans

Mix and sprinkle over sweet potato mixture and bake at 325° for 30 to 35 minutes.

Martha Hatcher, Montgomery Council

SWEET POTATO PUFFS

3 or 4 medium to large	1 pkg. grated coconut
baked sweet potatoes	1 pkg. large marshmallows
3/4 stick margarine	1/4 tsp. vanilla
3/4 c. sugar	Chopped nuts (optional)

While potatoes are still hot, peel and mash with margarine. Add sugar, vanilla and nuts. Mix well. Wetting hands with cold water, roll mixture around marshmallow and roll in coconut. Bake at about 400° just long enough to brown coconut. Serve hot.

Christine Johnson, Birmingham West Council

ARMENIAN RICE

1 stick butter	2 cans beef consomme
1 c. rice	Optional: 1 small jar
1 medium onion	mushrooms

Brown rice in butter; add onion. Put consomme in covered Pyrex dish, then add the other ingredients. Bake at 350° for 1 hour. Serves 6 to 8. Halve ingredients to serve 2 to 4. Goes well with steak.

Mrs. Sharon Davis, Montgomery Council

GREEN RICE

2 Tbsp. chopped onion	1/2 c. finely chopped parsley
1/4 tsp. minced garlic	1 1/4 c. milk
(optional)	3 eggs, slightly beaten
2 Tbsp. butter	1 c. grated Cheddar
2 c. cooked rice	cheese

Saute onion and garlic in butter; add rice, parsley and

milk. Blend in beaten eggs and cheese. Pour into buttered casserole and bake in pan of hot water at 350° for 40 minutes or until firm.

Jeannie Riddles, Riverchase Council

RICE DRESSING OR DIRTY RICE

1 lb. ground meat
1 c. rice
1 can cream of mushroom
  soup
1 can onion soup
1 dash of red pepper
1 dash of salt

1 stalk celery, diced
1/4 bell pepper
2 pods of garlic, chopped
  fine, or garlic flakes
1/4 c. onion tops (green
  onions)
1/4 c. parsley or parsley
  flakes

Mix all together. Pour in a 2 quart covered dish and cook at 350° for 1 hour.

Bertha Ross, Decatur Council

RICE LOAF (WITH MUSHROOM SAUCE)

2 c. cooked rice
1 1/2 c. grated cheese
1/4 c. melted oleo
1 c. hot milk
3 eggs, beaten
1/2 c. dried bread crumbs
1 Tbsp. chopped onion

1 Tbsp. chopped green
  pepper
1 Tbsp. chopped pimento
1 Tbsp. chopped parsley
1/2 tsp. salt
1 can cream of mushroom
  soup

Combine all ingredients except mushroom soup. Put mixture in greased baking pan; bake at 350° for 45 minutes. Heat undiluted cream of mushroom soup to use as sauce over the Rice Loaf. Serves 8-10.

Elaine Rindt, Riverchase Council

SPANISH RICE

3/4 c. rice, partially cooked
1/2 c. chopped celery
1/2 c. chopped bell pepper

1/4 c. chopped onion
1 small jar pimento
1 c. chicken stock or bouillon

Brown celery, onion and pepper in butter. Combine with cooked rice, chicken stock and pimento in casserole dish and bake at 350° about 30 minutes.

Miriam Stokes, Montgomery Council

SPANISH RICE

1 can Spanish rice
1 small onion, chopped
  up
1/2 c. bell pepper,
  chopped up

Spices (nutmeg or allspice)
  (a dash)
1 tsp. sugar
1 Tbsp. vinegar
1 small can tomato sauce

Cook in 300° or 350° oven for about 45 minutes.

Margaret Hare, Anniston Council

WINE RICE

1 1/2 c. Uncle Ben's long
  grain rice, uncooked
6 Tbsp. butter
3/4 c. onion, chopped fine
2 c. beef or chicken
  stock (hot)

3/4 c. dry white wine
1 tsp. curry powder
1/8 tsp. mace
1/4 tsp. paprika
Salt and pepper to taste
2 Tbsp. grated Parmesan
  cheese

Saute onion in 4 tablespoons butter until tender. Sprinkle with paprika and small amount of salt and freshly ground pepper; add 2 more tablespoons butter and stir in uncooked rice. Stir and cook rice until golden. Add other ingredients except Parmesan cheese. Cover tightly and bake at 375° F. for 50 to 60 minutes or until rice is done. Top with Parmesan cheese and bake 3 minutes or run under broiler.

Betty Parker, Montgomery Council

SAUERKRAUT BALLS

8 slices bacon
1/2 c. onion, finely
  chopped
1/2 c. mashed potatoes*
1 tsp. parsley flakes
2 tsp. caraway seeds
2 eggs, beaten

1 clove garlic, finely
  chopped
1 (16 oz.) can sauerkraut,
  drained
1 1/2 c. Special K cereal,
  crushed
Oil

*Can use instant potatoes.

Fry bacon in large skillet until crisp; drain and crumble. Pour off all but 2 teaspoons fat. Saute onion and garlic until tender; stir in bacon, sauerkraut, potatoes and parsley. Drop by rounded teaspoonfuls onto waxed paper lined baking sheet and form into balls. Cover with waxed paper lined baking sheet and form into balls. Cover with waxed paper and refrigerate until firm. Dip sauerkraut balls into mixture of cereal and caraway seed. Fry balls until golden brown in oil heated to 375°. Drain on paper towel.

Beverley Piatkowski, Riverchase Council

SPINACH PIE

1 box frozen spinach	Pepper to taste
2 1/4 c. seasoned bread crumbs	1 c. grated Parmesan cheese
Salt to taste	3 eggs

Boil spinach until done; drain well. In mixing bowl combine spinach, bread crumbs, salt and pepper to taste and grated cheese. In separate bowl beat eggs and add to other ingredients. Mix well (with hands). Heat small amount of oil in skillet and pour mixture in and flatten out to cover bottom. Fry until golden, then place a plate on top of skillet to cover top. Remove from heat and flip to other side and cook until golden. Place on flat dish; cut into pie pieces and serve.

Marian R. D'Anna, Future Pioneer,
Birmingham East Council

HELEN CRIK'S SPINACH

3 pkg. frozen chopped spinach	1 regular size container sour cream
1 pkg. Lipton dry onion soup	Buttered bread crumbs

Cook spinach; don't drain. Add Lipton dry onion soup mix; stir and let stand at least an hour; longer is better. Drain well. Mix with sour cream; top with buttered bread crumbs. Bake at 350° till hot.

Anne Spragins, Birmingham East Council

CREAMED SPINACH (MICROWAVE STYLE)

1 (10 oz.) pkg. chopped spinach (unfrozen)	1 (3 oz.) pkg. cream cheese
1/4 c. margarine	1/2 tsp. salt
	1/4 c. Parmesan cheese

Press extra moisture out of spinach while still in box. Mix cream cheese, margarine and spinach together and microwave for 4 minutes at 70% power, covered with plastic wrap.

Dina Johnson, Birmingham South Council

BAKED SQUASH

2 pkg. frozen crookneck
  squash (or fresh)
2 Tbsp. butter or
  margarine

1 c. dairy sour cream
1/2 c. finely chopped onion
1/2 tsp. salt
1/4 tsp. pepper

Cook squash (do not cook until done). Drain off water and mash squash. Add remaining ingredients and put into an ungreased 1 quart casserole. Sprinkle with bread crumbs or crumbled cheese crackers, if desired. Bake at 400° for 30 minutes. Makes 6-8 servings.

Sara Lindsey, Riverchase Council

BAKED SQUASH

1 to 1 1/4 lb. squash
1 medium onion, chopped
2 slices bread, soaked in
  milk
1 egg, beaten slightly

2 to 3 Tbsp. butter
1 tsp. salt
Dash of pepper
1 1/2 c. grated cheese
  (sharp)

Cook squash until tender; drain. Mash with butter, salt and pepper. Add slightly beaten egg, bread and onion; mix well. Pour half mixture in casserole dish; top with half of cheese. Add remaining mixture and top with remaining cheese. Bake at 350° for 30 minutes.

Eloise Bennett, Decatur Council

BAKED ACORN SQUASH

Use 2 acorn squash. Mix all together:

3 Tbsp. brown sugar
2 Tbsp. butter
3 Tbsp. applesauce

1 Tbsp. chopped pecans
1/4 tsp. cinnamon

Wash. Pierce squash with a fork. Place on paper towel in microwave oven. Cook 8 minutes on high power. Turn halfway through cooking time. Cut in half; remove seeds. Fill each cavity with ingredients. Return to cook for 4 minutes on high power. Turn halfway through cooking time. Yield: 4 servings.

Linda L. Unger, Riverchase Council

ACORN SQUASH (MICROWAVE)

Use high power, 1/2 squash 5 to 8 minutes, 1 squash 8 1/2 to 11 1/2 minutes, 2 squash 13 to 16 minutes.

Halve 1 1/2 pound acorn squash lengthwise; scoop out seeds. Fit squash halves together again, or cover each with plastic wrap. Microwave for 1/2 the time. Turn over whole squash or rotate and rearrange halves. Microwave remaining time. Place 1 tablespoon butter and 1 tablespoon brown sugar in each squash half before standing. Sprinkle with chopped nuts, if desired. Cover with plastic wrap. Let stand 5 to 10 minutes.

Terry Dillard, Riverchase Council

SQUASH CROQUETTES

5 lb. squash	2 oz. margarine
1 qt. bread crumbs	Salt and white pepper to taste
4 1/2 oz. onions	Accent to taste
3 large eggs	1 pt. corn bread crumbs

Steam squash until well done. Mash fine; chop or grind onion fine. Saute in margarine until tender. Mix all ingredients together. Chill overnight or until very cold. Form into oblong croquettes and roll in soft bread crumbs. Cook in deep fat until brown.

Viola Vines, Huntsville Council

SQUASH CROQUETTES

1 small onion, cut up	2 Tbsp. butter
Salt to taste	1/2 c. grated cheese
4 or 5 yellow squash, cut up	1 c. cracker crumbs
1 egg, beaten	

Cook onion and squash in small amount of salted water; drain and mash. Add egg, butter, cheese and 1/2 the cracker crumbs. Mix well. Shape into balls and roll in remaining cracker crumbs. Fry in deep fat.

Mrs. John Pilling, Decatur Council

SQUASH HUSHPUPPIES

2 c. ground corn meal (plain)	1 tsp. baking powder
1 Tbsp. flour	1 Tbsp. salt
1 tsp. soda	2 eggs
1 1/2 to 2 c. buttermilk	6 Tbsp. instant minced onions
	2 c. grated yellow squash

1567-82

Mix dry ingredients; add onion, buttermilk and eggs. Mix well. Stir in squash. Drop by spoonfuls into deep hot grease. Drain on brown paper or paper towels. For best results, mix and let stand for a few minutes. Do not stir again before dropping into hot grease. Good with seafood, vegetables and soup.

Bobby Blair, Birmingham East Council

SAUSAGE STUFFED SQUASH

6 medium size yellow
  squash
1/2 lb. bulk pork sausage
1/4 c. finely chopped onion

1/2 c. herb seasoned stuffing
1/4 tsp. salt
2 1/2 Tbsp. grated Parmesan
  cheese

Wash squash thoroughly; cook in boiling, salted water to cover 8 to 10 minutes, or until tender but still firm. Drain and cool slightly; trim off stems. Cut squash in halves lengthwise; remove and reserve pulp, leaving a firm shell.

Cook sausage and onion in a skillet over medium heat until sausage is browned, stirring to crumble. Remove from heat and drain off pan drippings. Stir in squash pulp, herb seasoned stuffing and salt. Place squash shells in a 13x9x2 inch baking dish. Spoon sausage mixture into shells; sprinkle with Parmesan cheese; bake at 350° for 30 minutes or until lightly browned. Yield: 6 servings.

Mary C. Martin, Birmingham East Council

YUMMY SQUASH

2 c. cooked squash
  (yellow crookneck)
1 Tbsp. sugar
1 egg

1 Tbsp. margarine
Salt and pepper to taste
1 c. corn bread crumbs
1/2 can French fried onions

Mix all together. Pour into baking dish. Pour remaining onions on top and bake for 30 minutes at 350°.

Kay Atkisson, Montgomery Council

SQUASH DELIGHT

1 qt. squash
1 tsp. sugar
1/2 c. chopped onions
1/4 c. chopped green
  peppers

2 eggs, beaten
1 c. herb seasoned stuffing mix
1 can creamy chicken and
  mushroom soup

1/2 c. chopped nuts or
  slivered almonds
1/2 c. mayonnaise
1/2 c. grated cheese

1/2 stick margarine
Salt and pepper to taste
1/2 can evaporated milk

Cook onions and pepper in butter. Cook squash and drain. Mix cheese in until melted. Mix sugar, eggs, mayonnaise, nuts, salt, pepper, onions, stuffing mix, soup and milk. Pour into casserole, alternating mixture with stuffing mix; top with cheese. Bake in 400° oven for 35 to 40 minutes or until cheese and casserole bubbles. Better if made night before and stored in refrigerator overnight.

Kay Boyett, Montgomery Council

BACON-FLAVORED SQUASH

4 slices bacon
4 large yellow squash, sliced
2 green onions, sliced
1 egg, beaten
1/2 c. commercial sour cream

1/2 c. (2 oz.) shredded
  Swiss cheese
3/4 c. (3 oz.) shredded
  Cheddar cheese

Cook bacon in a large skillet until crisp; drain on paper towels. Crumble and set aside, reserving drippings. Saute squash and onion in drippings 8 to 10 minutes. Combine egg and sour cream; add to squash mixture. Stir in half the bacon. Spoon half the squash mixture into a greased shallow 2 quart casserole. Sprinkle Swiss cheese over top; spoon remaining squash mixture over cheese. Sprinkle Cheddar cheese over surface; top with remaining bacon. Bake at 350° for 20 minutes or until bubbly. Yield: 6 servings.

Regina Cash, Anniston Council

DEEP FAT FRIED SQUASH

5 squash in small amount
  of water, cooked down
1 grated onion
3 c. bread or cracker
  crumbs

Small amount of pimento
2 eggs
1/2 tsp. salt
1/2 tsp. black pepper

Mix well and deep fat fry.

Joyce Lawley, Anniston Council

FRIED SQUASH

5 small squash
1 c. corn meal
1 c. corn oil

Salt
Pepper

Slice squash into 1/8 inch slices. Batter in corn meal and salt and pepper to taste. Heat corn oil in skillet until bubbling. Fry slices in single layer until golden brown.

Verndale Bolton, Anniston Council

SQUASH-FRIED YELLOW

6-8 medium size squash
1/2 c. vegetable oil

1 c. flour

Thinly slice squash; add to 1/2 cup vegetable oil heated in 9 inch skillet. Cover and steam until tender. Sprinkle with flour and fry uncovered until brown. More oil may be added if needed.

E. H. Gearhart, Montgomery Council

SQUASH PATTIES

2 c. grated squash
  (yellow)
2 eggs
2 tsp. grated onion

1/4 c. and 2 Tbsp. flour
1/2 tsp. salt
1/8 tsp. pepper
2 tsp. sugar

Melt 2 tablespoons butter in skillet, using medium heat. Drop squash into butter by tablespoonfuls. Fry until brown.

Faith Kirby, Anniston Council; Mary Ann Davis, Anniston Council; "Mike" Buckner, Birmingham Central Council

SQUASH SOUFFLE

1 lb. squash
8 or 10 crackers, crushed
1/4 c. butter
2 eggs

1 large onion
1 c. grated sharp cheese
1/2 c. milk
Salt and pepper

Cook squash and onion together until tender; drain off water and mash squash and onions until fine. Add salt, pepper, cheese, butter, egg yolks and crackers, crumbled fine. Beat egg whites until stiff; fold into mixture. Bake in a buttered casserole until brown. Serve hot.

Marcella James, Tri-Cities Council
Sara Taunton, Montgomery Council

OLD SOUTH SUCCOTASH

2 c. fresh lima beans
  (about 1 lb.)
4 c. fresh corn, cut from
  cob (about 8 ears)

3 Tbsp. butter or margarine
1/2 c. whipping cream
1/2 tsp. salt
1/8 tsp. pepper

Cook beans in boiling, salted water about 15 minutes or until almost tender; drain. Add corn, butter, whipping cream, salt and pepper; mix well. Cook over low heat, stirring often, 7 to 10 minutes, or until corn is done. Yield: 6 servings.

Betty Floyd Parker, Montgomery Council

BAKED TOMATOES

Cut tomatoes in halves. Make topping of onion, fine bread crumbs, salt, pepper, oregano and basil. Mix together with plenty of melted butter. Put crumb mixture on top of each tomato half; sprinkle with Parmesan cheese and bake at 350° for 25-30 minutes. Great even with winter tomatoes!
Unknown

ESCALLOPED TOMATOES

1 (No. 2) can tomatoes
  or 4 large fresh
2 c. soft bread crumbs,
  toasted

1 medium onion, chopped
3/4 tsp. salt
1 Tbsp. sugar
2 Tbsp. butter

Combine tomatoes with the toasted bread crumbs and stir in onion, salt and sugar. Pour into buttered casserole. Bake at 375° for 15 to 20 minutes or until hot through. Makes 5 servings.

Pauline Woodham, Mobile Council

FRIED GREEN TOMATOES

3 or 4 large firm green
  tomatoes
1 egg
1/2 c. milk

1/2 c. corn meal
1/4 c. flour
Shortening

Wash and slice tomatoes about 1/8 to 1/4 inch thick. Beat egg and milk in bowl. In another bowl combine flour and corn meal. Dip each slice individually in the milk and egg mixture and then in the flour and meal mixture. Have shortening about 1/2 inch deep in heavy skillet. When short ening is hot, place tomatoes in and fry (not too fast) till brown on both sides. Salt to taste.

Marcia Freeman, Birmingham East Council

FRIED GREEN TOMATOES

6 large firm green tomatoes   1 c. corn meal
Salt and pepper to taste   Bacon drippings or shortening

Cut tomatoes into 1/4 inch slices; season with salt and pepper. Dredge in corn meal. Heat bacon drippings in a heavy skillet; add tomatoes and fry slowly until browned, turning once. Yield: 6 to 8 servings.

Betty F. Parker, Montgomery Council

GRILLED TOMATOES

4 medium tomatoes   1/4 c. shredded sharp
Salt, pepper   American cheese
1/2 c. soft bread   2 Tbsp. margarine, melted
  crumbs   2 Tbsp. chopped parsley

Halve tomatoes. Sprinkle cut surfaces with salt and pepper. Mix bread crumbs, cheese and margarine. Sprinkle crumb mixture over tomatoes. Trim with parsley. Heat tomatoes, cut side up, on grill about 5 minutes or until hot through.

Juanita Erdman, Mobile Council

TURNIP GREENS

2 large bunches turnip   4 Tbsp. bacon grease
  greens   or pure lard
1/2 lb. lean salt pork

Wash greens well to remove dirt; rinse at least 3 times in an abundance of water. Put small leaves in pot and strip larger leaves from stems. Before adding to pot container 1 quart cold water, cut salt pork into strips about 1 inch thick and drop into pot. Add bacon grease (or lard). Cover pot and bring to boil. Periodically stir greens in pot so as to allow those on top to go to the bottom. Then push down so leaves are covered with water. Lower heat and boil slowly for 2 hours (the longer the better), adding water to keep greens covered. Actual cooking time depends on tenderness of greens. Juice from greens is good served over corn bread and laced with pepper sauce.

708   Phillip McMillan, Montgomery Council

TURNIP CUSTARD

2 lb. turnips, pared,
  cooked and mashed
1 egg, well beaten
1/4 c. finely crushed
  crackers

2/3 c. undiluted evaporated
  milk
1 tsp. salt
1 c. shredded sharp
  Cheddar cheese

Blend mashed turnips with egg, crumbs, evaporated milk, salt and few grains of pepper. Turn mixture into a buttered 1 1/4 quart baking dish; set dish in a shallow pan of water in 350° oven. Sprinkle over top with cheese; bake 5 minutes, or until custard is set. Serves 6.

Mrs. Wallace Mintz, Anniston Council

CHINESE VEGETABLES

1 (No. 2) cans French
  style beans
Almonds

1 can water chestnuts
1 can LeSueur English peas
1 (No. 2) can Chinese
  vegetables

Boil and cool:
1/2 c. tarragon vinegar
1 c. sugar

1 c. celery
1 onion
Salt and pepper to taste

Pour over vegetables and chill.

Emma Rousseau, Huntsville Council

GERMAN FRIED VEGETABLES

1 c. cubed green tomatoes
1 c. cubed squash
1 c. thinly sliced okra
1 c. cubed potatoes

1/2 c. chopped onions
1/2 c. chopped green
  pepper
Salt and pepper to taste

Toss all vegetables with equal amounts of flour and meal. Fry as you would fry okra, using half shortening and half butter. Very good.

Louise Bonds, Life Member,
Birmingham Central Council

1567-82

COLACHE OR VEGETABLE MEDLEY
(MICROWAVE STYLE)

1/2 c. chopped onion
1/4 lb. green beans
1 Tbsp. butter
1/2 c. chopped green
  pepper

1 ear corn, cut in small pieces
3 zucchini, sliced
1 large tomato, sliced
1/4 tsp. salt
Dash of pepper

Microwave onions, green beans and butter for 3 minutes on high, covered. Add green peppers and corn. Microwave for 2 minutes on high; add tomatoes. Microwave on high till tender, about 2 minutes. Add zucchini; microwave on high till tender, about 3 minutes.

Dina Johnson, Birmingham South Council

VEGETABLE ROMANO

3 c. zucchini slices
1 c. onion rings
3 Tbsp. Parkay margarine

1 c. chopped tomatoes
Kraft grated Romano cheese

Saute zucchini and onions in margarine 10 minutes; add tomatoes. Continue cooking over low heat 5 minutes. Sprinkle with Romano. Makes 4 servings.

Bonnie Summers, Huntsville Council

MARINATED VEGGIES

1 can chicken broth
1 1/2 c. sliced carrots
2 c. cauliflowerets
2 small zucchini, thinly
  sliced

1/2 lb. sliced mushrooms
1/4 c. wine vinegar
1 env. Italian salad
  dressing mix

Heat broth to boiling in a large saucepan; add carrots and simmer 2 minutes. Cool. Stir in all other ingredients. Chill 6 hours or more, stirring occasionally.

Debbie Tucker, Birmingham East Council

HAWAIIAN YAMS

4-5 large sweet potatoes
1 c. sugar
1/2 can Angel Flake
  coconut

1 egg
1 tsp. vanilla
1 c. Pet milk
1/2 tsp. salt

Topping:

1 large can crushed
  pineapple
1 c. sugar

3 Tbsp. cornstarch
1 (10 oz.) jar cherries

Cream potatoes; add other ingredients. Bake at 350°
for 30 minutes.

Topping: Mix all ingredients together; cook until thick.
Spoon on top of potatoes.

Mary McCully, Birmingham East Council

ZUCCHINI STIR FRY
(Surprisingly good)

Wash and slice thin 2 cups zucchini. Use 1 small onion,
chopped fine. Melt 2 tablespoons butter in skillet on medium
heat. Add vegetables and stir fry until tender.

Sherry Lonnergan, Anniston Council

FRIED ZUCCHINI

1 lb. zucchini, cut into
  1/2 inch slices
Salt and pepper to taste

2 eggs, well beaten
About 1 c. corn meal
Hot vegetable oil

Sprinkle zucchini with salt and pepper. Dip into egg,
and dredge in corn meal. Fry zucchini in hot vegetable oil
over medium heat until golden brown, turning once. Serve
hot. Yield: 4 to 6 servings.

Linda Mitchell, Decatur Council

ITALIAN ZUCCHINI

4 c. thinly sliced zucchini
1 c. chopped onion
1/2 c. margarine
1/2 c. chopped parsley
1/2 tsp. salt
1/2 tsp. pepper
1/2 tsp. garlic powder

1/4 tsp. basil
1/4 tsp. oregano
2 eggs, beaten
8 oz. shredded Mozzarella
  cheese
1 (8 oz.) can crescent
  dinner rolls
2 tsp. mustard

Cook zucchini, onion and margarine for 10 minutes; stir
in parsley, salt, pepper, garlic, basil, oregano, eggs and
cheese. Place the separated crescent triangles into an ungreased 10 inch pie pan; press over bottom and up sides to
form crust. Spread mustard over crust. Pour vegetable

1567-82

mixture into crust. Bake in preheated 375° oven for 18-20 minutes. (Cover crust with foil during last 10 minutes of baking.) Let stand 10 minutes before serving.
Sandra Herndon, Birmingham South Council

ZUCCHINI AND TOMATO BAKE

4 medium zucchini, sliced
1/2 tsp. soy sauce
1/4 tsp. salt
1/4 tsp. garlic salt
1/4 tsp. pepper

2 medium tomatoes, cut
  into wedges
1 medium onion, sliced
1 1/2 c. shredded Cheddar
  cheese
3 Tbsp. butter

Place zucchini in a 2 1/2 quart casserole; sprinkle with 1/2 each soy sauce, salt, garlic salt and pepper. Layer tomatoes and onion over zucchini; sprinkle with remaining seasoning. Top with cheese and dot with butter. Cover and bake at 350° for 40 minutes. Serves 8 to 10.
Betty Floyd Parker, Montgomery Council

ZIPPY ZUCCHINI SKILLET

2 Tbsp. vegetable oil
4 medium zucchini,
  thinly sliced
1 medium onion,
  chopped
1 (16 oz.) can whole
  kernel corn, drained

1 (4 oz.) can chopped
  green chiles
2 tsp. seeded chopped
  jalapeno peppers (optional)
1/4 tsp. salt
1/8 tsp. garlic powder
1/2 c. (2 oz.) shredded
  Cheddar cheese

Heat oil in a large skillet. Saute zucchini and onion 10 minutes or until tender. Stir in remaining ingredients except cheese; cook, stirring occasionally, until thoroughly heated. Remove from heat; stir in cheese. Yield: 6 servings.
Regina Cash, Anniston Council

RICE STUFFED VEGETABLE

6 medium green peppers,
  or 6 large zucchini
3 Tbsp. salad oil
1/2 c. chopped onion
1 garlic clove, crushed
1/2 lb. pork sausage
  or ground chuck

1/2 lb. fresh mushrooms,
  sliced
2 c. hot cooked rice
1/4 c. chopped parsley
1/2 tsp. salt
1/8 tsp. pepper

712

Place in boiling water pepper, tops cut off, seeds and membrane removed or, for zucchini, ends cut off and cut into 3 inch lengths and cored. Boil for 5 minutes. Add 1 teaspoon salt to water, then drain well. In large skillet heat oil; add onions and garlic; saute until translucent. Add meat and cook until brown. Add mushrooms and cook until tender. Remove from heat; stir in rice, parsley, salt and pepper. Set aside. Preheat oven to 350°. Spoon rice stuffing into each vegetable. Place in baking dish; bake 20 minutes or until heated through and tender. Makes 6 servings (340 calories each).

Kathleen Wilson, Birmingham East Council

THANK GOD FOR DIRTY DISHES

Thank God for dirty dishes,
They have a tale to tell.
While others are going hungry
We're eating very well.
With home and health and happiness,
I shouldn't want to fuss.
For by this stack of evidence,
God's very good to us.

I SAID A PRAYER FOR YOU TODAY

I said a prayer for you today
    And know God must have heard -
I felt the answer in my heart
    Although He spoke no word!
I didn't ask for wealth or fame
    (I knew you wouldn't mind) -
I asked Him to send treasures
    Of a far more lasting kind!
I asked that He'd be near you
    At the start of each new day
To grant you health and blessings
    And friends to share your way!
I asked for happiness for you
    In all things great and small -
But it was for His loving care
    I prayed the most of all!

** NOTES **

INDEX OF RECIPES

1567-82

1567-82

CAKES, FILLINGS, FROSTINGS

1567-82

726

SALADS

734

1567-82

1567-82

Need additional copies of *Calling All Cooks* (soft cover)?
Visit swphmarketplace.com, email customerservice@swpublishinghouse.com, or call 800-358-0560 to order.

If you love *Calling All Cooks,* you will want to check out the other cookbooks from the AT&T Pioneers, Alabama Chapter. Complete and mail this form along with a check or money order to the address below. If you would like to pick up your books, please call 205-848-4748 for pickup locations.

AT&T Pioneers
Alabama Chapter 34
3196 Hwy 280 E., Room 316S–Desk 639
Birmingham, Alabama 35243

		Quantity	Total
Calling All Cooks one (Special Hard Cover Edition)	$23.00 ea.	_____	$ _____
Calling All Cooks one (soft cover)	$18.00 ea.	_____	_____
Calling All Cooks two	$18.00 ea.	_____	_____
Calling All Cooks three	$18.00 ea.	_____	_____
Calling All Cooks four	$18.00 ea.	_____	_____
Celebrations	$13.00 ea.	_____	_____
Calling All Kids	$13.00 ea.	_____	_____

Total (All prices include postage and handling.) $ _____

Name   (Please print clearly)

Address

City   State   Zip

(   )
Area code/Telephone number

Email address

Please make checks payable to **AT&T Pioneers Chapter #34.**
For more information,
visit our website at **attpioneervolunteers.org** (click on **Chapters** link).